P9-DDW-262

Introduction to Law Enforcement and Criminal Justice

FOURTH EDITION

Introduction
to Law Enforcement
and Criminal Justice FOURTH EDITION

Henry M. Wrobleski
Normandale Community College
Bloomington, Minnesota

Kären M. Hess
Normandale Community College
Bloomington, Minnesota

WEST PUBLISHING COMPANY

Minneapolis/St. Paul ■ New York ■ Los Angeles ■ San Francisco

Text Design: Roslyn Stendahl, Dapper Design
Indexes: Christine M. Hess
Composition: Carlisle Communications

WEST'S COMMITMENT TO THE ENVIRONMENT

In 1906, West Publishing Company began recycling materials left
over from the production of books. This began a tradition of
efficient and responsible use of resources. Today, up to 95
percent of our legal books and 70 percent of our college and
school texts are printed on recycled, acid-free stock. West
also recycles nearly 22 million pounds of scrap paper annually—
the equivalent of 181,717 trees. Since the 1960s, West has
devised ways to capture and recycle waste inks, solvents, oils,
and vapors created in the printing process. We also recycle
plastics of all kinds, wood, glass, corrugated cardboard, and
batteries, and have eliminated the use of styrofoam book
packaging. We at West are proud of the longevity and the scope
of our commitment to the environment.

Production, Prepress, Printing and Binding by West Publishing Company.

Copyright ©1979,
1986, 1990   By WEST PUBLISHING COMPANY
COPYRIGHT ©1993   By WEST PUBLISHING COMPANY
                                    610 Opperman Drive
                                    P.O. Box 64526
                                    St. Paul, MN 55164-0526

All rights reserved

Printed in the United States of America

00 99 98 97 96 95 94 93   8 7 6 5 4 3 2 1 0

Library of Congress Cataloging-in-Publication Data

Wrobleski, Henry M., 1922-
    Introduction to law enforcement and criminal justice / Henry M.
Wrobleski, Kären M. Hess. — 4th ed.
        p.   cm.
    Includes bibliographical references and index.
    ISBN 0-314-01241-9 (acid-free paper)
    1. Law enforcement—United States.   2. Crime—United States.
I. Hess, Kären M., 1939-   II. Title.
HV8138.W76 1993
363.2'3'0973—dc20   92-40380
                                                                    CIP

About the Authors

Henry M. Wrobleski

Henry M. Wrobleski, LLB, is coordinator of the Law Enforcement Program at Normandale Community College. He is a respected author, lecturer, and consultant with 30 years of experience in law enforcement. He is also Dean of Instruction for the Institute for Professional Development and is a graduate of the FBI Academy.

Kären M. Hess

Kären M. Hess, PhD, has written extensively in the field of law enforcement. She is a member of the English department at Normandale Community College as well as the president of the Institute for Professional Development.

Contents in Brief

Contents

SECTION FOUR
In Search of Justice: Our Criminal Justice System in Action
501

18 *Our Courts: Seeking the Truth—Innocent Until Proven Guilty*   *503*

21   Critical Issues in Criminal Justice: Challenges of the 1990s   593

List of Cases

List of Figures

List of Tables

List of Acronyms and Initials

ADA	Americans with Disabilities Act
ADL	Anti-Defamation League
AIDS	Acquired Immune Deficiency Syndrome
AFIS	Automated Fingerprint Identification System
ATF	Bureau of Alcohol, Tobacco, and Firearms
AVM	Automatic vehicle monitoring
AYM	Aryan Youth Movement
BAC	Blood Alcohol Concentration
BATF	Bureau of Alcohol, Tobacco, and Firearms
BJS	Bureau of Justice Statistics
BNDD	Bureau of Narcotics and Dangerous Drugs
BFOQ	bona fide occupational qualification
CAD	Computer-Assisted Dispatch
C.A.P.E.	Computer-Assisted Police Effectiveness
CASP	Comprehensive Alcohol Safety Project
CAT	Combat Auto Theft
CCRP	Citizen Crime Reporting Program
CDC	Center for Disease Control
CHP	California Highway Patrol
CPI	California Psychological Inventory
CPTED	Crime Prevention Through Environmental Design
CRB	Civilian Review Board
D.A.R.E	Drug Abuse Resistance Education
DBMS	Data Base Management System
DDP	Directed Deterrent Patrol
DEA	Drug Enforcement Administration
DNA	deoxyribonucleic acid
DPMA	Data Processing Management Association
DUF	Drug Use Forecasting System
DUI	Driving Under the Influence
DWI	Driving While Intoxicated
EEOA	Equal Employment Opportunity Act
ETS	Evidence Tracking System
FBI	Federal Bureau of Investigation
FDEA	Federal Drug Enforcement Administration
FLETC	Federal Law Enforcement Training Center
FTO	Field Training Officer
HIV	Human Immunodeficiency Virus
IACP	International Association of Chiefs of Police
INS	Immigration and Naturalization Service
IRS	Internal Revenue Service
LARS	LoJack Auto Recovery System
LEAA	Law Enforcement Assistance Administration

LEEP	Law Enforcement Education Program
LWOP	Life Without Parole
MADD	Mothers Against Drunk Driving
MDC	Mobile digital communications
MDT	Mobile Data Terminal
MICA	Mentally ill, chemically addicted, or both
MMPI	Minnesota Multiphasic Personality Inventory
NCIC	National Crime Information Center
NCS	National Crime Survey
NORML	National Organization for Reform of Marijuana Laws
NOVA	National Organization for Victim Assistance
NRA	National Rifle Association
OJJDP	Office of Juvenile Justice and Delinquency Prevention
OSHA	Occupational Safety and Health Administration
PAL	Police Athletic League
PC	Personal Computer
PSA	Public Service Announcement
PTSD	Post-Traumatic Stress Disorder
RCS	Regional Communication System
RFLP	Restriction Fragment Length Polymorphism
RICO	Racketeer Influenced and Corrupt Organization Act
ROR	Released on Recognizance
SADD	Students Against Driving Drunk
UCR	Uniform Crime Reports
VCAN	Victims Constitutional Amendment Network
VIS	Victim Impact Statement
VOCA	Victims of Crime Act
VSO	Victim Statement of Opinion

Preface

The future of our lawful, democratic society depends in large part upon those of you currently in the field of law enforcement and those of you preparing to enter this field. The law enforcement officer is responsible for assisting those in distress, providing services to persons who request them, preserving peace and order in the community, preventing unlawful acts, and apprehending those who violate the law. These complex responsibilities must be met under constantly changing conditions and in a manner that assures the rights of the individual. Increased technology, industrialization, urbanization, and mobility have brought new problems to law enforcement, requiring the law enforcement officer to be knowledgeable in a wide variety of areas.

Introduction to Law Enforcement and Criminal Justice provides basic information that should serve as an overview of the entire field as well as a solid foundation for future course work. The content in each chapter could easily be expanded into an entire book or course, but the basic concepts in each area have been included.

You will be introduced to the history of law enforcement, including how our laws have evolved and the basic rights all American citizens have. You will also look at the distinction between criminal and civil offenses.

Then you will look at police operations as they exist in the 1990s, including the roles and responsibilities of the modern law enforcement officer. Next you will look at the specific problems and people involved, including crime, criminals, gangs, and victims.

The text concludes with a discussion of the total criminal justice system, the role of the courts and corrections, the juvenile justice system, and some critical issues and challenges facing the criminal justice system in the 1990s.

Important court cases and decisions are presented throughout the text rather than isolated in a single chapter. Likewise, modern advancements in law enforcement are integrated into chapters rather than presented as a separate subject. The content of the text is based on fifteen years of classroom research among law enforcement officers and preservice students as to what subject matter is most important and useful to the future police officer. The text itself has been classroom tested and reviewed by several experts in the field.

HOW TO USE THIS BOOK

Introduction to Law Enforcement and Criminal Justice is more than a textbook; it is a learning experience requiring your active participation to obtain the best results. You will get the most out of the book if you first familiarize yourself with the total scope of law enforcement: read and think about the Contents and what is included. Then follow these steps as you read each chapter:

1. Read the objectives at the beginning of each chapter:

Do You Know

What the basic instrument of government is?

Think about your current knowledge on each question. What preconceptions do you hold?

2. Read the chapter (underlining or taking notes if that is your preferred study style).

   Pay special attention to all information between rules:

The United States Constitution is the basic instrument of government and the supreme law of the United States.

The key concepts of each chapter are emphasized in this manner.

Look up unfamiliar words in the glossary at the back of the text.

3. When you have finished reading the chapter, reread the list of objectives given at the beginning of the chapter to make certain you are able to give a response to each question. If you find yourself stumped, find the appropriate material in the chapter and review it.

4. Read the Discussion Questions, think about possible responses, and be prepared to contribute to a class discussion.

5. Finally, define the terms set out at the end of each chapter. All terms are in the glossary at the back of text.

Good reading and learning!

ACKNOWLEDGMENTS

We would like to thank the following individuals and organizations for their contributions to *Introduction to Law Enforcement and Criminal Justice.*

Thank you to Larry Gaines, Eastern Kentucky University; Professor George Green, Mankato State University; Robert Ingram, Florida International University; Glen Morgan, Lincolnland Community College; Professor Frank Post, Fullerton College; Jack Spurlin, Missouri Southern State College; and Larry Tuttle; Palm Beach Junior College for their helpful reviews of the manuscript and their suggestions for changes. A special thank you to Professor Post for his valuable additions, particularly in the areas of law enforcement agencies and the police career.

For their valuable suggestions for the third edition of *Introduction to Law Enforcement and Criminal Justice,* thank you to Robert Ives, Rockford Police Department; Sergeant James Walsh, Mount San Jacinto College; Paul H. Johnson, Murry State University; Roger Brown, Golden Valley Lutheran College; Dr. Jack Taylor, Oscar Rose Junior College; Lt. David A. Wilson, Turmbull Police Department; Professor Joseph Polanski, Sinclair Community College; Dr. David G. Epstein, Burnswick Junior College; Professor Kenneth Bowser, Westfield State College; Myron Utech, University of Wisconsin at Eau Claire; Dr. Steven Brown, East Tennessee State University; James Stinchcomb, Miami Dade Community College; Daniel Gunderson, Chippewa Valley Technical College; and Tim Vieders, Niagara County Community College.

For their excellent suggestions on modifications for the fourth edition, thanks to Vincent Del Castillo, John Jay College of Criminal Justice; Chris W. Eskridge, University of Nebraska; Larry A. Gould, Northern Arizona University; Burt C. Hagerman, Oakland Community College; Larry W. Hensel, Tallahassee Community College; Robert G. Huckabee, Indiana State University; Robert R. Ives, Rock Valley College; Sidney A. Lyle, Odessa College; E. W. Oglesby, Fullerton College; and Gary W. Tucker, Sinclair Community College. An extra thank you to E. W. Oglesby for his substantive contributions to the discussion of women in law enforcement and sexual harassment, reverse discrimination, the applicant selection process, and PCP.

Any errors in the text are, however, the sole responsibility of the co-authors.

Thank you to the administration and staff of Normandale Community College for their assistance and support during the classroom testing of the manuscript, to the students in Law Enforcement 050 for providing ideas and suggestions, and to Pamela Reierson, media specialist, for her invaluable assistance in locating sources and information.

Thank you to the Department of Justice; the Federal Bureau of Investigation; the Federal Drug Enforcement Administration; the International Association of Chiefs of Police; the Minnesota Attorney General's Office, Civil Service Department, County Attorney's Association, Governor's Commission on Crime Prevention and Control, and State Highway Department; the National Safety Council; and police departments of Minneapolis, Philadelphia, San Diego, and St. Louis Park; Keith Rodgers, Chief of the Criminal Investigation Training Division of the IRS; and the publishers for permission to include their materials in our text.

Thank you also to Robert J. Jucha, Diane Colwyn, and to Holly Henjum and Peggy Brewington, our editors, for their patience, their attention to detail, and their encouragement and support. It is largely through their efforts that this fourth edition has a new look.

Finally, thank you to our families and colleagues for their support and assistance during the development of *Introduction to Law Enforcement and Criminal Justice.*

Law Enforcement in Context

Our system of law enforcement did not magically appear. It has a rich heritage as well as a very complex system of laws on which it is based. The origins of law enforcement, from primitive and ancient times up through developments in English law enforcement, are the focus of chapter 1. Chapter 2 traces the evolution of law enforcement in the United States, from the time the colonists arrived, bringing with them their European customs and laws, up through the creation of our various levels of local, county, state, and federal governments.

Chapter 3 discusses how individuals are hired for positions in law enforcement, the legal restrictions and mandates on hiring, the progress of minorities and women in gaining employment in law enforcement, and what one might expect after being hired.

Chapter 4 discusses the foundation of our law enforcement system, our Constitution and Bill of Rights, which are the supreme law of this country and which have a profound effect on how law enforcement is practiced. In addition to constitutional law, police officers must also be familiar with the vast array of local, state, and federal statutes that have developed over the years. Chapter 5 looks at the various kinds of laws that have evolved and then focuses on the two most relevant to

law enforcement, criminal law and civil law. The elements of specific crimes such as murder, assault, rape, robbery, burglary, larceny/theft, auto theft, and arson are discussed. The chapter concludes with a look at the various areas frequently resulting in law enforcement officers being sued.

Everything a law enforcement officer does must be done with the realization that the profession is governed by laws and that all citizens, even if they are committing illegal acts, have certain rights that cannot be violated. Citizens, however, also have the right to be protected from those who would harm them—a precarious balancing act. As one yellowed piece of paper taped to the wall of a police roll-call room said:

> The policeman, he told us, is a mercenary: Society tries to make us out to be the Jolly Green Giants of the community. We're not. We're the barbed wire separating the wolves from the lambs.

The section closes with a discussion about crime in the United States (Chapter 6), including some of the special problems facing law enforcement such as white-collar crimes, computer crimes, organized crimes, bias crimes, and ritualistic crimes.

CHAPTER 1

Law Enforcement in the United States

The most visible component of the criminal justice system is law enforcement.

Law enforcement has changed considerably over the past decades. Changes include the addition of more officers from minority groups.

More women are also entering law enforcement and are found to perform as effectively as their male counterparts.

Most Americans over age sixteen have received, or know someone who has received a warning about speeding, or an actual speeding citation.

As our population ages, law enforcement officers will face new challenges. Here an officer assists an elderly citizen on Venice Beach.

Although infrequent, high speed chases are also a part of law enforcement. This is the scene of a police chase which ended with one civilian passenger killed and three other people injured. Such incidents have led to no-chase policies being established in some police departments.

Law enforcement also deals with crimes. Some crimes are quickly solved, such as the pursesnatching for which this D.C. youth is being arrested.

Other crimes, such as the homicide shown here, require long hours of investigation, and some may never be solved.

Police dogs help law enforcement officers find missing children, hidden suspects, drugs, and bombs.

Problems associated with prostitution and pornography still confront law enforcement in many cities, as here on 42nd Street in New York.

Another challenge is dealing effectively with gangs and gang members such as these in the "Zone" in Los Angeles.

Gangs are found across the country and include biker gangs such as those in the Red Hook Projects in New York.

Tremendous amounts of law enforcement resources are used in combatting the drug problem. Here an agent for the U.S. Customs Service examines a secret compartment in a Ford Tempo where 40 kilograms of cocaine were stashed.

Drug raids often coordinate efforts between local and federal agents. They require careful planning and teamwork.

Education is vital to dealing with the drug problem. Officers across the country participate in the D.A.R.E program, teaching elementary school-age children to say "no" to drugs.

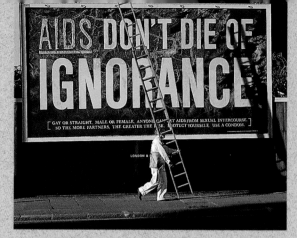

A relatively new problem confronting people is that of AIDS. This problem is directly related to unsafe sex practices and the sharing of hypodermic needles by drug addicts. Recently, during a hold-up at a Florida convenience store, the clerk ordered to empty the register was apparently too slow for one of the robbers. The robber stuck the clerk with a needle he claimed was tainted with the HIV virus, saying, "I have AIDS and now so do you."

Law enforcement agencies in many parts of the country are also conducting gun control programs.

Technology has been of great benefit to law enforcement, particularly in ease and rapidity of communication.

Another vital role of law enforcement is "keeping the peace" while simultaneously protecting citizens' civil rights. Protests can get out of hand and require police intervention.

Sometimes the mere presence of police in riot gear can deter further violence.

At other times use of police force is necessary. Although the use of force is authorized, such force must be reasonable.

The second component of the criminal justice system is the court. Courts operate at both the state and federal level. This trial in Milwaukee will rely heavily on the testimony of law enforcement officers.

The third component of the criminal justice system is corrections. As of June 30, 1991, prisons such as this housed a record 804,524 men and women found guilty of serious crimes.

Law enforcement is the foundation of our criminal justice system. Law enforcement officers protect law-abiding citizens and do their share to bring those who break the law to justice.

A Brief History: The Evolution of Law and Law Enforcement

History is a vast early warning system.

—**Norman Cousins**

Do You Know

What a law is?

When and why law enforcement began?

The origins of features of our law enforcement system such as:
The offices of constable, sheriff, and justice of the peace? General alarms and citizen's arrests? Separation between enforcing laws and judging offenders? Local responsibility for law enforcement? Division of offenses into felonies and misdemeanors? Jury by peers and due process? Paid law enforcement officers? Women in law enforcement?

The significance of the tithing system, the Frankpledge system, Leges Henrici, the Magna Carta, the Parish Constable system, and the Watch and Ward system?

How law enforcement has traditionally responded to increased crime?

What significant contributions to law enforcement were made by Sir Robert Peel?

Where and when the first police department was established in England and what it was called?

INTRODUCTION

A brief look into the history of laws and law enforcement will give you answers to many of the preceding questions. The heritage of law enforcement is a source of pride as well as a guide to avoiding mistakes in the future. Specific dates and events are not as important as acquiring a sense of the sequence or chronology of how present-day laws and our system of law enforcement came into existence.

Law is a body of rules for human conduct that are enforced by imposing penalties for their violation. Technically, laws are made and passed by the legislative branches of our federal, state, county, and city governments. They are based on customs, traditions, mores, and current need.

Law refers to all the rules of conduct established and enforced by the custom, authority, or legislation of a group, community, or country.

Notice that law implies both prescription (rule) and enforcement by authority. It might seem that the term *law enforcement* is redundant since law refers to both the rules and their enforcement. But, in the United States, those who enforce the laws are *not* the same as those who make them. Historically, however, in other countries, this was not the case. Often rulers both made and enforced the laws.

PRIMITIVE AND ANCIENT LAW

Law enforcement can be traced back to the cave dwellers. The cave dwellers had certain rules they were expected to follow or face death or banishment from the tribe. The customs depicted in early cave-dwelling drawings may well represent the beginning of law and law enforcement.

The prehistoric social order consisted of small family groups living together as tribes or clans. Group living gave rise to certain customs that everyone was expected to observe. The chief of the tribe had executive, legislative, and judicial powers and often appointed members of the tribe to perform special tasks such as serving as a bodyguard or enforcing edicts. Crimes committed against individuals were handled by the victim or the victim's family. The philosophy of justice was retaliatory, that is, punish the offender. A person who stole the game from a neighbor's traps could expect to pay for the crime by being thrown into a pot of boiling oil or a cage of wild beasts. Other common punishments for serious offenses were flaying, impalement, burning at the stake, stoning, branding, mutilation, and crucifixion.

A system of law and law enforcement began earlier than 2000 B.C. as a means of controlling human conduct and enforcing society's rules.

The earliest record of ancient people's need to organize and standardize rules and methods of enforcement to control human behavior dates back to approximately 2300 B.C. when the Sumerian rulers Lipitshtar and Eshumma set forth standards on what did and did not constitute an offense against society. A hundred years later, the Babylonian King Hammurabi established rules for his kingdom that designated not only offenses but punishments as well. In fact, Hammurabi established the oldest known building code. Although

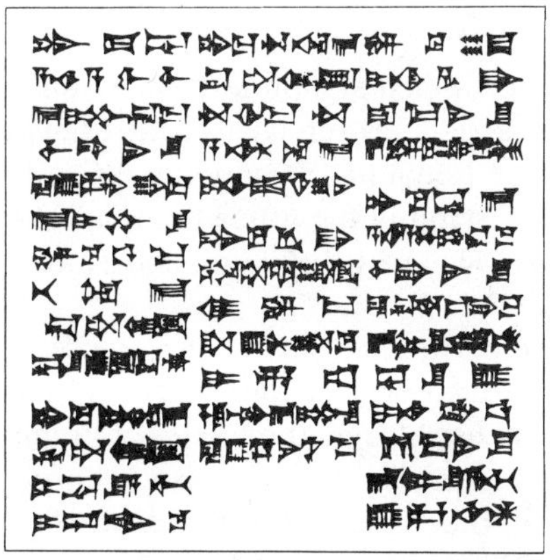

If a builder builds a house for a man and does not make its construction firm and the house collapses and causes the death of the owner of the house—that builder shall be put to death. If it causes the death of a son of the owner—they shall put to death a son of that builder. If it causes the death of a slave of the owner—he shall give the owner a slave of equal value. If it destroys property he shall restore whatever it destroyed and because he did not make the house firm he shall rebuild the house which collapsed at his own expense. If a builder builds a house and does not make its construction meet the requirements and a wall falls in—that builder shall strengthen the wall at his own expense.

Figure 1–1   From the Code of Hammurabi (2200 B.C.)
Source: Masonry Institute, 55 New Montgomery Street, San Francisco, Cal. 94105.

the penalties prescribed were often barbaric by today's standards, the relationship between the crime and the punishment are of interest. (See Figure 1–1.)

The Code of Hammurabi consisted of three hundred legal provisions concerning such matters as false accusations, witchcraft, military service, land and business regulations, family laws, tariffs, wages, loans, and debts. The main principle of the code was that "the strong shall not injure the weak." The code also established a social order based on individual rights. Hammurabi originated the legal principle of *lex talions*—an eye for an eye.

Egypt

The first accounts of a developing court system came from Egypt in approximately 1500 B.C. The sophisticated court system was presided over by judges appointed by the Pharaoh. About 1000 B.C. in Egypt, public officers performed police functions. Their weapon and symbol of authority was a staff topped by a metal knob engraved with the king's name. The baton carried by the modern police officer may have its origin in that staff.

Greece

Solon, the ancient lawgiver of Athens (638 to 559 B.C.) was asked to name the essential ingredient of the ideal community. His answer could be memorized by every law enforcement professional: "When those who have not been injured become as indignant as those who have."

The Greeks had an impressive form of law enforcement called the *ephori*. Each year at Sparta a body of five ephors was elected and given almost unlimited powers. They were the highest executive power in the land, being investigator, judge, jury, and executioner. These five men also presided over the Senate and Assembly, assuring that their rules and decrees were followed. One problem with this system, however, was that it promoted corrupt enforcement.

From the Greek philosopher Plato, who lived from 427 to 347 B.C., came the idea that punishment should serve a purpose rather than just being retaliation. Note the similarity between this concept and the relationship between the crimes and punishments set forth by Hammurabi in 2200 B.C. This relationship is the basis of equity and the basis of law in America, as will be discussed later.

Figure 1–2   Fasces
Source: Drawing by Ione Bell.

Rome

Like the Greeks, the Romans had a highly developed system for the administration of justice. The Twelve Tables were the first written laws of the Roman Empire. Drawn up by ten of the wisest men in Rome in 451 and 450 B.C., the Twelve Tables were fastened to the speakers' stand in the Roman Forum. The tablets dealt with legal procedures, property ownership, building codes, marriage customs, and punishment for crimes.

About the time of Christ, the Roman emperor Augustus chose members from his military to form the Praetorian Guard to protect the palace and the Urban Cohort to patrol the city. Augustus also established the Vigiles of Rome. Initially assigned as fire fighters, they were eventually also given law enforcement responsibilities; consequently, they are sometimes referred to as the first integrated police-fire service. As the first civilian police force, the Vigiles sometimes kept the peace very ruthlessly. It is from these Vigiles that we derive the word *vigilante.*

In the Roman Empire during the first century A.D., public officials (called *lictors*) acted as bodyguards for magistrates (judges). When the magistrate ordered, the lictor would bring criminals before him and carry out the magistrate's prescribed punishments, even the death penalty. Their symbol of public authority was a *fasces*, a bundle of rods tied by a red thong around an axe, which represented their absolute authority of life and limb. (See Figure 1–2.) Within the city of Rome itself, however, the fasces had no axe because there was a right to appeal a capital sentence (Hall 1974, p. 119).

Another important contribution from the Roman Empire was the Justinian Code. Justinian I, ruler of the Eastern Roman Empire from A.D. 527 to 565, collected all the existing Roman laws. They became known as the Corpus Juris Civilis, meaning body of law. The Corpus Juris Civilis consisted of all Roman laws and legal principles, illustrated by cases, as well as explanations of new laws under proposal.

ENGLISH LAW AND LAW ENFORCEMENT

The early beginnings of just laws and social control were destroyed during the Dark Ages as the Roman Empire disintegrated. Hordes of Germanic invaders swept into the old Roman territory of Britain, bringing with them their own laws and customs. These German invaders intermarried with conquered English, the result being the hardy Anglo-Saxon.

Anglo-Saxons—The Tithing System

The Anglo-Saxons grouped their farms around small, self-governing villages that policed themselves. When criminals were caught, the punishment was often severe, as in ancient times. Sometimes; however, the tribe would let an offender prove innocence through battle. And sometimes they allowed testimony by other tribespeople willing to swear that the accused was innocent. In addition, the practice of allowing a criminal to pay a fine for committing a crime or to work off the debt was beginning to come into vogue.

As time went on, the informal grouping of families became more structured. Alfred the Great (A.D. 849 to 899) first set down the guideline that all freemen should belong to an association that binds them with a certain group of people. The idea was that if one person in the group committed a crime and was convicted, all people in the group were responsible for the person's fine. Consequently, all members of the group were very careful to see that no one in the group broke the law. Every male, unless excused by the king, was enrolled for police purposes in a group of ten families known as a **tithing.** To maintain order in the tithing, they had a leader or chief tithingman who was the mayor, council, and judge all in one. Society was so basic at this time that they needed to enforce only two laws: laws against murder and theft.

The **tithing system** established the principle of collective responsibility for maintaining local law and order.

Any victim or person who discovered a crime would put out the "**Hue and Cry,**" for example, "Stop, thief." Anyone who heard the cry would stop any activity and help capture the suspect. This may be the forerunner of both the general alarm and the citizen's arrest.

The Hue and Cry may be the origin of the general alarm and the citizen's arrest.

When capture was made, the suspect was brought before the chief tithingman, who determined innocence or guilt plus punishment. Theft was often punished by civil restitution or working off the loss by bondage or servitude—the basis for civil law, restitution for financial loss (Lunt 1938).

If a criminal sought refuge in a neighboring village, that village was expected to return the criminal for punishment. This cooperation among villagers eventually resulted in the formation of **hundreds**, which were groups of ten tithings. The top official of the hundred was called a **reeve.**

The hundreds also elected a **constable** to lead them in pursuit of any lawbreakers. The constable was the first English police officer and, as such, had charge of the weapons and horses of the whole community. Finally the hundreds were consolidated into **shires,** or counties. The head of the shire was called, quite logically, the **shire-reeve,** which is the forerunner of our county sheriff.

Constables on duty during Anglo-Saxon times.

The shire-reeve acted as both police officer and judge for the territory, traveling from hundred to hundred. The shire-reeve had the power of *posse commitatus*, meaning he could gather all the men of a shire together when he needed assistance in pursuing a lawbreaker. This is the forerunner of our posse.

The Norman Frankpledge System

In 1066, William the Conqueror, a Norman, invaded and conquered England. As king of a conquered nation, William was too concerned about national security to allow the tithings to keep their own system of home rule. He established fifty-five military districts each headed by a Norman shire-reeve who answered directly to the crown. William also decided that shire-reeves should not try cases but should serve only as police officers. He selected his own judges who traveled around and tried cases. These were the forerunners of our circuit judges. Even more important, however, is that this separated the law enforcement and judicial roles.

Under William the Conqueror, the shire-reeves were limited to law enforcement and separate judges were appointed to try cases.

William established a highly centralized bureaucracy that also unified the country's law enforcement. He introduced the curfew, requiring that all fires be extinguished or covered during the night; and he developed a doomsday book, a tax roll listing the landowners and the extent of their land. The doomsday book was also a legal code with penalties for infractions—an idea formulated by King Alfred the Great 150 years earlier.

In addition, the Normans modified the tithing system into the **Frankpledge system,** which refers to the guarantee for peace maintenance that the king demanded from all free Englishmen.

The Frankpledge system required loyalty to the king's law and mutual local responsibility in maintaining the peace.

The Twelfth Century

William's son, Henry I, who ruled England from 1100 to 1135, also made significant contributions to law enforcement. In fact, he came to be known as Henry the Lawgiver after he issued the **Leges Henrici**, which established certain offenses such as arson, robbery, murder, counterfeiting, and crimes of violence as being against the king's peace. The Leges Henrici set the precedent that for certain crimes a person should be punished by the state rather than by the victim or by peers. It also divided crimes into felonies and misdemeanors.

The Leges Henrici made law enforcement a public matter and separated offenses into felonies and misdemeanors.

Henry I's reign ended in 1135 and was followed by many years of turmoil, which lasted until Henry II became king in 1154. Henry II's greatest contribution to law enforcement was the jury system. Called an inquisition, people were required to give information to a panel of judges, who then determined the guilt or innocence of the accused.

For the next hundred years kings appointed enforcement officers to meet their needs but who had no real control over their power. When John became king in 1199, however, he abused his power by demanding more military service from the feudal class, selling royal positions to the highest bidder, and increasing taxes without obtaining consent from the barons— actions all contrary to feudal custom. In addition, John's courts decided cases according to his wishes, not according to law.

In 1213, a group of barons and church leaders met near London to call for a halt to the king's injustices. They drew up a list of rights they wanted King John to grant them. After the king refused to grant these rights on two separate occasions, the barons raised an army and forced him to meet their demands. On June 15, 1215, King John signed the Magna Carta.

The Magna Carta

Our modern system of justice owes much to the Magna Carta, a decisive document in the development of constitutional government in England.

The **Magna Carta,** a precedent for democratic government and individual rights, laid the foundation for requiring rulers to uphold the law, forbidding taxation without representation, requiring due process of law, including trial by jury, providing safeguards against unfair imprisonment.

The Magna Carta contained sixty-three articles, most requiring the king to uphold feudal law. The articles initially benefited only the barons and other members of the feudal class, but they later became important to all people. Some articles granted the church freedom from royal interference, and a few guaranteed the rights of the rising middle class. Ordinary freemen and peasants, although making up the great majority of England's population, were hardly mentioned in the charter.

The charter required the king to seek the advice and consent of the barons on all matters important to the kingdom, including taxation. Later such articles supported the argument that no law should be made nor tax raised without the consent of England's Parliament. Article 13 restored local control to cities and villages, a fundamental principle of American law enforcement.

Other articles of the Magna Carta became foundations for modern justice. One article, for example, required that no freeman should be imprisoned, deprived of property, sent out of the country, or destroyed except by the lawful judgment of peers or by the law of the land. The concept of due process of law, including trial by jury, developed from this article.

The Next Five Hundred Years

Several interesting developments in law enforcement occurred in the following centuries. The **police des mouers** (police of the puters) was established to regulate prostitution. A register was maintained, and no prostitutes were permitted except in certain parts of the city. Thus, the origin of the **red light district**.

In 1285 King Edward I set up a curfew and night watch program that allowed for the gates of Westminster, then capital of England, to be locked.

This would keep the city's occupants in and unwanted persons out. Bailiffs were hired as night watchmen to enforce the curfew and guard the gates. Edward I also mandated that groups of one hundred merchants be responsible for keeping peace in their districts, thus making law enforcement a local responsibility. This system of law enforcement, called the **Watch and Ward**, provided citizens protection twenty-four hours a day. The term "Watch and Ward" originated from the name of the shifts, with the day shift called "ward" and the night shift "watch."

The Frankpledge system began to disintegrate by the thirteenth century. Inadequate supervision by the king and his appointees led to its downfall. As Frankpledge slowly declined, the Parish Constable system emerged to take its place.

With an ever-increasing population and a trend toward urbanization, society in England became increasingly complex. Law enforcement became truly a collective responsibility. If a man's next-door neighbor broke the law, the man was responsible for bringing the lawbreaker before the shire-reeve. This prompted the development of a system under which the hundred would decide yearly who would be responsible for maintaining law and order. Responsibility rotated among community members. It was inevitable that some people, not wanting to serve their turn, would seek other members of the hundred to serve in their place for pay. This was the beginning of the system of paid deputies appointed to be responsible for law and order. The paid deputy system was then formalized so that those whose turn it was to pay met and appointed the law enforcers. The abuse of citizen duty to serve as watchmen was pervasive, however, and led to the dregs of society, such as petty thieves and town drunks, serving as watchmen.

During the fourteenth century the office of justice of the peace was established to replace the shire-reeve. The justice of the peace was assisted by the constables and by three or four men knowledgeable of the country's laws. At first the justice of the peace was involved in both judicial matters and law enforcement, but later his powers became strictly judicial. He was responsible for settling matters of wages, prices, and conditions of labor and for pretrial hearings to determine if there was enough evidence to keep a man in jail to await trial. The justice of the peace eventually became the real power of local government (Lunt 1938).

During the fourteenth century, the shire-reeve was replaced by the justice of the peace.

With the passing of feudal times and the rise in the power of the church, the unit of local government in rural areas progressed from the hundred to the **parish,** that is, the area in which people lived who worshipped in a particular parish church. Once each year the parish appointed a person to be **parish constable** and to act as their law officer. This system of maintaining law and order in rural Britain lasted from the Middle Ages until the eighteenth century.

During the Middle Ages, the Parish Constable system was used for rural law enforcement; the Watch and Ward system was used for urban law enforcement.

Developments in urban England required a different system of law enforcement. With urbanization came commerce, industry, and a variety of buildings usually made of wood since England was primarily forest land. For purposes of fire prevention, the town guild appointed men (Watch and Ward) who patrolled at night on fire watch. They assumed the coincidental responsibility of preventing people from breaking into houses and shops.

In 1621 **habeas corpus** was established as the result of a wild party held in London. Habeas corpus is part of a Latin phrase that literally means "let the body be brought before the judge." The case making habeas corpus law in England involved a well-known rowdy lady, Alice Robinson, who threw a wild party. When the constable arrived and asked Alice and her guests to quiet down, she swore profusely at him. The constable arrested her, and a local justice of the peace committed her to jail. She was placed on a diet of black bread and water, forced to sleep on the bare floor, and was stripped and given fifty lashes. The worst of it was that Robinson was pregnant. When her case finally came to trial, the public was so indignant that Robinson was acquitted, the constable was sent to prison for arresting her without a warrant, and the justice of the peace was reprimanded. This case, in addition to several others, led to the passage of the Habeas Corpus Act in 1679.

In 1689, after numerous attacks on personal liberty, the English Parliament forced King James II to abdicate his throne. In addition, Parliament produced a Bill of Rights that contained the following provisions (Gardner 1985, p. 26):

> Suspending laws ... without consent of Parliament is illegal. Keeping a Standing Army within the Kingdom in Time of Peace unless it be with Consent of Parliament is against the law. Election of Members of Parliament ought to be free. Freedom of Speech ... ought not to be impeached or questioned.

In 1692, in response to steadily increasing crime, a system of *monetary reward* was instituted to encourage people to help apprehend thieves and bandits. The result was disappointing, however, for it led only to a great deal of blackmail and false accusations.

Although the Watch and Ward system was primitive and not too effective, it was adequate until the Industrial Revolution (1750) began. About the same time famine struck the rural areas, and large numbers of people moved from the country into the towns seeking work in weaving and knitting mills and in factories. Many, however, failed to find work, and England experienced much unemployment, poverty, and crime.

In addition, political extremists often aroused mobs and incited them to march upon Parliament. These mobs were usually unruly, destructive, and indifferent to the safety of local residents and their property. The government had no civil police force to deal with mob violence, so they ordered a magistrate to read the **riot act,** which permitted the magistrate to call the military to quell the riot.

The use of a military force to repress civil disobedience did not work very well. Soldiers hesitated to fire on their own townspeople, and the townspeople, who actually paid the soldiers' wages, resented being fired on by soldiers they had hired to protect them. Consequently, when the riot act was read and the military were called into action, citizen unrest usually mounted.

In addition to unemployment, poverty, and resentment against use of military force, the invention of gin and whiskey in the seventeenth century and the subsequent increase in the liquor trade also caused a great rise in violent crimes and theft.

The government responded to the increase in crime by improving street lighting, hiring more watchmen, and greatly increasing the severity of punishment for all kinds of crimes.

In 1736 a law was passed requiring every gin and whiskey seller and manufacturer to purchase exorbitantly priced licenses. This law did not stop the flow of gin and whiskey but instead greatly increased the corruption of the constables. Since the constables were often employed in the liquor trade, it was impossible for them to honestly enforce the regulations governing taverns and inns. Additionally, the London watchmen who were responsible for regulating the morals of the townspeople were highly susceptible to bribes and payoffs.

Henry Fielding and the Bow Street Runners

Around 1750 Henry Fielding, an English magistrate and novelist (author of *Tom Jones*), was instrumental in establishing the **Bow Street Runners,** the first detective unit in London and an indicator of the increasing problems faced by law enforcement officials.

The Bow Street Runners, first called "Thief-takers," were specially chosen men with reliable characters who were paid a weekly wage so they would not be tempted by bribes. Known for their incorruptibility, physical strength, and tenacity, they soon became the terror of all street gangs. Because of their skill and reputation, other agencies from throughout England often hired them. The most famous runner was Townsend, who was hired to guard the royal family and became a close friend of the king.

When these runners proved successful, other units were organized. Foot patrols of armed men guarded the city's streets during the day and a horse patrol combatted highway robbery on the main roads up to twenty-five miles from Bow Street.

Although the Bow Street Runners and patrols greatly improved control in the Bow Street area of London, other parts of London were overwhelmed by the impact of the Industrial Revolution. Machines were taking the place of many jobs, causing unemployment and poverty. The cities were developing into huge slums and the crime rate soared. Children were often trained to be thieves, and for the first time in England's history, juvenile delinquency became a problem. Citizens began to carry weapons, and the courts used long-term prison sentences, resulting in overcrowding in the jails and prisons. Punishments were also severe, with over 160 crimes punishable by death.

The Rookeries of London

As noted by Brantingham and Brantingham (1984, p. 298) the **rookeries** of London were dilapidated and teeming places (see Figure 1–3):

> London and other nineteenth-century English cities were marked by notorious criminal areas, some of which had been in place for centuries. These rookeries were slum criminal quarters, known to public and police alike as neighborhoods in which the homes of prostitutes, beggars, thieves, and killers were intermixed with those of the desperate urban poor. They were mazes of squalid hovels and houses carved into warrens of tiny rooms connected by secret doors, tunnels, catwalks, dark passages, and dank lanes. The rookeries sustained criminal social systems that provided schooling in crime for the young or the new-comers, fencing systems to purchase and resell stolen goods, and a protective code of silence in the face of police inquiries. . . .
>
> By the nineteenth century, the boundaries of the imperial metropolis lay far behind the ancient City limits: the City was just one of a number of municipalities

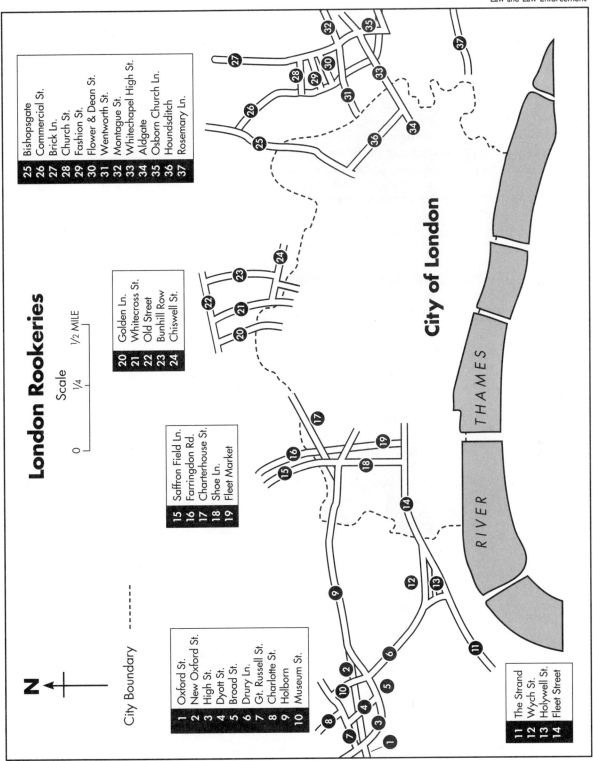

Figure 1–3   Distribution of the Principal London Rookeries

Source: J. J. Tobias, *Crime and Industrial Society in the 19th Century.* London: B.T. Batsford Limited, 1967,
p. 133. Reprinted with permission.

that together formed Greater London. Differences in the quality and character of public administration and the jealous way in which the different municipal constituents of the metropolis guarded their perogatives and liberties from encroachment by any of the others go far toward explaining this pattern.

Despite the rampant crime, however, most Londoners resisted an organized police force, seeing it as restricting their liberty. They had fought long and hard to overcome the historical abuse of military power by the English kings and resisted any return to centralized military power.

Then, in 1819 and 1820, two contrasting incidents occurred that helped people change their minds. The first incident was an attack by armed soldiers on a meeting of unemployed workers that left eleven people dead and hundreds injured. This incident, known as the Peterloo Massacre, was a vivid example of the result of using soldiers to maintain peace. In contrast, in the second incident the Bow Street Runners were able to break up a conspiracy to murder a number of government officials. When the conspirators were executed, people were well aware that actions by a group of professional peacekeepers could prevent a major insurrection.

In addition to rampant crime, Parliament was also justifiably concerned about poverty, unemployment, and general conditions. Five parliamentary commissions of inquiry met in London between 1780 and 1820 to determine what should be done about the public order. It was not until Sir Robert (Bobbie) Peel was appointed Home Secretary that the first really constructive proposal was brought before Parliament.

Peelian Reform

Sir Robert Peel, often referred to as the "father of modern policing," proposed a return to the Anglo-Saxon principle of individual community responsibility for preserving law and order. He proposed that London have a body of civilians appointed and paid by the community to serve as police officers. Parliament agreed and passed the Metropolitan Police Act of 1829, creating the Metropolitan Police of London.

The name *police*, introduced into England from France, is derived from the Greek word *polis* meaning "city." Originally, in continental Europe, the term included all state activities that had not been segregated into special administrative branches. By the middle of the eighteenth century, the scope of police activity had narrowed to two main classifications: security police, charged with preserving individuals from dangers threatening person or property, and welfare police, charged with fostering the public welfare by promoting interests beneficial to society.

Many of the fundamental principles of Peelian Reform are as applicable today as they were in 1829.

- Police must be stable, efficient, and organized militarily.
- Police must be under governmental control.
- The distribution of crime news is essential.
- The deployment of police strength by both time and area is essential.
- No quality is more indispensable to a policeman than a perfect command of temper; a quiet, determined manner has more effect than violent action.
- Good appearance commands respect.
- The securing and training of proper persons is at the root of efficiency.

- Public security demands that every police officer be given a number.
- Police headquarters should be centrally located and easily accessible.
- Policemen should be hired on a probationary basis.
- Police records are necessary to the correct distribution of police strength.

In addition, one of Peel's first steps was to introduce reform that abolished the death penalty for over one hundred offenses.

Peel's principles for reform called for local responsibility for law and order; appointed, paid civilians to assume this responsibility; and standards for these individuals' conduct and organization. His proposals resulted in the organization of the Metropolitan Police of London in 1829.

Although most of these principles make sense to us in the twentieth century, they were not readily accepted in nineteenth-century England. During the first few years of Peelian Reform, strong opposition was encountered. In addition to this opposition, Peel was faced with the problem of finding a building for the newly created London Police. He chose an abandoned building that had been built many years before for the Scottish nobility to use when they visited London. This building housed the London Metropolitan Police. It became known the world over as Scotland Yard, as immortalized by A. Conan Doyle in his Sherlock Holmes mysteries.

Peel eventually became a national hero, and his reforms led to increased status and prestige for all who entered a career in law enforcement. His principles also became the basis of police reform in many large cities in America.

Scotland Yard headquarters, 1890.

London Metropolitan Police (1829)

According to Dunham and Alpert (1989, p. 19):

> The London Metropolitan Police was a highly centralized agency. An extension of the national government, the police department was purposely removed from the direct political influence of the people. Furthermore, Sir Robert Peel recruited individuals who fit a certain mold. Peel insisted that a polite, aloof officer who was trained and disciplined according to strict guidelines would be best suited for the function of crime prevention.

As noted by Klockars (1985, p. 41), the entrance requirements for the "New Police" were minimal: "Candidates had to be at least 5'11" tall, under age 35, literate, reasonably healthy, and of good character." British police historian Critchley (1967, p. 52) suggests that: "From the start, the police was to be a homogeneous and democratic body in tune with the people, and drawing itself from the people."

Peel appointed Charles Rowan, an army officer, and Richard Mayne, a lawyer, to administer London's Metropolitan Police. To assure that the New Police would be politically neutral, Peel, Rowan, and Mayne imposed three major restraints on them (Klockars, p. 44): "They would be *unarmed* except for a small truncheon concealed beneath their coats; (2) they would be *uniformed*, and (3) they would be confined to *patrol* for the *prevention* of crime."

They were further controlled by the police administrators' ability to dismiss them, as frequently happened according to Lee (1971, p. 240): "Between 1830 and 1838 to hold the ranks of the New Police of London at a level of approximately 3,300 men required nearly 5,000 dismissals and more than 6,000 resignations, most of the latter not being altogether voluntary."

The London Metropolitan Police were uniformed for easy identification—top hats, three-quarter-length royal blue coats, and white trousers—and were armed only with truncheons. They were obviously not soldiers as they had no guns. They were (and still are) called "Bobbies" after Sir "Bobbie" Peel.

Unfortunately, the London Metropolitan Police were not popular. Soon after the force went on street duty in 1829, a London mob assembled, prepared to march on Parliament. A police sergeant and two constables asked the mob leaders to send their people home. The police, trained to be courteous but firm, did their job properly; however, the mob did not disperse. Instead they attacked the sergeant and constables, killing the sergeant and critically injuring the constables. A jury of London citizens, after hearing evidence clearly indicative of a cold, brutal murder, returned a verdict of justifiable homicide. In time, however, the effect of the police officers discharging their duties with professional integrity created a respect for the law that still exists in England.

City and Borough Police Forces (1835)

Broad public use of the steam engine and railways and better roads helped move many criminals from London to provincial cities such as Birmingham, Liverpool, and Manchester. Soon the citizens of these cities demanded some police organization similar to that of London. In 1835 Parliament enacted permissive legislation allowing (but not requiring) every city or borough (unincorporated township) over 20,000 people to form a police force. The act called for the town council, a body of elected representatives who administered the city's affairs, to appoint from its members a watch committee to (1) appoint a chief of police, (2) appoint the officers of the force, and (3) administer the force.

County Police Act (1839)

The counties had no collective system of local government larger than the individual parish, yet they, too, felt the need for an organized police force. This prompted Parliament to pass the County Police Act (1839) giving magistrates the responsibility to fix the strength of the force and to appoint and dismiss the chief constable. Unlike the borough counterpart, the parish magistrate, once appointed, had absolute rights of appointment over subordinates. The new force was paid for by citizens' taxes.

The County Police Act produced an uneven response. Only fifteen of the fifty-two counties had adopted it by the end of 1840. Reluctance to implement the legislation came from several sources, the most important being financial interests. The decision rested with the magistrates, the principal landowners in each county, and they had a vested interest in keeping taxes down.

Women Enter Law Enforcement

In 1883 the London Metropolitan Police appointed two women to supervise women convicts. Their numbers and functions later expanded.

In 1905 a woman was attached to the London Metropolitan Police force to conduct inquiries in cases involving women and children. Each year an increasing number of police matrons were hired.

Around 1914 considerable public concern arose in favor of employing women police as part of the organization to prevent and detect crime. The Penal Reform League passed a resolution urging the appointment of women police constables with powers equal to those of men constables in all county boroughs and the metropolitan boroughs of the County of London (Chapman and Johnston 1962).

Soon after, the Criminal Law Amendment Committee and the National Vigilance Association sent delegates to interview the secretary of state on the subject. Delegates were then appointed by the Women's Industrial Council to serve on the Parks Committee of the London Council.

Early in World War I, two separate movements for women police began. The Women Police Volunteers was formed and later came to be called the Women Police Service. In 1920 the group split into the Women's Auxiliary Service and the Women Patrols of the National Union of Women Workers of Great Britain and Ireland. The present official women police are largely a direct continuation of the Women Patrols (Chapman and Johnston 1962).

SUMMARY

Our current laws and the means by which they are enforced have their origins in the distant past, perhaps as far back as the cave dwellers. Law refers to all the rules of conduct established and enforced by the custom, authority, or legislation of a group, community, or country. A system of law and law enforcement began earlier than 2000 B.C. as a means of controlling human conduct and enforcing society's rules. Many features of our present system of law enforcement are borrowed from the Greeks, Romans, and particularly the English.

The English tithing system (groups of ten families) established the principle of collective responsibility for maintaining local law and order. If a law was broken, the Hue and Cry sounded. The Hue and Cry may be the origin of the general alarm and the citizen's arrest.

The constable was the first English police officer and, as such, had charge of the weapons and horses of the whole community. In response to a need for more regional law enforcement, the office of shire-reeve was established. The shire-reeve was the law enforcement agent for an entire county.

In 1066 William the Conqueror invaded England and changed the tithing system to the Frankpledge system, requiring loyalty to the king's law and mutual local responsibility for maintaining the peace. Under his rule the shire-reeves were limited to law enforcement, and separate judges were appointed to try cases. In effect, he separated the powers of law enforcement and the courts.

William's son, Henry I, became known as Henry the Lawmaker. His Leges Henrici made law enforcement a public matter and separated offenses into felonies and misdemeanors. Henry II established the jury system.

The next significant development was the Magna Carta, a precedent for democratic government and individual rights. The Magna Carta laid the foundation for:

- requiring rulers to uphold the law;
- forbidding taxation without representation;
- requiring due process of law, including trial by jury;
- providing safeguards against unfair imprisonment.

During the fourteenth century, the shire-reeve was replaced by the justice of the peace. Later, during the Middle Ages, the Parish Constable system was used for rural law enforcement; the Watch and Ward system was used for urban law enforcement. The government responded to an increase in crime by improving street lighting, hiring more watchmen, and greatly increasing the severity of punishment for all kinds of crime.

Of great importance to English law enforcement were the contributions of Sir Robert (Bobbie) Peel. Peel's principles for reform called for local responsibility for law and order; appointed, paid civilians to assume this responsibility; and standards for these individuals' conduct and organization. His proposals resulted in the organization of the first police force in England, the Metropolitan Police of London, established in 1829. In 1883 the London Metropolitan Police appointed two women to supervise women convicts. Their numbers and functions later expanded.

DISCUSSION QUESTIONS

1. What common problems have existed throughout the centuries for people in law enforcement?

2. How have these common problems been approached at different points in history?

3. Why was there no law enforcement during the daytime for many centuries?

4. Why did it take so long to develop a police force in England?

5. What parts of the Code of Hammurabi would not be applicable or accepted in contemporary society?

6. In today's society how has the power of the *posse commitatus* assisted and how has it worked against law enforcement?

7. The police des mouers was established to regulate prostitution. What methods do we use to control prostitution today?

8. At present, how does the government respond to increased crime in the United States in comparison to the responses in the seventeenth century?

9. The rookeries of London can be compared to what areas of cities in the United States today?

10. How many of Peel's principles still exist in today's police departments?

TERMS

Bow Street Runners, constable, Frankpledge system, habeas corpus, Hue and Cry, hundreds, law, Leges Henrici, Magna Carta, parish, parish constable system, police des mouers, red light district, reeve, riot act, rookeries, shire-reeve, shires, tithing, tithing system, Watch and Ward.

REFERENCES

Brantingham, P. and Brantingham P. *Patterns in Crime.* New York: Macmillan, 1984.

Chapman, S. G. and Johnston, Colonel T. E. St. *The Police Heritage in England and America.* East Lansing, Mich.: Michigan State University, 1962.

Critchley, T. A. *A History of Police in England and Wales.* Montclair, N.J.: Patterson Smith, 1967.

Dunham, R. G. and Alpert, G. P. *Critical Issues in Policing: Contemporary Issues.* Prospect Heights, Ill.: Waveland Press, 1989.

Gardner, T. J. *Basic Concepts of Criminal Law, Principles and Cases,* 3d ed. St. Paul, Minn.: West Publishing Company, 1985.

Hall, J. *Dictionary of Subjects and Symbols in Art.* New York: Harper & Row, 1974.

Klockars, C. B. *The Idea of Police.* Newbury Park, Calif.: Sage Publications, 1985.

Lee, M. *A History of Police in England.* Montclair, N.J.: Patterson Smith, 1971.

Lunt, W. E. *History of England.* New York: Harper & Brothers, 1938.

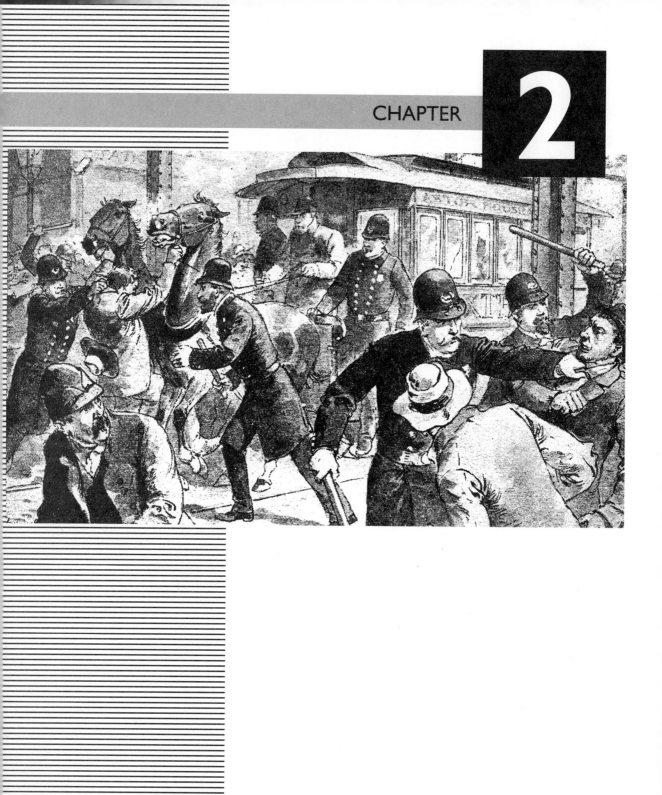

CHAPTER 2

The Evolution of Law Enforcement in the United States

The execution of the laws is more important than the making of them.
—**Thomas Jefferson**

Do You Know

What systems of law enforcement were brought from England to colonial New England and the South?

When and where the first modern American police force began and what it was modeled after?

What the vigilante movement was and why it occurred?

When and how state and federal law enforcement agencies originated in the United States?

Who the chief law enforcement officer at the federal and state level is?

What services the FBI provides?

What state agencies are involved in or offer assistance to law enforcement?

What functions state police often serve?

What two main types of county law enforcement are?

What the five levels of law enforcement are?

What three eras of policing have been identified? The main characteristics of each?

What effect the spoils system had in the 1900s?

What law enforcement organizational systems have been tried and have been most successful?

What the Pendleton Act accomplished?

How minority and women police officers were treated during the political era? What legislation caused this to change?

INTRODUCTION

When the English colonists came to America, they brought with them many traditions, including traditions in law enforcement. From the beginning they were concerned with avoiding anarchy. As noted by Gardner (1985, p. 26):

> As the *Mayflower* rode at anchor off Cape Cod, some of the passengers threatened to go out on their own, without any framework of government. To avoid this threat of anarchy, the *Mayflower Compact* [1620] agreed that: "We ... doe ... solemnly and mutually ... covenant and combine our selves together into a civil body politike for our better ordering and perservation ... and by vertue hereof to enact ... such just and equall lawes ... unto which we promise all due submission and obedience."

EARLY LAW ENFORCEMENT IN THE UNITED STATES

The early colonial American settlements relied heavily on self-policing to assure the peace. Communal pressure rather than formal policing was the backbone of law enforcement. The colonists were of similar background, most held similar religious beliefs, and there was actually little worth stealing. The seeds of vice and crime were present, however, as noted by political scientist David Perry (1973, p. 24):

> These colonists were far from the cream of European society; in many cases they represented the legal and religious castoffs. (Persons found guilty of criminal or religious offenses who were banished from Europe and exported to the New World.) Their migration served the dual purpose of removing socially undesirable persons from the Mother country and providing manpower for the outposts of imperial expansion. The governors of the new colonies were responsible for keeping such people in line.

Many features of British law enforcement were present in early American colonial settlements. In New England, where people depended on commerce and industry, the night watchman or constable served as protector of public order. In the South, where agriculture played a dominant role, the office of **sheriff** was established as the means of area law enforcement. Most watchmen and sheriffs were volunteers, but many were paid to serve in the place of others who were supposed to patrol as a civic duty.

New England adopted the night watchman or constable as the chief means of law enforcement; the South adopted the office of sheriff.

Many different types of law enforcement were tried in many different parts of the country. Almost all used some kind of night watch system, with little or no protection during the day. As might be expected, the fastest growing municipalities were the first to organize legal forces.

The First Police Forces

The first police forces in the United States were developed in Boston, New York, and Los Angeles.

Boston In 1631 the Boston court ordered a six-man force to be established to guard the city from sunset to sunup. This was the first night watch in

Judge Roy Bean dispensed frontier justice and cold beer in the Texas Territory west of the Pecos River.

colonial America. In 1636 a town watch was created. This watch consisted of a group of citizens appointed by the town council and stayed in effect for over two hundred years. During this time the services performed by the watch changed significantly. At first the primary function was to ring a bell in case of fire. In 1702 the police were to patrol the streets in silence; in 1735 they were required to call out the time of day and the weather.

In 1801 Boston became the first city in the United States to acquire a permanent night watch. These men were paid fifty cents a night. In 1807 the first police precincts were formed, and in 1838 a day force was created to supplement the night force.

New York   The first colonists in New York, then called New Amsterdam, were the Dutch. They settled on Manhattan Island's south end and were governed by Peter Minuit, director general of New Netherlands. In 1624 Minuit established the office of sheriff attorney to enforce the laws of the Dutch West India Company. The sheriff attorney was both police officer and prosecutor and was responsible for both civil and military laws. In 1632 Wouter van Tiller succeeded Minuit. Van Tiller instituted the whipping post from which lawbreakers were suspended to deter criminal activity.

In 1643 a "burgher guard" was formed to protect the colony. Then, in 1653 New Amsterdam became a city (population, eight hundred). The burgher guard was changed to a **rattle watch,** a group of night patrolling citizens armed with rattles to call for help. In 1658 the rattle watch was replaced by eight night watchmen who were paid to guard the city. These men were the first police force (Bailey 1989, p. 346).

In 1664 the British took over New Amsterdam and renamed it New York. Thirty years later the first uniformed police officers replaced the nighttime rattle watch, and four years after that New York's streets were lighted. In 1700 the mayor created a constable's watch.

The system of watchmen was very ineffective. Often the person on watch was sentenced to be a watchman as a form of punishment for a misdemeanor. In addition, citizens could avoid watch duty by hiring someone to take their places. This practice had its problems. Wealthy citizens came to rely on hiring others, and the men they hired were then hesitant to invoke their authority against the well-to-do. According to Richardson (1970, p. 10), by the mid-1700s New York City's night watch was described as follows:

> [a] parcel of idle, drinking, vigilant snorers, who never quell'd any nocturnal tumult in their lives; . . . but would, perhaps, be as ready to join in a burglary as any thief in Christendom.

Due to a continuing increase in crime during the daytime, New York City hired an assortment of watchmen, fire marshals, and bell ringers to patrol during the day and night. In 1844 a paid day watch was established, consisting of sixteen officers appointed by the mayor. At this time the night watch consisted of 1,100 watchmen and was completely separate from the day force. As might be expected, friction existed between the day and night forces, and it became an impossible arrangement, totally incapable of combatting the growing lawlessness in the city.

Legislators from New York City visited the London Metropolitan Police Department and were so highly impressed that, in 1844, New York City followed the pattern set in England fifteen years earlier by Sir Robert Peel and established a round-the-clock, paid police force.

In 1844 New York City established the first modern American city police force, modeled after London's Metropolitan Police Department.

Soon other police forces similar to that in New York developed, including forces in Chicago, Cincinnati, New Orleans, Philadelphia, Boston, Baltimore, and San Francisco.

In spite of patterning themselves after the London Metropolitan Police, New York police officers vigorously protested against wearing uniforms. Not until twelve years later did the New York police adopt a full police uniform and become the first uniformed law enforcement agency in the country. Likewise, although Henry Fielding established the Bow Street Runners (the first detective unit) in 1750, it was over a hundred years later before American police

In 1856 New York adopted a full uniform for each ward.

agencies recognized a need for detective units. In 1866 Detroit established the first detective bureau, followed by New York in 1882, and Cincinnati in 1886.

Other important differences from the London police were that police in the United States were armed and they were under local, not national, control. As noted by Dunham and Alpert (1989, pp. 19–20): "Unlike the London police, American police systems followed the style of local and municipal governments.... The police were an extension of different political factions, rather than an extension of city government."

Los Angeles   In 1850 California became a state and Los Angeles incorporated as a city with a population of 1,610. During its first year the city elected a mayor, a city marshal, and a sheriff. According to Bailey (1989, pp. 310–16):

> The duties assumed by the sheriff and marshal included the collection of local taxes. The sheriff's obligations required him to traverse a vast area on horseback, fighting bands of Indians and marauding desperadoes. Lacking paid assistants, the marshal was permitted to deputize citizens whenever necessary to maintain order.

In 1853 the city council established a police force of one hundred volunteers, the first official police officers, and called them the Los Angeles Rangers. Four years later they were replaced by the Los Angeles City Guards, who were charged with maintaining the peace. Finally, in 1869, the police force changed from a voluntary organization to a paid department.

The first mounted police force was formed in 1875, headed by Chief Jacob F. Gerkins. Bailey (1989, p. 310) described the duties of Chief Gerkins and his patrol officers as the following:

> The enforcement of laws prohibiting the grazing or herding of cattle in the streets, the sale of opium except for scientific or medical purposes and the speed of steam trains at more than six miles an hour within city limits. Officers were also instructed to pick up loose paper blown about the streets, lest it cause horses to run away.

Evolution of the City Police

When city police were first established, their only contact with their departments was face-to-face meetings or messengers. During the 1850s, however, telegraph networks linked police headquarters directly with their districts, making unnecessary the daily meetings between the captains and the commissioners. Several decades later a modified telegraph system linked the patrol officers directly to the station. A fire alarm system, first introduced in Boston, was adopted for police use. Call boxes placed on city street corners became a common sight. These boxes were equipped with a simple lever that signaled the station that the officers were at their posts. A bell system was then added that allowed the patrol officers to use a few simple signals to call an ambulance, a "slow wagon" for routine duties, or a "fast wagon" for emergencies. The introduction of a special "Gamewell" telephone into the call box in 1880 made this a truly two-way communication system, greatly improving the contact between the patrol officers and their station houses.

The Civil War brought new problems of social control. Municipal forces tried to meet these problems by organizing new divisions and specializing the force. As centers of population became increasingly urbanized and fringe areas became incorporated suburbs of the hub city, a trend developed to add forces to the police organization rather than to centralize or consolidate them. Consequently, newly developed fringe cities had their own forces, which fostered complex, uncoordinated relationships, compartmentalization, and inefficiency.

Although the cities in the United States developed police departments and maintained a certain level of law and order, this was not the case in many areas of the country, especially the frontiers. In such areas, Americans came to rely upon vigilante groups to maintain law and order.

The Vigilante Movement

Klockars (1985, p. 30) suggests: "American vigilante movements grew up in response to a typical American problem: the absence of effective law and order in frontier regions." He notes that at least 326 but possibly as many as 500 vigilante movements were organized between 1767 and 1900.

The **vigilante** movement refers to taking the law into one's own hands in the absence of effective policing.

The first American vigilante movement occurred from 1767 to 1769 in South Carolina. Unlike other areas along the Eastern seaboard where expansion was slow and orderly, the South Carolina Piedmont was newly settled and then devastated by the Cherokee Indian War. As noted by Brown (1991, p. 61):

> The disorder in the South Carolina back country of the 1760's was typical of later American frontier areas.... Outlaws, runaway slaves, and mulattoes formed their own communities where they enjoyed their booty.... By 1766 and 1767 the back country was in the grip of a "crime wave," and the outlaws were almost supreme.

Since there was no sheriff or court, "respectable settlers of average or affluent means" organized as **regulators** in 1767. These regulators attacked and broke up the outlaw gangs and restored order. Having accomplished their mission, they disbanded in 1769.

As noted by Brown (p. 60): "An American tradition had begun, for, as the pioneers moved across the Appalachian Mountains, the regulator-vigilanted impulse followed the sweep of settlement toward the Pacific." These South Carolina regulators were typical of the vigilante movements that followed. According to Brown: "Vigilante movements (as distinguished from ephemeral lynch mobs) are thus identifiable by the two main characteristics of (1) regular (though illegal) organization and (2) existence for definite (though possibly short) period of time."

Another characteristic of the vigilante movement was that usually the leader was one of the most powerful men in the community, thus making the movement highly respectable. According to Klockars (1985, p. 31): "Two presidents (Andrew Jackson and Theodore Roosevelt), eight state governors (including Leland Stanford, Sr., founder of Stanford University), and four U.S. Senators had either been vigilantes or expressed strong support for vigilante movements."

The vigilante tradition was strong, not only because of ineffective or non-existent law enforcement, but also because of an uneven judicial system and a lack of jails. According to Brown (p. 66):

> Whenever possible outlaws would obtain false witnesses in their behalf, pack juries, bribe officials, and, in extreme cases, intimidate the entire system; judges, juries, and law enforcement officials.... The guilty, when charged, utilized every loophole for the evasion of punishment. Compounding the problem was the genuinely heavy financial burden involved in maintaining an adequate "police establishment" and judicial system in a sparsely settled and economically under-developed frontier area.

To many pioneers, the only solution to these problems was vigilantism. W.N. Byers, a Denver, Colorado vigilante of 1860, is said to have reminisced (Brown, p. 66): "We never hanged on circumstantial evidence. I have known a great many such executions, but I don't believe one of them was ever unjust. But when they were proved guilty, they were always hanged. There was no getting out of it. No, there were no appeals in those days; no writs of errors; no attorneys' fees; no pardon in six months. Punishment was swift, sure and certain."

The vigilante movement was strong evidence of American value of law and order and the desire to be rid of those who would break the law. It was also evidence of a basic paradox in the illegal means used to the desired end. As noted by Brown (p. 72): "Perhaps the most important result of vigilantism has not been its social-stabilizing effect but the subtle way in which it persistently undermined our respect for law by its repeated insistence that there are times when we may choose to obey the law or not."

As the country grew and its society became more complex, federal and state agencies were established to meet needs which could not be met at the local level.

THE ESTABLISHMENT OF FEDERAL AGENCIES

Several federal law enforcement agencies were created by Congress to meet demands created by the changing conditions of the nation.

The oldest federal agency is the United States Marshals Office, created in 1789. Thirteen United States Marshals were assigned to President George Washington's attorney general. As the nation began to grow westward, the United States Marshals were the main law enforcement in the territories. When the Civil War ended (1865) and most of the territories had become states, the United States Marshals became the bailiffs of the United States District Courts, where violations of federal crimes are tried.

The Justice Department established other federal law enforcement agencies such as the Immigration and Naturalization Service (1891), of which the Border Patrol is a well-known division.

The Treasury Department established federal law enforcement agencies that are still well known today. The Secret Service was created in 1865 to control the flood of counterfeit currency bankrupting the war effort. After President McKinley was assassinated in 1901, the Secret Service was authorized to protect the president and his family.

Another well-known federal agency established within the Treasury Department was the Internal Revenue Service (1862). Its famous Intelligence Division agents' income tax evasion cases brought long prison sentences to such infamous criminals as Al Capone, Vito Genovese, and many others.

Among the earliest federal law enforcement agencies were the United States Marshals Office, the Immigration and Naturalization Service, the Secret Service, and the Internal Revenue Service.

Federal agents fulfill important responsibilities. Intelligence agents produce and disseminate information on foreign and domestic areas which affect national security. Investigative agents conduct investigations to determine compliance with federal laws. They carry guns, make arrests, and are usually enforcement oriented. Most federal agencies are attached to specific departments of the executive branch of government and have duties confined to the interests of the parent department.

The Department of Justice

The Department of Justice is the largest law firm in the country, representing the citizens in enforcing the law. It plays a significant role in protecting citizens through its efforts for effective law enforcement, crime prevention, crime detection, and prosecution and rehabilitation of offenders. It also conducts all suits in the Supreme Court that concern the United States.

The attorney general is head of the Department of Justice and the chief law officer of the federal government.

The Department of Justice's law enforcement agencies include the Federal Bureau of Investigation, the Federal Drug Enforcement Administration, United States Marshals, the Immigration and Naturalization Service, and the Bureau of Prisons.

The Federal Bureau of Investigation (FBI)   Created as the Bureau of Investigation, this agency was renamed the Federal Bureau of Investigation in 1935. Its national headquarters in Washington, D.C., maintains field offices in strategic cities in the United States and its possessions.

The FBI is the primary investigative agency of the federal government. Its special agents have jurisdiction over more than 200 federal crimes. They are responsible for general investigations, both criminal and civil, and for domestic intelligence dealing with the internal security of the nation. FBI agents are not subjected to the same demands for service that local police officers are: they do not handle drunks, answer domestic calls, respond to medical emergencies, or deal with deviant persons, which are the most frequent local problems of the community.

The Federal Bureau of Investigation's responsibilities include investigating espionage, interstate transportation of stolen property, kidnapping; unlawful flight to avoid prosecution, confinement, or giving testimony; sabotage, piracy of aircraft and other crimes aboard aircraft; bank robbery and embezzlement; and enforcement of the Civil Rights Acts.

The FBI's four investigative priorities are organized crime, foreign counterintelligence, white-collar crime, and terrorism. In addition to previous responsibilities, the FBI has been given further obligations under the Foreign Corrupt Practices Act of 1977, the Foreign Intelligence Surveillance Act of 1978, and the highly publicized Parental Kidnapping Prevention Act of 1980. Under this federal statute, the FBI's traditional jurisdiction over crimes involving unlawful flight to avoid prosecution has been extended to include parental kidnappers.

In 1982 the United States Attorney General assigned the bureau jurisdiction to investigate federal drug offenses. This significantly increased the FBI's involvement in major narcotic investigations and provided assistance to the Drug Enforcement Administration in a massive effort to deal with the serious drug problems in the United States.

In addition to these numerous responsibilities, the FBI provides valuable services to law enforcement agencies throughout the country.

The *Identification Division* was established in 1924 as a result of the tremendous value of fingerprint identification data. The FBI is the central repository for fingerprint information; over 22,000 agencies contribute to and may obtain information from it.

Data from the identification records are furnished to law enforcement and governmental agencies at the federal, state, county, and local levels for official use only. Wanted notices, periodically distributed by the FBI at the request of other law enforcement agencies, frequently result in the apprehension of dangerous criminals. The Identification Division is not restricted to criminal matters, however; many missing persons have been located, and victims of amnesia and homicides have been identified.

The Identification Division also maintains a disaster squad to assist in identifying victims of disasters such as explosions, storms, and plane crashes in which fingerprints are often the only means of identifying victims.

The *FBI Laboratory,* established in 1932, is the largest, most effective criminal laboratory in the world. Its facilities are available without cost to any city, county, state, or federal law enforcement agency in the country. Physical evidence obtained in a criminal investigation is examined not only to support evidence against a suspect but also to establish the innocence of accused persons. Included in the laboratory's services are identification of firearms, shoe prints, and tire prints; mineral analyses; and examination of blood, documents, hairs, fibers, and poisons.

The *National Crime Information Center (NCIC),* established in 1967, is a complex, computerized, electronic data exchange network developed to complement computerized systems already in existence and those planned by local and state law enforcement agencies.

Records on file in the **NCIC** concern wanted persons, stolen vehicles, vehicles used in the commission of felonies, stolen or missing license plates, stolen guns, and other stolen items that are serially identifiable such as television sets, boat motors, and so on. The reservoir of scientifically stored data on criminal activities gathered by federal, state, and local law enforcement agencies gives the street officer of any law enforcement agency in any part of the country up-to-the-minute information upon request in a matter of seconds.

Uniform Crime Reports (UCR) is another service provided by the FBI. Since 1930, by an act of Congress, the FBI has served as a national clearinghouse for United States crime statistics. States report their monthly crime statistics to the FBI, which in turn releases information semiannually and annually regarding all crimes reported to them.

Crimes are categorized by their seriousness and their frequency. Part I crimes consist of murder, forcible rape, aggravated assault, robbery, burglary, larceny/theft, arson, and motor vehicle theft. Part II crimes consist of forgery, prostitution, narcotics, and the like. Uniform Crime Reports give law enforcement administrators valuable information related to crime rates in similar communities, the number of arrests, and clearance rates. The FBI reports are valuable in assessing needed workers, equipment, and budget increases.

The FBI Uniform Crime Reports seek to (1) measure the reporting trends of serious crime, (2) record the volume of crime, and (3) determine significant police matters related to crime such as number of employees per thousand capita, the number of officers assaulted each year, the number of officers killed each year, and the types of action that caused the assaults or deaths.

The diverse character of the bureau's work makes it necessary to have regular contact with police at every level of government.

A forensic lab technician samples for blood and semen stain evidence. The stains are transferred to filter paper, chemicals are applied, and the stain color change is noted.

Federal Drug Enforcement Administration (FDEA) Before 1973, many fragmented government agencies pursued various courses of action in combatting dangerous drugs. In 1973 the Bureau of Narcotics and Dangerous Drugs (BNDD), the Office for Drug Abuse Law Enforcement, the Office of National Narcotics Intelligence, and the drug and investigative and intelligence units of the Bureau of Customs were merged into the Federal Drug Enforcement Administration.

Narcotics agents seek to stop the flow of drugs at their source, both domestic and foreign, and to assist state and local police in preventing illegal drugs from reaching local communities. They become involved in surveillance, raids, interviewing witnesses and suspects, searching for evidence, and seizure of contraband goods.

The FDEA is charged with the full responsibility for prosecuting suspected violators of federal drug laws. They have liaison with law enforcement officials of foreign governments and highly trained agents stationed in all major United States cities and in thirty countries throughout the world. The FDEA also regulates the legal manufacture of drugs and other controlled substances under the Controlled Substances Act of 1970.

The FDEA maintains six regional laboratories throughout the country to accumulate up-to-date information regarding drugs under its jurisdiction. This information is distributed to law enforcement agencies, allowing them to better cope with drug abuse problems and their related effects.

The federal government recognized the existence of a drug problem in this country nearly sixty-five years ago. Early government response, embodied in the Harrison Narcotic Act of 1914, was directed exclusively at controlling the supply of dangerous drugs. The Harrison Act established federal control over the supply, distribution, and use of narcotics. But almost no attention was given at the federal level to treating and rehabilitating drug users until the early 1930s, when the United States Public Health Service Hospitals at Lexington, Kentucky, and Fort Worth, Texas, were established to treat drug addicts.

The United States Marshals   In 1789 Congress created the office of United States Marshal. United States Marshals are appointed by the president with the approval of the Senate, as recommended by the attorney general, for a period of four years. The first marshals were appointed by President George Washington.

Each marshal's office has a staff of deputy marshals to carry out its functions and responsibilities. The functions of most deputy marshals are more enforcement than investigative. They are responsible for (1) seizing property in both criminal and civil matters to satisfy judgments issued by a federal court, (2) providing physical security for United States courtrooms and protection for federal judges, jurors, and attorneys, (3) transporting federal prisoners to federal institutions when transferred or sentenced by a federal court, and (4) protecting government witnesses whose testimony might jeopardize their safety. Such witnesses are protected by the government by being salaried, relocated in other cities, and provided with new identities. United States Marshals presently have some jurisdiction over federal fugitive investigations.

Immigration and Naturalization Service (INS)   The Immigration and Naturalization Service has border patrol agents who serve throughout the United States, Canada, Mexico, Bermuda, Nassau, Puerto Rico, the Philippines, and Europe. They conduct investigations, detect violations of immigrant and nationality laws, and determine whether aliens may enter or remain in the United States. It also has immigration inspectors who are responsible for detecting people who violate immigration and nationality laws. They work with border patrol agents and other investigators to determine if an applicant can enter the United States.

The extensive activities of the border patrol have resulted in many arrests for smuggling contraband and aliens into the United States. Searches for smuggled aliens are often made of automobiles, airplanes, and boats. The border patrol uses primarily airplanes, boats, and vehicles to deter illegal smuggling. Air-to-ground operations and searches of freight trains traveling between the United States and Mexico are common.

The Bureau of Prisons   The Bureau of Prisons is an integral part of the federal criminal justice system. It is responsible for the care and custody of persons convicted of federal crimes and sentenced to federal penal institutions. Correctional officers coordinate work assignments, enforce rules and regulations within institutions, and carry out plans developed for correctional treatment and modification of inmates' attitudes. The bureau operates a nationwide system of maximum, medium, and minimum security prisons, halfway houses, and community program offices.

The Department of the Treasury

The Department of the Treasury also has several agencies directly involved in law enforcement activities. Law enforcement agencies under the jurisdiction of the Department of the Treasury include the Bureau of Customs, the Internal Revenue Service, the Secret Service, and the Bureau of Alcohol, Tobacco, and Firearms Tax.

The Bureau of Customs   The Bureau of Customs has agents stationed primarily at ports of entry to the United States, where people and/or goods enter and leave. Customs agents investigate frauds on customs revenue and the smuggling of merchandise and contraband into or out of the United States. Customs agents have authority to conduct investigations and searches on all ships registered under United States laws.

Customs is active in suppressing the traffic in illegal narcotics and works in close cooperation with the Federal Drug Enforcement Administration. Customs patrol officers maintain uniformed and plainclothes surveillance at docks and airports.

The Internal Revenue Service (IRS)   The Internal Revenue Service, established in 1862, is the largest bureau of the Department of the Treasury. Its mission is to encourage the highest degree of voluntary compliance with the tax laws and regulations. Internal Revenue Service agents investigate willful tax evasion, tax fraud, and the activities of gamblers and drug peddlers.

The bureau has three divisions: Examination, Collection, and Criminal Investigation. Examination staff selects and audits tax returns of individuals and corporations. Collection staff includes revenue officers and field workers who contact delinquent taxpayers. Criminal Investigation staff includes special agents who conduct investigations, make arrests, provide armed escorts, protect other employees as well as government property, and assist Secret Service agents in protecting the president and other public officials.

The United States Secret Service   The Secret Service was established in 1865 to fight currency counterfeiters. In 1901 it was given the responsibility of protecting the president of the United States, the president's family members, the president-elect, and the vice-president.

The Secret Service has two major law enforcement functions: to suppress counterfeiting and to suppress forgery of government checks and bonds. It has other duties, too, such as investigating United States financial institutions. In their efforts to suppress counterfeiting and forgery, agents rely heavily on scientific investigation. To aid the agents, the Bureau of Engraving and Printing in Washington maintains a laboratory with modern scientific crime detection equipment. From the examinations conducted at the laboratory, the Secret Service gets valuable information that often leads its agents to the successful conclusion of cases.

The Secret Service is also responsible for investigating threats against the president. In 1976 the Secret Service became responsible for protecting presidential candidates as a result of threats against several of them and the actual shooting of presidential candidate, Governor George Wallace of Alabama.

One vital function of the Secret Service is to protect the president of the United States.

In addition to Secret Service special agents, two uniformed groups are under the control and direction of the service: the Secret Service Uniformed Division and the Treasury Police Force.

The *Secret Service Uniformed Division* protects the executive mansion and its grounds. Officers assigned to the Secret Service Uniformed Division are highly trained in techniques for identifying potential threats to the president and in self-defense tactics.

The *Treasury Police Force* protects the Treasury Building and the Treasury Annex in Washington. The Treasury Building has 475 rooms and covers the greater part of two city blocks. Beneath this building are safety vaults where the nation's money and valuable papers are kept. The Treasury Police Force is assigned to the continuous protection of the immense sums in the United States Treasury.

The Bureau of Alcohol, Tobacco, and Firearms Tax (BATF)   The Bureau of Alcohol, Tobacco, and Firearms Tax, an enforcement arm of the Department of the Treasury, is primarily a licensing and investigative agency involved in federal tax violations.

The Firearms Division enforces the Gun Control Act of 1968, which deals with the manufacture, sale, transfer, and possession of restricted firearms in the United States, including the illegal possession of automatic weapons, machine guns, and submachine guns by persons other than antique collectors.

The bureau also regulates interstate commerce in all types of guns to or from foreign countries. In addition, they collect the taxes of United States importers, manufacturers, and dealers of firearms. The bureau maintains a close relationship with other federal, state, and local enforcement agencies so that gun control laws are rigidly enforced.

The objectives of its criminal enforcement activity are to eliminate illegal possession and use of firearms, destructive devices, and explosives; to suppress the traffic in illicit distilled spirits; to enforce the criminal violation and forfeiture aspects of the federal wagering laws; and to cooperate with state and local enforcement agencies to reduce crime and violence (Office of the Federal Register 1976).

Other Federal Law Enforcement Agencies

Although the majority of federal law enforcement agencies are within the Department of Justice and the Department of the Treasury, other federal agencies are also directly involved in law enforcement activities such as the United States Postal Inspectors, the Coast Guard, military police of the armed forces, and investigators and intelligence agents and security officers for other federal agencies.

United States Postal Inspectors enforce federal laws pertaining to mailing prohibited items such as explosives, obscene matter, and articles likely to injure or cause damage. Any mail that may prove to be libelous, defamatory, or threatening can be excluded from being transported by the postal service. Postal inspectors protect the mails and recipients of mail. They also investigate any frauds perpetrated through the mails such as chain letters, gift enterprises, and similar schemes. The postmaster general is also authorized to prevent the delivery of mail to persons who might be using the mails to conduct a fraudulent business.

The *United States Coast Guard* assists local and state agencies that border the oceans, lakes, and national waterways. They have been actively involved in preventing the smuggling of narcotics into this country. A recent challenge of the Coast Guard has been dealing with the boat people attempting to land in the United States without authorization.

The *armed forces* also have law enforcement responsibilities. The uniformed divisions are known as the Military Police in the Army, the Shore Patrol in the Navy, and the Security Police in the Marine Corps and Air Force. Military police are enlisted personnel and officers; civilians do not serve in the uniformed military police units. Usually, these military police must not only meet all enlistment requirements of the service but also must show an aptitude for police work, must score well on the entrance examination, and must meet certain physical requirements. The military police are primarily concerned with the physical security of the various bases under their control. Within each operation, the security forces control criminal activity, court martials, discipline, desertions, and the confinement of prisoners. In time of war they are responsible for prisoners of war as well as custodial care and movement of refugees.

THE ESTABLISHMENT OF STATE AGENCIES

In 1835, when Texas was still a republic, the Texas provisional government established the Texas Rangers. The Texas Rangers were actually a military unit, established into three companies responsible for border patrol. The apprehension of Mexican cattle rustlers was a primary task (Folley 1980, p. 88).

In 1874 the Texas Rangers were commissioned as police officers in Texas. At that time there were 450 Rangers, and their duties included tracking down murderers, robbers, smugglers, and mine bandits.

The Texas Rangers were the first agency similar to our present-day state police.

Massachusetts was next to establish a state law enforcement agency by appointing a small force of state officers in 1865 to control vice within the state. The state also granted them general police powers; therefore, Massachusetts is usually credited with establishing the first law enforcement agency with general police authority throughout the state.

Most state police agencies established before the twentieth century were created in response to a limited need such as the control of vice. This was not the case in Pennsylvania.

The first modern state police agency was the Pennsylvania Constabulary, which originated in 1905 to meet several needs. As noted by Folley (1980, p. 66), the Pennsylvania Constabulary (1) provided the governor an executive arm to assist him in accomplishing his responsibilities, (2) provided a means to quell riots occurring during labor disputes in the coal regions, and (3) improved law enforcement services in the rural portions of the state where county officials were generally ineffective. Governor Pennypacker vividly describes the rationale for such a state agency (Mayo 1917, pp. 5–6):

> In the year 1903, when I assumed the office of chief executive of the state, I found myself thereby invested with supreme executive authority. I found that no power existed to interfere with me in my duty to enforce the laws of the state, and that by the same token, no conditions could release me from my duty so to do. I then looked about me to see what instruments I possessed wherewith to accomplish this bounden obligation—what instruments on whose loyalty and obedience I could truly rely. I perceived three such instruments—my private secretary, a very small man; my woman stenographer; and the janitor. . . . So I made the state police.

Humorous as it may sound, there was a large element of truth in the governor's thinking. Further, the labor riots were real and had to be faced. Perhaps most important, however, was the emphasis on rural law enforcement and the establishment of a uniformed mounted force offering protection in even the most remote areas of Pennsylvania.

The first modern state police agency was the Pennsylvania Constabulary, which originated in 1905 to meet several needs.

Although they were organized originally for the purpose of and functioned as strike-breakers, the Pennsylvania state police served as a model for other states and heralded the advent of modern state policing.

Many of the federal agencies have state counterparts.

State agencies with law enforcement responsibilities include state bureaus of investigation and apprehension and state fire marshal divisions as well as departments of natural resources, driver and vehicle services divisions, and departments of human rights.

Office of the State Attorney General

The attorney general is the chief legal counsel for the state. This office provides representation and advice to agencies in the executive branch of state government. The attorney general proposes and drafts legislation on a variety of subjects and assures that all state laws are adequately and uniformly enforced. This office also supervises district attorneys and sheriffs.

In addition to an antitrust division and a consumer protection division, the attorney general's office has a criminal division, which conducts criminal appeals, advises local prosecutors on the conduct of criminal trials, and helps develop and prosecute certain criminal cases, particularly those of organized crime and white-collar crime.

The attorney general's opinions office provides information to state and local officials on effects and requirements of state laws when laws either appear to conflict or are unclear in their application.

The state attorney general is the chief law enforcement officer at the state level. This office usually includes an antitrust division, a consumer protection division, a criminal division, and an opinions office.

State Bureau of Investigation and Apprehension

States vary in the organization and function of agencies that offer support to other law enforcement agencies in the state. They usually are organized to assist local law enforcement officials. The Bureau of Investigation and Apprehension places investigators throughout the state to help investigate major crimes and organized criminal activities; help investigate the illegal sale or possession of narcotics and prohibited drugs; conduct police science training courses for peace officers; provide scientific examination of crime scenes and laboratory analysis of evidence; and maintain a criminal justice information and telecommunications system. The bureau also provides statistical information on crimes and crime trends in the state.

State Fire Marshal Division

Designated state fire marshals investigate suspicious and incendiary fire origins, fire fatalities, and large-loss fires; tabulate fire statistics; and provide education, inspection, and training programs for fire prevention.

The *Fire Prevention Section* provides information on the state's Uniform Fire Code, removal of combustible materials, correction of fire hazards, fire prevention, and general information on smoke/heat detectors, fire alarms, fire extinguishers, and other fire protection appliances.

The *Inspection and Investigation Section* organizes investigation of all fires of suspicious and incendiary origin, large-loss fires, and fire fatalities. The section also conducts ongoing inspection of public and private schools, state hospitals, convalescent and other special purpose homes, hotels, rooming houses and other multiple dwellings, dry-cleaning establishments, motion picture theaters, places of assembly, and all installations where petroleum products, liquefied petroleum gas, and natural gas are manufactured, stored, or distributed.

The *Fire Prevention Awareness Section* identifies problem fire areas, inspects fires and buildings to guarantee fire safety standards, conducts public awareness programs, and maintains contact with local fire departments.

State Department of Natural Resources (Fish, Game, and Watercraft)

Some states combine fish, game, and watercraft under one division, a Department of Natural Resources, which enforces all laws and rules under its jurisdiction including hunting, fishing, and trapping laws and licenses and laws on the operation of watercraft. In some states the department is responsible for the firearms training laws. The division may hold auction sales to dispose of furs, firearms, and hunting, fishing, and trapping equipment confiscated from violators of fish and game laws.

Conservation officers investigate complaints about nuisance wildlife, misuse of public lands and waters, violations of state park rules, and unlawful appropriation of state-owned timber. Conservation officers also dispose of big game animals struck by motor vehicles, assist state game managers on wildlife census projects, enforce wild-rice harvesting rules, and assist in identifying needed sites for public access to lakes and streams.

The department also issues resident and nonresident boat licenses and licenses for hunting, fishing, and trapping.

Driver and Vehicle Services Division

The *Motor Vehicle Section* of the Driver and Vehicle Services Division registers motor vehicles, issues ownership certificates, answers inquiries, returns defective applications received through the mail, licenses motor vehicle dealers, supplies record information to the public, and in some states, registers bicycles.

The *Driver's License Section* tests, evaluates, and licenses all drivers throughout the state; maintains accurate records of each individual driver including all violations and accidents occurring anywhere in the United States and Canada; interviews drivers whose record warrants possible revocation, suspension, or cancellation; records the location of every reported accident; assists in driver education efforts; and administers written and road tests to applicants.

The Department of Human Rights

The Department of Human Rights enforces the Human Rights Act, which prohibits discrimination on the basis of race, color, creed, religion, national origin, sex, marital status, status with regard to public assistance or disability in employment, housing, public accommodations, public service, and education. It is also responsible for current affirmative action laws. It investigates and conciliates discrimination complaints. When conciliation is not possible, it settles the complaint through legal proceedings.

State Police and State Highway Patrol

The most visible form of state law enforcement is the state police, who often have general police powers and enforce all state laws, and state highway patrols, who focus their attention on the operation of motor vehicles on public highways and freeways.

Each state police agency differs, depending on its history and evolving law enforcement needs. From the Texas Rangers in 1835 to the present, new agencies have been formed and old agencies reorganized to meet the changing requirements of the states.

Some state police enforce all state laws; others enforce only traffic laws on highways and freeways and are usually designated as state highway patrol.

Usually *state police agencies* do not work within municipalities that have their own forces, except on request. These state forces generally do not enter local labor, political, or other mass disturbances or potentially disastrous situations unless asked by the local sheriff or police chief.

Most *highway patrol agencies* enforce state traffic laws and all laws governing operation of vehicles on public highways in the state. They usually operate in uniform, drive distinctively marked patrol cars and motorcycles, and engage in such activities as (1) enforcing laws regulating the use of vehicles, (2) maintaining preventive patrol on the highways, (3) regulating traffic movements and relieving congestion, (4) investigating traffic accidents, and (5) making surveys and studies of accidents and enforcement practices to improve traffic safety (Adams 1980).

The Michigan State Police and the Pennsylvania State Police are examples of agencies with general police powers. In contrast, Florida's Highway Patrol deals with traffic, while the Florida Department of Law Enforcement conducts investigations. Similarly, the Minnesota Highway Patrol directs its primary attention to enforcing traffic laws, while the Minnesota Bureau of Criminal Apprehension limits its function to investigative and enforcement functions at the state level.

In California, the Department of the California Highway Patrol is responsible for enforcing traffic laws, investigating traffic accidents, and rendering aid to motorists on the state and interstate highways. The California State Police are responsible for protecting only state property. They protect the state capitol and grounds as well as other state government buildings located throughout the state.

In addition, some highway patrol agencies coordinate the activity and maintain records on commercial vehicle enforcement, maintain public scales on the highways, inspect all school buses, and investigate accidents involving school buses throughout the state. Licensing or registration of official smog-control devices or headlights and other safety equipment installations, as well as inspection stations, may also be functions performed by a state highway patrol.

A governor may send state highway patrol or state police personnel to a locality to preserve the peace. This occurred in Mississippi and other southern states during mob actions prompted by efforts to racially integrate public schools. On two such occasions (Little Rock, Arkansas, in 1957 and Oxford, Mississippi, in 1962), National Guard units and regular United States Army military personnel were ordered by federal authorities to help state and local police maintain civil order.

The increasing responsibilities of state police are considerable. They often work in cooperation with the National Guard to restore order in mass disturbances. They have assumed responsibility from county sheriffs for policing traffic on major highways, and they assist the sheriff or small-town police officer in solving crimes requiring the use of specialized equipment. Further, many state police or highway patrol organizations administer the duties of the state fire marshal's office.

THE DEVELOPMENT OF COUNTY AGENCIES

The two main types of county law enforcement agencies are the county sheriff and the county police.

The County Sheriff

Many state constitutions have designated the sheriff as the chief law enforcement officer of the county. The sheriff is usually elected locally for a two- or four-year term. Qualifications are set by state law, and the salary is usually set by the legislature or the county board. As Folley (1980, p. 228) notes:

> The office of sheriff is probably the most obvious example of mixing police and politics. This office was integrated into the American police system with little change from what it was in England. Today the office of sheriff is subject to popular election in almost all counties throughout the United States . . . when a new sheriff is elected he will repay political debts by appointing new deputies and promoting others already employed. . . . This constant change of leadership and manipulation of the hierarchy has not been conducive to the provision of efficient police services.

The sheriff's powers and duties are also established by state law. Each sheriff is authorized to appoint deputies and, working with them, to assume responsibility for providing police protection as well as a variety of other functions including (1) keeping the public peace, (2) executing civil and criminal process throughout the county (such as serving civil legal papers and criminal warrants), (3) keeping the county jail, (4) preserving the dignity of the court, and (5) enforcing court orders.

The sheriff operates freely in the unincorporated portions of the county and works with the municipal police departments in incorporated areas. The sheriff also works closely with the state police or highway patrol and township personnel in unincorporated portions of the county.

The sheriff appoints deputy sheriffs to assist in fulfilling responsibilities. The hundreds of sheriff's departments vary greatly in organization and function. In some states the sheriff is primarily an officer of the court; criminal investigation and traffic enforcement are delegated to state or local agencies. In other states, notably in the South and West, the sheriff and deputies perform both traffic and criminal duties.

The sheriff's staff ranges in size from one (the sheriff only) to several hundred, including sworn deputies as well as civilian personnel. Likewise, a wide range of technical proficiency and expertise also occurs among a sheriff's personnel. Some departments have little equipment; others have fleets of patrol vehicles, airplanes, helicopters, and lavishly equipped crime laboratories.

Sheriffs' departments and highway patrols often work closely together. Both rely heavily on well-equipped patrol vehicles.

Holten and Jones (1978, p. 98) cite a major difference between sheriffs' offices and municipal police departments as "a greater emphasis by sheriffs on civil functions and operation of corrections facilities. There are often, for example, separate divisions or bureaus within sheriffs' departments for performing the civil functions of process serving and/or operating the county jail and caring for prisoners."

There are an estimated 3,340 county sheriff departments in the United States.

The County Police

The county police, not to be confused with the county sheriff and deputies, are often found in areas where city and county governments have been merged, such as in Florida. County police departments are headed by a chief of police, usually an administrator appointed from within the department, who is accountable to a county commissioner, prosecutor, manager, or director of public safety.

There are about seventy-five such county police departments in the United States. Pursley (1984, p. 169) states: "Many counties that have adopted the county police department have given this agency full authority and responsibility to perform all law enforcement functions."

Overlap Between the County Sheriff and County Police

Pursley goes on to note that when county police departments are established, they are often forced to retain the sheriff. He cites Georgia as an example of a state that recognizes the sheriff as a constitutional officer yet allows counties to establish independent police agencies. Pursley suggests:

> This duplication is costly, and people do not know whether to call the sheriff's department or the county police. A great deal of political acrimony has also been apparent between the heads of these two agencies as well as among political supporters and elected officials who either side with the sheriff or the county police. This results in charges and counter-charges of incompetence, poor service, corruption, and a host of other claims being leveled at one agency by supporters of the other.

The Coroner or Medical Examiner

Another officer of the county is the coroner or medical examiner. Adams (1980, p. 150) points out that the office of coroner has a history similar to that of the sheriff and comes to modern law enforcement from ancient times. The principal task of the coroner is to determine the cause of death and to take care of the remains and personal effects of deceased persons. According to Adams: "The coroner is required by law to investigate and sign the death certificate in all circumstances where a violent death has occurred, a sudden or unusual death, an unattended death, and any death that may have suspicious circumstances surrounding it whether it be associated with a crime, a public hazard, or a disease."

The coroner need not be a medical doctor or have any legal background to be elected; in some jurisdictions, however, the coroner has been replaced by the medical examiner, a physician, usually a pathologist who has studied forensic science.

In some states the coroner or medical examiner is, by statutory provision, the chief law enforcement officer of the county. When this occurs, a sheriff's department usually has the traditional combination of criminal and civil duties to perform. In Illinois, for example, the coroner is the only one who can serve subpoenas on the sheriff. If the sheriff becomes incapacitated and cannot function, or if the sheriff is arrested (which can be done only by the coroner), the coroner becomes sheriff until one is elected.

THE DEVELOPMENT OF LOCAL AGENCIES

Township and Special District Police

The United States has approximately 19,000 townships, which vary widely in scope of governmental powers and operations. Most townships provide a very limited range of services for predominately rural areas. Some townships, often those in well-developed fringe areas surrounding a metropolitan complex, perform functions similar to municipal police.

Not all townships have their own police forces. Many rural townships have few law enforcement problems and purposely avoid appropriating funds for local police protection, relying instead on the sheriff or state police (or both) for preventive patrol and criminal investigation.

When small, essentially rural townships enter the policing field, a variety of difficulties arise. In addition to jurisdiction conflicts and the resulting diffusion of responsibility, a general lack of coordination results from having two or more government agencies, at different levels, actively policing the same area. The small township department, with its limited financial support, cannot offer complete police services, provide specialized services, nor police the area continually, but if there is a township police force, regardless of its adequacy, township residents and officials cannot exert as much pressure on the county governing body to expand the sheriff's force to bring about better general county police protection.

Many townships have only a one-person police force similar to the resident deputy system frequently found in sheriff's departments in which one person must police vast, sparsely populated regions. This person serves as a "jack-of-all-trades" and is on emergency call day and night. This individual's home may serve as headquarters.

The Constable

Approximately twenty states have established the office of constable, especially in New England, the South, and the West. The constable is usually an elected official who serves a township, preserving the peace and serving processes for the local justice court. The constable may also be the tax collector or be in charge of the pound, execute arrest warrants, and transport prisoners. In some jurisdictions, the constable is under the direction of the sheriff.

Municipal Police

The United States has over 40,000 police jurisdictions and approximately 450,000 police officers, all with similar responsibilities but with limited geographical jurisdictions. The least uniformity and greatest organizational complexity is found at the municipal level due to local autonomy, that is, the independence of local governmental units to control their own police departments.

The majority of these police forces consist of fewer than ten officers, who provide resident deputy-type police service rather than emergency-oriented service. Some personnel of very small forces are appointed with little attention to their mental or physical fitness for the work, and many such personnel have never received any formal police training and lack proper supervision and discipline.

In contrast are police agencies in large metropolitan areas such as New York City, which have over 30,000 officers highly qualified and trained to perform demanding duties. Likewise, many suburban areas are now hiring career-minded, progressive police officers who bring with them dedication, education, and a high degree of competency in human relations and technical skills.

Suburban police departments have different policing problems than small towns and large cities, just as a small-town police department is far different from that of a city of several million people in terms of organization, structure, and discipline.

The Marshal

In some parts of the United States, a marshal serves as an officer of the court, serving writs, subpoenas, and other papers issued by the court and escorting prisoners from jail or holding cells in the courthouse to and from trials and hearings. The marshal also serves as the bailiff and protects the municipal judge and people in the court. In some jurisdictions the marshal is elected; in other jurisdictions the marshal is appointed.

OVERLAP

American police forces may be classified according to the level of government that each serves, but no uniform pattern of police administration exists at any of the five levels of government, and no mechanism exists to coordinate the activities and goals of the agencies, which differ greatly in size, jurisdiction, and operational methods.

The five levels of government authorized to have law enforcement agencies result in the presence of (1) township and special district police, (2) municipal police, (3) county police, (4) state police, and (5) federal police.

Police agencies of the five governmental levels can be found operating in any given spot in America. For example, you can find (1) several federal police establishments operating as much as 4,000 miles from Washington, D.C., (2) one or more statewide police services, (3) the county sheriff and county police force, (4) the township constables and town police constables or marshals, (5) village police or marshals, (6) city police forces that range in size from 10 to 39,000 officers, (7) special park and turnpike police, (8) special district police, (9) independent state and county detectives, identification, communication, and records agencies, and (10) numerous others of less direct relationship to the official police function.

Overlapping jurisdictions and potential competition when two (and often many more) forces find themselves investigating the same offense pose serious problems to law enforcement and highlight the need for education and professionalism. In addition, specialized police personnel may sometimes be involved, further complicating jurisdiction.

Specialized Police

Specialized police are in abundance in Washington, D.C., called by Hoffmann (1992, p. 56) "America's most policed city." He describes the following police forces operating alongside the Metropolitan Police, the city's main police force with 4,900 members: the Uniformed Division of the Secret Service (1,100 officers), the U.S. Capitol Police (1,265 officers), the Federal Protective Service Police (250 uniformed officers and 20 detectives), the Supreme Court Police (76 officers), the Library of Congress Police (152 officers), the Smithsonian Institution-National Zoo Police (20 officers), the Metro Transit Police (274 officers), and the Amtrak Police (35 officers).

The evolution of policing is much more than a history of agencies that have emerged to meet society's needs. Policing itself has evolved in how it views itself, its responsibilities, and the most effective means to meet those responsibilities.

THE THREE ERAS OF POLICING

Kelling and Moore (1991, pp. 3–25) describe three eras of policing: the political era, the reform era, and the community era.

The Political Era (1840–1930)

Recall that one basic difference between England's "New Police" and those in the United States was that in England, the bobbies could be fired. In the United States, this was not the case, as described by Klockars (1985, p. 42):

> In New York, for example, the first chief of police could not dismiss officers under his command. The tenure of the chief was limited to one year. Consequently, any early New York cop who was solidly supported by his alderman and assistant alderman could disobey a police superior with virtual impunity. So while the British were firing bobbies left and right for things like showing up late to work, wearing disorderly uniforms, and behaving discourteously to citizens, American police were assaulting superior officers, refusing to go on patrol, extorting money from prisoners, and releasing prisoners from the custody of other officers. . . .
>
> Perhaps the only good thing about the corrupt, inefficient, ineffective, and disobedient early American police is that as an institution it could not be well controlled by anyone—not even the local politicians.

The **political era** was characterized by:

- Authority coming from politicians and the law.
- A broad social service function.
- Decentralized organization.
- An intimate relationship to the community.
- Extensive use of foot patrol.

During the political era, police got their authority from politics and the law. This close tie to politics was not without its problems.

The Problem of Corruption   As in other countries, corruption became a problem in United States law enforcement. One primary factor underlying this corruption was the prevelant **spoils system,** whose motto, "To the victor go the spoils," resulted in gross political interference with policing. The winning party felt that its members should be immune from arrest, given special privileges in naming favorites for promotion, and assisted in carrying out vendettas against their political opponents. This system led politicians to staff many of the nation's police forces with incompetent people as rewards for support, "fixing" arrests or assuring that arrests were not made, and securing immunity from supervision for certain establishments or people.

The spoils system encouraged politicians to reward their "friends" by giving them key positions in police departments.

As noted by Walker (1983, p. 7):

The quality of American police service in the 19th century could hardly have been worse. The police were completely unprofessional and police work was dominated by corruption and inefficiency. The source of these problems was *politics.* Local government was viewed primarily as a source of opportunity—for jobs, for profit, for social mobility, for corruption. ... Selection standards for police personnel were nonexistent. Officers obtained their jobs through political contacts. ... In 1880 most big cities paid their police $900 a year; a factory worker could expect to earn only about $450 a year.

Reform movements began early but moved slowly against the solidly entrenched political "untouchables." Cities sought to break political control by a variety of organizational techniques, including the election of police officers and chiefs, administering forces through bipartisan lay boards, asking states to assume local policing, and instituting mayor-council or council-city manager municipal government.

The election of the municipal chief of police was common with the establishment of local departments. Remembering the corrupt officials who served as long as they pleased the king, the people elected police officials to serve short terms so they would not have time to become too powerful or corrupt. But this system had its drawbacks. Not only were the officials not in office long enough to become corrupt, they were not in office long enough to gain proficiency in their jobs. In fact, officials would just get to know their own officers and have enough experience to run the police department when their terms would expire. Additionally, since terms were so short, officials kept their civilian jobs and generally devoted most of their time to them, giving only spare time to running the police force. This system lacked professionalism; the position of police chief became a popularity contest. Therefore, it was decided that a permanent police chief, with experience and ability, was the best way to have effective law enforcement. Today the elected police chief system remains in only a few cities.

In the mid-1800s administrative police boards or commissions were established. These boards were made up of judges, mayors, and private citizens and served as the head of the police department with the police chief following its orders. The rationale was that the chief of police should be a professional and keep the job continuously, but that civilian control was necessary to maintain responsibility to community needs. This system lasted many years, but it had serious weaknesses. The board members often proved more of a hindrance than a help, and the system fostered political corruption.

As a reaction against local boards, and in an attempt to control corrupt police agencies, state control of local agencies was developed in some areas of the country. It was believed that if the state controlled local agencies, citizens would be assured of adequate and uniform law enforcement. While some cities still operate within this framework, most cities and states found this was not the answer to the problem because the laws were not equally enforced. In some areas the laws were underenforced and in other areas overenforced. The system also lacked responsiveness to local demands and needs. Therefore, control was again given to the local government in most instances.

The next system to be tried was the commission government charter. Commissioners were elected and charged with various branches of city government. This sytem, also on the decline, was as inadequate as the administrative police board.

The most efficient and prevalent current local system is the mayor-council or council-city manager government. The former is very efficient when the mayor is a full-time, capable administrator. The latter assures more continuity in the business administration and executive control of the overall operations because a professional, nonpolitical administrator manages the affairs of the community. Either way the chief of police is selected on the basis of merit.

Cities sought to break political control by a variety of organizational techniques, including the election of police officers and chiefs, administering forces through bipartisan lay boards, asking states to assume local policing, and instituting mayor-council or council-city manager municipal government—which has proved to be the most effective thus far.

In 1883, a major step toward reducing corruption within the police department occurred when Congress passed the Pendleton Act. Prior to this act, most government positions were filled by political appointment. Frequently the people appointed were incapable of performing their tasks well. One government worker who was going to be replaced by President Garfield shot and killed the president. This incident caused a public outcry and resulted in passage of the Pendleton Act.

The Pendleton Act created the civil service system for government employees and made it unlawful to fire or demote a worker for political reasons.

The act established a Civil Service Commission to enforce its provisions. The new laws called for a test open to all citizens and for new workers to be hired on the basis of who had the highest grades. The act also made it unlawful to fire or demote workers for political reasons and relieved government workers from any obligation to give political service or payments.

During the political era, police served a broad social service function. As noted by Kelling and Moore (p. 7): "Police ran soup lines; district or precinct stations were designed to provide brief lodging for immigrant workers when they arrived in cities; police assisted ward leaders in finding work for immigrants, both in police and other forms of work; and police provided a wide variety of other services."

The department organization during the political era was decentralized, primarily because of lack of effective communication. Toward the end of this era the call box made communication easier and helped to centralize the police organization.

During this era, police were usually close to their community. Foot patrol was the most common strategy used, and this brought the beat officer into contact with the people in the community. Most police officers lived in the area they policed and were of the same ethnic background.

Minorities Little has been published about minority police officers in the early history of the United States. According to Sullivan (1989, p. 331) African Americans first served as police officers as early as 1861 in Washington, D.C. Most were first hired in large cities, and around 1900 made up 2.7% of all watchmen, policemen, and firemen. That number declined until about 1910 when less than one percent of police officers were African American.

During this era many African American police officers rode in cars marked "Colored Police" and as noted by Sullivan (p. 331): "Often, black officers were hired exclusively to patrol black areas and were allowed only to arrest other black citizens." In addition, few were promoted or given special assignments.

During the political era, African American officers were often segregated and discriminated against.

Women Initially women were restricted to processing female prisoners and to positions as police matrons. Many misconceptions about the female's ability to perform certain "masculine" tasks were dispelled as a result of changing social attitudes; yet room for improvement remained.

Just before the turn of the century, a movement to employ women as regular police officers gained support. The first woman police officer in the United States was Marie Owen, appointed in 1893 by the Detroit Bureau of Police. In 1910 the first regular policewoman under civil service was appointed in Los Angeles. Shortly thereafter, in 1912, in New York, the first woman chief of police was appointed by the mayor of Milford, Ohio. By the end of World War I, over 220 cities employed policewomen.

A major reason for this relatively rapid acceptance of female peace officers was a change in the public's view of the police function. The acceptance of women paralleled the newly accepted emphasis on citizen protection and crime prevention rather than exclusive concentration on the enforcement of laws and detection of crimes.

Women were welcomed into police departments where they were assigned to handle cases involving children and women. As noted by Hale (1992, pp. 126–127):

> There is little doubt that early policewomen were assigned to handle children and their problems because of the female nuturing role. This role coincided with societal values that made mothers responsible for insuring that children grew up to be good citizens. Furthermore, the early policewomen's movement (1910–1930) received support from both national women's groups and prestigious civic and social hygiene associations.

Hale cites examples from two California police departments illustrating the role of policewomen:

> The Los Angeles Police Department created the City Mother's Bureau in October 1914 and hired policewomen to handle "cases of delinquent and pre-delinquent children whose parents desired informal intervention from a law enforcement agency but were reluctant to file a formal report against their children to the police."…. Policewomen were [also] used to monitor, investigate, and punish young girls whose behavior flouted social and sexual conventions.
>
> In 1925 August Vollmer opened the Crime Prevention Division in the Berkeley, California Police Department. This unit was headed by policewoman Elizabeth Lossing, a psychiatric social worker.

According to Hale (p. 127): "The separate roles of policemen and policewomen were emphasized by the International Association of Chiefs of Police (IACP) at its meeting in 1922 where it was recommended that policewomen meet higher education and training standards than policemen…. The IACP stated that policewomen were essential to police work and recommended that police departments establish separate units.

During the political era, the roles of policewomen were clearly separated from policemen, with women serving a protective and nurturing role.

Many departments established Women's Bureaus and delegated to it cases involving children, youth, and women. Policewomen were seen as assisting policemen.

The Wickersham Commission and Police Professionalism   In 1929 President Herbert Hoover appointed the national Commission on Law Observance and Enforcement to study the American criminal justice system. The commission, named after its chairman, George Wickersham, devoted two of its fourteen reports to the police. Report 11, *Lawlessness in Law Enforcement,* delineated the problem of police brutality. The report concluded that "the third degree—the inflicting of pain, physical or mental, to extract confessions or statements—is extensively practiced." Report 14, *The Police,* concentrated on police administration and called for expert leadership, centralized administrative control, and higher personnel standards; in short, police professionalism.

The Reform Era (1930–1980)

According to Kelling and Moore (p. 6): "The reform strategy developed in reaction to the political. It took hold during the 1930's, thrived during the 1950's and 1960's, began to erode during the late 1970's, and arguably, gave way to the community strategy during the early and mid-1980's."

The **reform era** was characterized by:

- Authority coming from the law and professionalism.
- Crime control as the primary function of police.
- A centralized, efficient organization.
- Professionally remote from the community.
- Emphasis on preventive motorized patrol and rapid response to crime.

Kelling and Moore describe the reform strategy as a "remarkable construction—internally consistent, rigorous, and based on the most advanced organizational and tactical thinking of the time." As early as the 1920s, August Vollmer was calling for reforms in policing. It was his protege, O.W. Wilson, who became the primary architect of the reform era and the style of policing known as the **professional model.**

The reformers sought to disassociate policing from politics. They were to become professionals whose charge was to enforce the law, fairly and impartially. The social service function became of lesser importance or even nonexistent in some departments as police mounted an all out war on crime. Two keys to this war were preventive patrol in automobiles and rapid response to calls. This is the style of policing with which most Americans are familiar and have come to expect.

Unfortunately, the war on crime was a losing war. Crime escalated. And other problems arose as well. In the 1960s, violent ghetto riots caused millions of dollars in damages, thousands of injuries, and many deaths. According to Sullivan (p. 333):

Most of these riots were triggered by incidents in which white officers were policing in black ghetto areas. The national Advisory Commission on Civil Disorder was formed to study the situation. The resulting Kerner Report (1968) was comprehensive and scathing, and placed a large part of the blame for the riots on racism in society and the severe under-representation of blacks in police departments.

As a result of this report and other studies, many cities began to actively recruit minorities for their police departments.

The Law Enforcement Education Program (LEEP)   Following publication of the Presidential Crime Commission's recommendation that by 1984 all police officers be required to have at least a bachelor's degree, Congress created and funded the Law Enforcement Education Program (LEEP). This program poured thousands of dollars into police education and by the mid-1970s over 1,000 academic institutions had police-related courses being offered to thousands of students nationwide. Eventually, however, LEEP was phased out of the federal budget.

Another relatively short-lived federal boost to the professionalization of law enforcement was the Law Enforcement Assistance Administration.

The Law Enforcement Assistance Administration (LEAA)   In 1968 Congress enacted the Omnibus Crime Control and Safe Streets Act; Title 1 of this act established the Law Enforcement Assistance Administration. When the act was amended in 1970 the LEAA program was expanded. The Crime Control Act of 1973 further strengthened the agency and extended its authorization through 1976. The Crime Control Act of 1976 extended the program through September of 1979.

Pursley (1984, p. 165) notes:

> Although the Law Enforcement Assistance Administration (LEAA) was never a federal law enforcement agency, it deserves special attention because it may well have brought about the most important developments in the annals of American criminal justice. During its relatively brief period of existence, no other American crime control agency appears to have produced the far-ranging improvements that LEAA brought to American criminal justice.

LEAA worked in partnership with state and local governments, which have historically assumed the primary responsibility for crime reduction and law enforcement. Congress affirmed this historical responsibility in the Omnibus Crime Control and Safe Streets Act: "Crime is essentially a local problem that must be dealt with by state and local governments if it is to be controlled effectively."

On the other hand, as noted by Richard W. Velde, former LEAA administrator: "Crime control is everyone's business. It is not just the business of the criminal justice system—of police, courts, and corrections—but of all citizens who want to live in harmony and peace."

Realizing the national significance of the crime problem, Congress created the LEAA to join state and local law enforcement agencies in their efforts to combat crime. Under the anticrime partnership, the federal government supplied financial resources, technical advice, and leadership; however, states and localities set their own crime control priorities, devised specific action programs, and allocated LEAA funds according to their carefully developed plans.

LEAA awarded more than $9 billion to state and local governments to improve police, courts, and correctional systems; to combat juvenile delinquency; and to finance innovative crime-fighting projects.

Major Achievements   Every state and locality felt the impact of LEAA's nationwide anticrime program. Tens of thousands of programs and projects were supported with LEAA funds, and millions of hours were applied to identify effective, efficient, economical ways to reduce crime and improve criminal justice. Projects were developed to reduce crime and improve criminal justice, to improve the management and administration of courts, to deploy police officers more effectively, to find jobs for ex-offenders, to sharpen the skills of criminal justice personnel, to give prosecutors better tools to fight crime, and to break the jail-street-crime-jail cycle of the drug addict.

Advances for Women and Minorities   A boost was given to women and minorities when the Supreme Court ruled in *Griggs v. Duke Power Company* (1971) that any tests used for employment purposes must be job-related. Another boost was the passage of the Equal Employment Opportunity Act (EEOA) in 1972.

The Equal Employment Opportunity Act prohibits discrimination on the basis of sex, race, color, religion, or national origin in employment of any kind, public or private, local, state, or federal.

This act was an important advance not only for minorities, but also for women. That same year, women began to seek positions as patrol officers. Tension and conflict resulted. Whereas they had been accepted as assistants to the policemen, they were seldom accepted as partners on patrol. As noted by Hale (1992, p. 128): "There was little resistance to their [women's] role in police work until the time that they went on patrol. It was then that they encountered many newly created obstacles challenging their capabilities to perform what was perceived by both their peers and supervisors—as well as the public—as 'men's work.'" Hale stresses:

> Clearly, policewomen on patrol have faced many obstacles from both their peers and management, who believed that they cannot perform patrol duties because they have neither the physical strength to do the job; the authoritarian presence to handle violent confrontations; nor the ability to serve as backup to their partners in high-pressure situations. Attempts by supervisors to either overprotect policewomen, or keep them from areas with high violence further reinforce the view that women are not capable of performing patrol. One of the concerns which has caused stress for policewomen is an expressed fear, on the part of both wives and public officials, of sexual misconduct between policemen and policewomen.

Studies have shown these stereotypes and fears to be unfounded, as will be discussed in Chapter 8.

During the reform era, minorities and women obtained legal equality with white male officers, but still often encountered discrimination.

Another event during 1972 had a great impact on eroding the reform strategy—the classic *Kansas City Preventive Patrol Experiment,* which called into serious question the effectiveness of preventive patrol or rapidity of response—the basic strategies of the reform era. As noted by Klockars (1983, p. 130), the Kansas City Experiment showed that "it makes about as much sense to have police patrol routinely in cars to fight crime as it does to have firemen patrol routinely in fire trucks to fight fire."

The inability of "traditional" approaches to policing to decrease crime; the rapidly escalating drug problem; the pressing problems associated with the deinstitutionalization of thousands of mentally ill, many of whom became homeless; the challenge of dealing with thousands of immigrants, some legal, some illegal, many speaking no English; the breakdown of the family unit—Toffler and Toffler (1990, p. 2) summarize the results of the preceding:

> We are witnessing the massive breakdown of America as we knew it and the emergence of a strange, new 21st-century America whose basic institutional structures have yet to be formed. The 1990s will either see a further deterioration of old systems and the social order that depends on them, or a serious effort to restructure America for the 21st century....
>
> More and more individuals are being freed from the social constraints that kept them on the straight and narrow. These individuals are multiplying, and that fact alone suggests further social turbulence in the years ahead.
>
> We all know that law enforcement is society's second line of defense. Crime, drug abuse, and sociopathic behavior generally are first held in check by social disapproval—by family, neighbors, and co-workers. But in change-wracked America, people are less bonded to one another, so that social disapproval loses its power over them.
>
> It is when social disapproval fails that law enforcement must take over. And until the "social glue" is restored to society, we can expect more, not less, violence in the streets, more white-collar crime, more rape and misery—and not just in the inner cities.

The feeling of many in law enforcement and the entire criminal justice system is that the police and the system cannot do it alone. As noted by Klockars (1991, p. 250): "All of the major factors influencing how much crime there is or is not are factors over which police have no control whatsoever. Police can do nothing about the age, sex, racial, or ethnic distribution of the population. They cannot control economic conditions; poverty; inequality; occupational opportunity, moral, religious, family, or secular education; or dramatic social, cultural, or political change. These are the 'big ticket' items in determining the amount and distribution of crime. Compared to them what police do or do not do matters very little."

To attack these causes of crime, many are turning to the concept of community-oriented policing.

The Community Era (1980–Present)

Paralleling changes being made in the business world, many police departments are beginning to become "customer-oriented," viewing the people within the community as consumers of police services. And, just as in business it is important to know what the customer really wants and needs, so in policing, it is important to know what the citizens of a community want and need.

The **community era** is characterized by:

- Authority coming from community support, law, and professionalism.
- Broad provision of services, including crime control.
- Decentralized organization with more authority given to patrol officers.
- An intimate relationship with the community.
- Use of foot patrol and a problem-solving approach.

In contrast to policing during the reform era which was **reactive,** responding to crime after it was committed; policing during the community era is more **proactive,** seeking to find the causes of crime and to rectify those problems, thereby deterring or even preventing crime. The community-oriented approach to policing is the focus of Chapter 8.

Largely because of civil service and a grassroots-inspired groundswell of general reform, most police forces have shaken the influence of corrupt politics. In contrast to conditions at the turn of the century, appointment to the forces and police administration generally is vastly improved. Police recruitment, discipline, and promotion have been removed from politics in most cities.

Communications involving police service have also greatly improved. The radio and patrol car transformed the relationship between the police and the public and offered increased protection for everyone. The continuous expansion of the telephone in the 1960s and 1970s made it easier for people to call the police. Police dispatchers were added to tie radio systems directly into telephone networks. The use of fingerprint systems and the increased employment of women as police officers as well as many other advances occurred at an accelerated pace.

Despite advanced technology, which greatly improved police officers' abilities to respond to requests for aid and increased their mobility, the basic strategy of police has not altered. Crime waves in metropolitan areas prompt cities to improve their street lighting, increase the number of police officers on the streets, and demand more severe punishment for the convicted criminals.

The human factor has assumed greater importance as police agencies cope with the tensions and dislocations of population growth, increasing urbanization, developing technology, the civil rights movement, changing social norms, and a breakdown of traditional values. These factors have enormously complicated law enforcement, making more critical the need for truly professional police officers.

Today's local police officers must be law enforcement generalists with a working knowledge of federal, state, county, and municipal law, traffic law, criminal law, juvenile law, narcotics, liquor control, and countless other areas. But this accounts for only approximately 10 percent of what a modern police officer does. Today's police officers spend 90 percent of their time providing a variety of services while protecting life, property, and personal liberty. They must be aware of human factors and understand the psychological and sociological implications of their work for the community. They must deal with all citizens, rich and poor, young and old, in ways that maintain the community's support and confidence. This is no small responsibility.

THE WAVES OF CHANGE

It has been said that change is the only constant. In his classic work, *Future Shock,* Alvin Toffler described three major revolutions that have changed the world: The Agricultural Revolution, the Industrial Revolution, and the Technological Revolution. In 1980 Toffler wrote a sequel, *The Third Wave,* in which he draws the analogy between the three revolutions and waves in the ocean. FBI Special Agent in the Behavioral Science Instruction/Research Unit at the FBI Academy, William Tafoya (1990, p. 15) notes:

> A rough correspondence to Toffler's wave analogy can be drawn with respect to the historical changes in law enforcement. Passage of the Metropolitan Police Act

of 1829 in England marked the beginning of the "first wave" of major law enforcement reform. Robert Peel and Charles Rowan were two visionaries who
brought order and the military model to policing.

A century later, in the 1930s, August Vollmer and O.W. Wilson, two American
police pioneers, advanced the goal of "professionalizing" law enforcement. Their
efforts ushered in the "second wave" of major law enforcement reform. Stan-
dardization, specialization, synchronization, concentration, maximization, and
centralization, dominated law enforcement during this era . . . .

The civil unrest of the mid-1960s through the mid-1970s was the impetus for
the advocacy of the "third wave" of major law enforcement reform.

This third wave is now. The question is, will it bury us or carry us boldly
forward into the twenty-first century.

SUMMARY

The early American settlers brought with them several features of English law
and law enforcement including those found in Leges Henrici, which made law
enforcement a public matter, and in the Magna Carta, which provided for due
process of law. Law enforcement in colonial America was frequently patterned
after England's Watch and Ward system and later after the London Metropolitan Police and the principles for reform set forth by Sir Robert Peel. The first
modern American police force, modeled after London's Metropolitan Police,
was the New York City Police Department, established in 1844. The vigilante
movement refers to taking the law into one's own hands in the absence of
effective policing.

Although law enforcement was generally considered a local responsibility,
the early beginning of state law enforcement agencies occurred with the establishment of the Texas Rangers and the early beginning of federal law enforcement agencies with the establishment of United States Marshals. After the
turn of the century other state agencies, notably the Pennsylvania Constabulary, and other federal agencies, notably the Federal Bureau of Investigation,
were established.

At the federal level several law enforcement agencies are under the jurisdiction of the Departments of Justice and the Treasury. The United States
Attorney General, as head of the Department of Justice, is the chief federal law
enforcement officer. Within this department are the Federal Bureau of Investigation, the Federal Drug Enforcement Administration, United States Marshals,
the Immigration and Naturalization Service, and the Bureau of Prisons.

The FBI, in addition to its numerous investigative responsibilities, provides
assistance to law enforcement agencies throughout the country through its
Identification Division, the FBI Laboratory, its National Crime Information
Center, and its Uniform Crime Reports.

Law enforcement agencies within the Department of the Treasury include
the Bureau of Customs, the Internal Revenue Service, the Secret Service, and
the Bureau of Alcohol, Tobacco, and Firearms Tax.

Other federal law enforcement agencies include the United States Postal
Inspectors, the Coast Guard, and the military police of the armed forces.

State law enforcement agencies include state bureaus of investigation and
apprehension, state fire marshals divisions, state departments of natural resources, driver and vehicle services divisions, departments of human rights,
state police, and state highway patrol.

At the county level, the two main types of law enforcement agencies are the
county sheriff and the county police.

Law enforcement in the United States is, indeed, a cooperative effort among local, county, state, federal, and specialized law enforcement officers. Each has something to offer and to gain from the other.

The three eras of policing are the political era, the reform era, and the community era. The political era was characterized by authority derived from politics and law, a broad social service function, a decentralized organization, an intimate relationship to the community, and use of foot patrol. During the political era, African American officers were often segregated and discriminated against. The roles of policewomen during this era were clearly separated from policemen, with women serving a protective and nurturing role.

The spoils system encouraged politicians to reward their friends by giving them key positions in police departments. Cities sought to break political control by a variety of organizational techniques, including the election of police officers and chiefs, administering forces through bipartisan lay boards, asking states to assume local policing, and instituting mayor–council or council–city manager municipal government—which has proved to be the most effective thus far. In addition, in 1883 the Pendleton Act created the civil service system for government employees and made it unlawful to fire or demote a worker for political reasons.

The reform era was characterized by authority derived from law and professionalism; crime control as the primary function of police; a centralized, efficient organization, professionally remote from the community; emphasis on preventive motorized patrol and rapid response to crime. During this era, in 1972, the Equal Employment Opportunity Act was passed. This act prohibits discrimination on the basis of sex, race, color, religion, or national origin in employment of any kind, public or private, local, state, or federal. This gave minorities and women legal equality with white male officers and prompted many women to seek patrol assignments. Despite the passage of the Equal Employment Opportunity Act, many minorities and women still often encountered discrimination.

The community era is characterized by authority derived from community support, law, and professionalism; the broad provision of services; a decentralized organization with more authority given to patrol officers; an intimate relationship with the community; and use of foot patrol and a problem-solving approach.

DISCUSSION QUESTIONS

1. Why did it take so long to develop a police force in the United States?
2. Should police chiefs be appointed or elected?
3. What demands are made on the modern police officer that were not present twenty or thirty years ago?
4. How do different law enforcement agencies relate to each other?
5. Which departments have jurisdiction over other departments?
6. Why aren't all the federal law enforcement agencies under the Department of Justice?
7. How well are women and minorities represented on your police force?
8. What state law enforcement agencies do you have? Which are most important in assisting your local law enforcement agency?
9. What form of county law enforcement do you have?
10. Where is your regional FBI office? What facilities and services does it offer?

TERMS

community era, political era, proactive, professional model, rattle watch, reactive, reform era, regulators, sheriff, spoils system, vigilante.

REFERENCES

Adams, T. F. *Introduction to the Administration of Criminal Justice.* 2d ed. Englewood Cliffs, N.J.: Prentice-Hall, 1980.

Bailey, W. G. (Ed.) *The Encyclopedia of Police Science.* New York: Garland Publishing, 1989.

Brown, R. "The American Vigilante Tradition." In *Thinking About Police: Contemporary Readings.* 2d ed., edited by C. B. Klockars and S. D. Mastrofski. New York: McGraw-Hill, 1991.

Dunham, R. G. and Alpert, G. P. *Critical Issues in Policing: Contemporary Issues.* Prospect Heights, Ill.: Waveland Press, 1989.

Folley, V. L. *American Law Enforcement.* Boston: Allyn and Bacon, 1980.

Hale, D. C. "Women in Policing." In *What Works in Policing,"* edited by G. W. Gardner and D. C. Hale. Cincinnati, Ohio: Anderson Publishing Company, 1992.

Hoffmann, J. "Washington D.C.: America's Most Policed City." *Law and Order* (February 1992): 56–60.

Holten, N. G. and Jones, M. E. *The System of Criminal Justice.* Boston: Little, Brown, 1978.

Kelling, G. L. and Moore, M. H. "From Political to Reform to Community: The Evolving Strategy of Police." In *Community Policing: Rhetoric or Reality,* edited by J. R. Greene and S. D. Mastrofski. New York: Praeger Publishers, 1991.

Klockars, C. B. *The Idea of Police.* Newbury Park, Calif.: Sage Publications, 1985.

Klockars, C. B. "The Rhetoric of Community Policing." In *Community Policing: Rhetoric or Reality,* edited by J. R. Greene and S. D. Mastrofski. New York: Praeger Publishers, 1991.

Klockars, C. B. *Thinking About Police: Contemporary Readings.* New York: McGraw-Hill, 1983.

Mayo, K. M. *Justice to All: The Story of the Pennsylvania State Police.* New York: G. P. Putnam's Sons, 1917.

Office of the Federal Register, National Archives and Records Service, General Sevices Administration. *U.S. Government Manual: 1976–77* (Revised 5–1–76). Washington, D.C.

Perry, D. C. *Police in the Metropolis.* Columbus, Ohio: Charles E. Merrill, 1973.

Pursley, R. D. *Introduction to Criminal Justice.* New York: Macmillan, 1984.

Richardson, J. F. *The New York Police.* New York: Oxford University Press, 1970.

Sullivan, P. S. "Minority Officers, Current Issues." In *Critical Issues in Policing: Contemporary Readings,* edited by R. D. Dunham and G. P. Alpert. Prospect Heights, Ill.: Waveland Press, 1989.

Tafoya, W. L. "The Future of Policing." *FBI Law Enforcement Bulletin* (January 1990): 13–17.

Toffler, A. and Toffler, H. "The Future of Law Enforcement: Dangerous and Different." *FBI Law Enforcement Bulletin* (January 1990): 2–5.

Walker, S. *The Police in America: An Introduction.* New York: McGraw-Hill, 1983.

CHAPTER 3

The Law Enforcement Career: A Close-Up Look

No one is compelled to choose the profession of a police officer, but having chosen it, everyone is obliged to perform its duties and live up to the high standards of its requirements.

—Calvin Coolidge

Do You Know

What qualities are essential for good police officers?

What steps are involved in officer selection?

What qualifications are required of police officers?

What most physical fitness tests are like?

What is most important in the medical examination?

What information is sought during oral interviews?

What occurs during the background investigation?

What legal considerations in hiring practices are mandated by the Omnibus Civil Rights Law and the Equal Employment Opportunity Act?

What the benefits of having a police department whose racial makeup reflects that of the community are?

What the length and purpose of probation are?

What restrictions are sometimes placed on police officers' off-duty employment?

The dominant characteristic of the police culture?

How stressful police work may be?

INTRODUCTION

For years society has sought more effective law enforcement and a criminal justice system to meet its needs. Concurrently, criminologists, psychologists, sociologists, police practitioners, and scientists have worked to solve the crime problem in America. Despite some disillusionment and cynicism, progress has been made, and the future offers encouragement.

The most visible signs of progress in the vast criminal justice system have been in the field of law enforcement, and the most notable advancement within this field has been in the professionalization of the police officer.

This is, in part, because 86 to 90 percent of most police agencies' budgets are allocated for personnel, and, therefore, they are demanding higher quality performance from them. This goal is sometimes difficult to achieve, however, because most police departments are understaffed. The attrition rate through-out the country—approximately 100,000 officers per year—compounds this problem and creates a constant demand for training.

An equally important force behind the professionalization of the police officer is the realization that to a large degree the future of law enforcement, its success or failure, is contingent on the quality and effectiveness of its police officers, their status in the community, and their ability to serve its residents. Members of minority groups and women are now perceived by most departments as necessary and valuable individuals in the department. Although members of minority groups and women have had a long, difficult battle in achieving equal employment rights, not only in the field of law enforcement but also in most other fields as well, great advancements have been made in the past decade. Today law enforcement offers excellent opportunities for all who are interested in a law enforcement career. (See Figure 3–1.)

The Police Executive Research Forum (1992, p. 6) reports: "The number of full-time state and local police officers increased 5.4 percent, or 28,500, from 1987 through 1990 to bring the total numbers in the United States to 556,800

Women and members of minority groups add an important dimension to policing.

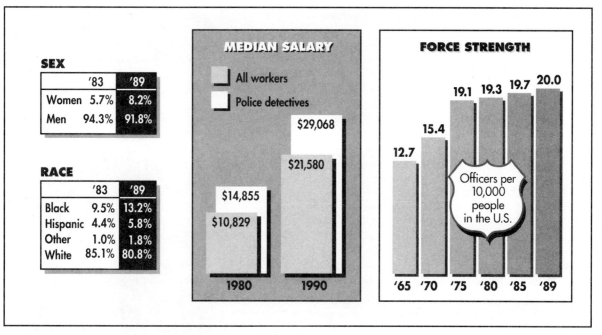

Figure 3-1   Who Are the Police?
Sources: *F. B. I. Uniform Crime Reports, Labor Department, Census Bureau.*

according to the Bureau of Justice Statistics (BJS) 1990 Law Enforcement Management and Administration Statistics survey.... The number of local police officers increased 2 percent to 363,000 and the number of state police officers grew by 4 percent to 52,400." Figure 3-2 depicts the "typical police officer."

Going beyond statistics, Starr (1991, p. 64) asks: "What kind of police officer do we want?" And answers: "The typical policeman, though he always carries a gun, may never have occasion to fire it outside the practice range. The typical policeman is not a hero; he calls for backup in dangerous situations. The typical policeman doesn't pick fights, nor run from them. The typical policeman suffers no illusions—he knows he will not stamp out crime, he knows the bad guys will sometimes get away. But he also knows this: Without him, the law-abiding would lead miserable lives."

DESIRED QUALITIES OF LAW ENFORCEMENT OFFICERS

If the citizens of a community were asked what traits they felt were desirable in police officers, a compilation of their responses might read something like the following: police officers should be able to work under pressure, to accept direction, to express themselves orally and in writing; they should have self-respect and the ability to command respect from others; they should use good judgment; and they should be considerate, compassionate, dependable, enthusiastic, fair, flexible, honest, humble, industrious, intelligent, logical, motivated, neat, observant, physically fit, prompt, resourceful, self-assured, stable, tactful, warm, and willing to listen and to accept change.

Unfortunately, no one possesses all these traits, but the more of these traits police officers have, the more likely they are to be effective in dealing with not only the citizens of the community but lawbreakers as well.

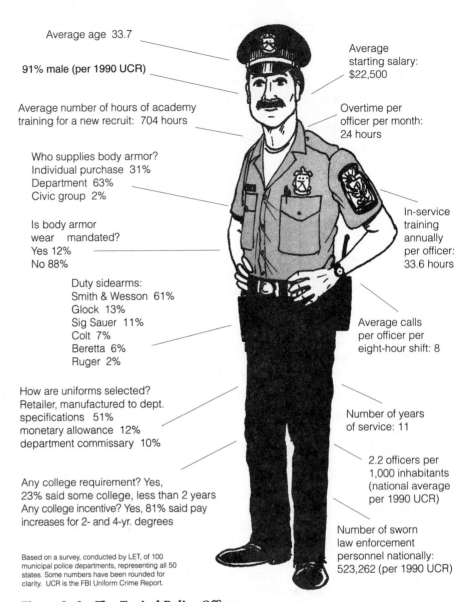

Average age 33.7

91% male (per 1990 UCR)

Average number of hours of academy training for a new recruit: 704 hours

Who supplies body armor?
Individual purchase 31%
Department 63%
Civic group 2%

Is body armor
wear mandated?
Yes 12%
No 88%

Duty sidearms:
Smith & Wesson 61%
Glock 13%
Sig Sauer 11%
Colt 7%
Beretta 6%
Ruger 2%

How are uniforms selected?
Retailer, manufactured to dept.
specifications 51%
monetary allowance 12%
department commissary 10%

Any college requirement? Yes,
23% said some college, less than 2 years
Any college incentive? Yes, 81% said pay
increases for 2- and 4-yr. degrees

Based on a survey, conducted by LET, of 100
municipal police departments, representing all 50
states. Some numbers have been rounded for
clarity. UCR is the FBI Uniform Crime Report.

Average
starting salary:
$22,500

Overtime per
officer per month:
24 hours

In-service
training
annually
per officer:
33.6 hours

Average calls
per officer per
eight-hour shift: 8

Number of years
of service: 11

2.2 officers per
1,000 inhabitants
(national average
per 1990 UCR)

Number of sworn
law enforcement
personnel nationally:
523,262 (per 1990 UCR)

Figure 3–2   The Typical Police Officer
Source: Law Enforcement Technology (October 1991), p. 32. Reprinted by permission.

A study conducted at Indiana University ("Indiana University Develops Police Selection Procedure" 1977, p. 1) identified twelve characteristics that separated good police officers from poor ones:

- Reliability.
- Leadership.
- Judgment.
- Persuasiveness.
- Communication skills.
- Accuracy.
- Initiative.
- Integrity.

- Honesty.
- Ego control.
- Intelligence.
- Sensitivity.

Qualities of a good police officer include reliability, leadership, judgment, persuasiveness, communication skills, accuracy, initiative, integrity, honesty, ego control, intelligence, and sensitivity.

Finding individuals qualified to become police officers is no easy task. The process of recruiting and screening candidates is a continuous and critical function of all police agencies in the country. By examining personnel selection developments over the past years, police administrators can evaluate the effectiveness of their personnel selection procedures. They can assess the recommendations made by the personnel branch and whether they are implemented, and they can assess whether their procedures conform with federal guidelines and regulations.

RECRUITING POLICE OFFICER APPLICANTS

The most common law enforcement recruitment practice is to place want ads in local newspapers, including minority newspapers to attract more minority candidates. This method of recruiting is not as effective as it formerly was, however, as found in a comparative study conducted by Slater and Reiser (1988, pp. 168–176). This comparison analyzed responses on a study for the Los Angeles Police Department in 1966 which determined what advertising sources were most influential in applying for a position. (More than one source could be identified.) A similar study was conducted in 1987. As noted by Slater and Reiser (p. 174) newspaper advertisements sharply decreased as a means of attracting police candidates from being in the first place in 1966 (43%) to being in seventh place in 1987 (8%). According to their study, in 1987 police officers influenced 50 percent of those applying, relatives and friends influenced 42 percent, a college or high school influenced 21 percent, pamphlets or brochures 17 percent.

EVALUATING AND SELECTING AN AGENCY FOR EMPLOYMENT

Individuals seeking employment in law enforcement should consider several factors, including, but not limited to, the advantages and disadvantages of the following:

- Employment with municipal, county, state, or federal agencies.
- Working in a small, medium, or large agency.
- Working in an environment with a high rate of crime versus an environment with little crime and, therefore, limited police enforcement activity.
- Working in a community where one was raised or currently resides.

Other factors to consider include the salary, pension and fringe benefits, the opportunities to work varied assignments in the broad spectrum of law enforcement, and the potential for promotion. What are the agency's current needs? Is there a hiring freeze? Do they have serious budget constraints?

Once an agency is selected, the individual wanting to become a police officer must usually go through several steps in the selection process.

THE SELECTION PROCESS

When applicants come to the designated place, they are given a fact sheet containing a brief job description, the salary range, fringe benefits, and an application to be filled out and submitted. They are also given a time and place to report for the written examination. Candidates who cannot personally appear may call or write to have the information sent to them.

Most police agencies and civil service commissions accept applications even though no openings are presently listed. The application is placed on file, and when an examination is to be conducted, the applicant is notified by mail or phone.

Although procedures differ greatly from agency to agency, several procedures are common to most selection processes, such as a formal application, a written examination, a physical agility test, a psychological examination, a medical examination, an oral interview, and a background investigation. Failure at any point in the selection process may disqualify a candidate.

Police officer selection usually includes:

- A formal application.
- A written examination.
- A physical agility test.
- A psychological examination.
- A medical examination.
- An oral interview.
- A background investigation.

The order in which these occur may vary from department to department. Figure 3–3 illustrates a typical selection process.

The Formal Application—Basic Requirements to Become a Police Officer

Usually anyone who wishes to become a police officer completes a formal application. A careful examination of this formal application shows several factors that are evaluated in a candidate: driving record, any criminal record, visual acuity, physical, emotional, and mental condition, and education.

Most agencies require that a police officer:

- Be a citizen of the United States.
- Have or be eligible for a driver's license in the state.
- Not have been convicted of a felony.

Requirements related to education and residency are also frequently stated.

Education   Opinions differ as to how much education a candidate for police officer should have. Most police agencies require a minimum of a high school education or equivalency certificate. On the other hand, some jurisdictions require at least two years of college and some a four-year degree.

Most police agencies require a minimum of a high school education.

Some administrators use set educational standards to attain professionalism and upgrade the service. However, police chiefs are at odds as to whether

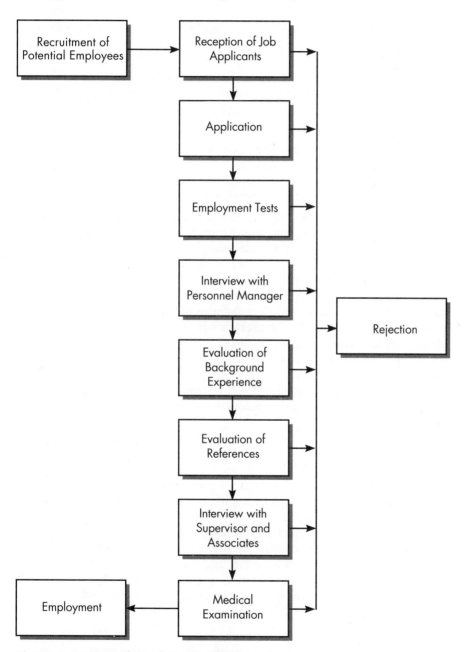

Figure 3–3   Typical Employment Process
Source: Reprinted by permission from page 205 of *Supervision,* 2d ed., by Stan Kossen; Copyright © 1991 by West Publishing Co.

education contributes significantly to the fight against crime. Unquestionably, a college-educated police officer contributes significantly to the quality of police service. On the other hand, some police chiefs feel that too much education makes social service officers of personnel who ought to be fighting crime in the streets. Some surveys indicate that the more education police officers have, the less likely they are to become involved in physical confrontations. Others feel that to require a degreed officer to perform such mundane tasks as issuing traffic tickets and parking tickets, making money runs, and carding juveniles in liquor stores is demeaning, and that such routine tasks soon diminish the highly educated officer's interest in law enforcement. Besides, they argue, most police officers see themselves as crime fighters, not social engineers. The legality and practicality of increasing educational requirements is discussed later in this chapter.

Residency Requirements   Over the years, cities and municipalities have waived residency requirements to obtain better candidates. Though generally not required, cities are again beginning to accept only candidates who reside within their boundaries.

It is always preferred and sometimes required that police officers live in the community they serve.

Sometimes compromises have been made whereby candidates are given one year to move into the community they serve. City and municipal politicians feel that by living in the community, a police officer becomes more closely identified with that community, more sensitive to its crime problems, and more readily participates in community activities.

The value of living in the community served cannot be disputed. Police officers are better able to understand the problems and needs of the community. They also develop relationships with the professional groups in the community and can better understand the life-style of the citizens. This is particularly important for those departments who are instituting community-oriented policing. Additionally, politicians' self-interests dictate that their police officers live in the community so they can contribute their fair share of taxes. Some officers, however, may not be able to afford the cost of housing in their community.

The Written Examination

Some departments use a civil service examination. Others use examinations designed specifically for their department. In either case, the examinations do not usually test on knowledge of police work or procedures.

Written examinations are usually multiple-choice tests lasting two to three hours and testing various abilities and aptitudes. Their primary function is to screen out those who do not have the "basic material" to be a police officer. They may test reasoning ability, reading comprehension, or ability to process information. They may test spelling, grammar, and mathematical ability. As noted by Kolpack (1991, p. 28):

> Written tests are popular for a number of reasons: they are easy to administer, quick to score, very economical and apparently objective. Finally, there is a widespread agreement that police officers must be intelligent and possess common sense and good judgment; written tests are generally believed to be capable of measuring these important qualities.

Most written examinations are a straight pass/fail situation, serving as an entry into the next phase of the selection process. Some agencies, however, factor in the score on this examination into their final selection decision. Many reference books and study guides are available to assist in preparing for taking written examinations in law enforcement.

Those candidates who do well on the written test go on to the next step which may include physical agility testing, psychological testing, a medical examination, an oral interview, and a thorough background check.

Physical Agility Tests

Physical fitness tests are usually administered to determine a candidate's co-ordination and muscular strength and to ascertain whether the candidate is in good or poor physical condition. The type of test varies with police agencies throughout the country.

A candidate may be required to run a designated number of yards and while doing so hurdle a three-foot barrier, crawl under a twenty-four inch bar, climb over a four- or six-foot wall with both hands on top of the wall, and sprint the remaining distance—all within a designated time period monitored by a police officer with a stopwatch.

Candidates may also be required to climb ropes or fire ladders, do chin-ups, or push-ups. Other variations of the physical agility test may be required, but usually only a minimum of strenuous activity is obligatory.

Figure 3–4 illustrates the physical agility course used at the Criminal Justice Institute of Broward Community College in Ft. Lauderdale, Florida.

Physical agility tests are necessary because they simulate what an officer may have to do on the street—jumping over a fence, climbing a wall, or chasing someone through backyards or streets. Candidates who are consider-ably overweight rarely pass the physical agility test.

Physical agility tests evaluate a candidate's coordination, speed of movement, and strength. The most common physical agility tests are similar to a military obstacle course, which must be completed in a designated time.

A candidate can prepare for the physical agility test through a regular sys-tem of workouts. Running is an excellent general conditioner because it de-velops endurance and strengthens the legs. Sit-ups, leg-lift exercises, push-ups, and lifting light weights are also helpful in preparing for the physical agility test. Like knowledge, physical fitness does not develop overnight; it develops gradually over an extended period.

Psychological Testing

Psychological tests are administered not to determine if an applicant is normal, but rather to determine if the person is emotionally suited for a career in law enforcement. According to Harr and Hess (1992, p. 82): "Psychological tests are a tool employers use to learn about the applicant's present state of mind, what is important to that person, and how that person is likely to respond to certain stimuli." Several such tests are available and commonly used.

The Minnesota Multiphasic Personality Inventory (MMPI) The MMPI is used primarily for emotional stability screening and is the most widely used paper-and-pencil personality test being used in the country—in all fields, in-

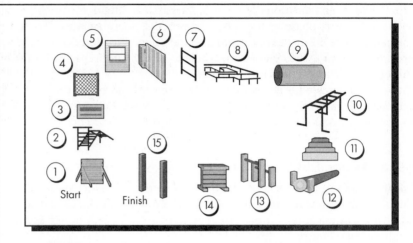

START

1) 6' Wall
2) LADDER CLIMB – Run across flat landing and down ramp
3) HURDLE – Use hands only!
4) CHAIN LINK FENCE CLIMB – Reach, lift and climb over fence
5) WINDOW CLIMB THROUGH
6) WOODEN GATE – Open fence gate door, go through and close door
7) HURDLE – Climb over
8) RUNNING MAZE – Enter at left. DO NOT touch siding
9) TUNNEL CRAWL – Crawl through. DO NOT dive!
10) HAND BAR WALK – Reach with hands, walk across
11) HIGH STEPPER – Lift feet high
12) LOG WALK – Slanted, walk across
13) HORIZONTAL HAND WALK – Use hands, push off ground and walk across bars
14) SHORT WALL – Jump up and over
15) POLE RUN – Run to your right, go 1 1/2 times around. DO NOT touch poles!

FINISH

Figure 3–4   Physical Agility Course

Source: Criminal Justice Institute, Broward Community College, Ft. Lauderdale, FL, July 1989. Reprinted by permission.

cluding law enforcement. It is a self-report questionnaire containing 550 statements to which individuals respond "true," "false," or "cannot say." As noted by Tsushima (1984, p. 386):

> The test items consist of a wide variety of psychological characteristics such as health, social, sexual, political, and religious values; attitudes about family, education, and occupation; emotional moods, and typical neurotic or psychotic clinical manifestations such as obsessive-compulsive behavior, phobias, delusions, and hallucinations.

The California Psychological Inventory (CPI)   This is the second most popular personality test. This multi-level self-administering questionnaire is designed to "identify and reveal the status of certain highly important factors in the personality and social adjustment" (Mitchell, 1985, p. 254). According to Mitchell (p. 252):

> Each scale is designed to forecast what a person will say or do under defined conditions, and to identify individuals who will be described in characteristic ways by others who know them well or who observe their behavior in particular contexts.

Gough (1988, p. 45) describes the CPI as "a multi-purpose questionnaire designed to assess normal personality characteristics important to everyday life."

The Myers-Briggs Type Indicator™   The Myers-Briggs is a widely used measure of people's disposition and preferences. It is becoming increasingly popular in business and is likely to do so in law enforcement also. According to the authors (Briggs and Myers, 1976, p. 1):

> There are no "right" or "wrong" answers to these questions. Your answers will help show how you like to look at things and how you like to go about deciding things. Knowing your own preferences and learning about other people's can help you understand where your special strengths are, what kinds of work you might enjoy and be successful doing.

It asks such questions as: "Are you more likely to speak up in (a) praise or (b) blame?" "If you were a teacher, would you rather teach (a) fact courses or (b) courses involving theory?" The test results describe an individual as being one of sixteen personality types based on their stated preferences on four indexes:

- Extroversion-Introversion.
- Sensing-Intuition.
- Thinking-Feeling.
- Judgment-Perception.

The Watson-Glaser Critical Thinking Appraisal   This test consists of five subtests: inference, recognition of assumptions, deduction, interpretation, and evaluation of arguments. The test has eighty items and must be completed in forty minutes. According to Mitchell (1985, p. 1692):

> The exercises include problems, statements, arguments, and interpretations of data similar to those that are encountered on a daily basis at work, in the classroom, and in newspaper and magazine articles.

The Strong Interest Inventory   This inventory has 325 items covering a wide range of occupations, occupational activities, hobbies, leisure activities, school subjects, and types of people. According to Strong et al. (1988, p. 4):

> The Strong compares a person's interests with the interests of people happily employed in a wide variety of occupations. It is a measure of interests, not of aptitude or intelligence. . . .
>
> And because the consistency of occupational interests from one culture to the next—the likes and dislikes of engineers, art teachers, bankers, police officers— has been demonstrated, it is used in translation in similar settings abroad.

The Medical Examination

Medical requirements vary from jurisdiction to jurisdiction, but the purpose is the same. With the modern emphasis on health care, more and more importance is being placed on the medical examination. Citizens, concerned about the possibility of early retirements due to poor health, are demanding physically fit officer candidates.

The medical standards usually include a variety of factors with some— vision, hearing, and the cardiovascular-respiratory system—being more important than others.

Good eyesight is of great importance. Candidates who wear glasses that correct their vision to meet the agency's requirements can qualify in some departments. Likewise, candidates who wear hearing aids that correct their hearing to meet the agency's requirements can qualify.

Because of the stress of the job and the hypertension that frequently accompanies it, the cardiovascular system is thoroughly checked. The respiratory and cardiovascular system play a critical role in fitness. To a great degree, endurance, the ability to continue exertion over a prolonged time, is directly related to the capacity of the cardiovascular-respiratory system to deliver oxygen to the muscles.

Vision, hearing, and the cardiovascular-respiratory system are of prime importance in the medical examination.

Other medical screening tests often used are the ratio of total cholesterol to HDL cholesterol to identify cardiovascular risk factors, blood pressure, smoking status, drug use, and blood sugar level for diabetes.

A physician who feels a candidate has a functional or organic disorder may recommend disqualification of that candidate.

The Oral Interview

Oral boards usually consist of three to five skilled interviewers knowledgeable in their fields. They may be staff officers from the agency doing the hiring or from other agencies, psychologists, sociologists, or representatives of a community service organization. The entire interviewing board may consist of members of a police or civil service commission. In smaller jurisdictions, oral boards are sometimes replaced by an interview with the mayor, a member of the council, or the chief of police.

The oral interview usually evaluates appearance, ability to present ideas, social adaptability, alertness, judgment, emotional stability, interest in the job, and communication ability.

The interviews, whether structured or unstructured, are designed to elicit answers revealing the candidates' personalities and suitability for police work, *not* to determine their technical knowledge in the police field. The candidate should be prepared to answer questions such as the following:

- Why do you want to be a police officer?
- What have you done to prepare for a career in law enforcement?
- What do you feel are the causes of crime?
- What are your favorite hobbies?
- Have you talked with your wife/husband about this position of police officer?
- What does she/he think about it?
- What is the last book you have read?
- What was your favorite subject in school?
- When did you last get drunk?
- What does the term "professionalization" of a police officer mean to you?
- What do you think will be the "toughest" responsibility of being a police officer?
- Are citizen volunteer units more of a hindrance than an asset to law enforcement?

- What type of situations cause you the most anxiety?
- Do you have any questions of us?
- Why did you select this department to apply to?

The oral interview seeks information about the candidate's personality and suitability for police work.

The oral interview will also test the candidate's ability to use good judgment in specific situations such as the following:

- A person is standing on the corner making a speech regarding the overthrow of the government. He is drawing a crowd, and a certain amount of animosity is being shown toward the speaker, indicating future trouble. How would you handle this situation?
- You are working radar and you clock the mayor going 39 mph in a 30 mph zone. How would you handle this situation?
- You are walking a beat and a juvenile thrusts a stick between your legs causing you to fall to the pavement and tear your pants. What would you do?

The oral interview is a critical phase of the selection process and should be thoroughly prepared for. Applicants should research the department to which they are applying and should also be familiar with the community. On the day of the oral interview, they should be well groomed and dress professionally. They should arrive on time and have an opening and closing statement carefully prepared. It is critical to be well prepared since the oral interview generally disqualifies more candidates than it qualifies.

The interview usually lasts about thirty minutes. The same questions are asked each candidate to allow comparison of answers. After the interview, the qualifications of each candidate are evaluated. Each candidate is given an overall rating, which is combined with the scores of the other examinations to yield a composite (total) score.

The Background Investigation

The applicant's background is one of the most critical factors considered in recruitment. In most police agencies an applicant must submit a personal history. The background investigation serves two purposes: (1) it examines the past work and educational record of the candidate, and (2) it determines if anything in the candidate's background might make him or her unsuitable for police work. The extensiveness of the background investigation is limited only by the number of candidates being investigated and time available.

Normally all information given by the applicant on the history sheet must be verified. Birth and age records are verified through vital statistics and driving records through the drivers' license bureau. Adverse driving records containing drunken driving, driving after suspension or revocation of license, or a consistent pattern of moving violations may cause disqualification.

Candidates are fingerprinted, and the prints are sent to the Federal Bureau of Investigation in Washington to determine if the candidate has a criminal record. The candidate's criminal record is also checked on the local and state levels, usually through fingerprints, name, and date of birth. Juvenile records are normally discounted unless a person has committed a heinous crime.

Ironically, because of the transient nature of our population, persons wanted on warrants in one part of the country have applied for a police officer's position in another part of the country. The criminal record check has sometimes resulted in the apprehension of such individuals.

Military records are usually checked to verify service and eligibility under the veteran's preference acts of some states. The check also determines if the candidate was involved in any court martials or disciplinary actions.

All personal and professional references listed on the history sheet are interviewed. Interviewing of references is sometimes criticized because candidates obviously will list only those who see them favorably; however, these references may lead to others who know the candidates and have a different view of them. When candidates list out-of-town references, letters or questionnaires are usually mailed.

Neighbors of the candidate, past or present, are an excellent source of information about a candidate's character and reputation. No department wants police officers who have had prior association with the criminal element, who have been addicted to narcotics or drugs, or who abuse alcohol. Their reputation in the community should be high.

Previous employers are contacted to determine the applicant's work record. An inability to hold continuous employment may indicate trouble getting along with supervisors. A high absentee rate may indicate lack of interest or initiative or health problems.

The financial status of the candidate is also determined, usually through a credit records check. Individuals whose expenditures exceed their total incomes may be candidates for bankruptcy or bribery. Good credit indicates the person can live within his or her means and possesses self-control. The candidate may be required to submit a financial statement.

Educational records from high school, college, and any other schools attended are usually checked through personal contact. The education record may indicate interests, achievements, accomplishments, and social life-style while attending school. The scholastic record reflects not only intelligence but also study habits. Any degrees, certificates of achievement, or awards are usually noted.

The use of the polygraph examination as a follow-up to the background investigation is a widely increasing means of verifying the background of a candidate. Although some states have banned its use for preemployment purposes, where it is used to screen police candidates it is necessary to determine why it is being given. Some departments use the polygraph extensively, especially if they have many transient applicants from other parts of the country. Some agencies use it to determine if the candidate has ever engaged in criminal activity and was ever apprehended. Some want to know if the candidate has any sexually deviant behaviors. Others use it to verify the written information the candidate has given on the application and history sheet.

The background investigation includes the following:

- Verification of all information on the application and history sheet.
- Check on driving record.
- Fingerprinting and a check on any criminal record.
- Check on military records.
- Interviews with personal references, acquaintances, past employers, neighbors, and teachers.
- Check on financial status.
- Check on past performances at school and previous jobs.

After all required tests are completed, they are analyzed and a composite score is given for each candidate. A list is made of eligible candidates, and they are called as openings occur in the police department. Some larger police departments keep their eligibility lists one to two years, depending on civil service requirements or other requirements mandated by states or municipalities.

TESTING OR ASSESSMENT CENTERS

Some police departments use a testing or assessment center in the selection process. Fralicx (1990, pp. 66–69) describes the testing conducted by Stanard & Associates, an industrial psychology firm specializing in testing police candidates. Their process involves four steps.

- A basic skills test that determines if candidates can read, solve arithmetic problems and handle writing assignments.
- A physical agility test using simulations to determine if the candidate is physically able to do police work. Set standards exist for strength, flexibility, endurance, and body fat composition.
- A psychological assessment, including a paper-and-pencil cognitive ability test and the MMPI.
- A background information check covering educational background, job experience, strengths, career objectives, and personal characteristics.

Candidates who successfully pass these four tests are then scheduled for an oral interview with the departments interested in hiring them.

An alternative to the traditional forms of testing is that being used in Appleton, Wisconsin: **situational testing** in an assessment center. Kolpack (1991, p. 28) states that, to be considered an assessment center, the following minimal requirements must be met:

1. The dimensions, characteristics and qualities to be evaluated are determined by an analysis of job behaviors.
2. Multiple assessment techniques must be used, at least one of which must be a simulation to showcase the participant's behaviors as he responds to a situation related to the target job.
3. Simulations exercises are job-related and pretested to ensure validity and reliability. These exercises must be scored objectively and indicate the relevant behavioral information.
4. Multiple assessors—"content experts" who have received prior training in these techniques—must be used.
5. Judgments on the behaviors must be based on pooled information from both the assessors and the exercises.
6. The final integration of information by the group of assessors occurs at a separate time from the observation of the behavior.

Kolpack (p. 28) contends: "The assessment center technique has not only gained considerable acceptance among candidates and management personnel, but has also satisfied the legal requirements regarding fair employment and promotion practices. Such requirements are becoming increasing complex.

FEDERAL GUIDELINES AND REGULATIONS

The basic rule of thumb is that all requirements must be clearly job-related. A **bona fide occupational qualification (BFOQ)** is one that is reasonably necessary to perform the job. It may, on the surface, appear to be discrimination. For example, in law enforcement, applicants may be required to have normal or correctable-to-normal hearing and vision because they are required to perform the job.

In 1964 Congress enacted the Omnibus Civil Rights Law. Title VII of this law concerns employment opportunities and prohibits discrimination because of sex, race, color, religion, or national origin. The law also established the Equal Employment Opportunity Commission (EEOC) to administer the law and gave this commission authority to establish guidelines. This law affected only private business, not state and local governments; therefore, it had little impact on police agency practices.

The 1964 Omnibus Civil Rights Law prohibits discrimination in employment opportunities in private business.

In 1972 Congress passed the Equal Employment Opportunity Act, which modified Title VII to include state and local units of government. This law was passed because six years after the EEOC published guidelines for employment and promotion testing, few state or local central personnel selection agencies had taken positive steps to meet the guidelines.

The 1972 Equal Employment Opportunity Act prohibits discrimination due to sex, race, color, religion, or national origin in employment of any kind, public or private, local, state, or federal.

The EEOC legislation restricts the type of information that can be gathered from job applicants. All questions must be relevant to the job for which the applicant is applying. Bittel (1989, p. 135) suggests the following information should not be asked about on application forms or during interviews: race or color, religion, national origin, age, marital status or ages of children, or if the person has ever been arrested. Applicants may be asked if they have a present disability that will interfere with the job to be performed, but not about past disabilities or illnesses. They may be asked if they have ever been convicted of a crime and, if so, when and where it took place. Questions about education and experience are largely unrestricted.

The Affirmative Action Amendment (signed by President Nixon in 1973) further strengthened the power of the EEOC. Affirmative Action refers to special endeavors by employers (including law enforcement agencies) to recruit, hire, retain, and promote minority group members and to eliminate past and present employment discrimination.

Further complicating the selection and employment process is the Americans with Disabilities Act (ADA) which President Bush signed into law in July of 1990. The purpose of this act, according to Scuro (1992, p. 59), is "to provide qualified individuals with disabilities equal employment opportunities and equal access in the private and public employment sectors." According to Scuro (p. 61): "The act defines a disability as a 'physical or mental impairment' that has the effect of 'substantially' limiting one or more of the 'major life activities' of an individual seeking employment." Clearly excluded from protection are "current users of illegal drugs, sexual behavior disorders, compulsive gambling, sexual dysfunctions (homosexuals, bisexuals, transsexuals, transvestites), pedophilia, voyeurism, kleptomania, pyromania, exhibitionism, and psychological disorders resulting from the current use of illegal drugs."

Litchford (1991, p. 11) lists the following significant provisions of the act:

- Employers will be prohibited from discriminating against otherwise qualified employment applicants based on a condition of handicap, provided the individual can perform the "essential functions" of the job.
- One of the key factors in determining which job functions are "essential" will be the contents of any written job description, provided that the description was prepared before the job was advertised or applicants were interviewed.
- Employers will be required to make "reasonable accommodations," including restructuring of job requirements and workspace configurations, when these modifications can be made without undue hardship.
- Pre-employment medical inquiries, medical exams and psychological testing will be prohibited, except that a job offer may be conditioned on successful completion of a *post-offer* medical or psychological exam.
- Current users of illegal drugs are *not* protected under the act.

Litchford notes that precluding medical and psychological examinations until *after* a conditional offer of employment "will have a significant adverse impact on most law enforcement selection procedures." She suggests, for example, that "pre-offer physical agility testing and polygraph testing, both of which normally involve some preliminary medical inquiries, may violate the provisions of the act."

Scuro (1992, p. 61) concurs with this assessment: "The biggest impact on law enforcement hiring practices appears to deal with preliminary medical and psychological screening examinations to potential applicants."

EDUCATIONAL REQUIREMENTS

Educational requirements have long been a source of controversy in law enforcement. Chapter 2 discussed the case of *Griggs v. Duke Power Company* (1971) and the need for tests to be clearly job related. Another factor in this case was Griggs' contention that the requirement of a high-school diploma was discriminatory. A similar case occurred in *Davis v. City of Dallas* (1978) where the department's requirement that applicants have completed forty-five semester hours of college credit with a "C" average was challenged. In this case, the court ruled in favor of the police department:

> The City introduced evidence which supports the educational requirement. Numerous nationwide studies have examined the problem of setting the education requirement for police departments with favorable conclusions. A college education as a condition of hiring as a police officer has been recommended by the National Commission on Law Observance in 1931; by the President's Commission on Law Enforcement and Commission on Intergovernmental Relations in 1971; by the American Bar Association in 1972; and by the National Advisory Commission on Criminal Justice Standards and Goals in 1973.
>
> Defendant's experts established the relationship between college education and performance of police officers. A study by one expert relied upon factual data from two large metropolitan areas that took two years to complete, showing significantly higher performance rates by college-educated officers. A persuasive point was made that a high school diploma today does not represent the same level of achievement which it represented 10 years ago.

Mahan (1991, pp. 285–286) stresses that law enforcement agencies establish a policy regarding educational requirements and that such a policy consider the following arguments supporting a requirement for college credits (from the *American Journal of Police*):

- It develops a broader base of information for decision making.
- It allows for additional years and experiences for maturity.
- Course requirements and achievements inculcate responsibility in the individual.
- Both general education courses and course work in the major (particularly a criminal justice major) permit the individual to learn more about the history of the country, the democratic process and an appreciation for constitutional rights, values and the democratic form of government.
- College education engenders the ability to flexibly handle difficult or ambiguous situations with greater creativity or innovation.
- In the case of criminal justice majors, the academic experience permits a better view of the "big picture" of the criminal justice system and both a better understanding and appreciation for the prosecutorial, courts, and correction roles.
- Higher education develops a greater empathy for minorities and their discriminatory experiences through both course work and interaction within the academic environment.
- A greater understanding and tolerance for persons with differing lifestyles and ideologies which can translate into more efficient communications and community relationships in the practice of policing.
- The college-educated officer is assumed to be less rigid in decision-making in fulfilling the role of the police while balancing that role with the spirit of the democratic process in dealing with variable situations; a greater tendency to wisely use discretion to deal with the individual case rather than applying the same rules to all cases.
- The college experience will help officers communicate and respond to crime and service needs of the public in a competent manner with civility and humanity.
- The educated officer is more innovative and flexible when dealing with complex policing programs and strategies such as problem-oriented policing, community policing, task force responses, etc.
- The officer is better equipped to perform tasks and make continual policing decisions with minimal, and sometimes no supervision.
- College helps develop better overall community relations skills including the engendering of respect and confidence of the community.
- More "professional" demeanor and performance is exhibited by college-educated officers.
- The educated officer is able to cope better with stress and is more likely to seek assistance with personal or stress-related problems, making the officer a more stable and reliable employee.
- The officer can better adapt his/her style of communication and behavior to a wider range of social conditions and "classes."
- The college experience tends to make the officer less authoritarian and less cynical with respect to the milieu of policing.
- Organizational change is more readily accepted by and adapted by the college officer.

As noted by Bennett and Hess (1992, p. 229): "Despite all these supposed advantages, others contend that many good officers could be lost if educational levels are set too high." Hinkle (1991, p. 105) puts it more strongly:

Requiring a college degree as a prerequisite to police work is impractical in the extreme. It fails to answer the basic question, Would a degree help in the preponderance of situations a street officer has to face? . . .

The facts are, effective street cops learn their street skills on the job, not in the classroom. . . . My FTO [field training officer] was a man who never saw the inside of a college classroom, but he remains in many ways the best cop I've ever known, and certainly one of the best teachers.

In the intervening years, like most lawmen—especially in college towns—I have been spat on, kicked, punched, cussed out and shot at. Many of these encounters require interpersonal skills that caused me to ask myself, How would Jerry defuse this? That is teaching at its finest—and it wasn't learned in a college classroom.

Thomas Edison didn't go to college but he filled hundreds of notebooks with his experiments. Ernest Hemingway never went to college, but he wrote some of the most compelling prose of the 20th Century. The list could go on, but the point is clear. A good cop must have certain attributes—compassion, courage, self-confidence, intelligence, a sense of humor, and a feeling for right and wrong. A college degree is not among them.

Other critics of a college education requirement contend that college graduates would be unlikely to seek employment in law enforcement, particularly women and minority college graduates. This requirement could undermine the progress that is being made in recruiting women and minorities. According to the Police Executive Research Forum (1992, p. 6): "Much of the growth in the number of local police officers was among persons of color and women."

MINORITY GROUP MEMBERS IN LAW ENFORCEMENT

To gain the community's general confidence and acceptance, police department personnel should be representative of the community as a whole. An integrated department helps reduce stereotyping and prejudice. Further, minority officers provide a department with an understanding of minority groups, their languages, and their subcultures, all with practical benefits to successful law enforcement. For example, a police officer with a knowledge of Spanish can help to prevent conflicts between the police and Spanish-speaking residents of the community.

A racially balanced and integrated police department both fosters community relations and increases police effectiveness.

The Police Executive Research Forum (1992, p. 6) notes that:

Among sworn personnel in local police departments, the overall representation of officers of color increased from 14.6 percent in 1987 to 17 percent in 1990, for a total of 61,700. The percentage of black officers in 1990 (10.5 percent) represented a slight increase over 1987 (9.3 percent). An increase also occurred for Hispanic officers (from 4.5 percent to 5.2 percent). In 1990, other ethnic groups, such as Asians and Native Americans, represented 1.3 percent, or 4,700, of local police officers, a 30 percent increase from the 1987 percentage of 0.8 or 2,850 officers.

As noted by Sullivan (1989, p. 332): "Nationwide, blacks and Hispanics have made enormous strides in recent years in terms of increasing the proportion of their members hired.... Blacks now comprise 12.5% of the general population and 13.5% of all police officers; similarly Hispanics were 6.4% of the population and 6.1% of the police. While both of these groups are now well represented among law enforcement agencies, other minority groups such as Asians and American Indians may remain under-represented." According to Sullivan (p. 333): "The departments that have the best records of promoting minority officers are those that are located in major cities with large minority populations."

While many minorities view police as the "enemy" and would never consider joining their ranks, others view law enforcement as a way to a better life. Sullivan (1989, p. 339) quotes an African American police lieutenant from Atlanta talking about why he became a police officer: "There were two ways to get out of my nieghborhood and not end up dead or in prison. You either become a minister or a cop. I always fell asleep in church so I decided to become a cop."

An important question related to minority officers is where they should be assigned. Many believe that minority neighborhoods should be policed by officers of the same background. However, as noted by Sullivan (1989, p. 341): "Others see this simply as a form of segregation. Ironically, many of those who during the 1960 riots demanded that only black officers be sent to black areas now are condemning the same practice."

Sullivan suggests that affirmative action has played a great role in the increasing number of minorities. For example, in March 1987 the U. S. Supreme Court upheld promotion quotas that required Alabama state troopers to promote one black officer for each white officer until blacks hold at least 25 percent of the top ranks.

Court-Imposed Quotas   In 1976, a federal court imposed a quota system on the Chicago Police Department which mandated that of the next 400 to 600 officers hired, 50 percent had to be African American or Hispanic males, 16.5 percent women, and 33.5 percent white males.

The Los Angeles Police Department has a similar order in effect which is in the form of a consent decree established in 1980. This order has set "appointment goals" for each police academy class of new officers. Those goals are 25 percent female, 25.5 percent African American, and 22.5 percent Hispanic. NOTE: Due to the long waiting list of qualified white male candidates, the oral score required for that group is currently 99 percent or better.

WOMEN IN LAW ENFORCEMENT

Deborah Lancaster (1983, p. 43) notes:

> In 1970, women constituted only 1 percent of sworn law enforcement officers. Today that figure is 4 percent and it continues to slowly rise each year. The men who are entering police work today are, for the most part, a new generation. They have been raised in an era of equal opportunity with the idea that women are equal and capable of performing just about any job. As these men rise through the ranks of police departments across the nation, I believe women will continue to enter and rise in the profession as well.

In 1986 the Police Foundation undertook a study of women in policing that paralleled one conducted in 1978. Questionnaires went to all 446 police departments serving areas with a population of over 50,000 and all state police agencies. Seventy-two percent of the questionnaires were returned. According to this study (Martin, 1989, p. 2): "The proportion of women among sworn police personnel has grown steadily since 1972," increasing from 4.2 percent in 1978 to 8.8 percent of all sworn officers in 1986. Other findings of the study include the following:

- The greatest increases were in departments in the largest cities.
- Minority women made up a disproportionately large share of all women in policing— 38 percent in 1978 and 40 percent in 1986.

■ In 1986 15 percent of the municipal agencies had court-ordered affirmative action hiring policies; 42 percent had voluntary affirmative action plans in effect; and 43 percent had none.

According to Martin (1989, p. 7): "The *pace* of change is, nonetheless, relatively slow; women still constitute less than 9 percent of all police personnel and 3.3 percent at the supervisory level. They thus continue to face the problems experienced by 'tokens,' e.g., performance pressures, heightened boundaries against 'outsiders,' and entrapment in stereotyped roles."

Although many women do not possess the upper-body strength and street-fighting abilities of many men, studies have shown that women are usually better at averting violence in the first place. Women officers are more likely to use verbal communication skills rather than force in confrontations with suspects. In response to the question "Are women better cops?" McDowell (1992, p. 70) says: "In some important ways, yes, especially as the job evolves. Cool, calm and communicative, they help put a lid on violence before it erupts."

On the other hand, some believe that when women become physically challenged, they will have more of a need (and justification) to use deadly force to protect themselves. However, according to McDowell (p. 71): "Studies consistently show that in situations in which force is needed, they perform as effectively as their male counterparts by using alternatives, such as karate, twist locks or a baton instead of their fists." McDowell (p. 72) notes:

> Because female cops are still relatively few in number, a woman answering a police call often evokes a mixed response. Reno officer Judy Holloday recalls arriving at the scene of a crime and being asked, "Where's the real cop?" Detective Burke, who stands 5 ft. 2 in. and has weighed 100 lbs. for most of her 23 years on the force, says she made 2,000 felony arrests and was never handicapped by a lack of physical strength. Burke recalls subduing a 6-ft. 4-in., 240-lb. robbery suspect who was wildly ranting about Jesus Christ. She pulled out her rosary beads and told him God had sent her to make the arrest. "You use whatever you got."

As of July 1991 women made up 13.3 percent of the 8,269 officers on the Los Angeles Police Department. The women in the city's overall work force made up 43.4 percent. The closest gender balance of any police department in the country was Madison, Wisconsin, where 19.2 percent of the officers were women (Oglesby, 1991). This department, incidentally, was a pioneer in community-oriented policing.

Reverse Discrimination

Although the increases in women and minorities in the ranks of the law enforcement agencies across the country is to be applauded, problems still exist. Sometimes these advancements are made at the expense of others—most notably white males. This is referred to as the problem of **reverse discrimination**—giving preferential treatment in hiring and promoting to women and minorities to the detriment of white males.

This issue has separated whites from minorities, men from women, and the advocates of affirmative action from those who believe in a strict "merit" principle for employment and advancement. A growing number of majority member workers are complaining bitterly about their own civil rights being abridged, and some are filing reverse discrimination suits in court.

The majority position has been summarized as a concern that for every deserving minority group member who is provided a job or promotion through preferential quotas, there is also a deserving, and often more qualified, nonminority person who is thereby deprived of a job or promotion. The courts themselves have been deeply divided over the constitutionality of the reverse discrimination that some believe is implicit in minority quotas and double standards.

PROBATION AND TRAINING

Some states have mandated that recruits must be given from 240 to 400 hours of police training within one year of employment. Coincidentally, one year is also usually the length of time the officers are placed on probation.

The probationary period is a trial period, usually one year, during which the officer is observed while obtaining training and applying this training on the streets.

Police officers may obtain their training in a state police academy, a city academy, or a specialized rookie school. The basic training of police officers varies with each jurisdiction and its needs, but most officers will be trained in constitutional law, laws of arrest, search and seizure, and in the various requests for service such as accident investigation, crisis intervention, and first aid.

While in training recruits may be required to return to the department and spend a specified number of hours on street patrol. Some jurisdictions alternate their training periods every two weeks, allowing an officer to apply on the street what was learned in basic recruit school.

While on the street the recruits ride with a field training officer or FTO, usually a sergeant, who monitors their movements and helps them apply principles learned in rookie school. While in school, the officers are evaluated and tested by their instructors, who periodically send progress reports to the chief

Classroom instruction helps keep officers abreast of the latest advances in policing.

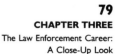

Connecticut State Police recruits practice self-defense drills at the state police school.

of police. After completing training, they continue to ride with one or more training officers who evaluate their street performance.

Following successful completion of the probationary period, they are full-fledged police officers. After probation some states license the person to be a police officer. Legislatures in Texas, Michigan, California, Oregon, Minnesota, and other states have adopted standards for police officers that must be met to satisfy the state's training requirements for licensing.

States have also mandated a certain amount of in-service training to keep the license current. Many of these in-service training requirements revolve around the behavioral sciences so police officers have a better understanding of the entire criminal justice system. Guest speakers from the corrections system, the court system, and on many occasions from minority groups present their philosophy and objectives to police officers.

SALARY AND BENEFITS

Salaries among police departments in the country have little uniformity. A variety of factors influence a police officer's salary. Of utmost consideration are the community's ability to pay, the cost of living in the area, and the prevailing wages of similar police departments in the surrounding area.

Normally position-classification plans are implemented under a personnel ordinance or department rule book. Steps on the salary scale are established in each position classification. New recruits start at the bottom of the salary scale and receive increment raises after six months and each succeeding year until they reach their maximum salary, usually after three to five years. They obtain more salary only if granted a cost-of-living raise; however, a promotion to the next rank would bring them into a different salary bracket. Sergeants, lieutenants, captains, and chiefs all have minimum and maximum starting levels with the top salary usually reached after three years in the position.

To compensate individuals who do not attain a rank during their police careers, many police departments have adopted longevity plans whereby non-ranking officers receive a certain percentage more of their salaries after the tenth year, the fifteenth year, and so on. This seniority system has been attacked, however, on the grounds that it discourages initiative and further education.

When salary schedules are formulated, fringe benefits such as hospitalization and dental plans, insurance, vacation, sick leave, and holidays are all considered. Police officers' indirect benefits from their employers are estimated to be approximately 33 percent, comparable to what business and industry currently allow their employees.

In addition to fringe benefits, most police departments give police officers a yearly clothing allowance to maintain their uniform wardrobe.

Policies vary regarding overtime pay for officers on the job, going to court while on duty, being required to attend training while off duty, and being called back to duty in an emergency. Some departments pay overtime; others give compensatory time off.

Police departments may belong to unions that bargain for them. Usually all conditions of employment are clearly spelled out in their contracts.

OFF–DUTY WORK LIMITATIONS

Moonlighting, working at a part-time job while fulfilling the obligations of a full-time position, has been a source of controversy in the police field for many years. Some administrators allow their officers latitude in the off-duty work performed and the number of hours worked. Other administrators are becoming more conservative as a result of poor work performance by some moonlighting officers and lawsuits against the officer and the city or municipality due to some incident while the officer was working off duty.

Most police departments restrict the type of work that can be done and the number of hours an officer can work while off duty.

Some cities allow their police officers to work off duty in only police-related areas; others allow them to work in only nonpolice-related areas. While there are advantages and disadvantages in allowing police officers to work off duty, most cities and municipalities have some limits on the officer's off-duty time.

THE POLICE CULTURE

Police officers work nights and weekends; they deal with highly confidential material that cannot be shared with friends; they must enforce the law impartially, whether it is a friend or a stranger who violates a law; and they frequently face public hostility, abuse, name calling, and biased reporting in the media. A combination of these factors largely accounts for the existence of a "police culture."

Individuals who become police officers frequently find that they lose their nonpolice friends within a few years. They work different hours—nights and weekends—and they may make some of their friends uneasy, especially their friends who drink and drive or who habitually speed. Police officers' friends often do not understand some of the actions police are forced to take in fulfilling their responsibilities.

Police officers not only frequently lose their nonpolice friends, they may also come to realize that they are now a part of a group that is isolated from the rest of society. Although they are highly visible, they are set apart. They may be feared, disliked, hated, or even assaulted by citizens. Thus they keep close ranks for protection and security. The closer they become, the greater the suspicion and fear on the part of the citizens, leading to even tighter ranks, and so the cycle goes. Police officers are expected to take the place of mother, father, church, and school—to be "family"—to those who will not accept them.

The police become the "in group" and everyone else is the "out group." As noted by Skolnick (1967, p. 52), social isolation produces a "we-they" view of the world. To a police officer the world consists of cops and civilians, or perhaps better phrased as cops versus civilians.

This "them versus us" attitude leads to defensiveness exhibited in such ways as reluctance to give up traditional police responsibilities (for example, traffic control on state highways) or reluctance to explain their actions to citizens. Official police silence is sometimes necessary to protect the rights of others or to safeguard an investigation, but sometimes it is, in reality, a defensive response.

The dominant characteristic of the police culture is isolationism. It may result in a "them versus us" situation.

Police officers who isolate themselves from the community and from their nonpolice friends frequently develop a "one-track" life with the central focus being law enforcement. They may have few outside interests, devoting their attention to reading articles and watching programs related to law enforcement and socializing only with other individuals in the law enforcement field.

STRESS AND BURNOUT

No discussion of the real life of a police officer would be complete without recognizing the highly stressful nature of this profession. Police officers deal with crisis daily, usually that of someone else. Sometimes, however, the demands of the roles and how they are expected to be performed create enough stress to put police officers themselves into a crisis situation.

A police officer's job is highly stressful and may result in a personal crisis for the officer.

Several writers and researchers have stated that police work is, indeed, stressful. Dash and Reiser (1978, p. 18) have noted: "Police work is a high stress occupation. It affects, shapes, and, at times, scars the individuals and families involved."

Stress can be either positive or negative. In ancient China the symbol for stress had two written characters—one for opportunity and one for danger. In fact, the excitement/stress of police work is one important reason many individuals enter the profession. According to Conroy and Hess (1992, p. 7): "One positive side of police stress is the excitement. The incredible feeling when the pulse quickens, the senses keen, and all energy focuses on crisis can translate into status for you. The more stress you're put under, the more exciting the job [is]."

Unfortuately, much of the stress experienced by police officers and, indeed, the general population, is negative. As noted by Bennett and Hess (1992, p. 446), daily living or general sources of stress include the following:

- Changes/transitions (marriage, separation, divorce, death, moving, job changes/loss).
- Relationships (continued conflicts, lack of support).
- Life-style (inconsistent, credit-card debt, poor investments).
- Loss of self-esteem (falling behind professionally, accepting others' expectations).
- Fatigue or illness (poor diet, lack of sleep, lack of exercise).

The importance of these daily stressors are noted by Noble (1989, pp. 38–39):

Very few of us [police officers] die in shoot-outs and high-speed chases. In truth, police work takes its toll in more insidious ways. Instead of going out in a blaze of glory, the average officer dies by inches. It is the daily stresses, often compounded by poor eating, irregular sleep, and a general lack of fitness, which erode our bodies and minds before helping us into early graves.

Other sources of stress are job related. Cope (1991, p. 1E) cites a poll conducted for Northwestern National Life based on "the growing realization that stress is caused by the organization itself." This poll found that one out of three people thought seriously about quitting their jobs because of stress. The stressors identified included the following circumstances:

- Mandatory overtime is frequently required.
- Employees have little control over how they do their work.
- Consequences of making a mistake on the job are severe.
- Workloads vary greatly.
- Employees must react quickly and accurately to rapidly changing conditions.
- Personal conflicts on the job are commonplace.
- Few opportunities for advancement are available.
- Employees deal with lots of red tape to get things done.
- Staffing, money, and/or technology are inadequate.
- Pay is below the going rate.
- Employees are rotated among shifts.
- Employees generally are isolated from one another.
- Employees have little or no privacy.
- Meal breaks are unpredictable.
- Work is either sedentary or physically exhausting.

It is rather amazing how closely the preceding stressors seem to be describing police work! Indeed, most individuals employed in law enforcement as well as those in the criminal justice system have these stressors and more. Monahan and Farmer (1980, p. 46) cite the following stressors frequently encountered by those in law enforcement:

- Courts—rulings and procedures.
- Top-level police administrators' decisions, lack of support, favoritism, etc.
- Departmental policies.

- Departmental procedures.
- Equipment—adequacy and state of repair.
- Dangerous life or duty situations.
- Public image of police.
- Repulsive situation (fatal accidents, death notifications).
- Changing shift routine.
- Negative encounters with supervisors.
- Non-police work duties.
- Lack of confidence in fellow officers.
- Multiple conflicting job demands.
- Departmental politics.
- External politics affecting the department.
- Boredom and isolation.
- Pay and job status.
- Promotional opportunities.
- Abuse by public.
- Feeling unappreciated.

As noted by Oglesby (1991):

Law enforcement officers are highly vulnerable to a variety of occupational pressures and stress factors, falling into two general categories, external and internal:

External—unfavorable court decisions, police media coverage, lack of community support, increase in violent crime, increased disrespect for law and order, and the increased potential to become the victim of an assault which may be fatal.

Internal—struggle for increased salary and benefits, highly competitive promotional practices, limited career advancement, affirmative action, sexual harassment, lack of administrative support, policies which adversely affect morale, rotating shifts, excessive paperwork, and poor quality, outdated, and limited equipment.

Terry (1981, pp. 61–65) discusses four sets of stressors functioning in police work:

External stressors include frustrations with the criminal justice system, particularly in terms of the apparent leniency of court decisions and the scheduling of court appearances, discontent with unfavorable media coverage, resentment of certain opinions arising out of minority communities, and dislike of the decisions and interests of government and administrative bodies affecting the performance of police work.

Internal stressors cover a large number of problem areas, many of which are organizational, including training that is felt to be inadequate, equipment that is thought to be substandard or in a state of disrepair, poor pay, and ambiguously defined reward structures, as well as inadequate career development guidelines, offensive departmental policies, excessive paperwork, and intradepartmental political favoritism.

Task-related stressors include role conflicts, the rigors of shift work, boredom, fear, danger, being exposed to the miseries and brutalities of life, and work overload.

Finally individual stressors include fears about job competence, individual success, and safety. Discussions of individual stressors also include consideration of stressors arising out of performing police work, particularly health problems, alcoholism, marital problems, divorce, and suicide.

One important stressor is the shift work often involved in law enforcement positions. As noted by O'Neill and Cushing (1991, p. 1):

The impact of shift work, particularly rotating shifts, has garnered national and international attention in recent years. As early as 1978, the National Institute of

Occupational Safety and Health issued the following warning in a report titled *Health Consequences of Shift Work*:

> "Rotating shift workers, who not only work at unconventional hours but who move from shift to shift, clearly encounter the most difficulty in adjusting their psycho-biological rhythms and patterns to their work schedules. Shift work may well pose a distinct health hazard for certain rotating shift workers."

O'Neill and Cushing (p. 10) note that: "Studies have shown that 20 percent of the population has no difficulty adjusting to shift work, 60 percent of the population has difficulty adjusting, and 20 percent is unable to adjust at all."

An extensive study of the effects of police work conducted in Chicago came to the following conclusion (O'Neill and Cushing, p. 67): "Shift work is deleterious to the physical and psychological health of the individual and to the well-being of the organization."

If the stresses become great enough, officers may burn out. According to Bennett and Hess (1992, p. 458): "**Burnout** occurs when someone is 'consumed, rendered unserviceable or ineffectual by maximum use; exhausted or made listless through overwork, stress, or intemperance.' Burnout is a problem resulting from long-term, unmediated stress.... Those most likley to experience burnout are those who are initially most committed. You cannot burn out if you have never been on fire."

Ellison and Genz (1978, pp. 4–5) examine some specific factors that might account for burnout. They first identify two specific types of particularly stressful situations: the first is the wounding or death of a fellow officer, especially one's partner; the second is the maiming or sexual assault of a child. They note that as long as only one kind of basic skill is required in a job, problems are minimal, but that when assignments require different, contradictory skills, problems do arise:

> When the necessity for interaction and sensitivity to human feelings and behavior is combined in an assignment with the necessity for dealing with situations which demand distancing because they [police officers] deal with basic human fears of mutilation, trauma, and death, the officer must attempt to perform the almost impossible balancing act of working appropriately with "clients" who are undergoing ego-threatening crisis and protecting his own ego.

Ellison and Genz (1978, pp. 4–5) feel that burnout is more of a problem when officers are required to handle large numbers of serious calls or when they are not equipped or trained to handle them. Further, they believe that "job-related stress is exacerbated, and indeed, may be caused by certain traditional police practices. One of the most devastating of these is the indiscriminate use of a military model. This model sees police skills as technological ones. It assumes that every assignment involves skills that do not vary greatly from individual to individual or with the setting. It views discretion as unimportant and inappropriate for all but top brass." Unfortunately, this model simply does not work in many situations.

Another serious problem related to stress is **post-traumatic stress disorder.** As noted by Fiscus (1991, p. 63):

> In 1980, the American Psychiatric Association formally recognized post-traumatic stress syndrome (PTSD) as a medical entity.... Law enforcement is custom made for this disorder as the very nature of the work fits the clinical description of the illness:
>
> "Post-traumatic stress disorder is characterized by recurrent nightmares, intrusive thoughts, or flash-backs of a traumatic event; phobic behavior or gener-

alized apathy; and hypervigilance and other symptoms of increased arousal lasting longer than one month. . . . Post-traumatic stress disorder often occurs after a highly stressful event that is outside the range of usual human experience and would be distressing to almost anyone."

Fiscus (p. 64) notes: "The illness generally happens after a highly stressful event or series of events and is most commonly associated with shooting incidents."

Recognizing the stress involved in the law enforcement profession is a first step in preventing burnout or other serious emotional or physical symptoms.

Individuals going into law enforcement should do so knowing fully what the job entails. In addition, they must know what powers they are granted and how they are restricted by the laws of the country, the focus of the next chapter.

SUMMARY

The future success (or failure) of our law enforcement system depends in large part on the effectiveness of our police officers. Therefore, valid recruitment, screening, testing, and selection procedures must be used to assure that only well-qualified candidates are hired. Qualities identified in good police officers include reliability, leadership, judgment, persuasiveness, communication skills, accuracy, initiative, integrity, honesty, ego control, intelligence, and sensitivity. Individuals possessing such skills are sought through a careful selection procedure.

Police officer selection usually includes (1) a formal application, (2) a written examination, (3) a physical agility test, (4) a psychological examination, (5) a medical examination, (6) an oral interview, and (7) a thorough background investigation. Most agencies require that a police officer candidate be a citizen of the United States, have or be eligible for a driver's license in the state, and not have been convicted of a felony. Additional requirements may specify educational level and residency in the community served.

In addition to local and state requirements for recruitment and selection of police officers, certain federal guidelines and regulations must be met. Most important are the 1964 Omnibus Civil Rights Law, which prohibits discrimination in employment opportunities in private business, and the Equal Employment Opportunity Act of 1972, which prohibits discrimination due to sex, race, color, religion, or national origin in employment of any kind, public or private, local, state, or federal. All individuals meeting the specific requirements of the department should be given the opportunity to apply for and successfully compete with other candidates.

Members of minority groups are highly beneficial in a police department. A racially balanced and integrated police department fosters community relations and increases police effectiveness.

Just as members of minority groups have a promising future in law enforcement, so do women. The acceptance of women into law enforcement paralleled the newly accepted emphasis on citizen protection and crime prevention rather than exclusive concentration on the enforcement of laws and detection of crimes.

Once candidates have passed all tests in the selection process, they usually enter a one-year probationary period during which they are observed while obtaining training and while applying this training on the streets. This probationary period allows for evaluation of the selected candidates. After the probation, the officers should continue to receive periodic in-service training to maintain already acquired skills and to achieve proficiency in new ones.

All police officers, be they white, black, brown, male, or female, are subjected to the hazards of police work, and all are expected to fulfill the responsibilities of the job. Each must be given an equal chance to become a police officer, to be adequately trained, and to be promoted. Each offers the profession an added dimension and one more means of fulfilling its mission.

The dominant characteristic of the "police culture" is isolationism, which may result in a "them versus us" orientation that does little to further good community relations. Stress and burnout are often a problem for police officers.

DISCUSSION QUESTIONS

1. What is the most common restriction for off-duty work for a police officer?

2. Where are the United States Civil Service Commission offices in your area?

3. Is a newspaper advertisement placed by a police department that requests that only women apply for a job opening fair?

4. What is the most common reason for rejection during the selection process?

5. What employment opportunities in law enforcement are available locally? In your county? Your state?

6. What is the percentage of minorities and women on your police force? Is this "balanced"? How did this situation come to be?

7. How do police officers deal with their own lives when they spend so much time with the worst of people?

8. What are some societal factors interfering with police work?

9. What is the dominant characteristic of the police culture?

10. Whose problem is it when the police and the community don't get along?

TERMS

bona fide occupational qualification (BFOQ), burnout, moonlighting, post-traumatic stress disorder (PTSD), reverse discrimination, situational testing.

REFERENCES

Bennett, W. W. and Hess, K. M. *Management and Supervision in Law Enforcement.* St. Paul, Minn.: West Publishing Company, 1992.

Bittel, L. R. *The McGraw-Hill 36-Hour Management Course.* New York: McGraw-Hill, 1989.

Briggs, K. C. and Myers, I. B. *Myers-Briggs Type Indicator*™. Palo Alto, Calif.: Consulting Psychologists Press, 1976.

Conroy, D. L. and Hess, K. M. *Officers at Risk: How to Identify and Cope with Stress.* Placerville, Calif.: Custom Publishing Company, 1992.

Cope, L. "Job-Stress Test Identifies Work Situations That Are Worst, Best." *Star Tribune,* May 1, 1991, 1E, 8E.

Dash, J. and Reiser, M. "Suicide among Police in Urban Law Enforcement Agencies." *Journal of Police Science and Administration* (1978): 18–21.

Ellison, W. K. and Genz, J. L. "The Police Officer as Burned-Out Samaritan." *FBI Law Enforcement Bulletin* (March 1978): 2–7.

Fiscus, C. A. "Post Traumatic Stress and Mandatory Retirement; Who Wins?" *Law and Order* (September 1991): 63–64.

Fralicx, R. "Better Quality Police Officer: The Result of Test-Oriented Selection Process." *Law and Order* (November 1990): 66–69.

Gough, H. G. "California Psychological Inventory: Proven Measure of Normal Personality." *1988 CPP Catalog.* Palo Alto, Calif.: Consulting Psychologists Press, 1988: 45–47.

Harr, J. S. and Hess K. M. *Seeking Employment in Law Enforcement, Private Security, and Related Fields.* St. Paul, Minn.: West Publishing Company, 1992.

Hinkle, D. P. "College Degree an Inpractical Prerequisite for Police Work." *Law and Order* (July 1991): 105.

"Indiana University Develops Police Selection Procedure." *Target* 6, no. 8 (September 1977): 1.

Kolpack, B. D. "The Assessment Center Approach to Police Officer Selection." *The Police Chief* (September 1991): 28–46.

Lancaster, D. A. "One Woman's Struggle." *Police* 7, no. 9 (September 1983): 42–43.

Litchford, J. M. "The Americans with Disabilities Act." *The Police Chief* (January 1991): 11–13.

Mahan R. "Personnel Selection in Police Agencies: Educational Requirements for Entry Level." *Law and Order* (January 1991): 282–286.

Martin, S. E. *Women on the Move? A Report on the Status of Women in Policing: Police Foundation Report.* Washington, D.C.: Police Foundation, 1989.

McDowell, J. "Are Women Better Cops?" *Time,* February 17, 1992, 70–72.

Mitchell, J. V., Jr. "California Psychological Inventory." *The Ninth Mental Measurements Yearbook.* Vol. 1. Lincoln, Neb.: University of Nebraska Press, 1985: 249–254.

Mitchell, J. V., Jr. "Watson-Glaser Critical Thinking Appraisal." *The Ninth Mental Measurements Yearbook.* Vol. 1. Lincoln, Neb.: University of Nebraska Press, 1985: 1691–1694.

Monahan, L. H. and Farmer, R. E. *Stress and the Police: A Manual for Prevention.* Pacific Palisades, Calif.: Palisades Publishers, 1980.

Myers, I. B. and Briggs, K. C. "Myers-Briggs Type Indicator™." *1988 CPP Catalog.* Palo Alto, Calif.: Consulting Psychologists Press, 1988: 30–32.

Noble, T. R. "Let's Get Physical." *Police* (May 1989): 38–41, 44.

Oglesby, E. W. Review of Third Edition, *Introduction to Law Enforcement and Criminal Justice* (October 1991).

O'Neill, J. L. and Cushing, M. A. *The Impact of Shift Work.* Washington, D.C.: Police Executive Research Forum, 1991.

Police Executive Research Forum. "BJS Releases Latest Data on Law Enforcement." In *Subject to Debate.* Washington, D.C.: Police Executive Research Forum, May/April 1992: 6.

Scuro, J. E., Jr. "The Americans with Disabilities Act." *Law and Order* (March 1992): 59–63.

Skolnick, J. H. *Justice without Trial: Law Enforcement in a Democratic Society.* New York: John Wiley and Sons, 1967.

Slater, H. R. and Reiser, M. "A Comparative Study of Factors Influencing Police Recruitment." *Journal of Police Science and Administration* (September 1988): 168–176.

Starr, R. "What Kind of Police Officer Do We Want?" *Insight,* February 25, 1991, 64.

Strong, E. K., Jr.; Hansen, J. C.; and Campbell, D. P. "Strong Interest Inventory." *1988 CPP Catalog.* Palo Alto, Calif.: Consulting Psychologists Press, 1988: 4–11.

Sullivan, P. S. "Minority Officers, Current Issues." In *Critical Issues in Policing: Contemporary Readings,* edited by R. D. Dunham and G. P. Alpert. Prospect Heights, Ill.: Waveland Press, 1989.

Terry, W. C., III "Police Stress: The Empirical Evidence." *Journal of Police Science and Administration* 9, no. 1 (1981): 61–65.

Tsushima, W. T. "Minnesota Multiphasic Personality Inventory." In *Encyclopedia of Psychology,* vol. 2, edited by Raymond J. Corsini. New York: John Wiley and Sons, 1984.

CHAPTER 4

The American Quest for Freedom and Justice: Our Laws

We hold these truths to be self-evident: that all men are endowed by their creator with certain unalienable rights; that among these are life, liberty, and the pursuit of happiness.

—Thomas Jefferson

Do You Know

What civil rights and civil liberties are?

What the Declaration of Independence says about civil rights and civil liberties?

How to define and differentiate law, social or moral law, common law, case law, and statutory law?

What law takes precedence if two laws conflict?

What equity is?

What the basic instrument of government and the supreme law of the land is?

What the Bill of Rights is?

What specific rights are guaranteed by the First, Second, Fourth, Fifth, Sixth, Eighth, Thirteenth, and Fourteenth Amendments?

Where police get their power and authority and what restrictions are placed on this power and authority?

When changes in our institutions and statutes are necessary?

INTRODUCTION

The Europeans' original immigration to the New World was heavily motivated by a desire to escape the religious, economic, political, and social repressions of traditional European society. North America was seen as a land where individuals could get a new start, free to make of themselves what they chose.

Sometimes, however, reality did not fully coincide with the **American creed** of individual freedom, as seen in the treatment of Native Americans, the importation of slaves, the establishment of state churches, and the repressiveness involved in episodes such as the Salem witchcraft trials. Nevertheless, the spirit of liberty and justice remained strong. As noted by Gunnar Myrdal (1944): the American creed is the national conscience; a body of beliefs about equality, liberty, and justice which most Americans believe in, in spite of the fact that America has, and always has had, multiple wrongs.

In the 1760s the British began taking away rights that Americans had come to feel were naturally theirs, and the American Revolution resulted. In effect, the United States was born out of a desire for—indeed, a demand for—civil rights and civil liberties.

Civil rights are those claims that the citizen has to the affirmative assistance of government. **Civil liberties** are an individual's immunity from governmental oppression.

Civil rights and civil liberties are recurring themes in America's development. Our initial institutions reflected an intense concern for the individual human spirit. Our founding fathers showed strong commitments to positively guarantee those rights that Americans had fought and died to protect in the American Revolution. These values were forcefully stated in our most basic document: the Declaration of Independence.

THE DECLARATION OF INDEPENDENCE

The Declaration of Independence is not only a statement of grievances against England, but it is also a statement of alternative basic premises underlying human freedom. As Thomas Jefferson phrased it in the Declaration, the United States was demanding "the separate and equal station to which the laws of nature and of nature's God entitle them." In powerful rhetoric, Jefferson asserted:

> We hold these truths to be self-evident:—That all men are created equal; that they are endowed by their Creator with certain unalienable rights; that among these are life, liberty, and the pursuit of happiness. That, to secure these rights, governments are instituted among men, deriving their just powers from the consent of the governed; that, whenever any form of government becomes destructive of these ends, it is the right of the people to alter or to abolish it, and to institute new government.

In other words, the purpose of government is to secure the people's unalienable rights, including life, liberty, and happiness—on an equal basis, since "all men are created equal."

The Declaration of Independence asserts that all individuals are created equal and are entitled to the unalienable rights of life, liberty, and the pursuit of happiness. It further asserts that governments are instituted by and derive their power from the governed.

The Declaration of Independence was an idealistic statement of philosophy. It broke our ties with England, but it did not establish how the United States should be structured or governed. As you saw in Chapter 2, each colony developed its own means of policing and protecting itself. The colonists relied heavily on laws they had brought with them from their homelands, England in particular.

TYPES OF LAW

Several types of law must be understood to appreciate the importance and complexities of law and to put the police role in proper perspective. Recall that this textbook began with a discussion of what law is. Law is a body of rules for human conduct that are enforced by imposing penalties for their violation. Laws define social obligations and determine the relations of individuals to society and to each other. The purpose of law is to regulate the actions of individuals to conform to the way of life that the people's elected representatives or the community consider essential.

Social or Moral Law

Often obedience to law is obtained through social pressure—ridicule, contempt, scorn, or ostracism. Such methods are called moral or social sanctions, and the laws they enforce are called moral or social laws.

Moral or **social laws** are laws made by society and enforced solely by social pressure.

Moral or social laws include laws of etiquette, "honor," and morality. When moral laws break down and social sanctions fail to obtain conformity, other laws may be enacted and enforced.

Precedents: Common Law and Case Law

The beginnings of law are found in social habit or custom. Custom is simply **precedent**—doing what has been done before. In early times custom, religion, morals, and the law were intermingled. Some early customs have, over the centuries, become law.

Some customs were enforced physically rather than morally, and the violator was expelled from the community, sacrificed to the gods, or hanged. Other violations of custom that were not felt to be harmful to the whole community were punished by the injured group or the injured individual with the aid of the family (self-help, vengeance, feud). As long as such acts of vengeance, although regarded as right by the victim, might lead to retaliation, the sanction behind the rules of custom were still purely moral. But when the community began to protect those who had taken *rightful* vengeance, these persons became agents of the community. This kind of self-help met early society's needs when the right to take vengeance or redress was clear. It did not provide a way to settle controversies. Therefore, courts were established to interpret customs and settle controversies.

Custom was replaced by judicial precedent. Legally, however, precedents or decisions are not law, but only evidence of the law. Even if the precedent or decision is written, the law in them is "unwritten."

In England, **common law** was the term applied to the laws and customs of the realm applied by the royal courts. It was defined as the customary law of

England set by the judges as disputes rose. This was in contrast to local custom, equity, or **ecclesiastical** (church) **law.** When Parliament supplemented and modified the existing legal principles, the term *common law* was used to describe the law in force before, and independent of, any acts of the legislature.

Common law refers to the precedents set by the judges in the royal courts in England.

The common law brought to the United States by the early settlers and established in the various colonies forms the basis of modern American law. The common law of the states has one exception, Louisiana, which established and kept the system of French civil law.

In a nontechnical sense, common law describes the precedent generally followed in the absence of a specific law. In the United States this has come to be known as **case law.**

Case law refers to judicial precedents; no specifiic law exists, but a similar case serves as a model to be followed.

According to Oran's *Dictionary of the Law:* "Case law summarizes how statutes and constitutional problems have been interpreted by judges in cases coming before them." When cases not covered by the law come before the courts, the judges' rulings on previous similar cases will, for all practical purposes, be treated as law.

Statutory Law

In an advanced society, legislation becomes an increasingly important agency of legal development. The United States, as well as many other countries, has largely succeeded in replacing common law (unwritten law) with **statutory law** (legislated and written law). Much of our law still rests upon judicial precedent, however; that is, common law and case law.

Statutory law is law passed by the legislature. It may be passed at the federal or state level, and at either level it includes **constitutional** and **ordinary law.**

Federal constitutional law is based on the United States Constitution, its amendments, and interpretations of the Constitution by the federal courts, as discussed shortly. Law enforcement officers must comply with constitutional law, which places numerous restrictions on their actions. Ordinary federal law consists of acts of Congress, treaties with foreign states, executive orders and regulations, and interpretation of the preceding by federal courts.

State constitutional law is based on the individual state's constitution, its amendments, and interpretations of them by the state's courts. State ordinary law consists of acts of the state legislatures, decisions of the federal courts in interpreting or developing the common law, executive orders and regulations, and municipal ordinances.

In addition, in most states, each county and city is given the right to make and pass laws for its local jurisdiction, providing the law does not conflict or preempt the state's laws. The basis of the local **ordinances** (laws) are primarily enacted to protect the individual community.

Order of Authority of Law

If two laws conflict, a set order of authority has been established.

The order of authority of law is the federal Constitution, treaties with foreign powers, acts of Congress, the state constitutions, state statutes, and finally, common law or case law.

Equity

Before leaving the general discussion of laws, one other concept is important; that is, the concept of **equity.**

Equity means to resort to general principles of fairness and justice whenever existing law is inadequate.

Neither the Roman praetors nor the English chancellors made rigid rules like legislators. Instead they found law in the decisions of single cases as judges do. They did not, however, regard themselves bound by precedents. The new rules were not regarded as law at first but rather as arbitrary assertions of governmental power. Both in Rome and in England, however, equity, following its own precedents, soon developed a new body of judicial custom recognized as law. In England and in the United States today, equity is recognized as judge-made law, that is, a legal ruling by a judge based on fairness. In the United States, equity describes a system of rules and doctrines supplementing common and statutory law and superseding laws that are inadequate for fair settlement of a case. In other words, equity requires that the "spirit of the law" take precedence over the "letter of the law."

Equity demands that the law change as society changes. In fact, our law has been called a "living law." Laws that once made good sense now appear ridiculous. Consider, for example, the following laws:

- An old law in Truro, Massachusetts, states that a young man may not marry until he has killed either six blackbirds or three crows.

- In Gary, Indiana, it is illegal to go into a theater within four hours of eating garlic.

- An old Minnesota law requires that men's and women's underwear may not be hung on the same clothesline at the same time.

- In Pine Island, Minnesota, a man must tip his hat to every passing cow.

- In Gurnee, Illinois, a two-hundred pound woman is not allowed to wear shorts when riding a horse.

Obviously, if every locality and state were left alone, our legal system would be in a terrible state. Fortunately, our founding fathers foresaw this danger and wrote the Constitution of the United States, a carefully drafted document to establish the workings of a democracy.

THE UNITED STATES CONSTITUTION

The **Constitution** was drafted by the Constitutional Convention of 1787 and, following its ratification by conventions in two-thirds of the states, became effective in 1789. It is the basic instrument of government and the supreme law of the United States.

The Constitution states that the legislative, executive, and judicial departments of government should be separated as far as is practical, and that their respective powers should be exercised by different individuals or groups of individuals. The legislature makes the laws, the executive branch, of which law enforcement is a part, enforces the laws, and the judicial branch determines when laws have been violated.

The Constitution is the basic instrument of government and the supreme law of the United States.

When the first Congress of the United States convened on March 4, 1789, it had before it 103 amendments to the Constitution submitted by the states, forty-two amendments proposed by minority groups within the states, and bills of rights submitted by two states. After deliberating on these proposed amendments, Congress reduced them to twelve to submit to the states for ratification. Two failed to be ratified; the others became the first ten amendments. They went into effect on December 15, 1791, and are known as the Bill of Rights.

THE BILL OF RIGHTS

The Constitution organized the government of the new nation but contained few personal guarantees. Consequently, some states refused to ratify it without

Congreſs of the United States :

Begun and held at the City of New-York, on Wedneſday the fourth of March, one thouſand ſeven hundred and eighty-nine.

THE Conventions of a number of the States having at the time of their adopting the CONSTITUTION *expreſſed a deſire, in order to prevent miſconſtruction or abuſe of its powers, that further declaratory and reſtrictive clauſes ſhould be added : And as extending the ground of public confidence in the government will beſt enſure the beneficent ends of its inſtitution—*

RESOLVED *by the* SENATE *and* HOUSE *of* REPRESENTATIVES *of the United States of America in Congreſs aſſembled, two thirds of both Houſes concurring,* That the following articles be propoſed to the legiſlatures of the ſeveral ſtates, as amendments to the Conſtitution of the United States, all or any of which articles, when ratified by *three fourths* of the ſaid legiſlatures, to be valid to all intents and purpoſes, as part of the ſaid Conſtitution, viz.

ARTICLES in Addition to, and Amendment of, the CONSTITUTION OF THE UNITED STATES OF AMERICA, *propoſed by Congreſs, and ratified by the Legiſlatures of the ſeveral States, purſuant to the fifth Article of the original Conſtitution.*

The first official version of the ratified Bill of Rights for circulation to the governors of the states was printed in February 1792 on order of the secretary of state, Thomas Jefferson.

a specific bill of rights. In 1791 ten amendments, with personal guarantees included, came into effect. They became known as the **Bill of Rights,** a fundamental document describing the liberties of the people and forbidding the government to violate these rights.

The Bill of Rights protects a person's right to "life, liberty, and the pursuit of happiness." It forbids the government to violate these rights.

Humans are considered to have inborn rights of which a government may not deprive them. Government has only limited powers, which are delegated by the people.

Individual constitutional rights are clearly specified in each amendment. Some are of more relevance to individuals in law enforcement than others. Of special importance are the First, Second, Fourth, Fifth, Sixth, Eighth, Thirteenth, and Fourteenth Amendments.

The First Amendment

Congress shall make no law respecting an establishment of religion, or prohibiting the free exercise thereof; or abridging the freedom of speech or of the press; or the right of the people peaceably to assemble and to petition the government for a redress of grievances.

The First Amendment guarantees:

- Freedom of religion.
- Freedom of speech.
- Freedom of the press.
- Freedom of peaceable assembly.
- Freedom of petition.

Freedom of Religion Two guarantees of religious freedom are provided: (1) no law can establish an official church that all Americans must accept and support or that favors one church over another, and (2) no law is constitutional that prohibits the free exercise of religion. In short, citizens are guaranteed freedom to worship as they see fit.

According to Gardner and Anderson (1992, p. 348), the Supreme Court defined the First Amendment freedom of religion in *Davis v. Beason* (1890):

The First Amendment was intended to allow everyone under the jurisdiction of the United States to entertain such notions respecting his relations to his Maker and the duties they impose as may be approved by his judgment and conscience, and to exhibit his sentiments in such form of worship, as he may think proper, not injurious to the equal rights of others, and to prohibit legislation for the support of any religious tenets or the modes of worship of any sect....

The First Amendment clearly separates church and state and requires that the government be neutral on religious matters, favoring no religion above another. The first guarantee of this amendment, called the Establishment Clause, was made applicable to the states in *Cantwell v. Connecticut* (1940) and *Murdock v. Pennsylvania* (1943).

Cantwell v. Connecticut ruled that it was religious censorship to require official county approval for a person to solicit house-to-house for religious or philanthropic causes.

Murdock v. Pennsylvania ruled that municipal license fees on transient merchants or book agents could not be applied to Jehovah's Witnesses who went door-to-door offering religious pamphlets for sale.

Gardner and Anderson (1992, p. 348) note that in *Cantwell v. Connecticut* the Supreme Court held:

> Thus the [First] Amendment embraces two concepts—freedom to believe and freedom to act. The first is absolute, but, in the nature of things, the second cannot be. Conduct remains subject to regulation for the protection of society.... The essential characteristics of these liberties [set forth in the First Amendment], is, that under their shield many types of life, character, opinion and belief can develop unmolested and unobstructed. Nowhere is this shield more necessary than in our own country for a people composed of many races and creeds.

The second guarantee of the First Amendment is called the Free Exercise Clause and is very closely related to the freedom of speech portion of the First Amendment. Important cases related to this law are as follows:

- *Pierce v. Society of Sisters* (1925) struck down on Oregon law requiring that all children attend only public schools for the first eight grades.

- *Lovell v. Griffin* (1938) protected Jehovah's Witnesses' rights to sell their literature door-to-door, on free-press grounds.

- *Niemotko v. Maryland* (1951) reversed the conviction of some Jehovah's Witnesses arrested for making speeches in a public park without a permit.

- *Kunz v. New York* (1951) struck down a New York ordinance requiring a police permit to hold public worship meetings on city streets.

Freedom of Speech   The Supreme Court has ruled that the First Amendment does not protect all forms of expression. Highly inflammatory remarks spoken to a crowd, which advocate violence and clearly threaten the peace and safety of the community, or present a "clear and present danger" to the continued existence of the government, are not protected.

Schenck v. United States (1919) established the "clear and present danger" doctrine and serves as a guide to the constitutionality of government restrictions on free speech (and free press). The Court held that: "The most stringent protection of free speech would not protect a man in falsely shouting fire in a theatre causing a panic. . . . The question in every case is whether the words are used in such circumstances and are of such a nature as to create a clear and present danger that they will bring about the substantive evils that Congress has a right to prevent."

Chaplinsky v. New Hampshire (1942) also established that use of **fighting words** likely to cause violence will not be tolerated. The Court ruled in this case that the states can ban the use of those "personally abusive epithets which, when addressed to the ordinary citizen, are, as a matter of common knowledge, inherently likely to provide violent reaction" (Lewis and Peoples 1978, p. 1074).

The ban on "fighting words" and words presenting a "clear and present danger" is counterbalanced by the concept of **pure speech,** a theory created by the Supreme Court. Pure speech is speech without any accompanying action. In *Watts v. United States* (1969) the Court reversed the conviction of a defendant who told a discussion group that he was not going to report for military induction and that: "If they ever make me carry a rifle, the first man I want to get in my sights is L.B.J." Watts was originally convicted under the federal law against knowingly and willfully threatening the president. When it was proved that Watts had no real intention of killing the president, the Court held Watts was exercising his right to free speech and that his statement was "political hyperbole" rather than a true threat. Another example of pure speech is the Americanism "Kill the umpire," heard throughout the country during the baseball season.

According to Gardner and Anderson (1992, p. 267):

> The requirements for the "fighting word" violation are (a) that a valid criminal statute or ordinance exist in that jurisdiction which clearly and specifically prohibits such language likely to cause a breach of the peace by the person to whom it is addressed; (b) that such language is used and addressed to a person on a face-to-face basis and that the words and the manner in which they were used could cause the average person to respond with an act of violence. The occasion, the manner, and the context in which the words were used do much to determine the offensiveness of the words. The words must be one step away from violence.

They provide the following example:

> A man walking down a street makes foul and insulting remarks to every girl and woman he meets, causing angry reactions. Persons complain to an officer who hears him make such remarks. . . . There would be ample justification for an arrest in jurisdictions having statutes or ordinances that forbid language or conduct tending to cause or provoke a disturbance or breach of the peace.
>
> "The test is what (persons) of common intelligence would understand would be words likely to cause an average (person) to fight" (*Chaplinsky v. New Hampshire*).

Some states have additional requirements before convicting on a "fighting word" violation if the words are spoken to a police officer. In the 1988 case of *Harrington v. Tulsa,* the Oklahoma court of appeals ruled that police officers must exercise a higher standard of restraint and that in the *Harrington* case the police officers were not likely to cause a fight. Other courts, however, have disagreed with this view. In 1989 in *Burgess v. City of Virginia Beach,* the court said it "shudder[ed] to think of the verbal abuse that law enforcement officers would be subject to" if this higher standard of restraint were used.

Table 4–1 summarizes the types of verbal offenses that might be specified in state statutes and what constitutes the verbal offense.

Unlike pure speech, a second type of speech called **speech plus** is not protected by the First Amendment. An example of speech plus is the action taken by people in a labor strike picket line. If the striking employees physically prevent other people from entering or leaving a commercial building, the police may be called upon to assure that those who wish to enter or exit the building are allowed to do so.

Courts have also recognized that **symbolic speech,** involving tangible forms of expression such as wearing buttons or clothing with political slogans or displaying a sign or a flag, is protected by the First Amendment.

Even burning of the American flag has been upheld by the Supreme Court as protected by the First Amendment. In both *Texas v. Johnson* (1989) and *United States v. Eichman* (1990), the Court held that states may not forbid flagburning if the person is burning his or her own flag and not committing another offense while doing so. As noted by Gardner and Anderson (1992, p. 294):

> Flag-burners could be punished if they burned the flag of another person without the consent of that person (criminal damage to the property of another). They

Table 4-1 **Verbal Offenses**

TYPE OF VERBAL OFFENSE	TO CONSTITUTE THE VERBAL OFFENSE, THERE MUST BE
"fighting words"	1. insulting or abusive language 2. addressed to a person on a face-to-face basis 3. causing a likelihood that "the person addressed will make an immediate violent response"
obscenity	1. a communication that, taken as a whole, appeals to the prurient (lustful) interest in sex, 2. and portrays sexual conduct in a patently offensive way, 3. and the communication, taken as a whole, does not have serious literary, artistic, political, or scientific value.
urging unlawful conduct (inciting)	1. language or communication directed to inciting, producing, or urging 2. **imminent** lawless action or conduct, or 3. language or communication likely to incite or produce such unlawful conduct
obstruction of a law enforcement officer (or of justice)	1. deliberate and intentional language (or communication) that hinders, obstructs, delays, or makes more difficult 2. a law enforcement officer's effort to perform his official duties (the scienter element of knowledge by the defendant that he or she knew the person obstructed was a law enforcement officer is required) 3. some states require that the "interference would have to be, in part at least, physical in nature" (see the New York case of *People v. Case*)
defamation (libel and slander)	1. words or communication that are false and untrue 2. and injure the character and reputation of another person 3. defamation must be communicated to a third person **When a public official is the victim, it must also be shown** that the words or communications were uttered or published with a reckless disregard as to the truth or falsity of the statement. (See also the case of *Falwell v. Hustler Magazine* as Rev. Falwell is a public figure.)
abusive, obscene, or harassing telephone calls	1. evidence showing that the telephone call was deliberate, 2. and made with intent to harass, frighten, or abuse another person 3. and any other requirement of the particular statute or ordinance
loud speech and loud noise	**Cities and States May:** 1. forbid speech and noises meant by the volume to disturb others 2. and forbid noise and loud speech that create a clear and present danger of violence

Source: T. J. Gardner and T. M. Anderson. *Criminal Law, Principles and Cases.* 5th ed. St. Paul, Minn.: West Publishing Company, © 1992, 292. Reprinted by permission.

could also be charged with trespass if they climbed a government building to take down the flag flying over the building (check the trespass statute in your state or city). If the burning occurred in the middle of a busy traffic intersection, or in a city that had an ordinance forbidding burning without a proper permit, charges could be considered.

Finally, the courts have frequently condemned censorship by requiring official approval or a license in advance of speaking. While citizens are free to make speeches on the public streets, they may be prevented from doing so when they use a loud, raucous amplifier in a hospital zone or when the location

Andrew Hamilton defends Peter Zenger in the famous libel case of 1735.

chosen for the address is likely to interfere with traffic. Thus, freedom of speech is not an absolute.

Freedom of the Press The First Amendment also guarantees the right to express oneself by writing or publishing one's views. The founding fathers recognized the importance of a free interplay of ideas in a democratic society and sought to guarantee the right of all citizens to speak or publish their views, even if they were contrary to those of the government or the society as a whole. Accordingly, the First Amendment generally forbids censorship or other restraint upon speech or the printed word.

As with speech, freedom to write or publish is not an absolute right of expression. The sale of obscene or libelous printed materials is not protected. The Supreme Court has ruled, however, that public figures cannot sue for defamation unless the alleged libelous remarks were printed with knowledge of their falsity or a reckless disregard for the truth.

Broadcasting, including radio, television, and motion pictures, receives the protection of the free press guarantee and is subject to its limitations. As Klein (1980, p. 141) notes: "The right of freedom of expression has come to a head-on collision with those proponents of pornographic literature, movies, and photos. The police are in a dilemma in enforcing statutes designed to inhibit or control this activity. . . . The Supreme Court has not been too helpful in offering precise guidelines as to what is constitutional and what is unconstitutional behavior." Several Supreme Court decisions have attempted to define obscenity.

Roth v. United States (1957) held that obscenity is not within the area of constitutionally protected freedom of speech or press and that the standard to be employed is "whether to the average person, applying contemporary community standards, the dominant theme of the material, taken as a whole, appeals to prurient interest, that is, having a tendency to excite lustful thoughts."

In *Memoirs v. Attorney General of Massachusetts* (1966) the Court stated that for material to be obscene it must be shown that (1) the dominant theme of the material taken as a whole appeals to a prurient interest in sex, (2) the material is patently offensive because it affronts contemporary standards for the description or representation of sexual matters, and (3) the material is utterly without redeeming social value.

Mishkin v. New York (1966) held that the First Amendment was not violated by a state criminal obscenity statute that covered only "hard-core pornography"—that definition being more stringent than the definition required by federal constitutional standards. The case of *Miller v. California* (1973) set forth the following guidelines to determine whether a particular material was obscene: (1) whether the average person, applying contemporary community standards, would find the work, taken as a whole, as appealing to prurient interests; (2) whether the work depicted or described, in a patently offensive way, sexual conduct specifically prohibited by the applicable state law; and (3) whether the work, taken as a whole, lacked serious literary, artistic, political, or scientific value. This case held that the "utterly without redeeming social value" test and the "national standards" test were no longer applicable. In essence, the Court held that local community standards determine what is obscene, and that a work having "some redeeming social value" could no longer be used as a defense.

Finally, *Jenkins v. Georgia* (1974) stated that in state obscenity prosecutions, juries could properly be instructed to apply "community standards" of obscenity without specifying which community.

Other Supreme Court cases have dealt with private use of obscene materials, using the mails to send obscene materials, and laws protecting minors from obscene material.

One area in which police officers may confront problems related to freedom of the press is during political elections. *Branton v. State* (1949) held that a statute forbidding candidates to distribute ballots used in the election to instruct voters to vote for them was constitutional. This problem should diminish, however, as use of voting machines becomes more common.

The police and the press often come into conflict. According to Pace (1991, p. 244): "The police are often at odds with the media because of the slow process of investigation. There is even an incongruity between constitutional guarantees. The First Amendment guarantees freedom of the press while the Sixth and Fourteenth Amendments guarantee the right to a fair trial and the protection of the defendant's rights." (Provisions of the Sixth and Fourteenth Amendments will be discussed shortly.) This same view of the constitutional conflict is noted by Kobel (1989, p. 1):

> In police jurisdictions throughout the United States, police become angry, adversarial and uncooperative with the press for a variety of reasons, including press criticism of the police agency, inaccurate reporting, publication of sensitive information, lack of press sensitivity, or the betrayal of an officer's trust....
>
> The specifics of police-press disputes can take many forms, but restricted access to police information is the common thread that runs through almost every case. Reporters, eager to beat their competition and earn the esteem of being first with the most information, aggressively seek out and publicize as much information as possible on police and crime matters. Police, on the other hand, are as likely as not to withhold information in the interest of protecting their cases and the privacy of those involved.
>
> The situation is one that pits the administration of justice against the public's right to know, fair trial and privacy against a free press, the Sixth Amendment against the First. At its simplest, the police-press standoff is a legitimate, necessary, constitutionally recognized and protected conflict of interests between two groups whose missions are to serve the public good.

Gardner and Anderson (1992, p. 294) stress balancing the need for a free press with the right to a fair trial:

> A free and unfettered press that seeks out and publishes the news is necessary to the functioning of a democracy. The people must be fully and adequately in-

formed in order that they may intelligently discharge their responsibilities as citizens. On the other hand, we as a nation have long cherished the fundamental principles that a defendant in a criminal case shall be afforded all the safeguards of due process of law and shall be given a fair and impartial trial. These two principles come into conflict when newspapers and other communication media publish detailed information before a defendant has been tried.

The potential for the press to try someone in the paper is illustrated in the murder trial of Sam Sheppard, found guilty of brutally murdering his pregnant wife, a case which received "massive, pervasive and prejudicial publicity" (Gardner and Anderson, p. 295). The Ohio Supreme Court in reviewing the case, *Sheppard v. Maxwell* (1966), ruled that the state trial judge:

> ... did not fulfill his duty to protect Sheppard from the inherently prejudicial publicity which saturated the community and (failed) to control disruptive influences in the courtroom....
>
> Murder and mystery, society, sex and suspense were combined in this case in such a manner as to intrigue and captivate the public fancy to a degree perhaps unparalleled in recent annals. Throughout the preindictment investigation, the subsequent legal skirmishes and the nine-week trial, circulation-conscious editors catered to the insatiable interest of the American public in the bizarre.... In this atmosphere of a "Roman holiday" for the news media, Sam Sheppard stood trial for his life.

Freedom of Peaceable Assembly   Americans have the right to assemble peaceably for any political, religious, or social activity. Public authorities cannot impose unreasonable restrictions on such assemblies, but they can impose limitations reasonably designed to prevent fire, health hazards, or traffic obstructions. The Supreme Court has emphasized that freedom of assembly is just as fundamental as freedom of speech and press. Thus, while no law may legitimately prohibit demonstrations, laws or governmental actions may legitimately restrict demonstrations to certain areas or prohibit the obstruction and occupation of public buildings.

Picketing has also been protected under the free speech guarantee; however, it may be reasonably regulated to prevent pickets from obstructing movement onto and from the involved property. Picketing on private property has been upheld but only where the property is open to the public and the picketing relates to the business being conducted on the property. Klein (1980, p. 137) points out the following:

> Police problems involving labor disputes are similar in some respects to that of the Parade Regulation. There are two competing constitutional rights that the police officer is confronted with: those who are on strike have a constitutional right to peacefully picket and those who may wish to go to work who have a constitutional right to peacefully conduct their business. ... The police administrator is often confronted with the problem of maintaining order when groups unlawfully and without applying for a permit take over the streets, parks, or public buildings. ... The prevailing rule now appears to be that so long as the gathering is reasonably orderly, notwithstanding the fact that the police may validly enforce a constitutional limitation, the demonstration is permitted in order to avoid a confrontation which might result in loss of life or injury to persons or property.

Supreme Court decisions related to balancing the rights of people who wish to assemble and those who want to pursue their normal routine include *Poulos v. New Hampshire* (1953). This case stated that a group of demonstrators cannot insist on the right to blockade a street or entrance to a public or private building and allow no one to pass who did not agree to listen to their exhortations. *Walker v. Birmingham* (1967) stated that the First Amendment does not give people the right to trespass and disrupt the normal operations of business and government during the course of social protest, while *Cameron v. Johnson* (1968) held that taking over buildings for the purpose of demonstration is not protected by the First Amendment.

Freedom of Petition The right of **petition** is designed to allow citizens to communicate with their government without obstruction. When citizens exercise their First Amendment freedom to write or speak to their senator or representative, they partake of "the healthy essence of the democratic process."

The Second Amendment

A well-regulated militia being necessary to the security of a free state, the right of the people to keep and bear arms shall not be infringed.

The Second Amendment guarantees the right to keep and bear arms.

Officers on horseback, such as this Boston policewoman, help to maintain order.

Citizens are guaranteed the right to protect themselves from disorder in the community and attack from foreign enemies.

The United States "gun culture" arose out of the *practical* need for the pioneers to protect themselves against thieves, bandits, and Native Americans whose land they were crossing, as well as the *philosophical* belief that they needed to protect themselves from political tyranny.

As noted in a *U.S. News and World Report* article, sociologist Herman Kahn believes that to take away a citizen's right to have guns is "hitting America in the teeth. You think it's making a minor change, just taking the gun away. It's right at the center of the culture." This same article notes that the National Rifle Association (NRA) contends that the Second Amendment says the government has no power over controlling weapons. Gun opponents, on the other hand, assert that the amendment governs only the state's right to maintain an army. As noted in the article, p. 25:

A complete reading of court interpretations raises questions about both approaches. Even the Supreme Court has not touched the question in 50 years, and neither gun-control advocates nor their opponents can take much comfort from the 1939 ruling. In that decision, the Court upheld a control on sawed-off shotguns because they were not ordinary military equipment explicitly protected by the Second Amendment. That kind of reasoning, in the current debate, might make skeet guns more controllable than AK-47s.

The article further suggests that:

The absence, not the excess of government control [has become] the most compelling practical reason to own guns. Some police experts believe the greatest growth in gun ownership in recent years has been among the people who want guns for self-protection. That fact underscores that they are increasingly an urban phenomenon, even though the greatest attraction for sporting purposes continued in the South and West, where rural roots remain strongest. Indeed, according to data cited as credible by both sides, fewer than half the handguns in circulation are primarily used for recreation.

This right to bear arms has become much less important in recent decades as well-trained military and police forces have been developed to protect citizens. No longer do citizens need to rely on having their own weapons available, yet attempts to limit this right are strenuously opposed by many citizens, as evidenced in the current gun control controversy. No matter what police officers' views are on gun control, they are obliged to enforce the laws passed by Congress.

The Supreme Court has ruled that state and federal governments may pass laws that prohibit carrying concealed weapons, require the registration of firearms, and limit the sale of firearms for other than military use. Thus, it is illegal to possess certain types of "people-killing" weapons such as operable machine guns and sawed-off shotguns of a certain length.

The right of the states to pass laws regulating firearms rests in the interpretation of the Second Amendment by the Supreme Court. In *United States v. Cruikshank* (1875) the Court stated that the amendment protected only the right of the states to maintain and equip a militia, and that unless a defendant could show that the possession of a firearm in violation of federal statutes had "some reasonable relationship to the preservation or efficiency of a well-regulated militia," that individual could not challenge a gun control statute on Second Amendment grounds. The American Bar Association has stated: "Every Federal court decision involving the amendment has given the amendment a collective, militia interpretation and/or held that firearms control laws enacted under a state's police power are constitutional" (*Handgun Facts*).

The Second Amendment is a continuing source of controversy, as discussed further in Chapter 21. Those who oppose gun control state that outlawing handguns would arm criminals and disarm law-abiding citizens. They say the criminals will get guns anyway. The question revolves around whether the government should regulate handguns—the number-one weapon of killers. Some twenty thousand murders occur every year in the United States, often committed by "law-abiding" people shooting other "law-abiding" people. In addition, an average of more than ninety police officers are slain by handguns every year.

Some polls consistently show that the majority of United States citizens support sensible handgun legislation. When Massachusetts held a referendum proposing to ban handguns, however, it was defeated by a 70 percent majority. Possibly they realized what New York's tough gun law has shown: if only one state outlaws guns, a person can easily get one in another state.

The Third Amendment

No soldier shall, in time of peace, be quartered in any house without the consent of the owner, nor in time of war but in a manner to be prescribed by the law.

Before the Revolution, American colonists were frequently forced to provide food and lodging for British soldiers. The Third Amendment prohibited continuing this practice.

The Fourth Amendment

The right of the people to be secure in their persons, houses, papers, and effects, against unreasonable searches and seizures, shall not be violated, and no warrants shall issue but upon probable cause, supported by oath or affirmation, and particularly describing the place to be searched, and the persons or things to be seized.

The Fourth Amendment requires probable cause and forbids unreasonable searches and seizures.

In some countries, even today, police officers may invade citizens' homes, seize their property, or arrest them whenever they see fit. In the United States such actions are prohibited by the Fourth Amendment, which protects individuals and their property from unreasonable search and seizure by law officers.

In most instances a police officer is not allowed to search the homes of private citizens, seize any of their property, or arrest them without first obtaining a court order—a **warrant.** Before a warrant will be issued, the police officer must convince a magistrate that there is **probable cause**—good reason—to believe either that the individual involved has committed a crime, or that the individual has in possession evidence related to a crime. Even with a warrant, police cannot typically break into a private home without first demanding entrance, unless such action is permissible under a **no-knock statute,** which authorizes such entry if it is reasonable to expect the evidence will be destroyed.

The courts have ruled that in some instances it is permissible to arrest a person or conduct a search without a warrant. For example, if a felony is committed in the presence of a police officer, the officer has the right to arrest the criminal immediately, without an arrest warrant. If police officers make such an arrest, they may search the suspect and a limited area surrounding the suspect to prevent the suspect from seizing a weapon or destroying evidence. Any evidence in plain view may also be seized.

The courts have permitted the police to search certain vehicles without a warrant on the grounds that the vehicle may be miles away by the time a police officer returns with a warrant.

The courts have frequently faced the problem of determining what constitutes probable cause for a search or an arrest. Generally speaking, the criterion has been common sense. On the available evidence, would a reasonable person consider there was a good basis to believe that the person to be arrested had committed a crime or that the place to be searched contained evidence of a crime?

The Supreme Court, in considering whether a police officer who stopped and frisked a citizen with reason to believe that individual had committed a particular crime, ruled that the Fourth Amendment did not prohibit such a search if it was reasonable on the basis of the police officer's experience and the demeanor of the individual who was frisked (*Terry v. Ohio,* 1968).

Listening in on a telephone conversation by mechanical or electronic means and electronic bugging are considered search and seizures under the Fourth Amendment, and, therefore, they also require probable cause, reasonableness, and a warrant for their use. Congress has passed legislation that limits the use of wiretapping and bugging to the investigation of specific crimes and restricts those officials permitted to authorize them. *Berger v. New York* (1967) established that electronic evesdropping was prohibited by the Fourth Amendment, but that under specific conditions and circumstances it could be permitted. *Katz v. United States* (1967) also established that evidence of conversations overheard through electronic surveillance of a telephone booth was inadmissible because the proper authorization had not been obtained.

Evidence secured by means of an unlawful search and seizure cannot be used in either a state or federal prosecution. Thus, the phrase "innocent until proven guilty" in practice means "innocent until proven guilty by evidence obtained in accordance with constitutional guarantees."

Numerous Supreme Court cases have interpreted restrictions imposed by the Fourth Amendment. For example, in *Boyd v. United States* (1886), the Court held that the Fourth Amendment applied "to all invasions on the part of the government and its employees of the sanctity of a man's home and the privacies of life. It is not the breaking of his doors, and the rummaging of his drawers, that constitutes the essence of the offense; but it is the invasion of his indefensible right of personal security, personal liberty and private property." The findings in *Boyd* clearly suggest that evidence gathered in violation of the Fourth Amendment should be excluded from Federal criminal trials and, consequently, contributed to the development of the Exclusionary Rule some thirty years later.

In *Weeks v. United States* (1914) the Court, considering evidence seized unconstitutionally, concluded:

> If letters and private documents can thus be seized and held and used in evidence against a citizen accused of an offense, the protection of the Fourth Amendment declaring his right to be secure against such searches and seizures is of no value, and, so far as those thus placed are concerned, might as well be stricken from the Constitution. The efforts of the courts and their officials to bring the guilty to

punishment, praiseworthy as they are, are not to be aided by the sacrifice of those great principles established by years of endeavor and suffering which have resulted in their embodiment in the fundamental law of the land.

The *Weeks* case established that "in a federal prosecution the Fourth Amendment bars the use of evidence secured through an illegal search and seizure." This is known as the **Exclusionary Rule.**

Mapp v. Ohio (1961) established that the Exclusionary Rule must be applied at the state level as well as the federal level—that any evidence seized in violation of the Fourth Amendment guarantees was not admissible in state criminal prosecutions.

Other important Supreme Court cases related to the Fourth Amendment include several related to searches:

- *Burdeau v. McDowell* (1921) held that evidence obtained by a government agency from an unlawful search and seizure conducted by a private citizen can be used in government prosecution, provided the government had not "connived" in the unlawful search and seizure.

- *Abel v. United States* (1960) found that there was no invasion of privacy if an abandoned room or property was searched.

- *Stoner v. California* (1964) established that a guest in a hotel room was entitled to constitutional protection against unreasonable search and seizure, and that evidence obtained without a warrant, even with the consent of the desk clerk, was not admissible.

- *Michigan v. Tyler* (1978) held that entry by police and fire officials to investigate fire-damaged private property was subject to the Fourth Amendment, but that no warrant was required in an emergency to enter a burning structure to extinguish the fire.

- *Nix v. Williams* (1984) adopted what is now known as the "inevitable discovery exception to the Exclusionary Rule."

Supreme Court cases concerning searches related to arrests include *Henry v. United States* (1959), which found that if police did not have reasonable cause to believe a crime had been committed at the time they stopped a defendant, any search incidental to arrest was not legal. *Beck v. Ohio* (1964) held that in determining the validity of a warrantless arrest, the court must first determine if the facts available to the officer at the time would cause a person of "reasonable caution" to believe a crime had been committed.

Terry v. Ohio (1968) established that if police officers believe a suspect is armed, they can stop and frisk that person as a safety precaution, and *Chimel v. California* (1969) held that a warrantless search incidental to lawful arrest must be limited to the suspect's immediate surroundings to prevent the suspect from obtaining a weapon or destroying evidence. Any search beyond this limit was unconstitutional.

Five other Supreme Court decisions relate directly to searches of automobiles:

- *Carroll v. United States* (1925) established that since automobiles and other conveyances were highly mobile, they could be searched without a warrant if they were suspected of containing contraband.

- *Chambers v. Maroney* (1970) held that police could search a vehicle at the police station after they had arrested the driver. They did not have to search it at the time of the arrest.

- *Coolidge v. New Hampshire* (1971) found that a warrantless search of a suspect's car parked in the driveway at the time the suspect was arrested inside the house was not constitutional; a warrant should have been obtained.

- *South Dakota v. Opperman* (1976) established that a routine search of vehicles impounded for traffic violations was constitutional.

- *United States v. Ross* (1982) held that the police may search a car, including containers, without a warrant as long as they have probable cause to believe contraband is somewhere in the car.

Strict interpretation of the Fourth Amendment frequently results in evidence being excluded from a trial and may greatly limit the police's investigatory powers. Consequently, support for the strict interpretation of the amendment has declined. In *Go-Bart Import Company v. United States* (1931), and in *United States v. Rabinowitz* (1950), the Court held that "what is a reasonable search must be resolved in the facts and circumstances of each case." In effect, the Court assumed the responsibility of deciding on a case-by-case basis whether the Fourth Amendment was violated. This has resulted in numerous exceptions to the warrant requirement implied by the Fourth Amendment.

The search and seizure provisions of the Fourth Amendment are critical to law enforcement officers and will be discussed in depth in Chapter 12.

The Fifth Amendment

No person shall be held to answer for a capital or otherwise infamous crime unless on a presentment or indictment of a grand jury, except in cases arising in the land or naval forces, or in the militia, when in actual service, in time of war or public danger; nor shall any person be subject for the same offense to be twice put in jeopardy of life or limb; nor shall be compelled in any criminal case to be a witness against himself; nor be deprived of life, liberty, or property, without due process of law; nor shall private property be taken for public use without just compensation.

The Fifth Amendment guarantees:

- Due process—notice of a hearing, full information regarding the charges made against him, the opportunity to present evidence in his own behalf before an impartial judge or jury, and to be presumed innocent until proven guilty by legally obtained evidence.

- Just compensation when private property is acquired for public use.

The Fifth Amendment prohibits:

- Double jeopardy.
- Self-incrimination.

Grand Jury   The Fifth Amendment requires that before individuals are tried in federal court for an "infamous" crime, they must first be **indicted** by a **grand jury;** that is, formally accused of a crime by a grand jury. The grand jury's duty is to assure that there is probable cause to believe the accused person is guilty. This prevents a person from being subjected to a trial when insufficient proof exists that he or she has committed a crime.

An **infamous crime** is a felony (a crime for which a sentence of more than one year's imprisonment can be given) or a lesser offense that can be punished by confinement in a penitentiary or at hard labor.

An indictment is not required for a trial by court-martial or by other military tribunals. Also, the constitutional requirements of grand jury indictment do not apply to trials in state courts.

Due Process   The words **due process of law** express the fundamental ideas of American justice. A due process clause is found in both the Fifth and Fourteenth Amendments as a restraint upon the federal and state governments respectively.

The due process clause protects against arbitrary, unfair procedures in judicial or administrative proceedings that could affect a citizen's personal and property rights. Due process requires notice of a hearing or trial that is timely and that adequately informs those accused of the charges against them. It also requires the opportunity to present evidence in one's own behalf before an impartial judge or jury, to be presumed innocent until proven guilty by legally obtained evidence, and to have the verdict supported by the evidence presented.

The due process clauses of the Fifth and Fourteenth Amendments provide other basic protections to prevent the state and federal governments from adopting arbitrary, unreasonable legislation or other measures that would violate individual rights. Thus, constitutional limitations are imposed on governmental interference with important individual liberties such as the freedom to enter into contracts, to engage in a lawful occupation, to marry, and to move without unnecessary restraints. Governmental restrictions placed on one's liberties must be reasonable and consistent with due process to be valid.

The United States Supreme Court has not given a precise definition of due process. Justice Frankfurter, in *Rochin v. California* (1952), stated: "Due process of law, as a historic and generative principle, precludes defining, and thereby confining, these standards of conduct more precisely than to say that convictions cannot be brought about by methods that offend a sense of justice."

Due process requires that during judicial proceedings, fundamental principles of fairness and justice must prevail, including both substantive and procedural due process. **Substantive due process** protects individuals against unreasonable, arbitrary, or capricious laws and limits arbitrary government actions. No court or governmental agency may exercise powers beyond what the Constitution authorizes.

In contrast, **procedural due process** deals with notices, hearings, and gathering of evidence. The vast majority of due process cases are in the area of procedural due process. Because the Fifth Amendment is so vague, hundreds of cases have been heard. Important Supreme Court cases involving due process include *Brady v. Maryland* (1963), which held that the suppression of evidence favorable to an accused by the prosecution violates due process. *In Re Gault* (1967) established that juvenile court proceedings must also meet the requirements of due process, and *United States v. Russell* (1973) found that it was not entrapment for an undercover agent to have supplied the defendant with a scarce ingredient required to manufacture an illicit drug.

In *Hampton v. United States* (1976) the court held that it was not entrapment for undercover agents to be both providers and purchasers of drugs involved in the case. *Manson v. Brathwaite* (1977) established that eyewitness identification could be made from a single photograph if "the totality of circumstances" made it reliable.

Double Jeopardy   The Fifth Amendment also guarantees that citizens will not be placed in **double jeopardy;** that is, they will not be tried before a federal or state court more than once for the same crime. A second trial can occur, however, when the first trial results in a mistrial, for instance, when the jury cannot agree on a verdict, or when a second trial is ordered by an appellate court.

Double jeopardy does not arise when a single act violates both federal and state laws and the defendant is prosecuted in both federal and state courts. Nor does a criminal prosecution in either a state or federal court exempt the defendant from being sued for damages by anyone who is harmed by the criminal act. Further, a defendant may be prosecuted more than once for the same conduct if it involves the commission of more than one crime. For instance, if a person kills three victims at the same time and place, he or she can be tried separately for each slaying. *Benton v. Maryland* (1969) stated that the double jeopardy clause also applies to state prosecutions.

Self-Incrimination   In any criminal case every person has the right not to be a witness against himself or herself; that is, individuals are not required to provide answers to questions that might convict them of a crime. This is referred to as **self-incrimination.** Such questions may be asked at the very earliest stages of an investigation; therefore, the Supreme Court has ruled that when an individual is interrogated in the custody of the police, the guarantees of the Fifth Amendment apply. **Custodial interrogation** can extend to questioning outside the police station and has even included police questioning of a defendant in his or her own bed.

In ancient times, self-incrimination was a standard means of justice. People convicted of crimes were put to various inhumane tests that few could pass. Those who did not pass were determined to be guilty. As noted by Klotter and Kanovitz (1985, p. 335): "Before the year 1236 the accused in a criminal case was required to be sworn, but there was no questioning by the judge. The act of taking the oath was a ritual, and the decision of guilt or innocence was determined not on what was said, but on the correct pronunciation of the oath."

In 1236 this changed when the ecclesiastical courts required an accused to answer specific questions under oath. In seventeenth-century England all ecclesiastical courts were forbidden to administer any oath whereby people might be obliged to accuse themselves. As the original states developed their constitutions, the principle that individuals could not be compelled to witness against themselves was entrenched in the common law.

To insure against self-incrimination the Court ruled, in the well-known *Miranda* decision, that citizens must be warned prior to custodial interrogation of their right to remain silent, that what they say may be used against them in court, and that they have a right to counsel, which will be furnished them. If these warnings are not given, any statements obtained by the questioning are inadmissible in later criminal proceedings.

Although accused persons may waive their rights under the Fifth Amendment, they must know what they are doing and must not be forced to confess. Any confession obtained by force or threat is excluded from the evidence presented at the trial. Further, if defendants or witnesses fail to invoke the Fifth Amendment in response to a question when on the witness stand, such a failure may operate as a waiver of the right, and they will not be permitted to object to a court's admitting their statement into evidence.

Courts have ruled that the guarantee against self-incrimination applies only to testimonial actions. Thus, handwriting samples, blood tests, and appearance, including repeating words in a police lineup, do *not* violate the Fifth Amendment.

Courts have also ruled that the Fifth Amendment prohibits both federal and state prosecutors and judges from commenting on the refusal of defendants to take the witness stand in their own defense. The refusal of witnesses to testify to matters that could subject them to criminal prosecutions at a later date has also been upheld. The courts have recognized, however, a limited right of the government to question employees about the performance of official duties and have upheld the dismissal of employees who refuse to answer such questions.

Important Supreme Court cases regarding self-incrimination include the following:

■ *Rochin v. California* (1952) held that pumping a defendant's stomach without a search warrant to obtain contraband was a denial of due process.

■ *Escobedo v. Illinois* (1964) said that when the investigative process shifts to accusatory, the adversary system starts to operate and the suspect must be allowed to consult with an attorney.

■ *Schmerber v. California* (1966) established that taking physical evidence such as blood samples despite the accused's objections did not violate the Fifth Amendment, and that the evidence was admissible.

■ *Miranda v. Arizona* (1966) held that suspects must be told of their right to remain silent, of the possibility of using what is said against them in court, and the right to a lawyer. Unless a suspect is advised of these rights, any statements, admissions, or confessions are not admissible in court.

■ *Gilbert v. California* (1967) established that requiring a suspect to give a handwriting sample without an attorney present did not violate the Fifth Amendment.

■ *Cupp v. Murphy* (1973) held that police may take incriminating samples from the fingernails of a suspect without a warrant where there was probable cause to arrest.

■ *United States v. Carter* (1981) stated that defendants who do not choose to testify in their own defense have the right to ask the judge to instruct the jury not to infer guilt because of this refusal to testify.

■ *New York v. Quarles* (1984) established a new public safety exception to the Exclusionary Rule in that in certain cases police may question a subject in custody without first advising of the right not to self-incriminate.

Creamer (1980, p. 367) suggests:

> The public sees the Fifth Amendment invoked by people they don't like and who they presume are dishonest—or worse. People perceive that crime by government officials and other white-collar types is a serious problem, and they assume that too many such criminals are hiding behind the Fifth Amendment. The rising use of the Fifth Amendment has brought with it a rising outcry that the Fifth isn't worth the trouble it causes. This shallow notion is appealing on the surface, but in substance it is a dangerous idea, much like setting fire to one's home in order to rid the house of termites.
>
> No principles of law are more misunderstood by Americans than those which encompass the Fifth Amendment. From the old Red-baiting days through the postwar anti-racketeering era and the anti-war dissent period and the Watergate age, the myth has grown that justice and virtue have been continually frustrated by public enemies hiding behind the Fifth.

To the contrary, the history of the Fifth Amendment is the history of human-kind's attempts to become civilized. In its origins it was a rejection of government torture as a means of solving governmental problems. Today it is all that stands between a citizen and our government's unlimited right to ask questions and demand answers.

The Fifth Amendment serves as a declaration of our centuries-old American distrust of public officials. That this distrust has been well founded is especially evident now, when we are still recovering from overzealous governmental assaults on war protesters, black militants and political dissidents coupled with government-sponsored burglaries, illegal wiretaps and illegal mind control experiments, all committed in the name of law and order. . . . The right to silence has long been with us. It stands for human dignity and self-respect. It prevents the government from probing the secrets of our conversations or our innermost thoughts. Former Supreme Court Justice William O. Douglas once observed, "The crucial point is that the Constitution places the right of silence beyond the reach of government."

The Sixth Amendment

In all criminal prosecutions, the accused shall enjoy the right to a speedy and public trial, by an impartial jury of the state and district wherein the crime shall have been committed, which districts shall have been previously ascertained by law, and to be informed of the nature and cause of the accusation; to be confronted with the witnesses against him; to have compulsory process for obtaining witnesses in his favor, and to have the assistance of counsel for his defense.

The Sixth Amendment establishes requirements for criminal trials. It guarantees the individual's right:

- To have a speedy public trial by an impartial jury.
- To be informed of the nature and cause of the accusation.
- To be confronted with witnesses against him or her.
- To subpoena witnesses for defense.
- To have counsel for defense.

The right to a speedy and public trial requires that the accused be brought to trial without unnecessary delay and that the trial be open to the public. Intentional or negligent delay has been grounds for dismissal of charges. The Supreme Court has ruled that delay in prosecution is not justified by the defendant's confinement on an earlier conviction; the defendant should be temporarily released for trial on the later charge.

The requirement that the jury have twelve members and that the twelve members must reach a unanimous verdict was derived from common law, not from the Constitution. The Supreme Court has ruled that state juries need not have twelve members and has approved state statutes that require only six. Moreover, the Court has ruled that jury verdicts in state courts need not necessssarily be unanimous.

The right to jury trial does not apply to trials for petty offenses, that is, those punishable by six months' confinement or less; examples are shoplifting or some traffic violations.

In all jury trials the jury members must be impartially selected. No one can be excluded from jury service because of race, class, or sex.

The Sixth Amendment requires that accused persons must be told how it is claimed they have broken the law so they can prepare their defense. The crime must be established by statute beforehand so all persons know it is illegal before they act. The statute must clearly inform people of the exact nature of the crime.

Generally, accused persons are entitled to have all witnesses against them present their evidence orally in court. **Hearsay evidence** cannot be used in federal criminal trials except in certain instances.

According to Oran (1985, p. 142): **Hearsay** is secondhand evidence. Facts not in the personal knowledge of the witness, but a repetition of what others said, that are used to prove the truth of what those others said. Oral or written evidence that depends on the believability of something or someone not available in court.

Accused persons are entitled to the court's aid in obtaining their witnesses. This is usually accomplished by **subpoena,** which orders into court as witnesses persons whose testimony is desired at the trial.

Finally, the Sixth Amendment provides a right to be represented by counsel. For many years this was interpreted to mean that defendants had a right to be represented by a lawyer only if they could afford one. The Supreme Court held in 1963, in *Gideon v. Wainwright,* however, that the amendment obligated the federal and state governments to provide legal counsel at public expense for those who could not afford it even for petty offenses if a jail sentence might result. The **indigent,** that is, people who are destitute, poverty-stricken, with no visible means of support, have such a right at any "critical stage of the adjudicatory process," including the initial periods of questioning, police line-ups, and all stages of the trial process.

In addition, indigents have the right to a free copy of their trial transcript for purposes of appeal of their conviction. Congress enacted the Criminal Justice Acts of 1964 and 1970 to implement this right to counsel by establishing a federal defender system to represent those defendants who could not afford legal counsel. Most state legislatures have enacted similar measures.

The Supreme Court's first modern ruling on the right to counsel was *Powell v. Alabama* (1932), a case involving nine young black males, ages thirteen to twenty-one, charged with raping two white girls. The trial was held in Scottsboro, Alabama, where community sentiment was extremely hostile toward the defendants. Although the trial judge appointed a member of the local bar to serve as defense counsel, no attorney appeared on the day of the trial, so the judge appointed a local lawyer who reluctantly took the case. The defendants challenged their conviction on the grounds that they did not have a chance to consult with their lawyer or prepare a defense, and the Supreme Court concurred.

Another Supreme Court case seems to fly in the face of the Sixth Amendment right to a lawyer. That is the case of *Faretta v. California* (1975) in which the Supreme Court held that defendants could reject appointed counsel and could, instead, represent themselves. Justice Potter Stewart stated: "It is one thing to hold that every defendant, rich or poor has the right to the assistance of counsel, and quite another to say that a state may compel a defendant to accept a lawyer he does not want."

Other important Supreme Court cases related to the Sixth Amendment include the following:

Right to a Speedy Trial

■ *Klopfer v. North Carolina* (1967) held that the right to a speedy public trial applies to the states.

- *Barker v. Wingo* (1972) found that whether or not a defendant has been denied the right to a speedy trial must be determined by considering the length of delay, the reason for the delay, and any prejudice resulting from the delay.

Right to an Impartial Jury

- *Parker v. Gladden* (1966) stated that the right to trial by an impartial jury applies to the states.

- *Duncan v. Louisiana* (1968) held that the states are bound by the Sixth Amendment requirement of a jury trial in criminal cases but not in cases involving petty offenses.

Right to Confront Witnesses

- *Pointer v. Texas* (1965) found that the right to confront witnesses applies to the states.

- *Illinois v. Allen* (1970) stated that the Sixth Amendment right to be present during the trial can be lost by a defendant who, despite warnings, disrupts the trial.

Right to Counsel

- *Massiah v. United States* (1964) stated that an indicted person cannot be questioned or otherwise persuaded to make incriminating remarks without the presence of counsel.

- *United States v. Wade* (1967) found that an accused's right to counsel included having counsel present during a lineup identification because the suspect had been indicted and it was a critical stage in the prosecution.

- *Kirby v. Illinois* (1972) held that there is no right to counsel during a police lineup for identification if a suspect has not been formally charged with a crime.

- *Argersinger v. Hamlin* (1972) stated that no person can be imprisoned for any offense, even a misdemeanor, unless represented by counsel at trial, or unless this right was knowingly and intelligently waived.

- *United States v. Ash, Jr.* (1973) found that a suspect is not entitled to counsel during postindictment display of photographs used for identification.

- *Brewer v. Williams* (1977) reaffirmed the *Massiah* rule that once defendants are formally charged with a criminal offense, they have the right to have a lawyer present when being interrogated.

- *Scott v. Illinois* (1979) held that a state defendant has the right to a state-paid attorney, if necessary, only in cases that lead to imprisonment, not in all cases where imprisonment is possible.

The Seventh Amendment

In suits at common law, where the value in controversy shall exceed twenty dollars, the right of trial by jury shall be preserved, and no fact tried by a jury, shall be otherwise re-examined in any Court of the United States, than according to the rules of the common law.

Whereas the Sixth Amendment guaranteed a jury trial in all criminal prosecutions, the Seventh Amendment establishes this right to a jury trial for all "suits at common law" where the value is over twenty dollars—a goodly sum in 1791 when the Bill of Rights was passed.

The Eighth Amendment

Excessive bail shall not be required, nor excessive fines imposed, nor cruel and unusual punishments inflicted.

The Eighth Amendment forbids excessive bail, excessive fines, and cruel and unusual punishments.

Bail **Bail** has traditionally meant payment by the accused of an amount of money, specified by the court based on the nature of the offense, to insure the presence of the accused at trial. An accused released from custody and subsequently failing to appear for trial forfeits bail to the court.

The Eighth Amendment does not specifically provide that all citizens have a right to bail, but only that bail will not be excessive. A right to bail has, however, been recognized in common law and in statute since 1791. In 1966 Congress enacted the *Bail Reform Act* to provide for pretrial release from imprisonment of indigent defendants who could not afford to post money for bail, and who were, in effect, confined only because of their poverty. The act also discouraged the traditional use of money bail by requiring the judge to seek other means as likely to insure that defendants would appear when their trial was held.

The leading Supreme Court decision on excessive bail is *Stack v. Boyle* (1951) in which twelve community leaders were indicted for conspiracy and bail was fixed at $50,000 per defendant. The defendants moved to reduce this amount on the ground that it was excessive, and the Supreme Court agreed. Chief Justice Fred M. Vinson stated that in the opinion of the Court:

> This traditional right to freedom before conviction permits the unhampered preparation of a defense, and serves to prevent the infliction of punishment prior to conviction. . . . Unless this right to bail before trial is preserved, the presumption of innocence, secured only after centuries of struggle, would lose its meaning.
>
> The right of release before trial is conditioned upon the accused's giving adequate assurance that he will stand trial and submit to sentence if found guilty. . . . Bail set at a figure higher than an amount reasonably calculated to fulfill this purpose is "excessive" under the Eighth Amendment.

The following spring, in *Carlson v. Landon* (1952), the Court held that the Eighth Amendment did not guarantee the right to bail.

Cruel and Unusual Punishment Whether fines or periods of confinement are cruel and unusual must be determined by the facts of each particular case. Clearly excessive practices such as torture would be invalid. The Supreme Court has held the death penalty itself to be cruel and unusual in certain circumstances if it is not universally applied. This issue is discussed in Chapter 21.

The clause also applied to punishment for a condition that the criminal had no power to change. For example, a law making narcotics addiction illegal was struck down by the Supreme Court as cruel and unusual since it punished a condition beyond the accused's control. Some courts have held laws punishing public drunkenness to be cruel and unusual when applied to homeless alcoholics, since they cannot usually avoid public places.

The Supreme Court has heard numerous cases concerning cruel and unusual punishment, including the following:

- *Furman v. Georgia* (1972) stated that the death penalty does violate the Eighth Amendment if the sentencing authority has the freedom to decide between the death penalty and a lesser penalty.

- *Gregg v. Georgia* (1976) held that the death penalty for murderers is not per se cruel and unusual punishment.
- *Proffitt v. Florida* (1976) reaffirmed the *Gregg* decision.
- *Jurek v. Texas* (1976) also reaffirmed the *Gregg* decision, refusing to declare the death penalty unconstitutional in all circumstances.
- *Roberts v. Louisiana* (1977) ruled that the statute requiring the death penalty for murdering a police officer engaged in performing his or her duty, with no consideration of mitigating circumstances, was unconstitutional.
- *Coker v. Georgia* (1977) stated that the death penalty for a person convicted of rape was cruel and unusual punishment.
- *Lockett v. Ohio* (1978) invalidated Ohio's death penalty for murder because it limited too strictly the factors that could be considered in the decision whether or not to impose the death penalty.
- *Rummel v. Estelle* (1980) ruled that a mandatory life sentence required by a state habitual offender statute was not cruel and unusual punishment.

The Ninth Amendment

The enumeration in the Constitution of certain rights shall not be construed to deny or disparage others retained by the people.

The Ninth Amendment emphasizes the founding fathers' view that powers of government are limited by the rights of the people, and that it was *not* intended, by expressly guaranteeing in the Constitution certain rights of the people, to recognize that government had unlimited power to invade other rights of the people.

Griswold v. Connecticut (1965), a case involving the Ninth Amendment, addressed the issue of whether the right to privacy was a constitutional right, and, if so, whether the right was reserved to the people under the Ninth Amendment or was only derived from other rights specifically mentioned in the Constitution.

Courts have long recognized particular rights to privacy that are part of the First and Fourth Amendments. Thus, freedom of expression guarantees freedom of association and the related right to be silent and free from official inquiry into such associations. It also includes the right not to be intimidated by the government for expressing one's views. The Fourth Amendment's guarantee against unreasonable search and seizure confers a right to privacy because its safeguards prohibit unauthorized entry onto property and tampering with a citizen's possessions or property including his or her very person.

The Court in *Griswold* ruled that the Third and Fifth Amendments, in addition to the First and Fourth, created **zones of privacy** safe from governmental intrusion, and, without resting its decision upon any one of these or on the Ninth Amendment itself, simply held that the right of privacy was guaranteed by the Constitution.

The Tenth Amendment

The powers not delegated to the United States by the Constitution, nor prohibited by it to the states, are reserved to the states respectively, or to the people.

The Tenth Amendment embodies the principle of **federalism,** which reserves for the states the residue of powers not granted to the federal government or withheld from the states.

██████████ **ADDITIONAL AMENDMENTS**

Since the ratification of the first ten amendments (the Bill of Rights) in 1791, other amendments have been passed.

The Thirteenth Amendment

Neither slavery nor involuntary servitude ... shall exist within the United States or any place subject to their jurisdiction.

██

The Thirteenth Amendment abolished slavery.

Before the Civil War, slaves were considered property. Article IV, Section 2 provided that slaves were to be counted as three-fifths of a person when determining representatives to the lower house of Congress (Klotter and Kanovitz 1985, p. 493). Even the Supreme Court placed its stamp of approval on slavery in the infamous *Dred Scott* decision (*Dred Scott v. Sandford,* 1856). Chief Justice Taney proclaimed that the dark race as a class was inferior and altogether unfit to associate with the white race, either in social or political relations, and whether enslaved or emancipated, the Negro could not be a citizen (Klotter and Kanovitz 1985, p. 495).

After the Civil War, in 1865, the Thirteenth Amendment was enacted, emancipating the slaves. According to Klotter and Kanovitz (1985, pp. 493–95):

Hostile Southern legislatures responded to the Thirteenth Amendment with the enactment of Black Codes which were designed to compel the newly freed slaves to return to the service of their former masters. . . . A period of racial turbulence and violent unrest followed as terrorist organizations like the Ku Klux Klan and the Knights of the White Camelia sprang up in numerous local communities.

To protect the newly emancipated slaves, Congress ratified the Fourteenth Amendment. Klotter and Kanovitz (1985, pp. 493–95) suggest: "The immediate object of the Fourteenth Amendment was to protect the newly freed slaves from arbitrary and unequal treatment at the hands of hostile state and local government officials."

The Thirteenth Amendment was enacted after the Civil War, while Abraham Lincoln was president.

The Fourteenth Amendment

1. All persons born or naturalized in the United States, and subject to the jurisdiction thereof, are citizens of the United States and of the state wherein they reside. No state shall make or enforce any law which shall abridge the privileges or immunities of citizens of the United States; nor shall any state deprive any person of life, liberty, or property without due process of law, nor deny to any person within its jurisdiction the equal protection of the laws. . . .

* * *

5. The Congress shall have power to enforce by appropriate legislation the provisions of this article.

The Fourteenth Amendment requires each state to abide by the Constitution and the Bill of Rights. It guarantees due process and equal protection under the law.

Due Process The Fourteenth Amendment limits the states' infringement upon the rights of individuals. The Bill of Rights does not specifically refer to actions by states but applies only to actions by the federal government.

Thus, state and local officers could proceed with an arrest without any concern for the rights of the accused. The Fourteenth Amendment, in essence, duplicates the Fifth Amendment, except it specifically orders state and local officers to provide the legal protections of due process.

Some important Supreme Court cases related to the Fourteenth Amendment include *Brown v. Mississippi* (1936), which stated that a criminal conviction based on a confession obtained by brutality was not admissible under the Fourteenth Amendment due process clause. In *Gideon v. Wainwright* (1963) the Court held that the Fourteenth Amendment requires states to provide indigent defendants with counsel in criminal cases, whether the offense is capital or noncapital. *Malloy v. Hogan* (1964) found that the Fourteenth Amendment gives state prosecutors the same privileges against self-incrimination as provided to federal prosecutors under the Fifth Amendment. *Argersinger v. Hamlin* (1972) extended the *Gideon* ruling to misdemeanor cases involving a possible jail sentence as well as the right to a court-appointed attorney in such cases.

Equal Protection The Fourteenth Amendment also prohibits denial of the **equal protection** of the laws. A state cannot make unreasonable, arbitrary distinctions between different persons as to their rights and privileges. Since "all people are created equal," no law could deny red-haired men the right to drive an automobile, although it can deny minors the right to drive. The state can make reasonable classifications; however, classifications such as those based on race, religion, and national origin have been held to be unreasonable. Thus, racial segregation in public schools and other public places, laws that prohibit sale or use of property to certain races or minority groups, and laws prohibiting interracial marriage have been struck down.

The Supreme Court has further held that purely private acts of discrimination violate the equal protection clause if such acts are customarily enforced throughout the state, whether or not there is a specific law or other explicit manifestation of action by the state.

The equal protection clause also means that citizens may not arbitrarily be deprived of their right to vote, and that every citizen's vote must be given equal weight. Therefore, state legislatures and local governments must be apportioned strictly in terms of their populations in a way that accords one person one vote.

POLICE POWER

Without means of enforcement, the great body of federal, state, municipal, and common law would be empty and meaningless. Recall that the term *law* implies not only the rule but also enforcement of that rule. All forms of society rely on authority and power. **Authority** is the right to direct and command. **Power** is the force by means of which others can be made to obey.

Police power is a term used to describe the power of the federal, state, or municipal governments to pass laws regulating private interests, to protect the health and safety of the people, to prevent fraud and oppression, and to promote public convenience, prosperity, and welfare.

Police power is derived from the United States Constitution, United States Supreme Court decisions, federal statutes, state constitutions, state statutes, state court decisions, and various municipal charters and ordinances.

Section 5 of the Fourteenth Amendment provides the authority for much of the civil rights legislation passed by Congress in the 1960s.

Police power was defined by the United States Supreme Court in 1887 as "embracing no more than the power to promote public health, morals, and safety" *(Mugler v. Kansas)*. Others have defined police power as the force used by the state to preserve the general health, safety, welfare, and morals.

For example, narcotics laws are passed to preserve the people's health. Individuals who abuse narcotics or drugs by taking them without medical prescription and in proper dosage jeopardize their own mental and physical health. Traffic laws are passed to preserve the general safety and to make the highways safe for the motoring public. Gambling laws are passed by the legislature to protect the individual and the family from financial loss. Likewise, juvenile laws are passed to protect juveniles from parents, guardians, relatives, or other people who would place the youths' physical and mental welfare in danger. Finally, legislation prohibiting prostitution and obscenity is passed to protect the public's morals.

All levels of government grant their legislative branches the authority and power to make laws. The executive branches of government are created to enforce these laws, while the judicial branches interpret what the laws mean and how they are to be enforced.

The police power of the federal government is based on authority granted by the United States Constitution. The general grants of power, such as the power of Congress, the legislative branch of government, to provide for the general welfare of the United States by law, are restricted by other provisions of the Constitution taken from the English Bill of Rights or from the political experience of England and America.

The police power of the states is delegated to them by the federal government in the Bill of Rights. The Tenth Amendment of our Bill of Rights gives the states those powers not delegated to the federal government. Since the power to organize police forces is not delegated to the federal government, this authority is given to the individual states and their subdivisions, that is, their cities, counties, and townships. Therefore, police power ultimately rests with the people, since their elected representatives create the laws that the police enforce.

Police power and authority are broad in scope. These New York City police officers may maintain order by their very presence.

Because each state is responsible for its citizens' health, safety, and general well-being, the usual procedure has been to assign these functions to municipal police departments in the cities and to sheriffs and constables in the rural areas of the state. Within the limits established by state constitutions, state legislatures may define the powers and duties of police officers in the state. However, police officers' authority and powers cannot conflict with the provisions in the Fourteenth Amendment of the Constitution, which guarantee citizens equal protection by due process of law. Therefore, police officers can exercise only the powers and authority specifically granted by legislative enactment.

The authority, powers, duties, and limits of the police officer are usually determined by each state for all police officers—state, municipal, and rural. Most states fulfill their responsibilities for preserving the public peace, detecting and arresting offenders, and enforcing the law by giving cities the authority to appoint municipal police officers. Although these municipal officers are concerned with enforcing city ordinances, enforcing state statutes is their most important job.

Police authority and power are broad in scope and include maintaining the peace, licensing trades and professions, regulating public service corporations' rates, and enforcing health regulations such as quarantines, compulsory vaccinations, and segregation of people with contagious diseases. State laws and judicial decisions also determine the civil and criminal liability of police officers who step beyond their legal powers in discharging the duties of their office.

Although the state legislature passes laws, the courts, the judicial branch of government, decide the purpose and character of the statutes as well as whether these statutes conflict with the Constitution or are contrary to proper public policy. Since the courts continuously review laws, police authority and power cannot easily be corrupted or controlled by private interests.

The courts determine what police authority and power is appropriate. Acceptable police power requires that the regulations are (1) reasonable, (2) within the power given to the states by the Constitution, and (3) in accord with due process of law.

Police power is restricted by the Constitution, by the Fourteenth Amendment, and by the courts.

Klockars (1991, p. 240) notes the paradox created by the existence of a police force in a society where peace is so highly prized:

> While no one whom it would be safe to have home to dinner argues that modern society could be without police, this situation places police in a most uneasy relationship with both the society and the state that authorize it. In their aspiration to eliminate violence as an acceptable means of conducting human affairs, both are forced to accept the creation of a core institution whose special competence and defining characteristic is its monopoly on a general right to use coercive force. Understood in this light, the police are not only fundamentally and irreconcilably offensive in their means to the core cultural aspiration of modern society, but an ever present reminder that all of these noble institutions, which should make it possible for citizens to live in nonviolent relations with one another and the state, often come up very short.

PRINCIPLE VERSUS PRACTICE

There is a vast difference between stating ideals and goals and achieving them. Our Constitution and the Bill of Rights were written on the premise that all people would obey the law. Time has shown that this is not always true. The ideals set forth in our Declaration of Independence, our Constitution, and our Bill of Rights have not been achieved automatically.

Civil rights and civil liberties must be consciously and actively sought and protected if the documents on which our government is founded are to be more than elegant words. Laws and institutions must parallel our goals and ideals of liberty, freedom, equality, justice, human dignity, individual self-determination, freedom from tyranny, and freedom of conscience.

These goals have motivated Americans since they first came to the New World. These same goals carried American pioneers west, looking for a new life, a Utopia. These goals have led men and women of all races and creeds, from all parts of the country, to invest tremendous energy in the civil rights movement, to risk their lives confronting violently irate traditionalists, in an effort to obtain new levels of human decency and equality and new levels of freedom and justice for millions of Americans who belong to minority groups.

In many respects the history of civil rights and civil liberties in the United States has been a fight for the attainment of the abstract values that our nation claims it is committed to achieving.

The history of civil rights and civil liberties is not simply struggle, confrontation, marching, picketing, and demanding; it is holding the government responsible for the principles that are its central purpose for existence. From the beginning, our institutions, our statutes, and our legal process were means to obtain fundamental civil liberties central to the American purpose: freedom of speech, freedom of the press, freedom of assembly, freedom of religion, due process of law, the right to privacy, the right to a fair trial, the right to vote and have that vote counted fairly, and the right to equal opportunity, education, housing, and employment.

The history of civil rights and civil liberties has been dynamic, reflecting constant change as new challenges emerged in the shift from a simple, homogeneous, agrarian, rural society to an advanced, highly complex, industrial, urban society. Although our principles have remained the same, our institutions and laws have continually changed. Thomas Jefferson recognized the necessity for such change in a letter he wrote in the nineteenth century:

> I am certainly not an advocate for frequent and untried changes in laws and constitutions. I think that moderate imperfections had better be born with because we accommodate ourselves to them and find practical means to correct their ill effects, but I know also that laws and institutions must go hand in hand with the progress of the human mind, as that becomes more developed, as more discoveries are made, new truths disclosed, and manners and opinions change with the changing circumstances, institutions must advance also, and keep pace with the times. We might as well require a man to wear still the coat which fitted him as a boy as civilized society to remain ever under the regiment of their barbarous ancestors.

Our institutions and laws must change as our society changes.

The history of civil liberties has not always been a pleasant one, nor does it show Americans in their best light. It is painfully clear in American history that at certain times and under certain circumstances individuals and groups have been deprived of their liberties and denied fundamental freedoms under the rationalization that such denial was in the public interest.

Granted, liberty is not license; if an individual abuses freedom, takes advantage of society, corrupts justice, or poses a threat to law and order, society has the right to take action on its own behalf. The problem is to know when and where to draw that line. When have the limits of freedom been exceeded? Conversely, when have the essential social controls of free society been imposed too arbitrarily? Does the majority have the right to temporarily suspend the rights of the minority in order to preserve liberty?

Examples of attempts to suspend the rights of members of minority groups are, unfortunately, recurrent in our history. Aliens, for example, have faced this problem since the Alien and Sedition Acts of 1798. In the turbulent years of the 1840s, Catholic immigrants were often treated with intolerance and as second-class citizens. The lack of equality in the treatment of Native Americans, slaves, free African Americans following the Civil War, and women is also evident in the treatment of labor agitators and political and economic radicals with allegedly dangerous ideas. Pacifists and conscientious objectors encounter great difficulties during war years. And we have had not only arguments, but also public policy, that called for placing American Communists in a deprived legal status.

The treatment of the Japanese Americans during World War II is an example of the complexity of civil rights and civil liberties. After the attack on Pearl Harbor many Americans honestly believed the Japanese Americans posed a serious national threat. Some 110,000 Japanese, the majority of whom were American-born citizens, were forced by government order to sell their homes and businesses and were herded into temporary barracks (internment camps).

Although at the time it was claimed that Japanese Americans were a threat to national security, if one group of citizens can be so treated during a period of national emergency, a precedent is created that should disturb every American. From the standpoint of civil liberties, the episode has long-range implications, for the denial of one individual's rights is a direct threat to the rights of all Americans.

In the 1930s the United States Supreme Court began to question whether justice was being attained for large numbers of Americans as a result of the

The first arrivals at the Japanese evacuee community in Manzanar, California. Some 120,000 people of Japanese ancestry were imprisoned in 1942-46 as "national security risks."

federal policy of keeping "hands off" local law enforcement. After careful examination, begun in 1932 and continuing for forty years, it was gradually and consistently concluded that local justice was *not* true justice. Often local courts offered no true justice for African Americans in the South. Likewise, there was often little justice for a stranger accused of a crime in a community. Local standards were often biased, prejudiced, and intolerant. Therefore, the Court came to insist that uniform national standards be applied in local courts and in police procedures. The Supreme Court, charged with interpreting our laws, established uniform national standards to be applied to local justice.

Unfortunately, however, value systems such as prejudices and resistance to change cannot be legislated out of existence

▬▬▬ SUMMARY

Just as our current methods of enforcing the laws have slowly evolved, so have the laws themselves. In the beginning most laws were set by a ruler or were moral or social laws, enforced by social pressure. This was followed by common law—law based on precedent. In the United States common law became known as case law. Statutory law has replaced most common and case law. Statutory law consists of laws passed by federal and state legislatures regarding both constitutional and nonconstitutional (ordinary) matters.

The history of civil rights and civil liberties reflects our values, national purpose, the American experience with government, and the need for flexibility within stability. If the fundamental values of our society are to be preserved and extended, citizens must understand and support those institutions and statutes that, in practice, reflect the principles set forth in the Declaration of Independence, the Constitution, and the Bill of Rights.

These documents established not only each citizen's civil liberties— freedom from government oppression—but also each citizen's civil rights— claims to affirmative assistance from the government.

To achieve the goals set forth in the Declaration of Independence, the United States Constitution was drafted, the basic instrument of our government and the supreme law of the land, which was signed in 1789.

Some states refused to ratify the Constitution if it did not contain personal guarantees. Ten amendments to the Constitution containing such guarantees were passed in 1791 and became known as the Bill of Rights. The Bill of Rights protects a person's right to "life, liberty, and the pursuit of happiness" and forbids the government to violate these rights:

- The First Amendment guarantees freedom of religion, freedom of speech, freedom of the press, freedom of assembly, and freedom of petition.
- The Second Amendment guarantees the right to keep and bear arms.
- The Fourth Amendment forbids unreasonable searches and seizures and requires probable cause.
- The Fifth Amendment guarantees due process and just compensation when private property is acquired for public use; it prohibits double jeopardy and self-incrimination.
- The Sixth Amendment guarantees the individual's rights in a criminal trial.
- The Eighth Amendment forbids excessive bail, excessive fines, and cruel and unusual punishments.

Since the Fifth Amendment was directed to federal officials, an additional amendment was later ratified, the Fourteenth Amendment, which requires each state and locality to abide by the Constitution and the Bill of Rights.

Without means of enforcement, the great body of federal, state, and municipal law would be meaningless. To insure enforcement, police have been given power and authority from local, state, and federal sources; but they are also restricted in their use of this power by the Constitution, the Fourteenth Amendment, and the courts. They have the power to enforce the laws so long as they do not violate the civil rights and liberties of any individual.

Although the principles of civil rights and civil liberties do not always prevail in practice, they remain the cornerstone of our democracy and our American creed. These principles directly affect how law enforcement officers fulfill their responsibilities. In addition, as our society changes, our institutions and laws must change accordingly.

DISCUSSION QUESTIONS

1. What specific restrictions are placed on police officers by the Bill of Rights?

2. Why has the Supreme Court said that state and federal governments can pass laws against carrying weapons when the Second Amendment specifically guarantees the right to bear arms?

3. Why were African Americans considered "unequal" until Lincoln was president? The Constitution existed; why did it not apply to African Americans?

4. What is the basic difference between civil rights and civil liberties?

5. In what well-known cases has the Fifth Amendment been repeatedly used?

6. What does police power and authority consist of?

7. The Declaration of Independence states that all people are created equal. Does this mean all people have the same opportunities?

8. Why is the general public so adamant about upholding the rights stated in the Fifth Amendment?

9. Should we do away with the jury system and replace it with a panel of professional judges to determine guilt or innocence in a trial?

10. Should Fourth Amendment rights be extended to include general searches?

TERMS

American creed, authority, bail, Bill of Rights, case law, civil liberties, civil rights, common law, Constitution, constitutional law, custodial interrogation, double jeopardy, due process of law, ecclesiastical law, equal protection, equity, Exclusionary Rule, federalism, fighting words, grand jury, hearsay, hearsay evidence, indicted, indigent, infamous crime, moral law, no-knock statute, ordinances, ordinary law, petition, police power, power, precedent, probable cause, procedural due process, pure speech, self-incrimination, social law, speech plus, statutory law, subpoena, substantive due process, symbolic speech, warrant, zones of privacy.

REFERENCES

Creamer, J. S. *The Law of Arrest, Search and Seizure.* 3d ed. New York: Holt Rinehart & Winston, 1980.

Gardner, T. J. and Anderson, T. M. *Criminal Law, Principles and Cases.* 5th ed. St. Paul, Minn.: West Publishing Company, 1992.

Handgun Facts. A pamphlet distributed by Handgun Control, Inc. (n.d.).

"Hitting America in the Teeth." *U.S. News and World Report,* (May 8, 1989): 24–25.

Klein, I. J. *Constitutional Law for Criminal Justice Professionals.* North Scituate, Mass.: Duxbury Press, 1980.

Klockars, C. B. "The Rhetoric of Community Policing." In *Community Policing: Rhetoric or Reality,* edited by J. R. Greene and S. D. Mastrofski. New York: Praeger Publishers, 1991.

Klotter, J. C. and Kanovitz, J. R. *Constitutional Law.* 5th ed. Cincinnati, Ohio: Anderson Publishing, 1985.

Kobel, R. "The Pen vs. the Sword: Do Police Determine the Rules and Tone of Press Relations?" *Law Enforcement News* (July 31, 1988): 1, 6, 13.

Lewis, P. W. and Peoples, K. D. *The Supreme Court and the Criminal Process: Cases and Comments.* Philadelphia: W. B. Saunders, 1978.

Myrdal, G. *The American Dilemma.* New York: Harper & Brothers, 1944.

Oran, D. *Law Dictionary for Nonlawyers.* 2d ed. St. Paul, Minn.: West Publishing Company, 1985.

Pace, D. F. *Community Relations Concepts.* Placerville, Calif.: Custom Publishing Company, 1991.

CHAPTER 5

Criminal and Civil Offenses: An Important Distinction for Law Enforcement

There is no man so good, who, were he to submit all his thoughts and actions to the laws would not deserve hanging ten times in his life.

—**Montaigne**

Do You Know

What criminal law does?

The difference between a felony and a misdemeanor?

How crime is defined?

What is usually necessary to prove that a crime has been committed?

What strict liability crimes are?

What the eight Index Crimes are?

How to define the following violent crimes against persons: murder, assault, rape, and robbery?

How to define the following crimes against property: burglary, larceny/ theft, motor vehicle theft, and arson?

What civil law refers to?

What a tort is?

What the basic differences are between a crime and a tort?

What Section 1983 of United States Code, Title 42, stipulates?

▓▓▓▓▓▓ INTRODUCTION

To assure each United States citizen the right to "life, liberty, and the pursuit of happiness," society has established laws that all are expected to obey. In Chapter 4 you were introduced to the supreme law of the land—the United States Constitution and its Bill of Rights.

Beyond that, however, each city, state, and the federal government has continued to pass laws governing citizen behavior. Our system of laws is extremely complex and may be classified as follows:

- *Type*—written or common law
- *Source*—constitutional, statutory, case
- *Parties involved*—public, private
- *Offense*—criminal, civil

The criminal/civil distinction is of most interest to law enforcement officers, for they must learn to deal with those who break criminal laws but at the same time not violate the "criminal's" civil rights. Officers who do not deal legally with criminal matters may find themselves the target of a civil lawsuit.

In addition, it is important that law enforcement officers be able to tell the difference between a criminal and a civil offense because they are responsible for investigating only criminal matters. Civil offenses are not within their jurisdiction.

Consider first criminal law and its importance for police officers.

▓▓▓▓▓▓ CRIMINAL LAW

Criminal law defines crimes and fixes punishment for them. Criminal law includes rules and procedures for investigating crimes and prosecuting criminals; regulations governing the constitution of courts and the conduct of trials; and the administration of penal institutions.

American criminal law has a number of unique features. In establishing criminal law, the federal government and each state government are sovereign within the limits of their authority as defined by the Constitution. Therefore, criminal law varies from state to state. Although there are many differences, most of them have a tradition derived from English common law. There is no federal common law jurisdiction in criminal cases, however (*United States v. Hudson,* 1812).

Criminal law defines crimes and fixes punishments for them.

The statutes that define what acts constitute social harm are called substantive criminal law, for example, a statute defining homicide. A substantive criminal law not only defines the offense but also states the punishment. The omission of the punishment invalidates the criminal law.

In most countries crimes and punishments are expressed in statutes. Punishments include removal from public office, fines, exile, imprisonment, and death. Unless the act of which a defendant is accused is expressly defined by statute as a crime, no indictment or conviction for the commission of the act is legal. This provision is important in establishing the difference between government by law and arbitrary dictatorial government.

Criminal law in the United States generally defines seven classes of crimes. It includes offenses against (1) international law, (2) the dispensation of justice and the legitimate exercise of governmental authority, (3) the public peace, (4) property, (5) trade, (6) public decency, and (7) persons. And, like English law, American criminal law also classifies crimes with respect to their gravity as treason, felonies, and misdemeanors.

Felony refers to serious crimes, generally those punishable by death or by imprisonment for more than one year in a state prison or penitentiary. The court may inflict a lesser punishment.

No crime is a felony unless made so by statute, or unless it is a felony under common law. Formerly a felony was a crime punishable by forfeiture of the criminal's lands, or goods, or both. In addition, other punishment might be added, according to the degree of guilt. In England for a long time most felonies were punishable by death.

Misdemeanor is a term applied to any minor offense, generally punishable by a fine or a short term, usually not to exceed one year, in a jail or workhouse.

The criminal codes of the states vary in their classification of offenses that are considered misdemeanors. Examples of crimes usually defined as misdemeanors include libel, assault and battery, malicious mischief, and petty theft.

In some states the distinction between felonies and misdemeanors is practically discarded, the punishment for each particular crime being prescribed by statute.

The same situation existed under common law. Although under common law a crime was generally classified as treason, felony, or misdemeanor, many offenses could not be defined exactly, so the rule was adopted that any immoral act harmful to the community was, in itself, a crime, punishable by the courts. Crimes were classified as *mala in se* (bad in itself), based to a large degree on religious doctrine, or as *mala prohibita* (bad because it is forbidden). A *mala in se* crime is one that is so offensive that it is obviously criminal, for example, murder or rape. A *mala prohibita* crime is one that violates a specific regulatory statute, for example, certain traffic violations. These would not usually be considered crimes if no law prohibited them.

A CLOSE-UP ON CRIME—WHAT MUST BE PROVEN

Haskell and Yablonsky (1983, p. ix) suggest that "crime exists in all societies. Wherever there are laws or moral prescriptions for behavior, there is always a segment of society that will violate these norms."

As noted by Monk (1991, p. xii): "By almost any measurement of 'what is important,' crime continues to rank at or near the top of America's priorities and concerns. Local, state, and federal crime fighting and crime control budgets often involve the highest expenditures—typically numbering in the billions of dollars—for the police, courts, and prisons."

The Bureau of Justice Statistics (U.S. Department of Justice 1988, p. 2) defines **crime** as follows: "We define crime as all behaviors and acts for which a society provides formally sanctioned punishment." Crimes are made so by law. State and federal statutes define each crime, the elements involved, and the penalty attached to each.

Crime is defined as any prohibited behavior for which society sanctions a punishment.

Wilson and Herrnstein (1991, p. 56) say: "A crime is any act committed in violation of a law that prohibits it and authorizes punishment for its commission." Senna and Siegel's (1990, p. 37) definition is among the most comprehensive:

> Crime is a violation of societal rules of behavior as interpreted and expressed by a criminal code created by people holding social and political power. Its content may be influenced by prevailing public sentiments, historically developed moral beliefs and the need to protect public safety. Individuals who violate these rules may be eligible for sanctions administered by state authority, which include social stigma, and loss of status, freedom, and even on occasions one's life.

Sutherland and Cressey (1978, pp. 12–14) have summarized seven interrelated and overlapping characteristics of crime delineated by Jerome Hall:

1. A crime has certain external consequences called a harm. Crime has a harmful impact on social interests; mere intention without resulting in such a harm is not a crime.
2. The harm must be specifically outlawed in advance.
3. Conduct must occur, either intentional or reckless action or inaction, to bring about the harmful consequences.
4. *Criminal intent* must be present. Criminal intent must not be confused with motivation. The motive might be "good," but if the intention is to perform an act specifically outlawed, it is still a crime. For example, if a person steals from the rich to give to the poor, his motives are "good," but his intention is still wrong.
5. The criminal intent and conduct must be related. For example, a salesperson who enters a home on business and then decides to steal something cannot be charged with breaking and entering.
6. A causal relation must exist between the outlawed harm and the intentional act. For example, if a person shoots someone and the victim suffocates while in the hospital recovering from the wound, the causal relation is not clearcut.
7. The punishment must be legally prescribed; the action must be punishable by law.

Another way of looking at crime is presented by Samaha (1983, p. 34), who suggests: "Every crime for which a law has been passed and punishment spelled out is comprised of several essential ingredients called *material elements.*" The five principal material elements are as follows:

- The actual act (*actus reus*—the forbidden act)
- The mental state of mind (*mens rea*—the guilty mind)
- Concurrence—the act and mental state occurring at the same time
- Harmful result
- Surrounding circumstances

All of these must be proven beyond a reasonable doubt for a person to be convicted of a crime.

To prove a crime has been committed, the following are usually necessary:

- Prove the criminal mental state *(mens rea)*—intent to do wrong.
- Prove the act itself *(actus reus)*—the elements of the crime.

Although in differing order, Samaha's five principal material elements parallel those of Sutherland and Cressey. Basic in both is the concept of ***mens rea*** — literally, the "guilty mind." According to Senna and Siegel (1990, p. 121):

> *Mens rea* is the element of the crime that deals with the defendant's intent to commit a criminal act and also includes such states of mind as concealing criminal knowledge (scienter), recklessness, negligence, and criminal purpose. A person ordinarily cannot be convicted of a crime unless it is proven that he or she intentionally, knowingly, or willingly committed the act.

Also basic to the commission of a crime is the concept of ***actus reus*** — literally the "guilty act." The *actus reus* must be a measurable act, including planning and conspiring. What constitutes this forbidden act is usually spelled out very specifically in state statutes and is called the *corpus delicti.*

Contrary to popular belief, the ***corpus delicti*** of a crime is not the body in a murder case. It is, quite literally, the body of the crime itself. As noted by Chamelin and Evans (1991, p. 18): "Every offense consists of distinctive elements, all of which must exist for a particular crime to be proven." These **elements of the crime** make up the *corpus delicti.* Chamelin and Evans explain:

> At common law, the *corpus delicti* of burglary consisted of the following elements: breaking, entering, dwelling house of another, in the nighttime with the intent to commit a felony therein. All these elements had to exist before the crime of burglary could properly be charged at common law. If, instead of a dwelling house a store had been broken into, then burglary had not been committed, because one element was not present. Instead, another crime had been committed and the case would have been thrown out of court. . . .

> The *corpus delicti* issue has gained its primary renown in homicide cases. To prove a felonious homicide (i.e. murder), one must prove that a person existed and that such person is now dead at the hands of a human agency.

Later in this chapter the elements of the most serious crimes police officers deal with are introduced.

Law enforcement officers are most responsible for proving that the actual act occurred — establishing the elements of a specific crime, which will be discussed shortly.

Much more difficult to establish is the mental state of the suspect. Gardner (1985 p. 34) suggests that the "mental requirement of criminal intent is embodied in criminal statutes in the following degrees: intentionally (the highest degree of mental fault), knowingly, recklessly, negligently." According to Gardner: "The U.S. Supreme Court has never drafted and announced a doctrine requiring proof of *mens rea* in all crimes . . . therefore, the states are free to create criminal laws that do not require proof of *mens rea* or to create criminal laws requiring different degrees of mental fault or mental guilt." Further, as Gardner notes: "A criminal intent without a criminal act is no crime. . . . To prove a true crime the state must show that the external physical act and the internal mental state essential to that crime occurred at the same time."

When criminal intent *is* an essential element of a crime, it is up to the state to prove it. How law enforcement officers can assist in this is discussed in Chapter 10.

In some crimes intent is not an element. These are known as **strict liability** crimes. These offenses generally involve traffic violations, liquor violations, and hunting violations. Individuals who break traffic, liquor, and hunting laws are not considered "criminals," and the penalties involved are usually less.

In strict liability crimes such as violations of traffic codes, hunting regulations, and liquor laws, the defendant is liable regardless of his or her state of mind when the act was committed.

As Gardner (1985, p. 41) notes:

> A bartender cannot ordinarily use as a defense the fact that the person to whom he sold liquor looked twenty-two when in fact the person was only seventeen. The driver of an overweight truck cannot argue that the company scales were faulty; nor can an adult male, in most, if not all, states, argue that he did not know the age of the fifteen-year-old girl with whom he had sexual intercourse.

Nor can the speeder claim ignorance of the posted speed limit or claim a faulty speedometer. Intent is not at issue—only the speed.

Intent is *not* to be confused with **motive.** Your motive for doing something is your *reason.* Motive is not an element of any crime, but it can help to establish intent. If police officers can show why a suspect would benefit from committing a certain act, this greatly strengthens the case. Gardner (1985, p. 40) illustrates that "the mother who kills her imbecile and suffering child out of motives of compassion is just as guilty of murder as is the man who kills for gain, since each intentionally takes another human life. Although motive is not relevant to the issue of guilt or innocence, it can be a factor in sentencing."

Another element of a crime that must sometimes be proven is *scienter. Scienter* is a "degree of knowledge that makes an individual legally responsible for the consequences of his or her acts" (Gardner 1985, p. 37). In other words, the person committing the act knew that it was a crime. For example, to be guilty of harboring a felon, the person harboring the felon has to know the person *is* a felon. Or the person who buys stolen property has to know that the property is, indeed, stolen.

Crimes can be categorized in many different ways. You have already seen one such classification—a criminal act can be either a misdemeanor or a felony. Another common classification is to differentiate between violent crimes or crimes against persons and property crimes. Crimes against persons include homicide, rape, assault, and robbery—actions that involve the use of force or the threat of force against a person. In contrast, property crimes do not involve such force. They include larceny, burglary, motor vehicle theft, and arson.

SOURCES OF INFORMATION ON CRIME

Much of what we know about crime comes from the media which, according to some, overdramatizes the seriousness of the problem. One such critic, Wright (1991, pp. 111–112) notes:

> The press—in newspapers, television, and magazines—keeps us apprised of the seriousness of the crime problem. . . .
>
> The broadcasting industry also engages in vigorous crime reporting. During the evening news, viewers are often taken to the scene of a violent crime. . . .
>
> The message . . . rings clear: Violent crime in America has risen to a crisis point. There is no adequate explanation for what is happening, and few pragmatic solutions to the problem exist. . . .

The United States has been through supposedly major crime waves every twenty years or so, and more than once Americans have been told that the social order stands in trembling peril.

Abadinsky (1987) suggests that our *perception* of crime is influenced by other sources in addition to the media coverage:

- Governmental decisions about law enforcement, for example increasing the number of police officers is likely to result in an apparent increase in crime since more criminals will be apprehended.
- Our definitions of what constitutes crime, for example, in New York private citizens can usually be arrested for possessing a handgun, a behavior that would not be a crime in a state such as North Carolina.

Information also comes from actual statistics gathered from around the country. In 1930 Congress assigned the FBI the responsibility to serve as a national clearing house for crime statistics, The National Crime Information Center (NCIC). Their program is called the Uniform Crime Reports (UCR), and the annual publication of this program is entitled *Crime in the United States.* According to Monk (1991, p. 85): "Approximately 15,000 agencies report crimes to the FBI. This is 98 percent of all law enforcement agencies, and thus the UCR is by far the most comprehensive source of crime statistics in the country."

The UCR divides offenses into two major categories: Part I and Part II, with Part I, also called **Index Crimes,** being those that are most serious in terms of either their use of violence or the value of the property involved.

The eight Part I crimes are (1) murder, (2) aggravated assault causing serious bodily harm, (3) forcible rape, (4) robbery, (5) burglary, (6) larceny/theft, (7) motor vehicle theft, and (8) arson.

An annual summary of the figures for the Part I crimes are depicted in the Crime Clock (Figure 5–1).

Crime statistics should always be interpreted with caution because although, as noted by Nettler (1978, p. 55): "The most popular measure of crime is official statistics of offenses 'known to the police,' " such statistics have some major problems. "Crimes known to the police are themselves a result of social processing. . . . Complaints to the police are subject to errors that result from mistakes and from lies." In addition, "Official statistics on crime are imperfect not only because of what is and is not included but also because of imperfections in those who do the counting" (Nettler 1978, p. 63).

This point is reiterated by the Brantinghams (1984, p. 56): "Criminal justice statistics do not enumerate all crimes. They enumerate only those crimes made known to the criminal justice system. A substantial number of crimes are never reported to the police or any other agent of criminal justice. The true number of crimes, called the **dark figure of criminality,** is unknown." In spite of these difficulties, police departments do make frequent use of the information from the Uniform Crime Reports.

Another source of data compiled every two years that interests the general public as well as criminal justice researchers and educators is the Bureau of Justice Statistics (BJS) document, *Report to the Nation on Crime and Justice.* This document brings together a wide range of data from the BJS's own statistical series, FBI Uniform Crime Reports, the Bureau of the Census, the Na-

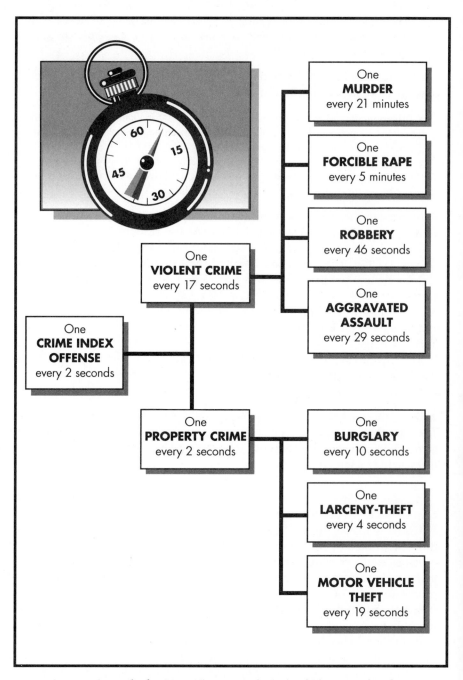

Figure 5–1 Crime Clock 1991 The crime clock should be viewed with care. Being the most aggregate representation of UCR data, it is designed to convey the annual reported crime experience by showing the relative frequency of occurrence of the Index Offenses. This mode of display should not be taken to imply a regularity in the commission of the Part I offenses; rather, it represents the annual ratio of crime to fixed time intervals.

Source: FBI Uniform Crime Reports.

tional Institute of Justice, the Office of Juvenile Delinquency Prevention, and many other research and reference sources. The report presents national data on crime and the criminal justice system and answers questions such as the following:

- How much crime is there?
- Whom does it strike?
- When?
- Where?
- Who is the typical offender?
- What is the government's response to crime?
- How differently are juveniles handled from adults?
- What are the costs of justice and who pays?

Data from both the Uniform Crime Reports and those of the BJS will be used throughout this text.

Now turn your attention to the specific crimes law enforcement officers must deal with. Remember, however, that since definitions of crimes and their penalties vary considerably on the local, county, state, and federal levels, law enforcement officers must be familiar with their area's criminal statutes and ordinances. These statutes and ordinances list specific conditions, called the **elements of the crime,** that must occur for an act to be called a specific kind of crime.

Knowing these elements is essential to a firm base in **substantive criminal law.** Later in the book you will look at **procedural criminal law**—how to lawfully carry out the responsibilities of law enforcement officers. For now, however, concentrate on recognizing the elements of each crime, which is essential to gathering evidence to prove that a crime has, in fact, been committed.

CRIMES AGAINST PERSONS—VIOLENT CRIMES

Statistics gathered by the U.S. Department of Justice indicate that violent crime is widespread in the United States. Table 5–1 summarizes their key findings.

The four Index Crimes against persons are murder, assault, rape, and robbery.

Murder (Homicide)

Murder or **homicide** is defined in the Uniform Crime Reporting Program as the willful killing of another person. Deaths caused by negligence, suicide, accident, justifiable homicide, attempts to murder or assaults to murder are *not* included.

Murder (homicide) is the willful killing of a human by another human.

The generally recognized levels of homicide are (1) first-degree murder, (2) second-degree murder, (3) manslaughter (or nonnegligent manslaughter), and (4) negligent homicide. The first three categories, considered to be willful acts, are classified as felonies. Negligent homicide, however, is usually considered a misdemeanor.

Table 5-1   Violent Crime in the United States

- Violent crime is more likely to strike the young than the elderly.[a]
- Except for rape, violent crime is more likely to strike men than women.[a]
- Persons who live in central cities are more likely to be violent crime victims than persons who live in suburban or rural areas. Persons who live in cities of 250,000 to 499,999 population have the highest violent victimization rates.
- On average, 2.2 million victims are injured from violent crime each year; 1 million receive medical care; half a million are treated in an emergency room or hospital.
- Among those victims injured in rapes, robberies, and aggravated assaults in recent years, an estimated 22,870 received gunshot wounds each year, 76,930 received knife wounds, and 141,460 suffered broken bones or teeth knocked out.

- Of all violent crimes, 55% are committed by strangers, 32% by acquaintances, and 8% by relatives. In 1989 persons not known to the victim committed 3.2 million violent crimes.
- Nearly 25% of all violent crime incidents are committed by two or more offenders; 13% are committed by three or more offenders. Crimes committed by strangers are more likely to involve multiple offenders than are crimes by known persons.
- Of murder victims in 1989, 15% were killed by relatives, 39% by acquaintances, 13% by strangers, and 33% in circumstances where the relationship was not known.
- Among all female murder victims in 1989, 28% were killed by husbands or boyfriends. Five percent of male victims were killed by wives or girlfriends.

- Violent crimes are more likely to be cleared by arrest than other crimes. In 1989 the clearance rate was—
  68% for murder
  52% for forcible rape
  26% for robbery
  57% for aggravated assault.
- When prior conviction offenses are taken into account, an estimated 66% of state prison inmates in 1986 were found to have had a current or past conviction for a violent crime.
- Violent offenses are most likely to be handled by the states and localities. In 1988 there were an estimated 99,900 violent convictions in state courts, as compared to 2,241 in U.S. district courts. In state courts, violent offenses represented a larger proportion of all convictions (15%) than they did in U.S. district courts (5%).

[a]The elderly and women take more precautions to avoid being victims of crime than do young men.
Source: U.S. Department of Justice, 1991, "Violent Crime in the United States."

First-degree murder is the willful, deliberate, and **premeditated** (planned) taking of another person's life. A homicide that occurs during the commission or attempted commission of arson, robbery, rape, or burglary is also usually classified as first-degree murder, even though it was not willful, deliberate, or premeditated. The question of premeditation is always left up to the jury.

Second-degree murder is murder that is *not* premeditated but the intent to kill is present. The charge of murder in the second degree or manslaughter often results from killings that do not involve weapons.

Manslaughter is differentiated from murder in that the element of **malice** is absent, that is, the death was accidental; there was no original intent, hatred, ill will, or disregard for the lives of others. In many states manslaughter is classified as either involuntary or voluntary. *Involuntary* manslaughter involves killing someone while doing some lawful act negligently or while negligently failing to perform some legal duty. Many deaths resulting from automobile accidents are classified as involuntary manslaughter. If there is no malice or intent to harm, and if the activity that led to the death is not a felony and would not usually cause bodily harm, most state statutes define it as involuntary manslaughter. In contrast, *voluntary* manslaughter is intentionally killing someone without previous malice but in the sudden heat of passion due to adequate provocation. For example, a man who kills another man whom he found in bed with his wife would probably be found guilty of voluntary manslaughter. If a store owner kills a robber in his store, his act and many other instances of self-defense are often defined as voluntary manslaughter.

Negligent homicide refers to an accidental death that results from the reckless operation of a motor vehicle, boat, plane, or firearm.

According to the UCR, 21,500 homicides are committed per year. The Bureau of Justice Statistics cites these facts regarding homicide:

- Homicide is the least frequent violent crime.
- Ninety-five percent of the victims were slain in single-victim situations.
- At least 55 percent of the murderers were relatives or acquaintances of the victim.
- Twenty-four percent of all murders occurred or were suspected to have occurred as the result of some felonious activity.

The elements needed for a crime to be called a homicide are as follows:

1. It causes the death of another human being;
2. It is premeditated;
3. Malicious intent exists;
4. Adequately provoked intent results in the heat of passion;
5. It occurs while committing or attempting to commit a felony or a crime not a felony;
6. Force or threat is used;
7. Culpable negligence or depravity exists;
8. There is negligence.

The elements present determine what degree of murder is charged.

Assault

Assault is the unlawful attack by one person on another to inflict severe bodily injury. Aggravated assault is usually accompanied by the use of a weapon or other means likely to produce serious bodily harm or death. Attempts are included since it is not necessary that an injury result when a gun, knife, or other weapon is used that could and probably would result in serious personal injury if the crime were successfully completed.

Assault is attacking a person. It may be aggravated or simple.

Aggravated assault is an unlawful attack on a person to inflict severe bodily injury or death. Assault can safely be classified as *aggravated* if a gun, knife, or other weapon is used and serious personal injury is inflicted. In most states aggravated assault is a felony and carries severe penalties because it would have been murder if the victim died. The intent of the act "appears" to be murder and not simply injury.

Simple assault, the most frequent type of assault, has no intent of serious injury. It may or may not be accompanied by a threat. Hands, fists, or feet are the most frequently used weapons. Most simple assaults result from emotional conflicts and are classified as misdemeanors. The mere pointing of a gun at a person or threatening a person with bodily harm may constitute simple assault in certain situations.

The UCR estimates that 900,000 aggravated assaults occur annually. The Bureau of Justice Statistics cites these facts about assault:

■ Assault is the most common type of violent crime.

■ Simple assault occurs more frequently than aggravated assault.

For a crime to be called aggravated assault, bodily injury must be intentionally inflicted and result in:

■ A high probability of death;

■ Serious disfigurement; or

■ Permanent or protracted loss or impairment of the function of any body member or organ, or other severe bodily harm.

The kneeling officer receives information from an assault victim after the victim's injuries have been attended to and an ambulance called. Another officer receives the card of a witness to the assault.

The elements needed for a crime to be called simple are as follows:

1. Intent to do bodily harm to another exists;
2. Present ability to commit the act exists; and
3. An overt act toward carrying out the intention is committed.

Whether an assault is aggravated or simple is determined by the prosecuting attorney and is based on the intent of the attacker. Some states include the term *battery* in their statutes; others omit the term and allow the term *assault* to refer to both the blow and threats of attack. Assaults are frequently committed in conjunction with rape, burglary, and robbery.

Rape

Rape, as defined in the Index Program, is the carnal knowledge of a female through the use of force or the threat of force. Assaults to commit forcible rape are also included in the definition; however, **statutory rape** (without force) is not.

Rape is having sexual intercourse with a female through the use or threat of force. Rape may be aggravated or simple.

Aggravated rape involves using force, threats of immediate use of force, or taking advantage of an unconscious or helpless woman or a woman incapable of consent because of mental illness or a defect reasonably known to the attacker.

Simple rape involves misleading a victim about the nature of the act being performed; for example, having intercourse under the guise of a medical examination or treatment or knowingly destroying the victim's will to resist by use of a drug or intoxicant.

According to the UCR, between 90,000 and 95,000 forcible rapes occur annually. Rape is a violent crime against the person, yet it is probably one of the most underreported crimes because the victim fears her assailant or is extremely embarrassed. The Bureau of Justice Statistics cites these facts about rape:

- Most rapes involved a lone offender and a lone victim.
- About 36 percent of the rapes were committed in the victim's home.
- Fifty-eight percent of the rapes occurred at night between 6 P.M. and 6 A.M.

The elements that constitute the crime of rape are as follows:

1. It is an act of sexual intercourse;
2. It occurs with a female other than a wife;
3. It is committed without the victim's consent; and
4. It is committed against the victim's will and by force.

It should be noted that some states have deleted the word *female* from their rape statutes and substituted the word *person*. This, in effect, includes males as potential victims of rape. Likewise, wives can be considered potential victims of rape. This not only has social significance, but it also indicates a problem with the figures included in the Uniform Crime Reports.

In some states, laws have been changed so that the defense cannot use the victim's previous behavior as a point of attack. This would apply to known prostitutes who are raped. Other significant changes which states have made in their sexual assault laws are summarized in Table 5–2.

Robbery

Robbery is stealing or taking anything of value from the care, custody, or control of a person by force or by threat of force. Assault to commit robbery and attempts are included in the definition. This violent crime frequently results in injury to the victim.

Robbery is stealing anything of value from the control, care, or custody of a person by force or threat of force.

In 50 percent of the cases, robbery is accompanied by an assault upon the victim. Sometimes labeled as the most brutal and vicious of all crimes, robberies occur in all parts of the country; its victims are people of all ages, incomes, and backgrounds. Robbers may shoot, assault, or torture their victims

---

Table 5–2 **Traditional Rape and the New Sexual Assault Laws**

OLD COMMON LAW RULES REGARDING RAPE	STATUTORY CHANGES ENACTED IN MANY STATES
▪ Only females can be the victims of rape.	▪ Any person (male or female) may be a victim.
▪ Only a male could directly commit the crime.	▪ Any person (male or female) can directly commit the crime. (See the 1986 case of *State v. Stevens,* 510 A.2d 1070, where it was held an adult woman could be charged with having sexual intercourse with a thirteen-year-old boy.)
▪ A husband could not rape his wife (under the common law, however, the husband could be charged with assault and battery).	▪ A husband can be charged with the rape of his wife under the law of states that have made this change from the old common law.
▪ Rape was defined in one (or at most a few) degree.	▪ A variety of degrees of criminal conduct are defined in more specific language.
▪ Rape was defined only as the insertion of the penis into a vagina by force and against the will of the female.	▪ "Sexual intercourse" is broadly defined not only as vaginal intercourse, but also "cunnilingus, fellatio, anal intercourse, or any other intrusion, however slight, of any part of a person's body or of any object into the genital or anal opening of another, but emission of semen is not required" (Section 940.225[5][c] of the Wisconsin Criminal Code).
▪ Common law rape did not include the crime of "offensive touching" (however, this could be charged either as disorderly conduct or assault and sometimes battery if there was an injury).	▪ Many modern sexual assault laws include the offense of "offensive touching" in that they forbid "sexual contact" (intentional touching of an intimate part of another person's body without consent).
▪ "Utmost resistance" and "resistance" was required under the old common law.	▪ Resistance is no longer an essential element of the crime of rape. Instead, many states require proof that the sex act was done "without consent" and "against the will" of the victim.
▪ Rape was classified as a crime against sexual morality.	▪ Sexual assault is more often classified as a crime against a person.

Source: T. J. Gardner and T. M. Anderson. *Criminal Law, Principles and Cases.* 5th ed. St. Paul, Minn.: West Publishing Company, © 1992, 543. Reprinted by permission.

to find where their valuables are located. Many victims who have refused to cooperate, and even some who have, have been ruthlessly killed. Further, robbery calls are the third-ranking cause of police fatalities.

The favorite weapon of most robbers is the handgun. Other weapons used include knives, acids, baseball bats, and explosives. Armed robbers frequently attack drug stores (often for narcotics), supermarkets, liquor stores, jewelry stores, gas stations, banks, residential homes, cab drivers, and pedestrians.

The classic image of a robber is a masked man pointing a gun at a lone pedestrian on a city street or in a small grocery store at night, but in actuality many do not wear masks or carry guns. Frequently the victims are old people who are robbed of a small amount of money and are knocked to the ground, sometimes suffering permanent injuries or even death.

Robbery produces millions of dollars for criminals and is the most frequently reported crime. Approximately 10 percent of all willful homicides are the result of robbery attempts. But statistics do not reflect the human loss and tragedy often involved in robbery.

Not all robberies are aggravated, however. Some states have a category of simple robbery where no force or threat is used. A usual element of the crime of robbery is force and fear, not stealth. If a thief jostles a victim in a crowd to divert attention and picks his or her pocket, the crime is robbery. A normal pickpocket operation or purse snatching is larceny, not robbery, unless there is resistance or bodily contact.

Nationally about 55 percent of the robberies committed are street robberies. Large cities commonly have twenty to thirty robberies reported in a twenty-four-hour period on Fridays and Saturdays.

According to the UCR, 575,000 robberies are committed annually. The Bureau of Justice Statistics cites these facts about robbery:

- Robbery is a violent crime that typically involves more than one offender (in about half of all cases).
- Slightly less than half of all robberies involved the use of a weapon.
- Less than 2 percent of the robberies reported to the police were bank robberies.

The elements of the crime of robbery are as follows:

1. It is the wrongful taking of personal property;
2. It involves taking property from the person or in the person's presence; and
3. It is committed against the person's will by force or threat of force.

CRIMES AGAINST PROPERTY

The four Index Crimes against property are burglary, larceny/theft, motor vehicle theft, and arson. Although these crimes do not usually involve violence, they can leave their victims feeling violated.

Burglary

The Uniform Crime Reporting Program defines **burglary** as the unlawful entry into a structure to commit a felony or theft. The use of force to gain entry is not required to classify the crime as a burglary. Burglary has three subclassifications: forcible entry, unlawful entry where no force is used, and attempted forcible entry.

Burglary is unlawful entrance into a building to commit theft or other felony.

Many dictionaries have as their first (most common) definition of burglary, "the act of breaking into a house at night to commit theft or other felony." This definition reflects what burglary was historically (under common law)— breaking and entering a dwelling of another in the night. Modern-day statutes reflect numerous changes in that definition, broadening its scope considerably.

Some states, for example, have eliminated the word *breaking* and require only a trespass. Burglaries can occur by forcible or attempted forcible entry, unlawful entry, or without force as when a burglar opens an unlocked door or window or remains in a building without the consent of the person in charge with the intention of committing a crime. Department stores often have been the victims of burglars who hide in the store at closing time and wait until everyone else has left, take what they want, and then break out of the store to escape.

State statutes often restrict *building* to a dwelling or other structure suitable for human shelter or connected to such a structure. Warehouses, barns, garages, and some types of shelters have also been defined by the courts as dwellings. California defines burglary as the entry of a *structure* for the specific purpose of committing theft or some other felony. A structure is anything having continuous walls, a floor and roof, windows, and doors included.

State statutes also vary as to whether the crime must occur at night to be a burglary. Some states say it may occur at any time of the day or night. If entry occurs during the night, breaking may not be an essential element of the crime.

Punishments are usually most severe if the burglar has an explosive or tool in possession, if the building entered is a dwelling and the burglar has a dangerous weapon when entering, or if the burglar assaults someone while committing the burglary.

Some states have a modified charge of "breaking and entering," which is a lesser charge than burglary. The intricacies in defining burglary are interesting. For instance, if a salesperson pockets a diamond ring while making a sales call in a home, it is not burglary. If a person poses as a salesperson to get into a home and then steals a diamond ring, however, it is burglary in most states.

The UCR estimates between three and three and one-half million burglaries are committed annually. The Bureau of Justice Statistics cites these facts about burglary:

- Forty-five percent of all household burglaries occurred without forced entry.
- In the burglary of more than three million American households, the offenders entered through an unlocked window or door or used a key (for example, a key hidden under a doormat).
- About 34 percent of the no-force household burglaries were known to have occurred between 6 A.M. and 6 P.M.
- Residential property was targeted in 67 percent of reported burglaries; non-residential property accounted for the remaining 33 percent.
- Three-quarters of the nonresidential burglaries for which the time of occurrence was known took place at night.

The elements of the crime of burglary are as follows:

1. A structure is entered;
2. It occurs without the consent of the person in possession; and
3. There is the intent to commit a crime therein.

Larceny/Theft

Larceny/theft is the unlawful taking or stealing of property or articles without the use of force, violence, or fraud. It includes shoplifting, pocket picking, purse snatching, thefts from motor vehicles, thefts of motor vehicle parts and accessories, and bicycle thefts. The category does not include embezzlement, "con" games, forgery, and passing worthless checks, all Part II crimes. It also does not include motor vehicle theft, which is a separate offense.

Larceny/theft is unlawfully taking and removing another's personal property with the intent of permanently depriving the owner of the property.

Larceny/theft may be classified as either a misdemeanor or a felony. It differs from robbery in that it does not involve force, threats of force, or violence. The severity of punishment usually depends on the value and type of property taken, whether it was taken from a building or a person, and the specific circumstances of the case.

Most theft statutes indicate situations where the value of the article is immaterial in determining whether the offense is a felony or misdemeanor. These situations include stealing from the person of another or a grave or a corpse, stealing public records or public funds, looting, and stealing articles representing trade secrets.

Some states categorize larceny into degrees. **Grand** and **petty larceny** are common identifications for value of property taken and punishment. First-, second-, and third-degree larceny also indicate a certain minimum value of the property taken and various degrees of punishment.

The most common type of theft is the theft of items from motor vehicles and motor vehicle parts and accessories. The files of police departments throughout the country are filled with reports of losses such as CB radios, stereo tape decks, clothing, and photographic equipment taken from motor vehicles.

Other common forms of larceny are thefts from buildings such as under-ground garages where maintenance equipment such as lawnmowers, snow-blowers, lawn hoses, and fertilizers are the target. Bicycles are also a common target for thieves. Because they are easily removed and lack serial number markings, bicycle theft has become big business for many criminals. Police departments find that in some cities dealers specialize in the sale of stolen bicycles.

Thefts from coin-operated vending machines, pocket picking, purse snatching, and shoplifting are other common forms of larceny/theft. Shoplifting accounts for an estimated two billion dollars lost each year. Shoplifters range in age from five to eighty-five. The great majority are amateurs, but there are professional shoplifters (called **boosters**) as well as itinerant schools for professionals. The vast majority of shoplifters apprehended are not prosecuted because merchants do not want to alienate good customers or spend the time involved in prosecution, so the customers pay for the shoplifting losses in higher prices.

The UCR estimates approximately eight million larceny/thefts annually in the United States. The Bureau of Justice Statistics cites these facts about larceny/theft:

- Pocket picking and purse snatching most frequently occur inside nonresidential buildings or on street locations.

Although warning signs can be humorous, the problem of shoplifting is serious, resulting in higher prices for customers.

- Unlike most other crimes, pocket picking and purse snatching affect the elderly as much as other age groups.
- Most personal larcenies with contact occur during the daytime, but most household larcenies occur at night.

The elements of the crime of larceny/theft are as follows:

1. Felonious stealing, taking, carrying, leading, or driving away of another's goods or property;
2. Value of the property is above (grand) or below (petty) a specified amount;
3. There is an intent to permanently deprive the owner of the property or goods.

FORMS OF THEFT

Theft is a term that can refer to several different crimes, depending upon state statutes. It can describe a type of larceny, a theft from the person, a theft by force, or a burglary. The most commonly referred to forms of theft are summarized in Table 5–3.

A new phenomena and swindle has been victimizing discount retail establishments. Using sophisticated equipment and targeting new clerks in discount stores, thieves are clearing $6,000 to $7,000 daily through barcode swindles. The thieves are often part of an organization consisting of many teams of male and female couples who buy items at reduced prices and later return them for full value. For example, a couple might alter the bar code on a television set valued at $199 to be on sale for $99. They would then pick out the least experienced cashier. After making their purchase and leaving the store, the couple would arrange with their operations base for a falsified receipt and return the television for the original price.

In a class by itself is motor vehicle theft.

Table 5–3 **Forms of Theft**

THEFT/LARCENY	THEFT FROM THE PERSON	ROBBERY (THEFT BY FORCE OR THREAT OF FORCE)	BURGLARY (TRESPASS WITH INTENT TO STEAL OR TO COMMIT A FELONY)
▪ ordinary theft (usually done secretly) ▪ snatch and run theft ▪ shoplifting ▪ theft from autos ▪ theft from buildings ▪ theft by fraud (con game) ▪ embezzlement ▪ theft by bailee ▪ fraud on innkeeper, restaurant ▪ "looting"—taking property from building that has been destroyed by disaster, riot, bombing, fire, tornado, etc.	▪ purse snatching ▪ pickpocketing ▪ "rolling a drunk" (taking valuables from an intoxicated person or person in stupor) ▪ taking valuables from injured, dead, or disabled persons	▪ mugging or yoking (strong-armed robbery) ▪ armed robbery ▪ robbery in which the victim is placed in apprehension that the criminal is armed with a dangerous weapon ▪ masked robbery (identity is concealed) ▪ purse snatching and pickpocketing in which such force is used against the person that it constitutes strong-armed robbery ▪ "home invasion" robbery	▪ ordinary burglary (some states punish burglary committed at night more severely) ▪ armed burglary ▪ burglary in which an occupant of the building is injured ▪ "break and run" burglary (breaking store window and running off with property) ▪ newspapers use the term "cat burglary." Some states do have this crime.

Source: T. J. Gardner and T. M. Anderson. *Criminal Law, Principles and Cases.* 5th ed. St. Paul, Minn.: West Publishing Company, © 1992, 467. Reprinted by permission.

Motor Vehicle Theft

In Uniform Crime reporting, **motor vehicle theft** is defined as the unlawful taking or stealing of a motor vehicle, including attempts. This definition excludes taking a vehicle for temporary use by those persons having lawful access to the vehicle. Motor vehicle theft includes automobiles, trucks, buses, motorcycles, motorized boats, and aircraft.

Motor vehicle theft is the unlawful taking or stealing of a motor vehicle without the authority or permission of the owner.

Motor vehicle theft rates show this crime to be primarily a large city problem; the highest rates appear in the most heavily populated sections of the country.

It is difficult to obtain a conviction for auto theft unless witnesses see the person drive the vehicle away and make positive identification later. It is also difficult to prove if the suspect intended to permanently deprive the rightful owner of its use. Therefore, another category of auto theft has been created called "Unlawful Use of a Motor Vehicle," which applies to suspects who merely have possession of a vehicle reported stolen.

Auto thefts represent a great monetary property loss. The police are not only charged with the recovery of stolen vehicles but with the apprehension of the guilty parties.

Of the many motives for auto theft, joyriding leads the list. Young people steal a car, take it for ride, and then abandon it. Joyriding is often a separate charge where intent to permanently deprive is not in evidence. Autos are also stolen for revenge, for transportation, for commercial use, and for use in committing other crimes such as kidnapping, burglary, and bank robbery. Autos are stolen and stripped for such parts as transmissions, engines, and seats. Sale of stolen auto parts is one of the fastest growing businesses today because of the high cost of replacement parts and the unavailability of parts for foreign-made cars. Automobiles are also stolen, modified, given altered serial numbers and fraudulent titles, and sold to an unsuspecting public.

Table 5–4 illustrates the fate of most stolen cars and vehicles.

With the increased number of foreign students attending our universities, a relatively new scheme has caused millions of dollars of losses to American banks. The fraudulent car scheme has accelerated to a new high under the guise of car loans from banks. Foreign students buy new cars, obtain loans on them, and then ship them to foreign countries, which require no proof of ownership. In addition, many vehicles reported as stolen are actually driven into lakes and rivers or buried by their owners to defraud insurance companies.

The UCR estimates one million five hundred thousand motor vehicle thefts are reported annually. The Bureau of Justice Statistics reports the following:

■ Motor vehicle theft is relatively well reported to the police because reporting is required for insurance claims, and vehicles are more likely than other stolen property to be recovered.

■ About three-fifths of all motor vehicle thefts occur at night.

The elements of the crime of unauthorized use of a motor vehicle are as follows:

1. There is an intent to take or drive a motor vehicle; and
2. There is no consent of the owner or the owner's authorized agent.

Arson

Arson is intentionally damaging or destroying or attempting to damage or destroy property by means of fire or explosion. It is a felony in all fifty states. It was not until 1978 that Congress made arson a Class I (Part I) crime. Arson has increased over 400 percent in the past ten years. An estimated 1,000 people, including 45 firefighters, die each year in arson fires, and 10,000 people are injured annually. Annual damage estimates are as high as $15 billion. Insurance losses exceed $3 billion. New York's arson task force estimates that New York loses about 300–400 buildings a month by fire, the majority of which are arson.

Arson is intentionally damaging or destroying or attempting to damage or destroy by means of fire or explosion the property of another without the consent of the owner or one's own property, with or without the intent to defraud.

Table 5–4   **Car and Vehicle Theft**

The crime of car and vehicle theft has risen sharply in recent years. It formerly caused the largest property loss of any crime. The savings and loan scandal in the United States has now probably taken first place.

What happens to stolen cars and vehicles?
In 1989, 1.5 million vehicles were stolen and 2.9 million vehicles were illegally entered for valuables or accessories.

Chop-shop operations, in which professionals cut up the vehicle for parts. As nothing is left of the vehicle, the criminals are called "buzzards." Chop-shop operations are generally believed to be under the control of organized criminal groups.

Strippers who "strip" cars for some of the easily resalable parts: tires, wheels, doors, fenders, hoods, radios, stereos, spark plugs. Strippers are considered semiprofessionals; some are dope addicts who sell car parts to finance their habits. Stripped cars are generally recovered by owners.

Exported from the United States—The National Automobile Theft Bureau estimates that 200,000 vehicles are exported to other countries, where the vehicles or the parts sell at prices much higher than in the United States. (See "Motor Vehicle Theft Investigations" in the Sept. 1990 *FBI Law Enforcement Bulletin.*)

Abandoned or Returned or Recovered
- after use by a "joy-rider" (once the biggest offender but now estimated to be responsible for 10 percent of missing cars)
- after being used for a crime
- after being abandoned by strippers
- after a breakdown or being damaged

Phony car thefts—Car owners hide or abandon their vehicles and then falsely report them stolen in hopes of collecting insurance. Estimates range from 15 percent to as high as 30 percent of reported thefts are phony.

Used on Streets and Highways of United States
- with original VIN numbers and different plates
- with identification numbers salvaged from similar model cars in junkyards ("salvage and switch" operations)

It is estimated that car theft and vehicle looting costs the American public $7 billion a year in out-of-pocket expenses, plus the costs of higher insurance and the additional cost of law enforcement expenses. The National Automobile Theft Bureau (a private group) suggests the following: 1. Lock your car to avoid car theft. 2. Do not leave valuables in plain view in the car. 3. Leave only the ignition key when parking in a commercial garage. 4. Park in well-lighted areas. 5. Close your garage door and lock it. 6. Do not leave your license or registration in the car.

Source: T. J. Gardner and T. M. Anderson. *Criminal Law, Principles and Cases.* 5th ed. St. Paul, Minn.: West Publishing Company, © 1992, 449. Reprinted by permission.

One of the most serious problems often encountered in arson investigations is the joint jurisdiction of firefighters and law enforcement officers. All too frequently this results in duplication of effort and inefficiency.

The Uniform Crime Reports carry only trend and clearance tables for arson, stating that sufficient data is not available to estimate totals for this offense. The Bureau of Justice Statistics states the following regarding arson:

- Single-family residences were the most frequent targets of arson.
- Fifteen percent of all structures where arson occurred were not in use.

The elements of the crime of arson include:

1. Willful, malicious burning of a building or property of another or of one's own to defraud; or

2. Aiding, counseling, or procuring such a burning.

PART II INDEX CRIMES

The Part II offenses consist of several other crimes that can be either misdemeanors or felonies. They are as follows:

- Other assaults (intimidation, coercion, hazing, etc.)
- Forgery and counterfeiting
- Fraud (confidence games, etc.)
- Embezzlement
- Stolen property: buying, receiving, possessing
- Vandalism
- Weapons: carrying, possessing, etc.
- Prostitution and commercialized vice
- Sex offenses (except forcible rape, prostitution, and commercialized vice)
- Drug abuse violations
- Gambling
- Offenses against the family and children (child abuse, neglect, nonsupport)
- Driving under the influence
- Liquor laws (liquor law violations, bootlegging, etc.)
- Drunkenness
- Disorderly conduct
- Vagrancy
- Curfew and loitering (juveniles)
- Runaway (juveniles)
- All other offenses (abortion, bigamy, contempt of court, the list goes on and on)

Statistics on Part II offenses are based on the number of arrests recorded by law enforcement agencies rather than the complaints received by these agencies. Part II offenses do not meet the test of frequency of occurrence or seriousness, or they may be victimless crimes.

CRIMINAL LAW AND CRIME—IN REVIEW

You've looked at what constitutes a crime, at the various classifications of crime, and at the elements of the major crimes. You've also seen statistics on the prelevance of the eight serious Part I Index Crimes. The nature of crime in the United States, including white-collar crime and organized crime is the focus of the next chapter. Before leaving the discussion of crime, however, consider the question posed by Reiman (1991, p. 65): "What's in a name?" His answer is thought-provoking:

If it takes you an hour to read this chapter, by the time you reach the last page, two of your fellow citizens will have been murdered. *During that same time, at least 4 Americans will die as a result of unhealthy or unsafe conditions in the workplace!* Although these work-related deaths could have been prevented, they are not called murders. Why not? Doesn't a crime by any other name still cause misery and suffering? What's in a name?

The fact is that the label "crime" is not used in America to name all or the worst of the actions that cause misery and suffering to Americans. It is primarily reserved for the dangerous actions of the poor.

Table 5–5 summarizes reasons legislatures might and might not make certain actions crimes.

It is certainly true that many acts which most would consider wrong are not "crimes." Such actions often fall under the jurisdiction of civil law.

CIVIL LAW AND TORTS

Civil law refers to all noncriminal restrictions placed on individuals. Although laws vary from state to state, generally such actions as trespassing, desertion of family, slander, failure to make good on a contract, or similar actions against an individual would be covered under civil law.

Civil law refers to all noncriminal restrictions placed on individuals. It seeks not punishment, but restitution.

As Prosser notes (1955, p. 7):

A **tort** is not the same thing as a crime, although the two sometimes have many features in common. The distinction between them lies in the interests affected and the remedy afforded by the law. A crime is an offense against the public at large, for which the state, as the representative of the public, will bring proceedings in the form of criminal prosecution. ... A criminal prosecution is not concerned in any way with compensation of the injured individual against whom

---

Table 5–5   **Legislative Designations of Crime**

REASONS A LEGISLATIVE BODY MIGHT DESIGNATE SPECIFIC CONDUCT AS CRIMINAL	REASONS A LEGISLATIVE BODY MIGHT NOT DESIGNATE SPECIFIC CONDUCT AS CRIMINAL
To protect the public from violent or dangerous conduct	It is not within the power of the government to prohibit such conduct.
To protect public health	The conduct in question is constitutionally protected.
To maintain public order	
To protect the right of privacy of individuals	There is no demand by influential public or private groups or individuals for the regulation of such conduct.
To protect public morality	
Because there appears to be no other way in which to promote a desired public policy	It would not be economically feasible to enforce a law criminalizing such conduct.
	It would not be politically popular to pass a law criminalizing such conduct.

Source: T. J. Gardner and T. M. Anderson. *Criminal Law, Principles and Cases.* 5th ed. St. Paul, Minn.: West Publishing Company, © 1992, 8. Reprinted by permission.

the crime is committed. ... The civil action for a tort, on the other hand, is commenced and maintained by the injured person himself, and its purpose is to compensate him for the damage he has suffered, at the expense of the wrongdoer.

A tort is a civil wrong for which the court will seek a remedy in the form of damages to be paid.

Sutherland and Cressey (1978, p. 8) clarify the distinction between a tort and a crime:

The conventional view is that a crime is an offense against the state, while, in contrast, a tort in violation of civil law is an offense against an individual. A particular act may be considered as an offense against an individual and also against the state, and is either a tort or a crime or both, according to the way it is handled. A person who has committed an act of assault, for example, may be ordered by the civil court to pay the victim a sum of $500 for the damages to his interests, and may also be ordered by the criminal court to pay a fine of $500 to the state. The payment of the first $500 is not punishment, but payment of the second $500 is punishment.

It is important that law enforcement officers recognize when a matter is covered by criminal law and when it is covered by civil law (noncriminal matters). Sometimes police officers are asked to describe a citizen's rights in a noncriminal matter and what legal options are open.

The distinction between crimes and torts are as follows:

Crime

- Public wrong
- State prosecutes
- Seeks to punish
- Criminal intent is required

Tort

- Private wrong
- Individual prosecutes
- Seeks redress for injury
- Intent not necessary

THE LAW ENFORCEMENT OFFICER AND CIVIL LIABILITY

According to Harr and Hess (1990, p. 76): "Only naive or deluded police officers believe they would never be sued. The past two decades have produced an unprecedented increase in suits brought against the police. It is presently estimated that over thirty thousand lawsuits are initiated against law enforcement annually (Silver 1986, p. xi)."

One reason for the numerous lawsuits is the current interpretation of Section 1983 of the Civil Rights Act.

The Civil Rights Act (Section 1983)

The United States Code, Title 42, Section 1983, passed after the Civil War in 1871, states the following:

> Every person who, under color of any statute, ordinance, regulation, custom, or usage, of any State or Territory, subjects, or causes to be subjected any citizen of the United States or other person within the jurisdiction thereof to the deprivation of any rights, privileges, or immunities secured by the Constitution and laws, shall be liable to the party injured in an action at law, suit in equity, or other proper proceeding for redress.

Section 1983 of United States Code, Title 42, stipulates that anyone acting under the authority of local or state law who violates another person's constitutional rights—even though they are upholding a law—can be sued.

The two basic requirements for a Section 1983 action are that (1) the plaintiff must be deprived of a constitutional right and (2) the defendant must deprive the plaintiff of this right while acting under the "color of the law" (*Adickes v. Kress and Co.,* 1970). Like criminal law, civil law has levels of "intent."

- Strict liability—the wrongdoer is liable even if no harm was intended (for example keeping wild animals).
- Intentional wrong—the person knows the act was unlawful but did it anyway.
- Negligence—the person did not set out to do harm but acted carelessly.

The last two categories are the ones law enforcement officers most frequently find themselves involved with.

The intentional wrongs that may affect law enforcement include assault, battery, false imprisonment, false arrest, malicious prosecution, intentional infliction of emotional distress, trespass, illegal electronic surveillance, invasion of privacy, and defamation. Later chapters will introduce procedures to be followed to minimize the likelihood of a civil lawsuit for an intentional wrong.

The second category of civil charges frequently filed against law enforcement officers and their agencies is **negligence,** defined as the failure to use due care to prevent foreseeable injury. The routine police duties that most frequently lead to negligence lawsuits are care of incapacitated persons, duty to render emergency aid, caring for arrestees, aiding private citizens, investigating unusual circumstances, and operating emergency vehicles carelessly, for example, high-speed chases.

Procedures discussed elsewhere in this text should help to lessen the probability of a civil lawsuit. According to Gallagher (1990, p. 18):

> What police officers do is inherently dangerous. They carry weapons that can injure and kill. They drive cars at high speeds. They must constantly enforce (and obey) laws, statutes and ordinances, whose variety and intricacies confuse most people.
>
> Yet if an officer makes a mistake, or if his actions lead to unnecessary injury, a lawsuit and an adverse judgment can follow. The results can be disastrous. In fact, the fallout from a major lawsuit can be damaging, even if the lawsuit is won.

Scogin and Brodsky (1991) undertook a study of law enforcement officers' fear of litigation, technically known as **litigaphobia,** a combination of *litigation* and *phobia.* Participants in the study were ninety men and eleven women at a regional law enforcement academy. The average age was 28.4 years, the mean educational level 13.5 years, and about half came from agencies with less than twenty employees. This study found that:

- These officers worried moderately about work-related lawsuits.
- Sixty-nine percent take specific actions to prevent lawsuits.
- The officers reported moderate to severe distress when hearing of another officer being sued.
- The great majority did not think that their fears of litigation were irrational or excessive.

In response to the question as to what they did to prevent lawsuits, many responsed "going by the book" and "treating people fairly."

Law enforcement officers can avoid lawsuits if they are knowledgeable of criminal and civil law and act within that law. As noted by Thomas and Means (1990, p. 41):

> The U.S. Supreme Court has repeatedly held that state and local government officials will *not* be held liable in lawsuits brought under 42 U.S.C. § 1983 as long as they had an objectively reasonable belief in the lawfulness of their conduct. As the Court itself has said, this immunity shields "all but the plainly incompetent or those who knowingly violate the law."

As noted by delCarmen (1991, p. ix): "Law enforcement officers must know the basics of civil liabilities in hopes that such knowledge will minimize the possibility of their being sued or, if sued, of being held liable." delCarmen (p. 2) summarizes the results of a 1986 survey of police chiefs from the twenty largest cities and dozens of other municipalities with populations over 100,000 which "revealed that most of the police chiefs, their officers, and their agencies have been sued in the past and expect to be sued in the future." The lawsuits that were brought most frequently were, in descending order of importance, use of force, auto pursuits, arrests/searches, employee drug tests, and hiring and promotion.

delCarmen suggests (pp. 16–18) that civil liabilities under state law may be against persons or against property and include the following:

- Excessive use of force. The general rule is that nondeadly force may be used by the police in various situations as long as such force is reasonable.
- False arrest and imprisonment. False arrest usually refers to an arrest without probable cause or a valid arrest warrant. False arrest and false imprisonment are similar in that in both cases the individual is restrained or deprived of freedom without legal justification. They differ, however, in that false arrest leads to false imprisonment, but false imprisonment is not necessarily the result of false arrest.
- Assault and battery. Assault is the intentional causing of an apprehension of harmful or offensive conduct; it is the attempt or threat, accompanied by the apparent ability, to inflict bodily harm on another person. In contrast, battery is the intentional, undesired, and unprovoked infliction of a harmful or offensive body contact on another person.
- Wrongful death. This tort arises whenever death occurs as a result of an officer's unjustified action. The safest rule is that deadly force may be used only in cases of self-defense or when the life of another person is in danger and the use of deadly force is immediately necessary to protect that life.
- Intentional infliction of emotional or mental distress. This tort is usually filed in connection with other torts such as false arrest or assault and battery.
- Misuse of legal procedure. This tort includes malicious prosecution and abuse of process. It occurs when the officer uses the legal process for reasons other than that intended by law.

- Invasion of privacy. This tort refers to the violation of the plaintiff's right to be "let alone." Examples include unauthorized publication of somebody's picture, the unauthorized obtaining of evidence from a person's home, or the unauthorized publication of the details of a person's private life.
- Illegal electronic surveillance. Any form of electronic monitoring by the police that fails to comply with the provisions of federal and state law may lead to liability, particularly if specific penalties are imposed.
- Defamation. The publication of any false material injurious to a person's good name or reputation.
- Malicious prosecution. The wrongful prosecution of a person without reason to believe that the person has committed a crime.

Police officers may also be sued for negligence. As noted by delCarmen (p. 16): "Negligence is the breach of a common law or statutory duty to act reasonably toward those who may foreseeably be harmed by an officer's conduct. The most common suits brought against police officers are for negligent operation of a motor vehicle and negligent failure to protect."

As noted by Spector (1992, p. 8): "It is now well settled law that a police officer who fails to intervene to prevent a constitutional violation may be liable under 42 U.S.C. § 1983." He cites the leading case of *Byrd v. Brishke* (1972), in which the plaintiff claimed to have been surrounded by about a dozen Chicago police officers who repeatedly struck him. The plaintiff could not identify the specific officers who had beaten him, but his claim was that all those present were liable since they did nothing to stop the beating. The court concurred:

> We believe it is clear that one who is given the badge of authority of a police officer may not ignore the duty imposed by his office and fail to stop other officers who summarily punish a third person in his presence or otherwise within his knowledge. The responsibility obviously obtains when the nonfeasor is a supervisory officer to whose direction misfeasor officers are committed. So, too, the same responsibility must exist as to nonsupervisory officers who are present at the scene of such summary punishment, for to hold otherwise would be to insulate nonsupervisory officers from liability for reasonably foreseeable consequences of the neglect of their duty to enforce the laws and preserve the peace.

Spector also cautions that: "In addition to stopping the actual constitutional violation, officers must be made aware that they have to honestly come forward with information regarding misconduct of other officers. Evidence of a code of silence is sufficient to state a civil rights claim against a municipality." In any departments where such a **code of silence** exists, civil liability is greatly increased.

Sometimes the police are the ones wronged. When this occurs, they have the same rights as private citizens and can take the case to court. As noted by Manak (1989, p. 16):

> Public safety personnel, be they prosecutors, firefighters, police, sheriff's deputies or emergency medical personnel, are entitled to the same right to recover for wrongful injury as any other citizen. In increasing numbers, public safety personnel are themselves becoming plaintiffs in lawsuits filed against individuals who assault them or otherwise put them in danger. And in a good number of instances, they are successful in recovering.

Good Samaritan Laws

Law enforcement officers should be familiar with the **Good Samaritan laws** and which are applicable in their jurisdiction. Gardner and Anderson (1992, p. 13) identify three general categories into which Good Samaritan laws may be classified. The first is instances in which doctors and other health practitioners are encouraged to aid injured or ill strangers. The statutes do not encourage acts of heroism or require a duty to aid, but rather remove the fear of malpractice suits.

The second type of Good Samaritan law requires people to help victims if they can do so without endangering themselves. This might be simply calling the police or 911. Failure to do so could result in a fine.

The third type of Good Samaritan law allows people witnessing a violent assault to come to the aid of the victim. It does not, however, require that this be done.

SUMMARY

The law enforcement officer functions in a society where the citizens enjoy great freedom. Sometimes, however, this freedom is viewed by citizens as license to do as they please, to ignore the laws of society. State and federal statutes have defined actions that are not to be tolerated— crimes—and have set specified penalties for each. Although state statutes vary in their definitions of and penalties for crimes, certain generalizations can be made. Generally, a crime is an intentional action that is prohibited by law, and for which punishment is legally prescribed, that directly causes an actual harm.

The crimes most frequently reported to police, the most serious crimes in the nation, are called Part I Index Crimes. They include murder, assault, rape, robbery, burglary, larceny/theft, motor vehicle theft, and arson.

Crimes may be classified as felonies or misdemeanors. A felony refers to serious crimes, generally those punishable by death or by imprisonment for more than one year in a state prison or penitentiary. The court may, however, inflict a lesser punishment. A misdemeanor refers to any minor offense, generally punishable by a fine or a short term, usually not to exceed one year, in a jail or workhouse.

To prove a crime has been committed, it is usually necessary to prove the act itself (*actus reus*)—the elements of the crime—and to prove the criminal's mental state (*mens rea*)—intent to do wrong. In strict liability crimes, however, such as traffic violations, the defendant is liable regardless of intent.

Part I Index Crimes are described as follows:

- Murder (homicide) is the willful killing of a human by another human.
- Assault is attacking a person. It may be aggravated or simple.
- Rape is having sexual intercourse with a female through the use or threat of force. Rape may be aggravated or simple.
- Robbery is stealing anything of value from the control, care, or custody of a person by force or threat of force.
- Burglary is unlawful entrance into a building to commit theft or other felony.
- Larceny/theft is unlawfully taking and removing another's personal property with the intent of permanently depriving the owner of the property.
- Motor vehicle theft is the unlawful taking or stealing of a motor vehicle without the authority or permission of the owner.
- Arson is intentionally damaging or destroying or attempting to damage or destroy by means of fire or explosion the property of another without the consent of the owner or one's own property, with or without the intent to defraud.

Civil law refers to all noncriminal restrictions placed on individuals. It seeks not punishment but restitution. A tort is a civil wrong for which the court will seek a remedy in the form of damages to be paid. Section 1983 of United States Code, Title 42, states that anyone acting under the authority of local or state law who violates another person's constitutional rights—even though they are upholding a law—can be sued.

DISCUSSION QUESTIONS

1. If a person's reckless driving of a car injures another person who dies two weeks later as a result of the injuries, could the reckless driver be charged for a crime, sued for a tort, or both? How would the type of charge affect the possible consequences faced by the reckless driver?

2. Why is motor vehicle theft in a different category than larceny/theft?

3. Why are some crimes divided into categories or degrees?

4. Who should investigate arson offenses: the fire department or the police department?

5. Is fear of punishment a deterrent to criminal activity?

6. Would a law making the reporting of all crimes to the police mandatory, be a good deterrent to future criminal activity?

7. Should a mandatory sentence be imposed for all Part I offenses of the Uniform Crime Report?

8. Torts are a civil wrong. What purpose do they serve? Give an example.

9. Should law enforcement officers be immune from tort action?

10. How do the main concepts of this chapter relate to the Rodney King trial and verdict?

TERMS

actus reus, aggravated assault, aggravated rape, arson, assault, boosters, burglary, civil law, code of silence, *corpus delicti,* crime, criminal intent, criminal law, dark figure of criminality, elements of the crime, felony, first-degree murder, Good Samaritan laws, grand larceny, homicide, Index Crimes, intent, larceny/theft, litigaphobia, malice, manslaughter, *mens rea,* misdemeanor, motive, motor vehicle theft, murder, negligence, negligent homicide, petty larceny, premeditated, procedural criminal law, rape, robbery, *scienter,* second-degree murder, simple assault, simple rape, statutory rape, strict liability, substantive criminal law, theft, tort.

REFERENCES

Abadinsky, H. *Crime and Justice.* Chicago, Ill.: Nelson-Hall Publishers, 1987.

Brantingham, P. and Brantingham, P. *Patterns in Crime.* New York: Macmillan, 1984.

Chamelin, N. C. and Evans, K. R. *Criminal Law for Police Officers.* 5th ed. Englewood Cliffs, N.J.: Prentice Hall, 1991.

delCarmen, R. V. *Civil Liabilities in American Policing.* Englewood Cliffs, N.J.: Brady, A Prentice Hall Division, 1991.

Gallagher, G. P. "Risk Management for Police Administrators." *The Police Chief* (June 1990): 18–29.

Gardner, T. J. *Criminal Law, Principles and Cases.* 3d ed. St. Paul, Minn.: West Publishing Company, 1985.

Gardner, T. J. and Anderson, T. M. *Criminal Law, Principles and Cases.* 5th ed. St. Paul, Minn.: West Publishing Company, 1992.

Harr, J. S. and Hess, K. M. *Criminal Procedure.* St. Paul, Minn.: West Publishing Company, 1990.

Haskell, M. R. and Yablonsky, L. *Crime and Criminality.* Boston: Houghton Mifflin, 1983.

Manak, J. P. "The Police Plaintiff: Making the System Work *for* Law Enforcement." *The Police Chief.* (September 1989): 16–19.

Monk, R. C. "Are Official Statistics Meaningful?" pp. 84–85 In *Taking Sides: Clashing Views on Controversial Issues in Crime and Criminology.* 2d ed., edited by R. C. Monk. Guilford, Conn.: The Dushkin Publishing Groups, 1991.

Monk, R. C. "Introduction: The Study of Crime and Criminology," pp. xii–xvii in *Taking Sides: Clashing Views on Controversial Issues in Crime and Criminology.* 2d ed., edited by R. C. Monk. Guiford, Conn.: The Dushkin Publishing Groups, Inc., 1991.

Nettler, G. *Explaining Crime.* 2d ed. New York: McGraw-Hill, 1978.

Prosser, W. L. *Handbook of the Law of Torts.* 2d ed. St. Paul, Minn.: West Publishing Company, 1955.

Reiman, J. H. "A Crime by any Other Name." In *Taking Sides: Clashing Views on Controversial Issues in Crime and Criminology.* 2d ed., edited by R. C. Monk. Guilford, Conn.: The Dushkin Publishing Groups, 1991.

Samaha, J. *Criminal Law.* St. Paul, Minn.: West Publishing Company, 1983.

Scogin, F. and Brodsky, S. L. "Fear of Litigation Among Law Enforcement Officers." *American Journal of Police* X:1 (1991): 41–45.

Senna, J. J. and Siegel, L. J. *Introduction to Criminal Justice.* 5th ed. St. Paul, Minn.: West Publishing Company, 1990.

Silver, Isidore. *Police Civil Liability.* New York: Matthew Bender, 1986.

Spector, E. B. "Nonactor Liability: The Duty to Not Look the Other Way." *The Police Chief* (April 1992): 8.

Sutherland, E. H. and Cressey, D. R. *Criminology.* 10th ed. Philadelphia: Lippincott, 1978.

Thomas, B. and Means, R. "The Qualified Immunity: How to Never Lose a s.1983 Lawsuit." *The Police Chief* (June 1990): 41.

U.S. Department of Justice. Bureau of Justice Statistics. *Report to the Nation on Crime and Justice.* Washington, D.C.: U.S. Government Printing Office, 1988.

Wilson, J. Q. and Herrnstein, R. J. "Crime and Human Nature." In *Taking Sides: Clashing Views on Controversial Issues in Crime and Criminology.* 2d ed., edited by R. C. Monk. Guilford, Conn.: The Dushkin Publishing Groups, 1991.

Wright, K. N. "The Overdramatization of Crime in America." In *Taking Sides: Clashing Views on Controversial Issues in Crime and Criminology.* 2d ed., edited by R. C. Monk. Guilford, Conn.: The Dushkin Publishing Groups, 1991.

CHAPTER 6

Crime in the United States: Special Problems Facing Law Enforcement

No man is above the law and no man is below it; nor do we ask any man's permission when we require him to obey it.

—**Theodore Roosevelt**

Do You Know

What white-collar crime is?

What the most common types of white-collar crime are?

What computer crime may involve?

What three key characteristics of computer-related crime are?

What types of computer-related crime are most frequently committed?

How organized crime is usually defined?

What two characteristics of organized crime set it apart from other crimes committed by a group of individuals?

What types of crime are most frequently engaged in by members of organized crime?

What specific threats organized crime poses to the United States?

What major federal legislation has been enacted to deal with organized crime?

What special problems organized crime presents to law enforcement?

What bias crime is?

What types of bias may be involved?

What a ritual is?

What a ritualistic crime is and what must be investigated in it?

▬▬▬▬▬▬ INTRODUCTION

Chapter 5 discussed the major Index Crimes, the crimes most familiar to law enforcement and to the general public. Each state has its own specific statutes to define these crimes and assess penalties for them. But a whole other arena of crime is pervasive in the United States, an arena where the laws and the procedures for law enforcement officers to follow are not so clear. This arena includes white-collar crime, computer-related crime, organized crime, bias crime, and ritualistic crime.

▬▬▬▬▬▬ WHITE–COLLAR CRIME

White-collar crime is an occupational or business-related crime. The Part I offense of larceny/theft and several of the Part II offenses can also be classified as white-collar crimes. These crimes often involve billions of dollars and pose an extremely difficult challenge to law enforcement officers.

White-collar crime is occupational or business-related crime.

A special Report of the Bureau of Justice Statistics (1987, p. 1) states:

Although white-collar offenses are less visible than crimes such as burglary and robbery, their overall economic impact may be considerably greater. Among the white-collar cases filed by U.S. Attorneys in the year ending September 30, 1985, more than 140 persons were charged with offenses estimated to involve over $1 million each, and 64 were charged with offenses valued at over $10 million each. In comparison, losses from all bank robberies reported to police in 1985 were under $19 million, and losses from all robberies reported to police in 1985 totaled about $313 million.

In a large southern city, a grand jury brought indictments on thirty-two counts against a vice-president of a bank for embezzling funds. Outstanding community leader, father of several children—a respectable individual in the community was suddenly disgraced. At the same time in a western city, a grand jury brought indictments on twelve counts against a warehouse employee who had taken merchandise from his employer's warehouse, loaded it on a friend's truck, sold it, and divided the profits. The warehouse employee, a family man who attended church regularly, was shunned by his friends and fired by his employer.

Although most people in business are honest, corruption does exist. Security abuses, tax frauds, embezzlements, bribes, and kickbacks frequently occur, often the result of a "look the other way" attitude of co-workers and employers. Not only do employees and employers frequently ignore dishonesty within their businesses, they frequently engage in such practices themselves, rationalizing that they are acquiring something to which they really were entitled. For example, employees who make long-distance calls on an employer's phone or who pad expense accounts may tell themselves that since they are underpaid, this is simply one way of getting what they have coming to them.

When stealing from the boss (company, firm, business), most employees do not consider what they are doing as theft but merely a fringe benefit of the job. Going across the street and taking the same thing from another firm would be considered dishonest—but not when taken from one's own employer.

White-collar crime includes (1) credit card and check fraud, (2) securities theft and fraud, (3) insurance fraud, (4) consumer fraud, illegal competition, and deceptive practices, (5) bankruptcy fraud, (6) embezzlement and pilferage, (7) bribes, kick-backs, and payoffs, and (8) receiving stolen property.

Criminals involved in fraudulent schemes of all types are usually extremely mobile, moving from city to city and state to state, ruining individuals and small businesses.

Credit Card and Check Fraud

The billions of checks and millions of credit cards in circulation each year present limitless opportunity for crime. Unauthorized use of credit cards (found, stolen, or counterfeited) results in losses of millions annually. Credit card numbers obtained by various means, including discarded carbon copies of credit sales or by deceptive telephone schemes, are also used illegally.

Check fraud costs billions annually, including checks passed with insufficient funds or with no account, forged checks, counterfeit checks, stolen travelers' checks, money orders, and payroll checks.

As with insurance fraud, many white-collar crime experts exclude credit card and check fraud since they are not typically done in the course of a white-collar occupation.

Securities Theft and Fraud

Securities theft and fraud may be perpetrated by clerks acting independently, by individuals who rob messengers and steal from the mails, or by well-organized rings, one of which was reported as stealing approximately five million dollars worth of stock monthly. Most security thefts involve cooperation of dishonest employees ("inside" people) and may involve counterfeit and bogus securities as well.

Insurance Fraud

Insurance fraud losses lead to higher premiums for consumers. Since insurance is important to businesses and individuals, false claims for life, health, and accident benefits affect almost everyone.

Especially prevalent are fraudulent auto accident claims seeking compensation for treatments for personal injury, time lost from work, and automobile repairs. Many white-collar crime experts exclude insurance fraud since it is not typically done in the course of a white-collar occupation.

Consumer Fraud, Illegal Competition, and Deceptive Practices

Thousands of different schemes have been reported to defraud the public, including offers for "free" articles, advice, vacations, mailing or unordered merchandise, phony contests, recommendations for unneeded repairs, "going-out-of-business" sales, unqualified correspondence schools, and price fixing. Hundreds of other schemes undoubtedly exist but have not been reported because although the victims may realize the swindle, they do not want to admit having been "taken in."

Bankruptcy Fraud

Bankruptcy fraud, also called planned bankruptcy, scam, or bust-out, involves purchasing merchandise on credit from many different suppliers, selling the merchandise for cash that is "hidden," and then claiming bankruptcy, and not paying the creditors. A small business that has extended a large amount of credit to a company that declares bankruptcy (legitimately or not) may be forced out of business. Such an owner may then decide to use the same tactic, rationalizing the fraud as a justified effort to save his or her debt-ridden business.

Embezzlement and Pilferage

Many businesspeople consider embezzlement and pilferage to be their most serious problem. Both are, in effect, theft. To **embezzle** is to steal or use for oneself money or property entrusted to the person. To **pilfer** is basically the same, but on a much smaller scale. As noted by Gordon (1990, p. 12): "According to the latest figures from the U.S. Department of Commerce, employees walk off with $40 billion in goods every year. And they forecast that amount to increase 15 percent annually." She also notes that "The American Management Association has some equally appalling statistics: They estimate employee theft causes 20 percent of all business failures." The pilferer usually takes such things as office supplies, spare parts, and materials rather than money, but the result is the same. Cumulatively, the losses from pilferage may be much greater than what some other dishonest employee might embezzle. Equally dishonest is unauthorized use of company equipment, personnel, and time.

Bribes, Kickbacks, and Payoffs

Bribes, kickbacks, and payoffs are pervasive in the business world and are frequently used to obtain new clients, to keep old clients, to influence decisions, or to obtain favors. They can involve anyone from the custodian to the company president, and they can occur in any aspect of a company's operation.

Receiving Stolen Property

Although classified as a white-collar crime, receiving stolen property frequently occurs in conjunction with crimes such as robbery and burglary. The individual who buys and sells stolen property is of vital importance to the success of most burglars, robbers, and hijackers. Criminals depend upon a **fence** (a professional receiver and seller of stolen property) to convert what they have stolen to cash.

Other Types of White-Collar Crime

Police officers may also be called upon to investigate such white-collar crimes as crimes by businesses, as well as violent white-collar crimes such as selling dangerous products or intentional violation of safety codes. Investigating such crimes is difficult because usually individuals in top management are suspects and, consequently, uncooperative.

The seriousness of the problem of computer crime is emphasized by Black (1986, p. 31) who suggests:

> Unprecedented levels of sophistication are being advanced daily in ways to commit conventionally defined crimes, which were nonexistent prior to the widespread acceptance of computers in business, and are now being committed at an alarming increasing rate. These crimes are potentially more devastating in their effect, can be technically complex, and require a higher degree of preparedness by the agency charged with the responsibility for their investigation.

According to Manning and White (1990, p. 46): "The number of crimes involving computers is increasing dramatically throughout the country. There are documented offenses of every type—theft, fraud, burglary, prostitution, murder, child pornography—in which a computer was used in some way." Bennett (1987, p. 4) concurs: "Experts agree that computer crime in all its colorful variations—'data diddling,' 'superzapping,' 'logic bombs,' 'salami slicing,' 'Trojan horses'—will be the single greatest crime generator we face in the future."

Computer fraud may involve the input data, the output data, computer time, or the program itself.

Input data may be altered; for example, fictitious suppliers may be entered, figures may be changed, or data may be removed. Some universities have experienced difficulties with student grades being illegally changed. In a case cited by Dickey (1985, p. 29) the following occurred:

> A fifteen-year-old hacker with an inexpensive personal computer (PC) and modem [telephone hook-up] accessed patient files in the database of a hospital in California. Purely for self-amusement, he altered case histories and prescriptions. As a result of his interference, a patient suffered a massive allergic reaction, went into shock and nearly died. Eventually the hacker was traced and apprehended. He was a brilliant student—much admired by his teachers—and the son of a bank vice president. When the hacker's case was heard in juvenile court, the judge said that, as serious as the consequences *might* have been, no one had actually died. He also said that the hospital should not have relied on its computer to the extent that it had. Consequently, the sentence was suspended; since juvenile court records are closed, the hacker has no criminal record.

Output data may be obtained by unauthorized persons through such means as wiretapping, electromagnetic pickup, or theft of data sheets. An article in the *Las Vegas Review Journal* (March 2, 1986) cited the case of a Charles County, Maryland, teenage hacker who used a home PC to access a list of credit card account numbers and then charged $2,000 worth of computer equipment from seven computer firms in California, Georgia, Michigan, Minnesota, New York, Ohio, and Wisconsin. The crime was discovered when one of the computer firms became suspicious of fraud because several orders were received using different names but the same mailing address. The firm contacted the United States Secret Service in Baltimore. The youth was subsequently charged with seven counts of theft. Typically, however, output data is misused by an employee, not an outsider.

Computer time may be used for personal use, an example of pilferage to be discussed shortly. Some employees have even used their employer's hardware and company time to set up their own computer services for personal profit.

Computer-related crime is a growing type of white-collar crime that is especially difficult for law enforcement officers to investigate.

The computer program itself might be tampered with to add costs to purchased items or to establish a double set of records. According to Siegel (1983, pp. 332–33):

A number of common techniques are used by computer criminals. In fact, computer theft has become so common that experts have created their own jargon to describe theft styles and methods:

The Trojan horse. One computer is used to reprogram another for illicit purposes. In a recent incident, two high-school-age computer users reprogrammed the computer at DePaul University, preventing that institution from using its own processing facilities. The youths were convicted of a misdemeanor.

The salami slice. An employee sets up a dummy account in the company's computerized records. A small amount—even a few pennies—is subtracted from customers' accounts and added to the account of the thief. Even if they detect the loss, the customers don't complain, since a few cents is an insignificant amount to them. The pennies picked up here and there eventually amount to thousands of dollars in losses.

Super-zapping. Most computer programs used in business have built-in antitheft safeguards. However, employees can use a repair or maintenance program to supersede the antitheft program. Some tinkering with the program is required, but the "super-zapper" is soon able to order the system to issue checks to his or her private account.

The logic bomb. A program is secretly attached to the company's computer system. The new program monitors the company's work and waits for a sign of error to appear, some illogic that was designed for the computer to follow. Illogic causes the "logic bomb" to kick into action and exploit the weakness. The way the thief exploits the situation depends on his or her original intent—theft of money, theft of defense secrets, sabotage, and so on.

Impersonation. An unauthorized person uses the identity of an authorized computer user in order to use the computer in his or her stead.

Data leakage. A person illegally obtains data from a computer system by leaking it out in small amounts.

Bennett and Hess (1987, p. 392) describe two classic examples of computer fraud:

> Two computer programmers for an oil company plant who were responsible for the company's purchasing files created a fictitious supply company. They altered the company's computer database so that the oil company bought its supplies twice, once from the real supplier and once from the fictitious supply company, resulting in an embezzlement of several million dollars over a two-year period. The crime was discovered during a surprise audit, but the company declined to prosecute, not wanting to publicize how vulnerable its database was or how long it took to discover the embezzlement. Ironically, rather than being dismissed, the two embezzlers were promoted and placed in charge of computer security.
>
> In another instance, a New York bank hired an outside consultant to work with its computer technicians on transferring funds electronically. In the course of his work the consultant observed the access code being used to transfer the funds. He later used this access code to transfer a large sum of money to his own bank account. When the loss was finally discovered, management insisted that everyone in the section take a polygraph test, including the consultant. All except the consultant complied, and all passed. Although management was convinced the consultant had stolen the money, they did not prosecute; they simply changed their access code.

These cases illustrate three key characteristics of computer crimes.

Characteristics of computer-related crime are as follows:

- Computer crimes are relatively easy to commit and difficult to detect.
- Most computer crimes are committed by "insiders."
- Most computer crimes are not prosecuted.

The Data Processing Management Association (DPMA) in Park Ridge, Illinois, conducted a study of one thousand data processing executives in *Fortune* 1000 companies and found that only 2 percent of discovered computer abuses were reported to management or the authorities. The survey also found that only 2 percent of these abuses were committed by people outside the firm (Dickey 1985, p. 30).

As noted by Bennett and Hess (1987, p. 393):

> Enormous sums of money and tremendous quantities of information are electronically transferred by computers throughout the nation daily. These transfers present a unique opportunity for the computer thief. In October of 1986, President Reagan signed a bill modernizing the federal wiretap law to protect the privacy of high tech communications. This bill makes it illegal to eavesdrop on electronic mail, video conference calls, conversations on cellular car phones, and computer-to-computer transmissions. Other federal statutes relevant to computer-related crimes include patent laws, espionage and sabotage laws, trade secret laws, the Copyright Act of 1976, and the Financial Privacy Act of 1978.

At the state level, computer crime statutes exist in thirty-seven states (Dickey, 1985, p. 34), some being stringent. For example, disclosing the password of a computer system without the owner's consent is considered "unlawful use of a

Table 6–1   Current Statutes and Computer-Related Crime

Arson	Intentionally setting fire to a computer center
Burglary	Entering a computer center illegally with the intent to commit a crime therein
Extortion/Blackmail	Making threats against the operator(s) of a computer center to obtain money
Collusion	Working with others to commit a crime
Conspiracy	Several persons agreeing to commit an illegal act
Counterfeit	Copying or imitating computer documents
Embezzlement	Fraudulently converting property to personal use
Espionage	Stealing secret documents or information
Forgery	Issuing false documents
Fraud	Altering accounts or illegally transferring funds
Larceny	Theft of computer parts and materials
Malicious Destruction of Property	Destroying computer hardware or software
Murder	Tampering with life-sustaining computerized equipment resulting in the death of a patient
Receiving Stolen Property	Accepting any goods or information stolen by computer, knowing they were stolen
Sabotage	Intentionally destroying computer information, programs, or hardware
Theft	Stealing goods or money by use of a computer or stealing computer parts and materials

computer." Additionally, in many instances, existing state statutes are applicable to crimes involving computers. (See Table 6–1.)

The DPMA survey (Dickey 1985, p. 30) mentioned previously revealed the following:

Misuse of computer services made up nearly half of all incidents . . . . (Misuse could be anything from game playing or using the computer for personal work to diverting funds or altering records.) Program abuse—copying or changing programs—was the next most prevalent area (24 percent). Data abuse—diverting information to unauthorized individuals— was third (22 percent), and hardware abuse—damaging or stealing computer equipment—was last (5 percent).

The most common types of computer-related crime are misuse of computer services, program abuse, and data abuse.

Because use of computers in homes, small and large offices, businesses, and government installations will steadily increase, it can be expected that computer-related crimes will be a serious police investigative problem.

Unfortunately, as noted by Manning and White (p. 49): "Most law enforcement agencies are not currently prepared to effectively investigate computer crime. But criminals today are more intelligent and sophisticated than ever before, and if we are to avoid losing ground, we must be able to use this new technology to our *own* advantage."

Thirty-one states have enacted legislation addressing computer crime. The following specific violations are often included:

■ Publishing access codes through the use of a computer.

■ Theft of computer data.

- Unauthorized interruption of computer service.
- Computer tampering.
- Unauthorized access to a computer system.

Prosecuting computer crime cases is also difficult, according to Black (1986, p. 33): "especially when the jury consists of people who believe that a floppy disk can be corrected by a good chiropractor."

Also exceedingly difficult to prosecute are offenses committed by organized crime figures.

ORGANIZED CRIME

Organized crime has many names including the mob, the syndicate, the rackets, the Mafia, and Cosa Nostra. According to the National Advisory Committee on Criminal Justice Standards and Goals (1976, p. 7):

> Organized crime exists in both urban and rural areas.... Organized crime income is presently invested in a variety of businesses, including liquor establishments, nightclubs, health spas, travel agencies, massage parlors, motels, real estate agencies, nursing homes, and pornographic book stores and films. There are no "safe" enterprises, for organized crime may choose to infiltrate and take over wherever there is potential profit. Tactics adopted by organized crime include homicide, arson, and intimidation.

Organized Crime Defined

Definitions of **organized crime** vary from lengthy, detailed statements to simple eleven-word definitions. California's definition of organized crime is one of the most detailed (Committee on Criminal Justice Standards and Goals 1976, p. 214):

> Organized crime consists of two or more persons who, with continuity of purpose, engage in one or more of the following activities:
>
> 1. The supplying of illegal goods and services, that is, vice, loansharking, etc....
> 2. Predatory crime, for example theft, assault, etc....
>
> Several distinct types of criminal activity fall within this definition of organized crime. The types may be grouped into five general categories:
>
> 1. Racketeering.
> 2. Vice operations (narcotics, prostitution, loansharking, gambling).
> 3. Theft/fence rings (fraud, bunco schemes, fraudlent document passers, burglary rings, car thieves, truck hijackers).
> 4. Gangs (youth gangs, outlaw motorcycle gangs, prison gangs).
> 5. Terrorists.

A New York Conference on Combatting Organized Crime (Office of the New York Counsel to the Governor, 1966) defined organized crime as follows:

> Organized crime is the product of a self-perpetuating, criminal conspiracy to wring exhorbitant profits from our society by any means—fair and foul, legal and illegal. Despite personnel changes, the conspiratorial entity continues. It is a malignant parasite which fattens on human weakness. It survives on fear and corruption. By one or another means, it obtains a high degree of immunity from the law. It is totalitarian in its organization. A way of life, it imposes rigid discipline on underlings who do the dirty work while the top men of organized crime are generally insulated from the criminal act and the consequent danger of prosecution.

Rhodes (1984, p. 46) cites a 1967 Task Force Report that describes organized crime as a "society":

> Organized crime is a society that seeks to operate outside the control of the American people and their governments. It involves thousands of criminals, working within structures as complex as those of any large corporation, subject to laws more rigidly enforced than those of legitimate governments. Its actions are not impulsive, but rather the result of intricate conspiracies, carried on over many years and aimed at gaining control over whole fields of activity in order to amass huge profits.

And, as noted by Rhodes (1984, p. 47), by 1971 the National Advisory Committee recognized the wide variety of types of organized crime in its definition.

> Organized crime is a type of conspiratorial crime, sometimes involving the hierarchial coordination of a number of persons in the planning of illegal acts or in the pursuit of a legitimate objective by unlawful means. Organized crime involves continuous commitment by key members, although some individuals with specialized skills may participate only briefly in the ongoing conspiracies.

The Task Force on Organized Crime (National Advisory Committee, p. 7) notes:

> In nonlegal terms, organized crime has been called everything from non-existent to a vast conspiracy. As one observer of the organized crime scene noted, "For most purposes the term 'organized crime' has no precise legal configuration, although some specific attributes of syndicated criminal operations can be accurately defined."

Another problem encountered in discussing the problem of organized crime and possible solutions to it is the fact that organized crime itself is not illegal. According to Cressey (1969, p. 229):

> It is not against the law for an individual or group of individuals rationally to plan, establish, develop, and administer an organization designed for the perpetration of crime. Neither is it against the law for a person to participate in such an organization. What is against the law is bet-taking, usury, smuggling and selling narcotics and untaxed liquor, extortion, murder, and conspiracy to commit these and other specific crimes. Because "organized crime" is merely a social category, rather than a legal category, police and other governmental agencies cannot even routinely compile information on it as they do for other categories of crime.

Organized crime is a type of conspiratorial crime, sometimes involving the hierarchial coordination of a number of persons in the planning and execution of illegal acts or in the pursuit of a legitimate objective by unlawful means. Organized crime involves continuous commitment by key members, although some individuals with specialized skills may participate only briefly in the ongoing conspiracies.

Says Rowan (1986, p. 24):

> Crime pays. Annual gross income from the rackets will probably exceed $50 billion this year. That makes the mob's business greater than all U.S. iron, steel, copper, and aluminum manufacturing combined, or about 1.1% of GNP.... They [the figures] do not include billions more brought in from the mob's diversification into such legitimate enterprises as entertainment, construction, trucking and food and liquor wholesaling ... the mob's hold on the economy stifles competition and siphons off capital, resulting in a loss of some 400,000 jobs.... Since

organized-crime members cheat on taxes, the rest of the population will pay an estimated $6.5 billion more to the Internal Revenue Service this year.

Distinctive Characteristics of Organized Crime

All crime is a threat to our country, but organized crime poses a unique threat. Two features of organized crime, corruption and enforcement powers, set it apart from other types of crime and make it especially threatening, not only to police officers, but to our entire democratic process. (See Figure 6–1.)

Organized crime is distinct from other forms of crime in that it is characterized by corruption and enforcement powers.

Corruption   The President's Commission on Law Enforcement and Administration of Justice (1967, p. 241) drew the following conclusions about organized crime in the United States:

> In many ways organized crime is the most sinister kind of crime in America. The men who control it have become rich and powerful by encouraging the needy to gamble, by luring the troubled to destroy themselves with drugs, by extorting profits from honest and hardworking businessmen, by collecting usury from those in financial plight, by maiming or murdering those who oppose them, by bribing those sworn to destroy them. Organized crime is not merely a few

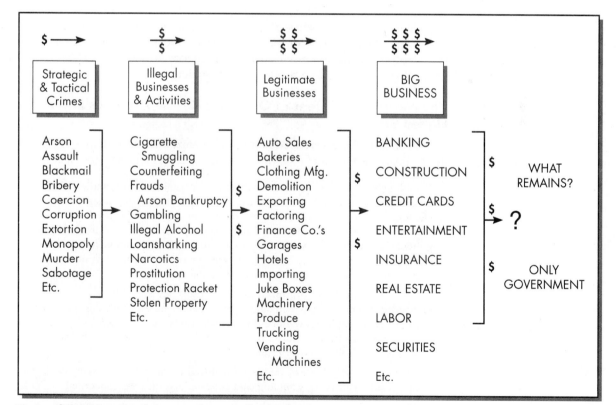

Figure 6–1   The Classic Pattern of Organized Crime

Source: R. Salerno and J. Tompkins. *The Crime Confederation.* Copyright © 1969. Reprinted by permission of Doubleday & Company: New York.

preying on a few. In a very real sense, it is dedicated to subverting not only American institutions, but the very decency and integrity that are the most cherished attributes of a free society. As the leaders of Cosa Nostra and their racketeering allies pursue their conspiracy unmolested, in open and continuous defiance of the law, they preach a sermon that all too many Americans heed: The government is for sale; lawlessness is the road to wealth; honesty is a pitfall and morality a trap for suckers.

Although written a quarter of a century ago, this characterization still rings true.

Corruption poses an extremely serious threat to police professionalism, discipline, and efficiency; the greatest source of that corruption is organized crime. (The types of corruption associated with organized crime are illustrated in Table 6–2.)

Enforcement Powers   A second unique characteristic of organized crime is the use of enforcement activities. Perhaps the gravest threat of organized crime is this assumption of enforcement powers. In our society, only legitimate government has the power to coerce its citizens through due process and the criminal justice system. When another group, such as organized crime, usurps that coercive power, it nullifies our legitimate government.

Organized crime usually has one or more fixed positions for "enforcers," who maintain organizational integrity by arranging for the maiming and killing of recalcitrant members and those who oppose them.

Unfortunately, organized crime's violent tactics seem to have caught the public's fancy, as evidenced by the tremendous success of books and movies about the Mafia. The public interest in gangsters' activities implies an element of voyeurism in participating vicariously in something illegal, yet exotic and tacitly approved. Because of the popularity of books and movies concerning organized crime, many Americans are much more aware of its existence, but few realize the true threat it poses to our society.

The Nature and Extent of Organized Crime Activities in the United States

The diversified yet interrelated nature of organized crime activities is evident in the Task Force Report (National Advisory Committee, pp. 10–12):

> Gambling has long been a traditional arena for organized crime, and is one area law enforcement officials fear that there may be attempts by organized crime elements to take over any gambling operations that may be legalized in the future. As for other activities, the drug business (notably cocaine trafficking) is growing; pornography also is showing astronomical distribution profits. Loan-sharking is found to be tied into several other activities, including gambling, and arson and fraud are tied into insurance irregularities.
>
> There are also large, organized hijacking rings, armed robbery groups, and increasing vehicle losses, including heavy equipment. Untaxed cigarettes are another major problem. Credit card and stock frauds, sale of stolen and counterfeit securities, and the manufacture and distribution of counterfeit money are among prevalent white-collar crimes.
>
> There apparently is a link between organized crime and street crime where drug operations, fencing, gambling, and certain burglaries are concerned.
>
> Drug addicts pose a major problem in terms of burglaries. Some law enforcement people believe that most established crime figures began their careers in street crime operations. They also point to ties between organized crime and

Table 6–2 **A Typology of Organized Crime Payoffs**

PARTICIPANTS	HOW OBLIGATIONS ARE INCURRED	HOW THE DEBTS ARE PAID
Elected officials (federal)	Support in political campaigns Trips, vacations on company expense accounts, cash through foundations, and cash bribes through lobbyists, etc.	Political appointments Contracts Personal favors Paroles, pardons
Appointed staff	Campaign workers Liaison with revenue sources Cash payoffs	Hired as staff worker Retains contact with revenue sources Conducts business for elected official
The elected official	*State* Campaign contributions Trips on private accounts Cash through lobbyists Tips on investments, i.e., public franchises and licenses *Local* Campaign contributions Promise to self-interest groups—gamblers, etc. Money to citizens' committees during preelection campaign Cash payoffs through lobbyists	Contracts Allocations of franchises Granting license such as liquor Contracts for local service—garbage, ambulance, towing, etc. Abstain from enforcing certain type of laws
The judge	*All Levels* Campaign contributions Cash payoffs	Favorable decisions Probation, parole and select court assignment
The lawyer	Client contacts and referrals Campaign workers Liaison with business and criminal clientele Cash payoffs (fees)	Appointments to positions to keep contacts with proper clients Consultants on contracts, crime commissions, etc.
The police	*All Levels* Political patronage Campaign contributions to elected offices Budget manipulation Cash payoffs	Select enforcement methods Preferential treatment in the degree of enforcement Lack of enforcement

Source: D. F. Pace and J. C. Styles. *Organized Crime: Concepts and Control.* Copyright © 1975, 31. Reprinted by permission of Prentice-Hall, Inc.: Englewood Cliffs, New Jersey.

thefts of credit cards, airline tickets, securities, and money. They believe that channels controlled by organized crime are used to launder stolen money and to distribute stolen credit cards.

The relationship between corruption and street crime also is important, with elements creating a subculture in which certain people believe they are above the law. In some communities their impact is so strong that they in fact become the law, maintaining a well-insulated position and buying official protection.

Legitimate businesses are not only infiltrated or manipulated, but also are taken over by organized crime. For example, the liquor industry is a primary

Many books depict organized crime factually, but many others glamorize the life of organized crime figures.

arena for organized crime operations—one often ignored in crime reports and one that benefits from weaknesses in law enforcement. Alcoholic beverage outlets are the underworld's retail market for all its goods and activities, and tax fraud is a frequent occurrence in connection with liquor operations.

Another vulnerable area is the vending machine industry—whether the machines are operated for services, entertainment, or other purposes. Because they involve large cash flows, these machines are a growing operational area for organized crime.

Organized crime figures are believed to have influence over the banking industries, grand juries, and some members of the legal profession.

Organized crime is heavily involved in gambling, drugs, prostitution, pornography, loansharking, and infiltration of legitimate businesses.

Gambling Illegal gambling (placing bets with bookmakers) is a billion-dollar business in the United States. It occurs throughout the country, with organized crime maintaining control by violence and by providing services including protection, sharing of financial risk (layoffs), legal assistance, and financial aid.

Wagers on football are most popular. Organized crime often either controls gambling operations or takes a cut of someone else's operation. The "street people" (bookies) are part of the organized crime network, but they are not part of organized crime itself, and they know little about it.

Organized crime is also involved in legal gambling, such as the casinos in Las Vegas, race tracks throughout the country, and even legal charity games. Only lotteries seem to have escaped the infiltration of organized crime.

Without participation of "law-abiding" citizens, organized crime would lose billions of dollars and much of its power. Unfortunately, countless millions of citizens contribute to the wealth and power of organized crime by making illegal bets. The benefits to the bettor are numerous, even when legitimate games are available. Illegal games offer greater variety, better odds, regular service, and a fast, guaranteed payoff. The bettor can phone in bets, charge them, preserve anonymity, and avoid having to pay taxes on winnings. These advantages offset the risks of getting caught or becoming indebted to organized crime.

Drugs   Organized crime's involvement in drugs concentrates on heroin and cocaine, a trade made to order because of its large demand, substantial profit, and need for an efficient organization with a good deal of capital as well as street-level protection.

The sale of narcotics is usually organized like a legitimate import business. Organized crime purchases large quantities of drugs from Europe, Asia, or Mexico and then distributes it in smaller lots to middle-level wholesalers, who cut it further and sell it to dealers on the street.

Organized crime figures usually do not become directly involved beyond the middle level, thus protecting themselves from the authorities. They are primarily financiers, putting up capital for large-scale purchases. Frequently even import and distribution is taken over by others.

Prostitution   Prostitution, one of organized crime's rackets since the turn of the century, reached its peak during the Depression but since that time has declined. The Organized Crime Task Force of the President's Commission on Law Enforcement (National Advisory Committee, 1976) quoted from the 1952 Second Interim Report of the United States Senate's Kefauver Committee, which investigated organized crime:

> Before the First World War, the major profits of organized criminals were obtained from prostitution. The passage of the Mann White Slave Act, the changing sexual mores, and public opinion combined to make commercialized prostitution a less profitable and more hazardous enterprise. . . . Prostitution is difficult to organize and discipline is hard to maintain.

Pornography   The pornography industry consists of films, magazines, books, sexual devices, and various "service" establishments. A number of recent studies indicate that pornography is organized crime's latest business. As with gambling and the drug trade, pornography is a prohibited product with a large market, requiring good organization, money, muscle, and lax law enforcement.

Supreme Court decisions related to pornography have complicated the problem of law enforcement officers when dealing with the pornography industry. The Court has not extended First Amendment protections to pornog-

The pornography industry is a major source of income for organized crime.

raphy, so it is not automatically legal, but the Court's decisions have left unclear what constitutes pornography. At present three somewhat vague criteria exist (*Miller v. California,* 1973):

1. The dominant theme of the material must appeal to prurient interests;
2. The material must be utterly without redeeming social, political, literary, or scientific value; and
3. The material must be patently offensive in its depiction of sexual matters, in terms of contemporary standards.

Each state must pass its own legislation defining the standards, but a jury representing the community decides on individual cases.

The pornography issue was further complicated by a 1969 Supreme Court ruling (*Stanley v. Georgia*), which held that pornography for private use in one's home is legal.

Loansharking   **Loansharking,** lending money at higher than legally prescribed rates, is the second largest source of revenue for organized crime. Gambling profits often provide the initial capital for loanshark operations. Many types of individuals became involved with loansharks: gamblers to pay off gambling debts, drug addicts to obtain needed drugs, businesspeople to buy goods or to close deals.

Infiltration of Legitimate Business   Organized crime invests much of its money in legitimate business, thereby establishing a source of legal funds. Because business ownership is easily concealed, it is difficult to determine all the types of businesses that organized crime has penetrated. Control of businesses is usually acquired through one of four methods (Presidents' Commission on Law Enforcement and Administration of Justice, 1967, p. 190):

1. Investing concealed profits acquired from gambling and other illegal activities.
2. Accepting business interests in payment for the owner's gambling debts.
3. Foreclosing on usurious loans.
4. Using various forms of extortion.

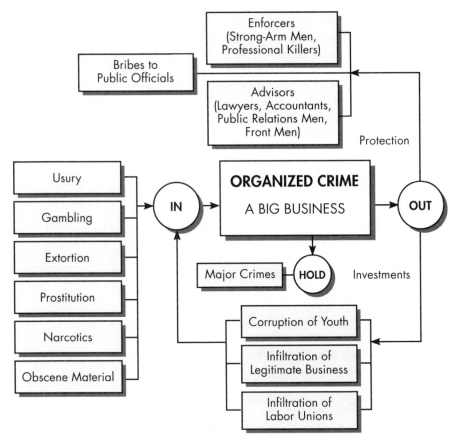

Figure 6–2   The Web of Organized Crime   The web of organized crime, a portion of which is shown above, reaches into every part of the nation and affects all levels of society.
Source: Courtesy of the Federal Bureau of Investigation.

The ordinary businessperson can seldom compete with organized crime, which has large amounts of ready cash, union connections, and "enforcers" to assure cooperation.

Figure 6–2 illustrates how organized crime has infiltrated our society.

The Threat of Organized Crime

The primary goals of organized crime, whether through illegal enterprises such as gambling or legitimate businesses, are making money and maximizing profit. Organized crime has found it expedient to invest large amounts of money in corrupting political figures from the local level to the federal level as well as figures within the law enforcement field. Cressey (1969) has stated that the goal of organized crime is "the nullification of government." Organized crime can flourish only if it can control police investigations, prosecutions, judicial proceedings, and the corrections process.

The direct national threat is that organized crime seeks to corrupt and control police officers, prosecutors, judicial proceedings, and the corrections process.

Federal Legislation Regarding Organized Crime

Siegel (1983, p. 392) points out that one of the first directly anti–organized crime measures was the Interstate and Foreign Travel or Transportation in Aid of Racketeering Enterprises Act (Travel Act— 18 U.S. 1952 [1976]). This act prohibits travel in interstate commerce or use of interstate facilities for promoting, managing, establishing, carrying on, or facilitating any unlawful activity.

The Organized Crime Control Act   The Organized Crime Control Act was passed by Congress in 1970. It has several important provisions, including the following (National Advisory Committee, 1976, p. 18):

> It provides for establishing a special grand jury in cities having major organized crime operations.
>
> It establishes a federal "use immunity" whereby witnesses can be ordered to testify in return for immunity from prosecution using any information so derived. Witnesses who fail to testify can be jailed for up to eighteen months.
>
> It provides protection for witnesses in organized crime cases and members of their families.
>
> It provides for perjury prosecution.
>
> It provides for taking and using pre-trial depositions when because of "exceptional circumstances it is in the interest of justice."
>
> It expands federal jurisdiction over illegal gambling operations.
>
> It prohibits using illegal profit from racketeering activity to take over legitimate businesses and unions (RICO).
>
> It provides for extended sentences for persons convicted of participating in continuing illegal businesses or who are habitual criminals.

RICO   The most important measure of the Organized Crime Control Act is Title IX, The Racketeer Influenced and Corrupt Organization Act (RICO) (Pub. L. No. 91–452, Title IX, 84 Stat. 922 [1970]). This act defines racketeering activity as involvement in two or more acts prohibited by twenty-four existing federal and state statutes. Siegel (1983, p. 392) states that the offenses listed in RICO include state-defined crimes such as murder, kidnapping, gambling, arson, robbery, bribery, extortion, and narcotic violations, as well as federally defined crimes such as bribery, counterfeiting, transmitting gambling information, prostitution, and mail fraud. Siegel goes on to note that RICO is designed

The Organized Crime Control Act provides protection for witnesses in organized crime cases.

rson is included in the list of RICO offenses. Here an officer examines evidence found at the scene of a suspicious fire.

to limit patterns of organized crime activity by defining racketeering as an act intended to:

1. derive income from racketeering or the unlawful collection of debts and to use or invest such income;
2. acquire through racketeering an interest in or control over any enterprise engaged in interstate or foreign commerce;
3. conduct business enterprises through a pattern of racketeering;
4. conspire to use racketeering as a means of making income, collecting loans, or conducting business.

The Organized Crime Control Act was passed in 1970. Title IX of this act, the Racketeer Influenced and Corrupt Organization Act (RICO), created new categories of offenses in racketeering activity.

A person found guilty of violating RICO is subject to twenty years in prison and a fine of $225,000. In addition, the person so convicted forfeits to the United States government any investment in a business that violates RICO.

To enforce the legislation, the federal government created a Strike Force Program in eighteen cities. This program coordinates the efforts of several state and federal law enforcement officers and prosecutors to work as a team against racketeering and organized crime.

The Police Officer and Organized Crime

Organized crime is everyone's problem. Unfortunately many people believe that sole responsibility rests with law enforcement—that it is up to the police officer to apprehend those involved in organized crime. However, police officers need the help of citizens and a judicial and political system free of corruption.

Some of the special problems the law enforcement officer encounters when dealing with organized crime are:

- The lack of citizen cooperation.
- The code of ethics of organized crime members, which prevents them from giving information.
- The tremendous wealth, power, and organization behind them.
- The corruption of other police officers, politicians, judges, jury members, and corrections officers.

Perhaps one of the most serious of the problems is lack of citizen cooperation. Citizens not only do not want to get involved. Many actually promote organized crime by engaging in illegal activities from which organized crime obtains its working capital, for example, illegal betting, buying stolen goods from fences, buying drugs, and so on.

The challenge is clear; however, it is also clear that law enforcement cannot do the job alone. A large part of the challenge rests in enlisting public support.

The Changing Nature of Organized Crime

According to Rowan (p. 24), organized crime has its problems: "In spite of its clout, organized crime is an industry in crisis. The leadership is old, and the next generation of managers seems to lack spirit, dedication, and discipline." In April of 1992, John Gotti, the nation's "top mobster" was found guilty on 13 counts and may be facing life in prison.

Indeed, organized crime is no longer limited to the Italian mafiosos groups. Traditional organized crime families are frequently loosing out to the Asian organized crime groups who now seem poised to take over. In addition, the drug cartels, the Yakua, the Chinese Tongs and Triads, the growing Nigerian mobs, the Jamaican Possee, the Puerto Rican connection, the Irish organized crime groups, the Israeli organizations, the Cuban connections—all present unique problems for the law enforcement community.

Yet another area of concern for law enforcement is the dramatic increase occurring in bias or hate crimes.

BIAS CRIMES

As noted by Lutz (n.d.):

Not a day has passed in the last seven years without someone in the United States being victimized by hate violence. Harassment, vandalism, arson, assault and murder motivated by racism, antisemitism or other forms of bigotry—such as homophobia—plague every section of our country. This violence is a largely unrecognized cancer eating away our communities and social institutions....
Ku Klux Klan and neo-nazi groups have increasingly targeted gay and lesbian people for physical attack and intimidation. In addition, a largely spontaneous wave of homophobic violence appears to be sweeping the nation....

The traditional targets of hate violence, black people and other people of color, as well as Jews, remain the single largest target of organized hate violence....

Bigoted violence has become a critical criminal justice issue of the late 1980s.

The Center for Democratic Renewal has documented nearly three thousand acts of bigoted violence between 1980 and 1986.

Bias crimes are crimes motivated by bigotry and hatred against a specific group of people.

Story (1991, p. 101) defines **bias** or **hate crimes** as "unlawful actions designed to frighten or harm an individual because of his or her race, religion, ethnicity, or sexual orientation. Such acts range from verbal intimidation and harassment to destruction of property, and even to physical violence."

The Southwest Regional Laboratory defines hate crime as follows (Bodinger-deUriarte, 1991, p. 2):

... any act, or attempted act, to cause physical injury, emotional suffering, or property damage through intimidation, harassment, racial or ethnic slurs and bigoted epithets, vandalism, force, or the threat of force, motivated all or in part by hostility to the victim's real or perceived race, ethnicity, religion, or sexual orientation.

Bodinger-deUriarte (1991, p. 2) notes that hate crimes differ from other assaults against persons and property in some important ways:

- *The relationship of the victim to the perpetrator.* Most assaults involve two people who know each other, but hate crimes tend to be "stranger" crimes.
- *The number of perpetrators.* Most assaults involve two people, the attacker and the victim. Hate crimes involve an average of four assailants for each victim.
- *The uneven nature of the conflict.* Hate crime perpetrators often attack younger or weaker victims, or arm themselves and attack unarmed victims.
- *The amount of physical damage inflicted.* Hate crimes are extremely violent, with victims being three times more likely to require hospitalization than "normal" assault victims.
- *The treatment of property.* In most property crimes, something of value is taken. In hate crimes, it is more likely that valuable property will be damaged or destroyed.
- *The apparent absence of gain.* In most hate crimes no personal score is settled and no profit is made.
- *The places in which hate crimes occur.* Hate crimes frequently occur in churches, synagogues, mosques, cemeteries, monuments, schools, camps, and in or around the victim's home.

Articles in *Law Enforcement News* describe the increase of bias/hate crimes in our country. "Grim News on Hate Crime: Survey Finds Sharp Rise in Anti-Gay Crime, Violence," states that "Anti-gay violence rose sharply in six U.S. cities during 1990 . . . with all of the cities showing double-digit increases over 1989." According to this article:

A total of 1,588 incidents of harassment, intimidation, physical assault, vandalism, arson, police abuse and murder were reported during 1990 to agencies in Boston, Chicago, Los Angeles, New York, Minneapolis/St. Paul and San Francisco.

A second article, "Hate Violence Grows More Frequent, Vicious, Random," notes: "1990 was marked by an unprecedented escalation of hate violence, including a dramatic jump in murders motivated by race or connected to the white supremacy movement."

Bodinger-deUriarte (1991, pp. 3–4) cites the following statistics:

- The National Gay and Lesbian Task Force reported more than 7,000 antihomosexual crimes in 1990.
- The Northwest Coalition Against Malicious Harassment found that hate crime motivated by a reaction against race, religion or sexual orientation rose 20% last year.

- Anti-Semitic incidents climbed to a record 1,685 in 1990, making it the fourth consecutive record-breaking year.
- In the first half of 1990, the 272 entries in the log of hate crime for Orange County, California, represented a 32% jump in reported incidents over the same period in 1989.
- Those groups most likely to be victimized by hate crimes are (in alphabetical order): African-Americans, Arabs, Asians, gay males, Jews, Latinos, lesbians, Native Americans, and white women in interracial relationships.

The rise of hate crimes on high school and college campuses is especially disturbing. According to Bodinger-deUriarte: "The New York City Police Department reports that 70 percent of all bias incidents are now committed by people under 19. . . . The Ku Klux Klan now considers high school and college campuses to be among its most fertile recruiting groups."

Randolph (1988, pp. 128–30) discusses the African American student's battle against racism on college campuses: "Racial prejudice is a daily fact of college life. This reality is particularly chilling since black students are attending predominantly white colleges in record numbers, while those attending historically black colleges have declined from 44 percent to 16 percent between 1965 and 1985. . . . America's college campuses are witnessing one of their most turbulent and disturbing periods since the racial unrest of the '60s."

As noted, African Americans are not the only target. An article in *Time* magazine, "Open Season on Gays" (Zuckerman 1988, p. 24), states: "AIDS sparks an epidemic of violence against homosexuals." The article claims that according to gay-rights groups, hate-motivated assaults have nearly tripled in recent years. As one person put it: "AIDS has provided a green light to the bashers and the bigots." The article suggests:

Victims who go to the police often find them insensitive or even hostile. . . .

A report released by the National Institute of Justice last fall concluded that "homosexuals are probably the most frequent victims" of hate-motivated violence, but the "criminal-justice system—like the rest of society—has not recognized the seriousness" of the problem.

Members of the Invisible Empire Knights of the Ku Klux Klan arrive at City Hall in Meriden, Connecticut, escorted by police in riot gear. The Klan was rallying support for local police.

Types of bias include racial, religious, national origin, sex, age, disability, and sexual orientation.

Offenses frequently involved in bias crimes include cross burning, swastika painting, bombing, hanging in effigy, disturbing a public meeting, graffiti, obscene letters or phone calls, or face-to-face oral abuse. Assault is becoming more frequent in bias crimes, some even resulting in death.

Neo–Nazi Skinheads

A special report of the Anti-Defamation League (ADL), *Young and Violent: The Growing Menace of America's Neo-Nazi Skinheads* (1988, p. 1), states:

> The Skinheads are shaven-headed youths who sport Nazi insignia and preach violence against Blacks, Hispanics, Jews, Asians and homosexuals. They range in age from about thirteen to twenty-five, with males outnumbering females. The typical skinhead has either a shaved head or closely cropped hair; is tatooed with Nazi and/or Satanic symbols; wears jeans, suspenders and "Doc Martens," a heavy boot of British make, sometimes used to kick or stomp on victims.

According to an ADL survey conducted through its thirty-one regional offices, the number of racist Skinheads has risen to about two thousand, located in twenty-one states. The ADL contends: "The rise in the number of Skinheads has been paralleled by an increase in the amount of violent crime they have committed, including two homicides and numerous shootings, beatings and stabbings, mostly directed against members of minority groups."

Figure 6–3 illustrates areas where the Skinheads have been operating.

One hate group with close links with the Skinheads is WAR, headed by Tom Metzger, a television repairman from California and a former Grand Dragon of the California Ku Klux Klan. Metzger's son John heads up WAR's affiliated Aryan Youth Movement (AYM). In addition to their links with Tom Metzger's organizations, Skinheads also participate in joint activities with other hate groups, especially the Ku Klux Klan.

The ADL (1988, p. 28) describes the Skinheads as "undisciplined, violence-prone, . . . obvious misfits. . . . Besides their tendency to commit violence against outsiders, the Skinhead gangs have severe internal problems. There is substantial evidence of drug use, Satanism, intragang violence, theft and all the other sociopathic tendencies to be found these days on the outer fringes of the youth culture." The ADL (1988, p. 29) states that Skinheads "typically promote their views through stickers, graffiti, the distribution of such hate publication as WAR, and records bearing lyrics of their 'white power' rock songs."

The ADL stresses that not all juveniles with shaved heads are neo-Nazis and that, in fact, some are very antiracist and have been targets of the neo-Nazi Skinheads.

The Effects of Hate Crimes

As noted in another report by the Anti-Defamation League of B'nai B'rith, *Hate Groups in America—A Record of Bigotry and Violence (1988):*

> Crimes motivated by bias can have a special emotional and psychological impact on the victim and the victim's community. . . . By making members of the minority groups fearful, angry, and suspicious, these incidents can cause an isolated incident to fester and explode into widespread community tension, perhaps leading to an escalating cycle of reprisals.

WEST	MIDWEST	SOUTH	EAST
Arizona	**Illinois**	**Alabama**	**Maryland**
Phoenix	Chicago	Birmingham	Baltimore
Scottsdale	**Michigan**	**Georgia**	Westminster
Tempe	Detroit	Atlanta	Washington D.C.
California	Grand Rapids	**Florida**	(suburbs)
San Diego	**Missouri**	Tampa	**New Jersey**
Riverside	Springfield	Clearwater	North Jersey
Orange County	**Ohio**	Miami Beach	Atlantic City
Ventura County	Cincinnati	Pinellas County	**Pennsylvania**
Salinas	**Wisconsin**	Broward County	Philadelphia
Hollister	Milwaukee	Orlando	
San Francisco		**Louisiana**	
Colorado		New Orleans	
Denver		**Oklahoma**	
Nevada		Oklahoma City	
Las Vegas		Tulsa	
Reno		**Texas**	
Oregon		Austin	
Portland		Dallas	
Salem		**Tennessee**	
Washington		Memphis	
Seattle			
Spokane			
Vancouver			

Figure 6–3   Locations Where Skinhead Groups Have Been Operating
Source: Anti-Defamation League of B'nai B'rith. *Young and Violent: The Growing Menace of America's Neo-Nazi Skinheads:* New York, 1988. Reprinted by permission.

According to Story (p. 101): "In addition to the devastating effect on the victim(s), these [bias] crimes threaten the democratic foundations of our society. Increased tensions and pressures occur within the neighborhoods or groups affected."

Bodinger-deUriarte (1991, p. 4) suggests that:

> ... the principal cause of bigoted violence ... is underlying social tensions.... Hate crime is a form of depersonalized vengeance in which strangers, by virtue of their membership in racial, ethnic, religious, or minority target groups, are scapegoated as the symbolic sources of broad social, economic, or political unease.

She further notes: "Americans often are poorly informed and suspicious of cultures and lifestyles outside their own." And yet, "as the demographic pattern of urban minority neighborhoods, ethnic enclaves, and white surburbs increasingly shifts to a pattern of multiethnic neighborhoods and diversified cities, daily exposure to those different from oneself becomes inevitable." In all too many instances, such exposure does not lead to understanding those different from oneself, but rather leads to efforts to drive them out.

Passage of the Hate Crime Statistics Act of 1990 directed the U.S. Justice Department to collect bias-crime data nationwide. The program is voluntary, however, and no budgetary provisions were made. Many states have also passed legislation mandating the collection of bias-crime statistics. In addition, the U.S. Department of Justice has created a hotline (1–800/347–HATE) which citizens can use to report bias crimes.

An additional area posing unique challenges to law enforcement is the investigation of ritualistic crimes.

▬▬▬ RITUALISTIC CRIME

Ritualistic crimes include unlawful activities performed by people involved with the occult, witchcraft, vodoo, Satanism, and black magic.

Rituals have a rich heritage. The Egyptians used amulets for good luck charms to ward off evil or to bring about good fortune. The Greeks practiced several forms of ritual, including hydromancy, similar to our wishing wells. They would throw bread onto a body of water: if it sunk they would have good luck, and if it floated they would have bad luck. Little wonder we throw pennies rather than bread into wishing wells. They also put much faith in astrology and the signs of the zodiac.

A **ritual** is a system of rites, a ceremonial act.

The Romans, too, practiced rituals, primarily fertility rites, including eating partridge flesh and fish eggs. Later in Europe and in the United States, witchcraft became a focus. In Europe over 200,000 witches were killed for their beliefs.

Most people have some sort of superstition they believe in, for example, breaking a mirror, or walking under a ladder bringing bad luck, finding a four-leaf clover bringing good luck, and the like. And many of us grew up with "supernatural" beings in our lives such as the tooth fairy, the Easter Bunny, and even Santa Claus.

Indeed, all recognized religions have rituals meaningful to their members.

Rituals may include symbols, artifacts, words, gestures, costumes, music, almost anything imaginable. They are heavily linked to a belief system.

Whether this belief system is a formal religion or not, it is protected by the First Amendment right to worship as one wishes.

When the rituals of a group involve crimes such as desecration of cemeteries, grave robbing, cruelty to animals, child sexual abuse, and even murder, it becomes a problem for law enforcement. As noted by Los Angeles Police Department Investigator Patrick Metoyer, "We don't investigate warlocks, satanists, vampires, Jews, Catholics, or Protestants. We investigate *crime.*"

Satanic Cults

The *Church of the Final Judgment* is an umbrella satanic cult believed to have members across the country. The *Church of Satan* was organized in 1966 in San Francisco by Anton LaVey, a former circus performer and police photographer. LaVey, who calls himself the High Priest of Satan, published *Satanic Rituals* and *The Satanic Bible,* a book that outsells the Christian Bible in many bookstores. The *Church of Satan* has grown to over fifty thousand members nationwide.

Cults such as these have one strong leader to whom all members give allegiance. Often the leader is worshipped as an anti-God—the embodiment of Satan and evil. The cult meets the needs of people who feel they have no self-identity and no power. One major drawing point of Satanism is that anything goes. Whatever one wants, one does.

Young people become involved in Satanism because it gives them a feeling of belonging, worth, and power. Members are often youths who do not fit in with their peers. In the cult they are accepted and given attention. They are often influenced by heavy metal music and may dress in a "punk" style. Members of cults frequently wear pentagrams and inverted crosses. Dark clothing is common, as is self-mutilation such as safety pins through nipples.

Chief Donald Story (1987, p. 81) warns that "ritualistic crimes are occurring with greater frequency in America. However, in many instances police officers do not realize that homicides, assaults, kidnappings, child abuse, animal mutilations or suicides are linked with the occult."

Graffiti may indicate the existence of a satanic cult or may be the work of a single person who is into Satanism.

Satanic Rituals Satanic rituals often include use of robes (red or black), daggers, candles, altars, and pentagrams. They often include chanting, occur at night, and are conducted in strict secrecy. According to Story (p. 83): "Satanists believe that there is a power of energy within the souls and bodies of animals and humans and that that power can be released and absorbed following rituals ranging from sexual activity to murder and cannibalism." He notes that the rituals often include sacrificing animals and that during the rituals the hearts, eyes, and tongues may be removed from goats, lambs, chickens, and doves. Drinking blood is also common.

Satanic rituals often include criminal actions. According to the National School Safety Center (1988, p. 21):

> Satanic references and symbols have been associated with the "Son of Sam" serial murders (New York, 1977), the McMartin Preschool child molestation case (Los Angeles, 1984), and, most recently, the "Night Stalker" homicides (Los Angeles and San Francisco, 1985). Animal mutilations, exhumation of bodies and church desecrations are becoming alarmingly prevalent.

Zorn (1986) states: "Devil worship was said to be involved in a series of multilation killings in Cook and DuPage Counties in 1981 and 1982, in which four men abducted and murdered up to eighteen young women. One of the men confessed to police that several parts of the women's bodies were used in sexual and cannibalistic rituals devoted to Satan."

And according to Stratford (1988, pp. 200–201), people who have escaped from satanic cults have "horror stories" to tell.

> One young man was a high priest in Satanism until he became a born-again Christian. On the "Oprah Winfrey Show" he said, "I started when I was at the age of five. I started out in what is known as the earth mother religion. Eventually I was told that it was Satan we were worshipping." He told about how four times a year his group performed human sacrifices. "The victims are easily picked up. They are wandering teenagers looking for a good time, runaways, skid-row bums, paper boys. . . ."

> On November 19, 1987, Geraldo Rivera interviewed a former Satanic priestess who identified herself only as Elain. "At seventeen, I saw my first sacrifice—a live baby," she said on the CBS network television program. "They carved the heart out of this child. I was told that if I said anything, I would be killed in such a manner or worse. These people mean what they say. They absolutely, totally control the children and the young, the teenagers, in absolute total fear."

Investigating Ritualistic Crime

Story (1987, p. 83) offers some specific suggestions for investigating ritualistic crime:

> At the crime scene, look for indications of a mockery of Christian symbols—items such as inverted crosses, candles or candle drippings, vandalized Christian artifacts and unusual drawings or a non-discernable alphabet used in writings or graffiti.

> Search for animal parts, blood, and books on Satanism. The presence of altars, bowls with colored salt, and skulls are very indicative.

> In homicide cases, pay close attention to the position of the body. Missing body parts and bodily mutilation are important characteristics to note. The location of wounds and the type of wounds may have a strong bearing on determining if the crime was satanic in nature.

> Other indicators at a crime scene include oils or incense found on the body or close by, and human or animal feces found on the body, or in the body during

a post mortem examination. The stomach contents can be of vital importance in determining what occurred just prior to death.

In summary, look for symbolism, animal mutilation, candles, bones or anything out of the ordinary.

Ritualistic crime is a problem law enforcement must become aware of and skilled at investigating. (See Figure 6–4.)

A **ritualistic crime** is an unlawful act committed during a ceremony related to a belief system. It is the crime, not the belief system, that must be investigated.

Normal investigative techniques are not effective with ritualistic crime. Usually multiple victims and multiple suspects are involved, and often logic will not work. Horror stories of murders may in actuality be some sort of

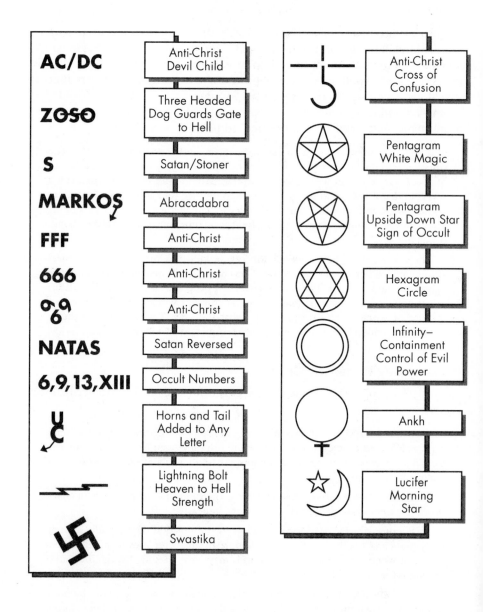

staged illusion to gain control of the cult members. Ritualistic crimes add yet another dimension to the challenge of law enforcement.

Ritualistic Child Abuse

Of great concern to law enforcement is growing evidence of rather widespread ritualistic abuse of children. In a newsletter, "Believe the Children," one "survivor" of ritualistic crime states:

> I must speak, for the children no one will believe, for the adults wandering in utter pain and confusion not knowing why they are in such agony, and for the boy whose life was taken in front of me, an innocent, precious life destroyed at the hand of evil and ruthless forces.
>
> Please, believe the children. This is no fantasy. It is happening, and it has been happening for many years. Satanic abusers are counting on the children never talking, and the adults not believing them if they do, which is why they make their rituals so bizarre.

A Caution

Some law enforcement professionals feel that the prevalence of ritualistic crimes is not as serious as the media would have the public believe. Jenkins (1992, p. 1), for example, says: "There is a strong suggestion that the threat of ritual crime has been massively exaggerated, and the phenomenon is largely a myth—part of what social theorists sometimes call a 'moral panic.'"

For example, television journalist Geraldo Rivera aired a NBC documentary, "Devil Worship: Exposing Satan's Underground" (October 25, 1988) in which he said:

> It is teenagers who are most likely to fall under the spell of this jungle of dark and violent emotions called satanism, and in some cases to be driven to committing terrible deeds.... There is no doubt that teenage satanic activity in this country is increasing....
>
> Many satanic crimes are not recognized as such.... These ritualistic crimes are everywhere, and yet in most communities they are either overlooked or under-reported.

Jenkins suggests: "The lesson for police agencies is that they should exercise restraint and skepticism in the face of 'satanic' claims. Otherwise they risk facing financial loss, together with public and political embarrassment."

FBI Agent Lanning (1989, p. 62) is also critical of the widespread attention to satanic crime given by law enforcement agencies. He suggests: "Any police executive contemplating spending scarce funds on a 'ritual' crime investigation, or even a seminar on the topic would do well to read one or all of the authenic sources available." Lanning notes that all these sources include the following themes:

- Claims about satanic crime are very poorly substantiated, and involve the rejection of accepted criteria of evidence and proof.
- On the occasions when we can check specific claims about satanic crime, they usually prove to be false.
- We can find no substantiation for the most serious charges—for example, about the existence of human sacrifice or ritual child abuse.
- The use of language by the claims-makers is usually vague in the extreme, and attempts at closer definition cause real doubts about the whole phenomenon of ritual crime.

- Charges about satanic crime can often be traced to religious fundamentalists, either individuals or groups, who consciously or otherwise use the occult panic as a vehicle to promote their social and political agenda.
- The spread of the satanism panic is often based on unsubstantiated rumors and urban legends, which reflect deeper social fears and concerns.

SUMMARY

White-collar crime—occupational or business-related crime—includes fraud involving credit cards, checks, securities, insurance, fraud of consumers by illegal competition, and deceptive practices, as well as bankruptcy fraud, embezzlement and pilferage, bribes, kickbacks, payoffs, and receiving stolen property. White-collar crime involves billions of dollars annually.

Computer fraud may involve the input data, the output data, computer time, or the program itself. Computer crimes are relatively easy to commit and difficult to detect. Most are committed by "insiders," and most are not prosecuted. The most common types of computer crime are misuse of computer services, program abuse, and data abuse.

Organized crime is heavily involved in gambling, drugs, prostitution, pornography, loansharking, and infiltration of legitimate businesses. Not only does organized crime cost the nation billions of dollars annually and ruin hundreds of lives, it also poses a direct national threat because it seeks to corrupt and control police officers, prosecutors, judicial proceedings, and the corrections process. In response to this threat Congress, in 1970, passed the Organized Crime Control Act. Title IX of this act, the Racketeer Influenced and Corrupt Organization Act (RICO), created new categories of offenses in racketeering activity. Nonetheless, many citizens actually promote organized crime by engaging in illegal activities, for example, buying stolen property, placing bets with bookies, and the like. Among the difficult problems the law enforcement officer encounters when dealing with organized crime are (1) lack of citizen cooperation, (2) the code of silence of family members, (3) their tremendous wealth, power, and organization, and (4) the corruption of other police officers, politicians, judges, jury members, and corrections officers.

Bias crimes are crimes motivated by bigotry and hatred against a specific group of people. Types of bias include racial, religious, national origin, sex, age, disability, and sexual orientation.

A ritual is a system of rites, a ceremonial act. A ritualistic crime is an unlawful act committed during a ceremony related to a belief system. It is the crime, not the belief system, that must be investigated.

DISCUSSION QUESTIONS

1. What are some reasons employees steal from employers?

2. Should all crimes committed through the use of a computer be violations of federal law?

3. Are there any methods police might educate computer owners about so that computer crime might be more preventable?

4. Should computer hackers pay a heavy penalty for their misdeeds?

5. What are some ways the average citizen can help stop or slow down organized crime?

6. Why is it so difficult for the police to deal with organized crime on a local level?

7. Describe what a bias crime might consist of.

8. Should additional penalties be imposed on people found guilty of committing bias crimes?

9. How should people guilty of participating in ritualistic crimes be treated in the criminal justice system?

10. What evidence would lead you to believe a satanic ritual may have taken place?

TERMS

bias crime, embezzle, fence, hate crime, loansharking, organized crime, pilfer, ritual, ritualistic crime, white-collar crime.

REFERENCES

Anti-Defamation League of B'nai B'rith. *Hate Groups in America—A Record of Bigotry and Violence*. New York, 1988.

Anti-Defamation League of B'nai B'rith/Civil Rights Division. An ADL Special Report. *Young and Violent: The Growing Menace of America's Neo-Nazi Skinheads*. New York, 1988.

Bennett, G. *Crimewarps: The Future of Crime in America*. Garden City, N.Y.: Anchor Press/Doubleday, 1987.

Bennett, W. and Hess, K. M. *Criminal Investigation*. 3d ed. St. Paul, Minn.: West Publishing Company, 1987.

Black, J. K. "Taking A Byte Out of Crime." *The Police Chief* (May 1986): 31–33.

Bodinger-deUriarte, C. "Hate Crime: The Rise of Hate Crime on School Campuses." Research Bulletin No. 10 of Phi Delta Kappa, Center for Evaluation, Development, and Research, December 1991.

Cressey, D. R. *Theft of the Nation: The Structure and Operations of Organized Crime in America*. New York: Harper & Row, 1969.

Dickey, S. "Is Getting in Getting out of Control?" *Today's Office* (September 1985): pp. 29–36.

Gordon, M. "Employee Theft." *Independent Business* (July–August 1990): 12–18.

"Grim News on Hate Crime: Survey Finds Sharp Rise in Anti-Gay Crime, Violence." *Law Enforcement News,* March 15, 1991, 5–6.

"Hate Violence Grows More Frequent, Vicious, Random." *Law Enforcement News,* March 15, 1991, 5–6.

Jenkins, P. "Investigating Occult and Ritual Crime: A Case for Caution." *Police Forum, ACJS Police Section,* 2, no. 1 (January 1992).

Lanning, K. V. "Satanic, Occult and Ritualistic Crime: A Law Enforcement Perspective." *The Police Chief* (October 1989): 62–85.

Lutz, C. "They Don't All Wear Sheets: A Chronology of Facist and Far Right Violence—1980–1986" (pamphlet), Center for Democratic Renewal. Published by the Division of Church and Society of the National Council of the Churches of Christ in the U.S.A. (no date).

Manning, W. W. and White, G. H. "Data Diddling, Salami Slicing, Trojan Horses . . . Can your Agency Handle Computer Crimes?" *The Police Chief* (April 1990): 46–49.

National Advisory Committee on Criminal Justice Standards and Goals. *Organized Crime: Report of the Task Force on Organized Crime*. Washington, D.C.: U.S. Government Printing Office, 1976.

National School Safety Center. *Gangs in Schools: Breaking Up Is Hard to Do*. Malibu, Calif.: Pepperdine University Press, 1988.

Office of the New York Counsel to the Governor 1966.

Pace, D. F. and Styles, J. C. *Organized Crime: Concepts and Control*. Englewood Cliffs, N.J.: Prentice Hall, 1983.

President's Commission on Law Enforcement and Administration of Justice. *The Challenge of Crime in a Free Society*. Washington, D.C.: U.S. Government Printing Office, 1967.

Randolph, L. B. "Black Students Battle Racism on College Campuses," *Ebony,* December 1988, pp. 126–30.

Rhodes, R. P. *Organized Crime: Crime Control vs. Civil Liberties.* New York: Random House, 1984.

Rowan, Roy. "The 50 Biggest Mafia Bosses." *Fortune,* November 10, 1986, 24–32, 34, 36.

Salerno, R. and Tompkins, J. S. *The Crime Confederation: Cosa Nostra and Allied Operations in Organized Crime.* New York: Doubleday, 1969.

Siegel, L. J. *Criminology.* St. Paul, Minn: West Publishing Company, 1983.

Story, D. W. "Hate/Bias Crimes: The Need for a Planned Reaction." *Law and Order* (August 1991): 101.

Story, D. W. "Ritualistic Crime: A New Challenge to Law Enforcement." *Law and Order* (September 1987): 81–83.

Stratford, L. *Satan's Underground.* Eugene, Or.: Harvest House Publishers, 1988.

"White Collar Crime." Bureau of Justice Statistics, Special Report, U.S. Dept. of Justice, September 1981, 1–8.

Zorn, E. "Satan Worship Called Dangerous, Growing." *The Chicago Tribune,* April 27, 1986.

Zuckerman, L. "Open Season on Gays." *Time,* March 7, 1988, 24.

SECTION 2

Police Operations: The Twenty-First Century Law Enforcement Officer

By this point you should have a good understanding of the total context within which present-day law enforcement officers function. They have a rich heritage dating back centuries. They must also enforce a vast array of complex laws while themselves staying within these laws.

This section looks at policing in the 1990s and into the next century. It begins with the roles and responsibilities of the modern law enforcement officer (Chapter 7). Police operations can usually be divided into three basic categories: patrol and traffic (Chapter 8), community service (Chapter 9), and investigation (Chapter 10). Although discussed separately, the three categories have considerable overlap. In some smaller agencies all three functions are performed by a single field service divi-

sion. In very small agencies they may be performed by a single police officer. Larger agencies, on the other hand, may have divisions within each of the three categories. In addition, larger agencies may have a separate division to deal with juveniles.

The section concludes with a discussion of how police officers obtain information (Chapter 11) and search and arrest suspects while staying within the law (Chapter 12).

CHAPTER 7

Policing in the 1990s: Roles and Responsibilities

The will of the people is the best law.

—Ulysses S. Grant

Do You Know

How the police officer's roles relate to the people?

What five basic roles the police officer must play?

What special skills are required of officers?

What two department organizational categories are?

What functions are handled in administration?

How officers receive their information?

What the NCIC is?

What types of records are used in law enforcement?

Why centralization of records is encouraged?

What is required by a data privacy act?

What functions are handled in field service?

What tasks occur in patrol? In a traffic division? In community relations programs? In investigation?

What specialized officers or departments may exist?

What basic styles of policing have been identified?

What discretion is and what role it plays?

How the police image arises?

What three ethics-check questions are?

What three areas can enhance police integrity and reduce corruption?

INTRODUCTION

The cover of a major city's annual police report dramatically shows two police officers reaching for their guns as they burst through the doors of a massive black and white police car which is screeching to a halt ... the flashing red lights and screaming siren complete the illustration. A less dramatic scene on an inside page of the report shows a police officer talking to a grateful mother whose lost child was returned. Which one of these illustrations most accurately describes the police role? ... The *New York Times* reports that policemen like to think of themselves as uniformed soldiers in an extremely dangerous war against crime ... in fact the police are more social workers and administrators than crime fighters. [John Webster, n.d., p. 94].

What is it about the police officer's role that makes the general public think of the law enforcement aspect of police work more often than the social service aspect when, in fact, approximately 90 percent of a police officer's time is spent in the social service function?

What does a police officer do? Most people have personal ideas about the role of police officers in the 1990s. As noted by Greene and Klockars (1991, p. 273): "The question of what police do, day in and day out, is the subject of a variety of 'conventional wisdoms.' There are visions of police as crime fighters, social workers, peacekeepers, street-corner politicians, traffic controllers, and recorders of important social events." Greene and Klockars suggest that how policing is viewed is the result of three factors: historical studies of police workload, ways to measure workload, and the values associated with police work.

Historical studies of police workload, conducted primarily in the 1960s and 1970s, suggest that 80 to 90 percent of police work is service related. The media, however, concentrates on the crime-fighting function of the police, including the "war on drugs." Greene and Klockars suggest that "we must attempt to reconcile gaps between actual and portrayed policing."

Ways of measuring workload is difficult because most of policing is done by individual officers, working alone or in pairs, carrying out their responsibilities as they were passed on to them by their field training officers (FTOs). This results in (p. 274) "a duality in policing, 'policing by the book' and 'policing in the streets,' and suggests a competing ideology in law enforcement, one dominated by street cops and the other by police administrators." Greene and Klockars further suggest that "the police themselves mystify their roles and selectively present themselves as engaged in crime-fighting, life-endangering, high-stress, dangerous, 'thin blue line' activity." Finally, they suggest: "Police attachments to the ideals of militarism, professionalism, bureaucracy, and, most recently, community policing underscore problems in defining and measuring what the police actually do."

Police work as values or ethics is the third factor influencing people's perceptions of what police do. According to Greene and Klockars (p. 276):

Police work means many things to many people. To some it represents identifiable law enforcement interventions such as making arrests for serious crime, enforcing the traffic code, and conducting criminal investigations. Such definitions emphasize the legal content associated with police decision making. For others, police work represents "handling situations and people" or resolving citizen-defined "something-that-ought-not-to-be-happening-about-which-something-ought-to-be-done-now" occasions. These portrayals of police work emphasize order maintenance and the peacekeeping functions of the police, and point our attention to the means-and-ends conflict often associated with public policing.

Still other descriptions of police work have characterized the police as change agents, street-corner politicians and problem solvers, emphasizing yet a broader role for the police as agents of municipal government.

In short, are the police primarily crime fighters, preservers of the peace, or providers of services? The answer varies by department, but in most departments the police serve all these functions. Where the emphasis is placed is increasingly influenced by the citizens within the jurisdiction. It is from them the police derive their power and to them that they are accountable. The importance of the community is stressed in the opening paragraph of the *Law Enforcement Code of Ethics* (see Figure 7–1) which was developed by the International Association of Chiefs of Police and has served as a statement of what policing is and how it should be done since 1957.

THE POLICE OFFICER AND THE PEOPLE

You learned earlier that **police authority** comes from the people—their laws and institutions. Police officers are ultimately responsible to the public they serve, and they usually recruit their officers from among local citizens.

Although the Tenth Amendment reserves police power for state and local governments, these governments must adhere to the principles of the Constitution and the Bill of Rights as well as to federal and state statutes. Police officers are not only a part of their community, they are also part of the state and federal government, which provides their formal base of authority, as well as a part of the state and federal criminal justice system, which determines society's course in deterring lawbreakers and rehabilitating offenders (Figure 7–2).

Note that in Figure 7–2 the arrows between the citizens, governments, and courts go two ways. Not only are the people ultimately responsible for estab-

---

As a Law Enforcement Officer, my fundamental duty is to serve mankind; to safeguard lives and property; to protect the innocent against deception, the weak against oppression or intimidation, and the peaceful against violence or disorder; and to respect the Constitutional rights of all men to liberty, equality and justice.

I will keep my private life unsullied as an example to all; maintain courageous calm in the face of danger, scorn, or ridicule; develop self-restraint; and be constantly mindful of the welfare of others. Honest in thought and deed in both my personal and official life, I will be exemplary in obeying the laws of the land and the regulations of my department. Whatever I see or hear of a confidential nature or that is confided to me in my official capacity will be kept ever secret unless revelation is necessary in the performance of my duty.

I will never act officiously or permit personal feelings, prejudices, animosities or friendships to influence my decisions. With no compromise for crime and with relentless prosecution of criminals, I will enforce the law courteously and appropriately without fear or favor, malice or ill will, never employing unnecessary force or violence and never accepting gratuities.

I recognize the badge of my office as a symbol of public faith, and I accept it as a public trust to be held so long as I am true to the ethics of the police service. I will constantly strive to achieve these objectives and ideals, dedicating myself before God to my chosen profession . . . law enforcement.

Figure 7–1 Law Enforcement Code of Ethics
Source: Reprinted by permission of the International Association of Chiefs of Police.

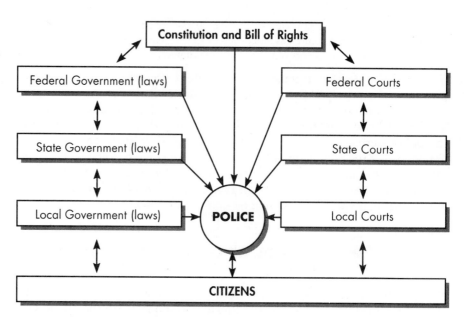

Figure 7–2   Sources of Police Authority

lishing governments and courts, they also elect the representatives who serve there. The citizens also directly influence the police. To a large extent, the specific goals and priorities of the police are established by what the community wants. For example, a community might want more patrols at night, stricter enforcement of traffic regulations during rush hour, or reduced enforcement for certain violations such as speeding.

Priorities are often more influenced by the desires of the policed than by any other consideration. Because the success of the police depends heavily upon public support, the wishes of the citizens must be listened to and considered.

The people largely determine the role of the police and give them their authority to fulfill this role. Their support is vital.

In addition, because the police are highly visible representatives of local government and are on duty twenty-four hours a day, people often call upon them for services that they are not specifically required to perform. Other agencies might be providing these services, but people do not know of them. For example, if a woman seeks help in dealing with a drunk husband (he is not abusing her; he is just drunk), a drug counselor, minister, or social worker might be the appropriate person to call. The woman, however, often does not know this. Since the police officers' reactions to requests for help affect the amount of respect received and promote a cooperative relationship with the public, police officers usually respond as helpfully as possible, even when the matter is technically civil and outside their responsibility (and sometimes their expertise).

BASIC ROLES OF THE POLICE OFFICER

Since the citizens of a community have such a great influence on the role of the police within the community, many differences exist in roles performed by police officers in different geographic localities. Generally, however, five basic roles are performed.

Five basic roles of most police officers are to:

- Enforce laws.
- Preserve the peace.
- Prevent crimes.
- Protect civil rights and civil liberties.
- Provide services.

These roles often overlap. For example, officers intervening in a fight may not only enforce a law by arresting a suspect for assault, they may also maintain order, prevent others from becoming involved in the fight, protect the civil rights and civil liberties of the suspect, the victim, and the bystanders, and provide emergency service to an injured victim.

Success or failure in fulfilling each role directly affects the success or failure of fulfilling the other roles. Although five roles normally performed by police officers are listed, in reality, policing is a single role comprised of numerous responsibilities.

Enforcing Laws

The term "law enforcement officer" underscores the central importance of this long-accepted responsibility. Historically, enforcement of laws has been the prime responsibility of police officers; however, this role has become increasingly complex. Not only must decisions be made as to what laws to enforce, but also the police are an integral part of the criminal justice system, responsible not only for apprehending offenders but for assisting in their prosecution as well.

Police officers are responsible for enforcing laws and for assisting in the prosecution of offenders.

As noted by Klockars (1991, p. 244): "So strong is the crime-fighting image of the U.S. police, that for the past 50 years virtually every purchase of equipment, every request for additional personnel, and every change in operating procedure has had to be promoted or defended in terms of its role in fighting crime."

The stereotype of the police officer emphasizes the role of "crime fighter," often to the exclusion of all others. In enforcing laws, police officers perform many functions: investigating offenses, interrogating suspects, interviewing witnesses, conducting searches, acting upon leads, participating in stakeouts, apprehending suspects, recovering stolen property, testifying in court, suppressing riots, combatting organized crime, and patrolling to discover crimes in progress.

Because each community and each state have numerous statutes to be enforced and limited resources, full enforcement of all laws is never possible. Even if it were, it is questionable whether full enforcement would be in keeping with legislative intent or the people's wishes. The police can, do, and must exercise discretion in which laws to enforce; that they cannot enforce all laws at all times must be accepted by both the police officer and the public.

Each police department must decide which reported crimes to actively investigate and to what degree, as well as which unreported crimes to seek out and to what degree. The law does not set priorities; it simply defines crimes, classifies them as felonies or misdemeanors, and assesses penalties for them. The police department sets its own priorities, based on citizens' needs.

Usually police departments concentrate law enforcement activities on serious crimes—those that pose the greatest threat to public safety and/or cause the greatest economic losses (the Part I Index Crimes). From that point on, priorities are usually determined by past police experience, the wishes and expectations of the citizens, and the resources available.

The police officer's responsibility does not end with enforcing a law and apprehending a suspect. In effect, when the police arrest an offender, they have initiated the criminal justice process. Police officers play a key role in assisting the prosecutor in preparing the case and often are called on to present evidence in court (the focus of Chapter 18). Unfortunately, since police are in the closest contact with the public, they are often blamed for failures in the criminal justice system. For example, an assault victim whose attacker is found innocent in court may feel resentment not only against the court but against the police.

The release of a suspect from custody for lack of sufficient evidence, the failure of a prosecutor to take a case to trial, or the failure of the corrections system to reform a convict prior to parole or release all directly affect the role police officers must play as well as their public image. And the public image of the police officer is critical when you consider that a large percentage of police work is in direct response to citizen complaints or reports. In fact, members of the community may be the single most important factor in the total law enforcement effort.

Preserving the Peace

The role of preserving the peace has also long been accepted by law enforcement officers. They have the legal authority to arrest individuals for disturbing the peace or for disorderly conduct.

Police are responsible for preserving the peace.

Police are often called upon to intervene in noncriminal conduct such as that which occurs at public events (crowd control), in social relations (domestic disputes), and in traffic control (parking, pedestrians) to maintain law and order. They frequently help people solve problems that they cannot cope with alone.

Often such problems, if unresolved, could result in crime. For example, loud parties, unruly crowds, or disputes between members of a family, business partners, landlord and tenant, or a businessperson and customer might result in bodily harm—assault. Studies indicate that domestic violence frequently leads to homicide. In addition, responses to domestic disputes are a leading cause of serious injury and fatal assaults on police officers.

The police officer's effectiveness in actually preserving the peace will largely be determined by public acceptance of this role. Often if a police officer simply asks a landlord to allow a tenant access to his or her apartment or asks the host of a loud party to turn down the stereo, this is enough. Mere police presence may reduce the possibility of a crime—at least temporarily. Here, as in the enforcement of laws, public support is vital.

Preventing Crime

Crime prevention is closely related to law enforcement and preservation of the peace. If the peace has been kept, crime has, in effect, been prevented. Crime prevention differs from peacekeeping and law enforcing in that it attempts to eliminate potentially dangerous or criminal situations.

A routine patrol might not only discover a crime in progress, but it might also deter or prevent crimes from being committed. If the police are very visible in a community, it is likely that many crimes will be prevented. This is extremely difficult to prove, however, since it is not known what crimes might have been committed if the police were not present.

Police officers are responsible for attempting to prevent a crime.

Notice the word *attempting*. These efforts will often be unsuccessful. Just as police officers cannot be expected to enforce all the laws at all times, they cannot be expected to prevent all crimes from occurring.

Klockars (1991, p. 244) suggests that: "The 'war on crime' is a war police not only cannot win, but cannot in any real sense fight. They cannot win it because it is simply not within their power to change those things—such as unemployment, the age distribution of the population, moral education, freedom, civil liberties, ambitions, and the social and economic opportunities to realize them—that influence the amount of crime in any society." He further notes (p. 250): "[The police] cannot control economic conditions, poverty, inequality; occupational opportunity, moral, religious, family, or secular education; or dramatic social, cultural, or political change. These are the 'big ticket' items in determining the amount and distribution of crime. Compared to them what police do or do not do matters very little."

This is where the idea of community policing comes from—the need for the police and the people within a community to work together as "coproducers of crime prevention" (p. 251). As noted by former New York City Police Commissioner Brown (1991, p. 20): "It is the citizens themselves who know best what the community's problems are and how they can be solved. They are on the front lines. They are the ones who know the pain of victimization, who see relatives and friends die at the hands of criminals, who clearly understand that one does not have to be a police officer to know what actions should be taken."

Crime prevention activities frequently undertaken by police officers include working with juveniles, cooperating with probation and parole personnel, educating the public, instigating operation identification programs, and providing visible evidence of police authority. In addition, many of the community services often provided by police departments (discussed in Chapter 9) aid considerably in crime prevention.

Not only are police charged with enforcing laws, preventing crime, and providing services, they are expected to do so as specified by the U.S. Constitution and the Bill of Rights.

Protecting Constitutional Rights

The first paragraph of the *Law Enforcement Code of Ethics* concludes with the statement that a law enforcement officer has a fundamental duty "to respect the Constitutional rights of all men to liberty, equality, and justice," described in Chapter 4.

As noted by the National Advisory Commission on Criminal Justice Standards and Goals (1973, p. 9): "Any definition of the police role must acknowledge that the Constitution imposes restrictions on the power of the legislatures to prohibit protected conduct, and to some extent defines the limits of police authority in the enforcement of established laws."

The commission, however, goes on to state (1973, p. 9): "Concern for the constitutional rights of accused persons processed by the police has tended to obscure the fact that the police have an affirmative obligation to protect all persons in the free exercise of their rights. The police must provide safety for persons exercising their constitutional right to assemble, to speak freely, and to petition for redress of their grievances."

Police are responsible for protecting citizens' constitutional rights.

Many citizens are angered when a suspect's rights prevent prosecution of the case. They begin to have doubts about the criminal justice system; however, should these same individuals find themselves in the position of being suspected of a crime, they, doubtless, would expect their rights to be fully protected. As Sir John Fortescue said, "Indeed, one would rather twenty guilty persons should escape the punishment of death than one innocent person should be executed." The United States must guarantee all citizens, even those perceived as unworthy of such protection, their constitutional rights or there is danger of a police state.

The authority, goals, and methods of the police must promote individual liberty, public safety, and social justice. The role of protecting civil rights and civil liberties is perceived by some as the single most important role of the police officer. As a case in point, the National Advisory Commission on Criminal Justice Standards and Goals states (1973, p. 9): "If the overall purposes of the police service in today's society were narrowed to a single objective, that objective would be to preserve the peace in a manner consistent with the freedoms secured by the Constitution."

Providing Services

In addition to enforcing laws, preserving the peace, assisting in preventing crime, and protecting civil rights and liberties, the police are often called upon to provide additional services to their community.

This role is acknowledged in the first sentence of the *Law Enforcement Code of Ethics:* "As a law enforcement officer, my fundamental duty is to serve mankind." Many police departments have as their motto: "Serve and Protect."

As society has become more complex, however, so have the types of service requested. Many new demands are made on the police because of their authority. Included among the numerous functions the police may perform in providing services are giving information, directions, and advice; counseling and referring; licensing and registering vehicles; intervening in domestic arguments; working with neglected children; rendering emergency medical or rescue services; dealing with alcoholics and the mentally ill; finding lost children; dealing with stray animals; and controlling traffic and crowds. In addition, many police departments provide community education programs regarding crime, drugs, safety, and the like.

Police are often responsible for providing services.

Considerable disagreement exists regarding what type and amount of services the police should provide.

The police are often inappropriately asked to perform functions that might better be performed by another agency of the government—usually because they are the only government representatives available around the clock and because they have the resources and the authority to use force if necessary. However, in many small cities and towns, the police services provided (even though considered by some to be inappropriate "social services") could not be provided by any other agencies.

Many police agencies have provided personnel with information to refer persons in need to the proper agency. For example, since New York City began using a citywide 911 emergency number, telephone calls for nonpolice municipal services have decreased dramatically. Police officers in Washington, D.C., use the *Referral Handbook of Social Services,* which indexes available governmental and private services by problem and agency. Police in Milwaukee, Wisconsin, have a comprehensive directory of almost five hundred community agencies and organizations.

What is of primary importance is that people who need help receive it; who provides the help is secondary. Since many people are likely to turn first to the police for help, however, police officers must be prepared either to provide the help or to refer the person to an agency that can provide it.

REQUIRED PROFICIENCIES

Look again at the two middle paragraphs of the *Law Enforcement Code of Ethics:*

> I will keep my private life unsullied as an example to all; maintain courageous calm in the face of danger, scorn, or ridicule; develop self-restraint; and be constantly mindful of the welfare of others. Honest in thought and deed in both my personal and official life, I will be exemplary in obeying the laws of the land and the regulations of my department. Whatever I see or hear of a confidential nature or that is confided to me in my official capacity will be kept ever secret unless revelation is necessary in the performance of my duty.

> I will never act officiously or permit personal feelings, prejudices, animosities or friendships to influence my decisions. With no compromise for crime and with relentless prosecution of criminals, I will enforce the law courteously and appropriately without fear or favor, malice or ill will, never employing unnecessary force or violence and never accepting gratuities.

Not only are police officers expected to enforce laws, preserve the peace, prevent crimes, protect constitutional rights, and perform community services, they are also expected to do so in an impeccable, professional manner. As noted by Dwight Dalbey of the FBI (James 1968, p. 104):

> We expect of a police officer the wisdom of Solomon in understanding the law, the strength of Samson in arresting a criminal, the gentleness of St. Francis of Assisi in repelling a riot, the patience of Job in dealing with each of us, and the moral purity of Caesar's wife in a nation whose public and private morals in areas outside police work are sometimes open to legitimate questions.

In spite of these expectations, police officers are human, with emotions, biases, and weaknesses. Their work is sometimes dangerous. They see suffering, injustice, and cruelty. They see people at their best and their worst. They are under constant pressure, even when things are momentarily calm. They must make rapid decisions, often without any guidelines. They frequently lack the necessary equipment and/or training. Their work is further complicated by people's conflicting expectations of them.

Police roles must be carried out skillfully and professionally. This requires mental, intellectual, physical, and personal proficiencies.

To perform in the manner expected by the department and the community, the police officer needs numerous proficiencies. The following list summarizes the results of a University of Chicago study of the behavioral requirements needed to perform police patrol duties (Saunders, 1970, pp. 17 – 18).

Mental   Police officers must:

- Endure a long period of monotony in routine patrol yet react quickly (almost simultaneously) and effectively to problem situations observed on the street or to orders issued by the radio dispatcher (in much the same way that a combat pilot must react to interception or a target opportunity).
- Have the facility to act effectively in extremely divergent interpersonal situations. A police officer constantly confronts persons who are acting in violation of the law, ranging from curfew violators to felons.
- Endure verbal and physical abuse from citizens and offenders (as when placing a person under arrest or facing day-in-and-day-out race prejudice) while using only necessary force in the performance of their functions.
- Tolerate stress in a multitude of forms, such as meeting the violent behavior of a mob, arousing people in a burning building, coping with the pressures of a high-speed chase or a weapon being fired at them, or dealing with a woman bearing a child.

Personal   Police officers must:

- Relate to the people on their beat—businesspeople, residents, school officials, visitors, etc. Their interpersonal relations must range up and down a continuum defined by friendliness and persuasion on one end and firmness and force at the other.
- Exhibit a professional, self-assured presence and a self-confident manner in their conduct when dealing with offenders, the public, and the court.
- Take charge of situations, for example, a crime or accident scene, yet not unduly alienate participants or bystanders.
- Be flexible enough to work under loose supervision in most of their day-to-day patrol activities and also under the direct supervision of superiors in situations where large numbers of officers are required.
- Exhibit personal courage in the face of dangerous situations that may result in serious injury or death.
- Maintain objectivity while dealing with a host of special interest groups, ranging from relatives of offenders to members of the press.
- Maintain a balanced perspective in the face of constant conflict, for example, refrain from accepting bribes or "favors," provide impartial law enforcement, etc.

Intellectual   Police officers must:

- Exhibit initiative, problem-solving capacity, effective judgment, and imagination in coping with the numerous complex situations they are called upon to face, for example, a family disturbance, a potential suicide, a robbery in progress, an accident, or a disaster. Police officers themselves clearly recognize this requirement and refer to it as "showing street sense."
- Make prompt and effective decisions, sometimes in life-and-death situations, and be able to size up a situation quickly and take appropriate action.
- Demonstrate mature judgment, as in deciding whether an arrest is warranted by the circumstances or a warning is sufficient, or in assessing a situation where the use of force may be needed.

- Demonstrate critical awareness in discerning signs of out-of-the-ordinary conditions or circumstances that indicate trouble or a crime in progress.
- Adequately perform the communication and record-keeping functions of the job, including oral reports, preparation of formal case reports, and the completion of departmental and force forms.
- Be capable of restoring equilibrium to social groups, for example, restoring order in a family fight, in a disagreement between neighbors, or in a clash between rival youth gangs.
- Be skillful in questioning suspected offenders, victims, and witnesses of crimes.
- Gain knowledge of their patrol areas, not only of its physical characteristics but also of its normal routine of events and the usual behavior patterns of its residents.

Physical   Police officers must:

- Exhibit a number of complex psychomotor skills, such as driving a vehicle in normal and emergency situations, firing a weapon accurately under extremely varied conditions, maintaining agility, endurance, and strength, and showing facility in self-defense and apprehension, as in taking a person into custody with a minimum of force.

Few roles in modern society are as demanding as that of the police officer.

ORGANIZATION OF THE DEPARTMENT

According to Arnold and Brungardt (1983, p. 232): "The organizational features of the United States police department exhibit a great deal of variation. The departments range from small, informally organized, small-town operations to highly bureaucratic metropolitan police departments with many subdivisions and thousands of employees."

Most police departments are organized into two basic units: field services and administrative services. Tasks and personnel are assigned to one or the other.

Field services (also called operations or on-line services) include patrol, traffic control, community services, and investigation. **Administrative services** (also called staff or support services) include recruitment and training, planning and research, records and communications, crime laboratories, and facilities including the police headquarters and jail. Teamwork is essential within and between field services and administrative services.

The chief of police oversees the operation of the entire department and coordinates the efforts of field and administrative services. Under the chief of police, depending on the size of the department, are captains, lieutenants, sergeants, and police officers.

Traditionally, most police departments have been structured in a militaristic pyramid, with the chief of police at the top as depicted in Figure 7–3.

Many departments are moving away from this structure to a more flattened structure with fewer officers in supervisory positions and more officers in the patrol division and an emphasis on teamwork rather than on blind obedience to higher authority. As noted by Nees (1990, p. 263): "Management, supervision and officers will develop a partnership. The line between management and officer ranks will become less clear." He also suggests that in the coming decade many police services will be consolidated and many will be provided by civilian services, including private policing agencies.

The specific organization within a police department is influenced by the department's size, location, and the extent and type of crime with which it must

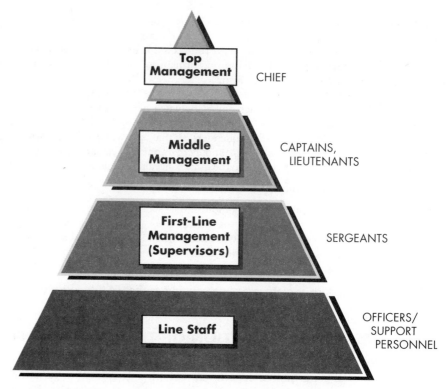

Figure 7–3   Typical Police Department Management Structure

deal. For example, a small police department often combines patrol, traffic, community services, and investigative tasks in a single division; a large police department usually has separate divisions for each. A community with a major freeway running through its business section faces different problems than a community located on a coast or on a border between the United States and Canada or Mexico. Communities with large groups of minorities face different problems than those that are homogeneous. For some communities, traffic control is a major problem; for others gambling, smuggling, or racial unrest may be priorities.

Whatever the size or configuration of the department, however, basic administrative and field services will be expected. The clear lines depicted in Figure 7–4 may become blurred as departments move to community policing and a team approach.

ADMINISTRATIVE SERVICES

Administrative services include communications and records, recruitment and training, and provision of special facilities and services.

Administrative services' two areas that most directly affect the efficient provision of field services are communications and records.

Communications

To properly serve the community, police officers must be kept currently and completely informed. They must know where and how much of each type of

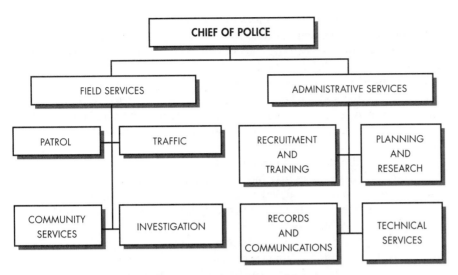

Figure 7–4   Typical Department Organization of Services

crime occurs, such as burglaries, car prowls, malicious destruction of property, and auto thefts. They also have to know what services are needed.

Current information is usually provided at roll call, by radio, and by computer.

Roll Call   One of the most important functions of the administrative division in its support of the other units of the police department is keeping members informed of daily police operations and providing administrative instructions and special assignments and tasks to be performed. This is usually done at a **roll call** session before the officers on the next shift go out into the street.

Up-to-date information is usually provided in a daily bulletin, which contains brief summaries of what has transpired in the previous twenty-four hours. Officers are given a synopsis of each complaint received and acted on as well as descriptions of missing and/or wanted persons, stolen personal property, and stolen autos.

Radio Communications   The information provided at roll call is continuously updated by radio. Data is available to officers in patrol cars or carrying portable radios. This immediate communication has improved the safety of law enforcement officers and has provided for better allocation of resources.

The introduction of the small hand-carried portable police radio and the beeper have extended the communications system so that officers on foot may be reached to assist mobile patrol units and vice versa.

The dependability of radio transmissions has improved steadily over the years and has resulted in a great reduction in response time to calls for service or criminal activity.

A typical radio system has four channels providing the capability of (1) contacting car to car in its own jurisdiction, (2) contacting its own dispatchers, (3) contacting another officer patrolling in a different geographical subdivision through a repeater system, and (4) placing emergency calls. The fourth channel is reserved for such emergencies as roadblocks, disasters, and civil defense messages.

Communications is the lifeline of the police department. The police dispatcher, or in some cases the telephone operator, receives all citizens' requests for police service. In some instances the calls come directly to the dispatcher, who must act upon them and determine their priority. Some agencies have telephone operators screen the calls prior to giving them to the dispatcher to segregate informational calls from service calls.

Dispatchers have the responsibility for dispatching patrol vehicles to requests for service and for knowing what patrol vehicles are ready for assignment. They may also have some records responsibility, for example, making out the original incident complaint report, noting the time the call was received, the time the patrol vehicle was dispatched, the time it arrived, the time it cleared, and the disposition of the call.

In addition, dispatchers may have to handle any walk-in complaints. Some dispatchers also have the added responsibility of monitoring jails through a closed-circuit television hookup. Such a system exists in many smaller and medium-sized departments today.

In larger agencies several dispatchers handle the incoming calls and give them priority according to their seriousness and the availability of officers to respond. Larger agencies may also have direct and complete integration of police radio with regular telephone service. In this system any call to the police emergency number is automatically channeled to the dispatcher who controls squad cars assigned to the area from which the caller is telephoning.

Some cities have a *911 system.* A person who wishes to call the police dials 911 on the phone, and a central dispatching office receives the call directly. The 911 system has been implemented in many cities in the United States. The eventual goal is to have this number as the emergency number to call for police service in any city in the United States.

Computers   Sharp (1991, p. 41) suggests that: "Computers have had a more significant impact on police operations in the last decade than any other single factor during the present century.... Computers have become such an important part of law enforcement operations that younger officers have a hard time imagining police work in the pre-computer era." Among the effects the use of computers have had are the following (p. 41):

> They have accelerated communications within and among departments, facilitated information searches, reduced officers' workloads, improved report and warrant writing procedures, enhanced statistical and data gathering and analysis techniques—in short, they have had a dramatic, positive effect on the way law enforcement agencies perform their duties.

Rubin (1991, p. 22) predicts: "Throughout the 1990s, we will see an explosion in the number of mobile data terminals (MDT's) installed in patrol vehicles." Minnesota State Troopers installed MDTs in their metro area squads in 1991 and found that (Matthews 1992, p. 8): "The MDT system has been a success for the two people who need it the most—the trooper on the road and the communications operator behind the desk." The Minnesota troopers' system allows transmission of administrative messages to a single car, a station, a district, or every vehicle with an MDT. All-point bulletins, weather reports, phone call messages, schedule changes, and even where the coffee stop is going to be are sent via the MDT system without using precious airtime. Adrian, a 20-year veteran of the metro area patrol, said the computer was "the best piece of equipment the state patrol ever issued me to help me do my job on a day-to-day basis" (p. 5).

As noted by Thibault et al. (1990, p. 136):

> Computer-aided dispatch (CAD) enhances calls for service from the public and the dispatching of police cars and personnel. The CAD system verifies addresses,

determines the beat of incidents, gives a case number and priority number to each call, and some systems report "dangerous" history. The computer automatically records all calls and can recommend to the dispatcher a choice of units to dispatch to the call. The time of dispatch is recorded as well as time on the scene and time the unit is free. Thus CAD provides real-time monitoring of vehicle status, a continuously updated incident file, and allows supervisors to monitor the incident status and provides telephone, radio, and digital activity in terms of incidences known to the police, provides statistics in terms of location and time of all types of crime, flag deviations and trends, automatically generate required data for resource allocation models, and on-line information can be available for line supervisors and administrators as well as line officers.

Fremont, California, is using a data-by-radio system that, according to Vinson (1992, p. 26): "equips its patrol cars with personal laptop computers plugged into a high speed data network utilizing sophisticated packet radio technology. The network lets patrol and field officers use the laptops to communicate directly with each other, exchange data with the department's host computers, and access law enforcement data bases across the country." Since the airwaves aren't used, messages are more secure and airwaves are freed up for other urgent police communications.

Further, the system facilitates officers' report writing. The laptops have a word processing program officers can use to write their reports and send directly in. According to Vinson (p. 28): "Time is saved; reports are more accurate. Money is saved, too. Fremont estimates its mobile data system will reduce its report writing costs by 50%."

Among the other types of computerized communication occurring in police departments are the following (Thibault et al. 1990, p. 138):

- Mobil digital communications (MDC)—provides a nonverbal means of transmitting dispatch and status messages between a law enforcement communications center and patrol units as well as accessing data files by both the communication center and the patrol units.
- Automatic vehicle monitoring (AVM)—provides the location and status of the vehicle, such as in pursuit, enroute to scene, door open, and so on.
- Regional communication system (RCS)—a plan whereby a number of law enforcement agencies cooperate in creating a common communications network.

One vital source of information for officers in the field is the FBI's computerized National Crime Information Center.

In 1967 the FBI implemented its computerized crime information storage system, the National Crime Information Center (NCIC). Under this system, each state has a number of computer terminals that interface with the FBI's main computer in Washington, D.C. The computer contains records of stolen property such as guns, autos, and office machines, and, in some cases, records of persons who are wanted on warrants.

The NCIC computer receives its information from other federal law enforcement agencies and from state and local law enforcement agencies. The NCIC makes it possible for a law enforcement officer in Texas who stops a suspicious person or car from California to contact the dispatcher by radio or teleprinter requesting information. The dispatcher can make an inquiry to the computer in Texas, which, in a matter of seconds, makes an inquiry on the status of the individual and/or the car to the NCIC terminal in Washington. The police officer can be quickly informed if the car has been stolen or if an arrest warrant is outstanding on the individual in the car.

The great volume of information contained in various state and federal computers is another aid given to police officers in maintaining up-to-date records systems.

The National Crime Information Center allows all police agencies in the country to
have access to the computerized files of the FBI.

As noted in the *NCIC Operating Manual* (1985: Intro–1), the following
goals have been accomplished by the NCIC:

- Enhancing the development of state, county, and metropolitan computerized
  criminal justice information systems, thereby making NCIC information more
  readily available to the officer on the street.
- Establishing uniformity of coding standards for the exchange of criminal justice
  information.
- Increasing the probability of criminal detection by providing law enforcement
  with the timely and accurate information necessary to combat today's highly
  mobile criminal population.

In December of 1991, the International Association of Chiefs of Police
(IACP) announced a new service for its members: the IACP NET—an information exchange for law enforcement professionals. This parallels the movement in the law enforcement field to go beyond crime statistics and information.
According to the IACP (December 1991, p. 23): "IACP NET will allow police
chiefs, sheriffs, commissioners, and other chief executives and their staffs to
quickly and conveniently exchange information with their colleagues throughout the United States and Canada. This interaction will bring top law enforcement experts closer together as a team and help each solve problems more
effectively than ever before." Subscribers to the IACP NET will be able to:

- Keep abreast of the latest events and trends affecting law enforcement.
- Base their actions on the experiences of and precedents set by others.
- Enjoy increased interactive communications with colleagues nationwide
  through private electronic mail and public conferences.
- Take advantage of greater exchange of information on topics of mutual
  interest.
- Receive assistance from others who have had similar experiences and
  problems.

With the enormous amounts of information police departments must receive, transmit, and be able to retrieve, an effective, efficient records system is
imperative.

Records

The quality of records maintained is directly related to the quality of communications and field services provided. To give proper direction, a police agency
must have a sound records system as well as an efficient communications
system. Police departments throughout the country vary in their reporting
systems and their needs in management control and effective operational control. The activities of a police department require keeping records not only of
criminal activity but of all essential activities of the department.

Types of Records

Police records may be categorized as (1) administrative records, (2) arrest records,
(3) identification records, and (4) complaint records.

Administrative records include inventories of police equipment, department memorandums, personnel records, evaluation reports, and all general information that reflects correspondence or services rendered.

Arrest records contain information obtained from arrested persons when they are booked as well as information about the control and/or release of prisoners and court procedures.

Identification records contain fingerprints, photographs, and other descriptive data obtained from arrested persons.

Complaint records usually contain information related to complaints and reports received by the police from citizens or other agencies as well as any actions initiated by the police. Since police work is public business, it requires accurate records of complaints received and the action taken by the police. Complaints may be criminal or noncriminal in nature; they may involve lost property, damaged property, traffic accidents, medical emergencies, or a missing person. Requests for police assistance may also involve robberies, murders, burglaries, vandalism, or children playing in the streets or cats up in trees. Although most complaints are minor, each must be treated with personal concern to the complainant and as a matter of importance to the police.

Most police agencies have a procedure for recording complaint information either on sheets or data processing cards. Initial complaint records are filled out on all complaints or requests for service received by the dispatcher or a police officer.

Information on the initial complaint record normally shows the complainant, victim, address of each, type of complaint, time of day, day of week, the officer handling the complaint or request, the area of the community where it occurred, the disposition, whether there was an arrest, and whether further follow-up reports or further investigation is justified by the investigative services division.

Benefits of Efficient Records Systems Efficient records systems are a vital management tool that aid in assessing department accomplishments, in developing budget justifications, in determining additional work force needs, and in evaluating the performance of officers as well as the attainment of objectives and goals.

Evaluation of carefully kept records will generally reflect needs in training, recruitment, public relations, allocation of resources, and general effectiveness. The continual or periodic evaluation of records by management in planning and research has allowed police agencies to provide better service to the public and, in turn, they have gained public support.

Centralized, integrated, and accurate systems of communications and records increase the effectiveness and efficiency of field services.

Computerized Information Many informational tools available to police agencies today are the result of the introduction of random-access storage and retrieval systems and computers into the police field.

The computer has revolutionized the record keeping system of many police departments. According to Sandona (1989, p. 73):

> The computerized records management system provides a tremendous increase in the amount of indexing information. . . . The system also makes it possible to achieve a vast increase in the quality of the information in terms of its completeness, integrity, accuracy and security.
>
> The speed of finding information is also greatly increased.

Rubin (1991, p. 24) notes another advantage of computerized records: "By the end of this decade, endless rooms filled with file drawers will be replaced with PCs with water cooler-sized optical memory devices."

As noted by Sharp (1991, p. 43): "Police agencies in general must utilize the capabilities available in the computer world in order to effectively manage their daily operations. The overall increase in police services requires the proper analysis of departments' workloads in order to effectively serve the citizens they are mandated to serve." Computers can also analyze crime data and identify trends that are vital to the problem-oriented policing approach being adopted by many departments nationwide.

Privacy of Records   The most sensitive aspect of computerized or manual records on persons arrested and related information about them is the possibility of including in the file unsubstantiated information that might contain derogatory, incomplete, or incorrect information—information that disseminated to the wrong person could prove damaging and provide cause for a civil action against the police agency. In addition, police agencies often tend to retain information longer than necessary.

As a result, by authority of the Omnibus Crime Control and Safe Streets Act of 1968, which was amended by the Crime Control Act of 1973, the Department of Justice issued regulations to assure that criminal history record information, wherever it appears, is collected, stored, and disseminated in a way that insures the completeness, integrity, accuracy, and security of such information and that protects individual privacy. The regulations apply to all state and local agencies and individuals collecting, storing, or disseminating criminal history information either manually or by computer.

A data privacy act regulates the use of confidential and private information on individuals in the records, files, and processes of a state and its political subdivisions.

Some law enforcement agencies have expressed dissatisfaction with provisions relating to law enforcement records and with the dissemination of criminal history information, particularly for employment purposes.

Because states have been slow in passing privacy act legislation, a certain amount of confusion often occurs among those who try to abide by the Department of Justice regulations. The effect of some state legislation has been that in the absence of an emergency classification, almost all information or data a police agency has kept on individuals legally must be made available to anyone requesting it. This unfortunate situation has been avoided in other states.

Administrative services are vital to the efficient functioning of any police department. But it must always be remembered that they are *support* for the field services. Without the field services, they would serve no purpose.

FIELD SERVICES

Sometimes field services are performed by one division; sometimes they are performed by separate divisions. They may be further specialized by the type of individual involved: juveniles, gamblers, prostitutes, burglars, drug dealers, and so on; by specific geographic areas (beats); or by specific times when the demand for service is highest, for example, holiday traffic or abnormal conditions such as strikes and protests.

Field services include patrol, traffic, community services, and investigation.

Traditionally, police departments have been generalist in organization; that is, most of their personnel is assigned to patrol and each officer is responsible for providing basic law enforcement services of all types to a specified geographic area. General patrol has been and is the backbone of police work in smaller departments. Larger departments tend to be more specialist oriented.

Patrol

Usually 60 to 70 percent of a department's police officers are assigned to patrol operations. Although other divisions may have more prestige, patrol officers are the first and primary contact between the public and the criminal justice system. They not only initiate the criminal justice system, they strongly influence the public's perception of this system.

Patrol is responsible for providing continuous police service and high visibility of law enforcement. Tasks include crime prevention, response to calls for service, self-initiated activity, and completing administrative functions.

The patrol function is discussed in detail in Chapter 8.

Traffic

Traffic may be a responsibility of patrol, or it may be a separate function. A well-rounded traffic program involves many activities designed to maintain order and safety on streets and highways.

Traffic officers are usually responsible for enforcing traffic laws, directing and controlling traffic, providing directions and assistance to motorists, investigating motor vehicle accidents, providing emergency assistance at the scenes of accidents, gathering information related to traffic, and writing reports.

The most frequent contact between the police and the noncriminal public is through traffic encounters; consequently, the opportunity for improving community relations by how traffic violations are handled must be considered. Although the traffic responsibilities of a police officer may not have the glamour of a criminal investigation, they are critical not only to the safety of the citizens in a community but also to the police image. It should be noted that a great number of criminal arrests result from traffic stops, for example, wanted persons and discovery of contraband.

The traffic function is discussed in detail in Chapter 8.

Community Service/Community Relations

In essence, every action of a police officer has an effect on community relations—either positive or negative. Many larger departments have established separate community relations divisions or community service divisions to strengthen communication channels between the public and its police department and/or to stress public education programs and crime prevention programs.

Every action of a police officer is, in effect, a part of community relations. Specific community relations or community service divisions seek to improve communications between the police and the public and/or to promote public education and crime prevention programs.

The importance of community relations and community service will be seen throughout the remainder of the book. Chapter 9 focuses on community relations and community service programs and approaches.

Investigation

Although some investigations are carried out by patrol officers, the investigation services division (also known as the detective bureau) has the responsibility for follow-up investigation. The success of any criminal investigation relies on the cooperative, coordinated efforts of both the patrol and the investigative functions.

The primary responsibilities of the investigator are to make certain the crime scene is secure, interview witnesses and interrogate suspects, photograph and sketch the crime scene, obtain and identify evidence, and record all facts related to the case for future reference.

Investigation is discussed in detail in Chapter 10.

Specialized Officers

In addition to the basic divisions that may exist within a police department, larger departments frequently train officers to perform highly specialized tasks.

Specialized officers may include evidence technicians, identification officers, intelligence officers, juvenile officers, vice officers, K-9-assisted officers, and tactical forces officers.

Evidence Technicians Some police agencies, such as suburban police departments with a complement of forty or more officers, have established the position of evidence technician. The evidence technician is usually a patrol officer who has received extensive classroom and laboratory training in crime scene investigation. In departments that have small detective bureaus and relatively inexperienced officers, this position fills a notable void. The officer has not been relieved of regular patrol duties but may be called upon to conduct a crime scene investigation. Use of evidence technicians provides better coordination of the preliminary investigation of crimes and increases the probability that the investigation will be successful during the preliminary stage because other patrol officers work with the evidence technician as a team.

Identification Officers Identification officers have had specialized training in taking, identifying, and filing fingerprints. Fingerprint identification is an extremely important form of positive identification used by the police in identifying people who break the law. Identification officers are highly trained in using scanners and computers in their work.

Intelligence Officers Most large cities have an intelligence division whose top officer reports directly to the chief of police and whose activities are kept secret from the rest of the police department. Intelligence units work in two areas. The first area is long-term, ongoing investigations into such criminal activity as illegal sale of guns, payoffs to police officers or politicians, major drug cases, and activities of organized crime. They often work on the same case in cooperation with county, state, and federal investigators.

The second area of intelligence work is investigation of fellow police officers in the department. For example, the intelligence unit may investigate a complaint of an officer drinking on duty, corruption, or other activities considered conduct unbecoming to police officers.

Intelligence officers do not wear uniforms or drive marked cars. They may even use assumed names and fictitious identities. To avoid identification problems, some large police agencies use officers who have just graduated from rookie school, as they are less known on the street.

Juvenile Officers The police officer is often the first contact for a child in legal trouble. Therefore, it is justifiable and logical to have juvenile police specialists to work primarily with juvenile offenders.

Because most juvenile work is informal and includes powers to release, refer, or detain, juvenile officers must be chosen from the most qualified officers in the department.

Juvenile officers can provide assistance to all other departments within their own agency when juveniles are involved. Since juveniles commit more than 50 percent of local crimes, all officers are juvenile officers much of the time, and it is the uniformed patrol division that has the most contact with these juvenile offenders.

Vice Officers Vice problems vary from community to community; for example, some sections of the country allow prostitution, but many sections of the country do not. Vice officers usually concentrate their efforts on illegal gambling, prostitution, pornography, narcotics, and liquor violations. Sometimes their work is coordinated with intelligence officers.

K-9-Assisted Officers Humans have used dogs in a variety of ways for thousands of years. Dogs have been used in police work in the United States,

A dog trained to detect blood scents assists the Dakota County, Minnesota, Sheriff's Department in its search along the Mississippi River for a 5-year-old girl, missing and presumed murdered.

Europe, and throughout the world for more than fifty years. Today K-9 units exist in more than three hundred towns and cities in the United States.

Today's police dog has had intensive schooling with one officer—the dog's partner. Both spend many weeks under a special trainer. The police dog's use in most cities falls into five categories: search, attack and capture, drug detection, bomb detection, and crime deterrence.

Tactical Forces Officers   Special crime tactical forces are immediately available, flexible, and mobile officers used for deployment against any emergency or crime problem. Tactical units supplement the patrol force and may operate selectively in high-crime areas. They may suppress burglaries, robberies, or auto thefts. They may be used in hostage situations and where persons have barricaded themselves. In such instances, the idea is to negotiate and reason with barricaded subjects, hostage takers, or the mentally disturbed rather than using force.

Miami Police Department SWAT Team during briefing (above) and in field exercises (below).

SWAT team members are highly trained in marksmanship, guerrilla tactics, patrolling, night operations, camouflage and concealment, and the use of chemical agents. They frequently participate in field exercises to develop discipline and teamwork.

Reserve Officers Some police departments have reserve units to help achieve the department's goals. The reserve officers patrol in uniform and are visible symbols of law enforcement although they cannot write citations. Reserve officers also help in public education programs, informing the public about such things as operation identification, in which valuables are marked for identification in case of theft, drugs, and bike safety. When a crime does occur, the reserves can guard the crime scene while the regular officers continue with their routine or specialized patrol.

You have looked at what policing is, how the police relate to the people they serve, the basic roles of police officers, and required proficiencies and desired qualities of law enforcement officers. You have also been introduced to the organization of typical police departments and the administrative and field services provided. Now turn your attention to something more personal—*how* individual officers interpret their responsibilities and how they carry out their specific roles, that is, officer style in policing.

STYLES OF POLICE WORK

As noted by Senna and Siegel (1990, p. 251):

> Policing involves a multitude of diverse tasks, including peacekeeping, criminal investigation, traffic control, and providing emergency medical service. Part of one's socialization as a police officer is developing a working attitude, or style, that is used to confront and interpret these various aspects of policing. For example, some police officers may view their job as well-paid civil service positions that stress careful compliance with written departmental rules and procedures. Other officers may see themselves as part of the "thin blue line" that protects the public from wrongdoers. They will use any means to "get their man."

Many studies have looked at styles of policing and have classified these styles into clusters called **typologies.** Although few police officers fall completely into a single typology, most tend to exhibit several behaviors that would place them into a specific typology.

Basic styles of policing include the following:

- The enforcer.
- The crime fighter/zealot.
- Social service agent.
- Watchman.

The first typology, the enforcer, according to Pursley (1987, p. 245), "places relatively high value on social order and 'keeping society safe,' and a relatively low value on individual rights and legal due process." Pursley suggests that such officers are highly critical of institutions such as the Supreme Court, of politicians, of police administrators, of minority interest groups, and of others viewed as "corrupt, incompetent, weak, criminal by nature, or simply naive." Enforcers have little time for minor violations of the law, seeing them as a waste of police time and resources.

The second typology, the crime fighter/zealot, is like the enforcer in that a primary goal is to "keep society safe." Officers with this style of policing tend to deal with all laws and all offenders equally. According to Pursley (1987): "This type of officer typically defines his or her role as a general law enforcement agent and is generally less critical than the enforcer. In fact, zealots tend to accept the diverse groups of society for what they are." They also are less critical of the social service aspects of policing than are enforcers.

The third typology, the social service agent, is much more accepting of the social service roles and much more attuned to due process. Frequently officers falling into this category are "young, highly educated, and more idealistic police officers" (Pursley 1987). Like the enforcer and the crime fighter, however, the social service agent is also interested in protecting society but is much more flexible in how this is approached.

The fourth typology, the watchman, is on the opposite end of the spectrum from the enforcer. The watchman is interested in maintaining the status quo, in not making waves. According to Wilson (1968, pp. 140–41):

> The police ignore many common violations, especially traffic and juvenile offenses, to tolerate, though gradually less so, a certain amount of vice and gambling, to use the law more as a means of maintaining order than of regulating conduct, and to judge the requirements of order differently depending on the character of the group in which the infraction occurs.

Table 7–1 summarizes these typologies as described by three sources.

No individual is purely one type or another and may change from one style to another depending on the situation. And, in any given police department it is likely that a variety of policing styles with some combination of the preceding typologies can be found.

Five similar styles of policing can be identified by considering whether the focus is on concern for civil rights or on control. Hageman (1985, pp. 24–25) suggests adopting Blake and Mouton's classic managerial grid to policing as illustrated in Figure 7–5.

In this figure a 1,1 style represents low concern for either citizen rights or control. A 1,9 style represents low concern for control, high concern for citizen rights; conversely, a 9,1 style represents high concern for control and low concern for civil rights. A 9,9 style would represent high concern for both.

As noted by Hageman (p. 25): "The officer's ability to choose styles of behaving means that he or she is able to do a (9,9) style when necessary and a (9,1) if need be, to protect himself or herself and/or others." She stresses (p. 26):

> The idea of this modern role grid is that the present-day role of agents in the criminal justice system mandates variety and flexibility. The argument should no longer be between those who demand "real police work" (as in concern for control) and those who have concern for people and their civil rights. Rather the

Table 7–1 **The Typologies of Policing Styles**

JAMES Q. WILSON (1968)	ROBERT PURSLEY (1987)	JOSEPH SENNA AND LARRY SIEGEL (1990)
Legalistic	Enforcer Zealot	Law enforcer Crime fighter
Service style	Social service agent	Social agent
Watchman	Watchman	Watchman

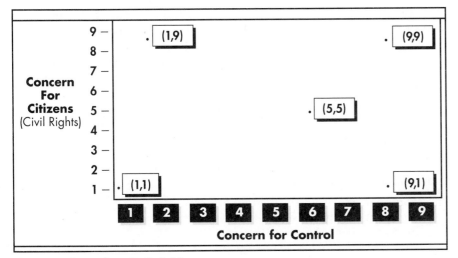

Figure 7–5   Police Work Grid
Source: M. J. Hageman. *Police-Community Relations.* Copyright © 1985, p. 25. Reprinted by permission of Sage Publications: Beverly Hills, Calif.

emphasis needs to be on when it is appropriate and beneficial to develop police-social work or other professional teams to handle communities' problems. Sniper or hostage situations usually do not call for community surveys.

One reason these styles exist within police departments is that police agencies and their officers have a great amount of *discretion* in how they carry out their roles and responsibilities.

DISCRETION

Just as citizens can decide to obey the laws or not, police agencies and their officers can decide which offenses to actively seek to control and which offenses to simply ignore.

Police **discretion** is the freedom of an agency or individual officer to make choices as to whether or not to act.

Any speeder who has talked a traffic officer out of issuing a ticket probably thinks that police discretion is good. The person who does receive a ticket, however, probably thinks the officer has erred in spending time chasing speeders rather than catching criminals.

Klockars (1983, pp. 262 – 67) uses the illustration of the speeding ticket to explain why discretion is necessary. One important reason is that most laws tend to "overreach." A posted speed limit, for example, applies to all situations, including people with valid reasons for exceeding the posted limit such as a volunteer firefighter on the way to a fire or a mother with a seriously injured child on the way to a hospital. As Klockars explains:

> Every law has the property of overreach, whether it provides penalties for traveling in excess of 35 mph on a certain stretch of road, gambling, assault, burglary, robbery, or the killing of another human being. Police exercise discretion in the enforcement of all these laws and every other law, because each criminalizes more than it intends. From the point of view of the law as written, the single most astonishing fact of police behavior is the extent to which police do not enforce the law when they have every legal right to do so.

A second important reason for the existence of discretion is that often the stop or confrontation with the law accomplishes its purpose and the punishment that might follow could be considered too severe. Klockars cites as examples a person who has never had a speeding ticket before and faints at the thought of it, the person whose insurance will be canceled, and the person who teaches driver's education at the local high school.

A third factor entering into the decision making of police officers is that they know that people will frequently lie to avoid "punishment" of any kind.

Yet another factor to be considered is that the police often cannot reveal their true reasons for issuing a ticket. Klockars says (1983):

Imagine a police officer saying . . .

Sorry, but I've got a quota of arrests to make.
Sorry, but the city depends on traffic fines for revenue.
Sorry, but I don't like people like you.
Sorry, but I don't think your excuse is good enough.
Sorry, but I don't believe you.

Any one of the preceding may, in fact, be the underlying reason for the ticket. But, since the officer cannot give any of these reasons, the most likely explanation will be: "I don't make the laws, I just enforce them," pretending to have no discretion at all.

Klockars (1983) also discusses the range of police discretion. He notes that it extends to such decisions as the following:

Resource allocation: patrol vs. detectives, drugs vs. juvenile aid, police academy vs. two officer cars, in-service training vs. internal affairs.
Whether to use police dogs, or use hollow point ammunition, or carry shotguns.
Whether to wear nameplates or bulletproof vests.
Whether to be allowed to moonlight.

Another interesting aspect of police discretion, as noted by Cole (1983, p. 141), is as follows:

Within the police bureaucracy, discretion has a special dimension: It increases as one moves down the organizational hierarchy. Thus, patrol officers, the most numerous and lowest-ranking officers and the ones who are the newest to police work, have the greatest amount of discretion.

One of the most important discretionary options police officers have is whether to arrest someone or not. If that decision is to arrest, then the discretionary powers of the rest of the criminal justice system come into play, as summarized in Table 7–2.

Discretion is used throughout the criminal justice system. It is usually most noticeable, however, at the patrol officer level. In those departments that change to a community-oriented philosophy of policing, even more discretion will be given to the patrol officers. As noted by Pratt (1992, p. 99): "Despite all the supervision and rules, officers make decisions all day, every day; whether to ignore or pursue, to arrest or merely 'chew out,' to stay cool or kick ass. These and many other decisions are made routinely by street officers, often in violation of the rules." Pratt notes that recent court decisions have increasingly recognized the role of discretion in police work, including the view that:

- Officers are more knowledgeable than most people in human (particularly criminal) behaviors.
- Assumes that officers, since they wear the badge, must be considered honest and their statements are more likely to be true than those made by a suspect.

Table 7–2   **Sources of Discretion in the Criminal Justice System**

Who exercises discretion?

THESE CRIMINAL JUSTICE OFFICIALS...	...MUST OFTEN DECIDE WHETHER OR NOT OR HOW TO—
Police	Enforce specific laws
	Investigate specific crimes
	Search people, vicinities, buildings
	Arrest or detain people
Prosecutors	File charges or petitions for adjudication
	Seek indictments
	Drop cases
	Reduce charges
Judges or magistrates	Set bail or conditions for release
	Accept pleas
	Determine delinquency
	Dismiss charges
	Impose sentence
	Invoke probation
Correctional officials	Assign to type of correctional facility
	Award privileges
	Punish for disciplinary infractions
Paroling authority	Determine date and conditions of parole
	Revoke parole

Source: U.S. Department of Justice. Bureau of Justice Statistics. *Report to the Nation on Crime and Justice.* (March 1988): 56–60.

■ Specialized training and experience enable officers to recognize suspicious actions not apparent to others.

■ Based on training and experience, officers can and should take any action reasonably necessary to investigate suspicious activity.

■ Officers are exposed to unusual dangers and must, at all times and under all circumstances, act to protect themselves from harm.

How officers use their discretion can have a great influence on the image they project to the public.

THE POLICE IMAGE

Recognize that each police officer is an individual. Police officers are fathers, mothers, sons, daughters, uncles, aunts, coaches of Little League teams, church members, and neighbors. As people, they like to be liked, but often their profession requires that they take negative actions against those who break the law. As a result, they are often criticized and berated for simply doing their jobs.

Although police officers are individuals just like those in the community they have sworn to "serve and protect," their behavior is very public. It may simply be that they are extraordinarily visible ordinary people.

The public's image of the police varies greatly. Some see police officers as saviors; others see them as militaristic harassers. The sight of a police officer arouses feelings of respect, confidence, and security in some citizens; fear, hostility, and hatred in others; and indifferences in yet others. The image of the police officer frequently portrayed on television has not been very helpful. The "Dirty Harry" tactics, with much violence and disregard for civil rights, are often presented as *the* way a police officer should behave.

The effects of television on both the police image and the fight against crime cannot be accurately measured. Certainly, it has an impact. Hardly an hour passes without an illegal search, a coerced confession, police brutality, and general violence dealt out by the police officers. Many modern-day police "heroes" are shown blatantly indulging in illegal and unconstitutional behavior, which in effect instills in the public the opinion that police misconduct is acceptable and, in fact, sometimes the only way to apprehend criminals. The same criticisms may be applied to our movies.

The police **image** results from the media portrayal and from everyday contacts between individual police officers and citizens.

In spite of what is written in books or portrayed on television and in movies, the abstraction called the "police image" is primarily the result of day-to-day contacts between police and citizens. It is the behavior of police officers at the patrol level rather than at the command level that is of greatest importance in establishing the police image. In turn, the individual behavior of the police officer who creates the police image is the result of several factors including length of service, the community served (ghetto or exclusive suburb), training, and experience.

In addition to easily identifiable and predictable factors such as experience, training, and locality served, numerous subtle factors influence police behavior and image, including the nature of police work itself, the police officer's unique relation to the criminal justice system, a confusion of identity, the democratic nature of our society, and the individual officer's personality.

The Nature of Police Work Numerous demands are placed upon the police officer. Police officers are under constant pressure and faced with rapidly changing conditions, sometimes life-threatening situations, with few guidelines and little supervision; they frequently must "play it by ear." The stressfulness of the situation in which police officers are placed is described by Remsberg (1986):

> Your day-to-day—sometimes minute-by-minute—contact with criminals, complainants and citizens alike who are crying, cursing, bleeding, puking, yelling, spitting, biting, fighting, lying, dying, dead, drunk, doped, dirty, scared, scarred, angry, vengeful, irrational, evasive, outlandish, grieving, manipulative, taunting, demanding, defiant, cruel, neurotic, hopeless, and just plain crazy subjects your system to repeated onslaughts of disturbance.... The question is—how many people could have had me today if they'd really wanted me?

Police officers must deal with people from all walks of life who are involved in criminal and noncriminal activities and must use broad discretion in a wide variety of situations with little supervision. They deal with crimes already committed, with people who are hurt, confused, angry, and upset; yet the officers must remain neutral, calm, and objective. They may appear indifferent or unsympathetic, but, much like physicians, they cannot become personally involved and still do a professional job. They must remain detached and objective.

The image resulting from the nature of police work might easily be compared to the image of a football referee. It is readily accepted that referees are necessary to the game. Without them chaos would reign. Despite their criticality, however, their image is frequently negative. No matter what call they make, a great many people are unhappy with them. They are usually perceived as being on the opponent's side. Defeats are frequently blamed on referees; however, seldom is a referee given credit for a team's victory. It is often a thankless, sometimes dangerous job. Fans have thrown pop bottles at and attempted to physically assault referees. Likewise, abusive names are frequently hurled at the referee. It often makes one wonder what type of individual could continue to work under such pressures.

Unique Relationship to the System   Another factor influencing the police image is the officers' relationship to the law. Although police officers frequently initiate the criminal justice system by investigating and apprehending criminals, they often feel like outsiders in the judicial system. They may feel their investigation and apprehension of criminals is hampered by legal restrictions and that suspects have more rights than victims.

Although police officers are frequently blamed for rising crime rates, their participation in the legal system is often minimized. They may be made to feel as if they were on trial during the court proceedings as the defense attorney cross-examines them. They are seldom included in any plea bargaining. And frequently defendants are found not guilty because of loopholes or legal technicalities. When a confessed robber is acquitted on a technicality or a known rapist is not brought to trial by the prosecutor, police officers may take this as a personal affront, as a criticism of their investigative expertise. In addition, citizens of the community may also blame the police officers for the unsuccessful prosecution of the suspect. Further, legal technicalities may even result in the police officer being sued for false arrest.

Role Conflict   The role conflict faced by many police officers has a direct influence on the image projected. Many police officers feel they are law enforcement officers, not social workers. They did not create nor can they control the social problems that exist and that prompt numerous service calls. When they do respond to such calls, their help is often perceived as interference; they may be berated or even assaulted.

According to Sparrow et al. (1990, p. 50):

> The police, we recognize, embrace an image of themselves as impartial professional crime fighters. This image lies at the heart of the police value system; indeed, it is its foundation stone. This image is what police chiefs talk of at award dinners and budget time; it is what police officers talk of with their "civilian" friends. It is the face policing wishes to present to the public. It is real, or at least honest.

Sparrow et al. (p. 51) list six "truths that officers feel in their bones":

- We are the only crime fighters. Crimefighting is what the public wants from us. Other agencies, public or private, only play at it.
- No one else understands the real nature of police work. That is, no one outside the police service—academics, politicians, and lawyers in particular—can comprehend what we have to do. The public is generally naive about police work.
- Loyalty to colleagues counts above everything else. We have to stick together. Everyone else—including the public, politicians, and especially senior officers—seems to be out to make our job difficult.
- It is impossible to win the war against crime without bending the rules. We are hopelessly shackled by unrealistic constraints foisted on us by civil liberties groups, thanks to the fickleness of politicians.

- Members of the public are basically unsupportive and unreasonably demanding. They all seem to think they know our job better than we do. They only want us when they need something done.
- Patrol work is the pits. The detective branch and other specialities are relatively glorious, because they tackle serious crime. Patrol work is only for those who aren't smart enough to get out of it.

For those officers who adhere to the preceding beliefs, unethical behavior might be expected. As noted by Sparrow et al. (p. 52): "[These beliefs] encourage and legitimize insensitive, unproductive, and even illegal behavior." In conjunction with the broad discretion of police officers, such beliefs can result in corruption.

POLICE ETHICS AND CORRUPTION

Ethics involves moral behavior, doing what is considered right and just. Lack of ethics may result in corruption. Pollock-Byrne (1989, p. 125) notes: "Police ethics involve a broad spectrum of behavior that includes not only corruption, but also malpractice, mistreatment of offenders, racial discrimination, illegal searching and seizures, suspect's constitutional rights violations, perjury, evidence planting, and other misconduct committed under the authority of law enforcement."

According to Walker (1980, p. 19): "Corruption is the oldest and most persistent problem in American policing. The history of law enforcement agencies is the story of repeated scandals over corrupt practices." Numerous definitions have been set forth for police corruption. One very plausible definition has been stated by Goldstein (1975, p. 3): "Police corruption consists of acts involving the misuse of authority by a police officer in a manner designed to produce personal gain for himself or for others."

The two key elements in the definition are: (1) the misuse of authority and (2) personal gain. Both elements must be present. The officer must be acting as a police officer, for example, using the authority of the badge to gain entrance to a building and then committing a theft. The act must also result in personal gain. Illegal acts of police officers such as excessive use of force or an illegal search do not constitute police corruption because they do not result in personal gain.

Walker (1983, p. 174) notes: "Police corruption is a problem of enormous magnitude." He contends that to deal with the problem effectively, it is necessary to understand the types of corruption that exist, why it exists, and how it might be controlled.

Police **corruption** is the misuse of authority by an officer for personal gain. It includes accepting gratuities and bribes as well as committing theft or burglary. The most common and extensive type of corruption is accepting small gratuities or tips.

Walker notes that a great difference exists between the officer who accepts a free meal and one who accepts, perhaps even encourages, a cash payment. In fact, many cities do not consider gratuities as corruption. A restaurant owner may sincerely want to do something extra for those who "serve and protect" and may also feel that police cars parked in the lot may deter crime in the area.

Although discounts and free service are usually not regarded as important, cash payments to police officers are quite another matter. The Knapp Commission (1973, p. 4) distinguished between "grass eaters" and "meat eaters," with the grass eaters being officers who passively accepted gratuities offered to them, in contrast to meat eaters who aggressively solicited payments.

Even more serious are outright bribes to avoid arrest or a fine. The most common instance of this occurs in traffic violations, particularly speeding. All too often a person who has been stopped for speeding may include a ten or twenty dollar bill along with the requested driver's license and end up with a warning rather than a ticket. In some instances, officers may actually suggest that a bribe be made, perhaps in the form of buying tickets to a police benefit.

Another form of extremely serious police corruption is appropriating material or money that comes into their possession in the line of duty, for example, detectives dividing their "scores" of narcotics and cash, sometimes amounting to thousands of dollars. Or property may be taken from the property room and then mysteriously "disappear."

Myron (1992, p. 27) quotes the statement made by a judge as he sentenced a police chief who pleaded guilty to being a drug addict:

> You were the chief of police of this community and it was you that the public trusted and it was you that everyone looked up to in this town to fight the problem that has been the scourge of this community. But you got caught up. . . . Let me tell you, there are police officers in this community and every community who [are] making maybe $30–40,000 a year and their kids need braces and they walk into a room and there's $100,000 on the table and there's a kilo of drugs on the table, and it's got to be awfully tempting, but they don't do it.

Although discretion is a "given" of law enforcement, there are, however, according to Myron (1992, p. 26), some absolutes:

> There can be no debate about the brutal violation of human and civil rights. . . .
>
> There can be no debate when it comes to planting evidence, obtaining retroactive search warrants or forcing people to sign disclaimers. . . .
>
> There can be no debate about lying on reports. . . .
>
> No criminal is so important that we must violate the Constitution or statutory law to make an immediate arrest.

At the beginning of this chapter you were introduced to the Law Enforcement Code of Ethics, a very idealistic code, but often extremely difficult to follow. The following listing of police values illustrates what is often encountered in real life (Sherman 1982):

1. **Discretion A:** Decisions about whether to enforce the law, in any but the most serious cases, should be guided by both what the law says and who the suspect is. Attitude, demeanor, cooperativeness, and even race, age and social class are all important considerations in deciding how to treat people generally, and whether or not to arrest suspects in particular.
2. **Discretion B:** Disrespect for police authority is a serious offense that should always be punished with an arrest or the use of force. The "offense" known as "contempt of cop" or P.O.P.O. (pissing off a police officer) cannot be ignored. Even when the party has committed no violation of the law, a police officer should find a safe way to impose punishment, including an arrest on fake charges.
3. **Force:** Police officers should never hesitate to use physical or deadly force against people who "deserve it," or where it can be an effective way of solving a crime. Only the potential punishments by superior officers, civil litigation, citizen complaints, and so forth should limit the use of force when the situation calls for it. When you can get away with it, use all the force that society should use on people like that—force and punishment which bleeding-heart judges are too soft to impose.

4. **Due Process:** Due process is only a means of protecting criminals at the expense of the law abiding and should be ignored whenever it is safe to do so. Illegal searches and wiretaps, interrogation without advising suspects of their Miranda rights, and if need be (as in the much admired movie, Dirty Harry), even physical pain to coerce a confession are all acceptable methods for accomplishing the goal the public wants the police to accomplish: fighting crime. The rules against doing those things merely handcuff the police, making it difficult for them to do their job.

5. **Truth:** Lying and deception are an essential part of the police job, and even perjury should be used if it is necessary to protect yourself or get a conviction on a "bad guy." Violations of due process cannot be admitted to prosecutors or in court, so perjury (in the serious 5 percent of cases that ever go to trial) is necessary and therefore proper. Lying to drug pushers about wanting to buy drugs, to prostitutes about wanting to buy sex, or to congressmen about wanting to buy influence is the only way, and therefore a proper way, to investigate these crimes without victims. Deceiving muggers into thinking you are an easy mark and deceiving burglars into thinking you are a fence are proper because there are not many other ways of catching predatory criminals in the act.

6. **Time:** You cannot go fast enough to chase a car thief or traffic violator, nor slow enough to get to a "garbage" call; and when there are no calls for service, your time is your own. Hot pursuits are necessary because anyone who tries to escape from the police is challenging police authority, no matter how trivial the initial offense. But calls to nonserious or social-work problems like domestic disputes or kids making noise are unimportant, so you can stop to get coffee on the way or even stop at the cleaner's if you like. And when there are no calls, you can sleep, visit friends, study, or do anything else you can get away with, especially on the midnight shift, when you can get away with a lot.

7. **Rewards:** Police do very dangerous work for low wages, so it is proper to take any extra rewards the public want to give them, like free meals, Christmas gifts, or even regular monthly payments (in some cities) for special treatment. The general rule is: take any reward that doesn't change what you would do anyway, such as eating a meal, but don't take money that would affect your job, like not giving traffic tickets. In many cities, however, especially in the recent past, the rule has been to take even those rewards that do affect your decisions, as long as they are related only to minor offenses—traffic, gambling, prostitution, but not murder.

8. **Loyalty:** The paramount duty is to protect your fellow officers at all costs, as they would protect you, even though you may have to risk your own career or your own life to do it. If your colleagues make a mistake, take a bribe, seriously hurt somebody illegally, or get into other kinds of trouble, you should do everything you can to protect them in the ensuing investigation. If your colleagues are routinely breaking rules, you should never tell supervisors, reporters, or outside investigators about it. If you don't like it, quit—or get transferred to the police academy. But never, ever, blow the whistle.

A conflict between the code of police ethics and the values often found within the police culture is evident. As noted by Pollock-Byrne (1989, p. 85):

Police routinely deal with the seamier side of society—not only drug addicts and muggers, but middle-class people who are involved in dishonesty and corruption. The constant displays of lying, hiding, cheating, and theft create cynicism and threaten even the strongest code of ethics, especially when these behaviors are carried out by judges, prosecutors, superiors, and politicians. The following are some rationales that might easily be used by police to justify behavior (Murphy & Moran, 1981, p. 3).

The public thinks every cop is a crook—so why try to be honest?

The money is out there—if I don't take it, someone else will.

I'm only taking what's rightfully mine; if the city paid me a decent wage, I wouldn't have to get it on my own.

I can use it—it's for a good cause—my son needs an operation, or dental work, or tuition for medical school, or a new bicycle. Given constant exposure to others' misdeeds, peer pressure to conform, and previously vague or nonexistent ideas about right and wrong, the question is not why some officers engage in corrupt practices but rather why more don't.

The seriousness of the problem cannot be ignored. According to Walker (1983, p. 187): "Corruption undermines the basic law enforcement function of the police. Whether the corrupt act involves a small bribe to ignore a traffic violation or a sizable and regular payoff to protect a gambling operation, illegal activity is being tolerated." And this communicates the message that criminal activity is acceptable behavior, undermining the basic mission of the police and damaging the reputation of the entire police department.

The effects of corruption within a department are illustrated in the following excerpts from the Philadelphia Police Department's white paper, responding to corruption problems within the department (Myron 1992, p. 28):

It is not enough that our personal integrity remain untarnished. Since our own reputations are tied so closely to the conduct of our brother and sister officers, we must ensure that those who work with us remain free from corruption. . . .

Each time an officer engages in an unethical or corrupt act, every officer in the department—in addition to our families—suffer injury whether that action is brought to official attention or not. Every improper, thoughtless, or unprofessional action taken by a Philadelphia police officer erodes the overall reputation and veracity of all police officers as held by the general public, judges, lawyers, and other agencies engaged in law enforcement—weakening our image, destroying their confidence in us and making our mission much more difficult.

According to Guthery (1990, p. 91), a recent Gallop poll finds that only 49 percent of Americans rate police officers' honesty and ethical standards in the high or very high category. He notes: "Funeral directors, reporters, and *even* lawyers, all receive higher average scores than we do." And yet, as noted by Delattre (1989, pp. 14–15): "The mission of policing can safely be entrusted only to those who grasp what is morally important and who respect integrity. Without this kind of personal character in police, no set of codes or rules or laws can safeguard that mission from the ravages of police misconduct."

Mangan (1992, p. 47) notes: "For law enforcement, more than any other branch of public service, integrity, ethics and credibility are the 'coin of the realm.' Law enforcement agencies can have the latest in technology—from high-speed satellite communications to mobile computer systems to the best in DNA-genetic fingerprint investigative resources—but if our citizens/clients do not trust us and believe in us, they will not talk to us and we will be out of business." He (p. 49) stresses:

Great strides have been made in terms of public trust since the problem days of the 1960s. Surveys during the recent decade show that law enforcement currently enjoys more public confidence and trust than at any other time in its history. This is a strength of incredible value to us, and yet one that is extremely fragile. We must work together—individually and collectively—to ensure that we do not lose this "bank account" of credibility that has been built up so painstakingly by those who have preceded us.

Unfortunately, the arrest and beating of Rodney King in March of 1991 and the May 1992 acquittal, on criminal charges, of all but one of the police officers involved has done tremendous damage to this trust. Individual officers and departments have much rebuilding to do, especially in areas with large minority populations.

Developing Personal Ethics

Blanchard and Peale (1988) have a bestselling book on the power of ethical management that provides direction for developing personal ethics as well. At the heart of their philosophy is the simple statement (p. 9): "There is no right way to do a wrong thing." They suggest (p. 20) three questions that can serve as personal "ethics checks."

The ethics-check questions are:

1. It is legal?

2. Is it balanced?

3. How will it make me feel about myself?

Obviously, those in the criminal justice field should always act legally and should follow established department policies and procedures. The question regarding balance asks if the decision or action is fair to everyone involved, both short- and long-term. Does it create a win-win situation? The third question includes such questions as: "Will it make me proud? Would I feel good if my decision was published in the newspaper? Would I feel good if my family knew about it?"

Blanchard and Peale (p. 79) also list five principles of ethical power for individuals:

1. *Purpose:* I see myself as being an ethically sound person. I let my conscience be my guide. No matter what happens, I am always able to face the mirror, look myself straight in the eye, and feel good about myself.
2. *Pride:* I feel good about myself. I don't need the acceptance of other people to feel important. A balanced self-esteem keeps my ego and my desire to be accepted from influencing my decisions.
3. *Patience:* I believe that things will eventually work out well. I don't need everything to happen right now. I am at peace with what comes my way.
4. *Persistence:* I stick to my purpose, especially when it seems inconvenient to do so. My behavior is consistent with my intentions. As Churchill said, "Never! Never! Never! Never give up!"
5. *Perspective:* I take time to enter each day quietly in a mood of reflection. This helps me to get myself focused and allows me to listen to my inner self and to see things more clearly.

Robinette (1991, p. 44) suggests that: "The best source of a moral perspective from which to derive principles of police behavior in a pluralistic and free society lies in the 'common promise' police make when they enter into service." She notes:

The common promise that all police officers make with their oath of office announces to the community that they are engaged in the bargain as agents, and from this bargain are derived five clear principles of fair conduct: fair access for all members of the public, respect for the public trust, a balance between enforcement efforts and the maintenance of order and security, coordination and cooperation among all members of the criminal justice system and objectivity in all dealings with the public.

An approach to enhance "morality" in police decision-making is suggested by Fair and Pilcher (1991, p. 25). They suggest that the following three values be considered in major decisions:

Rights—this includes both the human rights that we all have and also any special rights that we have because of some special relationship, such as being the recipient of a promise.

Excuses—one place to look for a good excuse is how the people involved in the decision will be affected—not just in the short term, but after they have had time to think. The happier they are, the easier it will be to explain the action; the more miserable and unhappy they are, the harder it will be to justify what was done.

Human flourishing—not just how people feel should be considered, but also how the decision will affect values needed for human beings to flourish as human beings.

With these values in mind, they suggest the following five-step process to ethical problem solving (pp. 25–27):

1. Recognizing that a problem exists—the first, absolutely essential step and one that can be particularly difficult in ethics.
2. Problem identification—thinking and data gathering to understand just exactly what the problem is.
3. Creating alternatives—part of making the problem more specific is to create an array of alternative responses.
4. Evaluating the alternatives.
5. Public justifiability of each of the alternatives—address the issue of whether the alternatives are the *kinds* of actions that a person could defend publicly.

The International Association of Chiefs of Police have also developed a "Police Code of Conduct" which goes into greater detail than their Code of Ethics. It includes the primary responsibilities of a police officer, how the duties are to be performed, use of discretion, use of force, confidentiality, integrity, cooperation with other police officers and agencies, personal-professional capabilities, and even private life. (See Figure 7–6.)

Building an Ethical Department

As noted by Mangan (1992, p. 47): "Well before the release of the now-famous videotape of the Rodney King beating in Los Angeles, the law enforcement profession had begun developing a more positive, creative approach to the issues of organization, professional, and personal ethics."

Brown (1991, p. 8) stresses that: "Ethical standards should be in the form of clear, unambiguous, written policies, disseminated to all personnel. Supervision and training are essential to ensure that the department's ethical principles are positively reinforced."

As noted by Braunstein and Tyre (1992, p. 30): "Ethically sound police officers are most likely to be found in an atmosphere that clearly gives high priority to ethical behavior and integrates ethics into every part of the department. . . . Ethical behavior must be seen as a primary goal of the administration and the department. If we are to expect officers to *behave* ethically, we must *treat* them—and the citizens they serve—ethically." They suggest that building an ethical police department can be broken into four categories: pre-hire, initial training, field officer training, and in-service training.

All law enforcement officers must be fully aware of the ethical responsibilities of their position and must strive constantly to live up to the highest possible standards of professional policing.

The International Association of Chiefs of Police believes it important that police officers have clear advice and counsel available to assist them in performing their duties consistent with these standards, and has adopted the following ethical mandates as guidelines to meet these ends.

Primary Responsibilities of a Police Officer

A police officer acts as an official representative of government who is required and trusted to work within the law. The officer's powers and duties are conferred by statute. The fundamental duties of a police officer include serving the community, safeguarding lives and property, protecting the innocent, keeping the peace and ensuring the rights of all to liberty, equality and justice.

Performance of the Duties of a Police Officer

A police officer shall perform all duties impartially, without favor or affection or ill will and without regard to status, sex, race, religion, political belief or aspiration. All citizens will be treated equally with courtesy, consideration and dignity.

Officers will never allow personal feelings, animosities or friendships to influence official conduct. Laws will be enforced appropriately and courteously and, in carrying out their responsibilities, officers will strive to obtain maximum cooperation from the public. They will conduct themselves in appearance and deportment in such a manner as to inspire confidence and respect for the position of public trust they hold.

Discretion

A police officer will use responsibly the discretion vested in his position and exercise it within the law. The principle of reasonableness will guide the officer's determinations, and the officer will consider all surrounding circumstances in determining whether any legal action shall be taken.

Consistent and wise use of discretion, based on professional policing competence, will do much to preserve good relationships and retain the confidence of the public. There can be difficulty in choosing between conflicting courses of action. It is important to remember that a timely word of advice rather than arrest— which may be correct in appropriate circumstances— can be a more effective means of achieving a desired end.

Use of Force

A police officer will never employ unnecessary force or violence and will use only such force in the discharge of duty as is reasonable in all circumstances.

The use of force should be used only with the greatest restraint and only after discussion, negotiation and persuasion have been found to be inappropriate or inef- fective. While the use of force is occasionally unavoidable, every police officer will refrain from unnecessary infliction of pain or suffering and will never engage in cruel, degrading or inhuman treatment of any person.

Confidentiality

Whatever a police officer sees, hears or learns of that is of a confidential nature will be kept secret unless the performance of duty or legal provision requires otherwise.

Members of the public have a right to security and privacy, and information obtained about them must not be improperly divulged.

Integrity

A police officer will not engage in acts of corruption or bribery, nor will an officer condone such acts by other police officers.

The public demands that the integrity of police officers be above reproach. Police officers must, therefore, avoid any conduct that might compromise integrity and thus undercut the public confidence in a law enforcement agency. Officers will refuse to accept any gifts, presents, subscriptions, favors, gratuities or promises that could be interpreted as seeking to cause the officer to refrain from performing official responsibilities honestly and within the law. Police officers must not receive private or special advantage from their official status. Respect from the public cannot be bought; it can only be earned and cultivated.

Cooperation with Other Police Officers and Agencies

Police officers will cooperate with all legally authorized agencies and their representatives in the pursuit of justice.

An officer or agency may be one among many organizations that may provide law enforcement services to a jurisdiction. It is imperative that a police officer assist colleagues fully and completely with respect and consideration at all times.

Personal-Professional Capabilities

Police officers will be responsible for their own standard of professional-performance and will take every reasonable opportunity to enhance and improve their level of knowledge and competence.

Through study and experience, a police officer can acquire the high level of knowledge and competence that is essential for the efficient and effective performance of duty. The acquisition of knowledge is a never-ending process of personal and professional development that should be pursued constantly.

Private Life

Police officers will behave in a manner that does not bring discredit to their agencies or themselves.

A police officer's character and conduct while off duty must always be exemplary, thus maintaining a position of respect in the community in which he or she lives and serves. The officer's personal behavior must be beyond reproach.

Figure 7–6   Police Code of Conduct

Source: Reprinted by permission of the International Association of Chiefs of Police.

The International Association of Chiefs of Police and the U.S. Department of Justice's Bureau of Justice Assistance (1991, pp. 27–41) note that in recent years, the United States has experienced an increasing number of scandals due to the sizeable temptations, the relaxation of standards in selecting police officers, and the decay of ethical standards throughout our society. They suggest that when examining police integrity and reducing corruption, three principal areas must be considered: the applicant selection process, the consistent reinforcement of values and standards among police officers, and an effective anti-corruption posture of checks and balances to reduce the opportunities and temptations for corruption.

Three areas to enhance police integrity and reduce corruption are:

- The applicant selection process.
- Consistent reinforcement of values.
- Anti-corruption posture of checks and balances.

The Applicant Selection Process   If the intent of a law enforcement agency is truly one of hiring the most qualified personnel, the applicant selection process is critical. All applicants must be screened, not for affirmative action or minority status, but for meaningful qualifications. This can be done through a pertinent written examination, a fair and impartial oral interview, and a challenging physical fitness evaluation. This must be followed by a recognized psychological exam and a very thorough and extensive background investigation. This may include a polygraph screening if anything of concern surfaces. Prior behavior, arrest records, drug use, and integrity must be aggressively researched.

Consistent Reinforcement of Values   Police officers hold a very powerful position in this country. Acceptable conduct should be the subject of regular, vigorous review for all police personnel of all ranks, sworn and civilian. Department personnel should regularly discuss and analyze the standards of conduct to strengthen their understanding of and commitment to such principles. Management's most important task is to create an environment in which every police officer can perform with integrity and professionalism. Such an environment can be achieved only through candid communication and by exemplary role models by those in management positions.

Anti-Corruption Posture of Checks and Balances   Management can reinforce integrity, detect corruption, and limit the opportunity for wrongdoing. The chief of police sets the level of integrity for the entire department. Supervisors must provide leadership and guidance when needed. This may mean that instead of spending the majority of their time on administrative tasks, first-line supervisors should spend more time in the field auditing their officers' activities. Every agency should have an internal affairs unit, and the commanding officer of that unit should report directly to the chief. All supervisors and staff members in the department must take responsibility for discipline. Discipline must be fair, impartial, instructive, and meant to promote personal and professional growth.

Blanchard and Peale (1988, p. 128) set forth the following principles of ethical power for organizations:

Purpose: The mission of our organization is communicated from the top. Our organization is guided by the values, hopes, and a vision that helps us to determine what is acceptable and unacceptable behavior.

Pride: We feel proud of ourselves and of our organization. We know that when we feel this way, we can resist temptations to behave unethically.

Patience: We believe that holding to our ethical values will lead us to success in the long term. This involves maintaining a balance between obtaining results and caring how we achieve these results.

Persistence: We have a commitment to live by ethical principles. We make sure our actions are consistent with our purpose.

Perspective: Our managers and employees take time to pause and reflect, take stock of where we are, evaluate where we are going and determine how we are going to get there.

The importance of integrity and ethical behavior is an underlying theme in all of police work and, indeed, in the entire field of criminal justice.

Police officers, even those assigned to patrol duties in a large city, are confronted with few serious crimes in the course of a single tour of duty. They tend to view such involvement, particularly if there is some degree of danger, as constituting "real" police work. It is apparent, however, that they spend considerably more time keeping order, settling disputes, finding missing children, and helping with medical emergencies than they do responding to criminal conduct that is serious enough to call for arrest, prosecution, and conviction.

This does not mean that serious crime is unimportant to police officers. Quite the contrary is true. But it does mean that they perform a wide range of other functions that are of a highly complex nature and often involve difficult social, behavioral, and political problems rather than major crimes.

Today's law enforcement officers need a broad background as well as broadening experiences to meet the complex challenges of a modern, changing, multiethnic, and multiracial society. On that point there is near-unanimous agreement.

SUMMARY

The people largely determine the role of the police and give them their authority to fulfill this role. Their support is vital if any law enforcement effort is to succeed.

Police officers must *enforce laws,* federal, state, and municipal, to protect the health and welfare of the community. For example, they enforce highway laws to make the streets safe for driving; they arrest people who unlawfully sell narcotics or who otherwise break the law.

They *preserve the peace* in a professional manner by patrolling troubled areas, intervening in domestic disturbances, and advising people in community disputes.

They attempt to *prevent crime* by being highly visible in the community, by educating the public about crime and crime prevention, and by involving them in programs such as operation identification.

They *protect civil rights and civil liberties* by living and enforcing the principles contained in the Bill of Rights.

They also *provide necessary services* such as rendering first aid in medical emergencies, and assisting in community programs.

These roles must be carried out skillfully and professionally, and require numerous mental, intellectual, physical, and personal proficiencies as well as discretion.

Although numerous federal and state agencies are directly involved in law enforcement, the ultimate responsibility is usually at the local level. It is here that the goals of law enforcement are initiated, based on what the citizens of the individual community perceive to be their most pressing needs.

Police officers work within the basic organizational structure of their department, which, most often, is divided into two sections: field services and administrative services. Tasks and personnel to accomplish them are assigned to one of these two sections.

Administrative services provide support for field services, including communications and records, recruitment and training, and special facilities and services. Most current information is conveyed to police officers at roll call, by radio or, more recently, by computers. Radio, for now, is still the primary method of transmitting and seeking information between headquarters and units in the field.

In addition to direct communication, police officers also rely upon information contained in various records depositories. The NCIC provides all police agencies in the country access to the computerized files of the FBI. Also, centralization of local police agencies' records allows the various line functions to be coordinated. Among the types of records the police officer may use are administrative, arrest, identification, and complaint records.

Access to information is not always unlimited, however. A data privacy act regulates the use of confidential and private information on individuals in the records, files, and processes of a state and its political subdivisions.

Within the field services provided in a police department are patrol, traffic, community services, and investigation . Sometimes these are specialized departments; sometimes the services are provided by a single department. In addition, many police departments, particularly the larger departments, have specialized officers such as vice officers and juvenile officers.

Patrol's continuous, highly visible service includes responding to calls for assistance and attempting to prevent crime. Traffic officers provide services such as providing direction to motorists and investigating motor vehicle accidents, and investigators gather information at crime scenes. In addition, specialized officers may include evidence technicians, vice officers, and juvenile officers.

With the varying roles and responsibilities police officers have, it is not surprising that distinct styles of policing have developed. Four major typologies have been identified: the enforcer, the crime fighter/zealot, the social service agent, and the watchman.

Also because of these varying roles and responsibilities, police agencies and their officers exercise a great deal of discretion, that is, they have the freedom to make choices as to whether or not to act—which often means to arrest or not.

Discretion plays a large role in the image created by police officers as well as their susceptibility to corruption. The police image results from the media portrayal and from everyday contacts between individual police officers and citizens. Police corruption is the misuse of authority by an officer for personal gain. It includes accepting gratuities and bribes as well as committing theft or burglary. The most common and extensive type of corruption is accepting small gratuities or tips. Three ethics-check questions are (1) Is it legal? (2) Is it balanced? and (3) How will it make me feel about myself? Three areas to enhance police integrity and reduce corruption are (1) the applicant selection process, (2) consistent reinforcement of values, and (3) anti-corruption posture of checks and balances.

DISCUSSION QUESTIONS

1. How has communication between the officer in the field and headquarters changed in the last hundred years?

2. How have the roles of police officers changed over time?

3. What services should police officers provide? Which are provided in your community?

4. What style of policing will you probably lean toward? Why?

5. Have you witnessed firsthand police discretion? Explain.

6. Do you feel police agencies and officers have too little, too much, or just the right amount of discretion?

7. What is *your* image of the police? What do you believe your community thinks of the police?

8. Have you seen examples of unethical behavior in police work? Of actual corruption?

9. What do you see as the greatest challenge of police officers in the 1990s?

10. How damaging to the police image and trust level were the jury verdict in the Rodney King case and the subsequent rioting? Is it fair that one part of the criminal justice system can so adversely affect the other parts?

TERMS

administrative services, corruption, discretion, ethics, field services, image, police authority, roll call, typologies.

REFERENCES

Arnold, W. R. and Brungardt, T. M. *Juvenile Misconduct and Delinquency.* Boston: Houghton Mifflin Co., 1983.

Blanchard, K. and Peale, N. V. *The Power of Ethical Management.* New York: Fawcett Crest, 1988.

Braunstein, S. and Tyre, M. "Building a More Ethical Police Department." *The Police Chief* (January 1992): 30–35.

Brown, L. P. "Policing in the '90s: Responding to a Changing Environment." *The Police Chief* (March 1991): 20–23.

Brown, L. P. "Values and Ethical Standards Must Flow from the Chief." *The Police Chief* (January 1991): 8.

Cole, G. F. *The American System of Criminal Justice.* 3d ed. Belmont, Calif.: Brooks/Cole Publishing Co., 1983.

Delattre, E. J. *Character and Cops. Ethics in Policing.* Washington, D.C.: American Enterprise Institute for Public Policy Research, 1989.

Fair, F. K. and Pilcher, W. D. "Morality on the Line: The Role of Ethics in Police Decision-Making." *American Journal of Police.* 10, no. 2 (1991): 23–38.

Federal Bureau of Investigation. *National Crime Information Center Operating Manual.* Washington, D.C.: Federal Bureau of Investigation, 1985.

Goldstein, H. *Police Corruption: A Perspective on its Nature and Control.* Washington, D.C.: Police Foundation, 1975.

Greene, J. R. and Klockars, C. B. "What Police Do." 273–332. In *Thinking About Police: Contemporary Readings.* 2d ed., edited by C. B. Klockars and S. D. Mastrofski. New York: McGraw-Hill, 1991.

Guthery, T. "The Percentages: Gallup Poll Rates Honesty and Ethical Standards of Police." *Law and Order* (May 1990): 91.

Hageman, M. J. *Police-Community Relations.* Beverly Hills, Calif.: Sage Publications, 1985.

International Association of Chiefs of Police. "IACP NET Facilitates Information Exchange for Members." *Police Chief* (December 1991): 23.

International Association of Chiefs of Police and the U.S. Department of Justice's Bureau of Justice Assistance. "Police Ethics: Building Integrity and Reducing Drug Corruption." *The Police Chief* (January 1991): 27–41.

James, H. *Crisis in the Courts.* New York: David McKay Company, 1968. (Copyright by the Christian Science Publishing Society.) Based on a series of weekly articles in *The Christian Science Monitor* (April to July, 1967).

Klockars, C. B. "The Rhetoric of Community Policing." In *Community Policing: Rhetoric or Reality,* edited by J. R. Greene and S. D. Mastrofski. New York: Praeger Publishers, 1991.

Klockars, C. B. *Thinking About Police: Contemporary Readings.* New York: McGraw-Hill, 1983.

Law Enforcement Code of Ethics. *The Police Chief* (January 1992): 15.

Mangan, T. J. "Organizational Integrity Critical to Law Enforcement Success." *The Police Chief* (March 1992): 47–49.

Matthews, K. "Mobile Data Terminals." *Minnesota Trooper* (May 1992): 5–8.

Myron, P. "Crooks or Cops: We Can't Be Both." *The Police Chief* (January 1992): 23–28.

National Advisory Commission on Criminal Justice Standards and Goals. *The Police.* Washington, D.C.: U.S. Government Printing Office (LEAA Grant Number 72–DF–99–0002, and NI 72–0200) 1973.

Nees, H. "Policing 2001." *Law and Order* (January 1990): 257–264.

Police Code of Conduct. *The Police Chief* (January 1992): 17.

Pollock–Byrne, J. M. *Ethics in Crime and Justice: Dilemmas and Decisions.* Pacific Grove, Calif.: Brooks/Cole Publishing Company, 1989.

Pratt, C. E. "Police Discretion." *Law and Order* (March 1992): 99–100.

Pursley, R. D. *Introduction to Criminal Justice.* 4th ed. New York: Macmillan, 1987.

Remsberg, C. *The Tactical Edge: Surviving High-Risk Patrol.* Northbrook, Ill.: Calibre Press, 1986.

Robinette, H. M. "Police Ethics: Leadership and Ethics Training for Police Administrators." *The Police Chief* (January 1991): 42–47.

Rubin, R. "Computer Trends in Law Enforcement." *The Police Chief* (April 1991): 20–24.

Sandona, R. "Arcadia Police Find a Cost-Effective Way to Computerize Records Management System." *Law and Order* (August 1989): 71–74.

Saunders, C. B., Jr. *Upgrading the American Police.* Washington, D.C.: The Brookings Institution, 1970.

Senna, J. J. and Siegel, L. J. *Introduction to Criminal Justice.* 5th ed. St. Paul, Minn.: West Publishing Company, 1990.

Sharp, A. G. "Computers Are a Cop's Best Friend." *Law and Order,* (November 1991): 41–45.

Sherman, L. "Learning Police Ethics." *Criminal Justice Ethics* 1, no. 1 (1982): 10–19.

Sparrow, M. K.; Moore, M. H.; and Kennedy, D. M. *Beyond 911, A New Era for Policing.* New York: Basic Books, 1990.

Thibault, E. A.; Lynch, L. M.; and McBride, R. B. *Proactive Police Management.* 2d ed. Englewood Cliffs, N.J.: Prentice Hall, 1990.

Vinson, C. "Data-by-Radio System Delivers Safer Traffic Stops." *Law and Order* (February 1992): 26–28.

Walker, S. *The Police in America: An Introduction.* New York: McGraw-Hill, 1983.

Walker, S. *Popular Justice.* New York: Oxford University Press, 1980.

Webster, J. A. "Police Task and Time Study." *Journal of Criminal Law, Criminology, and Police Science,* 61 (no date).

Wilson, J. Q. *Varieties of Police Behavior.* Cambridge, Mass.: Harvard University Press, 1968.

CHAPTER 8

Patrol and Traffic: Law Enforcement in Our Mobile Society

The patrol officer is the first interpreter of the law and in effect performs a quasi-judicial function. He makes the first attempt to match the reality of human conflict with the law; he determines whether to take no action, to advise, to warn, or to arrest; he determines whether he must apply physical force, perhaps sufficient to cause death. It is he who must discern the fine distinction between a civil and a criminal conflict, between merely unorthodox behavior and a crime, between a legitimate dissent and disturbance of the peace, between the truth and a lie. As the interpreter of the law, he recognizes that a decision to arrest is only the first step in the determination of guilt or innocence. He is guided by, and guardian of, the Constitution.

—**Task Force on the Police**

Do You Know

What the primary responsibilities of patrol are?

What five specific areas of responsibility are assigned to patrol?

How patrol has traditionally functioned? What changes are occurring in some departments?

What methods of patrol may be used?

What type of shift and beat staffing often lessens the effectiveness of preventive patrol?

What approaches have been tried to improve preventive patrol effectiveness?

How women on patrol perform compared with men?

What community policing is?

What the responsibilities of the traffic officer are?

What the primary goal of traffic law enforcement is?

What the most basic causes of motor vehicle accidents are?

How frequently alcohol is related to automobile accidents?

What implied consent laws are?

What specific tasks are performed by the police officer when responding to a traffic accident?

INTRODUCTION

Patrol is the most vital component of police work. All other units are supplemental to this basic unit. Patrol can contribute to each of the common goals of police departments, including preserving the peace, protecting civil rights and civil liberties, enforcing the law, preventing crime, and providing services.

Patrol is responsible for providing continuous police service and high-visibility law enforcement, thereby deterring crime.

In addition, patrol officers must understand the federal, state, and local laws they are sworn to uphold and use good judgment in enforcing them. The importance of the patrol function is emphasized by Hale (1981, p. 2):

In recent years, the police mission in contemporary society has become incredibly varied and complex, and law enforcement agencies are growing and evolving at a rapid pace. Patrol remains, however, the most important of all police functions. All other police services and activities exist for the exclusive purpose of supporting and enhancing the patrol effort. Patrol is the essence of the police function. Typically, the patrol force is the single largest element in the police organization, and the actions taken by patrol officers have a direct impact on citizen satisfaction and well-being and on the accomplishment of police goals and objectives.

Hale notes that the patrol function is the most visible form of police activity and that individual patrol officers are representatives of the entire police department. Their actions have "far-reaching consequences for the police agency, for the citizenry, and for the quality of justice in contemporary society."

According to Geller (1991, p. 59):

Patrol officers have remained "master generalists" and are still expected to handle competently a mind-boggling mix of calls. In the shorthand parlance of police dispatching and report writing, within a week's tour of duty a single officer might be dispatched to calls involving "lost and recovered property," "woman screaming," "assist an invalid," "deranged or disoriented person," "family fight," "missing person," "bar-room brawl," "crowd control," "shots fired," "abandoned car," "drug dealing in the school yard," "animal bite," "traffic accident," "prowler," "barking dog," "suspicious person," "speeding motorist," "wires down," "chemical spill," "loud noise," "terrorist threat," "intrusion alarm," and so forth. This crazy quilt constitutes the fabric of police work. . . .

Given the variety and importance of calls for service as well as the emphasis that television series and other police fiction put on violent crime, the layperson can be excused for thinking that patrol work is exciting. For most patrol offices, it is not. Violent crimes account for only about 1 percent of a municipal police department's dispatched workload. As for the rest, the grueling routine of answering call after call, taking report after report, and randomly driving the streets eventually become mind-numbing. . . .

In recent years, as our society has become more diverse and as many social controls have broken down, as information has exploded and technology has proliferated, the patrol function has become increasingly complex and critical to accomplishing the police department's mission. The majority of officers in a department are assigned to the patrol function, and the majority of the department's budget is usually spent here. In addition, as stressed by Geller (p. 59): "Patrol officers maintain closer contact with the public than any other section of the police department, and to a large extent the public's satisfaction with the police depends on how patrol officers handle these calls." To those departments instituting community policing, the patrol function is absolutely critical, as will be discussed later in this chapter.

Not only is patrol exceedingly important to the police function, it is also exceedingly challenging. According to Hale (1981, pp. 37–38):

> Police patrol is conducted in a world of contrasts, ranging from the skid row alleys of major cities to the quiet residential avenues of suburbia. ... In some settings they must be tough and uncompromising, while in others they can afford to be compassionate and relenting. They may be required to take a life one instant and help to bring another into the world the next. In some cases they are feared and mistrusted, while in others they are regarded in high esteem, ...
>
> Patrol officers often work alone and with little direct supervision.... While the good that they do goes unnoticed, their errors frequently do not.
>
> Patrol work can at times be challenging, exciting, emotionally exhausting, and quite satisfying. At other times it can be routine, monotonous, and boring. ... Patrol officers must learn to expect the unexpected; to respond calmly in the face of danger; to endure undeserved criticism; to show composure during times of crisis and hysteria; and to remain self-possessed when confronted with adversity and hostility.

Unfortunately in many departments, patrol officers not only have the position with the least prestige, but they also are the lowest paid, the least consulted, and the most taken for granted. Patrol officers strive to move "up."

DUTIES AND RESPONSIBILITIES OF PATROL OFFICERS

The two basic responsibilities of most police departments are to prevent criminal activity and to provide day-to-day police services to the community. The specific duties involved in fulfilling these responsibilities are varied and complex. The size of the department often dictates what functions are assigned to patrol.

Patrol officers may be responsible for:

- Preserving the peace.
- Protecting and serving the community.
- Enforcing the laws.
- Directing traffic.
- Investigating crimes.

As protectors, patrol officers promote and preserve order, respond to requests for services, and attempt to resolve conflicts between individuals and groups. Specific aspects of community service are covered in Chapter 9.

As law enforcers, the first duty of patrol officers is to protect constitutional guarantees (as described in Chapter 4); the second duty is to enforce federal, state, and local statutes. Patrol officers not only encourage voluntary compliance with the law but also seek to reduce the opportunity for crimes to be committed.

Patrol officers also serve important traffic control functions, described in detail later in this chapter, and important investigative functions, described in detail in Chapter 10.

Finally, patrol officers in any community are the most visible representatives of government, and although they are not supervisors in the organizational sense, they are responsible for the safety and direction of hundreds of people each day.

TYPES OF PATROL

Patrol is frequently categorized as being either general or specialized. Both general and specialized patrol seek to deter crime and apprehend criminals as well as to provide community satisfaction with the services provided by the police department. General patrol does so by providing rapid response to calls for service; specialized patrol does so by focusing its efforts on already identified problems. Whether general or specialized patrol is used depends on the nature of the problem and the tactics required to deal with it most effectively.

General Patrol

General patrol is also referred to as preventive patrol, random patrol, and routine patrol. Routine patrol, however, should not really be used as there is nothing "routine" about it. As Geller (p. 59) notes: "Every patrol officer knows that, in a split second the most inconsequential and routine activity can develop into a potentially hazardous attempt. Patrol work (at least as traditionally practiced) therefore consists of long periods of boredom punctuated by moments of terror."

The challenges of general patrol change constantly; the patrol officer may be pursuing an armed bank robber in the morning and rescuing a cat from a tree in the afternoon. It has been said that patrol consists of seven hours and fifty-nine minutes of boredom followed by one minute of sheer panic. As noted, patrol is the most basic unit of the police department, the primary means by which police departments fulfill their responsibility to the community.

Traditionally, patrol has been random, reactive, incident driven, and focused on rapid response.

These characteristics can be seen in the four main types of activities officers engage in during a typical patrol shift: random/preventive patrol, self-initiated activities, calls for service, and administrative duties.

Random/Preventive Patrol   Traditionally, patrol officers begin their shift on **random** patrol in hopes of detecting (intercepting) crimes in progress, deterring crime by their presence, or being in the area and consequently able to respond to crime-in-progress calls rapidly. Geller (p. 63) notes:

> The sight of continually roving patrol cars was intended to create an illusion of police omnipresence. It was assumed that the sight of patrol cars would heighten citizens' sense of security and that the cars' presence, like a "human scarecrow," would deter would-be offenders. This illusion of police omnipresence was a much-touted advantage when the patrol car was introduced.

As noted by the President's Commission on Law Enforcement and Administration of Justice (1967): "Preventive patrol, the continued scrutiny of the community by visible and mobile policemen, is universally thought of as the best method of controlling crime that is available to the police."

Preventive patrol is generally accomplished by uniformed officers moving at random through an assigned area. Since officers usually decide for themselves what they will do while on preventive patrol, this time is sometimes referred to as "noncommitted" time. It comprises between 30 and 40 percent of patrol time, but it is often broken into small segments due to interruptions by self-initiated activities, service calls, and administrative duties.

Often priorities for preventive patrol are identified and/or assigned during roll call. For example, patrol officers may be alerted to the presence of a known escaped criminal sighted in the area to watch for while on patrol.

According to Geller (1991, p. 62): "Random preventive patrol was found to be a high-cost, low-payoff strategy in terms of intercepting crimes in progress and deterring criminals and rapid response to calls had little effect on police ability to catch criminals." He notes that in recent studies conducted in Syracuse, San Diego, and Houston, patrol officers could expect to intercept fewer than 1 percent of street crimes. Geller suggests that the findings of research add credence to the popular saying: "Random patrol produces random results."

The serious challenge to random patrol began twenty years ago in the findings of the often-quoted Kansas City Experiment. Funded by a grant from the Police Foundation, the *Kansas City Preventive Patrol Experiment* was conducted in 1972 and is often referred to as the most comprehensive study of routine preventive patrol ever undertaken. The basic design divided fifteen beats in Kansas City into three different groups:

- Group 1 Reactive Beats—five beats in which no routine preventive patrol was used. Officers responded only to calls for service.
- Group 2 Control Beats—five beats maintained their normal level of routine preventive patrol.
- Group 3 Proactive Beats—five beats doubled or tripled the level of routine preventive patrol.

According to Kellings et al. (Klockars 1983, p. 160): "Given the large amount of data collected and the extremely diverse sources used, the overwhelming evidence is that decreasing or increasing routine preventive patrol within the range tested in this experiment had no effect on crime, citizen fear of crime, community attitudes toward the police on the delivery of police services, police response time or traffic accidents."

Klockars (p. 130) asserted that the results of the Kansas City Patrol Experiment indicated that "it makes about as much sense to have police patrol routinely in cars to fight crime as it does to have firemen patrol routinely in fire trucks to fight fire."

Although the Kansas City study found no significant differences in the incidence of crime resulting from varying the *level* of patrol, Goldstein (1977, p. 110) questioned whether the results would have been the same if they had varied the *form* of the patrol. Goldstein asked, "Specifically, would officers produce any different results if the time they devote to patrol was spent in more aggressive and intensive probing of individuals, places and circumstances?" Goldstein, credited with originating problem-oriented policing, suggested that patrol be **proactive** rather than **reactive,** directed rather than random.

Given the fact that street-wise criminals study police patrol methods and select targets that are not likely to be detected, and given the fact that many crimes are committed on the spur of the moment, particularly violent crimes such as murder and assault, and given the fact that much crime is committed inside buildings, out of the sight of patrols, Goldstein's question and sugges-

tions seem appropriate. His views were supported by Hale (1981, p. 11) who
stated:

> It should be the job of the police, then, to carefully analyze crime data, identify
> those types of crimes that are most likely to be prevented by police efforts, and
> design patrol strategies accordingly. The preventive efforts of the police must
> become more crime specific and target oriented.

This approach could greatly affect the second area of patrol activity, self-
initiated tasks.

Self-Initiated Tasks   Officer-initiated activities usually result from officers'
observations while on preventive patrol; that is, they encounter situations that
require their intervention. For example, an officer may see a crime in progress
and arrest the suspect. Usually, however, officer-initiated activities involve
community relations or crime prevention activities such as citizen contacts or
automobile and building checks. Officers may see a large crowd gathered and
decide to break it up, thereby preventing a possible disturbance or even a riot.
Or they may see a break in a store's security, take steps to correct it, and thus
prevent a possible burglary later.

Officers are sometimes hesitant to get involved in community services and
preventive activities because such duties make the officers unavailable for
radio dispatches and interfere with their ability to respond rapidly to service
calls. Hand-held radios and beepers have allowed patrol officers more freedom
of movement and have allowed them to initiate more activity.

Too often little attention is paid to the officer's use of noncommitted time,
which is often regarded as having no function other than to insure the availability of officers to quickly respond to service calls. Frequently noncrime
service calls interrupt a patrol officer's self-initiated activity that could prevent
or deter crime. Emphasis on rapid response to all service calls has sometimes
retarded the development of productive patrol services. Obviously, not all
service calls require a rapid response.

Call for Service   The two-way radio has made the service call an extremely
important element of patrol. It has also made it necessary to prioritize calls. A
radio dispatch almost always takes precedence over other patrol activities. For
example, if an officer has stopped a traffic violator (a self-initiated activity) and
receives a call of an armed robbery in progress, most department policies
require the officer to discontinue the contact with the motorist and answer the
service call.

In most departments, calls for service drive the department. This is known
as **incident-driven policing.** According to Brown (1990, p. 8): "Anyone in
policing today knows that an officer's day is structured by responding to 911
calls, each of which is treated as a separate incident." And, as Sumrall et al. note
(1981, p. 1): "When one considers that the major focus of this division [patrol]
is to respond to citizen calls for service and the fact that 40-60 percent of
patrol officers' time is spent responding to such calls, it becomes apparent that
the way police respond to calls for service significantly affects every facet of
their function." The response is usually reactive, incident driven, and as rapid
as possible. Given that fewer than 20 percent of dispatched calls for service
involve crime and that of these 75 percent are **cold crimes** (discovered after
the perpetrator had left the scene), such an approach is unlikely to make best
use of police resources. Many departments have found that **differential response strategies,** suiting the response to the call, are much more effective.

Factors related to the call to be considered include the type of incident and when it happened, that is, how much time has elapsed since it occurred. An in-progress major personal injury incident would be viewed differently than a minor noncrime incident that occurred several hours ago.

The response alternatives might range from an immediate response by a sworn officer to no response—not very effective from a community relations point of view. The chart in Figure 8–1 illustrates the general **differential response strategies** most often used.

Although police response time is often a cause of citizen complaints, Geller suggests (p. 65) that:

> Citizen satisfaction with response time was dependent on whether citizens perceived response time to be faster or slower than what the dispatcher had led them to expect.... Even long delays infrequently caused dissatisfaction, so long as the call was not an emergency and the victim knew what to expect.

In addition to using differentiated response strategies, patrol might also become more effective if it were less incident driven (reactive) and were, rather, more problem driven. Geller (p. 66) notes:

> Although it is now known that a very small percentage of locations (approximately 10 percent) continually account for about 60 percent of a department's call-for-service workload, officers are not routinely encouraged to identify, understand, or help resolve the underlying difficulties that give rise to repeat calls

TYPE OF INCIDENT/TIME OF OCCURRENCE

		MAJOR PERSONAL INJURY			MAJOR PROPERTY DAMAGE/LOSS			POTENTIAL PERSONAL INJURY			POTENTIAL PROPERTY DAMAGE/LOSS			MINOR PERSONAL INJURY			MINOR PROPERTY DAMAGE/LOSS			OTHER MINOR CRIME			OTHER MINOR NON-CRIME		
		IN-PROGRESS	PROXIMATE	COLD	IN-PROGRESS	PROXIMATE	COLD	IN-PROGRESS	PROXIMATE	COLD	IN-PROGRESS	PROXIMATE	COLD	IN-PROGRESS	PROXIMATE	COLD	IN-PROGRESS	PROXIMATE	COLD	IN-PROGRESS	PROXIMATE	COLD	IN-PROGRESS	PROXIMATE	COLD
SWORN	IMMEDIATE	●	●	●	●			●	●					●			●								
SWORN	EXPEDITE									●	●				●					●			●		
SWORN	ROUTINE					●	●												●		●				
SWORN	APPOINTMENT					●	●												●		●				
NON-SWORN	IMMEDIATE																								
NON-SWORN	EXPEDITE	●	●	●																					
NON-SWORN	ROUTINE																								
NON-SWORN	APPOINTMENT																								
NON-MOBILE	TELEPHONE					●	●					●	●					●	●			●		●	●
NON-MOBILE	WALK-IN																								
NON-MOBILE	MAIL-IN																								
NON-MOBILE	REFERRAL																						●	●	●
NON-MOBILE	NO RESPONSE																								

(Left axis label: RESPONSE ALTERNATIVES)

Figure 8–1   Example of Completed Differential Response Model
Source: R. O. Sumrall, J. Roberts, and M. T. Farmer. *Differential Police Response Strategies.* Copyright © 1981, 49. Police Executive Research Forum: Washington, D.C. Reprinted by permission.

at the same location or with the same actors. Even when repetitive offenses involving the same site or participants are documented, the criminal investigation that may follow often continues to address discrete incidents, and the cycle of incident-call-response continues.

Patrol might be more effective if it were proactive, directed, problem-oriented, and used differentiated response strategies.

Geller (pp. 68–69) recommends that: "To be effective, modern patrol officers must perform in three major spheres of activity—often simultaneously."

- Respond to emergency calls for service.
- Participate in tactical responses to apprehend perpetrators or to displace or disrupt problem patterns.
- Engage in strategic problem-solving efforts with the community.

Having time to engage in these three spheres of activity requires that patrol officers not be "swamped" responding to calls for service on a first-come-first-served basis.

In addition to preventive/random patrol, self-initiated tasks, and responding to calls for service, patrol officers have administrative duties.

Administrative Duties   Administrative work includes preparing and maintaining the patrol vehicle, transporting prisoners and documents, writing reports, and testifying in court. Efforts to make patrol more cost effective have often been aimed at cutting time spent on administrative duties. Some departments have greatly reduced the time officers spend maintaining their vehicles. Other departments have drastically reduced the amount of paperwork required of the patrol officers by allowing them to dictate reports, which secretaries then transcribe.

The types of reports police officers frequently use include Motor Vehicle Reports, Vehicle Recovery Reports, Offense Reports, Continuation Reports, Juvenile Reports, Juvenile Report Summaries, Missing Persons Reports, Arrest/Violation Reports, and Record Checks.

The importance of well-written reports cannot be overemphasized. In November of 1987 the Alexandria Technical Institute Law Enforcement Program mailed a questionnaire to all eighty-seven Minnesota county attorneys. The purpose of the survey was to learn the prosecutor's opinions about police reports and how these reports could be improved. Fifty-two county attorneys (60 percent) returned the survey.

Of those responding, 98 percent felt that police reports were either critically important or very important to the successful prosecution of criminal cases. Among their comments were the following:

> The police reports are often the first impression a judge or defense attorney has of an officer's competence, both generally and in regard to the specific elements of the offense charged. If the report is weak, defense attorneys and judges are inclined to require officers to testify and to scrutinize carefully the officer's testimony. A well-written report can often result in a settlement of the case without an Omnibus Hearing or trial.
>
> All prosecution is initiated by the reports submitted by the investigating agency. The decision to charge someone with a crime is based upon the police reports, usually alone.
>
> Good police reports help to speed up the entire system. Delays in prosecution often occur because of incomplete reports.

Poorly phrased reports or reports that are too brief have a tendency to blow up in your face at trial time.

If sloppy or incomplete, they will impeach the officer at trial.

A well-written report alone can settle a case.

As noted by Stokes (1991, Preface):

Most law enforcement officers submit their reports for prosecution with concern over the outcome, but without much thought about the wheels they've started in motion. This is understandable, for they've done their jobs and many more cases wait to be investigated. But what happens when they haven't really done their jobs—when their reports are distorted or incomplete (as many are) because of poor writing? The results not only cost the taxpayers in wasted man-hours, but they also breed disaster in the courtroom.

To cite an all-too-common example, in one recent criminal case, the reporting officer, using the passive voice, wrote the following in his report: "The weapon was found in the bushes where the suspect had thrown it." He did not clarify this statement elsewhere in his report. Expectedly, the prosecuting attorney subpoenaed the reporting officer to testify at the preliminary hearing. Unfortunately, the reporting officer's testimony revealed that his partner, not he, had observed the suspect's action and had retrieved the weapon. The partner was unavailable to testify on short notice. Without his testimony the necessary elements of the crime could not be established. The case was dismissed and had to be re-filed. The hours expended at the time of the dismissal—by witnesses, secretaries, clerks, attorneys, and the judge—were virtually wasted because the whole process had to be repeated. The reporting officer could have avoided the problem at the onset through use of the active voice, by writing: "Officer Jones found the weapon in the bushes." Sadly, this basic writing error is not an isolated example; such errors slip through the system daily, causing delays in the judicial process and depleting dwindling budgets.

Specialized Patrol

Specialized patrol, also called **directed** or **aggressive patrol**, is designed to handle problems and situations that require concentrated, coordinated efforts. Some patrol officers receive special training to deal with specific problems such as hostage and sniper situations, VIP protection, riot or crowd control, rescue operations, and control of suppressible crimes.

Suppressible crimes are crimes that commonly occur in locations and under circumstances that provide police officers a reasonable opportunity to deter or apprehend offenders. Included in the category of suppressible crimes are robbery, burglary, car theft, assault, and sex crimes. Such problems frequently involve a need for covert surveillance and decoys, tactics that cannot be used by uniformed patrol officers.

Specialized patrol operations are often used to saturate particular areas or to stake out suspects and possible crime locations. Countermeasures to combat street crimes have included police decoys to catch criminals—one of the most cost-effective and productive apprehension methods available. Officers have posed as cab drivers, old women, truck drivers, money couriers, nuns, and priests. They have infiltrated drug circles as undercover agents. Usually operating in high-crime areas, decoy officers are vulnerable to violence and injury. The results are considered worth the risk, however; an attack upon a decoy almost always results in a conviction of the attacker.

Patrol officers must take care that any stops they make during directed or specialized patrol are legal and not seen as harassment or discrimination.

METHODS OF PATROL

Patrol officers in the United States were originally on foot or horseback. Bicycles were introduced in policing in Detroit in 1897, and automobiles in 1910. Airplanes were first used by the New York City Police Department in 1930. At that time daredevil pilots were flying all over the city, sometimes crashing in densely populated areas. The New York Airborne police unit was created to control reckless flying over the city. These means of patrol and others can be found in the 1990s.

Patrol can be accomplished via foot, automobile, motorcycle, bicycle, horseback, aircraft, and boat. The most commonly used and most effective patrol is usually a combination of automobile and foot patrol.

Foot Patrol

The word *patrol* is derived from the French word *patrouiller,* which means, roughly, to travel on foot. Foot patrol, the oldest form of patrol, has the advantage of close citizen contact. Most effective in highly congested areas, it may help to deter burglary, robbery, purse snatching, and muggings. The 1980s saw a significant trend back to foot patrol. In the 1990s it has become almost synonymous with community policing. Foot patrol is relatively expensive and does limit the officer's ability to pursue suspects in vehicles and to get from one area to another rapidly. Used in conjunction with motorized patrol, foot patrol is highly effective.

According to the National Neighborhood Foot Patrol Center, Michigan State University School of Criminal Justice:

> Foot patrol is an exercise in communication—an attempt to develop rapport between the officer on the beat and the citizens he or she serves. Foot patrol officers constantly interact with the community. They instruct citizens in crime prevention techniques and link them to available governmental services. They are catalysts of neighborhood organizations.

Foot patrol is *proactive* rather than reactive. Its goal is to address neighborhood problems before they become crimes. The Center notes that "motorized patrolling has proven ineffective in certain key areas. Crime rates continue to rise, and even in areas where they are not high, vagrants, abandoned cars, and groups of juveniles on the street create an impression that the environment is violent and uncontrollable."

The Center cites a series of experimental programs conducted by criminal justice researchers to see if a modified version of foot patrol could contribute to modern policing. The intent was not to replace motorized patrol but rather to provide a combination of foot and motorized patrol, capitalizing on the strengths of each. One highly successful program was in Flint, Michigan, where in a three-year span crime was down 8.7 percent and calls for service were down 43.4 percent in areas where foot patrol was in force. Clear signs that police/community relations had dramatically improved were also evident. It was in part due to the success of this program that the Charles Stewart Mott Foundation provided funding for the National Neighborhood Foot Patrol Center.

According to Trojanowicz (1982, p. 86), the Flint program was highly regarded by the citizens: "Almost 70 percent of the citizens interviewed during the final year of the study felt safer because of the Foot Patrol Program."

A Newport Beach, California, parking police officer uses a computerized "ticket book" to issue a parking violation citation.

Automobile Patrol

Automobile patrol offers the greatest mobility and flexibility and is usually the most cost-effective method of patrol. It allows wide coverage and rapid response to calls—the vehicle radio provides instant communications with headquarters. The automobile also provides a means of transporting special equipment and prisoners or suspects. The obvious disadvantage of automobile patrol is that access to certain locations is restricted, for example, inside buildings. Therefore, officers may have to leave their vehicles to pursue suspects on foot.

In addition, while patrolling in a vehicle, officers cannot pay as much attention to details they might see were they on foot, for example, a door ajar, a window broken, or a security light out. The physical act of driving may draw attention away from such subtle signs that a crime may be in progress.

Another disadvantage of automobile patrol is a lack of community contact so necessary for effective police work. As one police officer said: "You're encapsulized in this car, and you're driving along. Usually the windows are rolled up because you're moving, so you're in this *steel cocoon*" (Conroy and Hess 1992, p. 120).

To counteract this isolation, officers in patrol cars might be considered foot officers who use cars for transportation from one point to another. Many officers, however, do not see it that way. Many resist getting out of their cars to talk to citizens; some even feel it is a degrading type of appeasement. In addition, the practice contradicts the tactical principle of preventive patrol, which requires the continual presence of moving, motorized street patrol. Some departments stress this principle to the extent that department regulations forbid unnecessary or unofficial conversations with citizens.

Recent research on the effectiveness of preventive patrol, however, indicates that a crime prevented by a passing vehicle can, and usually is, commit-

Automobile patrol provides the
greatest mobility and flexibility
for officers.

ted as soon as the police are gone. In effect, police presence prevents street
crime only if the police can be everywhere at once.

Some departments have gone to compact patrol cars to improve their fuel
efficiency, pursuit speeds, and maneuverability. The Texas Highway Patrol, for
example, according to Brand (1990, p. 36), has 400 Ford Mustangs in its
pursuit fleet of approximately 1,100 vehicles. Such cars usually also cost less,
but they are often cramped and usually have a rougher ride.

Harrison (1991, p. 65) suggests that "the traditional vehicle-based random
patrol is a luxury we soon may not be able to afford." He notes rising gas prices
as well as efforts by such groups as the Sierra Club to reduce the combustion
of all fossil fuels by 20 percent in the next fifteen years as contributing to the
need to look at alternative forms of patrolling. He (p. 67) concludes: "The days
of the traditional gas guzzler concept of random patrol will probably be rele-
gated to the stories recounted to rookies and grandchildren. 'Really? You just
drove around all day with no idea where the crooks were? No way ...'"

One-Officer versus Two-Officer Squads

Another factor of importance when using automobile patrol is whether to have
one or two officers assigned per squad. According to Hale (1981, p. 97): "It is
a very emotional subject since officer safety is an overriding concern. At the
same time, the police administrator must be concerned with the economic
aspect of the issue as a result of scarce resources and limited appropriations.
... It is safe to say that there are a number of valid arguments for both one-
officer and two-officer patrol units." Hale points out that sometimes it is necessary to use two-officer units to insure the officers' safety and to resolve the
problem involved satisfactorily; however, usually officer productivity and operational efficiency can be increased by using one-officer patrol units.

Circumstances should determine whether a one-officer or a two-officer unit
is more appropriate. Hale contends that the single-officer unit is the "rule

rather than the exception," and that most incidents can be handled by one officer. If two officers are required, two one-officer units can be dispatched to the scene. He feels two-officer units should be restricted to those areas, shifts, and types of activities most likely to threaten the officers' safety, for example, during the evening or in high-crime areas.

Several advantages are obtained by the one-officer unit including cost effectiveness in that the same number of officers can patrol twice the area, with twice the mobility, and with twice the power of observation. In addition, officers working alone are generally more cautious in dangerous situations, recognizing that they have no backup. And, officers working alone are generally more attentive to patrol duties, since they do not have a conversational partner. The expense of two cars compared to one, however, is often a mitigating factor.

Limited research has been done, and what is available is rather outdated. A study conducted by Chapman (1974, p. 145) found that two-officer patrol units did not enhance officer safety; nearly two-thirds of the officers suffering on-duty assaults were assigned to two-officer units; less than 15 percent of the reported assaults occurred with only one officer present.

Another study conducted in the San Diego Police Department (Boydstun et al. 1977), comparing one-officer and two-officer patrol units on several criteria, found the following:

- While overall performance for calls for service and officer-initiated activities were judged to be equal, more traffic citations were issued by two-officer units.
- Overall efficiency of one-officer units was judged to be higher than that of two-officer units, even though the former required most backup support.
- While citizens resisted arrest less frequently when dealing with one-officer units, overall safety was judged to be equal between both types of units. Assaults on officers, officer injuries, and vehicle accidents occurred at the same rate for both one-officer and two-officer units.

Although the San Diego study seems to support using single-officer patrol units strongly, authors of the study stress that the results of the study apply only to San Diego. Departments in other parts of the country should conduct their own studies.

Hale (1981, p. 100) notes: "Police unions have also supported the use of two-officer patrol units and have often managed to include provisions for two-officer units in their contracts with the local jurisdiction. In so doing, the unions have jeopardized the ability of management to make proper use of available resources and to make rational decisions concerning personnel deployment and scheduling."

Consider, however, the fact that of the 801 law enforcement officers feloniously killed in the line of duty from 1980 to 1989, of those killed while on patrol, 78 percent were assigned to one-officer vehicles, 10 percent to two-officer vehicles, and 2 percent to foot patrol. Fifty-three percent of the patrol officers were alone and unassisted at the time of their deaths (Major 1991, p. 2).

Motorcycle Patrol

Motorcycle patrol is similar to automobile patrol; however, it foregoes the advantage of transporting special equipment and prisoners to overcome the disadvantage of limited access presented by automobile. The motorcycle is also better suited to maneuver easily through heavy traffic or narrow alleys.

Motorcycles are used for traffic enforcement, escort, and parade duty. Motorcycles and automobiles have dominated traffic enforcement for the past

This state highway patrol officer can maneuver through traffic more easily than can an officer in an automobile.

seven or eight decades. The primary advantages of the motorcycle are its maneuverability in heavily congested areas and its ability to go where automobiles cannot.

Among the disadvantages of motorcycles are their relatively high cost to operate, their limited use in adverse weather, and the hazards associated with riding them.

Bicycle Patrol

Bicycle patrol is sometimes used in parks and on beaches or in conjunction with stakeouts and surveillance. It adds another dimension of patrol available in special circumstances such as in areas that are inaccessible for patrol vehicles and too large to be adequately patrolled on foot.

In addition to mobility, bicycles also provide a "stealth factor" since they can be ridden very quietly and do not attract attention.

Bicycle patrol is becoming increasingly popular. According to Harrison (1991, p. 66): "At least 80 departments, from San Diego to Toronto use bikes for general purpose patrol." Miller and Weston (1991, p. 30), in speaking of the Phoenix uniformed bicycle patrol, note: "The increased efficiency the bikes brought to the downtown walking beat had a dramatic effect on officer morale, and . . . the bicycle patrol's enthusiasm carried over into the officers' contact with the public."

Similar positive effects have been achieved in Tucson, Arizona where, as noted by McLean (1990, p. 24): "The element of surprise is just unbelievable, and the program is going fantastically well. . . . In one 11-month period, three Tucson bike cops made a whopping 1,886 arrests."

According to *Law and Order* (1991, p. 178):

Moving swiftly and silently through the shadowy areas between buildings, the all-terrain mountain bike has become the latest weapon in the anti-crime arsenal of the Los Angeles City Housing Authority Police Department. . . .

Because of the physical nature of the work and exposure to weather conditions, the bicycle patrol has had to change from regulation police uniforms to garments made of new, high-tech materials that are breathable, lightweight and waterproof. From shoes to helmets, including bullet-proof vests, everything is designed to keep the officers cool, comfortable, and agile.

Bicycles are also a part of the Palm Springs Police Department and, according to Slahor (1992, p. 81): "The bicycle unit is proving its worth in efficiency, visibility and better public relations."

Bicycles have some of the same disadvantages as motorcycles. One is that their use is limited by the weather. A second, more important disadvantage is that the officer is very vulnerable while riding a bicycle. Officers should have the proper safety equipment and follow all basic safety precautions while on bicycle patrol.

Mounted Patrol

Mounted patrol is decreasing in the United States, but it is still used effectively in larger cities such as New York City to quell civil disorders and riots, to patrol bridle paths and parks, and to control traffic. Although expensive, this method of patrol has a unique advantage—the size and mobility of the horse is more effective in an unruly crowd than an officer on foot or in a vehicle.

Mounted patrols were used in the search for Jacob Wetterling, an eleven-year old boy abducted in October of 1989. As noted by Hildreth (1990, p. 30): "Mounted sheriff's deputies from six counties were heavily involved. At the peak of the search 59 mounted deputies were involved. The mounted searchers covered about 20 square miles a day." Unfortunately, the search was unsuccessful. Hildreth (pp. 30–31) notes that mounted patrols have been called out to:

- Assist in evidence searches at crime scenes.
- Round up straying cattle after a truck tipped over.
- Search for lost children in tall corn or grass where searchers on foot would be ineffective.
- Provide horseback rides for retarded children in one of the county's schools.

An officer on horseback maintains order at a demonstration.

Air Patrol

Air patrol is another expensive yet highly effective form of patrol, especially when large geographic areas are involved, for example, a wide-spread search for a lost person, a downed plane, or an escaped convict. Helicopters and small aircraft are generally used in conjunction with police vehicles on the ground in criminal surveillance and in traffic control, not only to report tie-ups but to clock speeds and radio to ground units. Helicopters have also been used to rescue persons from tall buildings on fire and in other situations such as floods. In addition air travel is a cost-effective means of transporting prisoners over long distances.

Air patrol does have disadvantages, however, including the high cost of buying, operating, and maintaining planes and helicopters. Another disadvantage is that citizens may complain of the noise when the aircraft are used to patrol residential areas. And, some citizens feel they are being spied on—that the police are literally an "eye in the sky," and it makes them nervous. This disadvantage might be countered by public relations information stressing the purpose of the air patrol.

Boat Patrol

Boat patrol is used extensively on our coasts to apprehend gun and narcotics smugglers. Inland, boat patrols are often used to control river and lake traffic.

Water patrol units are very specialized and are used in relatively few cities in the United States. In those cities with extensive coasts, however, they are a vital part of patrol.

Yates (1991, pp. 52–53) explains that: "Police agencies use water craft that range in size from small inflatable boats to 25 to 30 foot cruisers equipped with lightbars, spotlights, sirens, rescue equipment and, of course, radar. They're used for routine enforcement such as exceeding 'No Wake' speed limits, intoxicated operators and safety inspections as well as search/rescue operations and emergency transportation in flooded areas." Watercraft can also be used for general surveillance as well as antismuggling operations.

Personal watercraft are also used by some police departments. As noted by Donaldson (1990, p. 43): "The useful characteristics most often cited by officers who use them are shallow draft, high maneuverability, stability and ease of operation." They are easy to load and unload, and they provide what several officers refer to as the "gotcha factor," that is, they can approach boating law violators, including speed and wake violators, and literally catch them in the act.

One disadvantage of water patrol is expense. Boats are expensive to buy, operate, and maintain. In addition, they must be moored, and they must be operated by officers with special boating skills.

Special-Terrain Patrol

Some police departments may require special-purpose vehicles to patrol. For example, areas that receive a lot of snow may have snowmobiles as part of their patrol fleet. These vehicles may be especially useful in rescue missions as well as on routine patrol.

At the opposite extreme, police departments operating in desert areas may require vehicles such as trail bikes and dune buggies. Police departments in remote parts of the country may use four-wheel drive vehicles. Departments with miles of beaches to patrol may use jeeps and dune buggies.

K-9-Assisted Patrol

K-9-assisted patrol is a specialized method of patrol usually found only in large departments. It has been used in crowd control, in searching out concealed suspects, and in identifying hidden narcotics. Police dogs are often used in place of a second officer on automobile and foot patrols. Dogs have also been trained and used extensively in major airports to locate bombs or narcotics on planes. Although expensive, K-9-assisted patrol may be cost effective by diminishing the number of officers required for a search.

It has been determined that a dog can recognize an odor 10 million times better than a human can (Frawley 1989, p. 115).

Spurlock (1990, p. 91) reports on a Lansing, Michigan study which found:

A single K-9 team was able to complete building searches seven times faster than four officers working together to search the same building. And while the dog team found the hidden suspect 93 percent of the time, the human officers found only 59 percent. . . .

A dog can also track a suspect or lost person through a field or wooded area more efficiently than a team of officers. The K-9 unit can also be used for controlling crowds, breaking up fights, recovering lost articles, or finding evidence discarded by fleeing suspects. And, yes, if the need arises, the dog will attack and subdue on command.

Benson (1991, p. 78) notes that: "U.S. Border Patrol K-9s sniffed out more than $46 million in narcotics and $5 million in drug contaminated currency in 1990."

Like other forms of patrol, K-9-assisted patrol also has some disadvantages. A K-9 program is relatively expensive. In addition, each dog works with only one handler. If that officer is ill or is transferred or promoted, problems can occur. Further, the dogs require special patrol cars.

Combination Patrol

Combination patrol provides the most versatile approach to preventing or deterring crime and apprehending criminals. The combination used will depend not only on the size of the police department but also on the circumstances that arise.

Table 8–1 summarizes the most common methods of patrol, their uses, advantages and disadvantages.

High Visibility versus Low Visibility

High-visibility patrol is often used in high-risk crime areas in hopes of deterring criminal activity. In addition, high-visibility patrol gives the citizens of a community a sense of safety, justified or not. Types of high-visibility patrol include foot patrol, especially with a canine partner, mounted patrol, marked police car patrol, and helicopter patrol.

Low-visibility patrol is often used to apprehend criminals engaged in targeted crimes. Many of the specialized patrol operations would fall into this category. Types of low-visibility patrol include unmarked police cars and bicycles.

The relative effectiveness of high-visibility and low-visibility patrol has not been determined. A combination of both high- and low-visibility patrol is often needed and most effective.

Table 8 — 1 **Summary of Patrol Methods**

METHOD	USES	ADVANTAGES	DISADVANTAGES
Foot	Highly congested areas Burglary, robbery, theft, purse snatching, mugging	Close citizen contact High visibility Develop informants	Relatively expensive Limited mobility
Automobile	Respond to service calls Provide traffic control Transport individuals, documents, and equipment	Most economical Greatest mobility and flexibility Offers means of communication Provides means of transporting people, documents, and equipment	Limited access to certain areas Limited citizen contact
Motorcycle	Same as automobile except for transporting individuals and limited equipment	Maneuverability in congested areas and areas restricted to automobiles	Inability to transport much equipment Not used during bad weather Hazardous to operator
Bicycle	Stakeouts Parks and beaches Congested areas	Quiet and unobtrusive	Limited speed
Mounted	Parks and bridle paths Crowd control Traffic control	Size and maneuverability of horse	Expensive
Aircraft	Surveillance Traffic control Searches and rescues	Covers large areas easily	Expensive
Boat	Deter smuggling Water traffic control Rescues	Access to activities occurring on water	Expensive
Special-terrain	Patrol unique areas inaccessible to other forms Rescue operations	Access to normally inaccessible areas	Limited use in some instances
K-9-assisted	Locating bombs, drugs, and concealed suspects	Minimizes officers' risks	Expensive

EFFECTIVENESS OF WOMEN ON PATROL

As with research on one-officer versus two-officer squads, research on the effectiveness of women on patrol is relatively dated. A seven-month study in New York City ("Women on Patrol" 1978, p. 43) found that women generally perform as well as men in police patrol work, although some small differences exist. The study, based on direct observation of 3,625 patrols and 2,400 police-civilian encounters, examined an equal number of men and women. It analyzed the actions required of the officers, their style of patrol, their methods of gaining control, their initiative, physical strength, and the reactions of the public.

The study found that the performance of policewomen is more like that of policemen than it is different, although the women made a better impression on the public. Citizens said women officers were more competent, pleasant, and respectful than the men. The women's performance created a better civilian regard for the New York City Police Department.

The study also found that women were less likely to join male partners in taking control of a situation or jointly making decisions. In the few incidents judged to be dangerous, however, men and women were equally likely to attempt to gain control. Women were neither more nor less likely than men to use force, display a weapon, or rely on a direct order. In addition, the behavior of women who patrolled with women was more active, assertive, and self-sufficient.

Other findings of the study were that women were slightly less physically agile in such activities as climbing ladders or steep stairs. Women took more sick leave than men—consistent with earlier research showing that, in general, women are absent from work more frequently than men, perhaps because they are more likely to stay home when family members are ill.

The report attributed the small but consistent differences to socially conditioned attitudes such as protectiveness, disdain, or skepticism by men and passivity by women. The study concluded: "The results offer little support either to those who hold that women are unsuited to patrol or to those who argue that women do the job better than men. By and large, patrol performance of the women was more like that of the men than it was different."

In 1972 the Police Foundation funded a comparison study of male and female recruits in Washington, D.C. Completed in 1974, the study concluded that from a performance viewpoint it was appropriate to hire women for patrol on the same basis as men. Among its specific findings were the following (Kiernan and Cusik 1977):

Both men and women officers obtained similar results in handling angry or violent citizens. No incidents cast serious doubt on a female officer's ability to patrol satisfactorily.

Women made fewer arrests and gave fewer traffic citations. However, they also had fewer opportunities to do so, as they were not given patrol assignments as often as men. Arrests made by women and men were equally likely to result in convictions.

Men were more likely to engage in serious misconduct than women, for example, to be arrested for drunk and disorderly conduct while off duty. Women, on the other hand, were more likely to be late for work.

A majority of Washington residents approved of the use of women in patrol work, although they were "moderately skeptical" of women's abilities to handle violent suspects.

There were no differences between men and women in the number of sick days used, number of injuries sustained, or number of days absent from work because of injuries.

Male and female partners shared driving equally, took charge with about the same frequency, and were about equal in giving each other instructions.

Resignation rates were also similar: 14 percent for women and 12 percent for men.

Studies have shown that women perform as well as men in police patrol work.

Perhaps the most graphic illustration of the equal role played by men and women on police patrol is that of Gail A. Cobb, who joined the Washington,

D.C. Police Department in 1973. She had been assigned to patrol duty for only five months when she responded to her last police call.

Around noon one Friday in September, Officer Cobb was patrolling downtown Washington when she was called to help search for two suspected bank robbers who had exchanged shots with police and then fled. Officer Cobb saw a man dash down a ramp into an underground parking garage and followed him. Then, moments after entering the garage, she was shot in the chest. Only twenty-four years old, Officer Gail Cobb became the first United States policewoman to be killed in the line of duty. As noted by Police Chaplain Reverend R. Joseph Dooley, her death "established the fact that the criminal makes no distinction between the sexes. It is the badge and the blue uniform that makes the difference."

STRUCTURE AND MANAGEMENT OF PATROL

Traditionally, patrol officers have been assigned a specific time and a specific geographic location to patrol. Typically, a three-shift structure is implemented and the beats are set up to be of equal geographic size. Such a structure poses obvious problems, because the workload is not the same at all hours of the day or in all areas.

The Chicago Police Lieutenants Association undertook a study of shift work by mailing a survey to 271 of their lieutenants. Of these surveys, 189 (70 percent) were returned. They also surveyed twenty-seven departments across the country. From that study, it was learned that the majority of calls were received between 4 P.M. and midnight, both in Chicago and the typical city (O'Neill and Cushing 1991, p. 52). Data from that survey are summarized in Table 8–2.

The major conclusion of this study was that (p. 67): "Shift work is deleterious to the physical and psychological health of the individual and to the well-being of the organization." These findings should be considered in any discussion of assigning patrol officers.

As noted by Williams, Formby, and Watkins (1982, p. 101): "Where equal shift staffing is used, the amount of preventive patrol time and the workload per officer are doubled, resulting in less preventive patrol to deter crime during times when the crime occurrence is highest." Likewise, some areas of a city or town are likely to have a higher demand for police service than others.

Equal shift and beat size staffing creates major problems and lessens the effectiveness of patrol during certain times and in certain areas.

Several attempts have been made to overcome the problems inherent in equal shift and beat size staffing. Some departments, usually larger ones, assign

Table 8–2 **Distribution of Calls for Service**

SHIFT	CHICAGO	TYPICAL CITY
Midnight— 8 A.M.	21%	22%
8 A.M.— 4 P.M.	33%	33%
4 P.M.—midnight	46%	45%

officers according to the demand for services, concentrating the officers' time where it is most needed. Union contracts, however, sometimes make this difficult.

Another problem with traditional approaches to organizing patrol is how the officers' time is structured. Recall that preventive patrol is usually broken up into short intervals of twenty to thirty minutes. Lack of a concentrated effort reduces the effects of preventive patrol.

Several attempts to improve the use of preventive patrol time have been implemented. Four such nontraditional preventive patrol strategies are described by Williams, Formby, and Watkins (1982, p. 101).

Their first example involves the Community-Oriented Policing concept and the Community Manager concept. Both approaches allow an officer to plan ahead for use of noncommitted time through the use of statistics on crime in the officer's allotted time and area. Officers are to use such crime analysis information to work with the community to devise methods to deter crime. Although such programs might be perceived as basically community relations, they do provide one approach to planning for more effective use of preventive patrol time.

A second approach, used primarily in and around New Haven, Connecticut, is the Directed Deterrent Patrol (DDP). Like the preceding example, DDP uses crime analysis information to organize the route and timing of preventive patrol. Officers are given the exact time, route, and duration of each preventive patrol activity, known as a D. run. When a D. run begins, the officers notify the dispatcher. From then until the run is completed, these officers do not receive any routine calls. Upon completion of the D. run, the officers again notify dispatch. This approach provides substantial time to be used for only preventive patrol.

A third example is the approach used in Wilmington, Delaware, called the Directed Apprehension or the Split-Force Patrol. In this approach, part of the patrol force undertakes only directed patrol activities; the remainder of the patrol force answers calls for service and performs traditional patrol activities.

The fourth example is the New York City Street Crime Unit, a unit of specially trained patrol officers using plainclothes surveillance and decoy tactics to apprehend offenders in the act of committing crimes. The officers, disguised as potential victims, patrol high-crime areas, watched by a backup team, also in disguise. Such specialized patrol teams were described earlier in this chapter.

Directed patrol uses crime statistics to plan shift and beat staffing, providing more coverage during times of peak criminal activity and in high-crime areas.

Other approaches to enhance the effectiveness of patrol include team policing and community-oriented policing.

TEAM POLICING

Team policing in the United States, patterned after a unique patrol experiment in Aberdeen, Scotland, in 1948, is designed to deliver patrol, investigative, and community services on a more informal basis, that is, neighborhood team policing combines the specialized services and equipment of large urban departments with the more personal community contact of small departments.

Police services are decentralized, with a team of officers assigned around-the-clock responsibility for crime control and police services in a specific area.

In many programs the officer's responsibilities are expanded to include investigative work as well as community relations services. As departments become decentralized, decision making becomes a product of teamwork, giving officers a voice in planning actions and policies that directly affect them. These features not only increase officer job satisfaction, but they also frequently improve the quality and quantity of police service delivered to the community.

Central features of team policing include the following:

- Combining patrol, investigative, and community relation services.
- Decentralization.
- Cooperative decision making.
- Permanent assignment to a team and a geographic area.

Although team policing means different things to different departments, most programs have three basic characteristics:

- Geographic stability of patrol.
- Maximum interaction among team members.
- Maximum communication among team members and the community.

The teams are organized in two different ways: shift teams and area teams. A shift team usually has no formal coordination of the various shifts serving a single area. The supervisor of the shift team reports to a watch commander, who is responsible for only a single shift within a twenty-four-hour period. This approach provides less continuity of service.

Area teams, in contrast, provide law enforcement services twenty-four hours a day. This around-the-clock responsibility allows a single team leader to coordinate all patrol activities in the same area and provides considerable flexibility in deploying officers to meet changing levels of service demands throughout the day.

Area teams have three distinct advantages over shift teams. First, they provide continuity of service to citizens; second, they allow for alteration of schedule; and third, they have a larger pool of officers from which to draw.

Team policing is found in small, medium, and large cities in equal numbers, not just in the big cities. It is found in both urban and suburban communities and in all parts of the country. Most team programs have replaced random roving patrol with objective-based patrol activities. Teams are assigned crime prevention, investigative, and community relations activities to perform when not responding to calls. Some departments place more emphasis on one of these activities than the others, and hence they can be classified by their primary focus.

More (1987, p. 13) notes that: "Team policing encourages close interactions between citizens and police. . . . It encourages police officer familiarity with community agencies and other resources. . . . Yet the implementation of this promising form of policing has been an elusive goal." He suggests the following reasons for the anticipated success of team policing to have not materialized:

- The **innovator effect** may be operating, that is, anything new tends to initially be greeted enthusiastically, but soon the "novelty wears off." In experimental psychology this is referred to as the **Hawthorne effect.**
- It represents a real threat to police departments' formal and informal power structure. Many at the top of the authority hierarchy are not willing to relinquish their power to the team.
- It is essentially incompatible with the present police orientation around rapid response to service calls.

It might well be that team policing was simply an idea ahead of its time. Many of the same ingredients of team policing may be found in community-oriented policing—an idea whose time seems to have come.

COMMUNITY-ORIENTED POLICING

Former New York Police Commissioner Brown (1991, p. 6) states:

> I believe that community policing—the building of problem-solving partnerships between the police and those they serve—is the future of American Law Enforcement. . . .
>
> In adopting community policing, we recognize that the problems of crime, fear and disorder can't be solved by the police department alone. Instead, we are building partnerships with citizens and other governmental agencies to get the job done. . . .
>
> We need to *solve* community problems rather than just *react* to them. It is time to adopt new strategies to address the dramatic increases in crime and the fear of crime. I view community policing as a better, smarter and more cost-effective way of using police resources.

Community-oriented policing is basically a philosophy that emphasizes a problem-solving partnership between the police and the citizens in working toward a healthy, crime-free environment.

Community-oriented policing goes by several names: **community policing, neighborhood policing, community wellness,** and the like. The concept of community-oriented policing was introduced in Chapter 2 and has been a recurrent theme throughout this text. It is discussed in more detail in Chapter 9.

THE RESPONSIBILITIES OF THE TRAFFIC OFFICER

Traffic is a complex responsibility, involving not only investigation but also service and interrelation with other agencies such as traffic engineering. According to *Accident Facts* (1988, p. 62):

> The first motor-vehicle death in the United States is reported to have occurred in New York City on September 14, 1899. . . . Since the first motor-vehicle death in the United States, slightly more than 2,700,000 persons have died in motor-vehicle accidents through the end of 1987. Based on historical figures, the 1,000,000th motor-vehicle death occurred sometime during 1952. The 2,000,000th motor-vehicle death will probably occur in the early 1990s.

According to Geller (1991, p. 162): "The principal goal of police traffic services is to increase safety on the streets and highways, largely by enforcing traffic regulations." In addition because police are on the streets so much of the time, they often are the first to know of problems in the transportation system and are in a "unique position to provide operational information as well as to advise on overall system planning" (p. 159).

All uniformed officers should be responsible for enforcing traffic laws and regulations because of the close interrelationship between traffic activity and all other police activities. It is not uncommon, for example, for a routine stop for a traffic violation to result in the arrest of the driver for a serious nontraffic offense. Abandoned vehicles may have served as getaway cars in a robbery or have been stolen for joyriding by teenagers.

Traffic officers may be responsible for:

■ Enforcing traffic laws.

■ Directing and controlling traffic.

■ Providing directions and assistance to motorists.

■ Investigating motor vehicle accidents.

■ Providing emergency assistance at the scene of an accident.

■ Gathering information related to traffic and writing reports.

The primary objectives of most traffic programs are to obtain the smoothest possible movement of vehicles and pedestrians consistent with safety and to reduce losses from accidents.

Enforcing Traffic Laws   Police officers seek to obtain the compliance of motorists and pedestrians with traffic laws and ordinances as well as driver license regulations and orders. They issue warnings or citations to violators. Traffic officers provide law enforcement action related to operating and parking vehicles, pedestrian actions, and vehicle equipment safety.

Directing and Controlling Traffic   Police officers frequently are called on to direct traffic flow, to control parking, to provide escorts, and to remove abandoned vehicles. They frequently are asked to assist in crowd control at major sporting events. They also are responsible for planning traffic routing, removal of traffic hazards, and emergency vehicle access for predictable emergencies.

Providing Directions and Assistance to Motorists   Police officers provide information and assistance to motorists and pedestrians by patrolling, main-

Directing traffic, especially in inclement weather, can be a tedious job. Nonverbal communication plays a vital part in traffic control.

taining surveillance of traffic and the environment, conducting driver-vehicle road checks, and being available when needed.

Investigating Motor Vehicle Accidents   Police officers gather and report the facts about accident occurrence as a basis for preventing accidents and providing objective evidence for citizens involved in civil settlements of accident losses. Police officers investigate accidents, including gathering facts at the scene and reconstructing the accident. They may also prepare cases for court and appear as prosecution witnesses when there has been a violation such as drunk driving.

Providing Emergency Assistance at the Scene of an Accident   At an accident scene the police officer may assist accident victims by administering first aid, transporting injured persons, protecting property in the victim's vehicle, and arranging for towing of disabled vehicles.

Gathering Information Related to Traffic and Writing Reports   The police officer reports on accidents, violations, citations and arrests, disposition of court actions, drivers' cumulative records, roadway and environmental defects, and exceptional traffic congestion. The reports assist the traffic engineer and traffic safety education agencies by providing information useful in their accident prevention programs as well as in planning for traffic movement or vehicle parking. Furthermore, traffic-related records, including registration records, drivers' licenses, traffic citations, and collision reports, may play an important role not only in traffic management but also in criminal investigations.

Sometimes police officers serve unofficially as the city's road inspectors as they discover problems in either road conditions or traffic flow. They may propose corrections to achieve safer, more effective motor vehicle and pedestrian travel and vehicle parking.

Violating traffic laws does not carry the social stigma attached to violation of other laws such as laws against murder and rape. Running a stoplight or speeding is not considered a crime, and people regularly and unconsciously violate laws designed to insure safe use of the streets and highways. Recall the distinction between crimes that are *mala in se* (bad in themselves) and *mala prohibta* (bad because they are forbidden). Traffic laws are excellent examples of *mala prohibita* crimes.

The primary goal of traffic law enforcement is to produce voluntary compliance with traffic laws while keeping traffic moving safely and smoothly.

A properly administered and executed police traffic law enforcement procedure is probably the most important component of the overall traffic program. If people obey the traffic laws, traffic is likely to flow more smoothly and safely, with fewer tie-ups and accidents. Effective traffic law enforcement usually consists of at least five major actions:

- On-the-spot instructions to drivers and pedestrians.
- Verbal warnings.
- Written warnings with proper follow-up.
- Citations or summonses.
- Arrests.

Each of these actions has importance to traffic law enforcement. The circumstances of each individual incident will determine which action is most appropriate. It is up to the traffic officers to decide which action to take, but their decisions will be more impartial and consistent if they have guidelines on which to base them.

A well-rounded traffic program involves many activities designed to maintain order and safety on streets and highways. Although the traffic responsibilities of a police officer may not have the glamour of a criminal investigation, they are critical not only to the safety of the citizens in a community but also to the police image. Traffic is the most frequent contact between police and law-abiding citizens.

In traffic contacts, officers should always act professionally. As noted by Geller (1991, p. 166): "In 'marketing' roadway safety to the public and to those caught violating traffic laws, police need to 'sell' their product in a way that their customers will ultimately support."

The question inevitably arises as to how much enforcement is needed to control traffic and reduce accidents. How many traffic citations will constitute the right amount to meet enforcement requirements and still retain public support for the police department? This is a local issue that must be determined for each jurisdiction; however, a nationally approved guide, called the *Enforcement Index*, has been developed to assist in this determination.

The Enforcement Index

The **Enforcement Index** is calculated by dividing the number of convictions with penalty for hazardous moving traffic violations during a given period by the number of fatal and personal injury accidents occurring during the same period.

$$\text{Enforcement Index} = \frac{\text{number of convictions for hazardous moving traffic violations}}{\text{number of fatal and personal injury accidents}}$$

Recommended Index Figure: 20 to 25

For example, if during January a city had 25 fatal or personal injury accidents and the police department had 300 convictions for hazardous moving traffic violations, you would divide 300 by 25 and arrive at an index figure of 12 —below the recommended level. This city should have from 500 to 625 convictions for hazardous moving violations rather than 300.

While not conclusive, this index provides one means of measuring the quantity of enforcement. The International Association of Chiefs of Police and National Safety Council, through statistical research, have suggested than an index of twenty to twenty-five is both obtainable and effective for most cities. In other words, for each fatal and personal injury accident there should be twenty to twenty-five convictions for hazardous moving traffic violations.

To attain an effective traffic program, the index value may have to be raised in some cities and lowered in others. The index is simply a management tool designed to measure general compliance of the motorists in the community.

In addition, any strategy that makes use of indexes or quotas must also take into account the "human equation," that is, the possibility that officers may fill the quota as quickly as possible and then do no more until the next period of evaluation. Effective supervision can eliminate this problem of substituting quantity for quality.

Selective Traffic Law Enforcement

Because numerous traffic violations occur every hour of every day, police departments cannot enforce all traffic regulations at all times. It is impossible to achieve 100 percent and almost always unwise to try to do so. **Selective enforcement** targets specific accidents and/or high-accident areas, for example, excessive speed around a school yard or playground where young children are present.

Selective enforcement is not only logical, it is practical, since most police departments' limited work forces require them to spend time on violations that contribute to accidents. Enforcement personnel, such as officers on motorcycles or assigned to a radar unit, are usually the officers assigned to selective traffic enforcement. The officers' activity is directed to certain high-accident areas, during certain days of the week and certain hours of the day or night.

Studies in city after city have proven a definite relationship between accidents and enforcement. In analyzing accident reports, one finds at the top of the list year after year the same traffic violations contributing to accidents and the same group of drivers being involved. Accidents will be discussed in greater detail later in the chapter.

Selective enforcement is based on thorough investigations of accidents, summarization, and careful analysis of the records. Adequate records are essential to the overall effectiveness of the selective enforcement program.

Quantity and quality of traffic law enforcement go hand in hand in any community. Many police departments have found that without quality, selectivity, or direction, their desired objectives in traffic supervision programs simply will not work. The public resents quantity goals that cause a police officer to issue many traffic citations and the court dockets to become overloaded with "not guilty" pleas. In departments where quality is emphasized, the public usually complies with safe driving techniques and acknowledges and supports safety programs.

Almost everyone has heard in exhaustive detail a friend's version of getting an "unfair" speeding ticket. The person will tell several people about it. In terms of quality and selective enforcement, this has the effect of informing the general public that the police are doing their job. It may also prevent others from speeding.

High-quality enforcement is not only supported by the public, it has an important effect on the would-be traffic violator. When the public is informed of the police department's enforcement program and it is understood and believed to be reasonable and fair, the public will usually accept and support it.

Traffic and Patrol

Detecting traffic violations is no different for a patrol officer than detecting vandalism, auto theft, burglary, or trespassing. The officers know general police methods, they appreciate the functions they have to perform while on patrol, and they know traffic laws and the department's traffic policies. A thorough knowledge of the department's overall traffic program, its objectives and operations, will make the patrol officers assigned to traffic responsibilities more effective.

While on patrol, police officers may also detect hazardous road situations and note locations where traffic control signs may be needed. In addition, they are readily available to respond to accident calls.

Public Education Programs

The police also seek to educate the public in traffic safety. Although not a primary function, they often participate in local school programs, private safety organizations, local service clubs, and state safety councils. The police know these programs are important and that they can contribute to the good of the community.

Traffic safety education also has high public relations value. An officer on the school grounds supervising the school crossing guards (patrols) or teaching youngsters bicycle safety contributes much to the police officers' image. It reflects their concern for the safety and welfare of the community's youth. Since safety education is a community responsibility, however, community agencies should assume their share of work and not rely solely on the police department for the entire effort.

▬▬▬▬ TRAFFIC ACCIDENTS

Motor vehicle accidents are a leading cause of death for people ages one to forty-four. During the hour in which you are reading this chapter there have probably been two hundred traffic accidents resulting in injury and five resulting in death. Billions of dollars are lost annually through motor vehicle accidents, and the cost in human suffering and loss is impossible to estimate.

Causes of Motor Vehicle Accidents—An Overview

Most accidents involve factors relating to the driver, the vehicle, and the road. The interaction of these factors often sets up the series of events which culminates in the mishap.

The basic causes of motor vehicle accidents are human faults, errors, violations, and attitudes; road defects; and car defects.

Good driving attitudes are more important than driving skills or knowledge, a fact frequently overlooked in driver education programs. Drivers who jump lanes, try to beat out others as they merge from cloverleafs, race, follow too closely, or become angry and aggressive account for many of our serious motor vehicle accidents. Negative driver behavior, such as illegal and unsafe speed, failure to yield the right of way, crossing over the center line, driving in the wrong lane, and driving while under the influence of alcohol, increases the number of accidents and causes traffic statistics to rise year after year.

Environmental factors cited as probable cause of accidents include view obstructions and slick roads.

Vehicular factors identified as causes include brake failure, inadequate tire tread depth, side-to-side brake imbalance, tire underinflation, and vehicle-related vision obstructions.

Vision and personality (especially poor personal and social adjustment) were also found to be related to accident involvement. Interestingly, knowledge of the driving task was not shown to be related.

Alcohol is a factor in at least 50 percent of fatal motor vehicle accidents.

Problems mount when the drinking age varies from state to state. In such instances, some teenagers may drive to neighboring states with lower drinking ages than their own and come home, usually during the late night hours, driving under the influence of alcohol. Overall, however, a study by the Insurance Institute of Highway Safety *Status Report,* September 23, 1981, reports that, on the average, a state that raises its drinking age can expect about a 28 percent reduction in nighttime fatal crash involvement among drivers to which the law change applies.

Law Enforcement and the Drunk Driver

Ross (1981, p. 632) contends:

> The problem of crashes caused by drivers influenced by alcohol has preoccupied public opinion and the law ever since the invention of the automobile in the late nineteenth century.... Vehicle codes initially forbade driving "while under the influence of intoxicating liquor," driving in an "intoxicated condition," or simply "drunk driving." These "classical" laws were directed against obviously blameworthy conduct and prescribed traditional criminal penalties and procedures.

Such laws were extremely difficult for police officers to enforce unless an accident resulted, and even then obtaining a conviction was difficult.

In the 1930s a new approach to drinking and driving emerged as a result of widespread dissatisfaction with existing laws. This approach, called the **Scandinavian-type law,** reflected the Scandinavian tendency at that time toward temperance. The Scandinavian-type laws prohibited driving with blood alcohol concentrations exceeding specific levels relative to body weight. According to Ross (1975, p. 303):

> Enforcement required chemical tests: a preliminary breath test that could be demanded by a policeman who suspected a driver of committing the offense, and an evidentiary quantitative blood test for those failing the first test. Penalties for violating the laws included license suspension and confinement in prison; the latter was made mandatory for blood alcohol concentration exceeding .05 percent in Norway and .15 percent in Sweden. In short, the Scandinavian laws introduced objective, nonclinical definitions of the drinking-and-driving offense, employing novel scientific criminal procedures and severe penalties. After World War II these laws were widely adopted throughout the developed, automobile-dependent world.

Scandinavian-type drinking and driving laws prohibit driving with blood alcohol concentrations exceeding specific levels and establish severe penalties for doing so. Such laws are effective if they are widely publicized and if the likelihood of punishment for noncompliance is high.

The effectiveness of Scandinavian-type laws in deterring drunk driving has been studied in England, France, and Canada, with the conclusion usually being that such laws are initially effective in deterring drunk driving, but that the effect eventually dissipates. The United States Department of Transportation conducted several campaigns called Alcohol Safety Action Projects, which all found that declines in the frequency of drinking and driving were limited to the period covered by the campaigns.

In addition to enforcement campaigns, punishment campaigns have also been attempted, greatly increasing the severity of the penalty for driving under the influence of alcohol. Such campaigns have been largely unsuccessful; however, an increased public perception of the likelihood of punishment *does* appear to deter drinking and driving. Unfortunately, it has been estimated that

the chances of a drunk driver being apprehended in the United States under a
Scandinavian-type law are between 1 in 200 and 1 and 2,000.

Since so many fatal automobile accidents involve drivers who have been
drinking alcohol, legislators and law enforcement agencies have tried to find a
valid way to determine if drivers are under the influence of alcohol. In 1953
New York enacted the first implied consent statute.

Implied consent laws state that any person driving a motor vehicle is deemed to
have consented to a chemical blood test of the alcohol content of his or her blood
if arrested while intoxicated; refusal to take such a test can be introduced in court
as evidence.

The alcohol content in a person's body can be determined through breath,
urine, or blood tests. The courts have held that this is *not* a violation of a
person's Fifth Amendment privilege against self-incrimination.

One of the first cases to test the constitutionality of forcibly taking blood
from an arrested person was *Breithaupt v. Abram* (1957). In this case the
conviction was upheld.

Then, in 1966, in the landmark case of *Schmerber v. California* the issue
was greatly clarified. The United States Supreme Court upheld the conviction
and stressed that taking a blood sample was not a violation of the privilege
against self-incrimination:

> We hold that the privilege protects an accused only from being compelled to
> testify against himself, or otherwise provide the state with evidence of a testi-
> monial or communicative nature, and that the withdrawal of blood and use of
> analysis in question in this case did not involve compulsion to these ends.

The Court did caution that the blood sample should be taken by medical
personnel in a medical environment. The Court also ruled that the blood test
did not violate the Fourth Amendment even though there was no warrant. The
Court reasoned that the blood alcohol content might have dissipated if the
officer had been required to obtain a warrant before taking the test.

Illegal Per Se versus Presumptive Levels Statutes often define two kinds of
blood alcohol concentrations (BAC): illegal per se and presumptive levels,
with the presumptive levels generally lower and requiring a different burden
of proof.

According to the Bureau of Justice Statistics (1983):

> Across the States, illegal per se blood alcohol levels cluster around .10, but
> several States define it as low as .08 and others as high as .15. Presumptive levels
> for DWI or DUI may range from .05 and up but also cluster at the .10 level. The
> President's Commission on Drunk Driving has recommended that a presumptive
> BAC of .08 be enacted by State legislatures.

A BAC level above .05 is described as "driving while impaired" by the
National Institute on Alcohol Abuse and Alcoholism Clearinghouse on Alcohol
Information.

Blood alcohol concentration can be influenced by many factors including
physiological differences, food consumption, the amount of ethanol ingested,
and the time elapsed between drinking and testing.

The DeKalb, Illinois, Police Department instituted a Comprehensive Alcohol Safety Project (CASP) in 1984. As noted by Usilton and McMorrow (1991,

p. 57), CASP officers, all volunteers, worked the hours when they were most likely to encounter drunk drivers. The results:

> More driving under the influence (DUI) arrests were made during the 3½ years CASP was operational than the DeKalb Police Department made in over 20 years. More importantly, during a time period that reflected a rising number of accidents statewide, the City of DeKalb registered decreases in accident rates during the program's operation.

Usilton and McMorrow (p. 59) conclude: "Target Patrol works. The officers pay for themselves. With money from fines, the program has more than paid for itself."

Sobriety Checkpoints   Many states use sobriety checkpoints to deter driving while under the influence of alcohol. In *Michigan Department of State Police v. Sitz* (1990) the Supreme Court ruled that "sobriety checkpoints are constitutional" because the states have a "substantial interest" in keeping intoxicated drivers off the roads and because the "measure of intrusion on motorists stopped at sobriety checkpoints is slight."

The California Supreme Court has outlined safeguards to assure that safety checkpoints are reasonable under the Fourth Amendment (Hannigan 1990, p. 52). The decision to set up a sobriety checkpoint, the site, and procedures must be established by supervisory law enforcement personnel, not officers in the field. The sites chosen must have a high incidence of alcohol-related accidents and/or arrests and yet be safe. The checkpoint must have high visibility. Safety for motorists and officers must be a primary consideration, including proper lighting, warning signs, and clearly identifiable official vehicles and personnel. A neutral formula must be used to decide who to stop, for example, every third car. Finally, each motorist should be detained only long enough for officers to briefly question the driver and to look for signs of intoxication such as alcohol on the breath, slurred speech and glassy or bloodshot eyes. A driver who displays no signs of impairment should be permitted to drive on without further delay.

Speed and Accidents

Legislation passed in April 1987 allowed states to raise the speed limit to 65 mph on interstate highways passing through areas with populations under 50,000. In 1987 thirty-eight states had implemented the 65 mph limit. The National Highway Traffic Safety Administration assessed the impact of the speed limit increase on highway safety and made the following conclusions in their May 1988 interim report:

> For the first thirty-seven states that raised rural Interstate speed limits, 1987 rural Interstate fatalities were 23 percent higher during the period after the speed limits were increased through September than for the identical period in 1986. In comparison, 1987 fatalities for the period from January 1 to the time the speed limit was raised, increased 10 percent over the identical 1986 period.
>
> In the first twenty-eight states that raised the speed limit, rural Interstate fatalities increased 18 percent during January to March 1987 versus 1986. In states that did not raise the speed limit, rural Interstate fatalities were stable January to March and increased 16 percent June to September.
>
> Four states, Arizona, California, Louisiana, and New Mexico, accounted for about 70 percent of the total 1987 increase in rural Interstate fatalities in the states that raised their rural Interstate speed limit.

Occupant Restraints and Accidents

According to National Highway Traffic Safety Administration studies, safety belts are 45 percent effective in preventing fatalities, 50 percent effective in preventing moderate to critical injuries, and 10 percent effective in preventing minor injuries. As of July 1, 1988, thirty-one states and the District of Columbia have enacted mandatory safety belt use laws. Five years before, in 1983, only New York had a mandatory seat belt law. All fifty states and the District of Columbia have mandatory child safety seat laws.

In a nineteen-city observation survey by the National Highway Traffic Safety Administration, driver restraint use was estimated to be 42 percent in 1987, a significant increase over the 11 percent observed using safety belts in 1982. Still, more than half the drivers in the United States are not wearing seat belts. Child safety seat use was estimated at 80 percent in 1987, up from 23 percent in 1982.

Beginning Minnesota's Buckle Down campaign, the Buffalo police chief ticketed costumed crash dummies Vince and Larry. The campaign aimed to increase seat-belt use to 70 percent by the end of 1992. (All drivers and front-seat passengers, as well as children under age 11, must wear restraints in Minnesota.)

The University of Michigan Transportation Research Institute evaluated the effects of *mandatory safety belt use laws* on motor vehicle fatality rates. The study showed a statistically significant decrease of about 9 percent in the fatality rates per vehicle mile traveled in the first eight states with seat belt laws. (The study was a time series analysis of fatalities occurring between January 1976 and June 1986.)

Enlisting Citizen Assistance

Geller (1991, p. 163) suggests that:

> Given an opportunity, many civic organizations in the community can aid the police traffic services program. Such groups include local safety councils, chambers of commerce, business groups, and service clubs such as Rotary and Lions. Groups such as Mothers Against Drunk Driving (MADD) and Students Against Driving Drunk (SADD) focus on specific aspects of traffic safety. Efforts should also be made to gain the support of ethnic and religious organizations and of senior citizens.

RESPONSIBILITIES OF THE OFFICER CALLED TO THE SCENE OF AN ACCIDENT

Frequently police officers are the first persons to arrive on the scene of a traffic accident who are equipped, trained, and legally responsible for providing services—perhaps lifesaving services if they act quickly and effectively. In addition to rendering first aid to accident victims, police officers have several other duties to perform such as protecting victims from further harm, reducing to the extent possible the involvement of other cars as they arrive on the scene, summoning emergency service for victims and, if needed, towing services for the vehicles involved, protecting the victims' personal property, locating witnesses, securing evidence and in other ways investigating the accident, and keeping traffic moving as though no accident had occurred.

The officer called to the scene of an auto accident should:

- Proceed to the scene rapidly but safely.
- Park safely and conveniently.
- Administer emergency first aid if required.
- Interview all persons involved as well as all witnesses.
- Provide needed assistance to victims.
- Accurately observe and record all facts related to the accident.
- Clear the scene as soon as possible to restore traffic flow.

It is important that all facts related to the accident are accurately observed and recorded. The time of day should be noted, as a setting or rising sun might have temporarily blinded one of the drivers. All marks on the road should be measured and recorded. The condition of the road should be noted: wet or dry; muddy, dusty, or sandy; dirt, asphalt, or cement. The width of the street and any obstruction to vision should also be noted.

An officer notes details of an accident. Accident reports are important for insurance claims as well as for compiling information on the safety of our streets and highways.

Traffic accident reports should include all relevant details, including information about the drivers, their actions, their vehicles, the type of accident, the manner of collision, the type of street, weather conditions, road conditions, light conditions, and existing traffic control.

IMPORTANCE OF ACCIDENT REPORTS

Accident reports provide important information for enforcement of laws, traffic engineering, and educational activities. Report writing is critical to a good traffic program. The best possible investigation serves little purpose if it is not accurately and completely reported.

Accident reports by police officers provide a guide for many other department activities as well as a guide for other agencies involved in traffic and safety. Accident reports provide important information for:

- Enforcement of laws.
- Traffic engineering.
- Educational activities.

In addition, a host of other agencies involved in traffic make use of the information contained in traffic accident reports. Public information agencies such as newspapers, television, and radio disseminate information about traffic, traffic conditions, road conditions, and traffic accidents. Attorneys and the courts use traffic accident reports in determining the facts in traffic accidents that result in lawsuits. The state motor vehicle department or state department of public safety, which has the power to suspend or revoke drivers' licenses, also uses information contained in these reports. Legislative bodies in each state may rely on traffic accident reports when they plan for providing funds, equipment, and personnel to effectively enforce traffic safety programs and when they determine what laws must be passed to control traffic.

Traffic accident reports may be used by engineers, both federal and state, who research ways to improve highway systems and by the National Safety Council and state safety councils that compile statistics related to accidents: Who is having them? Where? When? How? The reports may be used by insurance companies that base their automobile insurance rates on the accident record of the community.

Traffic accident reports serve as the basis of traffic law enforcement policy, accident prevention programs, traffic education, legislative reform of traffic laws, traffic engineering decisions, and motor vehicle administrative decisions.

In addition to effective reporting, police departments need an efficient traffic accident records system to evaluate the effectiveness of highway safety measures. Compilation of traffic statistics and records on major moving violations and frequent locations and causes of traffic accidents is also critical if a department is going to institute selective patrol and enforcement techniques.

In some smaller police departments, a police officer might be assigned to work with public works departments or city engineers in traffic engineering. Although not involved in the technical design, construction, or maintenance decisions and problems, the officer contributes information beneficial to mechanical operations such as routine maintenance by calling in hazardous road situations encountered while on routine patrol; inspecting facilities and making recommendations for the erection of traffic control signs, needed painting of street lines, cross-walks, and curbs; and performing similar activities of a nontechnical nature.

Although large cities usually have special traffic engineers, police officers still contribute expertise to those who make the final decisions. Police officers' most important contribution to traffic engineering is the research they compile related to accidents and congested streets. They also report hazardous conditions that need attention. In return, traffic engineers often furnish the police with advice and information to further their traffic supervision policies. This relationship can result in increased accident prevention and attainment of traffic control goals and objectives.

Reporting versus Investigating Accidents

Geller (1991, p. 174) warns that: "The distinction between reporting and investigating a traffic accident is not defined adequately by law, professional associations, or a uniform operational standard.... Confusion arises from the fact that what is usually referred to as 'accident investigation' is, in reality, accident reporting." Accident investigation is a topic beyond the scope of this text, but the distinction should be kept in mind.

ACCIDENT RECONSTRUCTION

A relatively new technique used to establish the facts of accidents and of help in lawsuits, insurance cases, and vehicular criminal cases is accident reconstruction using videotape.

In video construction scale models of the vehicles are used, often with a photo or video of the accident scene itself as the background. Speed calculations are made from the reporting officer's diagram and notes. Using time/

distance equations, the accident can be shot in segments of one-thirtieth of a second or one frame at a time. The only facility currently having the technology to do such accident reconstruction is the Minnesota State Patrol's Training Center.

HIGH-SPEED PURSUITS

A U.S. Department of Transportation study (Hannigan 1992, p. 46) reports over 50,000 pursuits annually in the United States. Research by the California Highway Patrol (CHP) suggests that the number of pursuits has increased significantly. Their statistics show that over 70 percent of those involved in CHP pursuits were wanted for felony or serious misdemeanor offenses. As noted by Hannigan, CHP Commissioner (p. 49):

> The CHP is not a proponent of damn-the-torpedoes, chase-'em-down-no-matter-what-the-circumstances school of pursuits. In our opinion, however, pursuits are necessary, as long as they are conducted in a responsible, controlled manner to enhance public safety through the apprehension of fleeing felons....
>
> Pursuits conducted by the CHP are regulated by an enforced written pursuit policy, which is reviewed every three months by all officers and supervisors....
>
> Officers acting *outside* the police guidelines are held accountable and provided remedial training; when necessary, they are subject to disciplinary action. Officers acting *within* policy guidelines are not—and should never be—held responsible for actions of the pursued, regardless of the consequences.

A study conducted by the Police Training Institute at the University of Illinois, "Police Pursuit Driving Operations in Illinois 1990," involved eighty-three law enforcement agencies and 286 pursuits. They found that four of every ten pursuits resulted in an accident involving either the officer, the suspect driver, or a citizen. Most commonly, the suspect lost control of his or her vehicle. The majority of pursuits occurred as the result of a police officer seeing a traffic violation. Approximately 70 percent ended with the arrest of the suspect driver, the majority for nonfelony violations (*Law and Order,* 1991).

Brewer and McGrath (1991, p. 63) contend: "Clearly any pursuit is potentially dangerous for the police, the pursued driver, and other (uninvolved) road users, and the financial and human costs of pursuit-related accidents have been well documented." Brewer and McGrath's study of offenders in high-speed pursuits found that only 44.7 percent held the appropriate full (car or motorcycle) license and that 76 percent tested recorded positive BACs, with 64 percent exceeding 0.08 BAC. Their study identified two major offender typologies (p. 67):

- Young, employed males with an appropriate driver's license who recorded high BACs.
- Young employed males who did not hold an appropriate driver's license, who recorded high BACs, and who had aberrant driving records and extensive petty criminal histories.

Dunham and Alpert (1991) looked at the dynamics of the age and gender of the pursuing officer and came to the following conclusions (pp. 57–60):

- Pursuits conducted by female officers and officers over forty years of age are more efficient than other pursuits in terms of the cost-benefit ratio.
- Chases by female officers were shorter and lasted an average of approximately four minutes; those involving male officers lasted approximately one minute more.

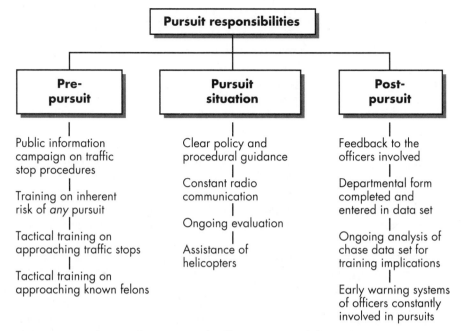

Figure 8–2   Phases of Pursuit and Officer Responsibility
Source: Adpated from J. O'Keefe. "High-Speed Pursuits in Houston." *The Police Chief* (July 1989): 32–40. Reprinted by permission.

- Pursuits by female officers averaged 56 mph; those by males 61 mph.
- Female officers were less likely to engage chases in the evenings or nights or on freeways.
- Pursuits conducted by officers over 40 lasted an average of seven minutes compared to about 4.5 minutes for those under 40.
- Older officers averaged 67 mph; younger officers 59 mph.

A committee of Houston Police Department patrol officers studied the pursuit issue and devised a three-phase approach, illustrated in Figure 8–2.

The pre-pursuit phase is both preventive and preparatory. It is a proactive approach to this phase of police work and involves both citizens and officers. The pursuit phase provides officers with clear guidelines as to acceptable practices should a pursuit occur. The post-pursuit phase assures that what occurs during any pursuit is learned from.

SUMMARY

Of all the operations performed by the police, patrol is the most vital. Patrol is responsible for providing continuous police service and high-visibility law enforcement, thereby deterring crime. Patrol officers may be responsible for preserving the peace, protecting and serving the community, enforcing the laws, directing traffic, and investigating crimes.

Traditionally, patrol has been random, reactive, incident driven, and focused on rapid response to calls. Patrol might be more effective if it were proactive, directed, problem-oriented, and used differentiated response strategies for calls.

Patrol can be accomplished via foot, automobile, motorcycle, bicycle, horseback, aircraft, and boat. The most commonly used and most effective patrol is usually a combination of automobile and foot patrol. Women have been found to be as effective as men on patrol.

Several factors are important in the structure and management of patrol. Equal shift and beat size staffing creates major problems and lessens the effectiveness of patrol during certain times and in certain areas. Directed patrol uses crime statistics to plan shift and beat staffing, providing more coverage during times of peak criminal activity and in high-crime areas.

Another approach to enhancing the effectiveness of patrol is use of community-oriented policing. Community-oriented policing is basically a philosophy that emphasizes a problem-solving partnership between the police and the citizens in working toward a healthy, crime-free environment.

Many hours are spent in traffic-related police work. Traffic officers have numerous responsibilities to fulfill and specific tasks to perform including enforcing traffic laws, directing and controlling traffic, providing directions and assistance to motorists, investigating motor vehicle accidents, providing emergency assistance at the scene of an accident, gathering information related to traffic, and writing reports.

The laws the officers enforce, the services they provide, and the information they compile are important to the total police department traffic program as well as to the image conveyed to the public.

The primary goal of traffic law enforcement is to produce voluntary compliance with traffic regulations and to provide maximum mobility with minimum interruption.

In spite of a highly effective traffic program, motor vehicle accidents will occur. The three basic causes of such accidents are (1) human faults, errors, violations, and attitudes, (2) road defects, and (3) car defects.

Drinking alcohol is indicated to be a factor in at least half the fatal motor vehicle accidents. One attempt at reducing the problem of the drunk driver has been establishing Scandinavian-type drinking and driving laws that prohibit driving with blood alcohol concentrations exceeding specific levels and establishing severe penalties for doing so. Such laws are effective if they are widely publicized and if the likelihood of punishment for noncompliance is high.

In an effort to determine if a driver is intoxicated, legislatures have enacted implied consent laws. These laws state that any person driving a motor vehicle is deemed to have consented to a chemical test of the alcohol content of his or her blood if arrested while intoxicated; refusal to take such a test can be introduced in court as evidence.

An officer called to the scene of an accident must proceed to the scene rapidly but safely, park safely and conveniently, administer emergency first aid if required, interview all persons involved as well as all witnesses, provide needed assistance to victims, accurately observe and record all facts related to the accident, and then clear the scene as soon as possible to restore normal traffic flow.

The responsibilities of the patrol/traffic officer in a mobile society are numerous, demanding, and vital.

DISCUSSION QUESTIONS

1. What type of patrol is used in your community?

2. Why doesn't patrol have as much prestige as investigation?

3. Why is patrol considered a hazardous assignment by some and a "drag" by others?

4. Which do you support, a one-officer or two-officer patrol unit? Why?

5. If you had your choice of patrol, what method would you select? Why

6. What kind of traditional patrol do you feel is effective? Which of the suggested changes do you support?

7. Have you ever been involved in a traffic accident? How would you evaluate the performance of the officer(s) responding to the call?

8. What can the public do to make the traffic officer's job easier?

9. Does your state have a seat belt law? If so, when was it passed and what kind of penalty does it impose?

10. When do you think police officers should issue warning tickets rather than citations for people who are speeding?

TERMS

aggressive patrol, cold crimes, community-oriented policing, community policing, community wellness, differential response strategies, directed patrol, Enforcement Index, Hawthorne effect, implied consent, incident-driven policing, innovator effect, neighborhood policing, proactive, random, reactive, Scandinavian-type law, selective enforcement, suppressible crimes.

REFERENCES

Accident Facts. 1983 and 1984 eds. Chicago: National Safety Council, 1988.

Benson, C. C. "K-9 Sniffers." *Law and Order* (August 1991): 78–81.

Boydstun, E. et al. *Patrol Staffing in San Diego: One- or Two-Officer Units.* Washington, D.C.: Police Foundation, 1977.

Brand, L. "Compact Patrol Cars." *Law and Order* (November 1990): 36–37.

Brewer, N. and McGrath, G. "Characteristics of Offenders in High-Speed Pursuits." *American Journal of Police* 10, no. 3 (1991): 63–68.

Brown, L. P. "Community Policing: Its Time Has Come." *The Police Chief* (September 1991): 6.

Brown, L. P. "The Police-Community Partnership." *The Police Chief* (December 1990): 8.

Bureau of Justice Statistics. Special Report Drunk Driving. U.S. Department of Justice. Washington, D.C.: U.S. Government Printing Office, November 1983.

Chapman, S. G. et al. *Perspectives on Police Assaults in the South Central United States.* Vol. 1. Norman, Okla.: The University of Oklahoma Press, 1974.

Conroy, D. L. and Hess, K. M. *Officers at Risk: How to Identify and Cope with Stress.* Placerville, Calif.: Custom Publishing Co., 1992.

Donaldson, J. "Personal Watercraft: Wave of the Future for Marine Law Enforcement." *Law and Order* (November 1990): 43–47.

Dunham, R. G. and Alpert, G. "Understanding the Dynamics of Officer Age and Gender in Police Pursuits." *American Journal of Police* 10, no. 3 (1991): 51–61.

Frawley, E. "Police Service Dog Work in Holland." *Law and Order* (September 1989): 115–117.

Geller, W. A. (Ed.) *Local Government Police Management, Municipal Management Series.* 3d ed. Washington, D.C.: International City Management Association, 1991.

Goldstein, H. *Policing in a Free Society.* Cambridge, Mass.: Ballinger Publishing, 1977.

Hale, C. D. *Police Patrol Operations and Management.* New York: John Wiley and Sons, 1981.

Hannigan, M. J. "California's Ongoing Battle Against DUI." *The Police Chief* (July 1990): 51–53.

Hannigan, M. J. "The Viability of Police Pursuits." *The Police Chief* (February 1992): 46–49.

Harrison, B. "Random Patrol: Days of Future Past?" *Law and Order* (July 1991): 65–67.

Hildreth, R. "The Modern Posse." *Law and Order* (June 1990): 30–33.

"Housing Authority Adds 'Stealth' Weapon to Arsenal." *Law and Order* (September 1991): 178.

Kiernan, M. and Cusik, J. "Women on Patrol: The Nation's Capitol Gives them High Marks." *Police Magazine* (1977): 45–53.

Klockars, C. B. *Thinking about Police: Contemporary Readings.* New York: McGraw-Hill, 1983.

Major, V. "Law Enforcement Officers Killed." *FBI Law Enforcement Bulletin* (May 1991): 2–5.

McLean, H. "Heat on the Pedals." *Law and Order* (December 1990): 24–29.

Miller, M. and Weston, A. P. "Phoenix Bicycle Patrol." *Law and Order* (January 1991): 30.

More, H. W., Jr. *Critical Issues in Law Enforcement.* Cincinnati, Ohio: Anderson Publishing Co., 1987.

National Neighborhood Foot Patrol Center (pamphlet). East Lansing, Mich.: Michigan State University (no date).

O'Neill J. L. and Cushing, M. A. *The Impact of Shift Work on Police Officers.* Washington, D.C.: Police Executive Research Forum, 1991.

President's Commission on Law Enforcement and Administration of Justice. *The Challenge of Crime in a Free Society.* Washington, D.C.: U.S. Government Printing Office, 1967.

"Police Pursuit Research." *Law and Order* (July 1991): 4.

Ross, H. L. "The Scandinavian Myth: The Effectiveness of Drinking-Driving Legislation in Sweden and Norway." *Journal of Legal Studies* 4 (1975): 285–310.

Ross, H. L. *Deterrence of the Drinking Driver: An International Survey.* National Highway Traffic Safety Administration Technical Report, DOT HS–805 820. Washington, D.C.: U.S. Government Printing Office, 1981.

Slahor, S. "Wheeling to Better Law Enforcement." *Law and Order* (March 1992): 79–81.

Spurlock, J. C. "K-9." *Law and Order* (March 1990): 91–96.

Stokes, F. *For the Record: Report Writing in Law Enforcment.* 3rd ed. Eureka, Calif.: Innovative Systems, 1991, Preface.

Sumrall, R. O.; Roberts, J.; and Farmer, M. T. *Differential Police Response Strategies.* Washington, D.C.: Police Executive Research Forum, 1981.

Trojanowicz, R. *An Evaluation of the Neighborhood Foot Patrol Program in Flint, Michigan.* East Lansing: Michigan State University, 1982.

U.S. Department of Transportation, National Highway Traffic Safety Administration, Interim Report on the Safety Consequences of Raising the Speed Limit on Rural Interstate Highways, May 1988, Washington, D.C.

Usilton, W. S. and McMorrow, R. "Target Patrol." *Law and Order* (February 1991): 57–60.

Williams, V. L.; Formby, W. A.; and Watkins, J. C. *Introduction to Criminal Justice.* Albany, N.Y.: Delmar Publishers, 1982.

"Women on Patrol." *Minnesota Police Journal* 50, no. 1 (February 1978): 43.

Yates, T. "Watercraft for Law Enforcement." *Law and Order* (July 1991): 52–56.

CHAPTER 9

Community Service: To Serve and Protect

The vocation of every man and woman is to serve other people.

—Leo Tolstoi

Do You Know

What community services the police department may provide its citizens?

What most public relations programs emphasize?

What most community relations programs emphasize?

What factors interfere with good community relations?

What single element is critical for any successful community relations program?

What types of youth programs have been developed?

What the two phases of community-oriented policing are?

What the four strategies of problem-oriented policing are?

What types of community service programs have been instituted to deter crime?

INTRODUCTION

Community service translates into customer service. As noted by Couper and Lobitz (1988, pp. 79–81):

> Our business is policing, our customers are the citizens within our jurisdictions, and our product is police service (everything from crime fighting and conflict management to safety and prevention programs). . . .
>
> The problems confronting the business world are the same problems we have in the police service. We approach our work with a short-term orientation (in our field, we seldom talk about five- or ten-year goals for our organizations), shallow thinking (if there is a problem in a particular neighborhood, we simply hurl more police officers at it and frequently push the criminal activity into the next neighborhood), and quick-fix expectations (like "street sweeping" prostitutes).
>
> We must start to pay attention to the new ideas and trends coming out of America's businesses: a commitment to people, the development of a people-oriented workplace, and the belief that leadership can and does make a difference.

Although speaking to management about how to effectively lead police officers, the same message applies to police officers as providers of service to the citizens in their respective neighborhoods. Effective police officers in the 1990s will be "customer oriented." As noted by Couper and Lobitz (1991, pp. 52–53):

> A customer orientation means listening to your customers. . . . Listening to and being responsive to citizens should be a goal. There are, of course, a number of parameters in being responsive—the law, ethics, and budgetary constraints. In this new era of community policing, listening to the customer is a vital part of the job. It is a change. Professionals today no longer have the exclusive market on knowing what is best for their patients, clients, or customers. Today, people want to be heard and participate.

Taking a page from the business world, customer oriented means:

- Providing the best service possible.
- Being courteous, honest, open, and fair.
- Treating each person as an individual, not as an object to be pushed aside or an inconvenience.
- Listening and being responsive to what each person wants.
- Keeping your promises.
- Knowing who to refer someone to if you cannot help them yourself.
- Thanking people when they are helpful.

Sometimes, of course, as in emergency situations, certain of these behaviors would be totally inappropriate and even counterproductive. Usually, however, police officers should be "consumer friendly" as the officers serve and protect. The types of service provided by the police take a variety of forms. Chapter 7 discussed these types of service and the controversy as to how much and what types are justified.

Police departments provide a wide variety of services including giving information, directions, and advice; counseling and referring; licensing and registering vehicles; intervening in domestic arguments; working with neglected children; rendering emergency medical or rescue services; dealing with alcoholics and the mentally ill; finding lost children; dealing with stray animals; controlling crowds; and providing community education programs on crime prevention, drug abuse, safety, and the like.

Although some police departments have a separate division assigned the responsibilities of community service and some have made community service a responsibility of a patrol team, in reality, community service is a vital part of every police officer's job.

PRESERVING THE PEACE AND SAFETY OF THE PUBLIC

As part of their role to preserve the peace and safety of the public, police officers may be called to handle disputes and disturbances, to quell civil disturbances, and to maintain order in labor/management disputes and strikes.

Disputes and Domestic Quarrels

One of the most common and most dangerous calls made to the police department is for assistance in settling a dispute, for example, a fight in a bar, or for resolving a domestic situation, for example, a husband beating his wife (or vice versa). Frequently alcohol is involved in such situations. Tempers are short, and the potential for violence is ever present. As noted by Levine, Husheno, and Palumbo (1980, p. 23):

> Diversity within cities creates the potential for all kinds of disputes and disturbances. Parties to traffic accidents get angry with one another; people imbibing at taverns get into fights; young people blasting stereos disturb neighborhood residents. One purpose of the criminal justice system is to moderate these tensions and keep hostilities from escalating. Indeed peacekeeping is one of the primary missions of the police and as important as this goal is, if it is pursued too zealously, the right of the people to be different may be impaired. There is a fine line between obnoxious conduct that intrudes into other people's lives and harmless behavior that merely defies common standards of propriety. Thus, neighbors may be annoyed when teen-agers "hang out" on the streets and use vulgar language, but it is arguable that they have the right to do so if they do not interfere with passersby. Likewise, demonstrators passing out political fliers often disturb people who disagree with their views, and the discarded sheets of paper can cause a mess, but to prohibit such activities would invade the constitutional right of freedom of speech. Too much emphasis on public peace can lead to social repression and an insistence on mass conformity.

Civil Disturbances

The civil disturbances on campuses throughout the country in the 1960s highlighted the role of the police in controlling civil disturbances. Although civil disturbances are not as prevalent, protest demonstrations continue throughout the country, for example, strong antiwar sentiment, disagreement with legislative decisions, strong sentiments for or against abortion, or protests against industries engaged in manufacturing war materiels.

In dealing with civil disturbances, police officers must always remember that our Constitution guarantees its citizens the right to *peacefully* assemble. This right must be protected. It is only when the assembly is no longer peaceful that officers have the responsibility to intervene. Determining what constitutes peaceful assembly places a large amount of discretionary power in the hands of police officers.

The primary responsibilities of police officers are to maintain order and to protect lives and assets. In the event of sit-in demonstrations, it may be necessary to forcibly remove participants. In such instances, the minimum amount of force necessary should be used.

The verdict in the trial of the
officers accused of beating Rodney King had repercussions
across the nation. Here, officers
arrest youths looting a store
during rioting in Crown Heights,
Brooklyn.

Riots

Although civil disturbances are not as prevalent as in the 1960s, they may
escalate to even greater destructive riots than in Watts, as evidenced by the
violence, brutality, and looting that occurred in Los Angeles in May of 1992
following the acquittal of three of the four officers involved in the Rodney King
beating.

Labor/Management Disputes and Strikes

Strikes are legal, but, as with the right to assemble, the strike must be peaceful.
If strikers physically restrict others from crossing the picket line, they are
acting illegally, and the police may be called to intervene. In such instances,
police officers must remain neutral. Their only responsibility is to prevent
violence and property damage or loss.

PROVIDING EMERGENCY SERVICES

Frequently patrol officers are the first on the scene of a situation requiring
emergency services.

Emergency First Aid

Police officers are often the first on the scene of a traffic accident and are
responsible for providing first aid to any persons injured in the accident. They
may also be called on to assist persons who have been injured in other ways
or who become seriously ill. Police officers should be thoroughly trained and
certified in CPR as well as in advanced first aid, including measures to stop

bleeding and to deal with fractures, shock, burns, and epileptic seizures. They should also recognize insulin coma and know how to treat it.

Ambulance Service

Closely related to providing emergency first aid, police officers may be required to transport accident victims or other persons who are gravely ill or injured to the nearest medical facility. In fact, in some communities, the police department is the sole ambulance service, and patrol cars are specially equipped to serve as ambulances. This policy of providing ambulance service tends to make the public more appreciative of the police department and may foster citizen cooperation; however, this can place a drain on a police department's resources. Local conditions should determine whether this service is routinely provided.

Natural Disasters

Floods, tornadoes, hurricanes, fires, and earthquakes can produce emergency conditions requiring action on the part of police officers. They may need to provide first aid to victims, provide crowd control, and protect the property of those involved.

Search and Rescue

Many departments are also actively involved in search and rescue operations that may or may not be necessitated by natural disasters.

Fire Control Service

In some departments, police and fire fighting are combined into a public safety department. In such instances, obviously, police officers must be trained in fire suppression techniques. In departments where the police are not primarily responsible for fire suppression activities, they may still be the first to arrive at the scene of a fire and can lend valuable assistance to the fire fighters.

The first action of police officers who come upon an uncontrolled fire is to call the fire department. Only then should any attempts be made to control or suppress the fire. Other functions the police may serve include traffic control, assuring that fire fighting equipment can arrive quickly at the scene, and helping search for and rescue people trapped by the fire. If children are trapped in a home that is burning, rescuers should check under beds and in closets because children frequently try to hide from the smoke and flames. Police officers can also provide crowd control, assist with first aid, transport injured persons to the nearest medical facility, and guard any personal property removed from the burning structure.

Bomb Threats or Incidents

If a bomb threat is made or a bomb is actually found, the police are usually the ones to be notified. In such instances the main responsibility of the police is to assure the safety of persons in the vicinity of the bomb and to call in experts to actually dispose of the bomb. Frequently a bomb disposal unit of a military installation is called in. Larger departments, however, may have their own bomb disposal teams.

Most major cities have sophisticated equipment to deal with
bombs.

In the event of an actual explosion, be it intentional or accidental as in an explosion at an industrial site, the police are usually responsible for crowd control and for investigating the incident.

OTHER COMMUNITY SERVICES

Several other services may or may not be provided by police departments, depending on local policy.

Missing Persons

Television programs have made the missing persons function of the police department seem a routine activity. In actuality, however, unless foul play is suspected or the person missing is retarded, mentally incompetent, or in need of medication, the police do not become involved in missing person cases. If no crime has been committed and the safety of the missing person is not in jeopardy, the police department performs an administrative function, recording the information to be used in helping to identify individuals who are unconscious, who are found wandering (senility), or who are found dead and have no identification on them.

Because of the mobility of individuals in our society, the need for a centralized, computerized system for recording information about missing persons was recognized and acted upon over a decade ago when the National Crime Information Center (NCIC) Advisory Policy Board approved establishing a Missing Person File. This file was added to the nationwide NCIC system in October 1975. The file has four specific categories and criteria for entry (Bishop and Schuessler 1982, p. 21):

> Disability—A person of any age who is missing and under proven physical and/or mental disability or is senile, thereby subjecting himself or others to personal and immediate danger.

Endangered—A person of any age who is missing and is in the company of another person under circumstances indicating that his physical safety is in danger.

Involuntary—A person of any age who is missing under circumstances indicating that the disappearance was not voluntary, that is, abduction or kidnapping.

Juvenile—A person who is missing and declared unemancipated as defined by the laws of his state of residence and who does not meet the entry criteria of the other three categories.

Damage to Property

Citizens who experience damage to their property are very likely to call the police. The first action of officers responding to such calls is to determine if any danger is inherent in the situation. If danger does exist, the police officers must take action to remove the danger. For example, if a tree has fallen on power lines and hot wires are on the ground, the police should rope off the area and call the power company. If no danger is inherent in the situation, the police officers should determine if the damage is the result of criminal or noncriminal actions. If it is criminal property damage, for example, the work of vandals, the officers should conduct a thorough investigation. If it is a noncriminal (and nondangerous) situation, for example, a tree has fallen on a home, the police officers should advise the complainant of alternatives in taking care of the damage. The complainant should usually also be advised to notify his or her insurance agent.

Lost and Found

People who find valuable property are likely to turn it in to the police department. Conversely, people who have lost items of value are likely to request assistance from the police department. In this situation, also, the police department plays primarily an administrative function, maintaining accurate records of property that has been found or lost. The department is responsible for protecting all found property and for attempting to locate the rightful owners. Of course, the owner also is responsible for checking with the police to see if the property has been found. Any unclaimed property is frequently disposed of through an open auction.

Missing and Stray Animals

Some police departments also have the responsibility for stray animals, especially unlicensed dogs. They may also be called upon to deal with dangerous animals such as bears or with trapped animals such as a raccoon up a chimney of a home. Department policy will determine whether such calls are responded to by the police department. If the department policy is not to handle animal problems other than unlicensed stray dogs (usually in violation of a leash law), officers should be prepared to offer advice to the person seeking assistance, for example, that the person should call the humane society.

Escort Services

Police may be called upon to provide escort service to extremely popular individuals, for example, rock stars, or for those who are extremely unpopular, for example, a politician the public greatly dislikes. They may also provide escort services for dangerous cargoes such as those containing highly flammable materials, hazardous wastes, and the like or for oversized cargoes. In addition, police may be asked to provide escort services for funeral processions or for very valuable cargoes such as large sums of cash.

Little agreement exists on when escort services are appropriate or on how they should be provided, that is, should they include red flashing lights and sirens, or proceed as though on general patrol? Local circumstances will largely determine the answers to these questions. The important thing in the area of escort services is that the department have a clearly established policy on the use of police escorts to avoid any charges of favoritism should a request for such services be denied.

Persons Locked Out

The police are frequently called to assist people who have locked themselves out of their car or home. In such instances it is usually preferable to have the civilian call a locksmith. If this is not possible, however, police officers should check the identity of the person requesting assistance. Imagine the predicament of a police officer who assists a burglar in breaking and entering.

If the police do assist in gaining entry to a car or home, headquarters should be fully informed prior to the action.

Transporting Civilians in Police Cars

As a general rule, most police officers are not allowed to transport civilians in their patrol cars unless they are on official business, for example, transporting a prisoner from one jail to another, a defendant to court for trial, or a witness to view a suspect.

In some departments, police officers are responsible for chauffeuring public officials and for transporting economically disadvantaged people to the welfare office to obtain assistance. Use of police vehicles for such purposes is usually not good practice; however, instances may arise when the police need to

Officers may assist people who have locked themselves out of their cars.

transport civilians in their squads. For example, a patrol officer may come upon a motorist whose car is totally disabled and the weather is extremely inclement. The patrol officer may, in such instances, give the civilian a ride to a service station or home, depending on the circumstances. In such instances, the patrol officer should notify headquarters of the situation.

Licensing

The police department is frequently involved in licensing handguns, understandably so since it is to their advantage to know who owns what kind of weapons in their locality. In addition, they are in a position to investigate the applicant for a license and to determine if such a license should be granted. They may also do background investigations on applicants for liquor licenses, for taxi licenses, and for tow truck licenses.

The police department is also frequently involved in other types of licensing such as licenses for holding a parade or for blocking off a street for a community function. When such licensing is provided by the police department, it is also responsible for activities such as blocking off streets and setting up detours, rerouting traffic, and the like.

Inspections

Because patrol officers routinely cover the entire area over which the police department has jurisdiction, many decision makers believe they should be responsible for inspections to insure adherence to fire codes, health codes, and building codes. This is another area of controversy because such activities are extremely time consuming. They do present the advantage of familiarizing the patrol officers with the people and buildings on their beats. On the other hand, such activities take patrol officers off the street and into buildings where they are no longer on preventive patrol but rather are serving a function that could easily be carried out by an inspector specifically hired for the job and, usually, at less cost.

In many areas, police are also responsible for checking the weight of trucks. Police are used in this capacity because they must be on the scene anyway to issue tickets to overweight trucks or to stop trucks who bypass the scales completely. Others contend, however, that the patrol officers in the vicinity could be called in for either of the preceding situations and that it might be more practical not to use patrol officers in this capacity.

PUBLIC RELATIONS PROGRAMS

Public relations programs frequently seek to enhance the image of the police officer by helping citizens gain an understanding and acceptance of the role of the police in the community. The programs are directed to groups or the entire community. The police officer may be portrayed as the friend of young and old, appear at school and church programs, sponsor little league teams or law enforcement days, or hand out bumper stickers encouraging people to support their local police.

The primary emphasis of most public relations programs is to raise the image of the police agency and its officials.

A state trooper shows children a squad car during an open-house. According to the officer, "We're not trying to influence how they think; we just want them to see we're human."

Such programs are usually geared to the needs of the police. Sometimes they are only cosmetic or token efforts to gain community approval. However, public relations is an accepted and healthy form of advertising used very successfully by major corporations and by many law enforcement agencies. There is nothing wrong with a police department using such tactics. The problem arises when a department institutes a special unit to "take care of the public image" and assumes that this is all that is required. No amount of bumper stickers or sponsorships will counteract negative actions by police officers. Respect must be earned; it cannot be bought or commanded. Always remember that the police image is primarily the result of daily contacts between police officers and citizens of the community.

Respect for and confidence in the police requires more than public relations programs. It requires, first and foremost, appropriate actions by police officers, and second, sound community relations programs.

POLICE–COMMUNITY RELATIONS PROGRAMS

While public relations programs are a one-way effort directed at raising the image of the police, police-community relations programs seek to provide means for police and citizens to work together to achieve their mutual goal of law and order.

The primary emphasis of police-community relations programs is to provide two-way communication between police and citizens to work toward achieving law and order in the community.

Over twenty-five years ago the president's 1966 Crime Commission, in *The Challenge of Crime in a Free Society* (1967, p. 100), stated:

A community relations program is not a public relations program "to sell the police image" to the people. It is not a set of expedients whose purpose is to tranquilize for a time an angry neighborhood by, for example, suddenly promoting a few Negro officers in the wake of a racial disturbance. It is a long-range, full-scale effort to acquaint the police and the community with each other's problems and to stimulate action aimed at solving those problems.

Many people are concerned about the relationship between police and citizens. Many people think they know the answer to the problem. Police officers feel that if citizens would only understand the responsibilities of law enforcement officers and would obey the law themselves, there would be no problem. Citizens, on the other hand, frequently believe that if the police would be more human and understanding, the problem would be solved. Both sides are partly right and partly wrong; however, their attitudes toward one another frequently interfere with working together to find answers to their mutual problems.

People tend to think in terms of the "ingroup"–the group to which they belong–and the "outgroup." The outgroup is everyone else and usually is perceived as being "bad." If citizens perceive police as members of the outgroup, citizens will be uncooperative and perhaps even hostile. Nobody wants to tell on a friend or sometimes even a total stranger who is a private citizen like himself or herself.

Group protectiveness interferes with communication and good relations.

Today it is more difficult to get a case through court, more dangerous to walk the streets at night, and more of a strain to get along with neighbors crowded in on all sides. Living in this generation requires more skill, knowledge, patience, and goodwill.

Police work also requires better training and more self-discipline than ever before. Law enforcement is no longer a job. It is a profession. Likewise, citizens must be willing to pay the price for living in this generation. One cost is personal involvement. To stand aside and expect others to carry the load is to default in a primary obligation of citizenship. As the Roman statesman and philosopher Seneca noted: "He who does not prevent a crime when he can, encourages it."

The police and public are bound together in a common destiny. What is good for one is inevitably good for the other. What is bad for one is bad for the other. If police work for low salaries, with inadequate training, or in hostile communities that provide little cooperation and frequent danger, they are not going to operate effectively. Citizens can do something to alleviate these conditions and thereby assure themselves of better and more professional police services.

As long as citizens live in fear of the police, believing them to be unfriendly mercenaries at best and brutal oppressors at worst, they will not provide the environment essential for effective law enforcement. Robert F. Kennedy once said: "Every society gets the kind of criminal it deserves. What is equally true is that every community gets the kind of law enforcement it insists upon."

Pace (1991, p. 4) says:

> **Community relations** is the sum total of activities by which the criminal justice system can become a part of the community, rather than being solely a punitive regulatory agency that is imposed upon the public it has been sworn to serve. The ability of the criminal justice system to function effectively is dependent upon community approval of its acts and public support of its programs.

Pace (p. 8) cites the following purposes of community relations:

- It allows agents of the [criminal justice] system to more fully understand the importance of human behavior.
- It lets the different components of the system know what kind of services the public desires.
- It is a vehicle to let the public know what they are getting in services, thus serving as an information and public relations media.
- It allows the agents of the system and the public to interact on common problems and to develop positive attitudes about one another.
- It allows the public and the system to work in a mutual endeavor to curb community problems. These problems are often not of a criminal nature, and the agency acts merely as a catalyst to resolve a social problem.

Approaches to Police-Community Relations

Several approaches have been taken to police-community relations programs. Bureaus have been established within police agencies. Community-wide citizen groups have been formed. Civilian review boards or advisory committees have worked with police agencies in establishing goals and priorities. Large-scale educational programs have been successful when they have promoted dialogue rather than simply conveying information (public relations). As noted by the President's Commission on Law Enforcement and the Administration of Justice (*The Police,* p. 159):

> Citizens who distrust the police will not easily be converted by information programs they consider to come from a tainted source. However, even for these groups, long-term education based upon honest and free DIALOGUE between the police and the public can have an effect. Indeed, this is one of the basic goals of the citizen advisory committees. On the other hand, citizens who are neutral or supportive can benefit from increased understanding of the complicated problems and tasks of the police. Informational programs can also generate support for more personnel, salary increases, sufficient equipment, and other resources to improve the efficiency of police work. It can help the cooperative citizen to avoid becoming a victim of crime and show him how to work more effectively with the police. And, to the extent that the police department is genuinely working at improved community relations, dissemination of this information to the press and other media does have a positive effect on community relations.

The police officer on the street is the community relations officer of the department. The officer's actions, demeanor, appearance, and empathy for people are all accountable for positive or negative community relations.

Community acceptance of crime prevention programs initiated depends on the overall effectiveness of all police operations. Hundreds of programs have aided the police in their efforts toward not only community relations but also improved law enforcement. As police officers' knowledge of the community and its citizens increases, so does their effectiveness as law enforcement officers. Their street contacts and sources of information are also vastly improved.

The police officer on the street is ultimately responsible for the success of police-community relations programs.

Community relations is a responsibility of both the police and the citizen. The police may contribute to improving two-way communication by the following:

- Understanding the problems of citizens and keeping an open mind; using good judgment.

- Paying attention rather than displaying a casual attitude. Police officers should listen attentively. If they disagree on a point, they should do so politely. They should show consideration rather than ignoring citizens. The problems citizens convey to the police may be of utmost importance to them.

- Using courteous words. Sarcasm in either words or attitude is readily apparent to citizens and hampers communication. Tone of voice can be as important as the words used. Tone can incite anger or instill confidence.

- Being patient. Police officers must exercise self-command and self-discipline. Although patience and kindness may be misperceived by some as a sign of weakness, this is not true.

- Giving time. Give citizens time to air their problems. Do not rush them.

- Showing enthusiasm. Officers should approach each contact with enthusiasm, believing in themselves and their communities. A lackadaisical attitude will thwart the objectives of any contact.

- Being helpful instead of hindering. Rendering aid is one of the most important functions of police officers.

- Showing sincerity. Mere words, in themselves, are not proof of sincerity. Police officers must be honest and straightforward in their citizen contacts.

- Being polite and friendly. A smile at the opportune moment is an asset to a police officer. It is hard for anyone to ignore a friendly smile.

YOUTH PROGRAMS

Brown (1991, p. 6), former president of the International Association of Chiefs of Police (IACP), emphasizes the critical importance of the youth of our country:

> When I was inaugurated as IACPs president, I dedicated my presidency to the children of the world, because I am concerned about *their* future. If our children are *our* future, what kind of citizens will they grow up to be if they are regularly

exposed to violence, drugs, crime, alcoholism and physical abuse during their formative years? Will they even have a *chance* to grow up?

It is important to understand that the complex problems that face our children cannot be solved through the efforts of law enforcement alone—they are everyone's responsibility—but the law enforcement community certainly has an important role to play.

Programs for youth include PAL programs, school-liaison officers, Officer Friendly, McGruff, explorer posts, and the D.A.R.E. program.

The PAL Program   Police Athletic League (PAL) programs have been in operation for over fifty years. These programs were developed to give youth opportunities to interact with police officers in sports. In Portland, Oregon, the police department has adopted the program to deal with increasing gang violence and street sale of drugs. Sports in their program include boxing, wrestling, football, soccer, martial arts, basketball, racquetball, track and field, volleyball, and speed and quickness training. Austin and Braaten (1991, p. 36) list the following goals for the Portland area PAL:

- Reduce the incidence of juvenile crime, substance abuse, and gang violence.
- Provide positive alternative activities for boys and girls.
- Guide boys and girls to make responsible decisions in life.
- Foster better understanding between youth and the police.

Austin and Braaten (p. 38) note: "Through PAL, we are helping these kids build self-esteem, meet life's challenges, interact with positive role models, enhance their physical sports abilities, and make friends with police officers."

Police-School Liaison Programs   The first police-school liaison program was developed in Flint, Michigan, in 1958. A typical police-school liaison program places an officer, uniformed or not, inside a school to work with the administration, students, and parents to prevent crime and antisocial behavior and to enhance police-youth relationships.

Officer Friendly   As noted by Pace (1991, p. 254): "Designed for lower grades, this program discusses the basic concepts of good citizenship, responsibility, and general safety. The concepts are reinforced by coloring books, a second visit to the school, and an activity book for the teacher to supplement the regular social studies curriculum."

McGruff   The "McGruff Take a Bite Out of Crime" program began as a national media campaign using public service announcements (PSAs) from late 1979 to 1981. It was hoped McGruff would become to crime prevention what Smokey Bear was to fire prevention. Originally McGruff was aimed at people of all ages. As noted by O'Keefe (1986, p. 253), the campaign had four major objectives:

- To change unwarranted citizen feelings about crime and the criminal justice system, particularly feelings of frustration and hopelessness.
- To generate an individual sense of responsibility for reducing crime among citizens.

- To encourage citizens, working within their communities and with local law enforcement agencies, to take collective crime prevention action.
- To enhance existing crime prevention programs at the local, state, and national levels.

The program met its objectives. Today McGruff may be even better known than Smokey Bear. Over time, the program has become more youth focused.

Police Explorers   Police explorers are senior Scouts (boy or girl) who volunteer time with a police department. Most departments require three to six months probation and provide extensive training in personal conduct, first aid, police procedures, weapons familiarization, crime scene investigation, traffic control, radio procedures, interpersonal communications, criminal law, and specialized police duties. According to Lesce (1991, pp. 98–100):

> The program requires both work and dedication. Members must participate in 66% of activities to maintain active status. These include training activities and special events, such as the Easter Pageant, the 10-kilometer run, and various parades. Explorers assist officers in traffic control and other non-enforcement duties, relieving the burden on department personnel....
>
> Explorer programs serve two purposes; favorable community relations and early recruitment for law enforcement agencies. The program is cost-effective for the sponsoring agency because the value of the public service time Explorers provide outweighs the cost of the program.

D.A.R.E.   The well-known Drug Abuse Resistance Education (D.A.R.E.) program was developed jointly by the Los Angeles Police Department and the Los Angeles Unified School District. Its purpose is to teach elementary school age children to "say no to drugs," to resist peer pressure to experiment with drugs, and to find alternatives to drug use. Police officers go into the schools and teach seventeen classroom sessions dealing with self-esteem, the dangers of drugs, and how to resist peer pressure to try them. The Ridgecrest Police Department has added a unique touch to this program: D.A.R.E. cards. According to Narramore (1990, p. 23):

> The newest and biggest success we have had in promoting the program are the new D.A.R.E. cards.
>
> We even included photographs of the two police dogs and their handlers. Each card is numbered and has a safety tip on the reverse side of the card along with a job description of the person on the card.

(See Figure 9–1.)

Other Programs

Programs in the schools, such as lectures and videos about "Children and the Law," have aided police in their fight against vandalism and shoplifting. They reach a segment of society that represents future citizens, informing children of the problem of crime in our society and how they might help reduce this problem.

In addition to community programs to help combat crime, many police departments have instituted programs to promote safety and the general welfare of the public. Most such programs are aimed at children, such as bike safety programs.

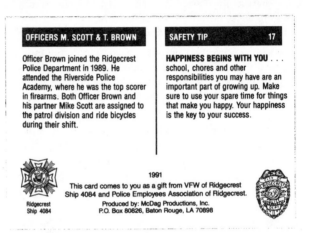

Figure 9–1   Ridgecrest Police Department D.A.R.E. Card

COMMUNITY SERVICE PROGRAMS TO DETER CRIME

Many police departments have instituted programs aimed at preventing crime in the community.

Crime prevention programs include neighborhood or block watch programs, operation identification programs, home security, store security, and automobile security.

Neighborhood or Block Watch Programs

Block watch programs have been initiated that instruct homeowners to form cooperative block groups to deter burglaries and thefts during the absence of homeowners and to provide places of safety for children who might be threatened on their way to or from school. Such neighborhood watch programs bring neighbors together in an effort to reduce the incidence of crime in their neighborhood. The program involves being aware of who your neighbors are,

Police department programs on safety are often aimed at children.

what their daily routines are, and of suspicious activities or persons in the neighborhood and reporting anything unusual to the police.

With cooperation and involvement of all citizens, such as sharing the responsibility of checking each other's homes when owners are on vacation, the neighborhood is a safer place in which to live. Most programs emphasize that residents should *not* try to apprehend suspects, so programs do not create "vigilante" actions.

These citizen crime reporting programs (CCRPs) are the most widely used police-community crime prevention programs in the country. As noted by Hageman (1985, p. 127): "Organized into groups such as block watches, auxiliaries, telephone relays, and citizen patrols, these groups serve as the 'eyes and ears' for the police, and they educate others in order to minimize their becoming victims of crime."

Signs are usually prominently displayed at curbside as well as on the homes or apartments themselves. Often such programs are instrumental in establishing property identification programs as well.

Operation Identification Programs

Police have also implemented operation identification programs in which citizens are provided tools and loaned markers to identify their property with a permanent identification number. If these items are lost or stolen and recovered by the police, the identification number provides a positive method of identifying the rightful owner. If the items are found in the possession of a burglar or thief, the number can aid the police in prosecuting and convicting the suspect.

Stickers and decals are furnished those citizens participating so that they can place a warning on their doors and window (see Figure 9–2). The warning labels and the marking of personal property with a permanent identification number are positive approaches to deter a burglar or thief from attempting to steal that property.

Figure 9–2   Operation I.D. Sticker
Source: Courtesy of Minnesota Crime Watch—Department of Public Safety.

A Neighborhood Watch notice posted in a Washington, D.C. neighborhood informs residents of a crime committed that day.

Home Security

Police departments may also provide home security inspections in which an officer goes to a citizen's home, evaluates its security, and suggests methods for making the home a less inviting target for crime. Recommendations may be made to install deadbolt locks, improve lighting, and so on. In some communities a subsidy is available for half the cost of making recommended changes.

Store Security

Police departments may assist store owners in their efforts to reduce losses from shoplifting by studying their stores and then recommending action. Recommendations might include hiring store detectives, implementing educational campaigns, installing convex, wide-angle mirrors in isolated areas, installing closed-circuit television cameras to watch shoppers from observation booths, or installing electronic systems using special magnetic or microwave-sensitive tags. The tags require a deactivating device or a special tool to remove them without damaging the merchandise. If a customer leaves an area of the store before a salesperson removes the tag or deactivates it, a sensor sounds an alarm and store personnel apprehend and detain the suspect for the police.

Often crime prevention through environmental design (**CPTED**) is an integral part of these programs. Based on Paul Newman's concept of "defensible space," CPTED uses access control, lighting, and surveillance as key strategies of **target hardening,** that is, making it more difficult for crime to occur.

Automobile Security

Because of the vulnerability of autos to theft, many antitheft programs and devices have been introduced to make it more difficult for a person to steal a car and more difficult for that person to use or sell it without its stolen nature being detected.

Automobile manufacturers have contributed by making the ignition switch mechanism lock the steering wheel and by having a separate steering post lock key and door lock key. Some police agencies have placed on every parking meter a sticker stating: "Have you locked your car?" and provided dashboard stickers that remind motorists: "Have you taken your keys and locked your car?"

Some cities have encouraged used-car dealers to fence in their lots or chain their entrances and exits. Public education campaigns have also been instituted using newspaper, radio, television, and placard publicity as well as bumper stickers with slogans reminding motorists to lock their cars.

Because 72 percent of the autos stolen are taken by persons under the age of twenty-one, extensive educational campaigns have been launched to educate youth about the seriousness of car theft and its consequences. Law enforcement agencies have also taken stronger measures to assure the immediate processing of persons apprehended.

An innovative anti-auto theft program using modern technology is the Lo-Jack Auto Recovery System (LARS). According to Nilson (1990, p. 36): "The primary component of the system is a homing device installed in a customer's car. . . . When the car is reported stolen, the homing device is automatically activated and a signal is transmitted."

A less expensive, less high-tech program is the Combat Auto Theft (CAT) program initiated in New York City in 1988. As noted by Hildreth (1990, p. 92): "The program [gives] police the right to stop any automobile that's marked with a special decal when observed traveling on city streets between 1 A.M. and 5 A.M." They do not need probable cause for the stop. In this voluntary program, car owners who normally do not operate their vehicles during these hours sign a consent form and are given the CAT decal to affix prominently on the inside of the car's rear window.

Evaluation of Crime Prevention Programs

Rosenbaum (1986, p. 7) notes in the foreword to *Community Crime Prevention: Does It Work?*:

> This volume contains some of the best evaluations of community crime prevention programs that have been implemented to date. . . . In general, the results of these evaluations are favorable, indicating that community crime prevention

programs can serve to reduce crime and fear, and at the same time improve the quality of life and the economic viability of urban neighborhoods and commercial settings. . . .

Overall, the results indicate that crime prevention programs need to be comprehensive in focus, mobilizing both citizen and police resources and promoting the effective collaboration of these efforts. In addition, program planners need to take the physical and social environment into consideration.

Despite these positive remarks, in the lead-off chapter, Rosenbaum (p. 11) says:

Crime, incivility, and fear of crime continue to plague American cities at unacceptably high levels relative to other countries. Since the "war on crime" began in the 1960s we have witnessed extensive research on the crime problem and billions of dollars spent to develop anticrime policies and programs at the local, state, and federal levels. Although the nature of this war on crime periodically changes with the winds of politics, there has been a steady and growing recognition that the police and the citizenry are on the front line of this battle and must do more than just react to the problem after the fact.

This need for proactive police-citizen partnerships is at the heart of community-oriented policing.

COMMUNITY–ORIENTED POLICING

Chapter 8 discussed briefly the impact of community-oriented policing on patrol. This movement has an even more profound impact on community service. As noted by Bayley (1991, p. 226): "When community policing rhetoric has been translated into novel programs, four elements tend to be associated: (1) community-based crime prevention, (2) proactive servicing as opposed to emergency response, (3) public participation in the planning and supervision of police operations, and (4) shifting of command responsibility to lower rank levels."

Examples of such programs, according to Brown (1991, p. 91), include the foot patrol experiments in Newark, New Jersey and Flint, Michigan; the problem-solving project in Newport News, Virginia; the fear-reduction programs in Houston, Texas and Newark, New Jersey; the Community Patrol Officer Program in New York City; and the Directed Area Responsibility Team Experiment in Houston. Brown notes that: "Often these programs had a curious fate. They were begun with fanfare, they produced important results, and then they faded within the departments that had initiated them." These programs were in the first phase of policing; they were a way of operating rather than an orientation or philosophy. Brown cautions (p. 91):

The ultimate demise of many of the programs showed the difficulty of trying to operate programs that embodied some of the important principles of community policing in the context of organizations whose administrative systems and managerial styles were designed for more traditional models of policing. It seemed clear that if the field as a whole or any police department within the field were to succeed in implementing community policing, it would have to be as an overall philosophy of the department.

Community-oriented policing should go from phase one, specific programs, to phase two, a basic approach or philosophy.

> Some law enforcement experts argue that community policing is simply a return
> to the 19th-century British and American systems built around officers on foot
> whose primary responsibility was to maintain order. But contemporary commu-
> nity policing is more than just "old wine in new bottles." It is really a new way
> of thinking about policing, suggesting that police officers are creative, intelligent
> individuals who can do more than just respond to incidents. By working with the
> people who live and work in an area, they can both identify the underlying
> problems and determine the best strategy to solve those problems.

Moving from community-oriented programs to a community-oriented philosophy is a large step. As noted by Couper and Lobitz (1991, p. 17), the
journey toward community-oriented policing philosophy begins with a vision
of your destination, a statement to your personnel and citizens of the direction
the department is going. For example, "We will be a police department devoted to maintaining customer satisfaction and getting closer to the people we
serve."

As noted by Vaughn (1991, p. 35): "Community oriented policing is a philosophy, a style, and a method of providing police service and managing the
police organization. It is value based and involves long-term institutional
change."

Components of a Community-Oriented Policing Philosophy

Brown (1991, pp. 92–94) outlines the following interrelated components of a
community policing philosophy:

- Results v. process—a problem-solving approach.
- Values—incorporating citizen involvement.
- Accountability—to a particular neighborhood's unique concerns and priorities.
- Decentralization—of authority and structure.
- Power sharing—by the police and the citizens.
- Beat redesign—to coincide with natural neighborhood boundaries.
- Permanent assignments—permanent rather than rotating shifts and beats.
- Empowerment of beat officers—encouraged to initiate creative responses to
  problems and given authority to make decisions.
- Investigations—decentralized, focusing on neighborhood or area-specific
  investigations.
- Supervision and management—roles at all levels change: patrol officer be-
  comes "manager" of the beat; first-line supervisor becomes trainer, coach,
  coordinator; management mobilizes needed resources.
- Training—in problem solving, leadership, etc. beginning at the recruit level.
- Performance evaluation—no longer a counting system (number of citations,
  arrests, etc.), but an assessment of problem-solving ability.
- Managing calls for service—using differentiated responses rather than seeking
  a rapid response on a first-come-first-served basis.

Brown (p. 95) feels that the benefits of this approach to policing to the
community include a commitment to crime prevention, public scrutiny of
police operations, accountability to the public, customized police service, and
involvement of community organizations. On the other hand, benefits of community policing to the *police* may include greater citizen support and increased respect, shared responsibility, greater job satisfaction, better internal
relationships, and support for organizational change. He concludes (p. 97): "In
the final analysis, community policing is emerging as the most appropriate

means of using police resources to improve the quality of life in neighborhoods throughout the country." This is assuming that most of the preceding
components are in place, that is, that community policing is not just a program, but the "dominant service-delivery style" and philosophy. All must be
integrated.

Couper and Lobitz (1991, p. 30) draw an analogy between neighborhood
police officers and the health care system: "Neighborhood officers are family
practitioners. The department encourages people to use neighborhood officers
for their long-term care and help. When an emergency arises, the department
will send motorized emergency care officers to the scene of the emergency."

This analogy is carried much further by Wadman and Olson (1990) who
advocate a **community wellness model.** Those in the medical profession
have found that rather than investing all its resources into curing disease, it is
much more effective to prevent disease in the first place. Such prevention
requires the skill and expertise of the professional as well as the willing,
responsible cooperation of the patient. As noted by Wadman and Olson
(p. 92):

> Community wellness is a sharing of responsibility and authority for the causes of
> crime, the fear of crime and crime itself. For too long, the police have accepted
> almost sole responsibility for crime and the fear of crime....
>
> Fighting crimes that have already been committed has proven to be ineffective
> in reducing crime. Much like fighting a forest fire, the wellness concept demands
> that personnel and equipment be diverted to create the "firebreaks" that reduce
> the opportunities for crimes to be committed. This is where the real risks come
> in. You have to take some personnel and equipment off the line in order to cut
> those firebreaks. You must take the risks; long-term gains demand it.

PROBLEM–ORIENTED POLICING

Problem-oriented policing and community-oriented policing are sometimes
equated. In actuality, however, problem-oriented policing is an essential component of community policing. Its focus is on determining underlying causes
of problems, including crime, and identifying solutions. Sulton (1990, p. 1)
notes that most theories of the causes of crime include "poverty, unemployment, substandard housing, inadequate education, racism, disease, inadequate
health care, physical deterioration, overcrowding, and drugs." Sulton suggests
that all the theories of the causes of crime share common threads:

> They assume that crime is a socially defined phenomenon caused by the failure
> of community institutions to constrain behavior so that it conforms to the law
> and does not threaten the rights, safety, and lives of others. According to this
> perspective, crime reduction depends on eradication of the social conditions that
> produce crime.

Sulton (p. 111) further suggests the urgency of eradicating these crime-
producing social conditions:

> To some, democracy is narrowly defined in terms of voting rights. To most, it
> refers to the ability to participate fully in the social, economic, and political life
> of their community. To the extent large segments of the population adhere to the
> latter definition and discover that they are unable to participate fully, the obvious
> result is that many people will view society as nondemocratic. The full conse-
> quence of this view is not readily apparent—the nation's ability to preserve its
> social, economic, and political system is seriously threatened. Crime and other
> forms of socially unacceptable behavior are the manifestations of that threat....

In other words, when large numbers of people are unable to participate fully in the life of their communities, the individual threads that are used to weave the fabric of this great nation are at risk of unraveling.

Problem-oriented policing, a vital component of community policing, requires that police move beyond a law-enforcement perspective in seeking solutions to problems.

As noted by Goldstein (1990, p. 2): "The dominant perspective of policing is heavily influenced by the primary method of control associated with the work—the authority to enforce the criminal law." He suggests that this view has "disproportionately influenced the operating practices, organization, training, and staffing of police agencies." It is like tunnel vision. Effective problem-oriented policing requires abandoning the "simplistic notion that the criminal law defines the police's role" and accepting that "policing consists of developing the most effective means for dealing with a multitude of troublesome situations." He suggests that "these means will often, but not always, include appropriate use of the criminal law."

Goldstein illustrates this change in perspective with the way the police have approached the drug problem; that is, with a law enforcement approach. Gradually the police and the public are coming to realize that this approach, arresting and prosecuting drug dealers, is ineffective. Goldstein contends:

> The challenge is to determine what use should be made by the police of the criminal law (given the difficulty of the process and limited resources); what other means are available to the police for dealing with the problem; and what the police (given their first-hand knowledge of the magnitude and complexity of the problem) should be urging others to do in responding to it.

In short, this is "a whole new way of thinking about policing" (p. 3).

Spelman and Eck (1987, p. 2) explain that problem-oriented policing is the result of twenty years of research into police operations converging on three main themes:

- *Increased effectiveness* by attacking underlying problems that give rise to incidents that consume patrol and detective time.
- *Reliance on the expertise and creativity of line officers* to study problems carefully and develop innovative solutions.
- *Closer involvement with the public* to make sure that the police are addressing the needs of citizens.

They note that problem-oriented policing uses four strategies.

The four strategies of problem-oriented policing are:

- Scanning—grouping individual incidents into meaningful "problems."
- Analyzing—collecting information from all available sources (not just police data).
- Responding—selecting and implementing solutions.
- Assessing—evaluating the impact of the solution.

Eck and Spelman (1987, p. 3) outline twelve requirements of a problem-oriented policing agency:

1. Focus on problems of concern to the public.
2. Zero in on effectiveness as the primary concern.

Table 9–1 Traditional vs. Community Policing: Questions and Answers

QUESTION	TRADITIONAL	COMMUNITY POLICING
Who are the police?	A government agency principally responsible for law enforcement.	Police are the public and the public are the police: the police officers are those who are paid to give full-time attention to the duties of every citizen.
What is the relationship of the police force to other public service departments?	Priorities often conflict.	The police are one department among many responsible for improving the quality of life.
What is the role of the police?	Focusing on solving crimes.	A broader problem-solving approach.
How is police efficiency measured?	By detection and arrest rates.	By the absence of crime and disorder.
What are the highest priorities?	Crimes that are high value (e.g., bank robberies) and those involving violence.	Whatever problems disturb the community most.
What, specifically, do police deal with?	Incidents.	Citizens' problems and concerns.
What determines the effectiveness of police?	Response times.	Public cooperation.
What view do police take of service calls?	Deal with them only if there is no real police work to do.	Vital function and great opportunity.
What is police professionalism?	Swift effective response to serious crime.	Keeping close to the community.
What kind of intelligence is most important?	Crime intelligence (study of particular crimes or series of crimes).	Criminal intelligence (information about the activities of individuals or groups).
What is the essential nature of police accountability?	Highly centralized; governed by rules, regulations, and policy directives; accountable to the law.	Emphasis on local accountability to community needs.
What is the role of headquarters?	To provide the necessary rules and policy directives.	To preach organizational values.
What is the role of the press liaison department?	To keep the "heat" off operational officers so they can get on with the job.	To coordinate an essential channel of communication with the community.
How do the police regard prosecutions?	As an important goal.	As one tool among many.

Source: M. K. Sparrow. "Implementing Community Policing." *Perspectives on Policing.* U.S. Department of Justice, National Institute of Justice, November 1988, 8–9.

3. Be proactive.
4. Be committed to systematic inquiry as the first step in solving substantive problems.
5. Encourage use of rigorous methods in making inquiries.
6. Make full use of the data in police files and the experience of police personnel.
7. Group like incidents together so that they can be addressed as a common problem.

8. Avoid using overly broad labels in grouping incidents so separate problems can be identified.
9. Encourage a broad and uninhibited search for solutions.
10. Acknowledge the limits of the criminal justice system as a response to problems.
11. Identify multiple interests in any one problem and weigh them when analyzing the value of different responses.
12. Be committed to taking some risks responding to problems.

These requirements mesh well with the overall community policing philosophy. Table 9–1 illustrates some of the most basic differences between traditional and community-oriented policing.

SUMMARY

Although the type and amount of community service provided by a police department varies from city to city, a certain level of community service is expected everywhere. The services provided include giving information, directions, and advice; counseling and referring; licensing and registering vehicles; intervening in domestic arguments; working with neglected children; rendering emergency medical or rescue services; dealing with alcoholics and the mentally ill; finding lost children; dealing with stray animals; controlling crowds; and providing community education programs on crime prevention, drug abuse, safety, and the like.

Community service should be differentiated from public relations and community relations. Public relations emphasizes building a positive image of the law enforcement officer. Community relations emphasizes improving two-way communication between citizens and the police, with the raising of image an anticipated side effect. Community service, in contrast, emphasizes actual police assistance or efforts to help citizens learn to help themselves in preventing crime and preserving individual safety and well-being.

Some police departments attempt to improve their image by instituting public relations programs—programs that emphasize raising the image of the police officer rather than opening channels of communications. Other departments concentrate on community relations programs to provide two-way communication between police and citizens to work toward achieving law and order in the community.

No matter what type of program is instituted, however, the fact remains that the police officer on the street is ultimately responsible for the success of the police-community relations program and for the image of the police held by the citizens of the community.

Programs for youth include PAL programs, school-liaison officers, the D.A.R.E. program, Officer Friendly, McGruff, and explorer posts.

Several community service programs focus on crime prevention, including operation identification programs, home security, store security, and automobile security.

Community-oriented policing should go from phase one, specific programs, to phase two, a basic approach or philosophy encompassing all segments of the police department's service delivery system.

Problem-oriented policing, a vital component of community policing, requires that police move beyond a law-enforcement perspective in seeking solutions to problems. The four strategies of problem-oriented policing are scanning (grouping individual incidents into meaningful "problems"), analyzing, responding, and assessing.

DISCUSSION QUESTIONS

1. What community services are available in your community? Which are most important? Which might be frivolous? Are any necessary services *not* provided?

2. What types of crime prevention programs are used in your community?

3. What types of safety promotion programs are used in your community?

4. What kinds of youth programs are available in your community? Are they sufficient?

5. Have you ever personally received service from a police officer? What were the circumstances? How would you evaluate the officer's performance? Have you ever needed a service that was not provided?

6. What do you feel are the greatest strengths of community-oriented policing?

7. What is the relationship of problem-oriented policing to community-oriented policing?

8. What do you predict the scanning strategy in the problem-oriented approach would reveal as major problems in your community?

9. What basic similarities and differences exist between community-oriented policing and systems such as the tithing system?

10. Might community-oriented policing dilute the power and authority of the police?

TERMS

community relations, community wellness model, CPTED, public relations, target hardening.

REFERENCES

Austin, D. and Braaten, J. "Turning Lives Around: Portland Youth Find a New PAL." *The Police Chief* (May 1991): 36–38.

Bayley, D. H. "Community Policing: A Report from the Devil's Advocate." In *Community Policing: Rhetoric or Reality,* edited by J. R. Greene and S. D. Mastrofski. New York: Praeger Publishers, 1991.

Bishop, D. R. and Schuessler, T. J. "The National Crime Information Center's Missing Person File." *FBI Law Enforcement Bulletin* (August 1982): 20–24.

Brown, L. P. "Community Policing: A Practical Guide for Police Officials." pp. 89–97 in *Criminal Justice 91/92.* Guilford, Conn.: Dushkin Publishing Group, 1991 (reprinted from *Perspectives on Policing.* U.S. Department of Justice, September 1989: 1–11).

Brown, L. P. "Making the Problems of Youth a National Priority." *The Police Chief* (June 1991): 6.

Couper, D. C. and Lobitz, S. H. "The Customer Is Always Right: Applying Vision, Leadership and the Problem-Solving Methods to Community-Oriented Policing." *The Police Chief* (May 1991): 17–23.

Couper, D. C. and Lobitz, S. H. "Quality Leadership: The First Step Towards Quality Policing." *The Police Chief* (April 1988): 79–84.

Couper, D. C. and Lobitz, S. H. *Quality Policing: The Madison Experience.* Washington, D.C.: Police Executive Research Forum, 1991.

Eck, J. E. and Spelman, W. *Problem Solving: Problem-Oriented Policing in Newport News.* Washington, D.C.: Police Executive Research Forum, 1987.

Goldstein, H. *Problem-Oriented Policing.* New York: McGraw-Hill, 1990.

Hageman, M. J. *Police-Community Relations.* Beverly Hills, Calif.: Sage Publications, 1985.

Hildreth, R. "The CAT Program." *Law and Order* (May 1990): 92–93.

Horne, P. "Not Just Old Wine in New Bottles: The Inextricable Relationship Between Crime Prevention and Community Policing." *The Police Chief* (May 1991): 24–29.

Lesce, T. "Police Explorers: A Learning Experience." *Law and Order* (September 1991): 97–100.

Levine, J. P.; Husheno, M. C.; and Palumbo, D. J. *Criminal Justice: A Public Policy.* New York: Harcourt Brace Jovanovich, 1980.

Narramore, R. "Cards for Kids." *Law and Order* (December 1990): 23.

Nilson, D. W. "Vehicle Recovery: New Technology Captures Chicago's Attention." *Law and Order* (February 1990): 36–37.

O'Keefe, G. J. "The 'McGruff' National Media Campaign: Its Public Impact and Future Implications." In *Community Crime Prevention: Does It Work?,* edited by D. P. Rosenbaum. Beverly Hills, Calif.: Sage Publications, 1986.

Pace, D. F. *Community Relations Concepts.* Placerville, Calif.: Custom Publishing Company, 1991.

President's Commission on Law Enforcement and Administration of Justice. Task Force Report. *The Police.* Washington, D.C.: U.S. Government Printing Office, 1967.

President's Commission on Law Enforcement and Administration of Justice. *The Challenge of Crime in a Free Society.* Washington, D.C.: U.S. Government Printing Office, 1967.

Rosenbaum, D. P. (Ed.) *Community Crime Prevention: Does It Work?* Beverly Hills, Calif.: Sage Publications, 1986.

Rosenbaum, D. P. "The Problem of Crime Control." In *Community Crime Prevention: Does It Work?,* edited by D. P. Rosenbaum. Beverly Hills, Calif.: Sage Publications, 1986.

Spelman, W. and Eck, J. E. "Problem-Oriented Policing." Washington, D.C.: National Institute of Justice, January 1987.

Sulton, A. T. *Inner-City Crime Control: Can Community Institutions Contribute?* Washington, D.C.: Police Foundation 1990.

Vaughn, J. R. "Community Oriented Policing . . . You Can Make It Happen." *Law and Order* (June 1991): 35–39.

Wadman, R. C. and Olson, R. K. *Community Wellness: A New Theory of Policing.* Washington, D.C.: Police Executive Research Forum, 1990.

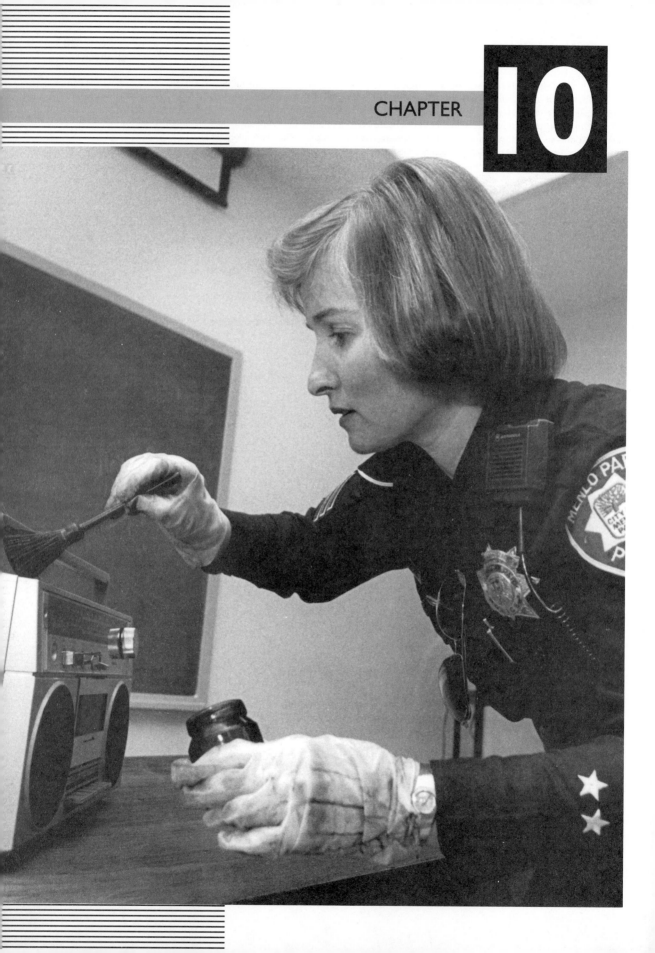

CHAPTER 10

Investigation: Processing the Crime Scene

Every fact that is learned becomes a key to other facts.

—E. L. Youmans

Do You Know

What the primary characteristic of an effective investigator is?

What the primary responsibilities of the investigator are?

What questions the investigator must seek answers to?

Why both sketches and photographs of a crime scene are usually needed?

How investigators must deal with evidence?

What types of evidence are likely to be found at the scene of a crime?

What DNA profiling is?

How computers are being used in investigation?

INTRODUCTION

To the general public, the term *criminal investigations* often brings to mind the image of the detective, as portrayed in novels, on the radio, in magazines, and on television. The "detective" AKA the "investigator" is the person who single-handedly digs out evidence, collects tips from informants, identifies criminals, tracks them down, and brings them to the bar of justice. Some police departments feel that solving crimes depends entirely on the detectives in the department. It is a prestigious assignment. In a great many departments throughout the country, the detective is a patrol officer—no special detective or investigative division exists. Throughout this chapter, when the term *investigator* is used, it may be interpreted as referring to either a patrol officer performing investigative duties or to a specialist assigned only investigative duties.

A large part of an investigator's role centers around obtaining information and **evidence.** The successful investigator obtains proof that a crime has been committed as well as proof that a particular person (the suspect) committed the crime. Investigators do *not* determine the suspects to be guilty; they remain objective in their investigation.

A primary characteristic of an effective investigator is objectivity.

The investigator seeks to find the truth, not simply to prove suspects guilty. As stated in Article 10 of the *Canons of Police Ethics* (International Association of Chiefs of Police):

> The law enforcement officer shall be concerned equally in the prosecution of the wrong-doer and the defense of the innocent. He shall ascertain what constitutes evidence and shall present such evidence impartially and without malice. In so doing, he will ignore social, political, and all other distinctions among the persons involved, strengthening the tradition of the reliability and integrity of an officer's word.
>
> The law enforcement officer shall take special pains to increase his perception and skill of observation, mindful that in many situations his is the sole impartial testimony to the facts of a case.

The relationship between investigators and patrol officers is a source of potential friction, yet the need for them to work together is critical, as noted by O. W. Wilson (1963, p. 293) some twenty-five years ago:

> The communication of information between patrol officers and investigators is a vital factor in the success of criminal investigations. Investigators should make every effort to foster the cooperation and enthusiasm of patrol officers through frequent personal contacts, by making certain that beat officers receive acknowledgement in reports and press releases, and by fostering preliminary investigations by patrolmen. One of the fastest ways to stop the cooperation between patrol officers and investigators is to have the latter rework the preliminary investigation as if the patrol officer were not to be trusted.

Wilson stresses: "In a sense, the investigation of a case is the responsibility of the entire department, and not just a single investigator. Effective investigation often depends on many people and on the organizational structure that governs what they do."

The Rand Corporation undertook an extensive study of the role of detectives in solving crimes. Waldron (1984, pp. 194–195) says of this study:

The single most important determinant of whether or not a case will be solved is the information the victim supplies to the immediately responding patrol officer. If information that uniquely identifies the perpetrator is not presented when the crime is reported, the perpetrator usually will not be subsequently identified. Of those cases that are ultimately cleared but in which the perpetrator is not identified at the time of the initial police incident report, almost all are cleared as a result of routine police procedures. Differences in investigative training, staffing, workload, and procedures have no appreciable effect on crime, arrest, or clearance rates.

This same interpretation of the Rand Study of Detectives is made by Klockars (1983, p. 131) who says the study shows that "all but about 5 percent of serious crimes that are solved by detectives are solved because a patrol officer has caught the perpetrator at the scene, because a witness tells the detective whodunit, or by thoroughly routine clerical procedures."

The Rand Study would seem to suggest that rapid response to a report of crime is extremely important. A study conducted by the Forum (Spelman and Brown 1981, pp. iii-xx) in Florida, Illinois, New York, and San Diego, however, found that, in the cities studied, arrests could be attributed to fast police response in only 2.9 percent of reported serious crimes. Spelman and Brown indicate this is so because about 75 percent of all serious crimes are **discovery crimes,** crimes discovered after they have been committed. It is in only the remaining 25 percent, the **involvement crimes,** that rapid response is critical. Klockars (1983, p. 130) rather humorously suggests: "Police currently make on-scene arrests in about 3 percent of the serious crimes reported to them. If they traveled faster than a speeding bullet to all reports of serious crimes, this on-scene arrest rate would rise no higher than 5 percent."

RESPONSIBILITIES OF THE INVESTIGATOR

To accomplish a successful investigation, police officers must (1) take their time, (2) use an organized approach that is efficient and methodical, because this may be their only chance to observe the scene, (3) recognize the issues and find facts to settle these issues, and (4) determine if a crime has been committed, and, if so, by whom and how.

Each of these responsibilities will be discussed in a few pages, but first a distinction should be made between the preliminary investigation and the follow-up investigation.

The **preliminary investigation** consists of actions performed immediately upon receiving a call to respond to the scene of a crime. This preliminary investigation is usually conducted by patrol officers.

The **follow-up investigation** may be conducted by the investigative services division, sometimes also known as the detective bureau. Therefore, the success of many criminal investigations relies on the cooperative, coordinated efforts of both the patrol and the investigative functions. In most smaller departments, however, the same officer handles both the preliminary and the follow-up investigations.

The International Association of Chiefs of Police (1970, p. 13) has developed an acronym around the meaning of PRELIMINARY as follows:

P   Proceed to the scene promptly and safely.
R   Render assistance to the injured.
E   Effect the arrest of the criminal.

L	Locate and identify witnesses.
I	Interview the complainant and the witness.
M	Maintain the crime scene and protect the evidence.
I	Interrogate the suspect.
N	Note conditions, events, and remarks.
A	Arrange for collection of evidence (or collect it).
R	Report the incident fully and accurately.
Y	Yield the responsibility to the follow-up investigator.

The preliminary investigative responsibilities are to:

- assure that the crime scene is secure;

- record all facts related to the case for further reference;

- photograph, measure, and sketch the crime scene;

- obtain and identify evidence;

- interview witnesses and interrogate suspects;

- assist in the identification of suspects.

SECURING THE CRIME SCENE

Any area that contains evidence of criminal activity is considered a crime scene, and it must be secured to eliminate **contamination** of the scene and outlying areas. The investigator in charge should limit the number of officers assigned to the crime scene, using only those required to do the work. Although some crimes do not have identifiable scenes (for example, embezzlement) or known scenes, the majority of crimes do; for example, bank robberies, burglaries, homicides, assaults, and bombings.

A police ribbon stretches around the restaurant where a Minneapolis police officer was gunned down while on break. Officers keep onlookers away as investigators search the area immediately around the pizza parlor.

The suspect may have left evidence such as fingerprints, blood, footprints, a weapon, a tool, strands of hair, fibers from clothing, or some personal item, such as a billfold, which may contain identification. No evidence should be touched or moved until photographing, measuring, and sketching of the scene are complete.

The first officer on the scene must protect it from any change. Although this officer may have little or nothing further to do with the case, this single responsibility may have far reaching effects on solving the crime. Physical evidence must be properly protected to have legal and scientific validity.

RECORDING RELEVANT INFORMATION

Investigators do not rely on memory. They record all necessary information by photographing, sketching, and taking notes to be used later in a written report of the investigation. Photographs, sketches, and notes are a permanent aid to memory and may be helpful not only in investigating the case and writing the report but also in testifying in court.

The notes should be written in a notebook, not on scraps of paper that might be lost or misplaced. They should be written in black ink because they are a permanent record and also because pencil may smear and become unreadable over time. The notes should be written legibly and be identified by the investigator's name, the date, and the case number. They should contain all relevant facts, especially the names and addresses of victims, witnesses, and possible suspects.

The investigator must obtain answers to the questions: who? what? where? when? how? and why?

Although each specific type of crime requires somewhat different information, most investigations require answers to such questions as the following (Hess and Wrobleski 1991, pp. 18–20):

When: did the incident happen? was it discovered? was it reported? did the police arrive on the scene? were suspects arrested? will the case be heard in court?

Where: did the incident happen? was evidence found? stored? do victims, witnesses, and suspects live? do suspects frequent most often? were suspects arrested?

Who: are suspects? accomplices?

Complete descriptions would include the following information: sex, race, coloring, age, height, weight, hair (color, style, condition), eyes (color, size, glasses), nose (size, shape), ears (close to head or protruding), distinctive features (birthmarks, scars, beard), clothing, voice (high or low, accent), other distinctive characteristics such as walk.

Who: were the victims? associates? was talked to? were witnesses? saw or heard something of importance? discovered the crime? reported the incident? made the complaint? investigated the incident? worked on the case? marked and received the evidence? was notified? had a motive?

What: type of crime was committed? was the amount of damage or value of the property involved? happened (narrative of the actions of suspects, victims, and witnesses; combines information included under "how")? evidence was found? preventive measures had been taken (safes, locks, alarms, etc.)? knowledge, skill, or strength was needed to commit the crime? was said? did the police officers do? further information is needed? further action is needed?

How: was the crime discovered? does this crime relate to other crimes? did the crime occur? was evidence found? was information obtained?

Why: was the crime committed? (was there intent? consent? motive?) was certain property stolen? was a particular time selected?

Answers to these questions are obtained by observation and by talking to witnesses, complainants, and suspects as discussed in Chapter 11. They are recorded in notes, photographs, and sketches or are in the form of actual physical evidence.

PHOTOGRAPHING, MEASURING, AND SKETCHING THE CRIME SCENE

In addition to taking notes, the investigator or crime-scene technician should photograph, measure, and sketch the crime scene. Photographic coverage of the scene must be done carefully. In addition to being technically competent and well equipped, the photographer must photograph objects that are related to the case and in such a way that no distortion occurs. The photographs should show the scene as it was found. They are usually taken in a series and "tell a story." In addition, they are usually taken from general to specific, that is, first an entire room, then one area of the room, then specific items within that area.

The evidence and location should be in their proper relationship and in a sequence that will orient a person unfamiliar with the scene. If a photograph is intended to show dimensional relationships, a suitable scale should be included. Photographs of evidence such as footprints, tire tracks, and tool marks must be done using close-up photography. DeAngelis (1980, p. 30) cautions:

> Unlike the studio photographer, the crime scene photographer has only one chance. If later he finds his photographs fail to show what is needed, then the opportunity is lost because the scene cannot be reconstructed. Crime scene photography is critical, with great consequences, and there are no arranged conditions. . . . All other processing of the crime scene must wait until the crime scene photographer's work is finished.

It is important that investigators not only know *how* to take photographs but that they know *what* to photograph. They should take enough photographs that the entire scene can be recreated for the jury.

In addition to traditional photography done at crime scenes, other types of photography such as ultraviolet, infrared, and aerial are also used. Videotaping has become increasingly common as a way to record a crime scene.

In addition to photographs, a sketch should be made of the crime scene before any evidence is moved. Sketches supplement photographs. They can be selective, and they can also show entire areas, for example, an entire layout of a home or business. The sketch need not be an artistic masterpiece as long as it includes all relevant details and is accurate and clear. The sketch should show the locations of all important evidence found during the crime-scene search. See Figure 10−1 for some common types of sketches.

Both photographs and sketches are usually needed. The photographs include all details and can show items close up. Sketches can be selective and can show much larger areas.

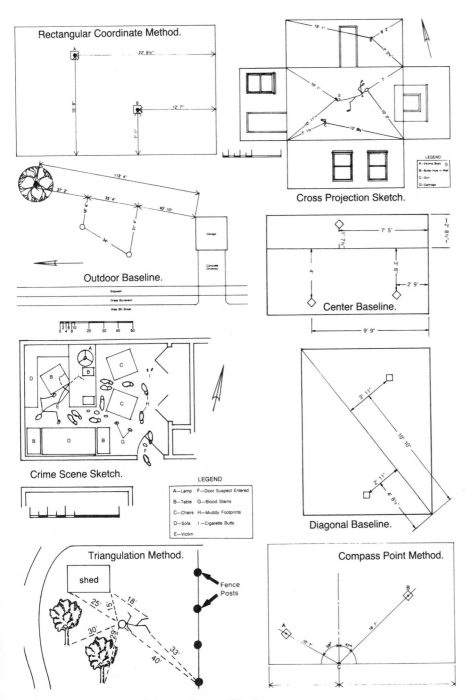

Figure 10–1 Types of Crime-Scene Sketches

Source: W. W. Bennett and K. M. Hess. *Criminal Investigation.* Copyright© 1991. Reprinted by permission of West Publishing Company. All rights reserved.

DeAngelis (1980, p. 9) stresses that "a crime scene sketch (drawn to scale) should usually be made because it can be a valuable aid in the presentation of most criminal cases."

O'Hara and O'Hara (1988, p. 66) define a crime-scene sketch as "a tool which is the simplest and most effective way of showing actual measurements and of identifying significant items of evidence in their locations at the scene."

Some rookie police officers do not see the need for sketches if photographs have been taken, but this is incorrect. Sketches and photographs complement each other. According to Bennett and Hess (1991, p. 110):

> Photographs present an overview of the entire scene; sketches present a detailed yet selective picture of relevant objects, omitting those that clutter or confuse the scene. . . .
>
> Photographs alone are insufficient for a number of reasons. They are not selective, do not show objects behind other objects, do not show measurements or true distances between objects and evidence, and may distort the scene because of the camera angle. Problems such as poor lighting or incorrect film may also cause pictures to be inaccurate. And errors can occur in developing.

OBTAINING AND IDENTIFYING PHYSICAL EVIDENCE

A primary responsibility of the investigator is to obtain and identify physical evidence. All important decisions will revolve around the available evidence and how it was obtained.

Effective investigators understand their functions as finders of facts and suppliers of proof that have both a scientific and a legal basis for presentation in court. Items of evidence found at the crime scene are usually routinely taken and held pending apprehension of a suspect. Frequently evidence is sent to a crime laboratory for analysis and comparison.

In the preface to the *Laboratory Manual for Introductory Forensic Science,* Walton (1979, p. vii) notes: "Today, the successful prosecution of criminal cases rests less upon confessions or eyewitness accounts and more upon the use of physical evidence. Even so, it is commonly conceded that a pitifully small fraction— 2 percent or less—of available evidence is properly recognized, collected, evaluated, and brought into court to tell its story to judge and jury." Walton contends that this is a "sorry situation" and that it must be corrected at the source, that is, the crime scene, "with properly trained and qualified personnel who know what to look for and how to collect, handle, and transport evidence so as to keep intact its legal and scientific integrity. At the crime laboratory the *criminalist* must evaluate what facts may be obtained from the evidence and be prepared to support his or her findings in a court of law."

The investigator must recognize, collect, mark, preserve, and transport physical evidence in sufficient quantity for analysis and without contamination.

Walton sees physical evidence as being the primary responsibility of two law enforcement agents: the crime-scene investigator (who may be a patrol officer, remember) and the criminalist. And he sees the single most important question in **criminalistics** as being related to identity: "Did this blood stain come from this victim? Did this automobile hit this pedestrian? Was this slug fired from this handgun?" Such questions are often answered by comparing one item to another, for example, fingerprints left at a crime scene with those taken from a suspect.

Physical evidence can be valuable in verifying that a crime has, in fact, been committed, identifying the person(s) who did it, and exonerating all other suspects. To realize its full potential, however, certain qualities of evidence must be attained and some minimum quantities collected before the crime lab can help. In the majority of cases, the police officers who protect and search the crime scene play a critical role in determining whether the evidence will be of value.

The kind of evidence to be anticipated is often directly related to the type of crime committed.

Crimes against the person include homicide, rape, robbery, assault, kidnapping, and sex crimes. These crime scenes frequently contain evidence such as blood, hair, fibers, fingerprints, footprints, and weapons.

Crimes against property include burglary, larceny, arson, and auto theft. These crime scenes are commonly characterized by forcible entry with tools leaving marks on doors, windows, safes, money chests, cash registers, and desk drawers.

Among the more common types of evidence found at the crime scene are fingerprints, blood, hair, fibers, documents, footprints or tire prints, tool fragments, tool marks, broken glass, paint, insulation from safes, bite marks, firearms, and explosives.

Specific Evidence and Scientific Aids

Fingerprints are often found at crime scenes. Fingerprint identification is currently the most positive form of identification accepted in court because the ridge arrangement on every finger of every person is different and unchanging, although as a person grows, the patterns enlarge slightly. A cut will alter the print until the healing is complete. A permanent scar may change the print, but it is usually still identifiable.

Experts in fingerprints look for nine basic patterns, which can occur in any combination (see Figure 10−2). The classification system used today in most

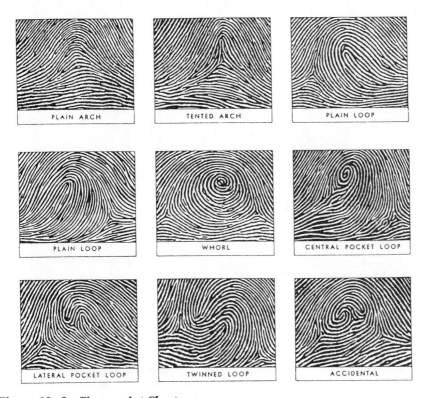

Figure 10−2 Fingerprint Chart
Source: Courtesy of Faurot, Inc. 26 Nepperhan Avenue, Elmsford, N.Y. 10523.

countries was developed in 1900 by Sir Edward R. Henry and is called the **Henry system.**

Latent fingerprints are made by sweat or grease that oozes out of the pores from little wells situated under the ridges at the ends of the fingers. When a person grasps an item with reasonable pressure, this grease takes the pattern of the person's fingerprints. This usually happens if the item grasped has a highly polished surface such as glass, polished metalware, highly glazed fabrics, or paper. It usually will not occur if the item grasped is soft, spongy, or has a rough surface.

Fingerprints may be found in an infinite number of places and under varied circumstances. Most crime scenes contain fingerprints of the suspect. Usually articles such as weapons, tools, documents, glass, metal, or any other objects that might have been touched or handled by the perpetrators have latent fingerprints on them.

Finding fingerprints is only half the job; they must be matched with the actual (inked) fingerprints of a suspect to be valuable as evidence.

The basic points of comparison are shown in Figure 10–3. Most experts require ten to twelve similar points to make a positive identification of a fingerprint, although no specific number is legally required. Any unexplainable difference, however, makes positive identification impossible.

Likewise, no set print size is required for positive identification. The print need be only large enough to contain at least ten to twelve points, a count that can be met by an area as small as the end of a pencil. As a general rule, if police officers develop an area and see a fingerprint that appears to have several ridges, regardless of the area size, the print should be lifted, marked, and submitted to the laboratory.

Points used for identification of fingerprints occur not only in the pattern area of the finger but also outside the pattern area, as well as on the first and

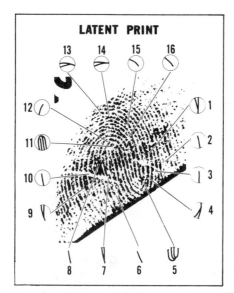 

Figure 10–3 Positive Identification of a Fingerprint Three men checked into a motel at 11:00 P.M. Shortly after midnight when a new desk clerk came on duty, the men went to the office and committed an armed robbery. Police investigating the scene went to the room occupied by the three men and found the latent fingerprint on an ashtray. This print was later matched up to one of the suspects, whose fingerprints were on file with the police department.

second joints of the finger and the entire palm of the hand. Patterns are also present on the toes and the entire sole of the foot.

Although fingerprints are perhaps the most common form of physical evidence and certainly one of the most valuable, they do have limitations. It is impossible to determine the age of latent prints. It is also not possible to determine the age, sex, race, or occupation of the person leaving the print. Nonetheless, latent prints are such valuable evidence that great effort should be made to recover them, recognizing that they are fragile, susceptible to complete destruction, and difficult to find.

Blood can be classified as having come from humans or animals. Human bloodstains can be classified into one of the four international blood groups: A, B, AB, or O. Bloodstains may be valuable as evidence in assaults, homicides, burglaries, hit-and-run cases, and rape. Although blood cannot be identified as having come from a particular individual, race, or sex, it can be helpful in eliminating suspects.

In addition, the physical appearance of the blood can sometimes be of help. For example, whether it is in the form of a pool, drops, stains, or splashes can tell investigators important information about the crime. Sometimes the appearance can also help to establish the approximate time the crime occurred.

Hair can also be classified as having come from humans or animals. Technology has not yet progressed to the point where it can be stated that a hair definitely came from a specific person, however. Currently, hair found at a crime scene can be examined and have one of three results:

- Inconclusive—it is neither similar nor dissimilar to the suspect's hair. This may result if the sample submitted was too small, if contamination or damage were present, or if there simply were not enough characterization.

- Exclusionary—the hair cannot be considered similar to the suspect's.

- Similarity—it is possible that the hair left at the scene came from the suspect. This result is **corroborative** only, never conclusive by itself.

It can be established that the hair was pulled out forcibly if the root end is present. In addition, the region of the body from which the hair was removed can be determined with considerable accuracy from the length, size, color, stiffness, and general appearance. Hair from the scalp, beard, eyebrows, eyelid, nose, ear, trunk, and limbs all have different characteristics. Hair from each racial group can be identified by its shape. The sex and age of a person cannot be determined from a hair examination with any degree of certainty except in the case of infant hair.

The possibility of hair evidence in any crime should never be overlooked. Hair is often valuable as a means of personal identification or as an investigative aid in cases such as hit-and-run, unusual death, and rape. Hair may be found from both the victim and the suspect on clothing, weapons, undergarments, blankets, sheets, seat covers, and the undercarriage of vehicles.

Fibers are excellent aids to investigators. It is possible to identify fibers as to type, such as wool, cotton, rayon, nylon, and so on. Sometimes it is possible to determine the type of garment from which the fibers came. In assault and homicide cases some contact usually occurs between the victim and the suspect causing clothing fibers to be interchanged. Fingernail scrapings and weapons may also contain fiber evidence. In burglaries, clothing fibers are frequently found where the burglar crawled through a window or opening. In hit-and-run cases, clothing fibers are often found adhering to the fenders, grill, door handle, or parts of the undercarriage of the automobile.

Document examination consists of a side-by-side comparison of handwriting, typewriting, or other written or printed matter. Age, sex, and race cannot be determined with certainty; however, in cases such as check forgery and alteration of wills, stocks, and bonds, conclusions based on examinations conducted by competent experts are positive and reliable. Such handwriting testimony has been accepted in United States courts for many years. Typewriter or printer samples may also identify the manufacturer, make, model, and age of a typewriter or printer.

A *footprint or tire impression* can be a "material witness" in locating a criminal and placing him or her at the scene of a crime. Such evidence is sometimes more reliable than an eyewitness. Impressions from feet or tires are often found where the perpetrator of the crime hastily entered or left the scene of the crime and overlooked the impressions. After photographing, measuring, and sketching, investigators carefully preserve such evidence by making a plaster cast of it. It often serves as a vital link to a criminal.

Footprints and tire prints are of two types: contamination prints and impressions. **Contamination prints** result when the footprint or tire has a substance on it, such as dirt or blood, that leaves a print on a hard surface. **Impressions,** in contrast, are prints left on a soft surface such as sand or mud.

Whether dealing with a footprint or tire print, of prime importance are individual characteristics such as nicks and scars. It is important to remember that it may be necessary to make a cast or photograph approximately seven feet long of tire prints to have a complete surface available to compare with the suspect's tires.

Tool fragments may be found at the crime scene. These pieces may later be matched to a broken tool in the possession of a suspect.

Tool marks may be left where windows have been forced with screwdrivers or pry bars, locks have been snipped with bolt cutters, or safes have been attacked with hammers, chisels, and/or punches. All these tools leave marks that, under favorable conditions, can be identified as definitely as fingerprints. Tool marks are most commonly found in the crime of burglary and malicious

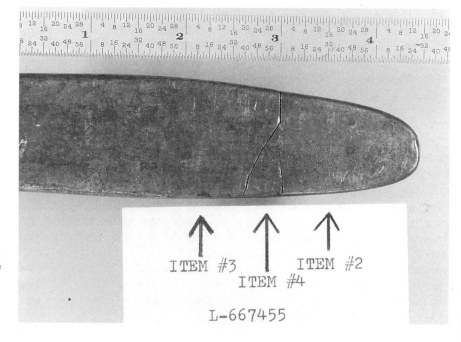

Pry tool used to open the rear door of a hardware store. Items 2 and 4 were found at the scene of the burglary. Item 3 was found in the suspect's car. The evidence led to the suspect's conviction for burglary.

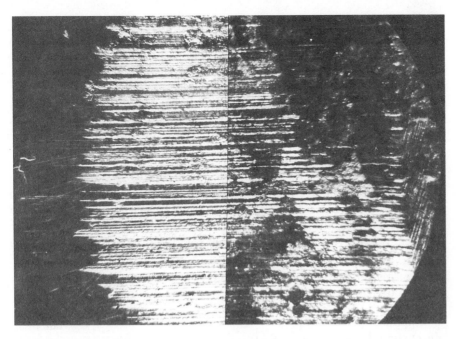

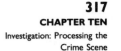

Striation patterns of a sledge hammer used to open a safe. The white marks are safe insulation. The left half of the photograph is evidence obtained at the scene of the crime. The right half shows the actual hammer seized from the suspect. The marks were matched up under a comparison microscope and magnified.

destruction of property. They may be found on windowsills, frames, doors, door frames, cash register drawers, file cabinets, or cash boxes.

Tool marks are of two types: impressions and sliding or cutting marks. For example, a hammer that has been pounded on a surface does not hit directly, so it leaves both some sliding marks and an impression.

In the past tool marks were frequently of more use because variations in the manufacture of the tools made each somewhat unique. Modern technology, however, has progressed to the point where many tools are identical to one another.

Glass is also an aid to the laboratory crime investigator. Glass is an excellent source of positive identification because two pieces of glass rarely contain the same proportions of sand, metal, oxides, or carbonates. Police officers frequently encounter glass from windows, automobiles, bottles, and other objects as evidence in burglaries, murders, assaults, and a large variety of other crimes.

When a criminal breaks a window, minute pieces of glass are usually found in his or her clothing, for example in pant cuffs, breast pockets, or, to a lesser extent, on the surface of clothing. Since these fragments are so small, they should be removed with a vacuum. Larger fragments should be carefully collected. The area adjacent to the actual break in a glass is critical in the examination. Fragments should not be overlooked.

Microscopic examination of glass fragments by an expert can determine the following:

- Whether a tiny glass fragment probably or definitely came from a particular broken glass object.
- If a large fragment came from a particular glass object that was broken.
- If a fragment came from a particular kind of glass object such as a window pane, an eyeglass lens, a bottle, etc.
- The origin of a fracture, its direction, and the direction of the force producing it.
- The order of occurrence of multiple fractures.

An investigator can determine whether glass was broken from the inside of a building by noticing where the fragments are. DeAngelis (1980, p. 123) describes the process of breaking glass as follows:

1. Pressure is applied to the surface of the glass.

2. The glass is pushed away from the direction of the pressure. As the elasticity of the glass reaches the maximum point, the glass starts to crack on the opposite side of the force.

3. A fracture results radiating away from the point of pressure. This is called a *radial* fracture.

4. If pressure continues, the glass then starts to break on the pie shaped portion, forming circular ridges around the point of pressure. This is called a *concentric* fracture.

5. Often there is significant backward fragmentation when glass fractures resulting from fragmentation on the force side of the breaking glass. Therefore, it is quite possible to find fragments on a suspect who has broken glass even though the glass flew in the opposite direction.

Summing up, the first fracture is called a **radial fracture** (radiating out of the center). The second fracture is called a **concentric fracture,** and it forms a circular pattern around the point of force and between the radial lines. Radial fractures start on the opposite side of a force, and concentric fractures start on the same side as the original force (see Figure 10−4).

Paint frequently is transferred from one object to another during the commission of a crime. Paint is often smeared on tools during unlawful entry. It may be chipped off surfaces during burglaries. It may flake off automobiles during hasty getaways following impacts. Paint has often proved to be a strong link in the chain of circumstantial evidence. It may have sufficient individual and distinct characteristics for significant examination or comparison. It often associates an individual with the crime scene, or it may eliminate innocent suspects.

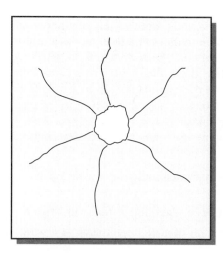

RADIAL FRACTURE

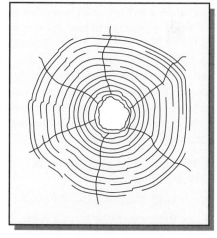

CONCENTRIC FRACTURE

Figure 10−4

Insulation from safes may also prove valuable as evidence. Insulations can be identified microscopically by composition, color, mineral content, and physical characteristics. Since few laypersons normally come into contact with this type of material, particles of safe or fireproof insulation material on the clothing or shoes of a suspect are a strong indication of guilt.

Bite marks are frequently overlooked in criminal investigations. According to DeAngelis (1980, p. 99): "Bite marks on the human body may last from a few seconds to several weeks, depending on the amount of pressure, the sharpness of the teeth, and the location of the bite. Also bite marks on a live body have different characteristics from those on a dead body." DeAngelis classifies bite marks into four degrees (see Table 10–1). Bite or teeth marks have individual characteristics matching the size and configuration of the teeth.

Firearms left at a crime scene may be traced to their owner through the serial number, the manufacturer's identification, or the dealer who sold the gun. The firearm might also contain the suspect's fingerprints or other marks that could lead to identification.

The make of the weapon is usually determined by the **riflings** in the barrel, which are spiral grooves cut into the barrel of a gun in its manufacture. The riflings vary considerably from manufacturer to manufacturer.

In addition, the entry of a bullet can be determined by the hole it makes. The bullet produces a cone-shaped hole, entering from the small point of the hole and emerging through the large end.

Before leaving the topic of firearms identification, it should be noted that sometimes the term *ballistics* is used to refer to this aspect of criminalistics, but this is not correct. **Ballistics** deals with the motion of the projectile, *not* with identification of the weapon from which it was fired.

Explosives may be of value as evidence in burglary; malicious destruction of property such as school buildings, churches, or public buildings; murder; or murder attempted by an explosive placed in an automobile or a home. The area around an explosion may contain such items as blasting caps, cap fragments, detonating wire, safety fuse, dynamite paper, cotton, soap, masking tape, primacord, or steel fragments. In some cases it is possible to find samples of unexploded materials.

Table 10–1 **Classification of Bite Marks**

DEGREE OF IMPRESSIONS	DEFINED	HOW FORMED	RESULT	LASTING DAMAGE
1	Clearly	Significant amount of pressure on skin	No cut or bruise	Minimal
2	Obvious	Increased first-degree pressure	Bruise	Lasts longer than first degree
3	Quite noticeable	Increased biting pressure; violent reaction	Breaks or cuts skin	Indefinite
4	Skin lacerated	Skin violently torn from body	Skin tissue missing	Unknown; medical treatment needed

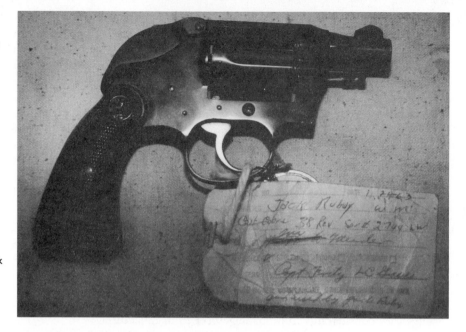

The gun supposedly used by Jack
Ruby to shoot and kill Lee
Harvey Oswald, the man ac-
cused of shooting President
John F. Kennedy.

DNA PROFILING

A new technique called *DNA profiling* holds great promise for forensic investigations. According to Kelly, Rankin, and Wink (1987, p. 105):

> The strength of the DNA technique rests in the intrinsic properties of Deoxyri-
> bonucleic Acid (DNA), the material of which chromosomes are made. Only tiny
> quantities are required for analysis, and each individual's DNA is unique. Under
> the correct circumstances DNA is remarkably stable and indeed has been ex-
> tracted from Egyptian mummies.

An article entitled "Getting Personal in Hunt for Clues" (1986, p. 5) states:

> It's found in the blood, in the hair, in saliva, semen, fingernail clippings—indeed,
> no part of the body is without it. More importantly to law enforcers, it may help
> revolutionize the identification of muggers, murderers and rapists as well as solve
> newborn baby mixups, aid in the identification of missing persons, alter immi-
> gration procedures, and establish parentage.

The article reports that researchers have made identifications from a four-
year-old bloodstain and from several weeks-old semen stains.

Whereas other tests of human tissues and secretions can only eliminate
suspects, DNA can positively identify an individual, with the exception of
identical twins. The implications for law enforcement are tremendous. According to Dodenhoff (1989, p. 1) the DNA breakthrough "promises to revolution-
ize forensic science."

As noted by Geberth (1990, p. 71): "It's like the criminal leaving his name,
address and social security number at the scene." (See Figure 10–5.)

Development of this new technique started in 1985, when Dr. Alec Jeffreys,
a British geneticist, developed a technique to analyze the genetic sequence of
DNA—the "blueprint of life"—from blood and human tissue. He was joined by
Dr. David J. Werrett, a British forensic scientist, and the two worked to apply
the technique to criminal investigations.

Kelly, Rankin, and Wink (1987, pp. 108–109) describe some applications of
the technique. In one instance in 1983 a young boy was refused entry into the

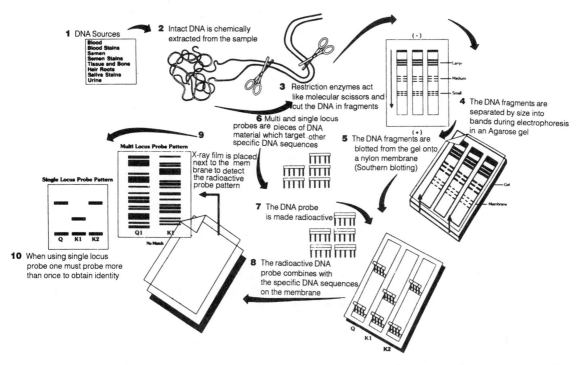

Figure 10–5   Restriction Fragment Length Polymorphism (RFLP); Multi and Single Locus DNA Probes
Source: Courtesy of Federal Bureau of Investigation.

United Kingdom because immigration officers doubted that his mother was a Ghanaian woman who held rights of settlement there. Immigrations officers believed the boy was her nephew, not her son. When DNA fingerprinting was done, however, statistical analysis established with virtual certainty that the boy was the woman's son. And in 1986 a youth who had been imprisoned for three months on a charge of murder was freed after DNA tests showed that he was not the murderer.

According to Dodenhoff (1989, p. 10): "In 1987 an Orlando jury convicted Tommie Lee Andrews of rape almost exclusively on the basis of DNA profiling. In late 1988, a state appellate court upheld the conviction and the use of the DNA evidence."

DNA profiling uses the material from which chromosomes are made to positively identify individuals. No two individuals, except identical twins, have the same DNA structure.

Geberth (p. 73) makes some strong claims for the importance of DNA analysis:

> DNA and genetic fingerprinting represent the most important breakthrough in crime detection since the discovery of the fingerprint. It is the future of forensic medicine, and the experts have only scratched the surface. It is a powerful tool which protects the innocent just as surely as it pinpoints the guilty. Genetic identification takes the "gamesmanship" out of the trial—it either is the defendant who committed the crime, or it is not.

Some disadvantages do exist, however. First, it is very expensive, costing an estimated $100,000 for a laboratory. At present only three labs exist: the FBI,

Lifecodes Corporation, and Cellmark Diagnostics. These labs could be over-whelmed with business if DNA profiling becomes popular in law enforcement. In addition it is very labor intensive and takes about two weeks to conduct each test. And, the technique has not yet received the "stamp of approval" from our justice system. Finally, the technique currently relies on a radioactive process, something scientists are trying to move away from.

PROTECTING AND STORING EVIDENCE

All evidence collected must be marked with the identifying mark of the investigator who collected it. It must be properly packaged and placed in the police evidence room until needed. If it is removed from the evidence room for any reason, strict check-out and check-in procedures should be followed. As noted by Bennett and Hess (1991, p. 207):

> Evidence is subject to chemical change, negligence, accident, intentional damage, theft, or alteration during handling. Protecting and storing evidence is often the weakest link in the **chain of evidence.** Some evidence requires more care than others.
>
> Improperly sealed containers can allow liquid evidence to evaporate or moisture to enter, causing rust. Envelopes can split open. Tags can fall off. Writing on labels can become smudged, blurred, or faded to the point of illegibility.
>
> Proper storage prevents theft, loss, tampering, contamination, and deterioration.

THE USE OF COMPUTERS IN INVESTIGATIONS

Computers have also become an integral part of the investigative responsibilities of police departments. As noted by FBI Director William Sessions (1990, p. 10): "Law enforcement and computers, two seemingly unrelated fields that even 40 years ago would not have been included in the same thought, today are partners in the war against crime. Computers have become a recognized weapon of the forensic scientist in this war."

Computers are being used to identify fingerprints, track evidence, analyze evidence, and aid in case investigation and management.

Computers and Fingerprints

One of the first uses of computers in law enforcement was to assist in identifying fingerprints. More and more departments are installing automated fingerprint identification systems (AFIS). According to Shonberger (1990, p. 86): "An AFIS computer is just a sophisticated filing system which has the ability to reduce a search down to a small number of possible matches." In June of 1990, for example, New York State Division of Criminal Justice began operating a $40 million AFIS system that should help them solve 10,000 crimes a year (*Law Enforcement News,* 1990, p. 4). Previously, when latent fingerprints were found at a crime scene, they had to be physically compared with the prints on file using a magnifying glass. This could take days, weeks, months, or longer depending on the number of prints on file. An AFIS can make this same comparison in seconds, selecting a limited number of prints to be physically examined by a fingerprint expert.

A more recent use of computers in fingerprinting has been the introduction of **biometrics**—measuring physical characteristics such as fingerprints or voice by computer. As noted by Zauner (1991, p. 22):

> The biological characteristics that make each of us unique—our fingerprints, our eyeballs, our voices, our signatures—have become the basis of systems so remarkable they can pick out an individual's characteristics from among millions of others, and with an error factor that is infinitesimal. Right now, biometrics foreshadows the end of ink pads as a means of acquiring and retrieving fingerprint identification.

The development of new technology by companies such as Identix, Fingermatrix, and Digital Biometrics, has resulted in computerized fingerprinters that can electronically scan and print superior quality fingerprints at the point of booking. These prints can be transmitted over phone lines to a computer system for identification matching in a fraction of the time it would take to physically match them.

According to a spokesperson from Digital Biometrics, the goal of the FBI is to "mandate that only electronic fingerprinting will be acceptable [for entry into their computerized AFIS]—possibly as early as the end of 1994" (Zauner 1991, p. 23).

Computers and Evidence

"Nearly every department has had to deal with items that are missing, lost, or stolen from the evidence room," says Hamilton (1991, p. 146). Barbour and Huestis (1990, p. 53) note: "The property control function is an important part of any law enforcement agency's duties, requiring constant attention to detail and careful documentation. A failure in this area is devastating to the reputation of an agency and the careers of the officers responsbile for the property control operation." To say nothing of the damage it can do to a case. Hamilton suggests that: "Automation of the evidence function can help prevent many of the problems inherent in managing evidence." What is needed is a computerized evidence tracking system (ETS).

Many such systems are available. Often they incorporate barcodes such as those used on merchandise in grocery stores. Barbour and Huestis (p. 53) contend that: "Barcodes have proven to be efficient and reliable adjuncts to the traditional property/evidence tags."

Barcodes can also be used in crime laboratories, as described by Hakanson (1991, p. 56):

> The Florida Department of Law Enforcement has installed a bar code system in each of the state's six regional labs to eliminate the cumbersome and unreliable process of manually tracking evidence undergoing forensic analysis.

Computers are also important in the laboratories for their analysis capabilities.

Computers and Laboratory Analysis

According to Sessions (1990, p. 10): "The FBI Laboratory in Washington, D.C. is using computers in almost every phase of its operations." For example, the automated mass spectrometers in the Chemistry/Toxicology unit allow technicians to separate and analyze components of samples to determine what substances they contain. These results can be projected onto the computer screen or produced as hard-copy printout. Either way, they can be rapidly compared to computerized libraries of over 42,000 known substances.

Computers and Case Management/Investigation

Sophisticated software packages have been developed to help with case management. One such program, HOLMES, according to Sutter (1991, p. 50): "is a complete case managment system which can receive, process, organize, recognize, interrelate and retrieve all aspects of information on a case. It also keeps track of ongoing progress, or lack of it, in the investigation."

Computer-aided design can also assist in understanding and critiquing incidents. As noted by Sessions (1990, p. 10):

> In direct support of bureau investigations, drawings can be constructed of crime scenes, objects, charts and numerous other devices. For instance, the computer may render a scale drawing of an improvised explosive device, or homemade bomb. The drawing can be manipulated and changed very easily within the memory of the computer. Court presentation to juries is extremely important and this attention-getting technique provides a very clear demonstration of modern technology.

A California corporation has developed a series of Computer Assisted Police Effectiveness (C.A.P.E.) products for the investigation of serious crimes that include the following:

- C.A.R.—automated drawing and calculations for Computerized Accident Reconstruction.
- Compuscene—for generating professional crime scene drawings without the drafting tedium.
- Compusketch—a composite sketch system for suspect ID, using police artist techniques.
- Quiksketch—a composite sketch system for suspect ID, replaces mechanical ID kit.
- Fotofile—to store and retrieve mug photos with existing computer and records systems.

It would appear that computer literacy may well be a requirement for investigators in the near future.

■■■■■■■■ SUMMARY

A large part of an investigator's role centers around *objectively* obtaining and presenting information and evidence. The preliminary investigative responsibilities are to (1) assure that the crime scene is secure, (2) record all facts related to the case for future reference, (3) photograph, measure, and sketch the crime scene, (4) obtain and identify evidence, (5) interview witnesses and interrogate suspects, and (6) assist in the identification of suspects.

Investigators, be they patrol officers or detectives, are responsible for securing the crime scene, which includes any surrounding area that contains evidence of criminal activity. They must obtain answers to the questions: who? what? where? when? how? and why? Usually they must obtain both photographs and sketches because although photographs include all details and can show items close up, sketches can be selective and can show much larger areas.

A primary responsibility of investigators is to recognize, collect, mark, preserve, and transport physical evidence without contamination in sufficient quantity for analysis. Such evidence may consist of fingerprints, blood, hair, fibers, documents, footprints or tire prints, tool fragments, tool marks, broken glass, paint, insulation from safes, bite marks, firearms, and explosives.

A relatively new technique, DNA profiling, uses the material from which chromosomes are made to positively identify individuals. No two individuals, except identical twins, have the same DNA structure.

Computers are being used to identify fingerprints, track evidence, analyze evidence, and aid in case investigations and management.

DISCUSSION QUESTIONS

1. What are the goals of an investigating officer?

2. What does a preliminary investigation consist of?

3. Name five relevant facts that may appear in an arson investigation?

4. What differences exist between a studio photographer and a crime-scene photographer?

5. What are some characteristics of crimes against property?

6. If you had a choice to present any type of evidence you wanted in a burglary case, what convincing evidence would you choose?

7. What type of evidence might you find at the scene of an assault? A forcible rape? A homicide?

8. In what types of crimes might you find bite marks?

9. Why is DNA profiling not more commonly used in criminal investigations?

10. Why are computers being used in investigations?

TERMS

ballistics, biometrics, chain of evidence, concentric fracture, contamination, contamination prints, corroborative, criminalistics, discovery crimes, DNA profiling, evidence, follow-up investigation, Henry system, impressions, involvement crimes, latent fingerprints, preliminary investigation, radial fracture, riflings.

REFERENCES

Barbour, G. R. and Huestis, R. P. "Barcodes: Technology Enhances Property Control Systems." *The Police Chief* (April 1990): 50–53.

Bennett, W. and Hess, K. M. *Introduction to Criminal Investigation.* 3d ed. St. Paul, Minn.: West Publishing Company, 1991.

DeAngelis, F. J. *Criminalistics for the Investigator.* Encino, Calif.: Glencoe Publishing, 1980.

Dodenhoff, P. "LEN Salutes Its 1988 Man-of-the-Year, Dr. David Werrett." *Law Enforcement News,* January 31, 1989, 1, 10–11.

Geberth, V. J. "Application of DNA Technology in Criminal Investigations." *Law and Order* (March 1990): 70–73.

"Getting Personal in Hunt for Clues: Scientists Eye DNA as New Key to Identifications." *Law Enforcement News,* April 7, 1986, 5.

Hakanson, W. P. "Bar Coding Preserves Evidence Chain of Custody." *Law Enforcement Technology* (October 1991): 56.

Hamilton, T. S. "Developing an Automated Evidence Tracking System." *The Police Chief* (April 1991): 146–149.

Hess, K. M. and Wrobleski, H. M. *For the Record: Report Writing in Law Enforcement.* 3d ed. Eureka, Calif.: Innovative Publications, 1991.

International Association of Chiefs of Police. *Criminal Investigation.* 2d ed. Gaithersburg, Md.: 1970.

Kelly, K. F.; Rankin, J. J.; and Wink, R. C. "Method and Applications of DNA Fingerprinting: A Guide for the Non-Scientist." *Criminal Law Review* (February 1987): 105–110.

Klockars, C. B. *Thinking About Police: Contemporary Readings.* New York: McGraw-Hill, 1983.

"New York Unveils AFIS." *Law Enforcement News,* June 15/30, 1990, 4.

O'Hara, C. E. and O'Hara, G. *Fundamentals of Criminal Investigation.* 5th ed. Springfield, Ill.: Charles C. Thomas, 1988.

Sessions, W. S. "Using Microcomputers to Enhance Police Productivity." *The Police Chief* (March 1990): 10.

Shonberger, M. F. "Miami Police and A.F.I.S. Complete First Decade." *Law and Order* (November 1990): 85–89.

Spelman, W. G. and Brown, D. K. *Calling the Police: A Replication of the Citizen Reporting Component of the Kansas City Response Time Analysis.* Washington, D.C.: The Police Foundation, 1981.

Sutter, S. H. "Holmes. . . . Still Aiding Complex Investigations." *Law and Order* (November 1991): 50–52.

Waldron, R. M. *The Criminal Justice System.* 3d ed. Boston: Houghton Mifflin, 1984.

Walton, G. *Laboratory Manual for Introductory Forensic Science.* Encino, Calif.: Glencoe Publishing, 1979.

Wilson, O. W. *Police Administration.* 2d ed. New York: McGraw-Hill, 1963.

Zauner, P. "Putting the Finger on Security." *Law and Order* (November 1991): 22–24.

Interviewing, Interrogating, and Identifying: The People Side of Investigation

You have the right to remain silent. Anything you say can and will be used against you in a court of law.

—Miranda Warning

Do You Know

What the Miranda warning is and when it must be given?

What the public safety exception is?

Why two people may see the same event yet report it differently?

What networks are? Why they are important to an interviewer?

How witnesses may be aided in making an identification?

What the three basic types of identification are?

When each is appropriate?

What rights the suspect has during the identification process?

What instructions and precautions should be taken to assure the legality and admissibility of an identification in court?

What relevance the *Wade* decision has to identification of a suspect?

What should be done if a suspect refuses to participate in a lineup?

INTRODUCTION

Police officers do not deal only with crime scenes and physical evidence. A large part of their investigative responsibilities is talking with people to obtain information. Sometimes people are very willing to talk, but other times they are very reluctant. In addition to gathering information about crimes that have been committed, police officers must determine the answer to the classic question: Who dunnit? Identifying suspects in a case is another critical investigative responsibility. Evans (1990, p. 90) notes:

> Only a small percentage of criminal cases are solved through the forensic sciences. Fingerprint identification, ballistic evidence, blood, hair and fiber samples are very useful when available, but they just don't play as big a role in everyday police work as television might have us believe. The vast majority of cases are solved simply through good interviewing techniques. They provide evidence that originates with people—namely, sworn statements from victims, witnesses, and the suspects themselves. Many cases fall short of being closed by arrest because of poor interrogation processes.

INTERVIEWING WITNESSES AND INTERROGATING SUSPECTS

The investigator must gain information by talking with victims, witnesses, friends, co-workers, neighbors, or immediate members of the family, as well as by talking with suspects in the case.

Witnesses

A **witness** is a person other than a suspect who has helpful information about a specific incident or a suspect. A witness may be a **complainant,** an accuser, a victim, an observer of the incident, a confidential or reliable **informant,** an expert, or a scientific examiner of physical evidence.

Most evidence at a trial is presented through witnesses. A person who is a qualified witness, who can perceive what was seen firsthand and can relate this experience, is an invaluable aid in the prosecution of the defendant. Witnesses are valuable because they may have seen:

- the suspect actually committing the crime;
- a tool, gun, or instrument used in the commission of the crime in the suspect's possession before or after the crime's commission;
- property that was stolen in the suspect's possession after the crime's commission;
- the suspect making preparations to commit the crime, or heard the suspect threatening to commit the crime, or knew that he or she had a motive for committing it; and
- the suspect going to or leaving the scene of the crime about the time the crime was committed.

In cases such as robbery, assault, or rape, the eyewitness testimony of the victim or a witness may be all that is necessary for a conviction. It is always preferable, however, to have physical evidence to corroborate the eyewitness testimony.

Suspects

Before interrogating any suspect, the police officer should give the Miranda warning, as established in *Miranda v. Arizona.* The United States Supreme

Court asserted that suspects must be informed of their rights to remain silent, to have counsel present, to a state-appointed counsel if they cannot afford one, and to be warned that anything they say might be used against them in a court of law. Many investigators carry a card that contains the Miranda warning to be read before interrogating a suspect. (See Figure 11–1.)

On the evening of March 3, 1963, an eighteen-year-old girl was abducted and raped in Phoenix, Arizona. Ten days after the incident, Ernesto Miranda was arrested by Phoenix police, taken to police headquarters, and put in a lineup. He was identified by the victim and shortly thereafter signed a confession admitting the offenses. Despite objections to the statement by the defense attorney, the trial court admitted the confession. Miranda was convicted and sentenced from twenty to thirty years on each count.

Miranda appealed on the grounds that he had not been advised of his constitutional rights under the Fifth Amendment. The Arizona Supreme Court ruled in 1965 that because Miranda had been previously arrested in California and Tennessee, he knowingly waived his rights under the Fifth and Sixth Amendments when he gave his confession to the Phoenix police. Justice Mc-Farland of the Arizona Supreme Court ruled that because of Miranda's previous arrests, he was familiar with legal proceedings and individual rights and made an intelligent waiver.

In 1966, upon appeal, the United States Supreme Court reversed the Supreme Court of Arizona in a 5–4 decision and set up precedent rules for police custodial interrogation. Chief Justice Warren stated: "The mere fact that he signed a statement which contained a typed-in clause stating that he had 'full knowledge of his "legal rights" ' does not approach the knowing the intelligent waiver required to relinquish constitutional rights."

The United States Supreme Court mandated that any time a person was in police custody police officers must give the Miranda warning so that persons being questioned can intelligently waive their right not to incriminate themselves as provided by the Fifth Amendment. If the warnings are not given, the prosecution cannot prove an intelligent waiver against self-incrimination, and any statement or confession will not be admissible against the suspect.

The Miranda rule applies not only to in-custody situations but to any instance in which a suspect is questioned and the questioning results in the individual being deprived of a substantial portion of his or her liberty. When police officers attempt to obtain a statement or confession from a suspect, they should usually first advise that person of the Miranda warning. This applies whether a suspect is questioned in the police station, in a police car, or on a street corner.

Miranda Warning

1. You have the right to remain silent.
2. If you give up the right to remain silent, anything you say can and will be used against you in a court of law.
3. You have the right to speak with an attorney and to have the attorney present during questioning.
4. If you so desire and cannot afford one, an attorney will be appointed for you without charge before questioning.

Waiver

1. Do you understand each of these rights I have read to you?
2. Having these rights in mind, do you wish to give up your rights as I have explained to you and talk to me now?

Figure 11–1 Miranda Warning

When the probable cause builds to such a point that no reasonable person could deny that an arrest would be imminent, the police officer should at that point give the Miranda warning to the suspect if it has not already been given.

When the *Miranda* decision was handed down in 1966, there was much controversy. Many police officers and citizens complained that the court was "handcuffing the police," hampering them in their duties; however, the Federal Bureau of Investigation had been advising suspects of their constitutional rights for several years before the *Miranda* decision.

The Miranda warning must be given to a suspect who is interrogated in the **custody** of the police, that is, when the suspect is not free to leave.

Two terms are key in this situation: *interrogated* and **in custody**. The circumstances involved in an interrogation and whether it requires a Miranda warning were expanded in *Oregon v. Mathiason* (1977) when the court said:

> Any interview of one suspected of a crime by a police officer will have coercive aspects to it, simply by virtue of the fact that the police officer is part of a law enforcement system which may ultimately cause the suspect to be charged with a crime. But police officers are not required to administer Miranda warnings to everyone whom they question. Nor is the requirement of warnings to be imposed simply because the questioning takes place in the station house, or because the questioned person is one whom the police suspect. Miranda warnings are required only where there has been such a restriction on a person's freedom as to render him "in custody." It was that sort of coercive environment which Miranda by its terms was made applicable, and to which it is limited.

According to del Carmen (1987, p. 263): "A lot of confusion can be avoided if the officer simply remembers that **'custodial interrogation'** takes place in two general situations: (1) when the suspect is under arrest and (2) when the suspect is not under arrest, but is deprived of his freedom in a significant way.' "

Sometimes both terms, *interrogation* and *in custody,* are issues, as was the case in *United States v. Mesa* (1980). In this case the FBI had an arrest warrant for a suspect charged with shooting his common-law wife and his daughter. The suspect barricaded himself in a motel room and was armed. Using a bullhorn, police tried to talk the suspect into coming out, but he refused. Finally he agreed to talk with them by phone. The FBI recorded the conversation, which included some incriminating statements by the suspect. The suspect finally surrendered peacefully and was arrested. The district court did not allow the statements made over the phone to be introduced, stating they were obtained in violation of the suspect's rights and that the Miranda warning should have been given. The circuit court of appeals reversed the decision, as noted by Inbau, Reid, and Buckley (1986, p. 302):

> The chief judge concluded that "where an armed suspect who possibly has hostages barricades himself away from the police, he is not in custody (within) the meaning of the Miranda rule." Another judge was of the view that the agent's conversation with the suspect had not constituted an interrogation. The third judge dissented because he concluded that there had been both custody and interrogation.

Perhaps the best guideline is, when in doubt, give the Miranda warning.

del Carmen (1987, pp. 266–268) lists nine instances when Miranda warnings are not normally required:

> No questions asked. [This is not interrogation.]
> General questioning at the crime scene.

Questioning witnesses.
Volunteered statements.
Statements made to private persons, for example, friends, cellmates.
Questioning in an office or place of business.
"Stop and frisk" cases.
Before a Grand Jury.
Noncustodial interrogations by a probation officer.

The **public safety exception** is an important consideration when discussing the *Miranda* decision. On June 12, 1984, in a landmark 5−4 decision in *New York v. Quarles,* the United States Supreme Court announced that in certain cases police may question suspects in custody without first advising them of their right not to incriminate themselves. Writing for the Court's majority, Justice Rehnquist cited the Supreme Court decision in *Michigan v. Tucker* (1974) and made the distinction that the Miranda warnings are: "Not themselves rights protected by constitution, but are measures to insure that the right against compulsory self-incrimination is protected. . . . On some facts there is a 'public safety' exception to the requirement that Miranda warnings be given before a suspect's answers may be admitted into evidence, and that the availability of that exception does not depend upon the motivation of the individual officers." Although the court set forth the "public safety exception," no attempt was made to determine in what situations this exception might apply.

The public safety exception allows police officers to question suspects without first giving the Miranda warning if the information sought sufficiently affects the officer's and the public's safety.

Knowledge of the background in the *Quarles* case helps in understanding when the public safety exception is relevant. In 1980, a young woman stopped two police officers and told them she had been raped. She described her rapist, who, she said had just entered a nearby supermarket armed with a gun. The officers located the suspect, Benjamin Quarles, and ordered him to stop. But Quarles ran, and the officers momentarily lost sight of him. When they apprehended and frisked him, the officers found an empty shoulder holster. When the officers asked Quarles where the gun was, he nodded toward some cartons and said, "The gun is over there." The officers retrieved the gun, arrested Quarles, and read him his rights. Quarles waived his rights and answered questions.

At the trial, the court ruled that the statement, "The gun is over there," and the subsequent discovery of the gun resulting from that statement were inadmissible at the defendant's trial.

The United States Supreme Court, after reviewing the case, ruled that if Miranda warnings had deterred the response to the officer's question, the cost would have been more than just the loss of evidence, which might lead to a conviction. As long as the gun remained concealed in the store, it posed a danger to public safety.

The Court ruled that in this case the need to have the suspect talk took precedence over the requirement that the defendant be read his rights. The Court ruled that the material factor applying this public safety exception is whether a public threat could possibly be removed by the suspect making a statement. In this case the officer asked the question only to insure his and the public safety. He then gave the Miranda warning before continuing questioning.

Waiving the Right   Suspects can *waive* their rights against self-incrimination and talk to police officers, but the **waiver** must be voluntary. Additionally, the suspect must fully understand what rights are being given up and the possible consequences.

If after hearing a police officer read the Miranda warning, suspects remain silent, this is *not* a waiver. To waive their rights, suspects must state, orally or in writing, that (1) they understand their rights and (2) they will voluntarily answer questions without a lawyer present.

Special care must be taken with individuals who do not speak English as their native language, who are under the influence of drugs or alcohol, who appear to be mentally retarded, or who appear to be hampered mentally in any way.

It is preferable to get the waiver in writing.

Caplan suggests these additional guidelines when conducting interrogations:

- Officers should honor a juvenile suspect's request to speak to a parent or guardian before waiving his rights. (p. 9)
- In major felony cases, the notification of rights, the waiver and the subsequent questioning should be videotaped. (p. 12)
- Any direct request for counsel requires all questioning to end. A request to speak to someone other than an attorney, such as a parent, friend, or even a probation officer is not an assertion of the right to counsel. (p. 14)
- When a suspect attempts to reach an attorney but is not successful, most courts hold that he has asserted his right and cannot be questioned. (p. 14)

WITNESS PERCEPTION

Experience has illustrated time and again that no two people will view the same situation in exactly the same way. How a witness describes what has happened is affected by many factors, some subjective (within the individual) and some objective (inherent in the situation). Because these factors vary from person to person, two people looking at the same thing may see something different. Take, for example, Figure 11–2. Whether the black surface projects toward the viewer or away depends completely upon the viewer's perception. In fact, the same person may see the black surface as projecting on first viewing, yet as receding on a second viewing.

Context, too, can alter how an object or event is perceived. For example, how do you "interpret" the following: 13

Now how do you interpret it? A 13 C   12 13 14

Another factor affecting perception is the amount of attention that is focused on an incident. When an incident barely catches the attention of a

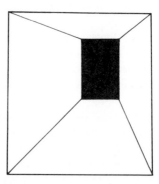

Figure 11–2   Perception

witness, perception is liable to be faulty. One reason for this is the human tendency to complete comprehension of a situation to make it meaningful. That is, people tend to organize their observations into a complete, meaningful picture. A witness may see a man with a mask on and his right hand extended as if holding a gun, and the witness may mentally *add* the gun in his perception of the incident, even though it did not actually exist. To overcome this tendency and obtain valid information, police officers must be aware of how and why people think and act in given situations. In other words, they should try to put themselves in the other person's position and use what is called "street sense" and empathy.

Perception of an incident is affected by the viewer's accuracy of observation, interpretation of what is seen, and attention paid to the incident.

As noted in the *Encyclopedia of Crime and Justice* (Yarmey 1983, pp. 749–755):

> Eyewitness identification is frequently much less reliable than the courts would generally believe. . . . Researchers have extensively investigated the perception and memory of faces. What is the application of this work to the criminal identification of suspects through the viewing of mug shots, artists' drawings, commercial composites, and corporeal lineups? Laboratory studies have indicated that subjects asked to identify faces in a recognition memory test did so accurately in about 75 percent of their selections. . . . More significantly, research is increasingly being conducted outside the laboratory in more naturalistic settings, for example, testing persons who witnessed mock crime performed in super markets and banks. . . . As indicated in *United States v. Nobles* (1975), it is now for the courts to decide whether expert testimony on eyewitness identification should be taken to assist the jury in understanding the evidence, or whether such evidence should be excluded on the ground that it invades the province of the jury.

From a biological perspective, it is almost impossible for two people to see the same thing exactly the same way. According to Hageman (1985, p. 40) the human eye is an energy transducer that can take in nearly five million bits per second. The eye itself does not "see," it transforms the bits into nerve impulses which go to the **sensorium,** the part of the human brain which translates the bits into what is seen. The sensorium can handle only about 500 bits per second. This means that much more goes "unseen" than "seen." The 500 bits one person sees will never be exactly the same as the 500 bits another sees. In addition, notes Hageman (p. 40):

> Perception is an active process. An individual looks at an object from a particular stance or perspective until he or she is able to give the picture some meaningful pattern or name. Oddly enough, once the pattern has been established in a person's mind, it becomes relatively stable. No matter how long one stays away from the pattern, the moment one returns to the figure, the pattern is recognized. In short, an individual, consciously or unconsciously, notices certain stimuli in the environment, chooses to give meaning to some of those stimuli (usually based upon past experience) and uses those stimuli to produce a response or a specific behavior. . . .

The technical name for this is the **phenomenological point of view.** According to Parker et al. (1989, p. 81): "The phenomenological point of view places emphasis on the fact that reality is very much the way a given person perceives it. Reality is therefore different for each person, just as each individual is unique. One needs to take cognizance of this fact when attempting to communicate with another as it is a power factor in establishing a relationship."

Two individuals may view the same scene and actually see different parts of it. Training can enhance perception, but such differences will always exist. These two Philadelphia officers will interpret what they view in their own unique ways.

Understanding the mechanisms of perception should help one to understand how witnesses to the same crime recall different versions of what happened and how one eyewitness's account differs so dramatically from that of another. Once a police agent can understand the selective perceptions of witnesses, then the agent may also be able to understand the differences in what he or she may perceive.

GENERAL GUIDELINES FOR FACILITATING COMMUNICATIONS

Parker et al. (1989, p. 77) suggest that police officers' "need to establish communication with citizens is paramount to successful pursuit of their job." Several specific techniques can be used to facilitate such communication.

First, it is important to have **empathy** or understanding of the person being communicated with. This is not the same as sympathy. It simply means trying to see things from their point of view. Parker et al. (p. 81) note: "Empathizing with another means communicating both verbally and nonverbally, and appreciating where the other person is at. It means letting that person know that you are able to 'hear' what he or she is really saying." They describe the following levels of empathy (p. 83):

- *Low empathy*—The communicator shows little or no understanding of the most basic part of what the other has communicated, seems out of touch with what the other has said, and responds only from her or his own frame of reference. In *Low Empathy* the first person *subtracts* from the interpersonal encounter.
- *Moderate Empathy*—The communicator grasps at least the essential part of the message, and sends a message that fits well with what the other is saying and is essentially interchangeable. The communicator shares with the other an

understanding of at least the surface feelings and main content of the message. This communicator has not completely missed the point as in *Low Empathy,* where there may not be even the slightest acknowledgement of what the person has communicated.

- *High Empathy*—In deep [high] empathy there is a consistent communication on the part of the communicator that indicates that she or he not only hears the surface message, but is able to sense the underlying feelings and concerns that are barely hinted at in the overt communication of the second person. In *High Empathy,* the communicator's responses are *additive* or expand on what the person has stated, and thus allow the second person to explore his or her feelings. In deep empathy, the recipient has a feeling of being able to elaborate on the discussion, and feels truly understood. Communication is opened up; there is an air of excitement about really being heard by the other. This is most important when the police officer . . . must communicate with distressed persons, as they are often required to do in their daily work.

Parker et al. (p. 86) gives the following example of the difference between low and high empathy:

> *Barricaded Man:* I haven't done a damn thing wrong. You get the hell out of here and get off my property before I blast you off!
> *(Low Empathy) First Officer (angrily and in a demanding tone):* Now look, you better cool it and come out, before we have to drag you out.
> *Barricaded Man:* I told you to get the hell out of here and I mean it; you make a move to come in here and you'll regret it.
> *(Low Empathy) First Officer:* Look, you've got to come out sooner or later, and if it isn't pretty damn quick, I'm going to have to come in and force you out.
> *Barricaded man:* Shove it!
> *(High Empathy) Second Officer (in a tentative tone):* It sounds to me like you're pretty angry about this whole mess, but I'm also hearing that you're a bit frightened about what's happening. Can we talk about it?

Other components of effective communication include openness, concreteness, immediacy, and positive regard or respect for the other person.

INTERVIEWING AND INTERROGATING TECHNIQUES

Witnesses who are pressured to give information may become antagonistic and refuse to cooperate. The following simple procedures (Hess and Wrobleski 1991, pp. 37–38) may help make an **interview** with a witness or an **interrogation** of a suspect more productive:

- Prepare for each interview in advance if time permits. Know what questions you need to have answered.
- Obtain your information as soon after the incident as possible. A delay may result in the subject's not remembering important details.
- Be considerate of the subject's feelings. If someone has just been robbed, or seen an assault, or been attacked, the individual may be understandably upset and emotional. Allow time for the person to calm down before asking too many questions. Remember that when emotions increase, memory decreases.
- Be friendly. Try to establish rapport with the subject before asking questions. Use the person's name; look at the person as you ask questions; respond to the answers.
- Use a private setting if possible. Eliminate as many distractions as you can, so that the subject can devote full attention to the questions you ask.
- Eliminate physical barriers. Talking across a desk or counter, or through a car window, does not encourage conversation.

- Sit rather than stand. This will make the subject more comfortable and probably more willing to engage in conversation.
- Encourage conversation. Keep the subject talking by:
  Keeping your own talking to a minimum.
  Using open-ended questions, such as "Tell me what you saw."
  Avoiding questions that call for only a "yes" or "no" answer.
  Allowing long pauses. Pauses in the conversation should not be uncomfortable. Remember that the subject needs time to think and organize his thoughts. Give the subject all the time needed.
- Ask simple questions. Do not use law enforcement terminology when you ask your questions. Keep your language simple and direct.
- Ask one question at a time. Allow the subject to answer one question completely before going to the next question.
- Listen to what is said, and how it is said.
- Watch for indications of tension, nervousness, surprise, embarrassment, anger, fear, or guilt.
- Establish the reliability of the subject by asking some questions to which you already know the answers.
- Be objective and controlled. Recognize that many persons are reluctant to give information to the police. Among the several reasons for this reluctance are fear or hatred of police, fear of reprisal, lack of memory, or unwillingness to become involved. Keep control of yourself and your situation. Do not antagonize the subject, use profanity or obscenity, lose your temper, or use physical force. Remain calm, objective, and professional.

The basic objective of an interview is to get the facts from a witness to eventually prove to the court that the suspect in question did, in fact, commit the crime. The interview itself must be carefully planned by the officer, with only relevant questions asked. In addition to seeking facts and evidence, the investigator is looking for honest witnesses, who demonstrate concern and cooperativeness.

Some witnesses are fearful, uninterested, or unwilling to get involved. With such witnesses, investigators must develop a rapport: be tolerant of the witness's position and thinking; eliminate misunderstanding, mistrust, and suspicion; and induce confidence. They must recognize that each individual will have a somewhat different view of the same incident.

Tables 11–1 and 11–2 summarize interviewing techniques and the types of questions that might be asked.

Pena (1986, p. 206) suggests that police officers should avoid using police terminology while interviewing/interrogating people as it will "increase the incriminating atmosphere" of the questioning. He suggests the following:

Avoid	**Better to Use**
- Murder	- Death
- Mayhem	- Injury
- Robbery	- Property taken
- Burglary	- Entered
- Rape	- Have sex
- Assault	- Scuffle
- Kidnap	- Move
- Conspiracy	- Arrangement
- Embezzle	- Use
- Life imprisonment	- Some time

Table 11-1 Interviewing Subjects

TYPES OF INDIVIDUALS	POLICE INTERVIEWING BEHAVIOR
Hostile Witness	Relieve anxiety and stress.
	Indicate what can and cannot be said.
	State the purpose of the interview.
	Exert control (nonthreatening).
	Develop trust and cooperativeness.
	Indicate potential outcomes of noninvolvement or silent behavior.
Nonhostile Witness	Listen closely to disclosures.
	Double-check all observations and perceptions.
	Avoid angering, confusing, frustrating, or silencing the interviewee.
	Record all descriptions.
	Seek specific details.
Victims	Check their mental and physical health.
	Conduct the interview when the victim has stabilized from shock or trauma.
	Be patient. Forgotten or confused recall may be brought out with careful questions.
	Reassure, calm, relax, protect victim.
	Seek appropriate help where necessary.
	Keep initial questions to a minimum.
	Encourage cooperation.
Indirectly Involved or Uninvolved Subject	Be polite, patient, understanding.
	Thoroughly canvas frequented locales.
	Listen carefully.
	Be perceptive.
	Observe nonverbal signals.
	Avoid antagonizing the general public.
	Persuade reticent individuals to disclose.
Suspects	Safety first. Monitor the suspect's behavior and likelihood of possessing a weapon.
	Gather information; avoid initial interrogation.
	Inform a suspect of appropriate rights.
	Avoid forming prejudgments.
	Avoid giving a suspect cause for alarm.
	Avoid signaling nervousness or anxiety.
	Be honest. Do not make false promises.
	Do not bully or ridicule.
	Never underestimate a suspect's behavior or testimony.
Angry Witness	Assess the interviewee's mental stability.
	Check for weapon.
	Call for assistance where necessary.
	Gain control of the interview.
	Demonstrate neutrality.
	Never argue or disagree.
	Defuse anger with questions.
	Do not allow a shouting match to develop.

Table 11–1   *continued*

TYPES OF INDIVIDUALS	POLICE INTERVIEWING BEHAVIOR
Excessively Verbal Subject	Redirect the interviewee's responses.
	Remind interviewee of the interview's purpose.
	Interrupt and ask closed-ended questions.
	Indicate specific topic areas for discussion.
Reticent Interviewee	Establish rapport.
	Compliment the interviewee.
	Reassure, reduce anxiety.
	Establish pleasant demeanor.
	Encourage talk.
	Avoid limiting response choices.
Uncooperative Interviewee	Exercise control.
	Remind interviewee of penalty for noncooperation.
	Reduce apprehension.
	Clarify unfounded fears.
	Provide incentives for disclosing.
Anxious and Stressed Interviewee	Direct stressed interviewee, when necessary, to professional counseling.
	Release tension in face and body.
	Establish a conversational climate.
	Clarify the nature of the interview.
	Allow opportunity for thinking.
	Do not rush responses. Double-check responses.
Interviewee of Different Race, Culture, Sex, or Ethnic Background	Be cognizant of how others communicate in interview situations.
	Understand the unique or specific verbal and nonverbal behaviors of people who differ from yourself.
	Repeat, reiterate, re-explain.
	Translate your meanings into the language of the interviewee.

Source: T. R. Cheatham and K. V. Erickson. *The Police Officers Guide to Better Communication.* Copyright © 1984. Reprinted by permission of Scott, Foresman and Company: Glenview, Ill.

Detecting Signs of Deception

It is a given that not all people will be honest with the police. Without becoming overly suspicious, police officers should become adept at determining when someone is probably being deceptive or truthful. Evans (1990, p. 94) suggests that interviewers/interrogators should be watchful for reliable indicators of lying:

Deceptive subjects often hesitate in order to gain more time to develop a lie. They use con words, such as "I swear to God," "Honestly," and "Believe me," to make their lies sound more believable.

Deceptive subjects are more likely to challenge minute details of factual information, such as the difference in a few minutes of time. People tend to look more while listening than speaking, and research shows that men engage in less eye contact than women. Still, a person will generally not look you in the eyes when making a deceptive response.

Table 11–2 Interview Questions

TYPE OF QUESTION	PURPOSE	CHARACTERISTICS	EXAMPLE
Open-Ended	To elicit a variety of responses To provide interviewee response choices To break the ice To reduce apprehension	No set response expected of interviewee No specific topic Found in nondirected interviews Interviewee centered Nonthreatening	"How is the weather today?" "How have you been?" "Will it be a good football year?" "Life treating you well?" "What do you think of politics?" "How is the economy affecting you?"
Closed-Ended	To limit interviewee response choices To gather specific information from subject To facilitate use of time	One-to three-word replies Specific answers sought Authoritarian Frequently appears in a series of closed-ended questions Brusque	"What did he say?" "Did you do it?" "What is your name?" "Where do you work?" "What time is it?" "What did she wear?" "Was it red or green?"
Probing	To force replies Explanation Clarification Elaboration Confrontation Repetition	Seeks additional information Requires respondent to be responsive to interviewer Clears up misunderstandings Reveals sensitive/disguised information	"Explain what you mean?" "Tell me again what you said?" "How is that possible?" "You don't believe that do you?" "Why did you do that?" "More details, please."
Mirror	To keep interviewee talking Clarification Explanation	Repeats or paraphrases interviewee's remarks Places burden of talk on interviewee	"So, you took the bike, huh?" "And then you left town?" "You say you like it?" "Which job are you talking about?"
Leading	To lead interviewee to particular response To reveal discrepancies in testimony To facilitate admissions To force a stand	Suggests or implies an appropriate answer Places words in respondent's mouth Leaves little room for interviewee explanation of responses Placed in a series of questions	"You didn't like her, did you?" "Do you think that was right?" "Can you really say that was the correct thing to do?" "You won't act like that again, will you?"

Source: T. R. Cheatham and K. V. Erickson. *The Police Officers Guide to Better Communication.* Copyright © 1984. Reprinted by permission of Scott, Foresman and Company: Glenview, Ill.

Truthful subjects, on the other hand, usually identify with the issue under investigation, respond without hesitation and are not afraid to discuss motive. Truthful subjects usually name individuals who might be guilty and eliminate others from suspicion. They tend to suggest harsher punishment than their deceptive counterparts.

Be conscious of body language. Body movements, gestures, facial expressions and eye contact can all be interpreted during the course of an interview to help determine whether or not a person is being truthful. Normally, lying causes anxiety and stress. To reduce anxiety, the body reacts by releasing energy through the shifting of body posture, bringing hands to the face, or picking lint from clothing.

Learn to evaluate body language—and consciously to look for it. You will find it useful during an interview to note when the body language reinforces and when it contradicts the feelings that are communicated verbally.

Remember, no single verbal statement or nonverbal behavior automatically means a person is lying or telling the truth. Each behavior must be considered in the context of the environment, the intensity of the setting, and in comparison to the subject's normal behavior patterns. An assessment of a subject's truthfulness should be based on clusters of behavioral characteristics, not on a single observation.

Networking an Interview

Most people are familiar with the concept of **networks,** that is, mutually beneficial personal contacts. What may not be familiar, however, is the importance of such networks to police officers conducting interviews or interrogations. According to Noose (1992, p. 101):

Networks represent relationships, links between people, and between people and their beliefs. Without an understanding of these relationships, these networks, it is often quite difficult, and sometimes even impossible, to understand an event or the circumstances that led to it. The answers obtained may have little in common with the questions asked.

All human beings act to create a personal reality, one that allows them to predict and control the world around them. Their associations with others and their own fundamental beliefs all become part of this unique construction of reality. In this way, these networks determine how people act and what they will relate when they are questioned. . . .

Networks produce the context within which a statement from a complainant, victim, witness, or suspect can be most clearly understood.

Networks are relationships, links, between people. They may be social, cultural, business, professional, political, or personal. They help explain a person's perception and mental state.

Noose (p. 103) explains: "Networks are complex pathways of human interaction that guide and direct an individual's perception, motivation and behavior. For police, networks define the context within which human behavior occurs. In order to understand an event, officers must understand the networks." This will become even more important as our society becomes more diverse culturally. Noose stresses that "the diverse nature of the social groups that will be encountered by police will widen and increase. To serve the public officers will have to be able to uncover the networks that are held by the citizens in their jurisdiction."

Networks color how the world is viewed. This officer and his son are establishing a bond. The boy will probably feel differently toward police officers than other children lacking such close ties.

Cognitive Interviewing

The **cognitive interview** is a technique to help victims or witnesses remember a specific incident. It guides the person back to the original memory using an established formula. Olsen and Wells (1991, p. 31) describe the four-step process of the cognitive interviewing technique to guide victims and witnesses:

1. *Reconstruct the circumstances.* Ask them to think about how they were feeling. Have them focus on the event in their minds' eye. Ask them to describe weather, surroundings, objects, people and smells.
2. *Report everything.* Ask them to focus on the event and tell everything; i.e., "Don't edit anything, even if you feel that it is unimportant." Make this an *uninterrupted* narrative.
3. *Recall the events in a different order.* Ask them to tell the story in reverse, beginning with the last thing that occurred and continuing to the first thing that happened.
4. *Change perspectives.* Ask them to assume the role of another person present or nearby. What would he have been able to see?

Follow the narrative with these five specific questions, asked slowly, when appropriate:

1. *Appearance:* Did the person remind you of anyone? Who? Why?
2. *Names:* Go through the alphabet. What was the first letter of the name you heard?
3. *Numbers:* How many numbers did you see? Were they high? Low? Mixed with letters?
4. *Speech:* Who did the voice(s) remind you of? Why?
5. *Conversations:* What was your reaction to what was said?

When this technique was tested in the Metro-Dade Florida Police Department, robbery detectives who interviewed crime victims and eyewitnesses elicited nearly 50 percent more information after being trained in the cognitive interview technique (*Law Enforcement News*, 1990, p. 1).

The Noncooperative Witness

A Witness Cooperation Study ("Witness Responses Misunderstood by Prosecutors", 1976) of almost three thousand randomly selected witnesses indicated that many citizens are incorrectly perceived as noncooperative. According to this study (p. 6): "Prosecutors were apparently unable to cut through to the true intentions of 23 percent or more of those regarded as noncooperative and recorded the existence of witness problems when this was a premature judgment at best and an incorrect decision at worst." The primary cause for this problem was attributed to faulty communication among police, prosecutor, and witness. Problems arise when witnesses are not contacted, when their role is not explained, when they are not told when and where to appear, when their participation is discouraged, and when they are given vague instructions.

The study showed that the police did not obtain the correct addresses for 23 percent of the witnesses at the time of the crime, that the prosecutors often did not insure that witnesses knew when and where to appear, that police sometimes asked for witness identification within hearing of suspects, and that witnesses often had no understanding of their role in the judicial process.

OBTAINING IDENTIFICATION OF A SUSPECT

If police officers do not actually witness the commission of the crime, eyewitness indentification plays an important part in the arrest as well as in the trial proceedings.

Aids to Witness Identification of Suspects

Rather than simply asking a witness to describe a suspect, it is often helpful if the investigator asks specifically about such items as the following:

- Sex
- Race
- Age
- Height
- Weight
- Build—stout, medium, slim, stooped, square-shouldered
- Complexion—flushed, sallow, pale, fair, dark

- Hair—color, thick or thin, bald or partly bald, straight, curly, wavy, style
- Eyes—color, close or far apart, bulgy or small
- Eyebrows—bushy or normal
- Nose—small, large, broad, hooked, straight, short, long, broken, pierced
- Beard—color, straight, rounded, chin whiskers only, goatee, long sideburns
- Mustache—color, short, stubby, long, pointed ends, turned-up ends
- Chin—square, broad, long, narrow, double and sagging
- Face—long, round, square, fat, thin, distinctive pimples or acne
- Neck—long, short, thick, thin
- Lips—thin, thick
- Mouth—large, small, drooping or upturned
- Teeth—missing, broken, prominent, gold, conspicuous dental work
- Ears—small, large, close to head or extended outward, pierced
- Forehead—high, low, sloping, bulging, straight
- Distinctive marks—scars, moles, amputations, tattoo marks, peculiar walk or talk
- Peculiarities—twitching of features, rapid or slow gait, eyeglasses or sunglasses, stutter, foreign accent, gruff or feminine voice, nervous or calm
- Clothing—mask: if so, color; did it have eye slits, ear openings, mouth openings? Did it cover the whole face, have any designs on it? Did the suspect wear a hat or cap (baseball, golf, etc.)? Any markings on the hat? Shirt and tie, sport shirt only, scarf, coat or jacket? Gloves, color of trousers, shoes, stockings, dressed well or shabbily, dressed neatly or carelessly? Any monogram on shirt or jacket?
- Weapon used (if any)—shotgun, rifle, automatic weapon, handgun. Was weapon readily shown or concealed? Taken with or left at scene?
- Jewelry—any noticeable rings, bracelets, or necklaces, earrings, watch?

In addition to questions related to the suspect's appearance, the investigator might also assist the witness by using a description sheet (see Figure 11–3).

Very specific questions and use of an identification diagram may aid witnesses in their identification of suspects.

Other information related to the suspect must also be obtained by the investigator. It is important to know how the suspect left the scene— running, walking, in a vehicle—and in what direction.

If the suspect escaped in a vehicle, the investigator should obtain information about the license number, make of the vehicle, number of passengers, direction of travel, the color and size of the car, as well as any other identifiable features such as racing stripes, hood ornaments, customized features, broken taillights or headlights, body damage, and so on. The car, if identified, may lead the investigator to the suspect.

If the witness knows the suspect, the investigator should ask about the suspect's personal associates, habits, and where he or she is likely to be found.

Usually, however, the witness does not know the suspect. If investigators can identify a suspect based on information given by the witness or on their own intuition as to who might be responsible for the crime, they must follow strict procedures in establishing that the individual is identified by the witness.

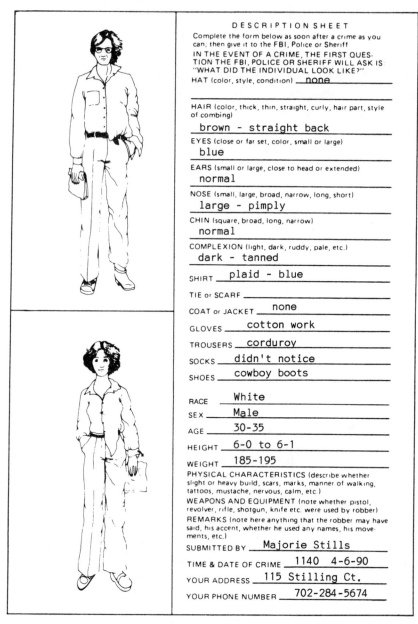

Figure 11–3   Witness Identification Diagram

BASIC TYPES OF IDENTIFICATION

The three basic types of identification are field identification, photographic
identification, and lineup identification. Each type of identification is used in
specific circumstances, and each must meet certain legal requirements to be
admissible in court. Sometimes more than one type of identification is used.

The three basic types of identification are:

- Field identification.
- Photographic identification.
- Lineup identification.

Field Identification

Field identification is at-the-scene identification and must be made within a reasonable time after a crime has been committed. Generally the suspect is returned to the crime scene for possible identification, or the witness may be taken to where the suspect is being held.

Field identification is generally used when a suspect matches the description given by a witness and is apprehended close to the scene of the crime. The critical element in a field identification is time.

Field identification is based on a totality of circumstances in which a witness identifies a suspect as being the person who committed a crime. **Totality of circumstances** takes into consideration the concentration a witness had upon the suspect at the time the crime was committed, the accuracy of the witness's description of the suspect, the certainty of the witness at the time of the confrontation, and the length of time between commission of the crime and the field identification. A reasonable basis for believing that immediate identification is needed must exist before using field identification, since the suspect does not have the right to have counsel present (*United States v. Ash, Jr.,* 1973).

The suspect does not have the right to have counsel present at a field identification.

Studies have shown a 60 percent probability of arrest if response time to crime calls was within one minute; however, the probability of arrest was considerably less when response time was longer. Rapid response greatly improves the officer's chances of apprehending suspects still at the scene. In such cases field identification is obviously justified. Even when the suspects have left the scene, however, if they are apprehended within a reasonable time (up to approximately fifteen minutes) after commission of the crime, immediate identification is justified.

Photographic Identification

Most people are familiar with the procedure of having victims and witnesses go through mug books in hopes of finding a picture of the person they saw commit a particular crime. This type of identification is time consuming and is profitable only if the suspect has a record.

If a suspect is not known, witnesses may make identification through mug shots.

Mug shots are not the only types of photographs used in suspect identification. Frequently officers know, or have a strong suspicion about, who committed a given crime. If the suspect is not in custody, or if it is not possible to conduct a fair lineup, officers may present photographs of people of similar general descriptions to victims or witnesses, who may identify the suspect from among the photographs.

Photographic identification is reserved for times when the suspect is not in custody or it is not possible to conduct a fair lineup. Photographic identification should use people of comparable race, height, weight, and general description.

Photographs used for suspect identification should not contain labels that reveal that a certain suspect has a criminal record. The identification is to be impartial, based on the witness's view of the suspect, and untainted by the suspect's past record. Witnesses should be instructed that they are not obliged to identify anyone from the photographs.

Both the United States Supreme Court and several state supreme courts have issued decisions recognizing the hazards in identification from photographs. Some state prosecutors require a minimum number of photos; however, each has stated that every case must be considered on its own facts. Admissibility in court is more probable if the witness was shown the photographs when he or she was alone and had had no communications with any other witnesses.

Lineup Identification

The basic idea of the lineup is to provide the opportunity for witnesses to observe several individuals, one of whom is the suspect, to see if that suspect can be identified. As with photographic identification, the prosecutor may require a minimum number of participants in the lineup.

The witnesses not only can see the people in the lineup, they also can hear them speak. A suspect may be asked to speak, walk, turn, assume a stance or a gesture, or put on clothing. If witnesses have described the suspect's clothing, then all those in the lineup or none should wear that type of clothing. Obviously if only one dressed the way witnesses described, the tendency would be to pick that individual. Some police departments have a small inventory of clothing and personal effects such as sunglasses, masks, scarves, gloves, and coats that they have the participants in a lineup wear, depending on the description of the witness(es).

A lineup is used when a suspect is in custody. It should contain individuals of similar race, height, weight, and general description. Witnesses must be instructed that no identification need be made.

A number of important court decisions have been made regarding lineup identification. One of the most important is *United States v. Wade* (1967), which affirms a suspect's right to have counsel present when participating in a lineup.

Although requesting participation in a lineup is not considered a form of self-incrimination under the Fifth Amendment, the lineup is considered a "critical stage" in the legal process. The *Wade* decision was based on a case in which Wade was convicted of robbing a Texas bank. His case went to the United States Supreme Court, which reviewed the proceedings and then sent the case back to an appeals court. In its review, the Supreme Court said: "The Sixth Amendment of the Constitution guarantees that every citizen shall have the right to counsel in criminal prosecution. When a citizen is suspected of a crime and required to participate in a lineup where witnesses attempt to identify him, then he has a constitutional right to have his lawyer present." The United States Supreme Court stated that "a lineup is just as critical a stage of the prosecution as the trial itself." It should be noted, however, that this particular constitutional right does not apply to field identification or to photographic identification.

The *Wade* decision states that "prior to having a suspect participate in a lineup, the officer must advise the suspect of his constitutional right to have his lawyer present during the lineup." Requesting a suspect to participate in the lineup is not a violation of the person's civil rights.

When using lineup identification, the officer must know the legal requirements accompanying such an identification as well as the composition of the lineup itself. A legal lineup should assure that:

- The suspect has been advised of his or her right to a lawyer.
- A lawyer has been secured if requested.
- The witnesses have been given impartial prelineup advice.
- The lineup is conducted fairly.
- The individuals in the lineup meet the requirements previously specified.

Generally, when an officer talks about "reading a suspect his or her rights," the officer means the Miranda rights protecting the suspect from self-incrimination. For a lineup, however, the officer is talking about the suspect's Sixth Amendment right to have a lawyer present as specified in the *Wade* decision. The *Miranda* decision is not relevant here.

When a suspect is in custody, a lineup should be used as long as it can be done without force and in a fair manner. If these conditions cannot be satisfied, photographic identification should be used.

If for any reason a suspect refuses to cooperate in a lineup, photographic identification may be used. The suspect's refusal to participate may be used against him or her in court.

If a lineup can be held, there is no reason to show pictures. If both are done in a short period of time, the officer destroys any doubt the witness might have that the person in the picture is the guilty party. A recent Midwest supreme court ruling reversed a guilty decision because a photo identification and lineup were held within minutes of each other.

Witnesses should not make photographic identification and then lineup identification within a short period of time.

SUMMARY

Investigators must interview witnesses and interrogate suspects. A witness may be a complainant, an accuser, a victim, an observer of the incident, a confidential or reliable informant, an expert, or a scientific examiner of physical evidence. A suspect, the person believed to have committed the crime, should not be interrogated without first being given the Miranda warning, which advises that he or she has the "right to remain silent . . . the right to speak with an attorney and to have the attorney present during questioning."

The Miranda warning must be given to a suspect who is interrogated in the custody of the police, that is, when the suspect is not free to leave. The public safety exception, however, allows police officers to question suspects without first giving the Miranda warning if the information sought sufficiently affects the officer's and the public's safety.

Information obtained from witnesses is usually critical to resolution of a case. Unfortunately, witnesses' perception of what happened often varies because perception is affected by the viewer's accuracy of observation, interpretation of what is seen, and attention paid to the incident.

Interviewers need to be aware of networks—relationships, links, between people. They may be social, cultural, business, professional, political, or personal. Networks help explain a person's perception and mental state.

In addition to physical evidence, eyewitness identification plays an important part in the arrest and in the trial proceedings. Very specific questions and use of an identification diagram may aid witnesses in their identification of suspects. Once this information has been obtained, the investigator may use three basic types of identification: (1) field identification, (2) photographic identification, or (3) lineup identification. Sometimes more than one type of identification is used.

Field identification is used when a suspect is temporarily detained or arrested. It is usually "at-the-scene" identification. Field identification is based on totality of circumstances in which a witness identifies a suspect as being the person who committed the crime. The suspect does *not* have the right to have counsel present at a field identification. The critical element in a field identification is time—it should usually occur within approximately fifteen minutes of the commission of the crime to be legally admissible.

Photographic identification may be of two types—mug shots or ordinary photographs. Mug shots are usually used when the suspect is not known to the witness or the police. Ordinary photographic identification is used when the police have a fairly good idea of who is involved in the crime and the suspect is not in custody or it is not possible to conduct a fair lineup. Photographic identification should use people of comparable race, height, weight, and general description.

A lineup is used when a suspect is in custody. The same legal requirements exist as for photographic identification: the lineup should contain individuals of similar race, height, weight, and general description. Witnesses must be instructed that no identification need be made.

The *Wade* decision states that "prior to having a suspect participate in a lineup, the officer must advise the suspect of his constitutional right to have his lawyer present during the lineup." Requesting a suspect to participate in a lineup is not a violation of the person's civil rights. If for any reason the suspect refuses to cooperate in a lineup, however, photographic identification may be used and the suspect's refusal to participate may be used against him or her in court. If both photographic identification and lineup identification are used, they should not be done within a short period of time.

DISCUSSION QUESTIONS

1. If there was a crime and the suspect was unusually tall or was a member of a minority group not common in the area, how could you hold a fair lineup?

2. In what crimes is eyewitness testimony all that is required for conviction?

3. Why would people not want to help put a stop to crime by being witnesses?

4. How do you convince witnesses to get involved when they really do not want to?

5. Can you force a witness to answer questions?

6. If two witnesses disagree on an identification, what happens?

7. If five witnesses are to identify a suspect in a lineup and four of them pick one person and one picks another, is it assumed that the majority are right, or is the lineup inconclusive?

8. How are participants in a lineup chosen?

9. How do empathy and perception interact? Why are they important to an interviewer/interrogator?

10. Why does the suspect not have the right to counsel at a field identification?

TERMS

cognitive interview, complainant, custody, custodial interrogation, empathy, field identification, in custody, informant, interrogation, interview, networks, perception, phenomenological point of view, public safety exception, sensorium, totality of circumstances, waiver, witness.

REFERENCES

Caplan, G. M. *Model Procedures for Polic Interrogation.* Washington, D.C.: Police Executive Research Forum (no date).

del Carmen, R. V. *Criminal Procedure for Law Enforcement Personnel.* Monterey, Calif.: Brooks/ Cole Publishing, 1987.

Evans, D. D. "10 Ways to Sharpen Your Interviewing Skills." *Law and Order* (August 1990): 90–95.

Hageman, M. J. *Police-Community Relations.* Beverly Hills, Calif.: Sage Publications, 1985.

Hess, K. M. and Wrobleski, H. M. *For the Record: Report Writing in Law Enforcement.* 3d ed. Eureka, Calif.: Innovative Publications, 1991.

Inbau, F. E.; Reid, J. E.; and Buckley, J. P. *Criminal Interrogation and Confessions.* 4th ed. Baltimore, Md.: Williams & Wilkins, 1986.

"Interview Style Pays Off." *Law Enforcement News,* February 14, 1990, 1, #6.

Noose, G. A. "Basic Investigative Interviewing Skills: Networking an Interview." *Law and Order* (March 1992): 101–107.

Olsen, L. and Wells, R. "Cognitive Interviewing and the Victim/Witness in Crisis." *The Police Chief* (February 1991): 28–34.

Parker, L. C., Jr.; Meier, R. D.; and Monahan, L. H. *Interpersonal Psychology for Criminal Justice.* 2d ed. St. Paul, Minn.: West Publishing Company, 1989.

Pena, M. S. *Practical Criminal Investigation.* 2d ed. Sacramento, Calif.: Custom Publishing, 1986.

"Witness Responses Misunderstood by Prosecutors." *Target* (LEAA Newsletter) 5, no. 1 (January 1976): 6.

Yarmey, A. D. "Eyewitness Identification." *Encyclopedia of Crime and Justice.* New York: The Free Press, 1983.

CHAPTER 12

Searching and Arresting: Staying Within the Law

Police arrest powers are indeed awesome, and even while they protect society, they can destroy a citizen.

—J. S. Creamer

Do You Know

The major provisions of the Fourth Amendment?

On what sources probable cause can be based?

The categories of informational probable cause?

What is established by the Exclusionary Rule?

What basic principles underlie stop and frisk and what differences distinguish them?

What significance the *Terry* case has in relation to the Fourth Amendment?

What a search warrant is and what it must contain?

When forcible entry is legal?

When nighttime and no-knock warrants are justified?

What an administrative warrant is? When it is required?

How one can challenge a warrantless search?

What authorities and restrictions are provided by the following cases: *Carroll, Chambers, Coolidge?*

What special conditions apply to search of autos?

What is meant by plain view evidence?

Whether open fields, abandoned property, or trash can be searched without a warrant?

What the authorities for lawful arrest are?

What the justifications for a reasonable search are and what limitations are placed on them?

When force can be used to make an arrest?

INTRODUCTION

Decency, security, and liberty alike demand that governmental officials shall be subjected to the same rules of conduct that are commands to the citizen. In a government of laws, existence of the government will be imperiled if it fails to observe the law scrupulously. Our government is the potent, the omni-present teacher. For good or ill, it teaches the whole people by its example. Crime is contagious. If the government becomes a lawbreaker, it breeds contempt for the law; it invites every man to become a law unto himself; it invites anarchy. To declare that in the administration of the criminal law the end justifies the means—to declare that the government may commit crimes in order to secure the conviction of a private criminal— would bring terrible retribution. Against this pernicious doctrine this court should resolutely set its face.

This synopsis was delivered by Supreme Court Justice Louis D. Brandeis in *Olmstead v. United States* (1928) and says, in effect, that government agents, including police officers, are subjected to certain restrictions in enforcing the laws. Those who are entrusted with the responsibility of protecting life and property must understand the principles of the federal and state constitutions and the duties that flow from their application as well as the numerous laws and statutes that have been enacted. In short, policing involves having to know the law without the benefit of having gone to law school.

THE FOURTH AMENDMENT

Arbitrary searches and/or seizures have no place in a democratic society. In fact, colonial grievances against unreasonable searches and seizures, in part, led to the revolt against English authority. The Fourth Amendment of the Constitution guarantees the right of citizens to be secure from such arbitrary searches and seizures.

The constitutional standards for searches and seizures, including arrests, are contained in the Fourth Amendment, which requires that searches and seizures be reasonable and based on probable cause.

The terms *reasonable* and *probable cause* provide a very fine, but significant, weight to balance the scales of justice, which measure the conduct of all people. Without what is referred to as probable cause, the laws that govern us might easily become unbalanced, that is, too permissive or too restrictive.

The second part of the Fourth Amendment, called the "warrant clause," states: "No warrant shall issue but upon probable cause." In other words, all warrants (search and arrest warrants) must be based on probable cause.

Reasonable

The rules for determining what constitutes a **reasonable search** or **reasonable seizure** result from interpretation of the first part of the Fourth Amendment, called the "reasonable search and seizure clause," which states, in part: "The right of the people to be secure in their persons, houses, papers, and effects, against unreasonable searches and seizures shall not be violated."

Reasonable also means possessing good sound judgment, well balanced. "Possessing good judgment" implies making decisions. Each case and situation is different from other cases and other situations; therefore, police officers must use their personal judgment as to what action to take. "Well balanced" applies to a built-in stability for justice. On the one hand there is the justification for an action, whether it be an arrest based on probable cause, or an arrest warrant, or stopping and frisking someone. On the other hand, the justification for the action must be balanced by observing the limitations on each action. When the limitations for any action are exceeded, we have gone beyond the reasonableness that made the action legal. Justification and limitation must always be considered together.

Probable Cause

According to Creamer (1980, p. 9):

> Probable cause for an arrest is defined as a combination of facts or apparent facts, viewed through the eyes of an experienced police officer, which would lead a man of reasonable caution to believe that a crime is being or has been committed.
>
> Probable cause for the issuance of a search warrant is defined as facts or apparent facts, viewed through the eyes of an experienced police officer, which would lead a man of reasonable caution to believe that there is something connected with a violation of law on the premises to be searched.

Probable cause requires more than mere suspicion; it requires facts or proof that would lead a person of reasonable caution to believe a crime has been committed or that premises contain evidence of a crime. Creamer goes on to note that according to Justice Rutledge (*Brinegar v. United States,* 1949): "The substance of all definitions of 'probable cause' is a reasonable ground for belief in guilt."

Further, in *Smith v. United States* (1949), probable cause is defined as: "The sum total of layers of information and the synthesis of what the police have heard, what they know, and what they observe as trained officers. We [the courts] weigh not individual layers but the laminated total."

Creamer also points out that the concept of probable cause is one of the oldest and most important in criminal law, having been in existence for more than two thousand years and occurring in both Roman law and the common law of England. According to Creamer (1980, p. 8): "This concept of probable cause has acquired its legal potency in the United States because it has constitutional dimensions and because it is interpreted in the final analysis by impartial judges rather than by the police. The severe penalty that the courts impose on police who fail to abide by the spirit of the Fourth Amendment is to declare the evidence they gathered inadmissible."

SOURCES OF PROBABLE CAUSE

Probable cause is "a state of facts that lead a man of ordinary care and prudence to believe and conscientiously entertain an honest and strong suspicion that the person is guilty of a crime." That strong suspicion may be founded on several sources.

Probable cause may be based on the following:

- Observation by officers.
- Expertise of officers.
- Circumstantial factors.
- Information communicated to officers.

More often than not, observational probable cause will be supplemented by expertise, circumstantial, or informational probable cause. In general, the officer has reason to believe a person is involved in a specific crime. For example, the officer sees a car weaving down the highway at 55 mph, the posted speed limit. Although the driver is not speeding, a car weaving from lane to lane would lead any reasonable person to entertain a strong suspicion that the driver was under the influence of alcohol or drugs. The officer not only has a right but also an obligation to stop the car because the driver is jeopardizing his or her own life as well as the lives of other people on the highway.

Suppose the officer stops the weaving car and discovers that the driver is suffering from a sneezing attack caused by a gust of wind blowing a cloud of dust into the car. Obviously an arrest would not be justified even though the probable cause strongly suggested the driver was drunk. On the other hand, if the driver had shown signs of drinking, such as the odor of an alcoholic beverage on his or her breath, red eyes, slurred speech, or incoordination, the officer would need additional corroboration by administering a sobriety test at the scene and further evidence such as a breath or urine test at the time of booking.

Police officers first have to justify an arrest by proving to themselves that a crime has been committed and that sufficient evidence exists to convince a jury "beyond a reasonable doubt" that the suspect was involved in the crime. Probable cause to stop a person in reference to a specific crime does not always mean that an arrest will occur.

Observational Probable Cause

Observational probable cause is what the officer sees, hears, or smells, that is, evidence that is presented directly to the officer's senses. This is similar to eyewitness testimony, and it is the strongest form of probable cause. The courts have generally recognized certain types of events as being significant in determining probable cause.

Suspicious activities are generally regarded as contributing to probable cause. For example, a car being driven slowly can be suspicious when (1) the car has circled a block several times, (2) the people in the car are carefully observing a building, (3) the building is closed, and (4) the building is located in a high-crime area. All four factors contribute to probable cause.

Familiar criminal patterns are also generally recognized as contributing to probable cause. The conduct of a person can be indicative of a familiar pattern associated with the sale of stolen property or narcotics or of someone who is casing a building.

Officers assemble factors that contribute to probable cause for arrest. Any one factor by itself may not be sufficient to establish probable cause, but collectively they provide justification—probable cause.

Expertise and Circumstantial Probable Cause

Expertise and **circumstantial probable cause** are often tied to observational probable cause. Police officers' knowledge of criminal traits and their ability to "put the pieces together" may also contribute to probable cause. For example, two police officers questioned two men seen driving from an alley at 2:00 A.M. The officers noted the license number of the car and the occupants' names and questioned the driver and passenger. The two men were allowed to continue, but a short time later, when the officers learned there had been a burglary in a nearby town, they forwarded the description of the car and its occupants to the local law enforcement officers. The suspects were apprehended, and a search of the vehicle revealed burglary tools as well as the property taken in two burglaries.

In the original confrontation with the suspects, the two officers were not satisfied with the suspects' explanation of why they were there at such an early hour, and even though they did not have sufficient evidence to establish probable cause for an arrest, their investigation of the suspicious circumstances eventually led to the arrest and conviction of the suspects, who later pleaded guilty to seven prior offenses, all felonies.

Arrest and conviction in this case were based on the officers' decision as to when there was sufficient reason to act on probable cause. To arrest without a warrant when a felony has been committed, the officers must have reasonable cause to believe that the person(s) arrested committed the crime.

Informational Probable Cause

Informational probable cause covers a wide range of sources. In the case previously described, the information about the two suspects forwarded by the police officers to the police in the nearby town constituted informational probable cause. In addition to official sources, victims of crime and citizen informants can be reliable sources of informational probable cause.

The major categories of reliable informational probable cause are (1) official sources, (2) victims of crimes, and (3) informants.

Official sources include police bulletins, police broadcasts, and roll-call information. This information can be relied upon because it is received through official police channels. Information coming from official sources is, in itself, generally sufficient to justify arrest. Although the police officer may arrest on the basis of information received through official channels, this does not relieve the prosecution from establishing that the original source of information was reliable; that is, the original source of information was sufficient to establish probable cause to arrest.

It is the source of information, not the manner of transmission, that will be considered at a trial. Police officers may testify that the information on which they acted was sent over the police radio, but the defendant has the right to demand to know where the information originated and who passed it on to the dispatcher. In other words, as in any other case, the original source of the information must be reliable. For instance, if police officers make an arrest based on information obtained directly from other police officers, the original officers may be required to testify at the trial as to their sources of information, and it is that source which must establish probable cause to arrest. The source may be a victim of a crime, a witness to a crime, or an informant.

Victims of crimes are also usually reliable sources of informational probable cause. Officers can be and are entitled to rely on the information supplied by victims of crimes committed against their person or property and to use this information in making the decision to arrest suspects. Their statements to police officers can be the source of the officers' belief that they have probable cause to look for a person or persons involved in the commission of a crime.

Informants quite often provide probable cause. Included in this category are citizens who actually witness a crime and openly aid in the apprehension of the suspect. **Eyewitnesses** are individuals who have observed a crime, who expect no favors from the police, and who do not exchange information for protection or act out of motives for revenge. Complete and otherwise credible information from a citizen informant, based on personal knowledge that a felony has been committed, is generally sufficient probable cause to justify a felony arrest or to obtain an arrest or search warrant.

THE EXCLUSIONARY RULE

Without procedures for enforcing the provisions of the Fourth Amendment, the impressive constitutional language would be meaningless. Consequently, the procedures and the power for their enforcement were vested in the courts. They must refuse to consider evidence obtained by unreasonable search and seizure methods, regardless of how relevant the evidence is to the case.

This rule, known as the **Exclusionary Rule,** is the direct result of the Supreme Court decision in the case of *Weeks v. United States* (1914). The Exclusionary Rule, defined in the *Weeks* case as a matter of judicial implications, was made applicable to the federal courts in 1914. In 1961 the Exclusionary Rule reached maturity when the Supreme Court, in the case of *Mapp v. Ohio,* extended the rule to every court and law enforcement officer in the nation.

Courts uphold the Fourth Amendment by use of the Exclusionary Rule, which demands that no evidence may be admitted in a trial unless it is obtained within the constitutional standards set forth in the Fourth Amendment. *Weeks v. United States* made the Exclusionary Rule applicable in federal courts. *Mapp v. Ohio* made it applicable to every court in the country.

On May 23, 1957, three Cleveland police officers arrived at Dollree Mapp's residence pursuant to information that a person wanted for questioning in connection with a recent bombing was hiding in Mapp's home and that there was also a large amount of gambling paraphernalia hidden there. After telephoning her attorney, Mapp refused to admit the officers without a search warrant. Three hours later the officers returned with reinforcements and again sought entrance. When she did not come to the door, the police officers gained entry by forcibly opening a door. Mapp demanded to see the search warrant. When a paper, claimed to be the warrant, was held up by one of the officers, she grabbed it and placed it in her bra. A struggle ensued in which the officers recovered the piece of paper and handcuffed Mapp. A thorough search was conducted of the entire apartment, including the basement of the building. Obscene materials, for the possession of which the defendant was ultimately convicted, were discovered as a result of that widespread search.

The state contended that even if the search were made without authority, it was not prevented from using the evidence at the trial because *Wolf v.*

Colorado (1949) had authorized the admission of such evidence in a state court. Furthermore, Ohio did not follow the Exclusionary Rule. After a discussion of other applicable cases, the Supreme Court decreed that henceforth evidence obtained by procedures that violated Fourth Amendment standards would no longer be admissible in state courts.

Since 1961 the Exclusionary Rule has applied to both the federal and state courts, and evidence secured illegally by federal, state, or local officers has been inadmissible in any court.

The Exclusionary Rule has important implications for the procedures followed by police officers, since neither the most skillful prosecutor nor the most experienced police officer can convince a jury of a defendant's guilt without adequate and lawfully obtained evidence. Police officers must obtain evidence that establishes that a crime has been committed, and they must obtain evidence that connects the defendant to the specific crime—usually long before the case comes to the prosecutor. Further, they must obtain such evidence without violating the rights of the defendant. Only if police officers obtain evidence that will be acceptable in court is there a probability of conviction.

STOP AND FRISK

One basic responsibility of police officers, and one heavily reliant on reasonableness and probable cause, is the responsibility to investigate suspicious behavior. Officers may simply talk to someone who is acting suspiciously and decide that no crime seems to be in progress or about to be committed. Or they may have their suspicions confirmed and decide to investigate further. The simple act of stopping someone may lead to a situation known in police terminology as a **stop and frisk.** The stop is also called a **field inquiry** or **threshold inquiry.**

The courts have stated that suspicious circumstances impose upon police officers the duty to investigate, that is, to stop and question suspects. The procedure of stopping and questioning suspects is directly regulated by the justifications and limitations associated with lawful searches and seizures.

The basic legal considerations in a stop and frisk situation were set forth in the landmark United States Supreme Court decision in *Terry v. Ohio* (1968). This case resulted from the following situation: One afternoon in 1963 Detective McFadden saw two men standing near a jewelry store. For all practical purposes they just seemed to be talking to each other, but to McFadden, a man of thirty years of detective work (thirty-nine years of police experience), "they just didn't look right." He had never seen the two before and could not say what first drew his attention to them, but he decided to take a post in a nearby store entrance and watch for a while.

The two men repeated a ritual nearly a dozen times. One man would walk to the window, pause, look into the window for a while, and then walk toward the corner. He would come back to look into the same window and then rejoin his companion. After a short conference, the man would repeat the entire pattern: walk to the store window, up to the corner, back to the store, and then back to rejoin the first man.

While this was going on, Detective McFadden continued to watch the two. At one point a third man joined them, talked with them briefly, then left. When he left, the other two spent several more minutes repeating the routine.

By this time McFadden suspected they were casing the store for a "stickup." As he made this decision, he also feared they might have a gun. He had already decided to investigate their activity further when the two men walked toward the store where the third man was waiting. At this point, the detective's knowledge was confined to what he had observed. He didn't know any of the three men by name or sight, and he had received no information on them from any other source.

McFadden approached the three, identified himself as a police officer, asked for their names, and then decided to act. He turned one man, later identified as John Terry, around, putting Terry between himself and the other two men. McFadden then made a quick "pat down" of Terry's outer clothing. He could feel a pistol in one of Terry's pockets but was unable to remove the gun. Keeping Terry between himself and the others, he ordered all three men to enter the store. As they obeyed him, McFadden removed Terry's coat and took a .38 caliber revolver from the pocket. Inside the store McFadden asked the owner to call for a police wagon while he patted the outer clothing of the others, taking another revolver from the coat of a man named Chilton. At the station Terry and Chilton were formally charged with carrying concealed weapons.

When Terry and Chilton were brought to court, their lawyers moved that the guns could not be used as evidence, claiming they were illegally seized. If the guns couldn't be used as evidence, there was no evidence and there was no charge or case.

The trial judge heard the two cases at the same time. He made two decisions that, at first, seemed to contradict each other. First, he rejected the defense motion that the evidence had been illegally seized. Then he rejected a prosecution contention that McFadden had established probable cause to arrest, and therefore, that officer had taken the guns in a search that was incidental to a lawful arrest. If neither theory applied, what did?

The judge said that on the basis of McFadden's experience, he had reasonable cause to believe that the defendants were conducting themselves suspiciously and some interrogation should be made of their actions. Purely for his own protection, the court added, McFadden had the right to frisk the men whom he believed to be armed. The judge said McFadden had stopped the suspects for the purpose of investigation, no arrest occurred at that point, and the "frisking of the outer clothing for weapons" was *not* a full search.

Both men appealed their conviction to the United States Supreme Court, but before the Court's decision was handed down in 1968, Chilton had died. Therefore, its review applied only to Terry.

The Court recognized Detective McFadden as a man of experience, training, and knowledge. McFadden was certainly "a man of reasonable caution." And, as a man of "**ordinary care** and prudence," he waited until he had strengthened his suspicions, making his move just prior to what he believed would be an armed robbery.

The United States Supreme Court upheld the Ohio court verdict; it said that McFadden had "acted reasonably" because (1) Terry's and Chilton's actions were consistent with McFadden's theory that they were contemplating a daylight robbery, (2) such a robbery would most likely involve the use of guns, and (3) nothing in the men's conduct, from the time the officer first noticed them until he confronted them, gave him any reason to doubt his theory.

The Court went on to say that McFadden had to make a quick decision when he saw the three gathered at the store and his actions were correct.

Although we associate a thoroughness to the terms *search* and *seizure* that does not seem to apply to the terms *stop* and *frisk,* the United States Supreme Court (*Terry v. Ohio*) says there is a **seizure** whenever a police officer restrains an individual's freedom to walk away; and there is a search when an officer makes an exploration of an individual's clothing even though it may be called a **"pat down"** or a **"frisk."**

A **stop** is a seizure if physical force or a show of authority is used. A frisk is a search.

Although stopping and frisking fall short of being a technical arrest and a full-blown search, they are definitely forms of search and seizure. Police officers stop citizens of their communities as part of their duties. This is daily practice, but most encounters cannot be considered "seizure of the person" because the officer does not restrain the individual's liberty. So an officer can stop a citizen without the action being considered a seizure of the person. Defining the term frisk, however, leaves no other alternative than to consider it a search.

The United States Supreme Court (*Terry*) had definite opinions about the type of search called a frisk: "It is simply fantastic," the Court stated, "to urge that such a procedure, performed in public by a police officer, while the citizen stands helpless, perhaps facing a wall with his hands raised, is a 'petty indignity.' . . . It is a serious intrusion upon the sanctity of the person, which may inflict great indignity and arouse strong resentment, and it is not to be undertaken lightly." The Supreme Court gave its own definition of stop and frisk by calling it a "protective search for weapons." As always, where there is a justification for taking specific action, there are also limitations. According to the Supreme Court, a protective seizure and search for weapons carries these limitations.

Stop and frisk is a protective search for weapons in which the intrusion must be limited to a scope reasonably designed to discover guns, knives, clubs, and other hidden instruments, which may be used for an assault of a police officer or others.

A frisk is conducted for officer safety. Here a sheriff's deputy pats down a suspect for concealed weapons.

Since some states do not have stop and frisk laws, when this type of protective search and seizure for weapons is referred to, it is on the basis of the opinion of the United States Supreme Court. The specific principles that arose from *Terry v. Ohio* (1968) can be applied to most stop and frisk situations.

1. Police officers have the right and duty to approach and interrogate persons to investigate crimes.

2. Police officers may stop and make a *limited* search of a suspect if they observe unusual conduct that leads them to reasonably conclude, in light of their experience, that criminal activity may be afoot and that the individual whose suspicious behavior the officers are investigating at close range is armed and probably dangerous.

3. The test of the officers' action is whether a "reasonably prudent man in the same circumstances would be warranted in the belief that his safety or that of others was in danger."

4. Officers may proceed to stop and frisk if nothing occurs to change the officers' theory that criminal activity may occur or that the suspect is armed.

5. The type of search in stop and frisk must be limited. It is a "protective seizure and search for weapons and must be confined to an intrusion which is reasonably designed to discover guns, knives, clubs, or other hidden instruments of assault."

6. If these conditions (principles 1–5) are met, the stop and frisk does *not* constitute an arrest.

7. Since stop and frisk actually involves a search and seizure, it must be governed by the intent of the Fourth Amendment of the Constitution, which forbids indiscriminate searches and seizures.

Terry established that the authority to stop and frisk is independent of the power to arrest. A stop is *not* an arrest, but it is a seizure within the meaning of the Fourth Amendment and therefore requires reasonableness.

While it is true that both the stop and the arrest are seizures and both must be justified by a showing of reasonableness, there are some important differences between a stop and an arrest.

On January 8, 1985, the United States Supreme Court ruled unanimously that the police may act without a warrant to stop and briefly detain a person they know is wanted for investigation by police in another city. In *United States v. Hensley* (1985) the Court extended the warrantless stop and frisk rules that it established in the 1960s for police who suspect that a crime is about to be committed or is imminent. Police may now sometimes stop, question, and even search people when there is less than probable cause to believe they were involved in a past crime.

The Supreme Court's opinion on stop and frisk and the rights and limitations for this type of action are illustrated in the case of *Henry v. United States* (1959), which involved an arrest made by officers who had observed Henry and another man stop twice in an alley and load cartons into a car. When the officers saw the two men driving off, they waved Henry's car to a stop, searched it, took the cartons, and later made the formal arrest. The men were convicted in Illinois courts of unlawful possession of stolen radios. The Supreme Court overruled the Illinois verdict, saying that an actual arrest had taken place when the officers stopped the suspect's car. The problem in this case was that the officers observed the transaction from a distance of some three hundred feet and could not determine the size, number, or contents of the cartons. The suspects were formally placed under arrest some two hours after they were taken into custody.

The issue in this case was whether there was probable cause for the arrest leading to the search that produced the evidence on which the conviction rested. Since probable cause to arrest had not been established at that time, the Court said the stolen merchandise could not be accepted as evidence. Future cases in many states were decided on this 1959 case, and the accepted opinion was that stopping a vehicle or an individual constituted an actual arrest.

Sobriety Checkpoints.   Recall that sobriety checkpoints, a form of stop, have been declared constitutional, provided they are conducted fairly and do not pose a safety hazard (*Michigan Department of State Police v. Sitz,* 1990).

Field Detention.   The courts have also upheld police officers' right to detain suspects with less than probable cause. Such **field detention** occurred in *Michigan v. Summers* (1981) where police officers arrived at Summers' home to execute a search warrant. They encountered Summers coming down the steps and asked him to let them in and wait while they conducted their search. They found narcotics in the basement and then searched Summers, finding heroin in his pocket. The Court ruled that it was legal to require the suspect to reenter his house and remain there until evidence establishing probable cause was found. The legality of field detention was upheld in *Michigan v. Chesternut* (1988), described by Senna and Siegel (1990, p. 294):

> While on a routine cruiser patrol, the police observed a car pull up to a curb and an individual exit and approach the defendant. When the defendant saw the cruiser he ran off and was observed to pull several packets from his pocket and discard them. The police examined the discarded packets and concluded that they contained cocaine. Chesternut was arrested and a search revealed other drugs including heroin. The Court rejected both the position that any pursuit is a seizure and the argument that no seizure can occur until the officer apprehends the person. Instead, the Court said that in view of all the circumstances, a reasonable person would not have felt free to leave the scene and therefore Chesternut's detention was not a seizure nor a violation of the Fourth Amendment.

Often searches and arrests are inseparable, with one leading to the other. That is, a search may result in an arrest, or after an arrest is made, the officers may conduct a search. Consider first, the laws governing searches.

LAWFUL SEARCHES

Creamer (1980, p. 58) defines a **search** as follows: "The looking into or prying into hidden places. The term search in the context of the Fourth Amendment involves a governmental invasion of privacy. Searches are intrusions into the privacy for the purpose of obtaining incriminating evidence. ... However, a search may never be justified by the incriminating evidence it turns up."

Guilty persons are convicted based on the facts that the court finds admissible. Police officers' reports must contain all the reasons for a search or seizure as proof of the reasonableness of their conduct. The questions most frequently asked by the prosecutor and the courts before admitting evidence are: Was the search reasonable? Was the arrest, if there was one, legal? There are rules to guide police officers in answering these questions on a day-to-day basis. The rules often seem contrary to what many people consider to be reasonable; however, these rules, contrary or not, *must* be considered when deciding whether a search or seizure is reasonable. The courts abide by these rules and base their decisions on them.

Since the word *unreasonable* is ambiguous, the courts have adopted guidelines to measure reasonableness and to assure law enforcement personnel that *if* certain rules are adhered to, their search or seizure will be acceptable—reasonable. The three principal justifications established by the court for the right to search are: (1) if the search is incidental to a lawful arrest; (2) if consent is given; (3) if a search warrant has been issued. These circumstances are the preconditions for a reasonable, legal search. A search that occurs under any one of these conditions is considered justified or reasonable.

The three principal justifications established by the court for the right to search are as follows:

1. If the search is incidental to a lawful arrest.

2. If consent is given.

3. If a search warrant has been issued.

Search Incidental to a Lawful Arrest

In a search incidental to a **lawful arrest** the search must be made simultaneously with the arrest and must be confined to the immediate vicinity of the arrest.

Chimel v. California (1969), involving a search incidental to an arrest, provides a definition of search of a person and a dwelling as well as the limitations of the search. Officers went to the Chimel home with a warrant to arrest Ted Chimel on a charge of burglarizing a coin shop. Mrs. Chimel admitted the officers, who then waited ten to fifteen minutes for her husband to come home. When the arrest warrant was handed to Chimel, he was told that the officers wanted to "look around." He objected but was informed that the officers had a right to search because it was a lawful arrest.

The officers opened kitchen cabinets, searched through hall and bedroom closets, looked behind furniture in every room, and even searched the garage. (Prior to this case, the courts had accepted fairly extensive searches incidental to an arrest.) On several occasions the officers had Mrs. Chimel open drawers and move the contents so they could look for items removed in the burglary. The search took nearly an hour and resulted in the officers finding numerous coins.

Chimel was convicted in a California court, but he appealed his conviction on burglary charges on the grounds that the evidence—the coins—had been unconstitutionally seized. The United States Supreme Court studied the principle of searches incidental to an arrest and determined the following:

> When an arrest is made, it is reasonable for the arresting officer to search the person arrested in order to remove any weapons that the latter might seek to use in order to resist arrest or effect his escape.
>
> It is entirely reasonable for the arresting officer to search for and seize any evidence on the arrestee's person in order to prevent its concealment or destruction and the area from within which the arrestee might gain possession of a weapon or destructible evidence.

The officers' justification for extending the search was based on the phrase that "It is entirely reasonable . . . to search . . . the area from within which the arrestee might gain possession of . . . destructible evidence."

In the *Chimel* case, the Supreme Court specified that the area of search could include only the arrestee's person and the area within his or her immediate control. The court defined **immediate control** as being that area within the person's reach, also called the person's **wingspan.**

Limitations on a search made incidental to an arrest are found in the Chimel Rule, which states that the area of the search must be within the immediate control of the suspect—that is, it must be within his or her reach.

The *Chimel* case resulted in a clear definition as to what, beyond the suspects themselves, could be searched when officers are using the authority of a search incidental to an arrest. The court pointed out that if an arrest is used as an excuse to conduct a thorough search, such as the search conducted in the *Chimel* case, the police would have power to conduct "general searches," which were declared unconstitutional by the Fourth Amendment over 200 years ago.

One can sympathize with the officers who had alerted Chimel's wife that they were looking for stolen coins and then felt they had to find them or face the possibility she would remove them. But the law allows only a limited search in this situation. Undoubtedly a magistrate would have issued a search warrant for the stolen coins if the officers had realized the limitations on their search and had requested the warrant.

Ironically, prior to the burglary, Chimel had wandered about the coin store, asked the owner where he kept his most valuable coins, inquired into the alarm system, and bragged that he was planning a robbery. Later he took exception to the owner's testimony that it was a "sloppy job," excitedly claiming that the burglary had been "real professional." But the Supreme Court reversed the California decision because the conviction had been based on evidence obtained in a search that was beyond reasonable limits.

An interesting sideline in the *Chimel* case is that three days after the initial search, officers again entered Chimel's house looking for evidence to support a separate charge of robbery. No evidence was seized on the second search, but Chimel was convicted and sentenced on the robbery charge.

Search with Consent

In a search where **consent** is given, the United States Supreme Court provides that the consent must be free and voluntary; therefore, it cannot be given in response to a claim of lawful authority by the officer to conduct the search at the moment. As with searches incidental to lawful arrest, a search with consent must be conducted only in the actual area for which the consent is given.

Consent must be free and voluntary, and the search must be limited to the area for which the consent is given.

As noted by the Maine Supreme Court in *State v. Barlow, Jr.* (1974): "It is a well established rule in the federal courts that a consent search is unreasonable under the Fourth Amendment if the consent was induced by deceit, trickery or misrepresentation of the officials making the search." A recognized exception to this general rule is when undercover operations are involved.

When a court is asked to determine if consent to search was "free and voluntary," it considers such things as the subject's age, background, mental condition, and education. The number of officers involved should not be a factor if no aggressiveness is displayed. As stated in *People v. Reed* (1975): "Where aggravating factors are not evident, the number of officers alone will not have an adverse effect on the consent. The presence of a large number of officers in an apartment does not present a situation which is per se coercive."

The time of day might also be a consideration. Officers should generally avoid seeking voluntary consent to search at night. In *Monroe v. Pape* (1961) Justice Frankfurter said: "Modern totalitarianisms have been a stark reminder, but did not newly teach, that the kicked-in door is the symbol of a rule of fear and violence fatal to institutions founded on respect for the integrity of man.... Searches of the dwelling house were the special object of this universal condemnation of official intrusion. Nighttime search was the evil in its most obnoxious form."

Perhaps most important is the way in which the request to search is made. It must, indeed, be a request, not a command.

Search Conducted with a Search Warrant

Recall the provision of the Fourth Amendment that the warrant must particularly describe "the place to be searched and the persons or things to be seized."

A search conducted with a warrant must be limited to the specific area and specific items delineated in the warrant.

We are all protected against unreasonable searches and seizures by the United States Constitution, which guarantees that probable cause, supported by **oath** or **affirmation,** shall be the basis for issuing a search warrant. Our courts have interpreted this guarantee to mean that any search or seizure other than one conducted with a warrant is technically unreasonable. The courts do, however, recognize that emergency situations will arise in which a police officer will not have the opportunity to secure a warrant.

A **search warrant** is an order issued by any court of record or by a justice of the peace in a county having no municipal court other than a probate court. The **magistrate** must have jurisdiction in the area where the search is to be made.

The warrant must contain the reasons for requesting the search warrant; the names of the persons presenting affidavits, for example, the officer who applied for the warrant, his or her colleagues, or others who have information to contribute; what specifically is being sought; and the signature of the judge issuing it.

A search warrant is a judicial order directing a police officer to search for specific property, seize it, and return it to the court. Probable cause is required for issuance of all warrants. Technically, all searches are to be made under the authority of a search warrant issued by a magistrate.

The procedures for obtaining and executing search warrants vary from locality to locality, but the following example illustrates what may be involved. Generally a search warrant may be issued for the following reasons:

- The property or material was stolen or embezzled.
- The possession of the property or material constitutes a crime, for example, stolen property or drugs.
- The property or material is in the possession of a person with intent to use them to commit a crime, for example, possession of burglary tools with intent to use them.
- The property or material was used in committing a crime, for example, a gun, knife, or burglary tools.
- The items or evidence tend to show that a crime has been committed or that a particular person has committed a crime, for example, letters, clothing.

When police officers present an **affidavit** to a magistrate, their facts must be sufficiently detailed to enable the magistrate to determine that probable cause to search exists. The affidavit need not be as polished as an entry in an essay contest, but it should not skimp on the facts.

The Constitution does not require all necessary information to appear on the face of the complaint, as long as a sworn affidavit made at the time the warrant was issued contains those facts.

A police officer must present adequate evidence for a magistrate to determine probable cause. If sufficient facts are contained in the application and supporting affidavit or supplementary facts are presented during questioning of an officer who applies for a warrant, a magistrate will issue the search warrant.

The use of search warrants has increased since the *Chimel* decision, which restricted the area that could be searched incidental to a lawful arrest. Prior to the *Chimel* case, some courts allowed extensive searches incidental to a lawful arrest. The *Chimel* ruling, however, makes it necessary for police officers to obtain a search warrant as well as an arrest warrant if they want to search a suspect's house incidental to the execution of the arrest warrant.

What May Be Seized

A search warrant must clearly specify or describe the things to be seized. The prosecution or the state must accept the burden of proof when items are seized that are not specifically stated in the warrant. This does not mean such items cannot be seized. They can, if a reasonable relationship exists between the search and the seizure of materials not described or if officers discover **contraband**—anything that is illegal for a person to own or have in possession, such as heroin or a machine gun.

Police may seize items not specified in the search warrant if they are similar in nature to those items described, if they are related to the particular crime described, or if they are contraband.

Consider this example. On two separate occasions, officers arrived at a private dwelling with search warrants authorizing them to seize items taken from burglaries. On both occasions their knock was unanswered, so they entered through a living room window. They seized many items on the search warrants as well as other similar items not specifically mentioned in the warrants. When the case came to court, the defense challenged those items introduced as evidence of the burglaries that were not specifically mentioned in the warrants. The lower court allowed the evidence to be used, and the state supreme court upheld the decision. The high court said the items seized in addition to those mentioned in the warrants were similar to items that the stores had on hand when the burglaries occurred.

In addition, contraband discovered during a search authorized by a warrant may also be seized. It is not necessary that the contraband be connected to the particular crime described in the search warrant.

Gaining Entrance

Police officers are usually required to announce their authority and purpose before entering a home. This protects the citizen's rights and avoids needless destruction of property where the owner or occupant is willing to voluntarily admit a police officer. Sometimes, however, the suspect will not allow entrance, or there may be no one home.

Police officers who arrive to execute a search warrant and find the house unoccupied may forcibly enter the house to search it. If the dwelling is an apartment, they could probably get a passkey from a caretaker, but this would still be considered a **forced entry.** Opening a closed but unlocked door or window is also considered a forced entry. Officers who are denied entrance to execute a search warrant may break an inner or outer door or window to gain entry.

Generally police officers must announce themselves. They may enter a house by force to execute a search warrant if they are denied entrance or if there is no one home.

Nighttime and No-Knock Search Warrants

A search warrant will normally be issued to be served during daylight hours, that is, from sunrise to sunset and will require that the officers knock and announce themselves. Sometimes, however, these usual procedures could render the police less effective. In such instances, special warrants may be issued.

Two special types of search warrants, nighttime and no-knock, must be authorized by a magistrate as a special provision of a search warrant.

Nighttime search warrants (also called **nightcap warrants**) may be justified and requested of the court by police officers. They must state the reasons, based on facts, for fearing that unless the search is conducted at night the objects of the search might be lost, destroyed, or removed.

Similarly, unannounced entries for the purpose of executing search warrants must also receive prior judicial authorization. The **no-knock search warrant** is reserved for situations where the judge recognizes that the normal cooperation of the citizen cannot be expected and that an announced entry may result in loss, destruction, or removal of the objects of the search; for example, surprise entries are often used in searches for narcotics and gambling equipment. In either of these instances, the court will usually acknowledge that evidence can easily be destroyed during the time required to give notice, demand admittance, and accept the citizen's denial of entry.

Administrative Warrants

Public safety personnel may enter structures which are on fire in order to extinguish the fire. After the fire has been extinguished, officials may remain a reasonable length of time to investigate the cause of the blaze (*Michigan v. Tyler,* 1978). After this time, if the police want to return to the scene to conduct an investigation into the cause of the fire, they may require an administrative warrant. According to Bennett and Hess (1991, p. 549):

> An **administrative warrant** requires an affidavit stating the location and legal description of the property, the purpose (to determine the fire's cause and origin), the area of the search, time of the search, use of the building, and measures taken to secure the structure or area of the fire. Searches are limited to the items specified in the warrant. Evidence found may be seized, but once the officers leave after finding the evidence, they must have a criminal warrant to return to the premises for a further search.

Emergency Situations/Extenuating Circumstances— Warrantless Search

As noted by Bruce (1990, p. 100): "Few areas of the law cause more confusion and uncertainty among law enforcement officers than questions about when a warrant is or is not needed to conduct a search."

When police officers follow the letter of the law and secure a search warrant, they receive an advance court decision that probable cause does exist. It was originally believed that the magistrate should be the sole judge of probable cause, but when **emergency situations** or **extenuating** or **exigent circumstances** became apparent, the courts decided there were times when reasonable searches and seizures could be based on the decisions of police officers.

In situations where police officers sincerely believe they have established probable cause and there is no time to secure a warrant, they can use their own discretion and act without a warrant. But it is here that the opportunity for a defense lawyer to challenge the legality of the search can be used. While a number of challenges can be raised, two occur most frequently. The defense may contend that a magistrate would not have issued a warrant had the officers presented the facts before the court (probable cause was not established), or that the officers had ample opportunity to secure a warrant and therefore had no justification to act without one.

If the defense raises one of these challenges in a case involving evidence seized as a result of a warrantless search, the burden of proof is on the officer and the prosecution. It must be proven that the officer was reasonable and prudent and had gathered sufficient facts to make the important decision that probable cause to search existed and that the search must be conducted immediately.

When police officers conduct a search without a warrant, they may be challenged on the basis that:

- Probable cause was not established.

- The officers had opportunity to secure a warrant and had no justification to act without one.

The Fourth Amendment says a great deal in only fifty-four words. It guarantees that United States citizens will not be unjustly searched or arrested and that their property will not be unlawfully seized. With added historical court decisions, most of the language of our present laws governing search and seizure is represented.

The Fourth Amendment was intended to interpose a magistrate between the police and the citizen—requiring a magistrate to study the evidence presented by the police and decide whether a warrant should be issued. The Constitution is a product of a period when authority had been badly misused, and it was presumed magistrates would be more objective than officers.

A strict interpretation of the Constitution requires that a magistrate decide whether probable cause exists. When the officer presents the facts to a magistrate and is granted a warrant, the defense lawyer cannot attack the decision of the individual officer. When the search warrant is issued, it becomes an order from the court, as the Constitution intended it to be. It is no longer the prosecution who has to defend its actions, but it is the lawyer for the accused who has to prove that a magistrate erred in issuing the warrant.

While the laws are still intended to provide protection, they are also designed to meet emergency situations not considered in the original amendment. There are rules to be observed in such situations; each must fall within the guarantees in the Fourth Amendment. The key is to protect all citizens against unreasonable searches and seizures.

The individuals who drafted the Constitution understood that other reasonable measures would have to be accepted to uphold the laws of the nation. The Supreme Court, therefore, surveys cases brought before it to determine whether the action taken in a particular situation was reasonable according to the Fourth Amendment. What may be reasonable in one situation may not be reasonable in another. For instance, you could justify a warrantless search of a vehicle by stating the reasons you believed it would be gone if you waited to obtain a search warrant. This same logic, however, cannot be applied to a search of a house or any other fixed object.

You have already looked at three types of warrantless searches:

- Searches connected with stop and frisk (limited to a search for weapons).
- Searches incidental to an arrest.
- Searches when consent has been given.

Although Supreme Court approval of warrantless searches incidental to an arrest was established in cases prior to 1920, it was the *Chimel* opinion in 1969 that confined the search to an area within the immediate control of the person arrested. This opinion did not apply to automobiles, however.

As noted, searches may be conducted without a warrant even though the search is not associated with stop and frisk, incidental to an arrest, or with consent; but when it is conducted under these circumstances, police officers must prove that an emergency existed that did not allow them to secure a search warrant. Very frequently this involves automobiles and other conveyances having **mobility.**

Warrantless Searches of Automobiles and Other Conveyances

When a vehicle is involved, the rules of reasonableness, although within the boundaries of the Constitution, are quite different. The courts have long recognized the need for separate exemptions from the requirement of obtaining a search warrant where mobility is involved.

The precedent for a warrantless search of an automobile resulted from *Carroll v. United States* (1925), which established two basic principles justifying warrantless searches of automobiles: (1) there is probable cause, and (2) the automobile or other conveyance would be gone before a search warrant could be obtained.

Carroll v. United States set the precedent for warrantless searches of automobiles provided there is probable cause for the search and provided the vehicle would be gone before a search warrant could be obtained.

The *Carroll* case did not involve a search incidental to an arrest. The concern was with probable cause for a search, not for an arrest.

During Prohibition in the 1920s, some 1,500 agents pursued bootleggers, many of whom brought liquor down from Canada. In addition to the imports, there was so much local production that the 9,500 stills raided in the first six months of Prohibition were known to be only a small fraction of the total.

Visualize a scene in a Michigan "honky-tonk" during the 1920s. Four men were sitting at a table holding a meeting; two were supposed buyers, and two were bootleggers. The "buyers" were actually federal Prohibition agents. Although the meeting seemed to go well, the two bootleggers, George Carroll and John Kiro, were somewhat suspicious. They indicated that the liquor had to come from the east end of Grand Rapids, Michigan. They would get it and return in about an hour. Later that day, Carroll called and said delivery could not be made until the next day. But the two did not return the next day.

The agents returned to their normal duty of watching a section of road between Grand Rapids and Detroit known to be used by bootleggers. Within a week after their unsuccessful attempt to make the "buy," the agents recognized Carroll and Kiro driving by. They gave chase but lost the car near East Lansing.

Two months later they again recognized Carroll's car coming from the direction of Detroit. They pursued the car and this time were successful in overtaking it. The agents were familiar with Carroll's car, they recognized Carroll and Kiro in the automobile, and they had reason to believe the automobile would contain bootleg liquor. A search of the car revealed sixty-eight bottles of whiskey and gin, most of it behind the upholstery of the seats where the padding had been removed. The contraband was seized, and the two men were arrested.

George Carroll and John Kiro were charged with transporting intoxicating liquor and were convicted in federal court. Carroll's appeal, taken to the United States Supreme Court, resulted in a landmark decision defining the rights and limitations for warrantless searches of vehicles.

The agents' knowledge of the two men and their operation, as well as the fact that the car was believed to be used in the transportation of liquor, produced the probable cause necessary to justify a search. So the first principle establishing this as an exception to the rule requiring a search warrant was met.

The *Carroll* decision established that the right to search an automobile is not dependent on the right to arrest the driver or an occupant, but rather it is dependent upon the probable cause the seizing officer has for believing that the contents of the automobile violate the law.

Regarding the mobility of such a conveyance, the court amplified its opinion to include some of the key reasons why an automobile can be exempted while a house or fixed object cannot:

- A vehicle or conveyance can be quickly moved out of the jurisdiction or locality in which the warrant must be sought.
- The occupants of the vehicle are immediately alerted.
- The vehicle's contents may never be found again if a police officer has to wait to obtain a search warrant before searching the car.

The Supreme Court saw each of these possibilities in the case against George Carroll and, consequently, provided a basis for making a similar judgment in a situation where these circumstances might occur.

The requirement of mobility is also present in the case of *Chambers v. Maroney* (1970). This case involved the armed robbery of a service station. The station attendant described the two men who held guns on him, and two boys provided officers with a description of a vehicle they had seen the men in circling the block prior to the robbery and again speeding out of the area. Within an hour officers spotted the vehicle and identified the occupants as the men the three witnesses had described. They stopped the car and arrested the men. The evidence seized and later used to convict Chambers and the other man included two revolvers and a glove filled with change they had taken from the service station.

Chambers based an appeal on the fact that the officers took the car to the police station before searching it. The defense contended that the search was illegal because it was made incidental to rather than simultaneous with the arrest. The defense was right. As a search incidental to an arrest, it would have been illegal. But the Court observed the same set of circumstances in relation

Officers can search a vehicle if they have probable cause to believe that its contents violate the law.

to the warrantless search of a vehicle; the seizing officers did have probable cause to believe that the contents of the automobile violated the law. Therefore, it was the right to search, not the right to arrest, that provided the officers with the authority for their actions.

The Supreme Court added another opinion to the *Chambers* case when it said that it was not unreasonable under these circumstances to take the vehicle to the police station to be searched. In other words, the probable cause to search at the scene continued to exist at the police station. Based on the facts, the Supreme Court said there was probable cause to search, and since it was a fleeing target, the Chambers vehicle could have been searched on the spot where it stopped. The Court reasoned that probable cause still existed at the police station, and so did the mobility of the car. The Court quickly pointed out that such actions must be confined to vehicles and other conveyances having mobility.

The *Chambers* case established that a car may retain its mobility even though it is impounded.

Yet another interpretation of mobility was provided in the case of *Coolidge v. New Hampshire* (1971). The *Coolidge* case, a homicide, tested the requirements of mobility. A fourteen-year-old girl disappeared in Manchester, New Hampshire, and her body was found eight days later. She had been shot. A number of errors were made in the case, including the fact that arrest and search warrants were drawn up and signed by the man who became the chief prosecutor.

A neighbor's tip led police to E. H. Coolidge, whom officers admitted was fully cooperative, even to the point of agreeing to a polygraph examination. The examination was conducted several days after Coolidge was first questioned. During the next two and a half weeks, evidence against Coolidge began to accumulate. The evidence included what the prosecution said was the murder weapon, which officers had obtained from Mrs. Coolidge. The arrest and search warrants were drawn up based on this evidence. The search warrant specifically designated Coolidge's car, which was in the driveway in plain view of the house at the time of the arrest. Mrs. Coolidge was told she was not allowed to use the car, and it was impounded prior to other officers dropping Mrs. Coolidge at a relative's home. During the next fourteen months the car was searched three times, and vacuum sweepings from the car were introduced as evidence.

Coolidge was convicted of the girl's murder. His appeal challenged the legality of the evidence seized from the car. Discounting the fact the warrants were invalid and the prosecution could not prove the search was incidental to an arrest, the prosecution contended the seizure of the car should be allowable based on the standards established by the *Carroll* and *Chambers* cases.

The Court considered the principles of the *Coolidge* case and weighed them against those of the precedent cases. Because testimony from witnesses and from Coolidge indicated that his car was at the scene of the murder, the Court accepted the fact that probable cause to search had been established. But was there sufficient cause to fear the automobile might be moved?

The Court said there was not. Coolidge could not have gained access to the automobile when the officers came to arrest him, and he had, in fact, received sufficient prior warning that he was a prime suspect to have already fled. The only other adult occupant, Mrs. Coolidge, was driven to a relative's home by other officers who were with her after the vehicle was actually taken to the station.

Coolidge v. New Hampshire established that the rule of mobility cannot be applied unless there is actually a risk that the vehicle would be moved.

Neither the *Carroll* nor the *Chambers* opinions could apply here because of the following differences:

- There appeared to be no criminal intent to flee.
- This was not a case of a fleeting opportunity to search on an open highway after a hazardous chase.
- There was no evidence of contraband, stolen goods, or weapons.
- There was no evidence of any friends of Coolidge's waiting to move the car and the evidence therein.
- The automobile in question was secured from intrusion when it was found.

Since the Coolidge premises were guarded throughout the night, and since Mrs. Coolidge was with officers until after the car had been towed in, the car was secure at all times. The Court could not accept the prosecution's contention that the Coolidge vehicle was included in the category of mobility.

Vehicles may also be searched without a warrant when they are used in the commission of serious crimes such as felonies. Such **instruments of a crime** may be seized and searched if the vehicle is an integral part of the defendant's apparatus for the commission of the crime. This generally includes getaway vehicles as well as automobiles, trailers, or similar conveyances used to secrete or transport stolen items.

Vehicles or other conveyances used in a crime may be seized and searched if the vehicle is an integral part of the defendant's apparatus for the commission of the crime.

United States v. Ross (1982) held that the police may search a car, including containers, without a warrant as long as they have probable cause to believe contraband is somewhere in the car.

Finally, *Colorado v. Bertine* (1987) ruled that police can inventory the contents of a vehicle that has been impounded. Police often routinely inventory the contents of impounded vehicles to accurately record an arrestee's possessions so they may be safely returned at the appropriate time. If during such a routine inventory, police find contraband or evidence of a crime, it is admissible in court. In this case Bertine was arrested for drunk driving, and the van he was driving was impounded. During a routine inventory search, police found canisters of cash and drugs. The cash and drugs were admitted in evidence, and Bertine was convicted. On appeal, the Supreme Court ruled that a warrant was not required since it was a routine inventory search. The *Ross* decision gave them the authority to open the cannisters.

Table 12–1 summarizes the limitations on searching vehicles.

Plain View

Plain view refers to evidence that is not concealed and that is inadvertently seen by an officer engaged in a lawful activity. Several factors determine what constitutes plain view. First, the police officer must be engaged in lawful activity prior to the discovery of plain view evidence. Such circumstances might occur while the officer is executing a warrant to search for another

Table 12–1 **Searching Cars**

METHOD OF SEARCH	LEADING CASE AUTHORITY	JUSTIFI- CATION FOR SEARCH	PERMISSIBLE SCOPE OF SEARCH	TIME OF SEARCH	PURPOSE OF SEARCH
Stop-frisk	*Terry v. Ohio,* 392 U.S. 1 (1968)	Officer's reasonable fear for his own safety	Person and area in his immediate control	At time of stop	Self- protection of officer
Arrest-search	*Preston v. United States,* 376 U.S. 364 (1964); *Chimel v. California,* 395 U.S. 752 (1969)	Probable cause to arrest someone in car	Person and area of car in his control	At time of arrest	Self- protection of officer and preservation of evidence
Search warrant	*Spinelli v. United States,* 393 U.S. 410 (1969)	Probable cause presented to judge	Entire car	Any time after warrant issued	Find and preserve evidence
Consent search	*Amos v. United States,* 225 U.S. 313 (1921)	Waiver of 4th Amendment rights by owner or driver	Entire car	Any time after consent	Find and preserve evidence
Custodial search of impounded car	*Cooper v. California,* 386 U.S. 58 (1967)	Police regulations to protect property in their custody	Entire car	Any time	Preserve car and contents
Probable cause search	*Chambers v. Maroney,* 399 U.S. 42 (1970)	Probable cause that car contains contraband, etc.	Entire car	Any time	Find and preserve evidence

Source: J. Shane Creamer. *The Law of Arrest, Search, and Seizure.* Copyright © 1980 by Holt, Rinehart, and Winston. Reprinted by permission of CBS College Publishing.

object, while in pursuit of a suspect, during a search incidental to a lawful arrest, during stop and frisk, or any other legitimate reasons justifying an officer's lawful presence.

Second, the seized items must not be concealed. As the name implies, they must be in "plain view." Third, the discovery of the evidence in plain view must be inadvertent, by accident. Police officers cannot obtain a warrant to search an automobile and fail to mention a particular object they are looking for and then justify its seizure pursuant to the plain view doctrine. If they were looking for it initially, it must be mentioned in the warrant. Fourth, plain view alone is not sufficient to justify the warrantless seizure evidence.

Plain view refers to evidence that is not concealed and that is inadvertently seen by an officer engaged in a lawful activity.

In the *Coolidge* case the Court could not accept the seizure of the car as being within plain view limitations because the officers intended to seize the car when they came onto Coolidge's property. So the rule that applied to *Coolidge* and to all plain view cases following is that the discovery of evidence in plain view must be inadvertent—by accident. The plain view doctrine applies even though the objects seized are not under immediate control of the suspect.

According to Wendt (1991, p. 98): "It is proper to augment the vision with binoculars, flashlights, etc." It is *not* proper, however, to move or pick up items without probable cause to believe the items are contraband, as established in *Arizona v. Hicks* (1987). del Carmen and Walker describe the background of this ruling (1991, p. 116):

> A bullet fired through the floor of Hick's apartment injuring a man below prompted the police to enter Hick's apartment to search for the shooter, weapons, and other victims. The police discovered three weapons and a stocking cap mask. An officer noticed several pieces of stereo equipment which seemed to be out of place in the ill-appointed apartment. Based on this suspicion, he read and recorded the serial numbers of the equipment, moving some of the pieces in the process. A call to police headquarters verified that one of the pieces of equipment was stolen. A subsequent check of the serial numbers of the other pieces of equipment revealed they were also stolen. A search warrant was then obtained and the other equipment seized. Hicks was charged with and convicted of robbery.
>
> ISSUE: May an officer make a "plain view" search with less than probable cause to believe the items being searched are contraband or evidence of criminal activity? NO. . . .
>
> This case holds that even after the officer has seen an object in plain view, he or she may not search or seize it unless there is probable cause to believe that the object is contraband or stolen property, or that it is useful as evidence in court. Therefore, if, at the moment the object is picked up, the officer did not have probable cause but only "reasonable suspicion" (as was the case here), the seizure is illegal. The "plain view" doctrine as the basis for warrantless seizure . . . may not be invoked based on "reasonable suspicion" or any other level of certainty that is less than probable cause.

Plain Feel/Touch

Closely related to the plain view doctrine is the **plain feel/touch doctrine** used in several states. As noted by Wendt (1991, p. 99): "A container search may be justified by what some courts have referred to as the 'plain feel' doctrine. These searches must arise out of a lawful Terry detention. Containers taken from suspects may be felt by the officer to determine if a weapon is present. If felt, a safety search is proper."

Open Fields, Abandoned Property, and Trash

According to Harr and Hess (1991, p. 166): "[Open fields and abandoned property] might be considered a natural extension of the plain-view doctrine. In effect, however, the courts have dealt with this area by extending the doctrine that anything held out to the public is not protected by the Fourth Amendment because there is no reasonable expectation of privacy."

If there is no expectation of privacy, the protection of the Fourth Amendment does not apply. This includes open fields, abandoned property, and trash.

The principles governing search and seizure of open fields and trash were established in *Hester v. U.S.* (1924). In this case police were investigating bootlegging operations and went to Hester's father's home. As they approached the house, they saw a man identified as Henderson drive up to the house, so the officers hid. They saw Hester come out and give Henderson a bottle, so the police sounded an alarm. Hester ran to a car parked nearby, took out a gallon jug, and he and Henderson ran across an open field. One officer chased them. Hester dropped his jug, and it broke, but about half its contents remained. Henderson threw his bottle away. Police found another broken jar containing liquid that appeared to be illegal whiskey. The officers seized the jars, even though they had no search warrant, and arrested Hester who was convicted of concealing "distilled spirits." On appeal, his lawyer contended that the officers conducted an illegal search and seizure. The Court did not agree, saying:

> It is obvious that even if there had been a trespass, the above testimony was not obtained by an illegal search and seizure. The defendant's own acts, and those of his associates, disclosed the jug, the jar and the bottle—and there was no seizure in the sense of the law when the officers examined the contents of each after it had been abandoned....
>
> The special protection accorded by the Fourth Amendment to the people in their "persons, houses, papers, and effects," is not extended to the open fields.

The **open fields doctrine** holds that land beyond what is normally associated with use of that land, that is, undeveloped land, can be searched without a warrant. **Curtilage** is the term used to describe the portion of property generally associated with the common use of land, for example, buildings, sheds, fenced-in areas, etc. As noted by Bruce (1990, p. 105): "Essentially, the curtilage is equivalent to the 'yard.' Thus, a house and the yard are both protected by the Constitution and cannot be searched without a warrant or one of the other exceptions." A warrant is required to search the curtilage.

Further, once a person throws something away, the expectation of privacy is lost. Therefore, something thrown from a car, discarded during a chase, or even garbage, once off the curtilage, may be inspected without a warrant.

Oliver v. United States (1984) strengthened the open fields doctrine by ruling that "No Trespassing" signs and locked gates do not constitute a "reasonable expectation of privacy." As noted by the Court:

> The test of a reasonable expectation of privacy is not whether the individual attempts to conceal criminal activity, but whether the government's intrusion infringes upon the personal and societal values protected by the Fourth Amendment. Because open fields are accessible to the public and because fences or "No Trespassing" signs, etc. are not effective bars to public view of open fields, the expectation of privacy does not exist and police are justified in searching these areas without a warrant.

California v. Greenwood (1988) established that garbage left outside the curtilage of a home for regular collection could be inspected. The Court noted: "Here we conclude that respondents exposed their garbage to the public sufficiently to defeat their claim to Fourth Amendment protection. It is common knowledge that plastic garbage bags left on or at the side of a public street are readily accessible to animals, children, scavengers, snoops, and other members of the public." If no expectation of privacy exists, Fourth Amendment protection does not exist either.

Some states, however, do not allow such searches. According to *Law Enforcement News* (1990, p. 4): "Flying in the face of a recent U.S. Supreme Court ruling, the New Jersey Court ruled 5–2 that garbage left on a curb is private property that police officials cannot search through without a warrant." The Court said:

> Garbage reveals much that is personal. We do not find it unreasonable for people to want their garbage to remain private and to expect that it will remain private from the meddling of the state.
>
> A free and civilized society should comport itself with more decency [than to allow] police to pick and poke their way through garbage bags to peruse without cause the vestiges of a person's most private affairs.

This case illustrates the criticality of police officers being knowledgeable not only of federal laws, but also the laws of their respective states. States can pass more restrictive laws, such as the preceding ban against searching through garbage without a warrant.

Aerial Searches

Another area closely related to the plain view doctrine and the open fields doctrine is that of aerial searches. In *California v. Ciraolo* (1986), as noted by Senna and Siegel (1990, p. 298): "The Court expanded the police ability to 'spy' on the criminal offenders":

> In this case the police received a tip that marijuana was growing in the defendant's backyard. The yard was surrounded by fences, one of which was ten-feet high. The officers flew over the yard in a private plane at an altitude of 1,000 feet to ascertain that it contained marijuana plants. On the basis of this information, a search warrant was obtained and executed, and using the evidence, Ciraolo was convicted on drug charges. On appeal, the Supreme Court found that the defendant's privacy had not been violated.

In *Florida v. Riley* (1989) the Court expanded this ruling when it stated that police do not need a search warrant to conduct even low-altitude helicopter searches of private property.

The Inevitable Discovery Doctrine

On June 11, 1984, the United States Supreme Court ruled that illegally obtained evidence may be admitted at trial if the prosecution can prove that the evidence would "inevitably" have been discovered by lawful means *(Nix v. Williams)*. From this case the Supreme Court adopted what is now known as "the inevitable discovery exception to the Exclusionary Rule."

Chief Justice Warren E. Burger wrote in the majority opinion: "Exclusion of physical evidence that would inevitably have been discovered adds nothing to either the integrity or fairness of a criminal trial." The point of the **inevitable discovery doctrine,** he said, was to put the police in the same, not a worse, position than they would have been in if no police error or misconduct occurred.

Limitations on Searches

A **reasonable search** involves more than justification by an arrest, consent, a search warrant, or extenuating circumstances. Limitations on the search itself are set as you have seen. After establishing the right to search, police officers must determine the limitations on that right—limitations imposed by law and interpreted by the courts. General searches are unconstitutional.

The most important limitation imposed upon any search is that the scope must be narrowed. General searches are unconstitutional.

Often what is found during a search provides the probable cause to make an arrest. As with searches, in an arrest the general rule is that a warrant is required.

LAWFUL ARRESTS

Laws of arrest are generally uniform in all fifty states and in federal criminal proceedings.

Statutes throughout the United States generally define **arrest** as the taking of a person into custody by the actual restraint of the person or by his or her submission to the custody of the officer that he or she may be held to answer for a public offense before a judge.

Black's Law Dictionary (1991, p. 72) defines *arrest* as follows:

To deprive a person of his liberty by legal authority. Taking, under real or assumed authority, custody of another for the purpose of holding or detaining him to answer a criminal charge or civil demand. . . .

Arrest involves the authority to arrest, the assertion of that authority with the intent to effect an arrest, and the restraint of the person to be arrested. All that is required for an "arrest" is some act by an officer indicating his intention to detain or take the person into custody and thereby subject that person to the actual control and will of the officer; no formal declaration of arrest is required.

Elements of Criminal Arrest

According to Creamer (1980, p. 56), the four elements of a criminal arrest are:

1. An *intent* by the peace officer to make an arrest.
2. Real or pretended *authority* to arrest.
3. A *seizure* or *restraint,* actual or constructive.
4. An *understanding* by the person being seized that he or she is being arrested.

Arrest Warrants

All states have a statute authorizing law enforcement officers to make arrests, but the Constitution stipulates that lawful arrests require an arrest warrant. Klotter and Kanovitz (1985, pp. 103–111) note: "Aside from constitutional considerations, there is a very practical reason why police officers should, wherever time permits, obtain a warrant before making an arrest. If the warrant is proper on its face and the officer does not abuse his authority in executing the arrest, he will be protected against civil liability for false imprisonment, even though it is later determined that the arrest was unjustified." Klotter and Kanovitz list eight requirements for a valid arrest warrant:

1. The warrant must be supported by probable cause. It will be up to the magistrate to determine if probable cause exists.
2. The affidavit for the warrant must be supported by oath or affirmation; that is, some individual must swear to the truth of the facts described in the affidavit.

3. The person to be seized (arrested) must be named.
4. The warrant must state the nature of the offense with sufficient clarity to advise the subject of the accusation.
5. The warrant must designate the officer or class of officers who are directed to carry out the court's order.
6. The warrant must be issued in the name of a state or the United States.
7. The warrant must be issued and signed by a neutral, detached judicial officer, including his/her title.
8. Additional state requirements may also be present.

Arrest without a Warrant

Lawful arrests require an arrest warrant. If, however, an emergency situation exists and the officers have probable cause to believe a person has committed a crime, they may make an arrest. The courts will determine its legality.

In *Draper v. United States* (1959) the United States Supreme Court stated: "Probable cause exists where the facts and circumstances within their (the arresting officers') knowledge and of which they had reasonable trustworthy information are sufficient in themselves to warrant a man of reasonable caution in the belief that an offense has been or is being committed." Creamer (1980, p. 57) notes:

> The exact moment when a warrantless arrest occurred is frequently the most important preliminary determination for a court. The legality of a warrantless arrest hinges, in large measure, on the probable cause or guilt-laden facts confronting the police officer up to and including, but never after, the actual moments of arrest. At the moment of arrest, probable cause ceases to build. Any after-the-arrest, guilt-laden facts that develop will not be considered by the courts as part of the probable cause necessary to justify the arrest.

If there is probable cause and an emergency situation exists, an officer may make an arrest without a warrant. The courts will determine whether the arrest was lawful.

Police officers may make lawful arrests without a warrant for felonies or misdemeanors committed in their presence or for felonies not committed in their presence if they have probable cause.

There are four authorities for arrest without a warrant. The first authority allows for an arrest for a public offense committed or attempted in the presence of an officer. **Public offense** includes both felonies and misdemeanors. To determine whether a public offense has been committed, ask this question: Would you be justified in seeking a complaint upon which an arrest warrant would be issued, and could you testify to all the elements of the crime?

"Committed or attempted in the presence of an officer" means the crime was apparent to the officer's senses, including sight, hearing, or smelling. A conversation over the telephone is within the officer's presence; therefore, a conversation lawfully overheard that might be indicative of criminal conduct is in the officer's presence. The odor of marijuana is evidence that a crime is being committed in the officer's presence and may constitute probable cause to effect an arrest. In most cases, however, the officer will actually see the crime committed, and this is where the first authority generally applies. A suspect can be arrested without a warrant for a misdemeanor only if the offense is committed in the officer's presence.

The remaining authorities allow an officer to arrest a suspect for a felony that was not committed in his or her presence. Any lawful arrest, with or

Table 12–2 Stop and Arrest		
	STOP	ARREST
Justification	Reasonable suspicion	Probable cause
Intent of Officer	To resolve an ambiguous situation	To make a formal charge
Search	Possibly a "pat down" or frisk	Complete body search
Record	Minimal	Fingerprints, photographs, and booking

without an arrest warrant, requires probable cause. Without an arrest warrant, police officers can arrest a suspect for a felony only if they have probable cause based on their own observations or on information provided to them. They cannot make this same type of arrest for a misdemeanor.

The four authorities for arrest without a warrant are as follows:

1. When a public offense is committed or attempted in an officer's presence.

2. When a person arrested has committed a felony, although not in an officer's presence, for example, an all-points bulletin on a bank robber before a warrant is issued.

3. When a felony has in fact been committed, and the officer has reasonable cause to believe that the person has committed it; for example, an officer answers a shooting call and the suspect is still at the scene.

4. On a charge made upon probable cause of the commission of a felony; for example, a person observed running down the street as a burglar alarm sounds is a likely suspect for the crime.

Creamer (1980, p. 64) emphasizes: "Police arrest powers are indeed awesome, and even while they protect society, they can destroy a citizen. The Fourth Amendment was designed to limit the chances of a citizen being harmed by an unjust arrest. The courts have the responsibility to make sure the Fourth Amendment works to protect the citizen and, at the same time, assure the security of society."

An arrest is never to be taken lightly. It can change a person's life forever. Officer discretion is critical when arrest decisions are made. It is also vital that officers clearly differentiate between a simple stop and frisk situation and an arrest. Table 12–2 (above) summarizes the important differences. Sometimes a stop and frisk situation leads to an arrest situation. And sometimes when an arrest is made, the person being arrested resists and the officer must use force to make the arrest.

THE USE OF FORCE IN MAKING AN ARREST

The Rodney King incident brought the issue of police use of force to national attention. As noted by Brown (1991, p. 6):

> Across the country, Americans have viewed repeatedly the horrifying event that took place in Los Angeles on March 3, 1991. The specter of some police officers beating Rodney King while others just stood by has cast a shadow over the entire policing community and has become the pre-eminent policing issue of the day.

What constitutes **reasonable force** is established in *Graham v. Connor* (1989):

> The reasonableness of a particular use of force must be judged from the perspective of a reasonable officer on the scene, rather than with the 20/20 vision of hindsight. . . . Not every push or shove, even if it may later seem unnecessary in the peace of a judge's chambers, violates the Fourth Amendment. The calculus of reasonableness must embody allowance for the fact that police officers are often forced to make split-second judgments—in circumstances that are tense, uncertain, and rapidly evolving—about the amount of force that is necessary in a particular situation.

According to del Carmen and Walker (1991, p. 133):

> This case gives police officers a "break" in civil liability cases involving the use of force. The old "substantive due process" test used by many lower courts prior to the *Graham* case required the courts to consider whether the officer acted in "good faith" or "maliciously and sadistically for the very purpose of causing harm." This meant that the officer's "subjective motivations" were of central importance in deciding whether the force used was unconstitutional. The *Graham* case requires a new test, that of "objective reasonableness" under the Fourth Amendment. This means that the reasonableness of an officer's use of force must be judged "from the perspective of a reasonable officer on the scene, rather than with the 20/20 vision of hindsight." This makes a big difference in determining whether or not such use of force was reasonable. This new test recognizes that police officers often make split-second judgments in situations that involve their own lives and must, therefore, be judged in the context of "a reasonable officer at the scene." This is a test most police officers welcome.

If there is no resistance, officers should use *no* force.

Clede (1990, p. 59) notes that use of force is on a continuum and that officers may move up or down that continuum, depending on the situation. Clede asks:

> What weapon does a police officer always have with him, even in a bar or at the beach? What device does an officer use in every encounter? What skills are appropriate under all circumstances? The answer to these questions is the same as to the one: in what skill is an officer the least trained? The answer is: his voice. . . .
>
> On the use of force continuum, a police officer's very presence is a force. When you request a driver's license, even politely, it's a forceful influence. When you issue a command, it's stronger force. When you raise your voice with an ultimatum, that's even more forceful.

The Use of Force Continuum

Connor (1991, p. 30) notes that the use of force continuum includes three varieties of force: no force—used with a cooperative person; ordinary force—used with a person who is resisting; and extra-ordinary force—used with a person who is assaultive. This use of force continuum is illustrated in Figure 12–1.

This continuum provides a perspective on whether handcuffs should be used on a person who is cooperative. Many police departments have a policy stating: "For the protection and safety of the officer, all individuals arrested and transported shall be handcuffed." This is often referred to as the **mere hand-**

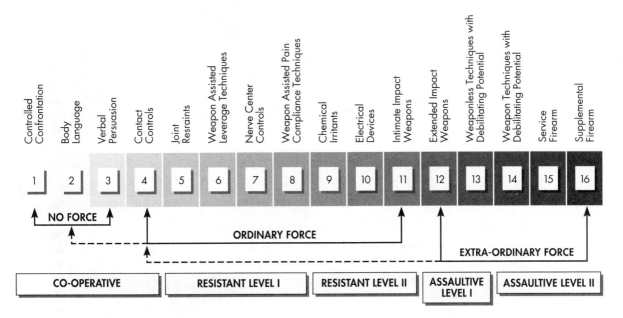

Figure 12–1. Use of Force Continuum

Source: Adapted from G. Connor. "Use of Force Continuum: Phase II." *Law and Order,* March 1991: 30. Reprinted by permission.

cuff rule. As noted by Allard (1991, p. 69): "Police department policies that require officers to handcuff all prisoners transported to headquarters are being questioned. . . . Courts are beginning to recognize claims against officers who knowingly display or threaten force which would create substantial fear in the average citizen, if the force threatened or displayed is not justified by the circumstances."

Graham v. Connor (1989) called into question the mere handcuff rule as being in conflict with the Fourth Amendment "objective reasonableness" standard for the use of force. As noted by Allard (1991, pp. 69–70): "The use of force must be necessary and in response to resistance offered. Accordingly, the least amount of force necessary in any situation is the greatest amount of force that is reasonable. Juries are instructed to give careful attention to the facts and circumstances of the case." According to the Court in *Graham v. Connor,* the facts and circumstances of the case include "the severity of the crime at issue, whether the suspect poses an immediate threat to the safety of the officers or others, and whether the suspect is actively resisting arrest or attempting to evade arrest."

PRISM: Police Response and Interaction with Suspect Model

The PRISM model goes beyond the use of force continuum, considering use of force within the entire dynamics of a given situation. As noted by Grossberg (1991, p. 34):

The PRISM concept is based upon the following premises:

1. *Police officers prevent crime.* Their decisions and actions are designed to control, contain, and hopefully deescalate a situation.
2. *Criminals create crime.* Unless they are in full compliance with an officer's commands, their decisions and actions are designed to maintain and/or escalate a situation.

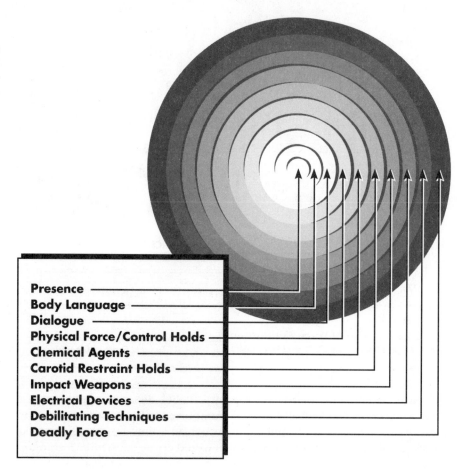

Figure 12–2. The PRISM Approach to Use of Force

Source: S. J. Grossberg. "PRISM: Police Response and Interaction with Suspect Model." *The Police Chief,* July 1991: 35. Reprinted by permission.

Grossberg (p. 34) suggests:

> Although experts will disagree on the specific order that force options should take (and, in fact, the force options in the PRISM diagram can be tailored to fit the specific policies of individual departments), this article will assume the following order: (1) presence, (2) body language, (3) dialogue, (4) physical force/control holds, (5) chemical agents, (6) carotid restraint holds, (7) impact weapons, (8) electrical devices, (9) debilitating techniques, and (10) deadly force.

Figure 12–2 illustrates the PRISM concept.

According to Grossberg (pp. 34–35): "The suspect's initial conduct is recorded on the appropriate circle with the code S1, while the police officer's response to that conduct is coded P1. This dual numbering continues action-by-action until the entire event is depicted. When complete, the diagram should show each of the suspect's actions along with a corresponding logical response by the officer (usually on the same level or one circle out). Such a diagram should be useful in any charges of police brutality and should help justify the amount of force used.

The FLETC Use-Of-Force Model

The Federal Law Enforcement Training Center (FLETC) also has a model for the use of force. As noted by Graves and Connor (1992, p. 56): "Progressive application of force encompasses three main elements of action: tools (i.e., curriculum topics such as weapons, procedures and behavioral perspectives,) tactics, and timing." They further note: "The model supports the widely accepted premise and practice of *progressive* application of force, which implies the appropriate selection of force options in response to the level of compliance from the individual to be controlled."

Color plays a large role in the model, with five colors depicting a "reasonable officer's perception" and corresponds with amount of activity on the color spectrum (Graves and Connor, p. 56):

Professional perception. The color blue (Level I), the lowest mode of activity on the color spectrum, represents the foundation of the perceptual process. This level of perception includes day-to-day law enforcement activities and the critical demands of the environment in which we function.

Tactical perception. At the second level of perception (Level II), color-coded green, the officer senses an increased threat within the confrontational setting and deploys specific safety strategies.

Threshold threat perception. The third level (Level III) of the model uses the color yellow to signal increased alertness due to the perception of threat and recognized danger.

Harmful threat perception. The color orange (Level IV) denotes an accelerated assessment of danger to the officer, who must now direct his energy and tactics toward defense.

Lethal threat perception. The highest level of threat (Level V) correlates the most intense color in the light spectrum, red. The officer must maintain the highest level of risk assessment and call upon his maximized survival skills.

These perceptions result in how a given person with whom the officer is interacting is perceived. Figure 12–3 illustrates the FLETC Use-of-Force Model.

Paralleling the officer's perception are responses a "reasonable officer" might make. At the professional perception level, the subject is seen as cooperative and only verbal control is used. At the next level the subject may

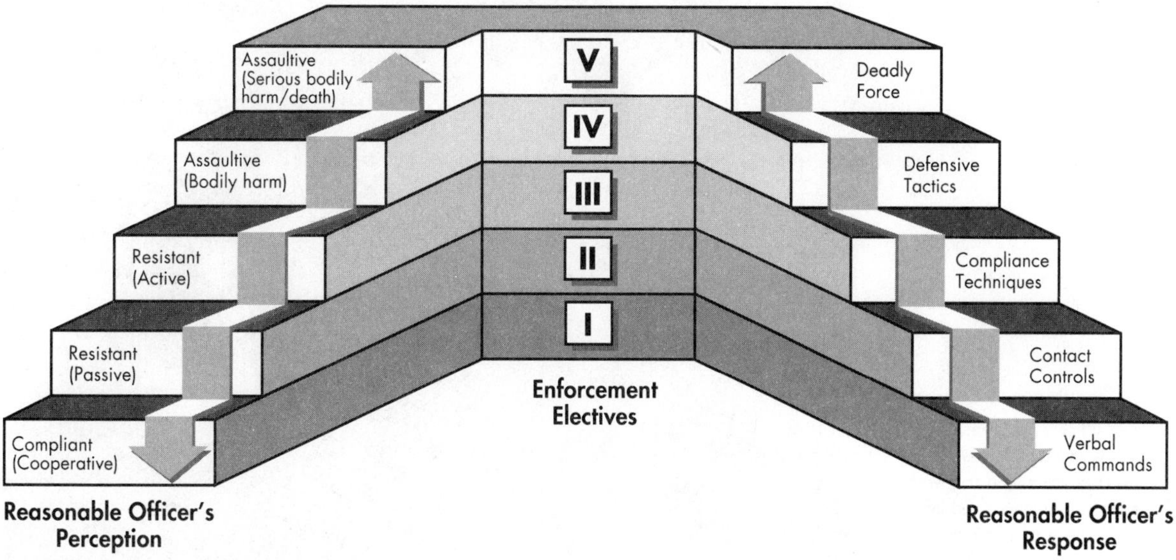

Figure 12–3. FLETC Use-of-Force Model

Source: F. R. Graves and G. Connor. "The FLETC Use-of-Force Model." *The Police Chief,* February 1992: 58. Reprinted by permission.

indicate lack of cooperation, but not physically. As the subject becomes less cooperative, more force is justified. As noted by Graves and Connor (p. 58): "Facing an assaultive situation that reaches the ultimate degree of danger, the officer must deploy absolute and immediate tactics to stop the lethal threat and secure conclusive compliance and control."

USE OF DEADLY FORCE

"The authority to use deadly force," says Waldron (1984, p. 198), "is the most critical and awesome responsibility that will ever be placed on a police officer. No other single government official has the right or the means to lawfully take another human life." Waldron goes on to caution:

> Make no mistake, a decision to use deadly force is irreversible. After the fact, the decision is final. . . . Similarly, a decision *not* to use deadly force may also result in an irreversible situation. A police officer who hesitates or decides not to employ deadly force may suffer his or her own death or the death of another person the officer is sworn to protect.

The amount of force police departments use and condone directly affects the public's attitudes toward the police. Excessive use of force has been a chronic complaint of minorities, particularly in the 1960s and the 1980s.

Pursley (1984, p. 244) notes: "An issue that has grown in importance in recent years has been the use of deadly force by the police. This issue is usually tied inextricably to the broader issues of police-minority relations and the supporting issues of police violence and/or police brutality."

When considering the justifiable use of **deadly force,** two interrelated rights are important: the legal right to use such force and the moral right compelling the officer to do so.

These officers are arresting a driver who "came out swinging" when they attempted to give him a ticket for running a red light. Using force is often a necessary part of a police officer's job, but the force must be reasonable.

State legislators have generally given the police very broad discretion in this area, with most politicians fearful of being labeled as "soft on criminals" if they did otherwise. Many state statutes authorize use of deadly force to prevent the commission of a felony or to prevent a fleeing felon from escaping. In fact, in one state, it is a felony to run from the police, thus making it legal for police to shoot the person. Although this is legally right, is it morally right?

To balance the legal and moral rights involved, several states have adopted penal codes that do not rely solely on a crime being classified as a felony. They focus instead on the danger posed by the suspect to the officer and society.

Justification for use of deadly force must take into consideration not only the legal right, but also the need to apprehend the suspect compared to the safety of the arresting officer and compared to the value of human life.

Pursley (1984, p. 245) concludes: "Like so many other concerns surrounding crime and criminals, discussion of such issues tends to be more emotional rather than logical. To minorities it is simply a means to further oppress and show disregard for Blacks or Chicanos; for many white Americans it is simply giving the robbers, the rapists, the murderers what they deserve—after all, they say, it's not our problem that a disproportionate number of them are Black or Chicanos. For the police themselves, it's an issue of perceived safety, and they naturally feel at 'greater risk' when confronting the more perceived prevalence of violence among minorities."

A landmark Supreme Court ruling, *Tennessee v. Garner* (1985), is of extreme importance in the issue of use of deadly force. This ruling bars police from shooting to kill fleeing felons unless there is an imminent danger to life. This ruling invalidates laws in almost half of the states that allow police officers to use deadly force to prevent the escape of a suspected felon. According to Nislow (1985, p. 1):

> The current ruling sprang from a 1974 incident in which a Memphis police officer fatally shot an unarmed fifteen-year-old, fleeing from police after having stolen ten dollars in money and jewelry from an unoccupied house.... The police officer who fired the fatal shot testified that he had fired because he believed the suspect would otherwise escape and because he had been trained that Tennessee state law permitted him, in such situations, to shoot a suspected fleeing felon.

The Supreme Court ruled that the Tennessee "fleeing felon" statute was unconstitutional insofar as it authorized the use of deadly force against fleeing suspects who are unarmed and pose no threat to the officer or third parties.

In effect, since taking a life is a "seizure" protected by the Fourth Amendment, any use of deadly force must be *reasonable.*

SUMMARY

The constitutional standards for searches and seizures, including arrests, are contained in the Fourth Amendment, which requires that searches and seizures be reasonable and be based on probable cause. As the word implies, *reasonable* means sensible, justifiable, logical, based on reason. Probable cause requires more than mere suspicion. It requires facts or proof that would lead a person of reasonable caution to believe a crime has been committed by a specific individual or premises contain evidence of a crime.

Probable cause may be founded on (1) observation, (2) expertise, (3) circumstantial factors, and (4) information conveyed to the officers, including official sources, victims of crimes, and informants.

The Fourth Amendment is reasonable in protecting the rights of the people while allowing law enforcement the right to investigate crime. It is strong enough to protect citizens but also flexible enough to enable police officers to uphold the Constitution.

The standards established by the Fourth Amendment are enforced by use of the Exclusionary Rule, which states that no evidence can be admitted in a trial unless it is obtained within the standards established in the Fourth Amendment. The federal precedent for this rule is found in the case of *Weeks v. United States.* The state precedent is found in the case of *Mapp v. Ohio.*

Stop and frisk is a form of search and seizure and, as such, is governed by the intent of the Fourth Amendment, which demands that all searches and seizures be based on reason. A stop is not an arrest; the authority to stop and frisk is independent of the power to search or arrest. A frisk, however, is a search. The type of search allowed under stop and frisk is limited to a protective seizure and search for weapons and is not a search for evidence of a crime.

Reasonable searches must also meet the standards set forth in the Fourth Amendment. The three principal justifications for a search are (1) it is incidental to a lawful arrest, (2) consent is given, or (3) a search warrant is obtained. The limitations placed on searches incidental to lawful arrest come from the case of *Chimel v. California,* which states that the scope of the search must be narrowed to the area within the suspect's immediate control. The limitations to a search made with consent are that the consent must be free and voluntary, not in response to an implied right to search, and the scope must be limited to the area for which consent has been given. The limitations to a search made with a warrant are stated within the warrant itself.

Most searches require a warrant. A search warrant is a judicial order directing a police officer to search for specific property, seize it, and return it to the court. Probable cause is required for issuance of all warrants. Technically, all searches are to be made under the authority of a search warrant issued by a magistrate. If a search is conducted with a warrant, the burden of proof as to admissibility of evidence seized is on the defense; if it is conducted without a warrant, the burden of proof is on the searching officer and the prosecution.

Police may seize items not specified in the search warrant if they are similar in nature to those items described, if they are related to the particular crime described, or if they are contraband.

When police officers execute a search warrant, they generally announce themselves. They may enter a home by force if they are denied entrance or if no one is home. Two special types of search warrants, nighttime and no-knock, may be requested if the officers fear the objects of the search might be lost, destroyed, or removed.

Warrantless searches, based on probable cause, have been justified in stop and frisk, incidental to a lawful arrest, with consent, in an emergency situation, and when mobility is involved.

The two most frequent challenges to such warrantless searches that may be raised by the defense are that (1) there was insufficient evidence to establish probable cause, so a search warrant would not have been issued by a magistrate, and (2) there was sufficient time to obtain a search warrant.

Special provisions have been made for warrantless searches of cars and other conveyances due to their mobility. Precedents for the warrantless search of an automobile were established by the *Carroll* case, which demonstrated that probable cause must exist along with mobility—the belief that the car or evidence would be gone by the time a search warrant was obtained. It also demonstrated that the right to search was not dependent on the right to arrest but rather on probable cause. The *Chambers* case demonstrated that a car may retain its mobility even though it is impounded. The *Coolidge* case demonstrated that the rule of mobility cannot be applied unless there is actually a risk the vehicle will be moved. A car may also be searched without a warrant if it is an instrumentality of a crime.

A special instance of legal seizure of evidence without a warrant exists in the plain view situation; that is, evidence that is not concealed is inadvertently seen by an officer engaged in lawful activity and is supported by other facts or evidence.

If there is no expectation of privacy, the protection of the Fourth Amendment does not apply. This includes open fields, abandoned property, and trash.

Even when the required conditions are met, certain limitations are placed on the search. The most important limitation imposed upon any search is that the scope must be narrowed. General searches are unconstitutional.

Citizens of the United States are also protected against unreasonable arrest (seizure) by the Fourth Amendment. An arrest is usually defined as the taking of a person into custody by the actual restraint of the person or by his or her submission to the custody of the officer so that he or she may be held to answer for a public offense before a judge. Such arrests must be reasonable, and they must be predicated on probable cause.

The Fourth Amendment requires that arrests be made by having a magistrate issue an arrest warrant, but police officers may make an arrest without an arrest warrant in an emergency; for example, for a felony or misdemeanor committed in their presence or for a felony not committed in their presence if they have probable cause. A person can be arrested for a misdemeanor only if (1) there is an arrest warrant or (2) the crime was committed in the officer's presence. A person can be arrested for a felony if (1) there is an arrest warrant, (2) the crime is committed in the presence of an officer, or (3) there is probable cause that the person committed a felony.

If there is no resistance, officers should use no force. Justification for use of deadly force must take into consideration not only the legal right, but also the need to apprehend the suspect compared to the safety of the arresting officer and compared to the value of human life.

DISCUSSION QUESTIONS

1. In popular television programs how are police officers portrayed in relation to protecting citizen's Fourth Amendment rights?

2. Why are the police not given total freedom to help stop crime? Why are they not allowed to use evidence that clearly establishes a person's guilt, no matter how they obtained this evidence?

3. In a state where stop and frisk is legal, can a police officer be sued for stopping and frisking someone?

4. According to Sir Arthur Conan Doyle, author of the Sherlock Holmes mystery stories: "When you have eliminated the impossible, whatever remains, however improbable, must be the truth." Discuss this quotation in light of what you know about lawful arrest.

5. What are the most important factors in determining if and when an arrest occurred?

6. Must all elements of probable cause exist prior to a lawful arrest?

7. Why is the presence of ten officers not considered intimidation when a request to search is made?

8. Have you ever been involved in a search and seizure situation? How was it handled?

9. From what you have learned about search and seizure, do you feel that the restrictions placed upon police officers are reasonable?

10. Compare and contrast the three models for use of force presented in this chapter.

TERMS

administrative warrant, affidavit, affirmation, arrest, circumstantial probable cause, consent, contraband, curtilage, deadly force, emergency situations, Exclusionary Rule, exigent circumstances, expertise, extenuating circumstances, eyewitnesses, field detention, field inquiry, forced entry, frisk, immediate control, inevitable discovery doctrine, informants, informational probable cause, instruments of a crime, lawful arrest, magistrate, mere handcuff rule, mobility, nightcap warrants, nighttime search warrants, no-knock search warrant, oath, observational probable cause, open fields doctrine, ordinary care, pat down, plain feel/touch doctrine, plain view, probable cause, public offense, reasonable, reasonable force, reasonable search, search, search warrant, seizure, stop, stop and frisk, threshold inquiry, wingspan.

REFERENCES

Allard, R., Jr. "Objectively Unreasonable Handcuffing: The Mere Handcuff Rule." *Law and Order* (April 1991): 69–72.

Bennett, W. M. and Hess, K. M. *Criminal Investigation.* 3d ed. St. Paul, Minn.: West Publishing Company, 1991.

Black's Law Dictionary. 6th ed. St. Paul, Minn.: West Publishing Company, 1991.

Brown, L. P. "Law Enforcement and Police Brutality." *The Police Chief* (May 1991): 6.

Bruce, T. A. "The Ten Exceptions to the Search Warrant Requirement." *Law and Order* (October 1990): 100–108.

Clede, B. "New Levels of Lethal Force." *Law and Order* (March 1990): pp. 59–60.

Connor, G. "Use of Force Continuum: Phase II." *Law and Order* (March 1991): 30–35.

Creamer, J. S. *The Law of Arrest, Search, and Seizure.* 3d ed. New York: Holt, Rinehart, and Winston, 1980.

del Carmen, R. V. and Walker, J. T. *Briefs of 100 Leading Cases in Law Enforcement.* Cincinnati, Ohio: Anderson Publishing Company, 1991.

Graves, F. R. and Connor, G. "The FLETC Use-of-Force Model." *The Police Chief* (February 1992): 56–58.

Grossberg, S. J. "PRISM: Police Response and Interaction with Suspect Model." *The Police Chief* (July 1991): 34–35.

Harr, J. S. and Hess, K. M. *Criminal Procedure.* St. Paul, Minn.: West Publishing Company, 1991.

Klotter, J. C. and Kanovitz, J. R. *Constitutional Law.* 5th ed. Cincinnati, Ohio: Anderson Publishing, 1985.

"New Jersey High Court Upholds Privacy of Curbside Trash." *Law Enforcement News,* July/August 1990, 4, 15.

Nislow, "Fleeing-Felon Rule Cut Down." *Law Enforcement News* 11, no. 8, April 22, 1985, 1.

Pursley, R. D. *Introduction to Criminal Justice.* 3d ed. New York: Macmillan, 1984.

Senna, J. J. and Siegel, L. J. *Introduction to Criminal Justice.* 5th ed. St. Paul, Minn.: West Publishing Company, 1990.

Waldron, R. J. *The Criminal Justice System.* 3d ed. Boston: Houghton Mifflin, 1984.

Wendt, B. "Container Searches, without Search Warrants." *Law and Order* (November 1991): 95–103.

One-on-One: The Problems and People Involved

Having looked at police operations in the 1990s and the responsibilities police officers face in the areas of community service, patrol/traffic, investigation, and preservation of civil rights, you are now ready to look at some of the very specific problems and people involved with law enforcement.

Police officers are faced with a rapidly changing public to be served and protected, including growing numbers of elderly, minorities, immigrants, and individuals with AIDS (Chapter 13). They must also deal with those

who commit the crimes discussed in the last section, especially those who are career criminals (Chapter 14). Police face an increasingly difficult challenge in the escalating drug problem in this country (Chapter 15) and an escalating gang problem (Chapter 16). Frequently criminals, drugs dealers, and gang members are one and the same, presenting tremendous challenges. In addition, police must assist the victims of those who break the rules of our society (Chapter 17).

CHAPTER 13

The Challenge of Serving and Protecting Our Changing Population

No man is an island.

—John Donne

Do You Know

How the population of the United States has changed in the past decades and how it is likely to continue to change?

What the "ghetto syndrome" is and why it is of importance to law enforcement?

How immigrants in the 1980s and 1990s differ from those of earlier decades?

What major challenges immigrants pose for law enforcement?

Who makes up the "homeless" population?

What major challenges the homeless pose for law enforcement?

What AIDS is? Who is most at risk of contracting AIDS? How it is transmitted?

What legislation has been passed related to AIDS?

INTRODUCTION

Our society has changed tremendously over the past decades, as have the challenges facing law enforcement. Technology has made the task easier, but the increasing diversity of our population has made it much more difficult. In addition, although there has always been poverty in the United States, the gap between those who live in poverty and those who are more affluent is widening. The acquittal on criminal charges of three out of the four police officers charged in the beating of motorist Rodney King led to riots in Los Angeles in May, 1992. The destructive rage, caused by the feeling that the justice system had failed, was as much a protest by those who feel they have been shut out of the American Dream as it was about civil rights. As noted by Mydans (1992, p. 1A): "Surrounded by burned-out buildings, the people who live there spoke with anger about a society that writes them off as hoodlums and gangsters and responds with more arrests to what they see as their cry for help."

The **American Dream,** that anyone can be successful who works hard and is willing to sacrifice for a while, is becoming much more difficult to attain, not only for members of minority groups, but also for middle class individuals of all ethnic and racial backgrounds. A college education, the traditional key to "getting ahead," is becoming prohibitively expensive for many youth. Jobs are harder to find. The high paying assembly line and factory jobs have been mechanized and computerized.

Our elderly population is increasing rapidly, as is our minority population. In addition hundreds of thousands of immigrants are pouring into the United States, and a great many of them speak no English. The homeless population is growing at an alarming rate, and the number of individuals who have AIDS is also escalating. Each of these populations may become frustrated and present a challenge to the police.

Our population is becoming older, has more minorities, more immigrants, more homeless, and more individuals with AIDS. In addition, the gap between those who live in poverty and those who are more affluent is widening.

THE GROWING ELDERLY POPULATION

Our elderly population is growing and will continue to do so. McCord and Wicker (1990, pp. 28–32) note: "In 1996 the first wave of 'baby boomers' will turn 50, marking the start of a "senior boom" in the United States. By 2010 one in every four Americans will be 55 or older."

In the twenty-first century the financial burden of caring for our elderly, the majority of whom are white, will fall to an increasing number of minority members who themselves may be struggling financially. Trojanowicz and Carter (p. 11) suggest: "Younger workers, many of whom will be minorities in lower-paying service jobs, increasingly will be asked to pay for the needs of primarily white retirees, whose health care costs alone may prove staggering."

Further, as the "graying of America" continues, more individuals with Alzheimer's disease will be in our communities.

THE GROWING MINORITY POPULATION

McCord and Wicker also note that: "By 2010 minorities will constitute the majority of children in New Mexico (77%), California (57%), Texas (57%),

New York (53%), Florida (53%), and Louisiana (50%)." Trojanowicz and Carter (1990, p. 7) agree: "According to **demographers** who study the characteristics of human populations, in less than 100 years, we can expect white dominance of the United States to end." They stress:

> Our past experience should also forewarn us that race constitutes the biggest barrier to full participation in the American dream. In particular, the black experience has been unique from the beginning because most African Americans did not come here seeking freedom or greater opportunity, but were brought to this country as slaves. And the lingering problem of racism still plays an undeniable role in preventing blacks from achieving full participation in the economic and social life of this country.

> **De facto segregation** persists in keeping many minorities trapped in decaying crime- and drug-riddled, inner-city neighborhoods. Though blacks constitute only 12 percent of the total U.S. population, as a result of "white flight," many of this country's major cities have minority majorities, while the suburbs that surround them remain virtually white.

> The role of race as an obstacle to full assimilation and participation is of obvious concern since almost one-half of all legal immigrants over the past decade have been Asians—Chinese, Filipino, Indian, Korean, Vietnamese, and Kampucheans (Cambodians)—and slightly more than one-third have been from Latin America. Though 9 out of 10 Hispanics are counted as "white," there is no doubt that they face discrimination because of their Hispanic ethnicity....

> Shortly after the turn of the 21st century, Asians are expected to reach 10 million. Today's 18 million Hispanics may well double by then....

> Because minorities are expected to continue to exhibit higher birth rates than whites, demographers expect minorities to constitute an even larger percentage of young people in this country in the near future.

Of particular concern is that many minority members live in **ghettos,** defined by Pace (1991, p. 43) as "an area of a city inhabited, often as a matter of involuntary segregation, by people of an ethnic or racial group who live in poverty and social disorganization." The frustrations experienced by those who live in ghettos, their sense of futility, and the great probability of failure has been described as the ghetto syndrome.

The **ghetto syndrome** is a vicious cycle of poverty and welfare dependency leading to inability to go to college or prepare for a well-paying job, leading to lack of motivation, leading to unemployment, poverty, welfare dependency. . . .

As one African American retired elementary school principal said in explaining why she had moved out of south-central Los Angeles (Mydans 1992, p. 1A): "Simply, I couldn't stand the depression, coming down and watching people fail, seeing kids go through school and knowing they're not going to make it." And when they don't make it, conflict is likely to be the result. As Pace (1991, p. 43) suggests:

> Logically, conflict between the criminal justice system and elements of the community comes from those segments of the community that are in conflict with the cultures, mores, and laws of the larger society. Because the ghettos of the cities are not in concert with the larger society, they become popularized as the breeding grounds of crime. Since ghettos house more than 70% of racial or ethnic minorities, the ghetto, minorities, and crime become interrelated and are the focus for most of the anti-crime efforts of the criminal justice system.

This focus is perceived by many as being racist, a perception those in law enforcement must be aware of and seek to eliminate.

Adding to the growing minority population is the ever increasing number of immigrants.

THE GROWING IMMIGRANT POPULATION

Trojanowicz and Carter (1990, pp. 6–7) suggest that:

> For many of us, the word "immigrant" evokes two vivid images: 1) the wave after wave of Europeans flooding through Ellis Island, and 2) the metaphor of the "melting pot." These two memories often converge in a romanticized view of the past as a time when those "poor, hungry, huddled masses" from other countries required only a generation or two for their offspring to become full-fledged Americans.

This picture has changed considerably.

Since 1980 only 12% of immigrants have been European. Recent immigrants tend to cluster in specific areas and many speak no English and fear the authorities.

According to Trojanowicz and Carter (1990, p. 8): "Many of today's new arrivals come from places where the police are feared, not respected, and the last thing they would be likely to do is ask an officer for help or share any information." The distrust and suspicion results, says Taft (p. 309), "from years of watching state-controlled thugs apply brutal sanctions in the name of law and order." This distrust and unfamiliarity with our customs can result in volatile situations. For example, the commonly used arrest position of having a suspect kneel, back to the officer with hands clasped behind the head, has resulted in some suspects attempting to run or to strike at the arresting officers. This is easier to understand when one realizes that our arrest position is the position used for executions in Vietnam.

They note that many immigrants will become victims, particularly victims of violent crimes. Being unfamiliar with our laws and customs, they become "easy targets for all kinds of predators." Not all immigrants fall within the "easy target" category, however, according to Trojanowicz and Carter:

> A small fraction of the immigrants coming in will be career criminals, eager to ply their trades here. The police have had to battle Asian drug gangs and Jamaican posses, as well as the alleged hardened criminals that entered this country as part of the Mariel Boat Lift.
>
> Moreover, there will always be the larger group that turns to crime when faced with economic hardship.

In addition to problems of crime, problems also arise when others in the community feel the new immigrants are taking their jobs. According to former St. Paul Chief of Police William McCutcheon (Taft 1991, p. 315): "We really have a cultural revolution going on, and it's brought the blacks and whites together, resisting the intrusion of the Hmongs. . . . If the competition for jobs becomes greater, we are going to see ethnic groups [banding together] and with all of them competing for the same jobs, it could mean violence."

Taft (1991, p. 308) cautions: "As the melting pot simmers and money grows more scarce, some observers are predicting racially motivated violence and an increase in mental health problems in the new immigrant ghettos."

The Law Enforcement Challenge

As noted by Taft (1991, p. 308): "The presence of new immigrants raises a host of problems both in practice and theory for the American police. The street patrol officer and investigator are confronted with alien languages and bewildering customs."

Major challenges presented by immigrants are language barriers and unfamiliar customs.

Often a major challenge is overcoming the language barrier. According to Taft (1991, p. 310): "Of all the problems faced by the officer patrolling the new immigrant ghettos, the language barrier is the most common and the most formidable." He gives as an example a situation in New York City where two patrol officers answered a call to a Brooklyn supermarket. A Korean man inside the store holding a gun shouted something in his native tongue to the two officers. The officers, not speaking Korean, shot and killed him. The Korean, it turned out, was a newly arrived immigrant who had just gotten a job as an armed security guard.

Some officers feel that as long as the immigrants have come to America, they should learn English. Perhaps so, but learning English takes time. In the interim, communication is often necessary. Many techniques for communicating with individuals who are hearing impaired would also be effective for communicating with individuals who speak little or no English. Some departments are encouraging their officers to become bilingual, learning the language of the main minority group in their area. Some are seeking to hire bilingual officers. Others seek assistance from the community, especially in instances when a college or university has language professors who might help.

An AT&T service, the **Language Line,** offers subscribers translation for over 140 languages. Officers who encounter language problems can call a toll-free number from almost any type of telephone and request the language translation needed. The service is available twenty-four hours a day, seven days a week. According to *Law Enforcement News* (1990, p. 3): "Police officers in departments subscribing to the service are issued language identification cards that list all of the languages the service can translate. The cards are designed so that non-English speakers are able to read the name of their language in their native script and point to it so the officer can connect with the required translator."

Even when language is not a barrier, customs may be. As noted by Taft (1991, p. 311): "Compounding the language problems are cultural gaps that can make police work among new immigrants tedious, unnerving, or even dangerous." Some Asian customs, such as coin rubbing to cure children of diseases, may be misinterpreted by teachers or police officers as child abuse. Taft describes the following misunderstandings:

> It is not odd for Vietnamese drivers to leave their cars when pulled over for traffic violations so they can bow in order to show the officer respect. Police who work in Korean communities are warned that handing a ticket or summons to a Korean with one hand instead of two can be interpreted as a sign of disrespect. In Hispanic communities juvenile officers are told not to be insulted if a Cuban youth looks down when facing police. It is a sign of deference to elders.

Taft (1991, p. 308) suggests: "Most of them [the rank-and-file officers] are lost when confronted with both the language and cultural barriers on the street. They complain that refugees are difficult and distant, and often complain that they're playing nursemaid to new arrivals rather than keeping the peace and catching criminals."

Because immigrants often cluster together in poor neighborhoods that have high crime rates, the tendency is to **stereotype** them as being involved in crime, when as often as not they are victims rather than perpetrators. Law enforcement officers must guard against such stereotyping. The great majority of immigrants are law-abiding individuals who are trying to build a new life and to fit into our society.

Trojanowicz and Carter (1990, p. 9) contend: "The primary challenge for law enforcement will be to find ways to meet their needs with special concern for their racial, ethnic, cultural, and religious diversity." This responsibility is reiterated by Taft (p. 309): "Police today remain the most accessible representatives of government for immigrant groups; they still serve as guardians, correcting inappropriate behavior and informally educating the newcomers about law and order."

Another challenge is that of the thousands of *illegal* immigrants entering the United States each year. These immigrants will avoid coming into contact with the police because they fear they will be deported. They are especially easy targets for those who would take advantage of them.

THE GROWING HOMELESS POPULATION

"The homeless in New York City have become a sight as familiar as the Empire State Building or the Statue of Liberty," says Clark (1992, p. 11). "They can be observed just about anywhere in the city—panhandling along pricey Fifth Avenue, setting up cardboard-box shantytowns across from the United Nations, dozing on park benches or on sidewalk heating and ventilation grates." Clark notes that: "Many homeless people say they endure these conditions because they feel safer than they would in the city's overcrowded, violence-ridden shelters, which have become breeding grounds for rampant tuberculosis."

New York City is not alone in its problem of homeless people. The problem can be found throughout the United States. Just who are the homeless? According to Grossman (1987, p. 39): "The word 'homeless' is almost meaningless because it is applied to so many different kinds of people who come from such varied backgrounds." Among the homeless are the following groups (pp. 39–40):

- *Veterans*—mainly from Vietnam, vets in some cities comprise 50 percent of the homeless male population.
- *Mentally ill*—about two decades ago, an estimated quarter-million of today's homeless would have been institutionalized.
- *Physically disabled* or *chronically ill*—those who do not receive any benefits or whose benefits cannot support permanent shelter.
- *Elderly*—the aged whose fixed incomes do not support their needs.
- *Men, women, families*—on the streets after losing a job.
- *Single parents*—usually women, without the resources or skills to establish new lives.
- *Runaway children*—often victims of abuse.
- *Alcoholics/drug abusers*—the troubles of this group often stem from extraneous conditions.
- *Immigrants*—both legal and illegal, who often are not counted among the homeless because they constitute a problem in their own right.
- *Traditional tramps, hobos, transients*—those who have taken to the road for whatever reason, and prefer to be there.

Among the three million plus homeless in the United States are veterans, the mentally ill, the physically disabled or chronically ill, the elderly, men, women, families, single parents, runaway children, alcoholics/drug abusers, immigrants, and traditional tramps, hobos, and transients.

According to Finn (1990, p. 1) 25–45 percent of the homeless are alcoholics and another 29 percent are mentally ill. The large number of mentally ill homeless individuals is partially the result of the **deinstitutionalization** policies of the mid-1960s and 1970s which discharged hundreds of thousands of mentally ill individuals from state psychiatric facilities. According to Murphy (1986, p. ix):

> A crucial element of this approach [deinstitutionalization] was to be the establishment of networks of public and private agencies to provide mental health care and assistance in developing basic living skills.
>
> What really happened, however, is that while large numbers of mentally ill persons were released or retained in the community, the networks of mental health and social services were slow to develop. Once developed, these services were frequently inadequate for the needs of the newly released, many of whom could not live at home, had few social skills, were difficult to treat, and had limited or no financial resources. Community-based mental health and social agencies were not geared to handle persons who were violent, suicidal or otherwise dangerous to themselves or others, the delivery of services was often impeded by bureaucratic obstacles, and the mentally ill population itself resisted treatment.
>
> The result was that persons unable to manage for themselves had no choice but to make it on their own.... With increasing frequency police found themselves called upon to "do something" with persons whose offense, if any, was minor but whose aggravation value was major.

Murphy (1989, pp. 1–10) notes that the police might be called by "Just about any citizen who feels threatened by bizarre behavior or the mere presence of a mentally disabled person. Family, friends or other citizens will request police assistance for one primary reason: 'make the problem go away.'"

Many are not mentally ill, however, but have recently lost their jobs or lost affordable housing (Finn p. 1): "An increasing number of intact families and women with children are homeless as a result of economic dislocation or eviction from their current residences."

Of particular concern are the homeless people who seek refuge in the subway system of New York City. As noted by Clark (1992, p. 11): "There, they face other dangers beyond the routine perils of homelessness—the possibility of being electrocuted by rails crackling with 600 volts of electricity, and the risk of being crushed by several tons of fast-moving subway train." Some 1,200 Port Authority police of New York and New Jersey attempt to deal with the hundreds of homeless people making the tunnels their home. Most, according to Clark, are males between the ages of 23 and 45, hardcore homeless who resist services, with up to 80 percent falling into what Transit Police call the "MICA" category—they're either mentally ill or chemically addicted or both.

Grossman (p. 38) notes: "In communities where sleeping on the streets is against the law, what begins as a social problem becomes a problem of criminal justice."

Officers drag a protester from a state-owned building. The man was among five advocates for the homeless who were arrested.

The Law Enforcement Challenge

As noted by Finn (1990, p. 1): "There are strong pressures on the police to 'do something' about this population, but officers are severely limited in what they can do." He notes several reasons why police may take action against street people:

> This population frequently breaks the law. By camping in public places, panhandling, or trespassing on private property, they may violate local ordinances. Fights among street people are not uncommon. Street people sometimes shoplift, sell drugs, mug passersby, and break into buildings.

> The presence of street people may give the impression that no one cares about a neighborhood, thus signaling to real criminals that they can enter the area and commit offenses with impunity.

> Even the most docile street people generate repulsion and fear among many residents, shoppers, and commuters.... Because many people will not frequent business and entertainment districts populated by the homeless, merchants lose business and employees lose jobs.

> There is frequently little police can do in these situations except to persuade street people to "move along." Police power to arrest the homeless is limited by court rulings with nationwide force and may be further restricted by local statutes or case law. Even when police have legal authority to detain the homeless, jail crowding in most jurisdictions discourages arrests.

> Not enough shelter and treatment facilities will accept police referrals....

> Detoxification facilities are also in short supply—and most available centers have do-not-admit lists for police referrals of chronic public inebriates.

The police response to the homeless problem ranges from strict enforcement of all laws to benign neglect.

While homeless protesters squat, the city and county squabble over the future of this public building. The city wants to build a jail there; the county wants to preserve the building for a youth center. Either way, the homeless will lose out.

According to Finn, in Santa Barbara the police enforce all laws strictly, routinely arresting street people for any infractions of the law, including public drunkenness. In Philadelphia, in contrast, street people are largely ignored except in the winter when they are encouraged to go to shelters.

Leepson (1992, p. 464) notes a widespread backlash against the homeless among the public at large as well as the government, with 1991 seeing budget cuts in state and local government homeless-aid programs and continued police crackdowns on homeless people living in public places. He also suggests a "growing antipathy among the public at street begging, antisocial acts committed by mentally ill homeless persons, and the homeless situation in general." Leepson describes three cities who have passed legislation aimed at helping the police crack down on the homeless:

> In July [1991], Atlanta passed a law giving police the right to arrest homeless persons for loitering in abandoned buildings and engaging in "aggressive panhandling." The previous year Atlanta had begun arresting homeless persons for loitering, public drunkenness, and blocking traffic in the city's downtown area. Police in New York City continued a tough crackdown on panhandling in the city's subways and mounted raids in June and October to dislodge hundreds of homeless persons living in makeshift encampments in a park and city-owned property in Manhattan's East Village. Washington, DC, officials closed two of the city's emergency shelters in August and announced plans for further cutbacks. In 1990 the nation's capital had weakened an ordinance that guaranteed shelter to any homeless person requesting it.

Finn contends that the homeless will continue to be a problem for four reasons (p. 5):

- There are not enough treatment facilities and shelters.
- Existing treatment facilities and shelters often are not attractive enough to interest many street people.

- We do not know how to "cure" chronic public inebriates and most severely mentally ill persons.
- There may always be a core of homeless who prefer to live on the streets and who will continue to create conflict for merchants, neighbors, commuters, and shoppers.

As with the newly arrived immigrants, homeless people are also a challenge to law enforcement because they are often victims. What limited possessions they have may be stolen. They may be assaulted. And they have no phone from which to call 911.

GROWING NUMBERS OF INDIVIDUALS WITH AIDS

"Between 1981, when it was first recognized, and late 1991, Acquired Immune Deficiency Syndrome **(AIDS),** a disease caused by HIV viruses, had claimed the lives of more than 126,000 Americans" (Tesar 1992, p. 350). The growing number of individuals with AIDS is of concern to law enforcement from two perspectives. As noted by Hammett (1990, p. 145):

> AIDS affects criminal justice professionals in two important ways. First, suspects and offenders are frequently people who engage in behavior that puts them at high risk for AIDS. As a result, many law enforcement officers and corrections workers are concerned that they are at increased risk of acquiring the AIDS virus through contact with these suspects and offenders. Second, law enforcement officers can serve a vital educational function in the community because they come into contact with many people who exhibit high-risk behavior—specifically intravenous drug abusers and prostitutes.

Aaron (1991, p. 35) suggests that "a high percentage of police officers are concerned about AIDS" and that "many officers have incorrect information about AIDS."

AIDS is a spectrum of reactions to the Human Immunodeficiency Virus **(HIV)** which infects and destroys specific white blood cells, undermining the body's ability to fight infection.

A person can be infected with HIV and remain symptom-free for years, but even without symptoms that person can transmit the virus to others. Table 13–1 describes the time from HIV infection to AIDS.

A positive result on the laboratory test for the HIV virus means the individual has been infected with HIV. It does *not* mean the person has AIDS or will get AIDS, although this may happen. A negative test result means the antibody to HIV is not detectable. It takes an average of six to twelve weeks after exposure for an infected individual to develop HIV antibody (Group Health, Inc., 1992, p. 5). It may take as long as six months to be detectable.

The Center for Disease Control (CDC) requires that for a patient to be diagnosed with AIDS, the person must have one or more "opportunistic infections" or cancers in the absence of all other known underlying causes of immune deficiency. Symptoms associated with AIDS include fever, weight loss, diarrhea, and persistently swollen lymph nodes.

According to Hammett (1990, p. 146): "The AIDS virus is difficult to transmit and is quite fragile outside the body. It can be destroyed by heat, many common household disinfectants and bleaches, and by washing with soap and water."

Table 13–1   **Time from HIV Infection to AIDS in 1991**

Date of HIV infection.	→	Six or more months for evidence of HIV infection to appear in blood test.	→	Medium latency from HIV infection to clinical AIDS is ten years. Some people, however, show signs of AIDS within a few years.	→	Death from infection or cancer within a year to five years.

Sources: "Testing for AIDS." *The New York Times,* May 5, 1991; and "Detecting the Next Pandemic." *Scientific American,* March 1991.

The AIDS virus is most commonly transmitted by exposure to contaminated blood, semen, and vaginal secretions, primarily through sexual intercourse and needle-sharing by intravenous drug users; from a mother to her fetus during pregnancy; and through infected blood transfusions.

The Occupational Safety and Health Administration (OSHA) has issued rules to protect employees, including police officers, from AIDS. According to Epps (1992, p. 14):

> Designed to prevent AIDS and hepatitis infections in workers who come into contact with blood or bodily fluids as part of their jobs, the mandatory rules require employers to provide workers with training and protective clothing, puncture-proof receptacles for contaminated needles and other medical wastes, and vaccination against the hepatitis virus. . . .
>
> Scope. Covers all employees who could be "reasonably anticipated" as the result of performing their job duties to face contact with blood and other potentially infectious materials. Infectious materials include semen, vaginal secretions, cerebrospinal fluid, peritoneal fluid, amniotic fluid, . . . any body fluid visibly contaminated with blood and all body fluids in situations where it is difficult or impossible to differentiate between body fluids.

Hammett (p. 145) stresses that: "AIDS is a disease of high-risk behavior, not high-risk groups. . . . In fact, everyone must be concerned with a few well-defined types of activities—specifically unprotected sexual intercourse, sharing of needles, and other activities where blood, semen, or vaginal secretions are exchanged." He suggests that:

> It is counterproductive to train staff to wear gloves, gowns, and masks for all contact with persons known or suspected to be infected with AIDS or persons who engage in AIDS high-risk behavior. Such precautions are not normally necessary and may encourage the incorrect view that the AIDS virus can be transmitted by casual contact.

Rather, specific responses to AIDS-related law enforcement concerns should be taught, as summarized in Table 13–2.

According to Gardner and Anderson (1992, p. 570), the U.S. Surgeon General has identified high risk groups as being "drug users using needles, homosexuals, and persons having sexual contacts with persons in these groups, which includes many prostitutes." They note that public officials have used one or more of the following to deal with the threat of AIDS from prostitutes (pp. 570–571):

1. Seek the maximum jail sentence for the offense for which the prostitute is being held. However, with a male prostitute, this could mean infecting other

Table 13–2   Possible Transmission of the AIDS Virus

ISSUE CONCERN	EDUCATIONAL AND ACTION MESSAGES
Human bites	Person who bites usually receives the victim's blood; viral transmission through saliva is highly unlikely. If bitten by anyone, milk wound to make it bleed, wash the area thoroughly, and seek medical attention.
Spitting	Viral transmission through saliva is highly unlikely.
Urine/feces	Virus isolated in only very low concentrations in urine; not at all in feces; no cases of AIDS or AIDS virus infection associated with either urine or feces.
Cuts/puncture wounds	Use caution in handling sharp objects and searching areas hidden from view; needle stick studies show risk of infection is very low.
CPR/first aid	To eliminate the already minimal risk associated with CPR, use masks/airways; avoid blood-to-blood contact by keeping open wounds covered and wearing gloves when in contact with bleeding wounds.
Body removal	Observe crime scene rule: Do not touch anything. Those who must come into contact with blood or other body fluids should wear gloves.
Casual contact	No cases of AIDS or AIDS virus infection attributed to casual contact.
Any contact with blood or body fluids	Wear gloves if contact with blood or body fluids is considered likely. If contact occurs, wash thoroughly with soap and water, clean up spills with one part water to nine parts household bleach.
Contact with dried blood	No cases of infection have been traced to exposure to dried blood. The drying process itself appears to inactivate the virus. Despite low risk, however, caution dictates wearing gloves, a mask, and protective shoe coverings if exposure to dried blood particles is likely (e.g., crime scene investigation).

Source: U.S. Dept. of Justice. National Institute of Justice Reports (December 1987).

male prisoners unless the male prostitute is segregated. After the prison terms expires, the person is released.

2. Use of the quarantine laws of the state that were written to protect public health but are not generally intended to regulate sexual activity.

3. Take the person to the local bus station and buy a ticket for the person to a city in another state. This practice has caused officials in other states to ship prostitutes back to the city of origin with loud complaints regarding the practice.

4. Release the person after urging and trying to convince him or her not to have sexual relations with others for fear of infecting them. This practice is often used when a prostitute permits testing for AIDS in return for a short jail sentence or no jail sentence.

Some states, such as California, have enacted statutes requiring testing for AIDS of persons convicted of prostitution. New York, in contrast, has a 1988 law expressly forbidding mandatory testing.

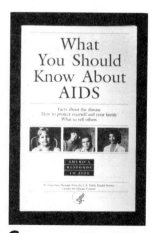

What
You Should
Know About
AIDS

Facts about the disease
How to protect yourself and your family
What to tell others

AMERICA
RESPONDS
TO AIDS

Combatting the AIDS problem requires a joint effort of the police and social service agencies. Education should be one key means to solving the problem.

Some states have passed laws making it a crime to knowingly transmit AIDS.

Although many states have laws forbidding knowingly transmitting venereal diseases, most states do not classify AIDS in this category. According to Gardner and Anderson (1992, p. 571):

Five or more states have created the new crime of knowingly transmitting AIDS. Alabama's statute requires that the offender act "in a manner likely to transmit" a sexually transmitted disease. Nevada's law has provisions for charging attempted murder for prostitutes who continue to sell their sexual services after learning they are infected with the AIDS virus.

Police Officers with AIDS

As noted by Blumberg (1989, p. 207): "Police departments generally employ relatively few individuals at high risk for AIDS." If an officer should contract AIDS, however, the department must consider if the officer poses a threat to other officers or the community as well as how the citizens might react to learning that an officer has AIDS. Blumberg asserts that: "Because AIDS is not spread by casual contact, there is no danger that infected officers will spread this disease to their colleagues." He cautions that: "Evaluating the risk to the public which an infected officer presents is slightly more tricky:"

> Police officers sometimes render assistance to accident victims or to individuals who have received gunshot or stab wounds. Consequently, there is a theoretical possibility, however small, that an infected officer with an open sore could transmit the virus to a citizen....
>
> Despite the small risk that an infected officer would pose to the community, police administrators must also take into account the likely attitude of the citizenry.

Blumberg suggests that community opposition might be extremely high and that the wisest course might be to assign the officer to non-operational duties.

SUMMARY

Our population is becoming older, has more minorities, more immigrants, more homeless, and more individuals with AIDS. People living in ghettos are caught in a vicious cycle of poverty and welfare dependency. In addition, the gap between those who live in poverty and those who are more affluent is widening.

Since 1980 only 12 percent of immigrants have been European. Recent immigrants tend to cluster in specific areas and many speak no English and fear the authorities. Major challenges presented by immigrants are language barriers and unfamiliar customs.

Among the three million plus homeless in the United States are veterans, the mentally ill, the physically disabled or chronically ill, the elderly, men, women, families, single parents, runaway children, alcoholics/drug abusers, immigrants, and traditional tramps, hobos, and transients. The police response to the homeless problem ranges from strict enforcement of all laws to benign neglect.

Another area of concern is the growing number of individuals with AIDS. AIDS is a spectrum of reactions to the Human Immunodeficiency Virus (HIV) which infects and destroys specific white blood cells, undermining the body's ability to fight infection. The AIDS virus is transmitted by exposure to contaminated blood, semen, and vaginal secretions, primarily through sexual intercourse and needle-sharing by intravenous drug users; from a mother to her fetus during pregnancy; and through contaminated blood transfusions. Some states have passed laws making it a crime to knowingly transmit AIDS.

DISCUSSION QUESTIONS

1. Does your community have a large minority population? Newly arrived immigrants? A homeless population?

2. What specific problems will the "graying of America" create for law enforcement?

3. How can law enforcement officers lessen the fear and distrust that immigrants often have for the "authorities"?

4. Which position do you favor for dealing with the homeless: strict enforcement, benign neglect, or somewhere in between?

5. If you were to suddenly become homeless, what do you think would be your biggest challenge?

6. How would you explain AIDS to an elementary-school age child?

7. Is AIDS a legitimate concern of law enforcement?

8. Which of the "growing populations" discussed in this chapter do you feel is the greatest challenge to law enforcement? Why?

9. Which of the "growing populations" do you think may become even more of a challenge in the years ahead? Less of a challenge?

10. Which of these growing populations are more often victims than victimizers? How can the police help reduce the victimization?

TERMS

AIDS, American Dream, de facto segregation, deinstitutionalization, demographers, ghettos, ghetto syndrome, HIV, Language Line, stereotype.

REFERENCES

Aaron, T. "AIDS Education in Law Enforcement." *Law and Order* (March 1991): 35–36.

Blumberg, M. "The Aids Epidemic and the Police." 207–209 in *Critical Issues in Policing: Contemporary Readings,* edited by R. D. Dunham and G. P. Alpert. Prospect Heights, Ill.: Waveland Press, 1989.

Clark, J. R. "Be It Ever So Humble: NY Transit Cops Reach Out to Those Who Would Make the Subways Their Home." *Law Enforcement News,* March 15, 1992, 11–12.

Epps, C. A. "OSHA Issues Regs on AIDS and Hepatitis." *The Police Chief* (March 1992): 14–15.

Finn, P. *Street People.* Washington, D.C.: U.S. Department of Justice, National Institute of Justice, 1990.

Gardner, T. J. and Anderson, T. M. *Criminal Law: Principles and Cases.* 5th ed. St. Paul, Minn.: West Publishing Company, 1992.

Grossman, A. "Homelessness in America." *Police* (August 1987): 38–42, 58–60.

Group Health. *AIDS and Lab Procedures for HIV Blood Tests.* Minneapolis, Minn.: Group Health, 1992.

Hammett, T. M. "Aids and the Law Enforcement Officer." 145–150 in *American Justice, Research of the National Institute of Justice,* edited by L. J. Siegel. St. Paul, Minn.: West Publishing Company, 1990.

Leepson, M. "Social Welfare." 462–464 in *The Volume Library: Yearbook 1992.* Nashville, Tenn.: The Southwestern Company, 1992.

McCord, R. and Wicker, E. "Tomorrow's America: Law Enforcement's Coming Challenge." *FBI Law Enforcement Bulletin* (January 1990): 28–32.

Murphy, G. R. *Managing Persons with Mental Disabilities: A Curriculum Guide for Police Trainers.* Washington, D.C.: Police Executive Research Forum, 1989.

Murphy, G. R. *Special Care: Improving the Police Response to the Mentally Disabled.* Washington, D.C.: Police Executive Research Forum, 1986.

Mydans, S. "Where It Started in LA: Life's Routines Return Feeling of Hopelessness." *(New York Times) Star Tribune,* May 15, 1992, 1A, 6A.

Pace, D. F. *Community Relations Concepts: Human Relations—Race Relations—Ethnic Groups Relations and Community Relations for Criminal Justice.* Placerville, Calif.: Custom Publishing Company, 1991.

"Parlez-vous Miranda Warnings? Language Line Gives Police Gift of Gab." *Law Enforcement News,* September 30, 1990, 3.

Taft, P. B., Jr. "Policing the New Immigrant Ghettos." 308–315 in *Thinking About Police: Contemporary Readings.* 2d ed. edited by C. B. Klockars and S. D. Mastrofski. New York: McGraw-Hill, 1991.

Tesar, J. "Medicine and Health." 348–352 in *The Volume Library: Yearbook 1992.* Nashville, Tenn.: The Southwestern Company, 1992.

Trojanowicz, R. C. and Carter, D. L. "The Changing Face of America." *FBI Law Enforcement Bulletin* (January 1990): 6–12.

Criminals: The Lawbreakers

The most conservative estimates suggest that thirty-six to forty million persons—16 to 18 percent of the total United States population—have arrest records for nontraffic offenses.

—Report to the Nation on Crime and Justice

Do You Know

What the three major sources of information about who commits crime are?

What the classical and the positivist theories of crime causation state?

What are some causes of criminal behavior?

What juvenile delinquency is?

How serious the delinquency problem is?

What status offenses are?

Who is responsible for most crime?

How our criminal justice system may actually be contributing to crime?

▮ INTRODUCTION

Just as since ancient times, society makes laws to protect its members, and there are those individuals who do not abide by the laws. Sometimes breaking the law is not considered criminal; for example, a person who breaks a traffic law by speeding would not be considered by most as a criminal. Other offenses, however, are serious enough that the person committing them is called a criminal or, if under legal age, a juvenile delinquent.

The Bureau of Justice Statistics (1988, pp. 41–51) answers the question, Who is the "typical" offender? with the following facts:

> Most crimes are committed by males, especially by men under age 20.
> Offenders described in arrest, jail, and prison data are predominantly male and disproportionately young and black.
> Participation in crime declines with age.
> Property crimes are more typical of youths than older offenders.
> Adults commit more serious crimes than juveniles.
> A few criminals commit many crimes.
> Juvenile delinquency often foreshadows adult criminal activity.
> The more serious the juvenile career, the greater the chances of adult criminality. Criminal history, age, and drug use are among the best correlates of future criminality.
> Relatively few offenders are female.
> Blacks were more likely than whites to be violent offenders.
> The proportion of Hispanics in prisons and jails is greater than in the total U.S. population.
> A high proportion of offenders grew up in homes with one parent.
> Many offenders have been victims of childhood abuse.
> Most offenders were not married.
> Most inmates have dependent children.
> The level of education reached by jail and prison inmates was far below the national average.
> Many offenders were unemployed.
> A high proportion of adult felons lacked steady employment.
> The proportion of blue-collar workers was higher in prison than in the general population.
> Few inmates had been working in their customary occupations.
> The average inmate was at the poverty level before entering jail.
> Drug use is far greater among offenders than among non-offenders.
> Prison inmates used alcohol more than their counterparts in the general population.
> Drug users are more involved in money-producing crimes.

▮ SOURCES OF KNOWLEDGE ABOUT WHO COMMITS CRIMES

Much crime is never reported. What is reported comes from three major sources.

The three major sources about crime are:

- Official records.
- Self-report surveys.
- Victim surveys.

Official records include data collected by the FBI and reported yearly in their *Uniform Crime Reports* and data collected by the Department of Justice,

Bureau of Justice Statistics, and published in their *Report to the Nation on Crime and Justice*. Such data must be interpreted cautiously, however, because they represent only *reported* crimes.

Self-report studies include one-to-one interviews, surveys, and anonymous questionnaires. In these studies people are usually asked whether they have committed certain crimes and if they were apprehended or not. These findings must also be interpreted cautiously, however, because people often exaggerate, conceal, or forget. In addition, many self-report surveys are conducted with people in correctional facilities.

Victim surveys such as the National Crime Survey (NCS) seek information from people who have been the victims of crimes. The NCS is conducted by the Bureau of Justice Statistics and the United States Census Bureau. They have surveyed about 100,000 individuals each year for the past ten years. According to the NCS, about 34 million crimes occurred in the United States in 1992, a much higher figure than "official" sources indicated.

The major sources do not give uniformly complete information about every kind of offender. In particular they tell us much more about common criminals who commit the offenses of greatest concern to the public: predatory crimes such as robbery and burglary, than they do about white-collar criminals.

WHY DO PEOPLE COMMIT CRIME?

The reason people commit crime has been debated since crime was first defined. Wilson and Herrnstein (1991, p. 58) note:

> Crime is caused, we are told, by the baby boom, permissive parents, brutal parents, incompetent schools, racial discrimination, lenient judges, the decline of organized religion, televised violence, drug addiction, ghetto unemployment, or the capitalist system. We note certain patterns in the proffered explanations. Our tough-minded friends blame crime on the failings of the criminal justice system; our tender-minded ones blame it on the failings of society.

Two philosophical theories have been set forth.

Classical versus Positivist Theory of Crime Causation

The **classical theory** was developed by the eighteenth-century Italian criminologist Cesare Beccaria. This view is held by Thimmesch (1984): "Who breaks the law are those who have convinced themselves that they are special and superior and that what they are doing is not wrong."

The classical theory sees people as free agents with free will. People commit crimes because they want to.

A refinement to the classical theory is the *routine activity theory* developed by Lawrence Cohen and Marcus Felson. This theory states that the volume and distribution of predatory crime (where the offender tries to steal an object directly) correlates highly with three variables found in everyday, routine American life:

1. The availability of suitable targets (homes/stores containing easily sold goods).
2. The absence of watchful guardians (homeowners, neighbors, friends, relatives, guards, security systems, etc.).
3. The presence of motivated offenders (unemployed individuals, drug abusers, etc.).

The presence of these three variables increases the chances of a predatory crime occurring. This theory gives equal weight to the role of victim and offender. It also suggests that the opportunity for criminal action depends on the victim's life-style and behavior.

The **positivist theory** was developed by Cesare Lombroso, an Italian criminologist, at the turn of the century. The studies of Lombroso (1911) support a biological causation for deviant behavior and, in fact, suggest that individuals who do not conform to society's laws and regulations are biologically inferior. *Biological theorists* suggest that how a person acts is basically a result of heredity. Richard Speck, convicted of killing eight Chicago nurses, for example, showed an unusual genetic structure. He had one extra male chromosome. Speck is not the only convicted criminal to display such a genetic abnormality.

The positivist theory sees criminals as "victims of society" and of their own biological, sociological, cultural, and physical environments.

Further, Herrnstein and Wilson (1983, p. 19) state: "Criminologists have long known about the correlation between criminal behavior and IQ, but many have discounted it for various reasons." Nonetheless the correlation does exist, and IQ is thought to be greatly influenced by heredity.

BIOLOGICAL CAUSES OF CRIMINALITY—CRIMINALS ARE BORN, NOT MADE

A medieval law states: "If two persons fall under suspicion of crime, the uglier or more deformed is to be regarded as more probably guilty." We've come a long way in our understanding of the causes of crime since the middle ages, but a person's physical makeup continues to be among those factors which many believe are correlated with criminality (Hess 1990, p. 1).

An individual's physical makeup, or **phenotype,** is a product of his or her genetic constitution or **genotype.** Some researchers contend that criminal behavior may be a product, to some degree, of that genotype. Among the most persuasive arguments supporting a genetic basis for criminal behavior are studies of twins and of adopted children.

Twin studies have lent great support to an active biological agent in criminal behavior. Wilson and Herrnstein (1985) note nine twin studies conducted by Karl Christiansen in which eight of the nine studies reported convincing evidence for a partial genetic basis to criminal conduct.

Rowe (1983) conducted a self-report survey of twins in eighth to twelfth grades in every school district in Ohio. The results strongly suggested genetic involvement in delinquent behavior. In addition, Rowe deduced that shared genes, rather than shared environments, were primarily responsible for the observed **concordances.** An interesting side finding of his survey suggested that the same genetic predispositions that gave rise to delinquent behavior also created the tendency for these youth to develop friendships with other delinquents, thereby reinforcing the behavior.

Adoption studies have also lent support for a biological basis for criminal behavior. A fairly powerful argument can be made for a biological basis of criminality when it can be shown that the adopted-away children of criminal biological parents grow up to display criminal behavior, especially when the adoptive (non-biological) parents are not themselves criminal.

A study by Mednick et al., reported the percentages of criminal adoptive sons with respect to the criminal status of the adoptive parents and the biological parents, as summarized in Table 14–1.

To be counted as criminal, only one of the two parents (if both parents were present) needed a criminal record, although often times both parents had been convicted of criminal activity. The highest percentage of criminal sons come from a situation where both the adoptive and biological parents are criminal—implying a "double-hit" condition, where the biological criminal parents provide the genetic predisposition and the adoptive criminal parents provide the environmental trigger.

The next highest percentage of criminal sons come from a situation where one or both biological parents were criminal, but neither of the adoptive parents was. These results point to genetic transmission of some factor linked to criminal conduct. In fact, Wilson and Herrnstein (1985, p. 97) state that "chronically criminal biological parents (three or more convictions) are three times more likely to produce a chronically criminal son than are biological parents with no convictions."

Table 14–2 summarizes the results of another aspect of the same Mednick study, this time looking at criminal tendencies of brothers adopted into separate homes.

Table 14–1 Adoptive Sons Convicted of Criminal Law Offenses

"Cross Fostering" Analysis: Percentage of Adoptive Sons Who Have Been Convicted of Criminal Law Offenses

| | ARE BIOLOGICAL PARENTS CRIMINAL? | |
	YES	NO
ARE ADOPTIVE PARENTS CRIMINAL?		
Yes	24.5%	14.7%
	(of 143)[a]	(of 204)
No	20.0%	13.5%
	(of 1,226)	(of 2,492)

[a]The numbers in parentheses are the numbers of cases in each cell, for a total sample of 4,065 adopted males.

Source: S. A. Mednick et al. "Genetic influences in criminal convictions: Evidence from an adoption cohort." *Science* (1984): 224.

Table 14–2 Male Siblings Placed in Separate Adoptive Homes

CONCORDANCE FOR CRIMINAL LAW CONVICTIONS IN MALE SIBLINGS PLACED IN SEPARATE ADOPTIVE HOMES

Degree of Genetic Relationship	Percent Pairwise Concordance
Unrelated raised apart	2.5
Half siblings raised apart	12.9
Full siblings raised apart	20.0
Half and full siblings raised apart; criminal father	30.8
Unrelated siblings raised together in adoptive home	8.5

Source: S. A. Mednick et al. "Genetic influences in criminal convictions: Evidence from an adoption cohort." *Science* (1984): 224.

Note that as the degree of genetic relatedness increases, so does the concordance for criminal behavior. Particularly noteworthy is the fact that, of the brothers, both half- and fully-related, who share a criminal father and were raised apart, there was a 30.8 percent pairwise concordance for criminal activity—the highest value of all scenarios. This provides convincing evidence for some underlying genetic mechanism.

The adoption studies, together with the twin studies, provide perhaps the most convincing evidence for a genetic link to criminal behavior.

Herrnstein (1990, p. 11) notes the correlation between criminality and IQ, suggesting that the offender population has an average IQ of about 91–93, compared to the average of 100 of the general population. It must be kept in mind, however, that this is the average IQ of offenders who are *caught*. It might well be that the higher an offender's IQ, the less likely that offender is of being apprehended.

Likewise, most of the studies have been done on "predatory" crimes such as robbery and burglary, not on white-collar crimes such as embezzlement and fraud. This may also greatly influence the findings related to IQ.

Personality, too, has been suggested as linked to criminality. According to Herrnstein (p. 13):

> Many studies have found that the average offender is distinctive, though not necessarily abnormal. He or she is likely to be impulsive, deficient in internal psychic experience and in emotional attachments to other people, mendacious, aggressive, unconventional, fatalistic—if not indifferent—about the future, drawn to adventure or danger, and emotionally disturbed or frankly psychotic. When these traits are sufficiently extreme, offenders are said to suffer from a psychiatric condition called "antisocial personality."

A counterposition to the biological theory is the *behavioral/environmental theory,* which suggests that criminals are *made,* not born.

ENVIRONMENTAL CAUSES OF CRIMINALITY—CRIMINALS ARE MADE, NOT BORN

According to Siegel (1990, p. 4):

> In the 1960s and into the 1970s it was generally agreed that crime was a social phenomenon. Most crime experts linked criminal activity to deteriorated neighborhoods, families in turmoil, lack of jobs and economic opportunities, and other social factors. The prevailing view held that if environment and family life could be improved most criminals would forego law violations and become productive citizens. Federal and state governments funded numerous programs to improve conditions in the inner city and provide legitimate alternatives to crime.

Families and Crime

Loeber (1990, p. 15) suggests that criminality runs in families. He notes that researchers have found the following:

- Parents of delinquent children often lack involvement with their children, provide poor supervision, and administer inadequate or erratic discipline.
- Some parents of delinquent youngsters are themselves not law abiding, thus providing examples of deviant behavior and values that their offspring may imitate.

- Many delinquent youngsters grow up in families that experience adversities, such as marital conflict, divorce, parental illness, poverty, or low socioeconomic status.
- Parents differ greatly in their childrearing skills. Some parents are too harsh, irritable and inconsistent. Others are too lenient, neglectful, or preoccupied with their own concerns.
- One feature of youngster's antisocial development is that they often direct antisocial behavior—particularly aggression and lying—against their parents. As a consequence, parents become less able to exercise their parental authority and may, in effect, especially with older children, abdicate their parental responsibilities.

Employment and Economic Conditions

McGahey (1990, p. 24) notes that many individuals who are arrested are unemployed and poor. In fact, he suggests: "Offenders and prisoners are much more likely to be poor and unemployed than the general population." However, McGahey also notes the following paradoxes:

> During the 1970s, Sun Belt cities had faster rates of economic growth than older cities in the Northwest, but the Sun Belt cities also had higher crime rates. Extremely poor rural areas traditionally have lower crime rates. Towns with rapid economic boom, like oil pipeline towns in Alaska or mining towns in Colorado, had rapid increases in crime as their economies grew.

Indeed, aggregate studies comparing national crime rates and economic indicators, studies of experimental programs to reduce unemployment and the effect on crime, and studies of individuals have all been inconclusive.

Alcohol and Crime

Jacobs (1990, p. 28) states: "There is a close relationship between alcohol and crime, and there is good reason to believe that consumption of alcohol causes crime." Beyond the obvious role it plays in drunk driving and public drunkenness, alcohol is also a factor in much violent crime, especially in intra family crime.

Jacobs cites Marvin Wolfgang's classic study of homicide in Philadelphia in which he found that the killer, the victim, or both were drunk in more than half the cases. Alcohol is also a factor in many cases of rape, aggravated assault, spousal abuse, child abuse, and child sexual abuse. The question remains as to whether people get drunk and then are uninhibited enough to commit crimes or whether they want to commit the crimes and drink to bolster their courage. This may vary from person to person.

Drugs and Crime

According to Siegel (1990, p. 81): "There is significant evidence that use of narcotics is strongly associated with criminality. One research effort found that about 75 percent of all arrestees test positively for drug use." This is the focus of the next chapter.

Siegel and Senna (1988, pp. 92–96) suggest other possible causes of delinquency including biochemical factors and neurological dysfunction. As noted by Drowns and Hess (1990, p. 77):

> Biochemical research focuses on the connection between youths' antisocial behavior and their biochemical makeup. Diet, blood chemistry, hormonal imbal-

ances, and allergies all affect body function and the central nervous system. These physical factors can influence behavior and have, in fact, been linked to anti-social behavior. Diet is of particular interest because an unusually high consumption of artificial food colorings, milk, and sweets may negatively affect behavior.

Neurological research focuses on the brain and nervous system.... A study of inmates on death row showed that a significant number had neurological handicaps due to head injuries they suffered as children.

Raloff (1983) suggests that "inborn chemical imbalances may underlie some of the severest criminal violence."
Timnick (1983) suggests:

The classic criminal's callousness, lack of remorse, inability to learn from experience or punishment, failure to anticipate the consequences of certain acts and seeming inability to "feel" is mirrored by objective physical measurements such as skin conductance tests, pulse rates, chemical levels in the blood, and brain wave tracings—all of which suggest that his nervous system is different, if not deficient.

It is likely that criminal behavior is the result of both heredity and life experiences.

Multiple Causes of Criminal Behavior

Rainwater (1974, p. 7) has identified five different perspectives on the causation of crime:

For the social pathologist, the problem is the defective character of individuals in society.... For the sociologist who focuses on social disorganization, the problem is in ineffectiveness of rules for organizing constructive social processes. For the value conflict theorist, the problem can be understood only as a result either of conflicts among groups in society or of conflicting interests held by a single individual. For the deviance theorist, the problem lies in the instigations to rule violation created by the unequal distribution of opportunities for self-realization in society. For the labeling theorist, the problem is very much in the eye of the beholder, and in the process by which society separates its members into the moral and the immoral, the conforming and the deviant.

Each perspective offers some insight into the complexity of the causations of crime, and each illustrates that there is no single factor responsible for the existence of crime, a fact long accepted by criminologists.

No definitive answer exists as to why people commit crimes. Of the several theories set forth, several suggest a combination of sociological, psychological, and biological factors.

According to the Bureau of Justice Statistics (1983, p. 30):

Historically, the causes of criminal behavior have included explanations ranging from the influences of evil spirits to the abnormal shape of the skull. Contemporary theories for the causes of crime still abound, but can be grouped into three general explanations:

The **sociogenic**—focuses on the environment's effect on the individual and places responsibility for crime on society. It identifies as the causes of crime such factors as poverty, ignorance, high unemployment, inadequate housing, and poor health. To these general environmental factors, it adds the impact of unstable homes, viewing their consequent discord, absence of affection and consistent discipline, and improper moral instruction as especially contributory to juvenile delinquency and youth crime. However, recent research has shown that these factors do not account for long-term fluctuations in crime. Moreover, these factors cannot explain why under certain circumstances, one individual commits a crime and another does not.

The **psychogenic**—focuses on psychological factors and understands crime to be the result of an individual's propensity and inducement toward crime. Propensity toward crime is determined by the individual's ability to conceptualize right and wrong, to manage impulse and postpone present gratifications, and to anticipate and take into account consequences that lie in the future as well as the individual's fondness of risk and willingness to inflict injury on others. Inducement relates to situational factors such as access and opportunity that may provide the individual with the necessary incentives to commit a crime. Under this explanation, while many environmental factors contribute to an individual's propensity to commit crime, the individual is responsible for his behavior. Further, inducement toward committing crime may be inherent in our technological age which, among other things, allows increased access through greater mobility.

The **biogenic**—focuses on biological functions and processes and relates human behavior, specifically criminal behavior, to such biological variables as brain tumors and other disorders of the limbic system, endocrine abnormalities, neurological dysfunction produced by prenatal and postnatal experience of infants, and chromosomal abnormalities (the XYY chromosomal pattern).

Numerous comparisons of groups of criminals with groups of noncriminals have failed to produce any single characteristic or "factor" that absolutely distinguishes the two groups. Further, since the concepts of crime, delinquency, deviant behavior, and the like apply to such a wide range of different kinds of behavior, having in common only the fact that they have been declared contrary to legal rules in various times and places, no single causal explanation can possibly cover this wide range of behaviors.

Many Americans have come to accept the existence of crime as a part of life, a price paid by a democratic society for its high standard of living where those who "have not" seek to get their fair share in any way possible.

Crime has always been a local problem and responsibility, yet it is a social problem that concerns the entire country. Its causative factors and effects have been studied by scientists and researchers for over a century. Its increase in the last quarter-century has so alarmed the country and cities that in the sixties and seventies politicians often dictated a "law and order" platform.

Many causative factors of crime are well beyond the control of the law enforcement officer. Included among these are the population, its density and size, that is, how many people live in a square mile; economics; the legal policies of prosecutors; the educational system of the community; the recreational areas and facilities available; and the religious characteristics of some communities. With a breakdown in discipline in many schools with open, permissive policies and a breakdown in the family value system, crime has become one of America's gravest social problems.

The high level of unemployment, especially among the young, increases the problem. With teenage unemployment in some large cities running 40 percent, attitudes and values may change considerably. The free enterprise system may appear to have little to offer a young person who cannot gain access to the system because no jobs are available. For some the logical alternative is to engage in crime. When frustration, emotional conflict, and desperation overcome individuals because of social and economic conditions, they frequently resort to a crime against property or persons. The result is that those individ-

A drug buy in process. For
some people, unemployment
makes crime look like an attractive way to make money.

uals who have been able to cope with the stresses of the free enterprise system
and are law abiding find themselves victimized by those who have turned to
crime.

Others, such as Sviridoff and Thompson (1983) argue that employment
does not stop crime: "They was making $200 a day in the street, $150 a day
gambling, stealing. And now they gonna work, ten hours a day; seven days a
week for $125?" Employment must be good enough (either pay enough or
offer the promise of advancement) to compete with life on the street.

Likewise, many do not feel that poverty is a cause of crime. Says Morriss
(1982): "Most poor people, in fact, do not steal; poverty does not compel
criminality. During the Great Depression, the streets, homes, parks, and subways were safe—at a time when college professors sold apples on the street
and all Americans were dreadfully deprived."

Senna and Siegel (1990, p. 105) note:

> Recent conceptualizations have tried to integrate a number of different views
> into a complex theory of crime causation. For example, James Q. Wilson and
> Richard Herrnstein have proposed a theory of criminality that holds that crime is
> a matter of personal choice (classical approach) influenced by a person's physical
> traits (biological theory) and family life (social process theory).

They have summarized the most commonly cited theories of causes of crime,
their major premises, and their strengths and weaknesses in Table 14–3.

What is operating in criminal behavior may be a complex *interaction* between predisposing biological/genetic factors and certain environmental
agents which trigger criminal tendencies. In fact, this relationship between
genes and the environment is often viewed as something synergistic—the
genes alone won't cause the behavior, nor will the environment alone. But

Table 14-3   Theories of Criminology: A Review

THEORY	MAJOR PREMISE	STRENGTHS	UNANSWERED QUESTIONS AND OTHER WEAKNESSES
Choice theory	People commit crime when they perceive that the benefits of law violation outweigh the threat and pain of punishment.	Explains how crime can be deterred. Can be empirically tested.	Assumes that crime is a rational choice. Does not explain why people break the law though harsh punishments exist.
Biological	People commit crime because of genetic, biochemical, or neurological deficiencies.	Explains the onset of criminality. Explains why crime is found in all levels of society. Explains why irrational violence occurs.	Does not account for geographic crime patterns. Has not been tested with adequate samples. Does not explain why the crime rates are linked to age, sex, race, income, etc.
Psychological			
Psychoanalytic	People commit crime because of personality imbalances developed early in childhood.	Explains the onset of crime. Explains middle- and upper-class crime.	Does not account for crime rates and patterns. Does not explain why juvenile delinquents do not necessarily become adult criminals.
Social learning	People commit crime when they model their behavior after others they see being rewarded for the same acts.	Explains such patterns as child abuse and family violence.	Does not account for the fact that many who are exposed to violence do not become violent themselves.
Social structure			
Cultural deviance theory	Citizens who obey the street rules of lower-class life (focal concerns) find themselves in conflict with the dominant culture.	Identifies more coherently the elements of lower-class culture that push people into committing street crimes.	Does not provide empirical support for the existence of a lower-class culture. Does not account for middle-class influence. Does not explain upper-class crime.
Strain theory	People who adopt the goals of society but lack the means to attain them seek alternatives such as crime.	Points out how competition for success creates conflict and crime. Suggests that social conditions and not personality can account for crime. Can explain middle- and upper-class crime.	Does not explain why people choose the crime patterns they do. Does not account for violent and senseless acts.
Subcultural theories			
Cohen's theory of delinquent gangs	Status frustration of lower-class boys, created by their failure to achieve middle-class success, causes them to join gangs.	Shows how the conditions of lower-class life produce crime. Explains violence and destructive acts. Identifies conflict of lower class with middle class.	Does not account for middle-class crime. Research efforts have been inconclusive. Ignores delinquency that is rational and profitable.
Cloward and Ohlin's theory of opportunity	Blockage of conventional opportunities causes lower-class youths to join criminal, conflict, or retreatist gangs.	Shows that even illegal opportunities are structured in society. Indicates why people become involved in a particular type of criminal activity. Presents a way of preventing crime.	Does not account for middle-class crime. Assumes that lower-class citizens have the same values as the middle class. Gang surveys indicate that delinquent gang boys do not specialize in one type of crime.
Social ecology theories			
Relative deprivation	Crime occurs when the wealthy and poor live in close proximity to one another.	Explains high crime rates in deteriorated inner city areas.	Does not account for noncriminals in poor areas. Is limited to explaining urban crime rates.
Social disorganization	The conflicts and problems of urban social life and communities control the crime rate.	Accounts for urban crime rates and trends.	Is limited to urban crime rates. Does not account for individual differences.

Table 14–3   (Continued)

THEORY	MAJOR PREMISE	STRENGTHS	UNANSWERED QUESTIONS AND OTHER WEAKNESSES
Social process			
Social learning theories			
Differential association theory	People learn to commit crime from exposure to antisocial definitions.	Explains onset of criminality. Explains the presence of crime in all elements of social structure. Explains why some people in high-crime areas refrain from criminality. Can apply to adults and juveniles.	Where do antisocial definitions originate? How can we measure antisocial definitions or prove that someone has been exposed to an excess of them? Fails to explain illogical acts of violence and destruction. Fails to discuss how to test theory adequately.
Neutralization theory	Youths learn ways of neutralizing moral restraints and periodically drift in and out of criminal behavior patterns.	Explains why many delinquents do not become adult criminals. Explains why youthful law violators can participate in conventional behavior.	Fails to show whether neutralizations occur before or after law violations. Does not explain why some youths drift and others do not. Cannot explain self-destructive acts such as heroin addiction.
Control theories			
Social bond theory	A person's bond to society prevents him or her from violating social rules. If the bond weakens, the person is free to commit crime.	Explains onset of crime; can apply to both middle- and lower-class crime. Explains its theoretical constructs adequately so they can be measured. Has been empirically tested.	Fails to explain differences in crime rates. Fails to show whether a weakened bond can be strengthened. Does not distinguish the importance of different elements of the social bond—for example, is attachment more important than commitment?
Social conflict			
Conflict theory	People commit crime when the law, controlled by the rich and powerful, defines their behavior as illegal. The immoral actions of the powerful go unpunished.	Helps explain the historical development of law and social control. Draws attention to the inequality in the law.	Has not been adequately tested. Cannot explain laws banning corrupt business practices that benefit the rich. Does not explain legal protections for the poor, such as public defenders, paid for by wealthy taxpayers.
Integrated	Youths who grow up in lower-class cultures are more likely to have weakened bonds to society and suffer other socialization problems.	Combines the strength of social process and social structure theory. Can account for higher crime rates in lower-class areas.	Has not been empirically tested.
Cohen and Felson's routine activities theory	Crime is a function of the availability of the victim, the presence of an offender, and the absence of an effective guardian.	Can explain fluctuation in crime rates; draws attention to the role of social control agencies in producing crime.	Does not explain individual motivations for committing crime.
Wilson and Herrnstein's human nature theory	People choose to commit crime when they are biologically and psychologically impaired.	Shows how physical traits interact with social conditions to produce crime. Can account for noncriminal behavior in high-crime areas.	Has not been empirically tested and relies on secondary sources. Does not adequately explain crime rates and trends.

Source: J. J. Senna and L. J. Siegel. *Introduction to Criminal Justice.* 5th ed. Copyright © 1990, pp. 103–105. West Publishing Company: St. Paul, Minn. Reprinted by permission.

functioning together, in the right combination, the individual will display criminal responses.

In effect, as suggested by Hess (1990, p. 10): "The causation of criminality is not a dichotomous either-or proposition, but an interaction of intrinsic and extrinsic, genetic and experiential components."

Problems with Explaining the Causes of Crime

Wilson and Herrnstein (1991, pp. 55–56) suggest three reasons why it is difficult to explain what causes crime:

- Crime is neither easily observed nor readily measured.
- Crime is very common, especially among males.
- The word "crime" can be applied to such varied behavior that it is not clear that it is a meaningful category of analysis.

They note (p. 56): "Crime is as broad a category as disease, and perhaps as useless." Wilson and Herrnstein (p. 57) suggest that a distinction be made between *crime* and *criminality:*

> *Crimes* are short-term, circumscribed events that result from the (perhaps fortuitous) coming together of an individual having certain characteristics and an opportunity having certain (immediate and deferred) costs and benefits....
>
> *Criminality* refers to stable differences across individuals in the propensity to commit criminal (or equivalent) acts.

One reason for focusing on criminality was the "discovery" of the chronic or career criminal by Marvin Wolfgang and his colleagues. The **chronic** or **career criminal** refers to a small group of offenders who are arrested five or more times as juveniles. Although most offenders "age out," chronic offenders continue on with a life of crime. It would seem that traditional programs aimed at rehabilitation have little effect on such criminals. These offenders are also considered *repeat offenders.*

CAREER CRIMINALS

As noted by the *Report to the Nation:*

> The term *career criminal* has been used to describe offenders who:
>
> - have an extensive record of arrests and convictions
> - commit crimes over a long period of time
> - commit crimes at a very high rate
> - commit relatively serious crimes
> - use crimes as their principal source of income
> - specialize (or are especially expert) in a certain type of crime
> - have some combination of these characteristics.

Such criminals are often described as "chronic, habitual, repeat, serious, high-rate, or professional offenders," and commit much of the nation's crime.

> The Chaiken's study of nearly 2,200 offenders coming into California, Michigan, and Texas jails and prisons found that 50 percent of the robbers committed an average of fewer than 5 robberies per year, but a robber in the most active 10 percent committed more than 85 per year. And, while 50 percent of the burglars averaged fewer than 6 burglaries per year, the most active 10 percent averaged more than 232 per year.

For career criminals, prison is the only home they know. Here inmates are being transferred from a New Mexico state penitentiary to prisons in other states.

A Washington, D.C. study reported that 24 percent of all the adult arrests were attributable to just 7 percent of the adults arrested. Similarly, a twenty-two-state study by the Bureau of Justice Statistics of young parolees revealed that about 10 percent of this group accounted for 40 percent of their later arrest offenses (Report to the Nation).

A few criminals commit many crimes. Repeat offenders, juvenile and adult, are responsible for much of our crime.

According to Sherman (1990, p. 6): "Repeat offenders are defined more generally as people who commit serious criminal offenses at a high rate and over a long period." Repeat offenders constitute approximately 15 to 20 percent of all criminals, but commit the majority of serious, detected crime. Sherman (p. 6) notes that of inmates convicted of robbery, half had committed fewer than five robberies per year, but 10 percent had committed over fifty per year. Likewise, of inmates convicted of burglary, half had committed fewer than five burglaries per year, but 10 percent had committed more than 150 per year, with some committing in excess of 1,000 per year. Sherman (p. 7) contends that:

> The criminal justice system may, and should, respond differently to offenders who have committed the same crime if one is believed especially likely to be a serious offender in the future. This view is reflected in "habitual offender" laws which permit "three-time losers" to be sentenced to life imprisonment or unusually long terms.

Garmire (1982, pp. 172–173) stresses that "special attention should be given to the career criminal as a part of a police agency's total investigative effort." Garmire suggests that most police administrators feel that about 10 percent of the criminals are committing the majority of crimes, including robberies, burglaries, larcenies, car theft, forgeries, and fraud. He points out the following:

> Often the career criminal is thought of as a member of organized crime—an invisible figure, highly sophisticated, possessing cunning and cleverness. Such is not, in fact, the case. The career criminal is often known to the police from prior offenses; he or she is most often an opportunist who will commit whatever crime is convenient. Often the career criminal is highly talented in one specialty, such as fraud, passing bad checks, or burglary. A single arrest is not sufficient to alter his or her pattern of crime.

A joint program of the Metro-Dade Police Department and the Bureau of Alcohol, Tobacco and Firearms (ATF) is "Project Achilles," so named because the offender's firearms possession is the targeted vulnerability point which allows the joint investigation. It is the result of two specific sections of the comprehensive Crime Control Act of 1984:

- Armed Career Criminal Act of 1984 (Section 924e).
- Use of a Firearm During a Federal Drug Crime or Crime of Violence (Section 924c).

The sections of this act call for mandatory imprisonment without parole and a discretionary fine for anyone possessing a firearm who has three previous state or federal convictions for a violent felony or serious drug offense.

The basic criteria of Project Achilles are simple, as noted by Farrell and Vince (1991, p. 40):

- A defendant not only must meet the past felony provisions, but must be a current, active violent criminal.
- Once a criminal is identified and designated as a career criminal, plea bargaining cannot be accepted.
- An immediate arrest warrant and pretrial detention must be sought.

Farrell and Vince contend that (p. 40):

> Programs such as Project Achilles, which selectively incapacitates offenders committing a disproportionate number of offenses, translate into economic common sense. In order to get the most bang for the criminal justice buck, imprisonment of the occupational felon is essential.
>
> In particular, with the extreme shortage of prison beds, hard choices must be made on selecting the violators who will fill them. We believe the decision is obvious: incarcerate the person for whom crime is a way of life. Our goal is to reduce crime and violence mandates it, and the economics of the times dictates it. . . .
>
> The firearm can truly be the chink in the criminal's armor that makes him vulnerable to this concerted effort.

In addition to targeting career criminals, police officers and the criminal justice system should focus attention on our youth, especially juvenile delinquents since this is frequently the beginning for the career criminal.

JUVENILE OFFENDERS

States vary as to the age of a juvenile, but most state statutes specify an individual under the age of sixteen or eighteen. **Juvenile delinquency** is behavior by a person not of legal age that violates a local, state, or federal law.

Drowns and Hess (1990, p. 426) define **delinquency** as "actions or conduct by a juvenile in violation of criminal law or constituting a status offense. An error or failure by a child or adolescent to conform to society's expectations of social order, either where the child resides or visits." A **delinquent** is "a child adjudicated to violate a federal, state, or local law; a minor who has done an illegal act or who has been proven in court to misbehave seriously. A child may be found delinquent for a variety of behaviors not criminal for adults (status offenses)."

Juvenile delinquency is behavior by a person not of legal age that violates a local, state, or federal law.

According to ten Bensel (*Child at Risk,* p. 41), national expert on child abuse and neglect, studies have shown that virtually "all violent juvenile delinquents have been abused children," that "all criminals at San Quentin prison . . . studied had violent upbringings as children," and that "all assassins . . . in the United States during the past 20 years had been victims of child abuse."

Juvenile delinquency presents a serious problem with an enormous number of youngsters involved. Self-report studies indicate that approximately 90 percent of all young people have committed at least one act for which they could be brought to juvenile court; however, many of these offenses are minor (for example, fighting, truancy, and running away from home), and state statutes often define juvenile delinquency so broadly that virtually all youngsters could be classified as delinquent.

Even though many offenses are minor, and even though many juvenile offenders are never arrested or referred to juvenile court, alarming numbers are. The Children's Bureau estimates that one in every nine youths and one in every six male youths will be referred to juvenile court for a delinquent act (excluding traffic offenses) before his or her eighteenth birthday.

Arrest statistics point out the severity of the problem, although such statistics may be somewhat exaggerated as juveniles are often more easily caught than adults, and they often act in groups when committing the crimes, thereby producing a greater number of arrests than crimes committed.

Table 14−4, from the Uniform Crime Reports, indicates the type and extent of crimes in which youth are involved. The seriousness of the problem is evident in the amount of relatively serious property crimes: burglary, larceny, and motor vehicle thefts. In addition, although juveniles account for more than their share of arrests for several serious crimes, such arrests are only a small part of all juvenile arrests. Juveniles are most often arrested for petty larceny, fighting, disorderly conduct, liquor-related offenses, and noncriminal conduct such as curfew violations, truancy, incorrigibility, or running away from home.

Youth is responsible for a substantial and disproportionate part of the national crime problem.

A special category of offenses has been established for juveniles, designating certain actions as illegal for any person under the state's defined juvenile age of sixteen or eighteen. These are **status offenses.**

Status offenses are violations of the law applying only to those under legal age. They include absenting from home, truancy, drinking alcoholic beverages, smoking, violating curfew, and incorrigibility.

Table 14–4 Type and Extent of Crimes in which Juveniles Are Involved

OFFENSE CHARGED	TOTAL ALL AGES	NUMBER OF PERSONS ARRESTED				PERCENT OF TOTAL ALL AGES			
		Under 15	Under 18	Under 21	Under 25	Under 15	Under 18	Under 21	Under 25
TOTAL	8,723,889	509,432	1,471,431	2,746,115	4,103,151	5.8	16.9	31.5	47.0
Murder and nonnegligent manslaughter	14,149	237	2,192	5,240	7,778	1.7	15.5	37.0	55.0
Forcible rape	23,246	1,240	3,563	6,690	10,484	5.3	15.3	28.8	45.1
Robbery	120,898	8,271	30,204	53,596	74,867	6.8	25.0	44.3	61.9
Aggravated assault	292,522	12,268	42,240	80,603	127,567	4.2	14.4	27.6	43.6
Burglary	257,486	34,770	85,010	127,794	163,180	13.5	33.0	49.6	63.4
Larceny–theft	1,055,699	149,626	324,533	468,506	592,491	14.2	30.7	44.4	56.1
Motor vehicle theft	134,914	16,753	60,092	84,520	101,363	12.4	44.5	62.6	75.1
Arson	10,935	3,411	5,150	6,209	7,203	31.2	47.1	56.8	65.9
Violent crime[1]	450,815	22,016	78,199	146,129	220,696	4.9	17.3	32.4	49.0
Property crime[2]	1,459,034	204,560	474,785	687,029	864,237	14.0	32.5	47.1	59.2
Crime Index total[3]	1,909,849	226,576	552,984	833,158	1,084,933	11.9	29.0	43.6	56.8
Other assaults	635,546	40,347	101,108	175,427	279,001	6.3	15.9	27.6	43.9
Forgery and counterfeiting	56,205	1,072	5,576	14,991	25,022	1.9	9.9	26.7	44.5
Fraud	170,990	2,225	8,135	27,533	58,514	1.3	4.8	16.1	34.2
Embezzlement	8,714	51	681	2,403	4,120	.6	7.8	27.6	47.3
Stolen property; buying, receiving, possessing	107,011	8,114	29,107	51,010	67,367	7.6	27.2	47.7	63.0
Vandalism	206,675	42,249	84,630	116,255	142,655	20.4	40.9	56.3	69.0
Weapons; carrying, possessing, etc.	143,610	7,304	28,056	54,841	79,133	5.1	19.5	38.2	55.1
Prostitution and commercialized vice	84,141	127	1,157	8,722	25,728	.2	1.4	10.4	30.6
Sex offenses (except forcible rape and prostitution)	63,241	5,165	10,140	15,722	23,557	8.2	16.0	24.9	37.2
Drug abuse violations	692,341	7,689	55,398	157,567	285,115	1.1	8.0	22.8	41.2
Gambling	12,678	141	731	1,813	2,974	1.1	5.8	14.3	23.5
Offenses against family and children	37,158	736	2,198	5,997	12,009	2.0	5.9	16.1	32.3
Driving under the influence	875,407	272	10,756	84,168	233,798	(4)	1.2	9.6	26.7
Liquor laws	438,378	8,482	95,123	288,939	355,036	1.9	21.7	65.9	76.4
Drunkenness	591,291	1,989	16,587	69,158	155,338	.3	2.8	11.7	26.3
Disorderly conduct	512,137	26,923	86,754	169,683	264,404	5.3	16.9	33.1	51.6
Vagrancy	29,306	713	2,173	5,099	8,574	2.4	7.4	17.4	29.3
All other offenses (except traffic)	1,961,488	61,216	205,946	487,299	837,109	3.1	10.5	24.8	42.7
Suspicion	16,264	959	2,732	4,821	7,305	5.9	16.8	29.6	44.9
Curfew and loitering law violations	61,506	17,692	61,506	61,506	61,506	28.8	100.0	100.0	100.0
Runaways	109,953	49,390	109,953	109,953	109,953	44.9	100.0	100.0	100.0

[1]Violent crimes are offenses of murder, forcible rape, robbery, and aggravated assault.
[2]Property crimes are offenses of burglary, larceny–theft, motor vehicle theft, and arson.
[3]Includes arson.

Source: Uniform Crime Reports, *Crime in the United States*, 1991.

According to the *Report to the Nation on Crime and Justice* (1988):

Most juvenile delinquents do not go on to become adult criminals, but many do continue to commit crimes.

In Marion County, Oregon, 30 percent of the juvenile boys convicted of serious crimes were later convicted of serious crimes as adults.

In Chicago, 34 percent of the boys appearing in juvenile court later went to jail or prison as adults.

The more serious the juvenile career, the greater the chances of adult criminality. In New York City, 48 percent of the juveniles who had only one year of juvenile activity had one or more adult arrests and 15 percent were serious adult offenders. In contrast, 78 percent of those with lengthy juvenile careers were arrested as adults and 37 percent were serious adult offenders.

A few criminals commit many crimes. Studies in Philadelphia, Pennsylvania; Racine, Wisconsin; and Columbus, Ohio, show that 23 to 34 percent of the juveniles involved in crime are responsible for 61 to 68 percent of all crimes committed by juveniles. In a national sample of United States youths ages eleven to seventeen, the 7 percent who were the most active offenders committed about 125 crimes per year each, whereas the 55 percent who were the least active committed an average of fewer than 8 per year.

THE ROLE OF OUR CRIMINAL JUSTICE SYSTEM

Although our criminal justice system may not actually cause crime, several people feel that it promotes crime.

Our criminal justice system, including plea bargaining, low conviction rates, lack of prison space, and lenient juvenile justice, may promote crime.

Oran (1985, p. 228) says: "**Plea bargaining** is discussions between a prosecutor and a criminal defendant's lawyer, in which the defense lawyer generally offers to have the defendant plead guilty in exchange for the prosecutor's agreeing to accept a *plea* to a less serious charge, to drop some charges, or to promise not to request a heavy sentence from the judge."

According to Rosenblatt (1981):

There are specific reasons for the nation's incapacity to keep its street crime down. Almost all of these reasons can be traced to the American criminal justice system. . . . It is not that there are no mechanisms in place to deal with American crime, merely that the existing ones are impractical, inefficient, anachronistic, uncooperative, and often lead to as much civil destruction as they are meant to curtail. . . . The majority of criminals go untouched by it [the system]. . . . Even when a suspect is apprehended, the chances of his getting punished are mighty slim.

These sentiments are echoed by Dershowitz (1982):

Incredible disparity makes the system a roulette wheel. It depends on where you commit a crime, which judge hears the case and whether you're smart enough to follow the first rule of crime. Commit it with somebody more important than you so that you can turn them in and make a plea bargain for yourself. The net result is that, however tough we may be in theory, the average criminal does not think he's going to do time for serious crimes. Criminals are gamblers by nature. They say to themselves, "If there's any chance that I might get off, I'll probably get off."

SUMMARY

The three major sources about crime are official records, self-report surveys, and victim surveys. Crimes are committed by youths and adults. Why? Two philosophies exist. The classical theory sees people as free agents with free will. People commit crimes because they want to. The positivist theory, in contrast, sees criminals as "victims of society" and of their own biological, sociological, cultural, and physical environments. It is likely that criminal behavior is the result of both heredity and life experiences. No definitive answer exists as to why people commit crimes. Of the theories set forth, several suggest a combination of sociological, psychological, and biological factors.

A few criminals commit many crimes. Repeat offenders, juvenile and adult, are responsible for much of our crime. Juvenile delinquency is behavior by a person not of legal age that violates a local, state, or federal law. Youth is responsible for a substantial and disproportionate part of the national crime problem. Many youth are guilty of status offenses, violations of the law applying only to those under legal age. They include absenting from home, truancy, drinking alcoholic beverages, smoking, violating curfew, and incorrigibility.

In addition, our criminal justice system, including plea bargaining, low conviction rates, lack of prison space, and lenient juvenile justice, may promote crime.

DISCUSSION QUESTIONS

1. What problems can arise in the legal definition of a juvenile delinquent and serious crimes such as murder?

2. Is there one single causative factor for crime today?

3. How can the personal biases of those in the criminal justice system be avoided in handling criminals in the community?

4. What are some high risk factors that contribute to a criminal career?

5. How long does one remain a criminal—until the crime has been "paid for" or for a lifetime?

6. What factors prevent most juvenile offenders from becoming adult criminals?

7. Why are more arrests among juveniles for theft than any other crime?

8. How reliable are self-report questionnaires given juveniles about their deviant behavior?

9. Are parents responsible for their children becoming criminals?

10. Have you ever known an adult convicted of a crime? If so, what was he or she like?

TERMS

biogenic, career criminal, chronic criminal, classical theory, concordances, delinquency, delinquent, genotype, juvenile delinquency, phenotype, plea bargaining, positivist theory, psychogenic, sociogenic, status offenses.

REFERENCES

Bureau of Justice Statistics. U.S. Department of Justice. *Report to the Nation on Crime and Justice.* Washington, D.C.: U.S. Government Printing Office, 1983, 1988.

Bureau of Justice Statistics. U.S. Department of Justice. *National Update,* vol. 1, no. 4. Washington, D.C.: U.S. Government Printing Office, April, 1992.

Dershowitz, *U.S. News & World Report,* August 9, 1982.

Drowns, R. W. and Hess, K. M. *Juvenile Justice.* St. Paul, Minn.: West Publishing Company, 1990.

Farrell, J. S. and Vince, J. J., Jr. "Cost-Effective Pursuit of the Career Criminal." *The Police Chief,* (March 1991): 39–40.

Garmire, B. L. (Ed.) *Local Government Police Management.* 2d ed. Washington, D.C.: International City Management Association, 1982.

Herrnstein, R. "Biology and Crime." In *American Justice, Research of the National Institute of Justice,* edited by L. J. Siegel. St. Paul, Minn.: West Publishing Company, 1990, 11–14.

Herrnstein, R. J. and Wilson, J. Q. "Are Criminals Made or Born?" In *Encyclopedia of Crime and Justice.* Vol. 4, edited by S. H. Kadish. New York: The Free Press, 1983.

Hess, C. M. *The Search for a Genetic Basis for Criminal Behavior.* Unpublished Paper. University of Minnesota (CPSY 5329) March, 1990.

Jacobs, J. B. "Crime File: Drinking and Crime." In *American Justice, Research of the National Institute of Justice,* edited by L. J. Siegel. St. Paul, Minn.: West Publishing Company, 1990, 28–31.

Loeber, R. "Crime File: Families and Crime." In *American Justice, Research of the National Institute of Justice,* edited by L. J. Siegel. St. Paul, Minn.: West Publishing Company, 1990, 15–18.

Lombroso, C. *Crimes: Its Causes and Remedies.* Montclair, N.J.: Patterson Smith, 1968. Originally published in 1911.

McGahey, R. "Crime File: Jobs and Crime." In *American Justice, Research of the National Institute of Justice,* edited by L. J. Siegel. St. Paul, Minn.: West Publishing Company, 1990, 24–27.

Mednick, S. A. et al. "Genetic Influences in Criminal Convictions: Evidence from an Adoption Cohort." *Science,* 1984, 224.

Morriss, F. "Lack of Virtue, Not Jobs, at Root of Social Unrest." *The Wanderer,* December 16, 1982.

Oran, D. *Law Dictionary for Nonlawyers.* 2d ed. St. Paul, Minn.: West Publishing Company, 1985.

Rainwater, L. *Inequality and Justice.* Chicago: Adline Publishing, 1974.

Raloff, J. "Locks—A Key to Violence?" *Science News,* August 20, 1983.

Report to the Nation on Crime and Justice. 2d ed. U.S. Department of Justice, Bureau of Justice Statistics, March 1988.

Rosenblatt, R. "Why the Justice System Fails." *Time,* March 23, 1981.

Rowe, D. C. "Biometrical Genetic Models of Self-Reported Delinquent Behavior: A Twin Study." *Behavior Genetics,* 13 (1983): 473–489.

Senna, J. J. and Siegel, L. J. *Introduction to Criminal Justice.* 5th ed. St. Paul, Minn.: West Publishing Company, 1990.

Sherman, L. "Crime File: Repeat Offenders." In *American Justice, Research of the National Institute of Justice,* edited by L. J. Siegel. St. Paul, Minn.: West Publishing Company, 1990, 6–9.

Siegel, L. J. (Ed.) *American Justice, Research of the National Institute of Justice.* St. Paul, Minn.: West Publishing Company, 1990.

Siegel, L. J. and Senna, J. J. *Juvenile Delinquency.* 3d ed. St. Paul, Minn.: West Publishing Company, 1988.

Sviridoff, M. and Thompson, J. W. *Crime and Delinquency,* April 1983.

ten Bensel, R. Testimony. Quoted in *Child at Risk,* 41. Office of Juvenile Justice and Delinquency Prevention. U.S. Department of Justice. Washington, D.C.: U.S. Government Printing Office (no date).

Thimmesch, N. *Human Events,* February 25, 1984.

Timnick, L. *The Los Angeles Times,* June 26, 1983.

Wilson, J. Q. and Herrnstein, R. J. *Crime and Human Nature.* New York: Simon and Schuster, 1985.

Wilson, J. Q. and Herrnstein, R. J. "Crime and Human Nature." In *Taking Sides: Clashing Views on Controversial Issues in Crime and Criminology.* 2d ed., edited by R. C. Monk. Guilford, Conn.: The Dushkin Publishing Group, 1991, 54–64.

CHAPTER 15

The Drug Problem:
A Nation of Users

Trouble, with a capital T that rhymes with D, that stands for drugs.
—Law Enforcement News

Do You Know

What act made it illegal to sell or use certain narcotics and dangerous drugs?

What narcotics and "dangerous" drugs are and what results they produce?

What exactly federal law prohibits in relation to narcotics and dangerous drugs?

What the most commonly observed drugs on the street, in possession of users, and seized in drug raids are and what the most frequent drug arrest is for?

What the most widely abused drug in the United States is?

If drug use and alcohol abuse are linked to crime?

What approaches to the drug problem have been suggested?

██████████ **INTRODUCTION**

"While police officials struggled to establish and maintain the innovations of recent years, such as community- or problem-oriented policing and the application of new technologies," says Rosen (1989, p. 1), "for the most part the criminal justice system found its attention [in 1988] riveted on three things: drugs, drugs, and more drugs." Rosen says that the "war on drugs" is "no longer a metaphorical catchphrase." Instead, it has "turned into an armed conflict of house-to-house fighting." According to Rosen, during 1988, "Prisons overflowed as an outgrowth of rising arrest rates, and police found themselves dealing more and more with recycled repeat offenders who carried increasingly powerful firearms." According to the director of the FBI, William Sessions (1989, p. 11):

> Our nation is facing the greatest law enforcement crisis in its history. It is a crisis of drug trafficking and drug use—and the enormous amount of violent crime caused by drugs.

Law Enforcement News (1991, p. 1) notes that: "As a nation, the United States spends almost as much on illegal drugs as it does to fight them. A recent Federal report places the retail value of illegal drugs at about $40.4 billion, as compared to $46 billion spent by the Federal, state, and local governments to fight drugs."

An ABC documentary, "Drugs: Why This Plague," pointed out that American history is filled with drug use, including alcohol and tobacco. As the early settlers moved west, one of the first buildings in each frontier town was a saloon. Cocaine use was also common by the 1880s. At the turn of the century cocaine was the "drug of choice," said to cure everything from indigestion to toothaches. It was added to flavor soft drinks like Coca-Cola in 1886. In effect, cocaine became the "all-American" drug.

In 1909 a presidential commission reported to President Theodore Roosevelt that cocaine was a hazard, leading to loss of livelihoods and lives. As the public became increasingly aware of the hazards posed by cocaine and other drugs, they pressed for legislation against the use of such drugs.

██████████████████████████

In 1914 the Harrison Narcotics Act was passed by the federal government, making it illegal to sell or use certain drugs.

In 1920 every state required that their students learn about the effects of narcotics. And in 1937, under President Franklin Delano Roosevelt, marijuana became the last of the drugs to be banned. For a quarter of a century the drug problem lay dormant.

Then came the 1960s, a time of youthful rebellion, a time of Haight Asbury and the flower children, a time to protest the war in Vietnam. A whole culture had as its theme: tune in, turn on, and drop out—often through marijuana and LSD.

By the 1970s, according to one survey, marijuana had been tried by 40 percent of eighteen to twenty-one-year-olds, and it was being used by many soldiers fighting in Vietnam. Many other soldiers, however, turned to heroin. At the same time, an estimated half a million Americans began using heroin back in the states. The peak of the drug culture came in the mid-1970s, and with it came the emergence of heavy cocaine use.

The United States became the most drug-pervaded nation in the world, with marijuana leading the way. One law enforcement student, in fact, wrote a term paper titled, "The United States: The World's Largest Drug Store." The 1980s saw a turnaround in drug use, with celebrities advocating, "It's not cool to do drugs," and "Just say no to drugs." But at the same time other advertisements advocated that where alcohol and smoking are is where the "fun is at." The United States remains a culture of pill poppers.

- Can't sleep?—take a pill.
- Want to lose weight?—take a pill.
- Want to quit smoking?—take a pill.
- Want to relax?—take a pill.
- Got a headache?—take a pill.
- Don't want children?—take a pill.

Sometimes the pills taken are legal, but other times they are not.

ILLEGAL POSSESSION, SALE, OR DISTRIBUTION OF NARCOTICS AND DANGEROUS DRUGS

Narcotics are drugs that produce sleep, lethargy, or relief of pain, including heroin, cocaine, crack, and marijuana. **Dangerous drugs** are addicting, mind-altering drugs such as depressants, stimulants, and hallucinogens.

It is a crime in most states to use or sell narcotics and dangerous drugs without a prescription. Additionally, the abuse of these substances is often closely connected to other types of crime. Homicide, rape, burglary, armed robbery, and shoplifting have been connected with the use of narcotics and dangerous drugs and with the drug abuser's need for money to support his or her habit.

The misuse and abuse of drugs and their illegal sale and disposition have become a national problem not limited to slum areas or to the use of hard narcotics. Consequently, new amendments by Congress, laws by state legislatures, and ordinances by local political subdivisions provide stronger regulation of the manufacture, distribution, delivery, and possession of many narcotics, depressants, stimulants, and hallucinogens.

In most states narcotics and dangerous drugs may not be used or sold without a prescription. Federal law prohibits sale or distribution not covered by prescription, but it does *not* prohibit possession for personal use.

Narcotics

Prohibited narcotics include heroin, cocaine, crack, and marijuana.

Heroin is a commonly abused narcotic. It is synthesized from morphine and is up to ten times more potent in its effects. Morphine comes from opium, which is derived from the dried resin from the base of the opium poppy grown in Afghanistan, Burma, Iran, Laos, Mexico, and Thailand. Heroin is physically addictive and expensive. It causes an easing of fears, followed by euphoria, and finally stupor. According to Kaplan (n.d., p. 1):

> Although heroin can be smoked or eaten, injection into a vein is the preferred means by which addicts in the United States take the drug....
>
> A primary reason for concern about heroin addiction in the United States today is the heroin addict's need to violate the law in order to raise sufficient funds to support the habit.... A rough estimate is that there are 500,000 addicts whose average daily consumption of heroin has a retail cost of about sixty dollars per day. The best estimates suggest that 60 percent of this roughly fifteen billion dollars per year is obtained from consensual crimes, such as prostitution and heroin sales, from welfare payments, and from occasional work. Most of the remainder, approximately six billion dollars, comes from the commission of property crimes, such as burglary, shoplifting, and other "hustles...."
>
> In all, the best estimate is that addicts commit about six times as many crimes while they are in a "run" of heroin use as when they are abstinent or using the drug irregularly.

Cocaine

Cocaine hydrochloride is a central nervous system stimulant narcotic. It is derived from the Erythroxylon coca bush of South America. Peruvian and Bolivian Indians chewed leaves of the coca bush for pleasure and also to enable them to do strenuous work. Sigmund Freud described the euphoric effects of cocaine and was supposedly one of its first abusers.

Peru and Bolivia are presently the main sources of cocaine. Cultivation of the bush is legal in these countries, with most of the product sold to flavor soft drinks and for medical uses.

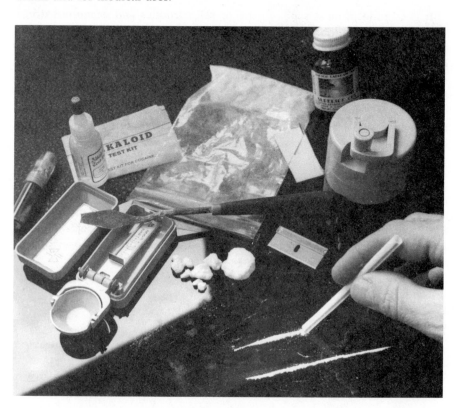

The paraphernalia used for preparing cocaine constitutes evidence of use of illegal drugs.

Coca leaves are soaked in a solution of water, potassium carbonate, and a petroleum distillate such as kerosene. This produces a doughlike sludge called *paste* that is dried and shipped to clandestine laboratories throughout Latin America. The cocaine that is extracted from the paste looks somewhat like rock sugar candy and is often called **rock.** Its purity varies from 70 to 80 percent. A more refined form of cocaine is called **flake.** It comes in flat crystals and is approximately 95 percent pure.

Cocaine smuggling is big business, run primarily by Colombians. They often are assisted by tourists and students, called **mules.** Larger quantities are brought in by professional smugglers, often using private planes and boats.

Cocaine may be inhaled or injected, producing euphoria, excitation, anxiety, a sense of increased muscular strength, talkativeness, and a reduction in feelings of fatigue. The pupils frequently become dilated, and the heart rate and blood pressure usually increase. Physical dependence on cocaine is possible, and psychological dependence can be extreme.

Crack

Crack is a relatively new form of cocaine first observed in Southern California in 1981. Traditional "freebasing" of cocaine converts cocaine hydrochloride (CH1) back to cocaine base for smoking. It uses solvents to remove dilutents, producing a powdery material. Danger of explosion or fire is high. In the crack procedure, only baking soda or ammonia and water are added to cocaine HC1. The mixture is heated and cooled, then filtered to collect the crystals. Eliminating use of flammable solvents eliminates risk of explosion and fire.

Crack is usually sprinkled on a marijuana or tobacco cigarette or mixed with marijuana or tobacco and then smoked in a pipe. It produces the same intense "rush" and euphoria that freebase cocaine does but at a greatly reduced cost.

Pellet-size bits or chunks of crack are often put into small plastic vials and sold for much less than a similar amount of cocaine. Because of its low price crack has been called the "equal opportunity drug."

Marijuana

Marijuana is probably the most socially acceptable of the illegal drugs; legislation lessening penalties for its use has frequently been proposed. Although it has been known for nearly five thousand years, it is one of the least understood, yet most versatile, of all natural drugs. Marijuana is derived from the cannabis plant, which still grows wild in many parts of the United States.

Marijuana is a hardy weed adaptable to most climates. It grows best in moderate moisture and direct sunlight, but this hemp plant can survive in extremely adverse conditions.

The marijuana plant is distinctive, resembling a poinsettia. It grows at a phenomenal rate from a seedling to a twenty-foot plant in one year. The leaves are then picked and dried in the sun, a stove, or even a clothes dryer. According to Peoples and Hahn (1991, p. 119):

> The drug of choice among abusers since the 1960s, marijuana is currently used by approximately 10 million Americans, making it the most abused drug in the country. Instead of the foreign-grown variety sought after in the '60s and '70s, however, today's abuser prefers the homegrown, highly potent **sinsemilla** variety....

Last year, over 1,600 reported indoor growing operations were seized by federal, state and local agencies. This represents a 20 percent increase over the previous year . . . It is currently estimated that 25 percent of cannabis consumed in the United States is produced domestically; it is anticipated that by 1995, 50 percent of the marijuana consumed in this country will be grown here.

Given the increase in "home-grown" marijuana, the Drug Enforcement Administration (DEA) has been conducting a special enforcement program targeted at the domestic indoor cannabis cultivation industry. Called "Operation Green Merchant," the program joins DEA, state, and local law enforcement agencies in identifying indoor growers, gathering evidence against them, and arresting them. Since the program's inception over 700 grow sites have been seized, along with millions of dollars in drug assets. Hundreds of violators have been arrested.

Marijuana is frequently used in the form of cigarettes, which have a distinctive odor like that of burning alfalfa. Its scent is clearly different from tobacco.

Marijuana cigarettes, also called joints, are usually rolled with two cigarette papers and crimped at both ends. They are usually smoked with the aid of a holder, called a roach holder or alligator clip.

When smoked, marijuana enters the bloodstream quickly, causing rapid onset of symptoms. The effects of the drug on the user's mood and thinking vary widely, depending on the amount and strength of the marijuana as well as the social setting and the effects anticipated. The drug usually takes effect in about fifteen minutes and lasts from two to four hours.

"Social" doses of one or two cigarettes may cause an increased sense of well-being; initial restlessness and hilarity followed by a dreamy, carefree state of relaxation; alteration of sensory perceptions including expansion of space and time; a more vivid sense of touch, sight, smell, taste, and sound; a feeling of hunger, especially a craving for sweets; and subtle changes in thought formation and expression. According to Bennett and Hess (1991, p. 578):

> Marijuana is variously classified as a narcotic, a depressant, and a hallucinogen and is the most controversial of the dangerous drugs. The use of marijuana was outlawed by the Federal Marijuana Tax Act of 1927.
>
> A wide spectrum of opinions exist regarding the harmfulness of marijuana. Some feel it should be legalized; others feel it is a very dangerous drug. Many surveys document psychological addiction from continued use of marijuana, as is true for most drugs. Research does not indicate that marijuana is physically addictive. However, some users claim withdrawal symptoms similar to those resulting from discontinuance of hard narcotics.
>
> Whether marijuana abusers continue on to hard narcotics or other controlled substances has not been totally researched. It is known that the vast majority of hard narcotics users once used marijuana, but how many marijuana users proceed to hard drugs is unknown. Marijuana is frequently used with alcohol, barbiturates, and amphetamines. The marijuana user may be more susceptible to experimenting with other drugs while under the influence of marijuana.
>
> Although research does not clearly establish or disclaim harmful results from continued use, marijuana is an illegal drug in all states, except Alaska, making its use or sale a violation of the law.

The Asian variety of marijuana provides the drug hashish, which has the same properties as marijuana but is four times more intoxicating.

Dangerous Drugs

Depressants (Barbiturates) Depressants, or **barbiturates,** are sedatives taken orally as a small tablet or capsule to induce sleep or to relieve tension. Homemakers are the most common abusers of barbiturates.

Small amounts of barbiturates make the user relaxed, sociable, and good-humored. Heavy doses cause sluggishness, depression, deep sleep, or coma. A barbiturate addict usually takes ten to twenty pills a day and often shows symptoms of drunkenness: speech becomes slurred and indistinct, physical coordination is impaired, and mental and emotional instability occurs. Many barbiturate addicts are quarrelsome and have a "short fuse." Overdoses are common and frequently cause intentional or accidental death.

Stimulants (Amphetamines) Stimulants, or **amphetamines,** are taken orally as a tablet or capsule, or intravenously, to reduce appetite and/or relieve mental depression. They are often taken by truck drivers, salespeople, college students, and businesspeople who want to stay awake for long periods and by people who want to lose weight.

Normal doses produce wakefulness, increased alertness and initiative, and hyperactivity. Large doses produce exaggerated feelings of confidence, power, and well-being.

Habitual users may take amphetamines for three or four days, eat nothing, and drive themselves until they black out from exhaustion. Heavy users may exhibit restlessness, nervousness, hand tremors, pupil dilation, dryness of mouth, and excessive perspiration. They may be talkative and experience delusions and/or hallucinations. Although small doses may produce cheerfulness and an unusual increase in activity, heavy and prolonged use may produce symptoms resembling paranoid schizophrenia. Handling this deviant behavior has always been a source of concern and danger for law enforcement officers.

Hallucinogens **Hallucinogens** may produce distortion, intensify sensory perception, and lessen the ability to discriminate between fact and fantasy. The unpredictable mental effects include illusions, panic, psychotic or antisocial behavior, and impulses toward violence and self-destruction. Probably the best known hallucinogen is LSD, which gets its name from the colorless, odorless substance lysergic acid diethylamide from which it is made.

Although hallucinogens are usually taken orally as a tablet or capsule, their physical characteristics allow them to be disguised as various commonly used powders or liquids. LSD has been found on chewing gum, hard candy, crackers, vitamin pills, aspirin, blotting paper, and postage stamps.

Other hallucinogens include DMT (dimethyltryptamine), a powerful drug similar to LSD; mescaline, a chemical derived from the peyote cactus; and psilocybin, a natural ingredient in a species of Mexican mushroom.

PCP (phencyclidine), another hallucinogen, was developed as an anesthetic and is still used as such by veterinarians. It appeared in San Francisco in the 1960s and was called the "Peace Pill." As its use spread across the country it was called by various other names, including angel dust, mist, zoom, super-weed, and angel weed.

Oglesby, Faber, and Faber (1982) stress that police officers should recognize the symptoms of PCP intoxication, understand the long-term effects of PCP use, and be aware of the aggression, violence, and super-human strength which may be experienced by users.

The *symptoms* of PCP intoxication vary greatly from individual to individual, depending on the dosage, previous use of the drug, and how it was ingested. Two symptoms, however, are almost always present in PCP intoxication: nystagmus and hypertension. **Nystagmus** is an uncontrolled, bouncing or jerking of the eyeball when the intoxicated person looks to the extreme right or left, and up or down. **Hypertension,** that is, elevated blood pressure, is present with the nystagmus.

PCP use has *long-term effects.* The chronic PCP user may experience emotional difficulties such as chronic depression, paranoia, auditory hallucinations, anxiety, and confusion. Social isolation and personality change may occur after extended use as may attempted suicide.

Much of the concern over the widespread use of PCP is the drug's ability to produce bizarre, sometimes tragic *aggressive, violent behavior.* Users often have hallucinations and disturbed thought patterns that may produce panic, which triggers aberrant or aggressive behavior. Police officers have often been injured when attempting to subdue a person under the influence of PCP. Another possible characteristic of PCP intoxication is preoccupation with death or death-like thoughts. There is often a feeling of being out of the body and having a lack of sensory perception, resembling the experience of death itself.

Finally, the evidence is overwhelming that some PCP users "freaked out" on the drug may exhibit *super-human strength* while showing aggression. One explanation for this phenomenon is that the mind completely controls the body and causes users to believe the hallucinations are real. Users believe what they see and panic. The adrenalin flows, and they fight desperately for survival using any and every method to escape the terrifying dilemma. The super-human strength is also directly related to the analgesic qualities of the drug under which users feel little or no pain.

A "bad trip" from any of the hallucinogens can be "more devastating than the most horrible nightmare."

Deliriants

Deliriants are volatile chemicals that include airplane glue, gasoline, lighter fluid, paint thinner, Freon, carbon tetrachloride, and other volatile commercial products. Although technically neither narcotics nor dangerous drugs, deliriants may be a prime cause of psychological dependency among young people.

Deliriants may be sniffed or inhaled either directly from a container or from a paper or plastic bag or cloth. Redness or irritation commonly occurs around the nostrils and lips. Other reactions vary according to the deliriant used and the amount inhaled; however, deliriants generally produce a "high" similar to that produced by alcohol.

Common Factors

In spite of numerous differences produced by use of various kinds of narcotics and dangerous drugs, certain common factors occur, the most important of which are (1) they are mind altering, (2) they may become addicting—either physically or psychologically, and (3) overdosage may result in convulsions and death. Table 15–1 describes the most common controlled substances uses and effects.

The most commonly observed drugs on the street, in possession of users, and seized in drug raids are heroin, opium, morphine, codeine, cocaine, crack, and marijuana. Arrest for possession or use of marijuana is the most frequent drug arrest.

Drug Abuse, AIDS, and the HIV Virus

An estimated 50 percent of intravenous drug abusers are infected with the HIV virus. And intravenous drug abusers comprise 17 percent of AIDS victims. Among new reported cases of AIDS, approximately one-third were intravenous drug abusers. According to the Centers for Disease Control (*Aids Policy and Law,* n. d.), "Researchers now see intravenous drug abuse as the major vehicle for the AIDS virus to be spread to the general public."

It is estimated that states have enacted more than six hundred pieces of AIDS-related legislation dealing with employment, health care, insurance liability, and criminal conduct. Some states are applying criminal punishment to those who knowingly spread AIDS.

Societal Effects

Although drug abusers may claim that it is their right to ingest, smoke, sniff, or inject whatever they want into their own bodies, the results of such actions do have serious implications for society. Users are no longer in control of what they think, say, or do and often pose a threat to other members of society.

The occasional user of marijuana may argue that no harm is being done to anyone, but researchers point out that a person predisposed to the abuse of one drug may be likely to abuse other, stronger drugs. Also users of one drug may be exposed to a variety of other drug users and sellers and, through this association, may be encouraged to experiment with more potent drugs. More importantly, however, is the expense involved in supporting a drug habit. Frequently this expense causes the addict to turn to crime to obtain money with which to purchase the needed drugs.

ALCOHOL

Although drinking alcohol is not illegal, laws have been established that regulate the age at which it becomes legal to drink as well as the amount that a person can drink and then operate a vehicle. The problem of the drunk driver is well known to police officers. Drunk drivers are a menace to themselves and to others. Drinking is a factor in at least half of all fatal motor vehicle accidents.

Alcohol is the most widely abused drug in the United States.

The widespread abuse of alcohol is partly due to its legality but also to its social acceptance. Alcohol is the drug of choice among teenagers.

DRUG ABUSE AND CRIME

The National Institute of Justice has recently implemented a Drug Use Forecasting (DUF) system. Under this system they are able to detect and track

Table 15–1 **Controlled Substances Uses and Effects**

DRUG	TRADE OR OTHER NAMES	METHODS OF USUAL ADMINISTRATION
Narcotics		
Opium	Dover's Powder, Paregoric, Parepectolin	Oral, smoked
Morphine	Morphine, Pectoral Syrup	Oral, smoked, injected
Codeine	Tylenol with Codeine, Empirin Compound with Codeine, Robitussin A-C	Oral, injected
Heroin	Diacetylmorphine, Horse, Smack	Injected, sniffed, smoked
Hydromorphone	Dilaudid	Oral, injected
Meperidine (Pethidine)	Demerol, Mepergan	Oral, injected
Methadone	Dolophine, Methadone, Methadose	Oral, injected
Other narcotics	LAAM, Leritine, Numorphan, Percodan, Tussionex, Fentanyl, Darvon, Talwin,* Lomotil	Oral, injected
Depressants		
Chloral Hydrate	Noctec, Somnos	Oral
Barbiturates	Phenobarbital, Tuinal, Amytal, Nembutal, Seconal, Lotusate	Oral
Benzodiazepines	Ativan, Azene, Clonopin, Dalmane, Diazepam, Librium, Xanax, Serax, Tranxene, Valium, Verstran, Halcion, Paxipam, Restoril	Oral
Methaqualone	Quaalude	Oral
Glutethimide	Doriden	Oral
Other Depressants	Equanil, Miltown, Noludar, Placidyl, Valmid	Oral
Stimulants		
Cocaine**	Coke, Flake, Snow	Sniffed, smoked, injected
Amphetamines	Biphetamine, Delcobese, Desoxyn, Dexedrine, Mediatric	Oral, injected
Phenmetrazine	Preludin	Oral, injected
Methylphenidate	Ritalin	Oral, injected
Other Stimulants	Adipex, Bacarate, Cylert, Didrex, Ionamin, Plegine, Pre-Sate, Sanorex, Tenuate, Tepanil, Voranil	Oral, injected
Hallucinogens		
LSD	Acid, Microdot	Oral
Mescaline and Peyote	Mesc, Buttons, Cactus	Oral
Amphetamine Variants	2,5-DMA, PMA, STP, MDA, MDMA, TMA, DOM, DOB	Oral, injected
Phencyclidine	PCP, Angel Dust, Hog	Smoked, oral, injected
Phencyclidine Analogs	PCE, PCPy, TCP	Smoked, oral, injected
Other **Hallucinogens**	Bufotenine, Ibogaine, DMT, DET, Psilocybin, Psilocyn	Oral, injected, smoked, sniffed
Cannabis		
Marijuana	Pot, Acapulco Gold, Grass, Reefer, Sinsemilla, Thai Sticks	Smoked, oral
Tetrahydrocannabinol	THC	Smoked, oral
Hashish	Hash	Smoked, oral
Hashish Oil	Hash Oil	Smoked, oral

*Not designated a narcotic under the CSA
**Designated a narcotic under the CSA

Table 15–1 (Continued)

POSSIBLE EFFECTS	EFFECTS OF OVERDOSE	WITHDRAWAL SYNDROME
Euphoria, drowsiness, respiratory depression, constricted pupils, nausea	Slow and shallow breathing, clammy skin, convulsions, coma, possible death	Watery eyes, runny nose, yawning, loss of appetite, irritability, tremors, panic, chills and sweating, cramps, nausea
Slurred speech, disorientation, drunken behavior without odor of alcohol	Shallow respiration, clammy skin, dilated pupils, weak and rapid pulse, coma, possible death	Anxiety, insomnia, tremors, delirium, convulsions, possible death
Increased alertness, excitation, euphoria, increased pulse rate and blood pressure, insomnia, loss of appetite	Agitation, increase in body temperature, hallucinations, convulsions, possible death	Apathy, long periods of sleep, irritability, depression, disorientation
Illusions and hallucinations, poor perception of time and distance	Longer, more intense "trip" episodes, psychosis, possible death	Withdrawal syndrome not reported
Euphoria, relaxed inhibitions, increased appetite, disoriented behavior	Fatigue, paranoia, possible psychosis	Insomnia, hyperactivity and decreased appetite occasionally reported

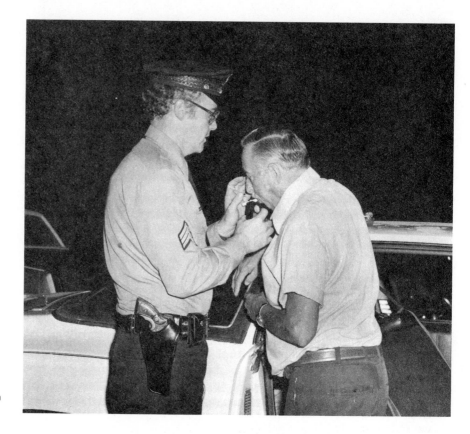

An officer administers a breath
test.

drug-use trends among people arrested for serious crimes. This voluntary program is in place in twelve major cities. Four times a year samples of arrestees in each city are interviewed and asked to provide urine specimens, which are tested for illicit drugs.

Initial tests showed a high level of drug use among the arrestees, with 50 to 80 percent of those arrested for serious crime testing positive. Their research also showed that criminals commit four to six times as much crime when they are actively using drugs as they do when they are drug free.

Clearly drug use is linked to criminal activity.

According to the National Institute most of those tested were charged with street crimes such as burglary, grand larceny, and assault. The most frequently found drugs were marijuana, cocaine, heroin, PCP, and amphetamines.

Tests conducted in New York City showed that cocaine use almost doubled during the three-year period. It more than tripled in the District of Columbia. The National Institute estimates that these rates are from two to nine times higher than in the general population.

In addition, alcohol abuse is common among criminals, with more than a third of all prison inmates indicating they drank heavily. Approximately 10 percent of the offenders indicated they were "very drunk" at the time of the offense.

As noted by Siegel (1990, p. 81): "One research effort found that about 75 percent of all arrestees test positively for drug use." Further, according to Graham (1990, p. 101): "Drug abuse has also been shown to be one of the best indicators of serious criminal careers. Institute-sponsored research found that a majority of the 'violent predators' among prison and jail inmates had

Table 15-2 **The Relationship Between Drugs and Violent Crime.**

- Researchers have identified three ways in which drugs are related to crime:
  psychopharmacological, in which a drug user commits crime because of drug-induced changes in physiological functions, cognitive ability, and mood
  economic compulsive, in which a drug user commits crime in order to obtain money to buy drugs
  systemic, in which violent crime occurs as a part of the drug business or culture.

- The actual number of drug-related acts of violence is difficult to measure. Three cities, however, have studied the amount of drug-related homicide in their jurisdictions:
  —Of 1,263 homicides reported in New York City in 1984, 24 percent were identified as drug-related.
  —Of 1,850 homicides recorded in Miami from 1978 to 1982, 24 percent were classified as drug-related.
  —In 1985, 21 percent of the homicides reported in the District of Columbia were identified as drug-related, increasing steadily to 34 percent in 1986, 51 percent in 1987, and to as much as 80 percent in 1988.

- Victims across the country reported that they believe their assailants were under the influence of drugs in about 12 percent of violent crime incidents in 1986–87. An additional 2 percent of the victims said their assailants were under the influence of drugs or alcohol, but they were not sure which. In 22 percent of the cases, the victims reported that the offenders were under the influence of alcohol alone.

- Incarcerated adults and youth report high levels of drug use. Among those incarcerated for violent crimes, a third of state prisoners and more than a third of the incarcerated youth said they had been under the influence of an illegal drug at the time of their offense. In the month before the violent offense for which they were incarcerated, 39 percent of state prison inmates reported daily drug use, and 16 percent reported daily use of a major drug (cocaine, heroin, PCP, LSD, and methadone).

  Among the violent offenders in state prison, those incarcerated for robbery were the most likely to have used a major drug daily, (23 percent); those incarcerated for rape and other sexual offenses were the least likely to report such use, 9 percent and 6 percent, respectively.

  Additional data from the surveys shed light on the relationship between drugs and crime, although not available separately for violent offenders.

- Overall, more than half of the state prisoners who had ever used a major drug (cocaine, heroin, PCP, LSD, or methadone) reported that they began their major drug use after their first arrest.

- Major drug use (cocaine, heroin, PCP, LSD, and methadone) is related to the number of prior convictions for state prisoners: the greater the use of major drugs, the more prior convictions the inmate was likely to report.

Source: U.S. Department of Justice. Office of Justice Programs. Bureau of Justice Statistics. *Violent Crime in the United States* (1991).

histories of heroin abuse, frequently in combination with alcohol and other drugs."

Table 15–2 indicates the relationship between drugs and *violent* crime.

THE DRUG USERS

Just who is taking these drugs and why? Authorities say that in New York City alone there are 400,000 drug addicts requiring an endless supply of drugs. Nationally there are about two million addicts out of forty million drugs users. The Federal Drug Enforcement Agency (FDEA) estimates that 5 percent of the population, or nearly ten million Americans, are involved in drug abuse of some sort.

Common symptoms of drug abuse include the following:

- Sudden and dramatic changes in discipline and job performance.

- Unusual degrees of activity or inactivity.

- Sudden and irrational flareups.

- Significant change in personal appearance for the worse.
- Dilated pupils or wearing sunglasses at inappropriate times or places.
- Needle marks or razor cuts, or long sleeves constantly worn to hide such marks.
- Sudden attempts to borrow money or to steal.
- Frequent association with known drug abusers or pushers.

Table 15–3 describes indicators of drug abuse.

An innocent population affected by drug use are the thousands of crack babies, children whose mothers were addicted to crack while pregnant. According to Rist (1990, p. 1): "The initial wave of crack babies, born after crack cocaine hit the streets in the mid-1980s, are kindergarten age today." Referred to in the literature as the **shadow children,** these crack babies are, according to one psychologist, "wired for 110 volts, living in a 220-volt world" (Rist, p. 1). Rist notes that: "Douglas Besharove, former director of the National Center on Child Abuse has called these children a potential 'bio-underclass'—a cohort of children whose combined physiological damage and extreme socioeconomic disadvantage could foredoom them to a life of permanent inferiority."

Why???

People do drugs and drink alcohol primarily for the "high" they get from it, for the escape from the trouble and tensions of the everyday world. In addition, it is often a very sociable thing to do. Teenagers, in particular, are greatly influenced by peer pressure, although some teenagers say they got the idea to drink or do drugs from watching their parents. In fact, many parents serve wine to their very young children along with Sunday dinner. Researchers have found that children of alcoholics are 70 percent more likely than of nonalcoholics to abuse drugs and alcohol at some point in their lives. And many children under age twelve say they learned to drink or do drugs from older brothers and sisters.

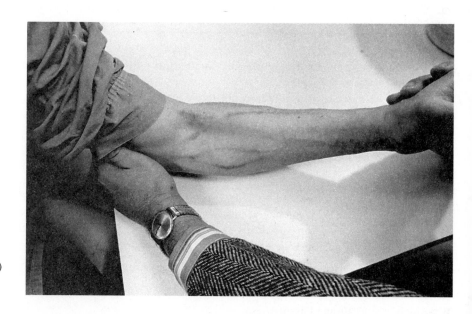

Needle marks (called "tracks") can be seen on the arms of intravenous drug users.

Table 15–3 **Indicators of Drug Abuse**

DRUG	PHYSICAL EVIDENCE	OBSERVABLE CONDITIONS
Morphine	Burning spoon, candle, hypodermic needle, actual substance	Needle marks, euphoria
Heroin	Burning spoon, candle, hypodermic needle, razor blade, eyedropper, actual substance	Needle marks or razor cuts, euphoria, starry look, constricted pupils, profuse perspiration
Cocaine	White or colorless crystalline powder, hypodermic needle, pipe	Needle marks, dilated pupils, increased heart rate, convulsing
Crack	Pellets, glass pipes, plastic bottle	Depression, euphoria, convulsions
Stimulants	Pills of various shapes and sizes	Restlessness, nervousness, hand tremor, dilated pupils, dry mouth, excessive perspiration
Depressants	Pills of various shapes and sizes	Resembles drunkenness: slurred, indistinct speech and loss of physical coordination
Hallucinogens	Hypodermic needle, eyedropper, spoon, bottle caps, tourniquets, cotton balls, actual substance	Needle marks on inner elbow, extreme emotionalism, noticeable dilation of pupils, often causing persons to wear dark glasses even at night
Marijuana	Roach holder, pipe with fine screen stuck halfway down bowl, actual substance	Sweet smoke odor; resembles mild intoxication: staring off into space, glassy eyes, sometimes passing into semiconsciousness or falling asleep

During the teenage years, fitting in is extremely important to most youth. They are growing fast, and some have what has been termed a "terminal case of the awkward." They are self-conscious and uncertain as to just who they are. Cocaine, especially, numbs such teenage anxieties. It helps anxious, awkward young people find an escape from a world that is frightening to them. It also gives them the illusion of membership, energy, and confidence. Unfortunately, many of the "innocent" drug users become involved in crime.

TYPES OF DRUG–INVOLVED OFFENDERS

Chaiken and Johnson (1988) studied the types of adolescent and adult drug-involved offenders, their typical drug use, problems, and contact with the justice system. Their results are summarized in Table 15–4, which represents a general progression in drugs and crime involvement.

THE DRUG DEALERS

American drug users pay drug traffickers an estimated $140 billion a year. Some dealers hand out free drug samples to hook new buyers. Illegal drugs are readily available, from marijuana to cocaine. Any buyer can find some kind of drug to meet his or her needs.

Table 15–4   **Types of Drug-Involved Offenders**

TYPE OF OFFENDER	TYPICAL DRUG USE	TYPICAL PROBLEMS	CONTACT WITH JUSTICE SYSTEM
Occasional users			
Adolescents	Light to moderate or single-substance, such as alcohol, marijuana, or combination use.	Driving under influence; truancy, early sexual activity; smoking.	None to little.
Adults	Light to moderate use of single substances such as hallucinogens, tranquilizers, alcohol, marijuana, cocaine, or combination use.	Driving under influence; lowered work productivity.	None to little.
Persons who sell small amounts of drugs			
Adolescents	Moderate use of alcohol and multiple types of drugs.	Same as adolescent occasional user; also, some poor school performance; some other minor illegal activity.	Minimal juvenile justice contact.
Adults	Moderate use of alcohol and multiple types of drugs including cocaine.	Same as adult occasional user.	None to little.
Persons who sell drugs frequently or in large amounts			
Adolescents	Moderate to heavy use of multiple drugs including cocaine.	Many involved in range of illegal activities including violent crimes; depends on subtype (see Table 15–5).	Dependent on subtype (see Table 15–5).
Adults	Moderate to heavy use of multiple drugs including heroin and cocaine.	Depends on subtype (see Table 15–5).	Dependent on subtype (see Table 15–5).

    The core of the American drug business is primarily in our inner cities. Dealing drugs is a way of making a very profitable living. Many decaying buildings are becoming crack "factories." In these buildings, powder cocaine is processed into rock cocaine, or crack, and pure heroin and cocaine are diluted with baking soda or sugar "stepped on" to increase the product, turning a thousand-dollar ounce of cocaine into two ounces worth two thousand dollars.

Street drug rings can be quite sophisticated, with a kingpin purchasing narcotics from foreign smugglers. Under the kingpin are leaders who oversee the packaging and distribution of the illegal drugs. Runners take the drugs to the street sellers. Lookouts get approximately two hundred dollars a day just looking out for the police. Enforcers, as the name implies, carry out the king-pin's orders, including killing people who get in the way of drug trafficking.

Profits for the dealers are very high, with a good week netting them thirty thousand dollars. According to a Ford Foundation study, drugs are often sold openly in inner cities, with inner-city residents resigned to drug dealing as a way of life. In some cities drug dealers have actually bought the cooperation of neighborhoods. Drug dealers come into a neighborhood, offer residents money or cars, and, in turn, use their homes for drug deals.

According to Kraar (1988, p. 19): "The illicit drug trade is probably the fastest-growing industry in the world and is unquestionably the most profit-able.... The global drug trade may run up to $500 billion a year.... The drug trade has created a breed of shadowy billionaires who seem as canny in business as they are vicious."

Siegel (1990, p. 81) suggests that: "The overwhelming problem associated with drug control is the enormous profits involved in the drug trade. A drug dealer can make 1.5 million in one shipment. An estimated sixty tons of cocaine are imported into the country each year with a street value of $17 billion. Government crackdowns simply serve to drive up the price of drugs and encourage more illegal entrepreneurs to enter the market.

Until the 1980s the drug industry was controlled by the Sicilian Mafia. They have lost ground since then. For example, as noted by Siegel (1990, p. 82): "The Hells' Angels motorcycle club has become one of the primary distributors of cocaine and amphetamines in the United States."

FDA agents have identified a new Bangkok heroin cartel that is as powerful as the notorious Medellin and Cali Colombian rings. Difficulties in prosecuting the cartel include Thailand's reluctance to crack down on drug trafficking and the ingenious smuggling used by the cartel. As noted in a *Star Tribune* article (1992, p. 10): "Drugs have been hidden in furniture, machinery, procelain and even the bellies of dead goldfish that were placed among live fish being shipped to the U.S."

Table 15–5 describes the types of dealers who sell drugs frequently or in large amounts.
As noted by Siegel (1990, p. 83):

> By far the most serious adolescent dealers are those who use multiple substances and commit both property and violent crimes at high rates. Only about 2 percent of all adolescents pursue serious criminality and use multiple types of illicit drugs. Such youths commit over 40 percent of the total robberies and assaults by adolescents. Additionally, they are responsible for over 60 percent of all teen-age felony thefts and drug sales....
>
> Although over two-thirds of drug-using juvenile delinquents continue to use drugs as adults, close to half stop committing crimes.... In general, youngsters are most likely to continue to be offenders as adults if:
>
> ■ They come from poor families.
> ■ They have other criminals in their family.
> ■ They do poorly in school.
> ■ They started using drugs and committing other delinquent and antisocial acts at a relatively early age.
> ■ They used multiple types of drugs and committed crimes frequently.
> ■ They have few opportunities in late adolescence to participate in legitimate and rewarding adult activities.

Table 15–5   **Types of Dealers Who Sell Drugs Frequently or in Large Amounts**

TYPE OF DEALER	TYPICAL DRUG USE	TYPICAL PROBLEMS	CONTACT WITH JUSTICE SYSTEM
Top-level dealers			
Adults (only)	None to heavy use of multiple types of drugs.	Major distribution of drugs; some other white-collar crime such as money laundering.	Low to minimal.
Lesser predatory			
Adolescents	Moderate to heavy drug use; some addiction; heroin and cocaine use.	Assaults; range of property crimes; poor school performance.	Low to moderate contact with juvenile or adult justice system.
Adult men	Moderate to heavy drug use; some addiction; heroin and cocaine use.	Burglary and other property crimes; many drug sales; irregular employment; moderate to high social instability.	Low to high contact with criminal justice system.
Adult women	Moderate to heavy drug use; some addiction; heroin and cocaine use.	Prostitution; theft; many drug sales; addicted babies; AIDS babies; high-risk children.	Low to moderate contact with criminal justice system.
Drug-involved violent predatory offenders: The "losers"			
Adolescents	Heavy use of multiple drugs; often addiction to heroin or cocaine.	Commit many crimes in periods of heaviest drug use including robberies; high rates of school dropout; problems likely to continue as adults.	High contact with both juvenile and adult criminal justice system.
Adults	Heavy use of multiple drugs; often addiction to heroin or cocaine.	Commit many crimes in periods of heaviest drug use including robberies; major source of income from criminal activity; low-status roles in drug hierarchy.	High contact with criminal justice system; high incarceration.
The "winners"			
Adolescents	Frequent use of multiple drugs; less frequent addiction to heroin and cocaine.	Commit many crimes; major source of income from criminal activity; take midlevel role in drug distribution to both adolescents and adults.	Minimal; low incarceration record.

Several options have been suggested as a way to combat the drug problem.

The drug problem might be approached by:

- Legalization.
- A two-market approach.
- Increased law enforcement.
- Asset forfeiture programs.
- Enlisting public support.

Legalization

Some people advocate legalizing marijuana and other drugs just as alcohol is, claiming that this would reduce the cost of maintaining a drug habit and, consequently, reduce the amount of crime that might be committed to obtain money to support the habit.

Proponents of legalization say that the prohibition on drug use has created "huge profits for drug dealers, overcrowded jails, a distorted foreign policy and urban areas terrorized by bloodthirsty gangs" (Church 1988, p. 12). Church cites the following arguments for and against legalization:

FOR:

- Costs. Some of the $8 billion spent on interdiction and local enforcement could be used for education and treatment, which receive less than $500 million.
- Organized crime. Cocaine and marijuana sales bring drug lords more than $20 billion each year. Legalization would wipe out their major source of funds.
- Foreign policy. The U.S. drug habit generates $2 billion in revenues for Latin American thugs. Crackdowns severely strain relations.
- Revenues. Treatment programs could be financed by taxes on drugs, like taxes on alcohol and tobacco.

AGAINST:

- Exposure. Cheap, available drugs would increase addiction; only 10 percent of drinkers become hooked, while an estimated 75 percent of regular drug users could become addicted.
- Exotics. Legalization could lead to the sale of synthetic drugs or derivatives like crack without any understanding of their effects.
- Medical costs. The health costs of drug abuse, estimated at $60 billion annually, would increase.
- Social mores. Removing the legal strictures could make drug use socially acceptable.

One strong argument against legalization has been set forth by John Lawn, head of the Drug Enforcement Administration, who says: "Drugs are not bad because they're illegal. They're illegal because they're bad. The legal production and sale of drugs would threaten all of society" (Church 1988, p. 18).

A Two-Market Approach

Under this approach, addicts would be supplied at clinics or other types of health facilities, but illegal drugs would not be available for nonaddicts. In the

"British system," heroin is provided to addicts at clinics specifically set up for that purpose. In more recent years, however, they have switched to using methadone, a synthetic opiate, as a maintenance drug.

Increased Law Enforcement

Efforts could be increased to stop illegal drugs from being produced in other countries, from being smuggled into the United States, and/or from being sold here.

Each approach has its problems. As far as preventing production of illicit drugs, Kaplan (n.d.) notes that preventing production of opium would require controlling poppy cultivation and international cooperation. Preventing smuggling is equally difficult. The United States has over 12,000 miles of coastline that must be patrolled. Kaplan suggests, for example, that the total heroin requirement of all American addicts for an entire year is probably less than 10 tons, yet 100 million tons of freight come into the United States yearly, and more than 200 million people cross American borders yearly.

Kraar (1988, p. 33) contends: "America's war on drugs is long on rhetoric and short on effectiveness. Busting drug dealers, as a Washington analyst puts it, 'is like trying to put General Motors out of business by knocking off used-car dealers.'"

Asset Forfeiture Program

Burden (1988, p. 29) notes that in the last fiscal year, the United States Justice Department approved payment of $24.4 million to state and local law enforcement agencies as their share of cash and property seized from organized crime and drug traffickers.

The Asset Forfeiture Program was enacted in 1984 and allows the Justice Department to share seized assets with state and local law enforcement agen-

SWAT teams are often involved in drug busts. Such an approach to reducing the drug problem is extremely expensive and often has limited success.

cies that participated in the investigations and arrests. Such forfeitures have included a recording studio, a Chevrolet dealership, a one-thousand-acre plantation, a horse farm with 210 Appaloosas including a stud horse worth $1.5 million, luxury homes, cars, boats, and planes.

Enlisting Public Support

As noted by Siegel (1990, p. 92–93):

> It is not reasonable to expect the police alone to put an end to sales of illicit drugs, given the diversity of people involved in using, selling, and distributing them; the low visibility of the sites in which most transactions are made, the early age at which children start using drugs, and the loose and shifting organization of drug-involved offenders. It is even less reasonable to expect the police to stop the use of illicit drugs. A large proportion of drug users and drug-involved offenders are youngsters. Achieving even a substantial reduction in the use and sales of illicit drugs will require long-term concerted efforts by the police, educators, health and mental health practitioners, and juvenile justice agencies to reduce availability of drugs, to counteract pressure for initiation of use, and to curtail continued abuse.

FBI Director William Sessions (1989, p. 11) urges police officers and administrators to become community leaders in fostering public support for the war against drugs:

> Police officials must use their skills and influence to help reshape public attitudes toward drug abuse. The fight against drugs is a war, and public support is needed for victory. . . .
>
> Police have a special responsibility to become fully engaged with the public to obtain their unflagging support.
>
> In their role as community leaders, the police must make the public recognize what is at stake—not only the hearts and minds of millions of adults and children, but their safety and lives, as well.

"Operation Broken Windows" Yonce (1992) describes a successful local program to stop drug sales in Wilson, North Carolina, when a specific area of the community, the 500 Block, became an "open air drug market," known throughout the city as a place where drugs could easily be bought. The name of the project is based on the **broken window** theory that if a window is broken in a car or building and is left unrepaired, it will send a signal that no one cares and that more damage can be caused without fear of punishment. It is an open invitation to crime.

In this program the police mobilized all the city's resources including input from the citizens who worked and lived in the 500 Block. The goals of the program were to (Yonce, p. 67):

- Force drug users to look elsewhere for drugs.
- Force drug dealers to move or change their method of operation.
- Attack social conditions feeding the drug problem.
- Make the area safer for residents and businesses.

Among the strategies used were undercover operations, a uniformed police presence, a crackdown on trafficking by assigning two K–9 units to the local bus station, and attention to social conditions: cutting the grass, removing the trash, repairing or installing streetlights, and inspecting buildings for code violations.

Educating Our Youth

In the preceding chapter it was suggested that the place to begin alleviating the problem of criminality was with our youth. The same is true with the drug problem our country faces. It is imperative to steer the youth of our country away from the devastation caused by drug use. Rosiak (1991, p. 122) suggests: "In structuring an educational campaign, focus on the immediate, tangible consequences of illicit drug, alcohol and tobacco use":

> This means, for example, emphasizing to preteens that smoking causes bad breath and makes their hair smell, or that getting drunk can mean real embarrassment if they throw up, and real humiliation and inconvenience if their parents find out and take their driver's licenses away. Similarly, teenagers can more readily see themselves dying in a crash than becoming alcoholics, so design an educational campaign that concentrates on the areas of greatest sensitivity.

SUMMARY

In 1914 the Harrison Narcotics Act was passed by the federal government making it illegal to sell or use certain drugs, including narcotics and dangerous drugs. Narcotics are drugs that produce sleep, lethargy, or relief of pain, including heroin, cocaine, crack, and marijuana. Dangerous drugs are addicting, mind-altering drugs such as depressants, stimulants, and hallucinogens.

In most states narcotics and dangerous drugs may not be used or sold without a prescription. Federal law prohibits sale or distribution not covered by prescription, but it does *not* prohibit possession for personal use. The most commonly observed drugs on the street, in possession of users, and seized in drug raids are heroin, opium, morphine, codeine, cocaine, crack, and marijuana. Arrest for possession or use of marijuana is the most frequent drug arrest.

Although legal, alcohol is the most widely abused drug in the United States. Drug use and alcohol abuse have been linked to criminal activity. The drug problem might be approached by legalization, a two-market approach, increased law enforcement, an asset forfeiture program, and enlisting public support.

DISCUSSION QUESTIONS

1. Where does alcohol fall in the discussions of drugs and crimes?

2. How does your city rank in the United States as far as occurrence of drug abuse?

3. Which drugs pose the greatest problem for law enforcement?

4. How effective is our court system in deterring sales and use of drugs?

5. Is imprisonment a good deterrent for those engaged in selling and using drugs?

6. If drugs were legalized, would law enforcement agencies benefit?

7. What can our government do to deal with the drug problem in the United States?

8. Should we establish trade embargoes on countries known to allow the transportation of drugs to the United States?

9. What is the best approach to combat drugs?

10. Should alcohol be banned in the United States?

amphetamines, barbiturates, cocaine, crack, dangerous drugs, deliriants, flake, hallucinogens, heroin, hypertension, marijuana, mules, narcotics, nystagmus, PCP, rock, shadow children, sinsemilla.

REFERENCES

AIDS Policy & Law (letter to "Executives"). Washington, D.C.: Buraff Publications, A division of The Bureau of National Affairs, Inc. (no date).

Bennett, W. W., and Hess, K. M. *Criminal Investigation.* St. Paul, Minn.: West Publishing Company, 1991.

Burden, O. P. "Finding Light at the End of the Drug War Tunnel." *Law Enforcement News,* December 15, 1988.

Chaiken, M. R. and Johnson, B. D. *Characteristics of Different Types of Drug-Involved Offenders.* Washington, D.C.: U.S. Department of Justice, National Institute of Justice, Office of Communication and Research Utilization, February 1988. NCH 108560.

Church, G. J. "Thinking the Unthinkable." *Time,* May 30, 1988, 12–16, 18–19.

"Federal Drug Agents Report New Thai Cartel Rivals Colombian Rings." *Star Tribune,* April 15, 1992, 10.

Graham, M. G. "Controlling Drug Abuse and Crime: A Research Update." In *American Justice: Research of the National Institute of Justice,* edited by L. J. Siegel. St. Paul, Minn.: West Publishing Company, 1990.

Jennings, P. "Why This Plague?" ABC Documentary, July 11, 1988.

Kaplan, J. *Heroin.* National Institute of Justice, Crime File Study Guide. U.S. Department of Justice. NCH 97225, (no date).

Kraar, L. "The Drug Trade." *Fortune,* June 20, 1988, 27–29, 32, 33, 36–38.

Oglesby, E. W.; Faber, S. J.; and Faber, S. J. *Angel Dust: What Everyone Should Know About PCP.* Los Angeles, Calif.: Charing Cross Publishing Company, 1982.

Peoples, J. T. and Hahn, L. M. "Indoor Cannabis Cultivation: Marijuana in the '90s." *The Police Chief* (October 1991): 119–120.

Rist, M. C. "The Shadow Children: Preparing for the Arrival of Crack Babies in School: Research Bulletin." Bloomington, Ind.: *Phi Delta Kappan,* July 1990, no. 9.

Rosen, M. S. "1988 in Review: Trouble, with a Capital T that Rhymes with D, that Stands for Drugs." *Law Enforcement News,* January 31, 1989, 1–2.

Rosiak, J. "Successful Drug Demand Reduction Strategies for Police Chiefs." *The Police Chief* (October 1991): 122–126.

Sessions, W. S. "Public Support Needed for Victory Against Drugs." *The Police Chief* (September 1989): 11.

Siegel, L. J. (Ed.) *American Justice: Research of the National Institute of Justice.* St. Paul, Minn.: West Publishing Company, 1990.

U.S. Department of Justice. Office of Justice Programs. Bureau of Justice Statistics. *Violent Crime in the United States.* Washington, D.C., 1991.

"U.S. Illegal Drug Tab Exceeds $40 Billion." *Law Enforcement News,* June 15/30, 1991, 1, 5.

Yonce, T. C. " 'Broken Window' Stops Drug Sales." *Law and Order* (April 1992): 67–70.

CHAPTER 16

Gangs: A Growing Menace

Gangs are now spreading through our society like a violent plague.
—Jackson and McBride, L.A.P.D.

Do You Know

How a gang is defined?

Whether gangs are racially or ethnically mixed?

What the distinguishing characteristics of gangs are?

How gang members might be identified?

What the role of most female gangs is?

What the most common reasons for joining gangs are?

Through what three stages a gang might evolve?

INTRODUCTION

"In October 1988, a Los Angeles Police Department (LAPD) officer was gunned down by gang members equipped with an AR–15 assault rifle while fleeing the scene of a drive-by shooting," according to Sessions (1990, p. 17). "A month later, other LAPD officers were attacked by suspected gang members armed with an AK–47 and .45 caliber semiautomatic pistol. . . . Throughout the 1970s and 1980s, gang members increasingly demonstrated their willingness to assault and murder law enforcement officers." According to Miller (1990, p. 263):

> Youth gangs of the 1980s and 1990s are more numerous, more prevalent, and more violent than in the 1950s, probably more so than at any time in the country's history. . . . The United States is one of the richest and most powerful nations in the world, with abundant resources in money and human talent. Why has its ability to secure a reasonable degree of safety and stability to millions of citizens in thousands of communities been frustrated for so long by a relatively small group of youthful males?

The gang problem has overwhelmed and intimidated huge segments of our population. The drug trafficking and drive-by shootings have proliferated in major cities. The spreading cancer of graffiti and other forms of destructive behavior have outstripped many neighborhoods' ability to contain it.

GANGS DEFINED

The *Encyclopedia of Crime and Justice (ECJ)* (1983, p. 1673) defines youth gangs as follows: "Youth gangs are self-formed associations of youths distinguished from other types of youth groups by their routine participation in illegal activities."

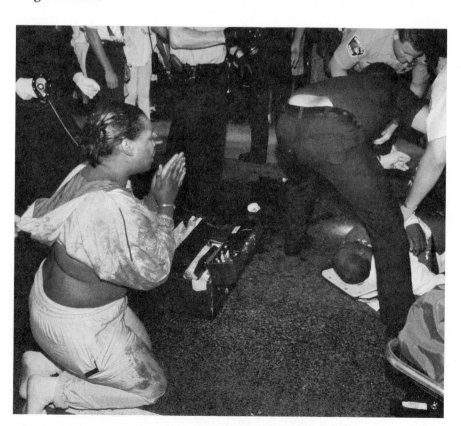

The victim's girlfriend kneels at the scene of an alleged gang-related killing.

Jackson and McBride (1985, p. 20) define youth gangs this way:

A **gang** is a group of people that forms an allegiance for a common purpose and engages in unlawful or criminal activity.

A definition commonly accepted by law enforcement is that a gang is any group gathered together on a continuing basis to commit antisocial behavior.

Los Angeles criminologists have divided gangs into two groups: **cultural gangs** and **instrumental gangs.** As noted by Sessions (1990, p. 17):

> Cultural gangs—LA's Hispanic gangs, for example—are neighborhood-centered and exist independently of criminal activity. Instrumental gangs, on the other hand, are formed for the express purpose of criminal activity and pose a greater threat because they provide for a higher degree of organization.

A BRIEF HISTORICAL PERSPECTIVE

Gangs have existed in nearly every civilization back through recorded history. Street gangs probably started in our country in Los Angeles about the turn of the century.

Hispanic Gangs

Davis (1982, p. 5) suggests that between 1910 and 1925 a great influx of immigrants from Mexico occurred. These immigrants tended to live with others from their native areas of Mexico, and rivalries developed that eventually resulted in the formation of gangs such as Bunker Hill, Mara Villa, and San Fernando. These Hispanic gangs lived in barrios that often could trace their heritage back several generations. They had a strong system of tradition and became known as **traditional gangs**.

The depression of the 1930s brought Latino families from Arizona, New Mexico, and Texas to Los Angeles. They fragmented into groups, each claiming its own territory and forming such gangs as Happy Valley, HoyoSoto, Alpine Hazard, and White Fence.

In the 1960s freeway displacement drove families from the central city eastward, where they created more new gangs such as Lomas and Bassett.

African American Gangs

African American street gangs also existed in the Los Angeles area for many years. They began as groups of young high school "thugs" who extorted money from students and terrorized teachers. One gang called itself the Crips. It had the reputation of being the toughest African American gang in Los Angeles. Other gangs started incorporating the word "Crip" into their names. Although they shared a common name, they were in reality independent, and rivalries developed. The African American gangs divided themselves into the **Crips** and the Non-Crips or **Bloods.** Since African American gangs have not existed as long as Hispanic gangs, they do not have generations of tradition and, consequently, are often referred to as "nontraditional" gangs.

Other Types of Gangs

Asian gangs known as Yu Li, Joes Boys, and Wah Chings exist in most of the major cities of the United States and Canada.

Table 16-1 Youth Gangs Characteristic Groups

Black Gangs	Origins in Los Angeles, Chicago, New York, Miami, and other major urban ghettos. Crips, Bloods, Players, Untouchables, and Vice Lords are some of the more prominent gangs.
Jamaican Posses	Immigrant Jamaicans in the U.S. with roots in Jamaica. Groups have been identified in New York, Boston, Philadelphia, Washington, D.C., Houston, Atlanta, Detroit, Seattle, and Anchorage among other locations.
Hispanic Gangs	Origins in Los Angeles, valleys of California, New York (Puerto Rico), Miami (Mariel Cubans, Dominicans), Washington, D.C., and other urban barrios. Tend to use highly stylized graffiti lettering.
Asian Gangs	Origins among recent emigres from Viet Nam, Hong Kong, and Philippines. Activity centered in New York, New Orleans, Los Angeles and Orange County, California, Portland, Oregon, Seattle, San Francisco, and Houston.
Pacific Islander Gangs	Primarily Samoans who have migrated to Western urban areas, i.e., Los Angeles, San Francisco, Portland.
White "Stoner" Gangs	Caucasian groups identified with Heavy Metal and Punk Rock music preferences and with some British working class gangs. Sometimes involved with Satanic rites and symbols.
Neo-Nazi Gangs	Tend to articulate white supremacy, racism, and Nazi symbols. Some call themselves "skinheads" and sport close-cut hair or shaved heads.
Motorcycle Gangs	Dominantly Caucasians, branches of Hell's Angels and other notorious motorcycle groups. Tend to be heavily involved with the manufacture and sale of methamphetamine.

Source: Metropolitan Court Judges Committee Report: *Drugs—The American Family in Crisis: A Judicial Response, 39 Recommendations,* August 4, 1988.

Filipino neighborhood street gangs are similar to Hispanic gangs and may gravitate toward Mexican gangs. The most common Filipino gangs are the Santanas, the Tabooes, and Temple Street.

The Korean community also has active gangs, the most well known being the Korean Killers.

Most gangs are racially or ethnically homogeneous.

Table 16-1 summarizes the origins and characteristics of the major youth gangs operating in the United States.

SPECIFIC CHARACTERISTICS OF YOUTH GANGS

Five general characteristics are often associated with gangs (*ECJ*, pp. 1671–73).

Distinguishing characteristics of gangs include leadership, organization, associational patterns, domain identification, and illegal activity.

Leadership

Gang leadership is usually quite well defined and may be one of three types: key personality, chain of command, or collective. As the name suggests, in the key personality leadership gang one particular gang member, often older than the others, is a strong and influential leader. He becomes a role model for other gang members.

In a gang with a chain of command form of leadership, the gang functions like a military unit or even a police department. Each member within the group has a specific rank, with authority going from the top down. As noted by Vetter and Territo (1984, p. 518):

> At the top is the "prez," who gains his or her position by being the most ruthless and violent member of the gang—and who remains on top only as long as he or she meets every challenge of authority. Under the "prez" is the "veep," who collects dues, supervises the recruitment and initiation of new members, and manages internal affairs.

In a gang with a collective leadership style, leaders change depending on the activity in which the gang is involved. If the gang is planning a crime, the best criminal mind is leader. If they are planning an attack on a neighboring gang, the best fighter is leader.

Organization

Gangs tend to be quite formally organized. One common organizational element is age. Gangs commonly have two to four age divisions. Another common organizational element is location, that is, two or more gangs may have localized versions of the same gang name, for example, the Southside Warriors and the Tenth Street Warriors.

Gangs also tend to have a hierarchical authority as described under leadership.

Associational Patterns

Gang members become very close to each other, hanging out together on street corners and in parks, school yards, and parking lots. They are, in effect, "family." As noted in the *ECJ* (1983), gangs in many cases take the place of family, school, and church. Concepts such as loyalty, ego strength, and camaraderie are all-important. An attack on a gang member is an attack on the entire gang.

Gangs often have specific criteria for membership and special initiation ceremonies. Often a person wanting to become a member may have to commit a crime before being admitted into the gang. According to Davis (1982, p. 10):

> One normally joins a street gang by either committing a crime or by being "jumped in." "Jumped in" is where the person being initiated is beaten, sometimes severely by fellow members to test his courage and fighting ability. The way to get out of a gang is not so easy as you have to be "jumped out." This is similar except they go to hurt you seriously, not to just see what you can do. This can discourage even the toughest gang member from leaving the gang.

Domain Identification

Typically gangs stake out a geographic territory, or **turf**, as their domain. This may be a specific facility such as a school or it may be an entire neighborhood. If one gang "trespasses" on another gang's turf, gang violence is likely.

Some gangs claim exclusive control over certain activities in an area such as the right to collect fees from students for using the restrooms or "insurance" payments from local merchants in exchange for protection.

Criminal Activity

As noted in the *ECJ* (1983, p. 1672): "The most distinctive form of gang offense is gang-fighting." Vetter and Territo (1984, pp. 571–618) claim: "Today, urban gangs are responsible for roughly one-quarter of all juvenile crimes committed each year. Gone are the knives, clubs, bicycle chains, and homemade 'zip' guns used as weapons in yesterday's 'rumbles.' The gang wars of today . . . feature sophisticated weaponry—AR–15s, M–16s, grenades, and plastic explosives— that would do credit to a military assault troop."

Acts of vandalism, arson, graffiti painting, stabbings, and shootings are common. Student extortion and teacher intimidation are also common. Davis (1982, p. 1) warns that gang activity "is more lethal today than at any time in the twentieth century. . . . They have indeed become our most pervasive threat to date relative to criminal victimization. Epidemics of murders, stabbings, drug sales and 'rip' offs by groups begin to identify a pattern. . . . [They] develop a lifestyle characterized by extortion, shootings, knifings, and dope deals. . . . Mutual excitement comes from pistol whippings or committing armed robberies."

According to the *ECJ* (1983, p. 1674) liberals and conservatives have opposing ideas as to why gangs engage in crime:

> Liberals generally ascribe gang crime to such unjust social conditions as poverty, inequality, bigotry, unemployment, discriminatory policies of criminal justice agencies, and inadequate resources for social services to the poor. Conservatives generally blame a progressive deterioration in social morality, including a weakening of self-discipline, individual responsibility, family solidarity, sexual restraint, and religion.

OTHER GANG CHARACTERISTICS

Other characteristics may help law enforcement officers identify gang members.

Gang members might be identified by their names, their symbols (clothing and tattoos), and how they communicate, including graffiti and sign language.

Gang *names* vary from colorful and imaginative to straightforward. They commonly refer to localities, animals, birds, royalty, and rebellion. As noted in the *ECJ* (1983, p. 1677):

> Localities can be streets (for example, the Tenth Streeters), neighborhoods (The Southsiders), housing projects (the Alazones Courts), and cities or towns (the Johnstown Gang). Popular animal names are the Tigers, the Panthers, the Cougars, the Leopards, the Cobras, the Eagles, and the Hawks. Royal titles include the Kings, the Emperors, the Lords, the Knights, the Barons, and the Dukes. Names denoting rebellion or lawlessness include the Rebels, the Outlaws, the Savages, and the Assassins. Gangs may be designated by the name of a leader or other important member such as "Joey and Them Kids" or "Garcia's Boys." A common combination is a local designation coupled with another category, for example, the West Side Majestic Warlords, the Third Street Rangers, and the Spring Hill Savages.

Gang *symbols* are also common. Clothing, in particular, can distinguish a particular gang. Perhaps best known is the typical attire of an outlaw motorcycle gang member: tattered Levis, scuffed boots, leather vests, and jackets with their own unique emblems. Sometimes "colors" are used to distinguish a

Gang members often may be identified by their clothing and their haircuts.

gang, as dramatized in the film *Colors*. Gang members also use jerseys, t-shirts, and jackets with emblems.

Tattoos are also symbols used by some gangs, particularly outlaw motorcycle gangs and Hispanic gangs. African American gang members seldom have tattoos.

Communications

Graffiti is a very common form of communication used by gang members. It is frequently used to stake out a gang's turf. Defacing, erasing, or substituting one gang's graffiti by a rival gang constitutes a challenge and usually results in violence and gang warfare. A Los Angeles White Paper on gang activity suggests:

> Much valuable information relative to police work may be gained from gang graffiti. For instance, one may be able to determine what gang is in control of a specific area by noting the frequency of the unchallenged graffiti because throwing a "placa" on a wall corresponds to claiming a territory. Writing left un-

changed reaffirms the gang's control. As one moves away from the center or core area of a gang's power and territory, the more rival graffiti and cross-outs are observed.

Contested areas are common when both gangs arrive at the same place at the same time. A confrontation occurs.

The White Paper also notes that African American and Latino styles of graffiti are vastly different, with the African American graffiti lacking the flair and attention to detail evidenced by the Latino gang graffiti. Much of the African American gang wall writing is filled with profanity.

Another form of communication typical of gang members is hand signals. These signs are often used to identify the person with a specific gang.

FEMALE GANGS

Female gangs are relatively rare.

Most female gangs are adjuncts or auxiliaries to a male gang.

A female gang may have a name affiliated with their male counterpart such as the Vice Ladies (from the Vice Lords). These auxiliaries usually consist of sisters and girlfriends of the male gang members. The females often assist the male gang, serving as decoys for rival gang members, as lookouts during the commission of crimes, or as carriers of weapons when a gang war is impending.

Campbell (1984, p. 266) studied the relationships among the girls in three New York gangs and found "intense camaraderie and strong dependency" on one another. According to Campbell, the "fundamental gang role of females has not altered substantially. Girl gangs exist as an adjunct to the male gang, and the range of possibilities open to their members is dictated and controlled by the boys."

WHY PEOPLE JOIN GANGS

The most frequently cited reason for people joining gangs is to *belong.* According to Sidney J. Harris, nationally syndicated columnist: "Gangs make martyrs of losers. . . . Gang members tend to be chronic losers, who can accomplish nothing individually, or who live in so depressed an environment that only by banding together can they exercise any influence over their lives."

The close ties of gang members is a major motive for membership. The membership provides both psychological and physical security. Most gang members are underachievers who come from broken homes or homes with no strong male authority figure. Davis (1982, pp. 9–10) cites four reasons people typically join gangs:

The most common reasons for joining a gang are for identity or recognition, for protection, for fellowship and brotherhood, or from intimidation.

As noted by Witkin (1992, p. 183): "For some kids, drugs, gangs and guns are simply vehicles through which to satisfy more basic yearnings." He describes the experience of fifteen-year-old Clarence and his motivation for dealing dope and carrying guns:

> I wanted to get paid. I thought money was the world. I'd spend it on my girlfriend, or I'd take all my homeboys out. If you made money that day, you'd pay, and that made me feel like I was the big daddy, the big man with the master plan. . . .
>
> If you had a gun, and you were with a girl, she'd be thinking, "He's bad." It made me feel macho, like nobody could touch me, like no one's going to mess with me.

Says Davis: (1982, pp. 9–10):

> Most gang members visualize themselves as warriors or soldiers protecting their barrio (community or neighborhood) from what they perceive to be a hostile outside world. You can see this in the gang murals painted on the walls throughout L.A. County.
>
> Many members join because they live in the gang area and are, therefore, subject to violence by rival gangs. Joining guarantees support in case of attack and retaliation for transgressions.
>
> To the majority of gang members, the gang is a substitute for a family cohesiveness lacking in the gang members' home environment. Many older brothers and relatives belong to or have belonged to the gang.
>
> Some members are forced into joining by their peer group. Intimidations range from extorting lunch money to beatings. If a particularly violent war is in progress, the recruitment tactics used by the gang can be extremely violent, even to the point of murdering one to cause others to conform.

According to Witkin (1992, pp. 183–184): "Today's kids are desensitized to violence as never before, surrounded by gunfire and stuffed with media images of Rambos who kill at will. . . . Disputes once settled with fists are now settled with guns."

According to the Los Angeles White Paper, family structure is probably the most important factor in formation of a gang member. Investigators have found certain common threads running through most families having hardcore gang members. The family is quite often a racial minority on some form of government assistance. It often lacks a male authority figure. This male figure may be a criminal or drug addict and, therefore, represents a negative role model. Typically neither adult has more than an elementary school education. Children live with minimal adult supervision.

When one child first encounters law-enforcement authorities, the dominant figure (usually the mother) makes excuses for the child, often in the form of accusations against society. Thus, children are taught early that they are not responsible for their actions and are shown how to transfer blame to society.

A second common type of family structure is one that may have two strong family leaders in a mother and father. Usually graduates from gangs themselves, they see little wrong with their children belonging to gangs. This is known as an assembly-line production of gang members.

A third common family structure is where the parents are non– English speaking. The children tend to adapt rapidly to the American way of life and in doing so, lose respect for their parents and the "old ways." They become experts at manipulating their parents, and the parents lose all control.

Many of these structures overlap.

THE PROGRESSION

The continual process of criminal experience and living is illustrated in Figure 16–1.

The challenge gangs present to law enforcement and the juvenile delinquency problem it fosters is well put by Sgt. Jackson, Los Angeles Police Department (National School Safety Center 1988, p. 15):

> How can you tell a kid who's making $500 a week guarding a rock house that he really ought to be in school or that he ought to be getting up at 4 a.m. every day to ride his bicycle around the neighborhood to deliver the morning papers?

Further, these youth do not fear the criminal justice system. In fact, in Austin, Texas, older gang members refer to their younger members as "minutemen" because if they do get "busted," they'll be out in a minute. Adults hire

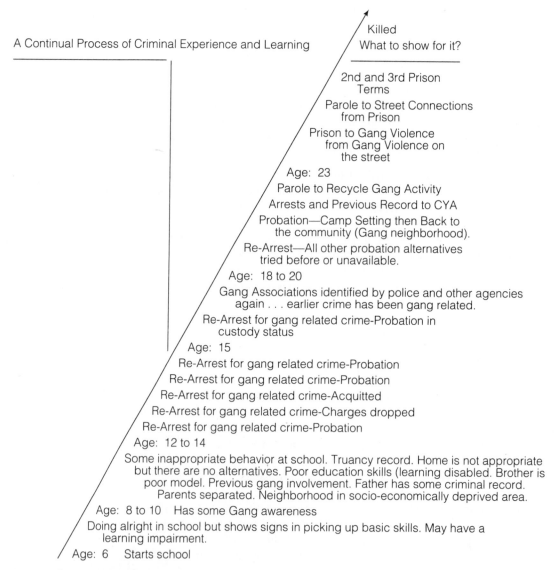

Figure 16–1 Symbolic Profile of a Gang Member's Life

Source: J. R. Davis. *Street Gangs.* Dubuque, Iowa: Kendall/Hunt Publishing, 1982, 4. Reprinted by permission.

kids to run their drugs for them, knowing that if the kids get caught, not much will happen to them.

RELATIONSHIP TO PRISON GANGS

Jackson and McBride (1985, p. 54) discuss the relationship between street gangs and prison gangs:

> Essentially there is no formal relationship between these two kinds of gangs, in the sense that one is an extension of the other. However, from the evidence available, it appears that the street gang members are potential raw material for the prison gang. The majority of prison gang members were at one time members of either barrio, ghetto, or motorcycle gangs. . . .
>
> Prison gang philosophy is very often diametrically opposed to that of the street gang. For example, although loyalty is a prime value for both groups, disagreements among prison gang members are many times settled by the murder of the offending member or members of his family. . . .
>
> The prison gang is cold, calculating, and purposeful. Individuals who break prison gang rules are punished ruthlessly and swiftly. The street gang, on the other hand, operates through pure emotion. Its planning is usually unsophisticated, its actions spontaneous.

Prison gangs are discussed in depth in Chapter 19.

THE EXTENT OF THE PROBLEM

Witkin (1992, p. 181) notes: "Gangs are growing like cancer." They now have affiliations in 32 states and 113 cities.

Authorities say members of two rival drug gangs from Los Angeles, the Crips and the Bloods, have infiltrated cities from Alaska to Washington, D.C., selling cocaine and its derivative, crack. Last year, 387 people died in gang-related violence in Los Angeles, about half of them innocent bystanders. As noted by Robbins (1988, p. 29A):

> With the entrepreneurial savy of MBAs, the Bloods and Crips are making their way across the United States, and officials say there are few states they haven't reached. . . . Two California gangs, fanning out along the interstate highway system, are spreading a sophisticated pattern of violence and drug-dealing across the country. . . . Humphrey [Minnesota Attorney General] said the arrival of the Bloods and Crips gangs makes tougher laws necessary. "These drug gangs are the organized crime families of the 1990s," he said.

And according to the findings of a California State Task Force on Youth Gang Violence (1986):

> Youth gang violence and its threat to innocent citizens are increasing in California.
>
> Heavy Metal, Punk Rockers and Satanic groups have emerged as new phenomena.
>
> Youth gangs are responsible for a disproportionate and growing share of the violence and vandalism in schools.
>
> California laws do not effectively deal with the violent crimes of youth gangs.
>
> Victim and witness intimidation is a major threat to gang case investigations and prosecutions.
>
> Narcotics involvement has become a major factor in gang violence and gang recruitment.

Witkin (1992, p. 29) suggests: "America has been caught up in a pincer movement: Los Angeles street gangs moved east and Jamaican posses moved west from the East Coast, and between them by the end of 1989, they had introduced much of the rest of the country to crack." He notes that "compared with Los Angeles, other cities were easy pickings." They spread across the country, following the interstate highway system.

According to Maxson and Klein (1990, pp. 71–72): "Research suggests higher levels of violence, greater numbers and sophistication of weaponry, broader age ranges among gang members, especially on the adult end, and increasing involvement of gang members in drug distribution systems." Taylor (1990, p. 103) also notes this increase:

> The increase and spread of youth gangs in today's United States constitute a movement that must be recognized and understood. Gangs can no longer be defined in traditional, preconceived terms. Social and economic factors have redefined them, and their imperialistic spread is a multidimensional movement. Illegal drugs play a significant part in this new imperialism. . . . Using fundamental economics, gangs are the suppliers of a continuing and increasing demand. Drugs, as a commodity, have become the same unifying economic force for gangs today (adult and juvenile) as alcohol was during Prohibition.

Taylor (p. 105) divides gangs into three types: scavenger, territorial, and corporate. Gangs may evolve through these three types.

Scavenger gangs have few goals and primarily provide an outlet for impulsive behavior and meet the need to belong. **Territorial gangs** establish turf and defend it. **Corporate gangs** have strong leaders and focus on illegal money-making ventures, often drug trafficking.

Taylor notes that scavenger gangs' crimes tend to be petty, spontaneous, and senseless. When scavenger gangs become serious about organizing for a purpose, they stake out a territory. Traditionally a gang's territory was limited to a neighborhood because most of the gang members did not have cars. Today, however, because gang members have mobility, a territory can be intrastate, interstate, or even international (Taylor, p. 108).

As noted in *Law Enforcement News* (1991, p. 3): "Highly organized and extremely vicious Vietnamese youth gangs are preying on their fellow Southeast Asian refugees, carrying out what police have dubbed 'home invasions,' extorting money from businesses and resorting to violence at whim, and authorities say their ability to stop the gangs is hampered by the unwillingness of victims to report the crimes."

A Cambodian immigrant who serves as a community relations officer with the Long Beach Police Department suggests that the Cambodian youth have asked the Asian gangs to help them in their battle against the Latino gangs. According to the community relations officer, the Vietnamese are "good teachers who have taught [the Cambodians] very well: extortion, armed robbery, rape and other things like drive-by shootings."

Native American gangs in Minneapolis—the Naturals and The Club—used to fight with each other, but now they are also fighting the Vice Lords and Disciples, gangs which have moved into the Minneapolis area. As noted by the president of the Minneapolis Urban League (Batson 1990, p. 12A): "Absolutely the worst thing that could happen in this community is for the conflict that seems to be emerging between Native Americans and African-Americans to explode."

Table 16–2 **Type of Gang Problem by Area (City, County, Site)**

CHRONIC PROBLEM CITIES/AREAS (*n* = 21)	EMERGING PROBLEM CITIES/AREAS (*n* = 24)
Albuquerque, NM	Atlanta, GA
Chicago, IL	Benton Harbor, MI
Chino, CA	Cicero, IL
Detroit, MI	Columbus, OH
East Los Angeles, CA	Evanston, IL
El Monte, CA	Flint, Mi
Inglewood, CA	Fort Wayne, IN
Long Beach, CA	Fort Worth, TX
Los Angeles City, CA	Hialeah, FL
Los Angeles County, CA	Indianapolis, IN
New York, NY	Jackson, MS
Oakland, CA	Louisville, KY
Pomona, CA	Madison, WI
Philadelphia, PA	Miami, FL
Phoenix, AZ	Milwaukee, WI
San Diego, CA	Minneapolis, MN
San Francisco, CA	Reno, NV
San Jose, CA	Rockford, IL
Santa Ana, CA	Sacramento, CA
Stockton, CA	Salt Lake City, UT
Tucson, AZ	Seattle, WA
	Shreveport, LA
	Sterling, IL
	Tallahassee, FL

CHRONIC PROBLEM-INSTITUTIONAL SITES (*n* = 2)	EMERGING PROBLEM-INSTITUTIONAL SITES (*n* = 4)
California Youth Authority[a]	Ethan Allen School (WI)
Sunrise House (CA)	Glen Mills School (PA)
	McClaren School (OR)
	Paramount School (CA)

[a] In much of the analysis, only the California Youth Authority is included as an area with cities or county areas. It has also dealt with the youth gang problem since before 1980.

Source: C.R. Huff. *Gangs in America.* Copyright © 1990, 292. Sage Publications: Newbury Park, Calif. Reprinted by permission.

Table 16–2 lists where gangs are a chronic problem and where they are an emerging problem.

WHAT CAN BE DONE?

The State Task Force on Youth Gang Violence (1986) of the California Council on Criminal Justice suggests that both short- and long-term solutions are needed for dealing with gangs and gang violence. Short-term approaches would rely on law-enforcement efforts, including stiffer penalties for hardcore gang members, and on special training for police, prosecutors, and judges. Long-term solutions would emphasize preventive and community-based counseling for both gang members and their parents.

The State Task Force (1986, p. 37) made the following long-term prevention and intervention solutions to youth gang problems:

Legislation should be enacted or policy should be established to

1. design and develop a statewide gang information system and clearinghouse;
2. implement a school-based gang/narcotic prevention program to operate co-operatively with local law enforcement agencies;
3. provide technical assistance to local law enforcement agencies for gang crime analysis;
4. establish a model project within the Department of the Youth Authority to identify youth gang members and intensify parole supervision;
5. establish or expand special units in probation departments to supervise gang members;
6. establish a Southeast Asian youth gang prevention and intervention program;
7. establish statewide standards within custodial institutions to restrict any activity encouraging or condoning gang membership;
8. establish a model gang intervention program using ex-gang members and community street workers.

Huff (1990, pp. 314–315) states: "A thorough review of the gang literature ... causes me to believe the following things about the gang problem in the United States":

1. We need more research on gangs, especially studies of gangs in the context of their social and economic milieu.
2. The research that we have suggests that gangs tend to be located in central cities and are composed primarily of poor, disadvantaged, culturally marginal youths. Many youths, however, who are ostensibly subject to the same living conditions do not become gang members.
3. Whether researchers adopt an urban underclass perspective or a subcultural perspective, we tend to be discussing the same *ecological* areas of our cities.
4. The solutions to the problems that cause gangs and the problems caused by gangs will require intervention strategies that involve community participants in efforts to counteract the decay of local institutions (families, churches, schools, recreational and job opportunities) by establishing ... functional communities ... Elitist, top-down policy formulation and implementation are doomed to failure because they are usually devoid of an understanding of the economic and sociocultural milieu of the target population and avoid establishing a sense of ownership or social investment on the part of those indigenous to the area.
5. Finally, I do not believe that the optimal public policy response to gangs and gang violence is to identify the problem in those terms. Rather, I believe we should view gangs as a manifestation of other problems endemic in our socioeconomic structure and in certain ecological areas of our cities. Whether one adopts a social disorganization (or other subcultural) perspective or an urban underclass (economic) perspective, it is likely that these ecological areas are generating the highest rates of crime, delinquency, incarceration, mental illness, public assistance, and other indicators of "social pathology."

Mobilizing the Community

As with the drug problem, the gang problem cannot be effectively dealt with by the police or legislation alone. It must be a total community effort. Some community organizational strategies that have been used to combat gang problems include the following (Spergel and Curry 1990, p. 295):

■ Cleaning up graffiti in the community.
■ Involving the schools.

Minneapolis gang members speaking to actor Jim Brown in his Hollywood home about channeling gang energy into improving conditions for the Afro-American community.

- Mobilizing the community.
- Building community trust.
- Involving parent groups in community programs.
- Educating the community.
- Changing the community.

Spergel and Curry (p. 309) conclude that:

The implication of our finding is that more resources alone for police or even human service programs would not contribute much to dealing effectively with the youth gang problem. It is more likely that community mobilization and more resources for and reform of the educational system and the job market, targeted at gang youth or clearly at-risk youth, would be more cost-effective as well as more effective in the reduction of the problem.

Policy recommendations emanating from these findings would not necessarily require a renewed war on poverty, but rather a series of programs targeted specifically at the youth gang problem addressing not only issues of economic deprivation and lack of opportunities but social disorganization and the mobilization of community institutions in a concerted attack on the problem.

SUMMARY

A gang is a group of people that forms an allegiance for a common purpose and engages in unlawful or criminal activity. Most gangs are racially or ethnically homogeneous.

Distinguishing characteristics of gangs include leadership, organization, associational patterns, domain identification, and illegal activity. Gang members might also be identified by their names, their symbols (clothing and tattoos), and how they communicate, including graffiti and sign language. Most female gangs are adjuncts or auxiliaries to a male gang.

The most common reasons for joining a gang are for identity or recognition, for protection, for fellowship and brotherhood, or from intimidation.

Scavenger gangs have few goals and primarily provide an outlet for impulsive behavior and meet the need to belong. Territorial gangs establish turf and defend it. Corporate gangs have strong leaders and focus on illegal money-making ventures, often drug trafficking.

DISCUSSION QUESTIONS

1. Are there gangs in your area? If so, in what are they involved?

2. Do you think the gang problem is as serious as authorities claim?

3. Are street gangs depicted realistically on television shows? In movies?

4. Do you personally know a gang member?

5. What do you think might be done to reduce the gang problem?

6. What are some distinguishing characteristics of gangs?

7. Do gangs have some value in society?

8. Why do people join gangs?

9. Is a hard or soft approach to gang activity the best approach to curtail criminal activity?

10. Are gangs a threat to the quality of life in your area?

TERMS

Bloods, corporate gangs, Crips, cultural gangs, gang, graffiti, instrumental gangs, scavenger gangs, territorial gangs, traditional gangs, turf.

REFERENCES

Batson, L. "Indian Gangs Battle New Enemies." *Star Tribune,* July 22, 1990, 12A.

Campbell, A. *The Girls in the Gang: A Report from New York City.* New York: Basil Blackwell, 1984.

Davis, J. R. *Street Gangs.* Dubuque, Iowa: Kendall/Hunt Publishing, 1982.

Drugs—*The American Family in Crisis: A Judicial Response, 39 Recommendations.* National Council of Juvenile and Family Court Judges, August 4, 1988.

Encyclopedia of Crime and Justice, vol. 4. New York: The Free Press, a Division of Macmillan, 1983.

"Growing in Power and Viciousness, Vietnamese Gangs Flex Their Muscles." *Law Enforcement News,* May 15/31, 1991, 3, 10.

Huff, C. R. (Ed.) *Gangs in America.* Newbury Park, Calif.: Sage Publications, 1990.

Jackson, R. K. and McBride, W. D. *Understanding Street Gangs.* Sacramento, Calif.: Custom Publishing, 1985.

Maxson, C. L. and Klein, M. W. "Street Gang Violence: Twice as Great, or Half as Great?" In *Gangs in America,* edited by C. R. Huff. Newbury Park, Calif.: Sage Publications, 1990, 71–100.

Miller, W. B. "Why the United States Has Failed to Solve its Youth Gang Problem." In *Gangs in America,* edited by C. R. Huff. Newbury Park, Calif.: Sage Publications, 1990, 263–287.

National School Safety Center. *Gangs in Schools: Breaking Up Is Hard to Do.* Malibu, Calif.: Pepperdine University Press, 1988.

Robbins, W. "California Gangs Staking Claims across the U.S." *Star Tribune,* December 4, 1988, p. 29A.

Sessions, W. S. "Gang Violence and Organized Crime." *The Police Chief* (November 1990): 17.

Spergel, I. A. and Curry, G. D. "Strategies and Perceived Agency Effectiveness in Dealing with the Youth Gang Problem." In *Gangs in America,* edited by C. R. Huff. Newbury Park, Calif.: Sage Publications, 1990, 288–309.

State Task Force on Youth Gang Violence. *Final Report.* California Council on Criminal Justice, January 1986.

Street Gangs of Los Angeles County: A White Paper.

Taylor, C. S. "Gang Imperialism." In *Gangs in America,* edited by C. R. Huff. Newbury Park, Calif.: Sage Publications, 1990, 103–115.

Vetter, H. J. and Territo, L. *Crime and Justice in America.* St. Paul, Minn.: West Publishing Company, 1984.

Witkin, G. "Kids Who Kill." In *Criminal Justice 92/93,* edited by J. J. Sullivan and J. L. Victor. Guilford, Conn.: The Dushkin Publishing Group, 1992. (Reprinted from *U.S. News & World Report,* April 8, 1991, 26–32.)

Witkin, G. "The Men Who Created Crack." In *Criminal Justice 92/93,* edited by J. J. Sullivan and J. L. Victor. Guilford, Conn.: The Dushkin Publishing Group, 1992. (Reprinted from *U.S. News & World Report,* August 19, 1991, 44–53.)

CHAPTER 17

Victimization: The Risks and Impact

Something insidious has happened in America: crime has made victims of us all. Awareness of its danger affects the way we think, where we live, where we go, what we buy, how we raise our children, and the quality of our lives as we age. The specter of violent crime and the knowledge that, without warning, any person can be attacked or crippled, robbed, or killed, lurks at the fringes of consciousness.

—**Statement of the Chairman, President's Task Force on Victims of Crime**

Do You Know

What percentage of all crimes against people and their households are not reported to police?

What groups of people are most likely and least likely to become victims of crime?

What households are at greatest risk of violent crime?

If a person is more likely to be victimized by a stranger or by a relative or acquaintance?

How victims of violent crime protect themselves?

How crime affects its victims?

What indirect or secondary victims are?

How many states have compensation programs to help victims of violent crimes and what these programs typically offer?

How victims may become involved in the criminal justice system?

INTRODUCTION

It is common knowledge that law enforcement officers must know how to deal with criminals. Equally important, however, is the officers' ability to deal with those who are victims of crime. This is critical, not only because this will enhance the image of the police officer as a professional, but also because personal concern and establishment of rapport will enhance communications, and consequently, result in the officers' ability to obtain more information related to the crime.

Waller (1990, p. 141) notes that: "Victims are the immediate source of 60% of common crime known to the police." Skogan et al. (1990, p. 9) suggest: "Crime victims could be key actors in the criminal justice process, but more often they are kept at the periphery." They further note: "Crime victims are the 'forgotten persons' of the criminal justice system, valued only for their capacity to report crimes and to appear in court as witnesses." As noted by Finn (1990, p. 39): "The single most important determinant of whether a case will be

Table 17–1 Reasons Given for Not Reporting Violent Crimes to the Police

PERCENT OF REASONS FOR NOT REPORTING

TYPE OF CRIME	REPORTED TO ANOTHER OFFICIAL	PRIVATE OR PERSONAL MATTER	OBJECT RECOVERED; OFFENDER UNSUCCESSFUL	NOT IMPORTANT ENOUGH	INSURANCE WOULD NOT COVER
All personal crimes	**15.4%**	**7.0%**	**24.8%**	**2.8%**	**2.0%**
Crimes of violence	10.6	20.3	19.8	5.4	0.1
Completed	8.8	18.3	12.9	2.8	0.4
Attempted	11.3	21.2	22.6	6.5	0
Rape	14.0	16.6	14.1	0	0
Robbery	7.8	13.2	24.1	1.8	0.4
Completed	5.5	10.3	16.9	0.8	0.8
With injury	7.3	14.2	8.8	0	2.5
From serious assault	8.3	0	4.3	0	0
From minor assault	6.4	26.1	12.5	0	4.6
Without injury	4.7	8.6	20.6	1.2	0
Attempted	10.4	16.4	32.3	2.9	0
With injury	13.2	8.0	27.5	3.0	0
From serious assault	5.8	12.4	6.1	7.1	0
From minor assault	18.7	4.7	43.4	0	0
Without injury	9.4	19.3	34.0	2.9	0
Assault	11.1	22.0	19.0	6.3	0.1
Aggravated	6.7	23.9	14.3	5.2	0.2
Simple	12.9	21.1	21.0	6.8	0
Crimes of theft	16.9	2.9	26.4	2.0	2.6
Completed	17.4	2.9	25.2	1.9	2.5
Attempted	8.2	3.0	43.2	4.2	3.0
Personal larceny with contact	11.8	3.7	17.0	1.6	0.9
Purse snatching	11.1	3.2	32.9	0	0
Pocket picking	12.0	3.9	12.2	2.0	1.2
Personal larceny without contact	17.1	2.8	26.8	2.0	2.6
Completed	17.7	2.9	25.7	1.9	2.6
Less than $50	20.3	2.6	38.5	2.5	1.4
$50 or more	15.3	3.2	12.2	1.1	3.9
Amount not available	14.2	2.6	25.1	3.2	2.6
Attempted	7.9	2.6	42.6	4.4	3.1

solved may be information supplied by the victim. Thus, it is not without reason that the most important person in the criminal justice system may not be the judge, the police officer, or the prosecutor—it may be the victim."

A great deal of crime is not reported to the police. Reporting rates have been found to vary by type of crime and by age and sex of the victim but not by the victim's race.

Kelly (1990, p. 173) states: "The National Crime Survey revealed that, at best, 50% of crimes were reported to police. A major reason for nonreporting was victims' apprehension as to how they would be treated and whether they would be believed."

One-half to two-thirds of all crimes are not reported to the police.

Reasons for not reporting violent crimes to the police were varied, with the most common being a private/personal matter (see Table 17–1).

Table 17–1 continued

PERCENT OF REASONS FOR NOT REPORTING

NOT AWARE CRIME OCCURRED UNTIL LATER	UNABLE TO RECOVER PROPERTY; NO ID NO.	LACK OF PROOF	POLICE WOULD NOT WANT TO BE BOTHERED	POLICE INEFFICIENT, INEFFECTIVE, OR BIASED	FEAR OF REPRISAL	TOO INCONVENIENT OR TIME CONSUMING	OTHER REASONS
4.5%	6.8%	9.9%	7.8%	2.9%	1.3%	3.9%	11.0%
0.2*	0.9	6.4	7.3	3.7	4.4	4.0	16.9
0*	3.0	9.0	8.3	5.2	7.4	4.1	19.7
0.3*	0*	5.4	6.8	3.1	3.2	3.9	15.7
0*	0*	11.3*	2.5*	4.0*	11.5*	9.6*	16.4*
0.4*	5.3	12.9	7.8	7.0	3.6	3.4	12.3
0*	9.8	17.0	8.0	7.2	6.7	2.7*	14.3
0*	7.4*	17.0	1.9*	6.6*	4.0*	6.5*	23.9
0*	9.0*	13.3*	0*	10.5*	8.9*	14.3*	31.4*
0*	6.0*	20.1*	3.4*	3.3*	0*	0*	17.6*
0*	10.9	17.0	10.8	7.5	7.8	0.9*	9.9
1.0*	0*	8.3	7.5	6.8	0*	4.3*	10.1
0*	0*	11.2*	5.8*	18.6*	0*	0*	12.6*
0*	0*	8.3*	0*	36.9	0*	0*	23.4*
0*	0*	13.4*	10.0*	5.0*	0*	0*	4.6*
1.3*	0*	7.2	8.1	2.7*	0*	5.8*	9.2
0.2*	0*	4.9	7.3	3.0	4.4	3.9	17.9
0.5*	0*	8.2	4.9	5.3	4.9	5.9	19.8
0.1*	0*	3.5	8.3	2.0	4.2	3.1	17.0
5.9	8.6	11.0	7.9	2.6	0.3	3.9	9.1
5.8	9.1	11.2	7.9	2.7	0.3	3.9	9.1
6.5	0.7*	8.5	7.8	1.1*	1.0*	3.7	9.3
8.3	10.4	18.1	7.4	3.3	0.7*	4.4	12.3
1.9*	9.6*	14.8	6.2*	6.9*	1.6*	4.6*	7.1*
10.3	10.6	19.1	7.7	2.2*	0.5*	4.3	13.9
5.8	8.5	10.7	7.9	2.6	0.3	3.9	9.0
5.7	9.0	10.8	8.0	2.7	0.3	3.9	8.9
3.3	6.0	7.5	6.5	1.4	0.2*	3.3	6.5
8.1	12.4	14.3	9.2	4.1	0.3	4.7	11.4
7.3	7.6	11.6	11.7	1.2*	0*	2.0*	10.9
6.9	0.8*	8.7	7.8	1.1*	1.1*	3.7	9.3

Note: Percents may add to more than 100% because some people gave more than one reason for not reporting.

Source: Criminal Victimization in the United States, 1989. U.S. Department of Justice, 1991.

VICTIMIZATION STATISTICS

The National Crime Survey (NCS) estimates that 35 million criminal victim-izations occurred during 1986 (Riggs and Kilpatrick 1990, p. 120). According to the Bureau of Justice Statistics (1988, p. 24): "The chance of being a violent crime victim, with or without injury, is greater than that of being hurt in a traffic accident." Table 17–2 compares the chances of being the victim of specific types of crimes with other life events.

The chances of becoming a victim are great. The U.S. Bureau of Justice Statistics estimates that 83 percent of children now twelve years old will become victims of actual or attempted violence if our crime rates continue at their present level. Further, according to Skogan et al. (1990, p. 7): "In recent years, one of every four U.S. households has been victimized by personal or property crime. At one time or another, crime will touch most Americans or affect the lives of their relatives, friends, and acquaintances."

According to National Crime Survey (NCS) victimization data:

- Age is one of the strongest correlates of victimization, with the elderly being victimized at a rate far less than that of younger people.
- The victimization rate for males is twice that for females.
- The rate of violent victimizations—especially aggravated assaults and rob-beries—is greater for blacks than whites.
- Those who live in urban areas suffer more victimizations than residents of suburban or rural areas.
- As income goes up, the risk of personal victimization goes down.

Sullivan and Victor (1990, p. 57) note: "The nation's crime siege has con-tinued through the 1980s despite predictions it would ease. . . . A violent crime is committed every 5 seconds, leaving an anguished victim and a scarred community." They cite the following statistics from a typical year:

- Fewer than half the crimes committed are reported to authorities.
- There are 8.1 million serious crimes like murder, assault, and burglary.

It is imperative that victims of and witnesses to crime report the information to the police.

Table 17–2 Comparison of Adult Crime Rates with the Rates of Other Life Events

EVENTS	RATE PER 1,000 ADULTS
Accidental injury, all circumstances	242
Accidental injury at home	79
Personal theft	72
Accidental injury at work	58
Violent victimization	31
Assault (aggravated and simple)	24
Injury in motor vehicle accident	17
Death, all causes	11
Victimization with injury	10
Serious (aggravated) assault	9
Robbery	6
Heart disease death	4
Cancer death	2
Rape (women only)	2
Accidental death, all circumstances	.5
Pneumonia/influenza death	.3
Motor vehicle accident death	.2
Suicide	.2
Injury from fire	.1
Homicide/legal intervention death	.1
Death from fire	.03

Source: U.S. Department of Justice. Bureau of Justice Statistics. *Report to the Nation on Crime and Justice.* 2d ed. (1988): 24.

- Only 724,000 adults are arrested.
- Only 193,000 of them are convicted.
- Only 149,000 of them go to prison.

The risks for criminals is low!

RISK FACTORS

The degree of risk people face is affected by individual factors as well as factors related to how and where they live, called **household risk factors.**

Individual Risk Factors

Certain individuals are at greater risk than others, as summarized in Table 17–3.

As noted by the Bureau of Justice Statistics:

- Victims of crime are more often men than women.
- Younger people are much more likely than the elderly to be victims of crime. (But the elderly have a greater fear of crime and may restrict their lives in ways that reduce their chances of being victimized.)
- Blacks are more likely to be victims of violent crime than whites or members of other racial groups.
- The divorced or separated and the never married are more likely than the married or the widowed to be victims of crime.

Table 17–3 **Victimization Rates per 1,000 Persons Age 12 and Older**

	PERSONAL CRIMES OF . . .	
	Violence	**Theft**
Total (U.S.)	29	69
Sex		
Male	37	72
Female	22	65
Age		
12–15	63	99
16–19	74	115
20–24	58	118
25–34	35	84
35–49	21	64
50–64	8	41
65 and older	4	20
Race and origin		
White	28	69
Black	36	69
Other	27	64
Hispanic	39	71
Non-Hispanic	28	69
Marital status by sex		
Males		
Never married	70	111
Divorced/separated	56	99
Married	17	48
Widowed	15	36
Females		
Never married	40	100
Divorced/separated	48	82
Married	11	52
Widowed	4	26
Family income		
Less than $7,500	50	71
$7,500–$9,999	32	52
$10,000–$14,999	35	62
$15,000–$24,999	29	66
$25,000–$29,999	28	70
$30,000–$49,999	23	68
$50,000 or more	20	78
Education		
0–4 years	17	23
5–7 years	45	67
8 years	30	53
High school graduate	30	61
1–3 years college	29	83
College graduate	25	85

Note: Personal crimes of violence include rape, robbery, and assault. Personal crimes of theft include larceny without contact, purse snatching, and pocket picking.

Source: BJS *Criminal victimization in the U.S.* 1991 for 1989.

- Violent crime rates are higher for lower-income people.
- Theft rates are highest for people with high incomes (more than $50,000 per year).
- Students and the unemployed are more likely than housewives, retirees, or the employed to be victims of crime.
- Rural residents are less often crime victims than are people living in cities.

Young, black, unemployed males living in the city have the highest victimization rates; elderly white females living in rural areas have the lowest victimization rates.

Risk of violent victimization drops significantly after age thirty-four. As might be expected risk is greatest in the central city and least in rural areas.

Both the Uniform Crime Reports and statistics from the Public Health Department indicate that the homicide rate has been rising since 1961. Reasons for the rise include the fact that babies born during the baby boom reached age sixteen in the early 1960s. Since violent victimization is more prevalent among people under age thirty, it might be expected that the homicide rate would increase as a large proportion of the population reached the victimization-prone ages.

- Homicide victims are more often men than women.
- Persons aged twenty-five to thirty-four are the most likely to be homicide victims.
- Blacks are five times more likely than whites to be homicide victims.

Table 17–4 summarizes homicide rates by sex, age, and race. Table 17–5 presents the lifetime risk of homicide by sex and race.

Household Risk Factors

Certain types of households also are more likely to be victims of crime than others. Included in the high-risk category are Hispanics, blacks, renters, house-

Table 17–4 **Homicide Rates**

Age	Total	SEX			RACE			
		Male	Female	Unknown	White	Black	Other	Unknown
Total	20,045	15,628	4,399	18	9,724	9,744	345	232
Percent distribution	100.0	78.0	21.9	.1	48.5	48.6	1.7	1.2
Under 18	1,970	1,362	607	1	942	971	38	19
18 and over	17,769	14,038	3,729	2	8,646	8,650	304	169
Infant (under 1)	264	148	116	—	159	98	5	2
1 to 4	317	176	140	1	169	136	10	2
5 to 9	118	51	67	—	61	51	2	4
10 to 14	270	162	108	—	138	125	7	—
15 to 19	2,348	1,994	352	2	918	1,376	28	26
20 to 24	3,472	2,923	549	—	1,485	1,911	52	24
25 to 29	3,405	2,736	669	—	1,519	1,818	40	28
30 to 34	2,773	2,140	633	—	1,307	1,386	53	27
35 to 39	2,051	1,615	436	—	991	994	44	22
40 to 44	1,400	1,108	292	—	774	575	29	22
45 to 49	894	695	199	—	537	322	21	14
50 to 54	586	469	117	—	358	206	17	5
55 to 59	451	332	119	—	271	159	18	3
60 to 64	422	322	100	—	261	152	5	4
65 to 69	284	195	89	—	180	98	5	1
70 to 74	234	129	105	—	167	61	5	1
75 and over	450	205	245	—	293	153	1	3
Unknown	306	228	63	15	136	123	3	44

Source: FBI *Crime in the United States 1990.*

Table 17–5 **Lifetime Risk of Being a Homicide Victim**

LIFETIME RISK OF HOMICIDE

1 out of:

179	White males
30	Black males
495	White females
132	Black females

Source: Updated data based on similar material from *The Risk of Violent Crime*, BJS Special Report, May 1985.

holds headed by younger persons, households containing six or more people, and households in urban areas.

Blacks are more often victims of household crimes than nonblacks.

- Renters have higher household crime rates than home owners.
- Household crime more often affects households headed by younger people.
- Household crime rates are highest for households with six or more people.
- Households in cities have higher crime rates than suburban or rural households.

OTHER FACTORS IN VICTIMIZATION

Beyond statistics, several other factors enter into understanding victimization, including the relationship between the victim and offender, the use of weapons, and how victims protect themselves—or attempt to do so.

The Relationship Between Victim and Offender

When people worry about crime, they are most often worried about being attacked by strangers. This fear is frequently justifiable: with the exception of murder and rape, most violent crimes are committed by strangers. Males, blacks, and young people face the greatest risk of violent crime by strangers and are victimized by violent strangers at an annual rate almost triple that of women. Blacks are more than twice as likely as whites to be robbed by strangers.

Most violent crimes except murder and rape are committed by strangers.

The risk of robbery is less for older people, but this may be because many older people are no longer physically able to move about outside their homes and many others may fear crime and, consequently, remain at home most of the time. It may be that older people who are active and mobile may be at as much risk as the general population.

Women are more vulnerable than men to assaults by acquaintances and relatives, with two-thirds of all assaults on divorced and separated women committed by acquaintances and relatives. Spouses or former spouses committed only 5 percent of the assaults by single offenders. In almost three-fourths of spouse versus spouse assaults, the victim was divorced or separated at the time of the incident.

More than half of all homicides are committed by someone known to the victim. Acquaintances commit more than 39 percent of all homicides; relatives commit 17 percent of all homicides.

It is of interest to note that victims and offenders are usually of the same race, as summarized in Figure 17–1.

Use of Weapons in Victimization

Except for homicide, most violent crimes do not involve the use of weapons (see Table 17–6).

One logical explanation for this is that victims will be less likely to resist a person armed with a gun or knife.

How Victims Protect Themselves

Victims rarely respond by wielding a weapon as summarized in Table 17–7. However, rape victims are more likely to use force, try a verbal response, or attract attention and are less likely than others to do nothing to protect themselves. In contrast, robbery victims are least likely to try to talk themselves out of being victimized and the most likely to do nothing.

Victims of violent crime can protect themselves by returning physical force, by verbal response, by attracting attention, by nonviolent evasion, or by brandishing a weapon.

Use of Deadly Force

Each state distinguishes when citizens may legally use deadly force compared to physical force to protect their dwellings. **Deadly force** refers to any force intended to cause death or serious physical injury. Physical force, in contrast, refers to all force directed to another person but not intended to be lethal, including confinement.

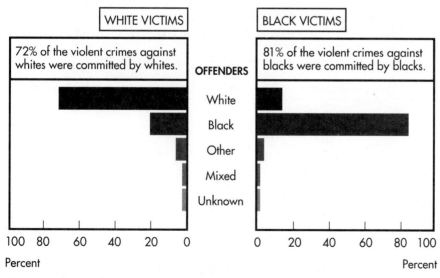

Figure 17–1 Relationship of Victims and Offenders by Race *Victims and offenders are of the same race in three out of four violent crimes.*

Table 17-6 Involvement of Weapons in Crime

Relationship and type of crime	Total	FIREARM Handgun	FIREARM Other gun	FIREARM Gun type unknown	Knife	Sharp object	Blunt object	Other weapon	Type unknown
All incidents									
Crimes of violence	31.7%	26.6%	5.0%	0.2%	26.7%	3.3%	17.7%	15.0%	5.4%
Completed	27.1	24.7	2.2	0.3	26.9	4.9	17.6	18.5	5.0
Attempted	35.1	27.9	7.0	0.2	26.6	2.2	17.9	12.5	5.7
Rape	26.4	26.4	0	0	39.7	6.3	14.0	13.6	0
Robbery	39.7	38.2	1.5	0	32.8	3.8	12.1	8.8	2.8
Completed	44.6	43.0	1.6	0	31.9	3.7	9.8	7.8	2.3
With injury	28.9	26.5	2.4	0	39.1	1.9	18.9	8.0	3.1
Without injury	53.5	52.3	1.2	0	27.8	4.7	4.6	7.6	1.8
Attempted	27.7	26.5	1.3	0	35.1	4.0	17.7	11.3	4.2
With injury	33.0	33.0	0	0	40.3	6.0	7.3	1.8	11.6
Without injury	26.0	24.4	1.7	0	33.4	3.3	21.0	14.3	1.9
Aggravated assault	28.9	22.3	6.3	0.3	24.2	3.1	19.9	17.4	6.5
Completed with injury	12.2	9.1	2.7	0.5	22.7	6.0	24.6	27.1	7.4
Attempted with weapon	36.5	28.3	8.0	0.2	24.9	1.8	17.8	13.0	6.1
Involving strangers									
Crimes of violence	35.5	29.9	5.4	0.1	25.4	3.7	15.9	13.8	5.7
Rape	19.6	19.6	0	0	43.4	6.8	15.3	14.9	0
Robbery	42.3	41.1	1.3	0	31.2	4.4	12.2	6.6	3.3
Aggravated assault	32.5	24.6	7.7	0.2	21.9	3.3	17.8	17.4	7.1
Involving nonstrangers									
Crimes of violence	23.3	18.9	4.0	0.4	29.7	2.4	21.9	17.8	4.9
Rape	100.0	100.0	0	0	0	0	0	0	0
Robbery	22.8	19.6	3.3	0	43.0	0	11.1	23.1	0
Aggravated assault	23.0	18.4	4.1	0.4	28.1	2.8	23.4	17.2	5.5

Note: Detail may not add to total shown because of rounding. Some respondents may have cited more than one weapon present.

Source: U.S. Department of Justice, *Criminal Victimization in the United States, 1989.*

Table 17-7 How Victims of Violent Crimes Protect Themselves. Personal crimes of violence, 1989: Percent distribution of self- protective measures employed by victims, by type of measure and type of crime

Self-protective measure	PERCENT OF SELF-PROTECTIVE MEASURES Crimes of violence	Completed violent crimes	Attempted violent crimes	Rape
Total	100.0%	100.0%	100.0%	100.0%
Attacked offender with weapon	1.4	1.7	1.1	0.8
Attacked offender without weapon	10.3	13.0	8.5	13.4
Threatened offender with weapon	1.4	1.2	1.6	0.9
Threatened offender without weapon	2.4	2.2	2.5	3.0
Resisted or captured offender	21.1	30.3	14.9	16.2
Scared or warned offender	8.5	8.6	8.3	10.6
Persuaded or appeased offender	14.7	11.3	17.0	14.2
Ran away or hid	16.3	11.6	19.5	11.2
Got help or gave alarm	10.7	9.4	11.6	9.7
Screamed from pain or fear	2.9	5.4	1.2	10.4
Took another method	10.3	5.3	13.7	9.5
Total number of self-protective measures	6,544,660	2,640,670	3,903,980	239,930

Note: Detail may not add to total because of rounding. Some respondents may have cited more than one self-protective measure employed.

Source: U.S. Department of Justice, *Criminal Victimization in the United States, 1989.*

In some states forced entry is enough to indicate that an inhabitant is in imminent, immediate danger justifying deadly force. In other states, the intruder must attack directly or threaten an inhabitant before deadly force is justified. Generally, a trespasser is not considered to pose a direct threat to life. Therefore, deadly force against trespassers is not usually justified.

If an assailant is attacking a third party, citizens are justified in using deadly force if the third party is in imminent, immediate danger of losing his or her life, provided the third party did not provoke the attack. Table 17–8 summarizes states laws that justify deadly force.

CRIME'S EFFECT ON ITS VICTIMS

National Crime Survey and UCR data suggest that losses from personal and household crime exceeded $13 billion in 1985 and that two million injuries or deaths resulted from violent crime.

Violent crime can affect its victim physically, economically, and emotionally.

The economic impact of crime must also take into consideration time lost from work, medical costs, and the introduction of security measures to prevent future victimization.

Most crime victims experience some combination of physical pain, financial loss, and emotional distress. Riggs and Kilpatrick (1990, p. 121) suggest:

> Victims experience problems that can be categorized loosely as immediate, short term, and long term in nature. The immediate reactions include shock, denial, anxiety, anger, depression, and feelings of vulnerability. These symptoms usually last for a period of hours to days. In the weeks and months that follow a criminal act the victims may experience mood swings, variously feeling fearful, angry, sad,

Table 17–7 *(Continued)*

| | ROBBERY | | | ASSAULT | |
Total	With injury	Without injury	Total	Aggravated	Simple
100.0%	100.0%	100.0%	100.0%	100.0%	100.0%
0.9	0.7	1.0	1.5	2.6	0.8
10.9	12.1	9.8	10.1	8.4	11.1
2.1	1.1	3.1	1.3	2.3	0.8
3.1	2.6	3.5	2.2	1.8	2.4
28.5	35.3	22.2	19.8	18.6	20.4
7.9	10.1	5.9	8.5	8.2	8.7
12.0	6.4	17.3	15.3	13.3	16.5
11.8	7.9	15.3	17.5	20.8	15.5
9.8	10.4	9.2	11.0	11.6	10.6
4.0	7.4	0.7	2.3	3.1	1.9
9.1	6.0	11.9	10.6	9.4	11.4
1,097,320	528,740	568,580	5,207,400	1,960,070	3,247,320

Table 17-8 State Laws that Justify Deadly Force

| State | EVEN IF LIFE IS NOT THREATENED, DEADLY FORCE MAY BE JUSTIFIED TO PROTECT: | | Specific crime against which deadly force may be justified |
	Dwelling	Property	
Alabama	Yes	No	Arson, burglary, rape, kidnaping, or robbery in "any degree"
Alaska	Yes	No	Actual commission of felony
Arizona	Yes	No	Arson, burglary, kidnaping, aggravated assaults
Arkansas	Yes	No	Felonies as defined by statute
California	Yes	No	Unlawful or forcible entry
Colorado	Yes	No	Felonies, including assault, robbery, rape, arson, kidnaping
Connecticut	Yes	No	Any violent crime
Delaware	Yes	No	Felonious activity
D.C.	Yes	No	Felony
Florida	Yes	No	Forcible felony
Georgia	Yes	Yes	Actual commission of a forcible felony
Hawaii	Yes	Yes	Felonious property damage, burglary, robbery, etc.
Idaho	Yes	Yes	Felonious breaking and entering
Illinois	Yes	Yes	Forcible felony
Indiana	Yes	No	Unlawful entry
Iowa	Yes	Yes	Breaking and entering
Kansas	Yes	No	Breaking and entering including attempts
Kentucky	No	No	—
Louisiana	Yes	No	Unlawful entry including attempts
Maine	Yes	No	Criminal trespass, kidnaping, rape, arson
Maryland	No	No	—
Massachusetts	No	No	—
Michigan	Yes	No	Circumstances on a case by case basis
Minnesota	Yes	No	Felony
Mississippi	Yes	—	Felony including attempts
Missouri	No	No	—
Montana	Yes	Yes	Any forcible felony

or elated. Victims often experience guilt, loss of self-esteem, vulnerability, anxiety, and depression, and they may reexperience the traumatic event in the form of nightmares or flashbacks.

According to Finn (1990, p. 39), emotional distress is often the most severe consequence of victimization and can include "feelings of fear, anger, shame, self-blame, helplessness, and depression. Sometimes long-term emotional disabilities also result, including sleeplessness, loss of concentration, and fear of being left alone."

INDIRECT OR SECONDARY VICTIMS

Family members and friends may become **indirect** or **secondary victims,** feeling the pain and suffering along with the **primary victim.**

Riggs and Kilpatrick (1990, p. 135) state: "It is important for the criminal justice system to recognize the difficulties faced by the friends and family

Table 17-8   (Continued)

State	EVEN IF LIFE IS NOT THREATENED, DEADLY FORCE MAY BE JUSTIFIED TO PROTECT: Dwelling	Property	Specific crime against which deadly force may be justified
Nebraska	Yes	No	Unlawful entry, kidnaping, and rape
Nevada	Yes	—	Actual commission of felony
New Hampshire	Yes	—	Felony
New Jersey	Yes	No	Burglary, arson, and robbery
New Mexico	Yes	Yes	Any felony
New York	Yes	No	Burglary, arson, kidnaping, and robbery including attempts
North Carolina	Yes	No	Intending to commit a felony
North Dakota	Yes	No	Any violent felony
Ohio	—	—	
Oklahoma	Yes	No	Felony within a dwelling
Oregon	Yes	—	Burglary in a dwelling including attempts
Pennsylvania	Yes	—	Burglary or criminal trespass
Rhode Island	Yes	—	Breaking and entering
South Carolina	No	No	—
South Dakota	Yes	—	Burglary including attempts
Tennessee	Yes	No	Felony
Texas	Yes	No	Burglary, robbery, or theft during the night
Utah	Yes	—	Felony
Vermont	Yes	—	Forcible felony
Virginia	No	No	—
Washington	No	No	—
West Virginia	Yes	No	Any felony
Wisconsin	No	No	—
Wyoming	No	No	—

Note: This table provides a summary of state statutes and should not be used by citizens in planning their protection. Legal advice that considers the specific situation and the State statute is advised.

Source: BJS update as of December 1986 based on data from Ronald Cruit, ed., *Intruder in Your Home* (New York: Stein and Day, 1983).

members of crime victims. Those involved in the criminal justice system should help indirect victims find legal and psychological assistance and prepare them for the stress that might result from contact with the criminal justice system."

Impact on the Community

When a violent crime occurs, the impact often goes further than the victim. Often the entire community suffers. If a small town youth murders his entire family, the community may go into shock. Everyone feels vulnerable. Fear sets in. Morale drops.

FEAR OF VICTIMIZATION

Public opinion polls have found that people do fear crime in general, but they generally feel their own neighborhoods are relatively safe. According to the Bureau of Justice Statistics (1988, p. 24): "about a third of the people in the United States feel very safe in their neighborhoods." This leaves, of course, two-thirds who do *not* feel safe. If someone in the neighborhood is victimized, however, the entire neighborhood may feel much more vulnerable. The Bureau also notes that the people with the highest risk of being victimized, that is young males, are not the ones who express the greatest fear of victimization. The people who express the greatest fear of being victimized are females and the elderly, and, as previously stated, they are at lower risk than other segments of the population. Whether they are at lower risk because they take measures to reduce their chances of being victimized is not known. If the elderly, for example, restrict their activities because they are afraid of becoming victims of crime, this fear is, in itself, a sort of victimization.

The Bureau also reports that "relatives, friends, and neighbors who hear about a crime become as fearful as the victim."

THE "SECOND WOUND": FURTHER VICTIMIZATION BY THE CRIMINAL JUSTICE SYSTEM

As noted by Maguire (1991, p. 365): "Victims' suffering is often exacerbated by official or community neglect." Newton (1988, p. 59) describes it as follows:

> For victims, the hazards and humiliations begin as early as the moment they are led dazed and limping in to a busy police station. There they discover the brutal truth—that their case is just one of many, and that there are long waits to be interviewed by detectives. For rape victims, there is an additional insult: They are told they must have hospital examinations—for which they will probably have to pay.
>
> Be prepared to be treated brusquely by jaded, overworked officials even at the scene of the crime, the experienced say.

Siegal (1983, p. 1271) characterizes the inequities of our criminal justice system and how it often treats victims as follows: "Vulnerable, angry, insecure, selfless, the victim who survives observes a criminal who is fed, housed, given legal, medical, psychological, and psychiatric aid—even education and vocational training. The victim ... suffers alone." The insensitive, often callous treatment of victims by the criminal justice system, according to Finn (1990, p. 39), may include the following:

- There may be insensitive questioning.
- There may be innuendos that the victim was somehow at fault. (There is a dilemma here—often the police do not know who was at fault and whether the apparent victim was the aggressor or somehow provoked the offender; aggressive questioning may be a necessary investigative technique.)
- The victim may have difficulty learning what is happening with the case.
- Property may be kept as evidence for a long time or may never be returned.
- Wages may be lost for time spent testifying in court.
- Time may be wasted as victims appear for court proceedings only to have the case postponed or dismissed.
- Victims may experience indifference to their fear of retaliation if they cooperate with the authorities.
- Victims may be anxious about testifying in open court and fearful of being questioned by defense attorneys.

It may be because of such treatment that many victims simply do not report crimes committed against them. Even when crime is reported, however, punishment of those who commit crimes is neither sure nor swift. As noted by Sullivan and Victor (1990, p. 57): "When a police officer does manage to collar a suspect, it may take more than a year in crowded urban court systems to dispose of the case." Up to 90 percent of the cases get plea bargained without

Table 17-9 **Rights of Criminals Compared to Rights of Victims**

CRIMINALS HAVE THE RIGHT TO ...	BUT VICTIMS ...
■ Be informed of their rights when arrested	■ Are given no warning before being selected as victims
■ Be represented by counsel—free of charge if they can't afford to pay	■ Are represented as "the people" in a case, not as individuals
■ Free food, clothing and medical care while in custody	■ May face financial ruin due to medical costs, time lost from work
■ Psychological counseling	■ Are counseled free only when limited state funds are available
■ Plea-bargain to a lesser charge in exchange for a guilty plea	■ Have no legal power to object to victimizers' plea bargains
■ A speedy trial (though they can ask for postponements)	■ Are subject to delays in court proceedings, sometimes as long as several years
■ Be present at proceedings and confront their accusers in court	■ May be excluded from trial; can confront their victimizers only if called as witnesses
■ Appeal to a higher court to overturn a ruling or lighten a sentence	■ Cannot appeal the acquittal of the victimizers

Source: E Newton. "Criminals Have All The Rights." *Ladies' Home Journal,* September 1986: 105. Reprinted by permission.

ever going to court. Even when cases do go to court, sentences may be lighter than most would perceive as just due to prison overcrowding. Or those who are imprisoned are released early for the same reason.

In addition, our legal system tends to pay more attention to the perpetrators than to their victims. According to Newton (1988, p. 57): "Once a crime has been committed, muggers and murderers have more rights than their innocent victims." Newton compares the rights of criminals to those of victims in Table 17-9.

Roberts (1990, p. 23) explains that: "During primitive times, 'social control,' restitution, and revenge were handled by individuals who took the law into their own hands and, in effect, made the law and carried out the punishment in the form of revenge. . . . By the end of the Middle Ages, it was generally recognized that the person harmed must have recourse through the common law, rather than taking the law into his or her own hands."

The tradition of concern for the rights of the defendant derive from traditions of English law that removed victims from the system and replaced them with the "State." Because the state is supposedly so much more powerful than the defendant, it is imperative that the civil rights of the defendant not be violated if justice is to be served. The victim simply had no place in the proceedings except perhaps as a witness.

EFFORTS TO IMPROVE TREATMENT OF VICTIMS

Recognition of the need to improve the way victims are treated led to two pieces of federal legislation and a presidential task force. The *Federal Victim and Witness Protection Act* (1982) seeks to protect and assist victims and witnesses by (Finn 1990, p. 39):

- Making it a felony to threaten or intimidate a victim or witness.
- Providing for inclusion of a victim impact statement in presentence reports.
- Furnishing explicit authority for Federal trial courts to order offenders to make restitution to victims.
- Requiring judges to state on the record the reasons for not ordering restitution.

Kelly (1990, p. 174) notes that in passing this act, Congress declared: "Without the cooperation of victims ... the criminal justice system would cease to function." She further contends (p. 174): "Studies revealed that a sense of participation was more critical to victims' satisfaction with the criminal justice system than how severely the defendant was punished."

Also in 1982 President Reagan appointed a special Task Force on Victims of Crime. As noted by Carrington and Nicholson (1991, p. 339): "Ronald Reagan was the first United States President to put the full weight and influence of that office behind the victims' movement." This task force heard testimony from almost two hundred witnesses, including sixty victims. They made sixty-eight specific recommendations, and as of 1989 seventy-five percent of the recommendation had been acted on. Among the recommendations were the following

- Police departments should develop and implement training programs to ensure that police officers are sensitive to the needs of victims and informed, knowledgeable, and supportive of the existing local services and programs for victims.

- Police departments should establish procedures for the prompt photographing and return of property to victims, with prosecutor approval.

- Police departments should establish procedures to ensure that victims of violent crime are periodically informed of the status and closing of investigations.

- Police officers should give a high priority to investigation of reports by witnesses of threats or intimidation and forward these reports to the prosecution.

The *Victims of Crime Act of 1984* (VOCA) established a Crime Victims Fund of up to $100 million a year, made up of fines collected from people convicted of crimes against persons. The money is made available through grants to the states to fund their victim compensation programs. According to Finn (1990, p. 39):

> Compensation is generally provided for unreimbursed medical expenses, funeral expenses, loss of earnings, and support of dependents of deceased victims. Property loss is not reimbursed. Only a few states provide compensation for psychotherapy. Most laws set a ceiling on the amount a victim can recover generally in the range of $10,000 to $15,000.

According to Muraskin (1992, p. 13) in 1988 Congress reauthorized VOCA for another six years, and each year the fund has increased. For 1991 the amount funded was raised from $144 to $150 million.

Not everyone is satisfied with the progress made, however, as noted by Elias (1991, p. 344): "Victims have progressed significantly in the last quarter century, but they have not yet shaken their second-class status. When victimized, they lack confidence in receiving the aid they need, and for good reason—they often must tolerate inadequate services, cultural insensitivity, political insignificance, and official maltreatment."

As noted by Carrington and Nicholson (1991, p. 340): "Until recently, the American legal system, including the United States Supreme Court, did not really recognize that crime victims *had* any legal rights."

IACP CRIME VICTIMS' BILL OF RIGHTS

Because victims are of such importance to police, the International Association of Chiefs of Police (IACP) has urged police forces to establish procedures and train their personnel to implement the "incontrovertible rights of all crime victims" which it defines as follows (IACP 1983):

1. To be free from intimidation.
2. To be told of financial assistance and social services available and how to apply for them.
3. To be provided a secure area during interviews and court proceedings, and to be notified if presence in court is needed.
4. To be provided a quick return of stolen or other personal property when no longer needed as evidence.
5. To a speedy disposition of the case, and to be periodically informed of case status and final disposition; and, wherever personnel and resource capabilities allow, to be notified in felony cases whenever the perpetrator is released from custody.
6. To be interviewed by a female official in the case of rape and other sexual offenses, wherever personnel and resource capabilities allow.

SPECIFIC VICTIMS' RIGHTS DURING THE CRIMINAL JUSTICE SYSTEM PROCEEDINGS

Kelly (1990, pp. 176–181) notes the following ways in which victims now participate in the criminal justice system in many states:

- Plea bargaining—twenty-three states now allow or mandate some form of victim participation in plea bargains.
- Court attendance—defendants' right to remain in the courtroom is guaranteed by the Sixth Amendment, but suspects have no such right in many states. The Victims Constitutional Amendment Network (VCAN) is working for state constitutional amendments to allow victims to be present and heard at all stages of the criminal justice system.
- Involvement in sentencing—as of August 1987, 96% of the states allowed some form of victim involvement in sentencing with the two most common methods being the victim-impact statement (VIS) and the victim statement of opinion (VSO).

Victims may become involved in the criminal justice system during plea bargaining, during the trial, and during sentencing.

As noted by Kelly (1990, p. 178):

> The VIS allows victims to detail the medical, financial, and emotional injuries that resulted from the crime. This information is usually provided to a probation officer, who then writes up a summary that is included in the defendant's presenting packet. The report then goes to the judge, who may give it as little or as much weight as he or she likes.

According to Elias (1990, p. 228) all but two states allow a **victim impact statement** and thirty-five states allow a **victim statement of opinion** (written or oral).

Wells (1991, p. 44) notes: "Perhaps the most powerful means of strengthening that bond [between investigators and crime victims] and making the victim an active participant in the administration of justice is the victim impact statement (VIS). Properly prepared and presented, a VIS helps prosecutors and judges to experience the real impact of crime, and often results in more stringent sentences."

Kelly further suggests (1990, p. 178):

> In contrast, the VSO is considered more subjective. VSO allows victims to tell the court their opinion on what sentence the defendant should receive. This can be

A mother clutches an envelope containing copies of a letter she wrote to the judge telling her feelings about her daughter's killer.

accomplished by speaking in court (**allocution**) or by a written statement to the judge.

In a Minnesota case, for example, the mother of a young girl who was murdered and whose murderer was found guilty, wrote a letter to the judge in the case which included the following statements (*Star Tribune* 1992, p. 12A):

> I just want to say that I have been hurting very very much and I'm in very bad pain. My Margaret meant the world to me and I miss and love her very much. . . .
>
> That monster John Jolley has to pay for what he did to my daughter. If anyone has had a child who has been murdered you know what I am going through. It's like somebody tore my heart out and he did it, that dirty low down monster with the black heart. He will never change. He will do it again. We have to think about our children.

THE IMPACT OF VICTIMS' RIGHTS ON OFFENDERS AND THE REST OF THE SYSTEM

As victims gain more rights, a price is often paid by offenders or by portions of the criminal justice system. Karmen (1992, p. 46) has classified some of the newly won rights of victims by asking, "At whose expense were they gained?" He notes:

> Given the conflicts between individuals, groups, and classes, the rights gained by one side strengthen their position vis-a-vis their real or potential adversaries. Some recently enacted rights of victims clearly were secured to the detriment of "offenders"—or more accurately: suspects, defendants, and prisoners. For exam-

Table 17–10 **Victim's Rights and at Whose Expense They Were Gained**

CHART ONE: PART A	CHART ONE: PART B
Informational Rights Gained At The Expense of Criminal Justice Agencies and Officials	**Participatory Rights Gained At The Expense Either of Offenders (Suspects/Defendants/Convicts) or Agencies and Officials**

CHART ONE: PART A

1. To be read one's "rights": to reimbursement of losses—from state compensation funds, court ordered offender restitution, insurance coverage, civil lawsuits, or tax deductions; to referrals—to counseling programs, self-help support groups, shelters for battered women, rape crisis centers, and other types of assistance; and to be told of one's obligations— to attend line-ups, appear in court, be cross-examined under oath, and to be publicly identified and the subject of media coverage.

2. To be informed of the whereabouts of the (accused) offender: at large; or in custody (jail or prison); escaped from confinement; or released back to the community (on bail, or due to dropped and dismissed charges, or because of acquittal after a trial, or out on appeal, probation, furlough, parole, or after an expired sentence).

3. To be kept posted about key decisions: arrests, the granting of bail, rulings at evidentiary hearings, negotiated pleas, verdicts at trials, sentences, and parole board deliberations.

4. To receive assistance in the form of intercession by an official in behalf of a victim with an employer or creditor; advance notification and facilitation of court appearances; and expeditious return of recovered stolen property.

CHART ONE: PART B

1. To be consulted when the terms and conditions of bail are being determined (as a protection against harassment and reprisals for cooperating with the prosecution).

2. To be consulted about the offers made during plea negotiations.

3. To be permitted to submit a victim impact statement, detailing how the crime caused physical, emotional, and/or financial harm, as part of the pre-sentence report, and to submit a statement of opinion suggesting remedies, for the judge's consideration.

4. To be permitted to exercise allocution rights in person, in court, detailing the harm caused by the offender and suggesting an appropriate remedy, before the judge imposes a sentence.

5. To be permitted to bring to the attention of the parole board, either in writing or in person, information about the harm caused by the offender and an opinion about an appropriate remedy.

Source: A. Karmen. *Issues in Justice,* Chapter 4. Copyright © 1990. Wyndham Hall Press: Bristol, Ind.

ple, under the so-called "Son of Sam" statutes, victims in most states are enabled to lay claim to any royalties and fees paid by movie producers or media outlets to convicts who profit from their notoriety by selling the rights to their "inside story." But other rights, such as the right "to be informed"—an obligation on the part of police departments and prosecutors' offices to keep victims posted on any progress and developments in their cases—come at the expense of the privileges and conveniences of criminal justice officials and the budgets of their agencies. The most widely enacted rights of this kind are listed in Part A [of Table 17–10]. A third group of rights that empower victims to directly participate to some degree in the criminal justice decision-making process, such as allocution before sentencing, may come at the expense of "offenders" or "officials", depending upon what victims seek as they exercise their new chance to have some input. The most common statutes of this sort are listed in Part B [of Table 17–10].

PROGRAMS FOR VICTIMS

According to McClenahan (1990, p. 104): "The most common needs among victims are access to case progress information, assistance with their safety concerns, compensation for losses, crime prevention information and feedback

on how their feelings compare to those of others in similar situations." Mc-
Clenahan suggests that victims also have several practical needs, including
"being in a safe environment, having funds to meet immediate expenses (e.g.,
bus fare, money for a meal) and having someone to talk to who is interested
not only in their recollection of facts, but also in their experience and its
emotional impact."

Such programs are becoming a reality in many states, as noted by Roberts
(1990, p. 13):

> After decades of neglect, crime victims are finally being recognized as a vulner-
> able and forgotten group of people who have rights and are in need of services.
> During the past 10 years, as a result of federal, state, and local initiatives, a host
> of victim service and witness assistance programs have been developed in cities
> and counties across the United States.

Davis and Henley (1990, p. 157) state: "The growth of service programs in
the United States has been nothing short of phenomenal. Whereas twenty years
ago there were none, today experts estimate the number of programs to be in
excess of 5,000." According to Skogan et al. (1990, p. 17): "There is good
reason to believe they have become a permanent part of the criminal justice
system." They also note, however, that the most common needs reported by
victims are for improved household security and financial assistance, yet relatively few programs provide such support.

Two main kinds of programs have been established—those that help victims
and witnesses deal with the criminal justice system and the trial itself and those
that provide them with moral and/or financial assistance to recover from their
victimization. As noted by Elias (1990, p. 227): "Victim services programs
emphasize financial aid, logistical support, and personal treatment."

Roberts (1990) reports on a survey of 184 victim service and witness
assistance programs conducted in 1986 asking about whether they provided
any of eleven specific services. The great majority of programs indicated that
they provided five or more of the eleven services listed in the questionnaire.
Table 17–11 summarizes the types of services and the number of programs
providing them.

Table 17–11   **Services Provided by Programs**

TYPE OF SERVICE	NUMBER OF PROGRAMS	PERCENTAGE
Explain court process	131	71
Make referrals	126	69
Provide court escort	120	65
Help with victim compensation applications	118	64
Public education	112	61
Assist with employers	111	60
Provide transportation to court	109	59
Provide crisis intervention	99	54
Provide child care	69	38
Provide emergency money	45	25
Repair locks	22	12

Note: 184 respondents supplied 1,063 responses.

Source: A. R. Roberts. *Helping Crime Victims: Research, Policy, and Practice.* Copyright © 1990, 47. Sage
Publications: Newbury Park, Calif. Reprinted by permission.

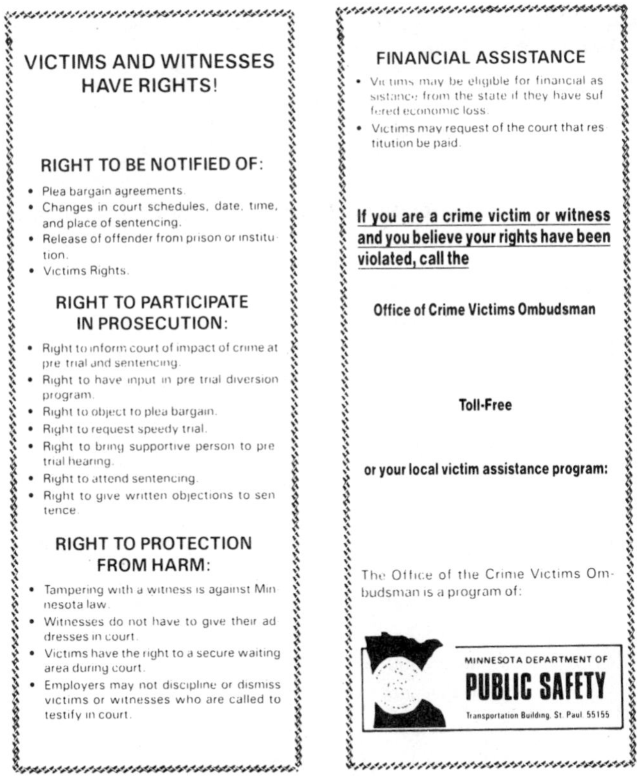
VICTIMS AND WITNESSES HAVE RIGHTS!

RIGHT TO BE NOTIFIED OF:

- Plea bargain agreements.
- Changes in court schedules, date, time, and place of sentencing.
- Release of offender from prison or institution.
- Victims Rights.

RIGHT TO PARTICIPATE IN PROSECUTION:

- Right to inform court of impact of crime at pre trial and sentencing.
- Right to have input in pre trial diversion program.
- Right to object to plea bargain.
- Right to request speedy trial.
- Right to bring supportive person to pre trial hearing.
- Right to attend sentencing.
- Right to give written objections to sentence.

RIGHT TO PROTECTION FROM HARM:

- Tampering with a witness is against Minnesota law.
- Witnesses do not have to give their addresses in court.
- Victims have the right to a secure waiting area during court.
- Employers may not discipline or dismiss victims or witnesses who are called to testify in court.

FINANCIAL ASSISTANCE

- Victims may be eligible for financial assistance from the state if they have suffered economic loss.
- Victims may request of the court that restitution be paid.

If you are a crime victim or witness and you believe your rights have been violated, call the

Office of Crime Victims Ombudsman

Toll-Free

or your local victim assistance program:

The Office of the Crime Victims Ombudsman is a program of:

MINNESOTA DEPARTMENT OF
PUBLIC SAFETY
Transportation Building, St. Paul 55155

Figure 17–2 Informational Brochure for Victims and Witnesses

When considering services to victims, one should keep in mind the statement of Maguire (1991, p. 363): "Although there is evidence of high levels of client satisfaction with victim services, research has not established that service provision greatly affects recovery from the effects of the crime." Some programs provide an informational brochure such as that illustrated in Figure 17–2.

Restitution Programs

Hillenbrand (1990, p. 195) describes the four basic types of restitution programs currently being offered to victims:

- Restitution components of victim assistance programs.
- Victim/offender reconciliation programs.
- Restitution employment programs.
- Restitution as a function of routine probation supervision.

Victim Compensation Programs

In 1965 California initiated the first statewide victim compensation program. These programs supplement existing programs that assist victims, such as rape crisis centers and prosecutors' victim assistance programs. According to the *United States Department of Justice* (1988) almost all states have established programs to assist crime victims and witnesses.

Forty-four states, the District of Columbia, and the Virgin Islands provide compensation for medical bills and lost wages for victims.

State	Victim Compensation Board Location[a]	Financial Award	TO QUALIFY, VICTIM MUST Show financial need	Report to police within	File claim within
Alabama	Alabama Crime Victim Compensation Commission	$ 0–10,000	No	3 days	12 mos.
Alaska	Department of Public Safety	$ 0–40,000	Yes	5	24
Arizona	Arizona Criminal Justice Commission	**	Yes	3	**
California	State Board of Control	$100–46,000	Yes	*	12
Colorado	Judicial district boards	$ 25–10,000	No	3	6
Connecticut	Criminal Injuries Compensation Board	$100–10,000	No	5	24
Delaware	Violent Crimes Board	$ 25–20,000	No	*	12
D.C.	Office of Crime Victim Compensation	$100–25,000	Yes	7	6
Florida	Department of Labor and Employment Security, Workmen's Compensation Division	$ 0–10,000	Yes	3	12
Hawaii	Department of Corrections	$ 0–10,000	No	*	18
Idaho	Industrial Commission	$ 0–25,000	No	3	12
Illinois	Court of Claims	$ 0–25,000	No	3	12
Indiana	Industrial Board	$100–10,000	No	2	24
Iowa	Department of Public Safety	$ 0–20,000	No	1	6
Kansas	Executive Department	$100–10,000	Yes	3	12
Kentucky	Victim Compensation Board	$ 0–25,000	Yes	2	12
Louisiana	Commission on Law Enforcement	$100–10,000	No	3	12
Maryland	Criminal Injuries Compensation Board	$ 0–45,000	Yes	2	6
Massachusetts	District court system	$ 0–25,000	No	2	12
Michigan	Department of Management and Budget	$200–15,000	Yes	2	12
Minnesota	Crime Victims Reparation Board	$100–50,000	No	5	12
Missouri	Division of Workmen's Compensation	$200–10,000	No	2	12
Montana	Crime Control Division	$ 0–25,000	No	3	12
Nebraska	Commission on Law Enforcement and Criminal Justice	$ 0–10,000	Yes	3	24

In general, victim compensation programs do the following:

- Provide financial assistance to victims and witnesses.
- Protect the rights of victims and witnesses.
- Complement existing efforts to aid special categories of victims such as rape victims and victims of family abuse.

Victim/witness services may also be provided by noncriminal justice agencies such as local or state departments of health or human resources. Additionally, many private organizations have developed programs such as rape crisis centers.

If a victim dies, payments may cover burial and related expenses, payable to dependent survivors. Often, people injured while trying to prevent a crime or apprehend an offender (Good Samaritans) are also eligible for payment.

Most states establish upper limits on payments, and most do not compensate for property losses. Usually payment can be made whether or not the offender is apprehended or convicted, but most states require that the crime

Table 17-12 (Continued)

State	Victim Compensation Board Location[a]	Financial Award	TO QUALIFY, VICTIM MUST		
			Show financial need	Report to police within	File claim within
Nevada	Board of Examiners and Department of Administration	$ 0-15,000	Yes	5	12
New Jersey	Executive Branch	$ 0-25,000	No	90	24
New Mexico	Executive Branch	$ 0-12,500	No	30	12
New York	Executive Department	$ 0-30,000[+]	Yes	7	12
North Carolina[b]	Department of Crime Control and Public Safety	$100-20,000		3	24
North Dakota	Workmen's Compensation Bureau	$ 0-25,000	No	3	12
Ohio	Court of Claims Commissioners	$ 0-25,000	No	3	12
Oklahoma	Crime Victims Board	$ 0-10,000	No	3	12
Oregon	Department of Justice/Workmen's Compensation Board	$250-23,000	No	3	6
Pennsylvania	Crime Victims Board	$ 0-35,000	No	3	12
Rhode Island	Superior court system	$ 0-25,000	No	10	24
South Carolina	Crime Victims Advisory Board	$ 100-3,000	No	2	6
Tennessee	Court of Claims Commission	$ 0-5,000	No	2	12
Texas	Industrial Accident Board	$ 0-25,000	No	3	6
Utah	Department of Administrative Services	$ 0-25,000	**	7	12
Virgin Islands	Department of Social Welfare	Up to $25,000	No	1	24
Virginia	Industrial Commission	$ 0-15,000	No	5	24
Washington	Department of Labor and Industries	$ 0-15,000[+]	No	3	12
West Virginia	Court of Claims Commissioner	$ 0-35,000	No	3	24
Wisconsin	Department of Justice	$ 0-40,000	No	5	12

[a]If location of the board is not indicated in the state statute, the board itself is noted.
[b]North Carolina's program is administratively established but not funded.
*Must report but no time limit specified.
**No reference in statute.
[+] Plus unlimited medical expenses.

Source: Bureau of Justice Statistics. *Report to the Nation on Crime and Justice* (1988): 37.

be reported to the proper authorities. The 1984 Federal Victims of Crime Act provides federal grants to help states with established qualifying victim compensation programs.

Many states also allow victims to recover crime-related losses, including property damages, if a court requires restitution by the offender as a sentencing condition. Such payments are available only if the offender is convicted and is financially solvent.

Many states also require that any profits earned by an offender in publicizing details of a crime be escrowed and, if the offender is convicted, be used to cover crime-related costs incurred by the victim, including, in some cases, legal fees.

Table 17-12 summarizes characteristics of the existing victim compensation programs.

State laws and the 1984 Federal Victim and Witness Protection Act also protect crime victims and witnesses against physical and verbal intimidation. Many states also require that victims be notified of the progress in a case, that they be notified of the release or escape of an offender, and that they be advised of any scheduling changes as well as any available funds to cover court appearances.

In some states victims may participate in sentencing, parole, and other custody decisions. "Victim Impact Statements" describing the financial and emotional effects of a crime on the victim are required in many state and federal cases as part of the presentence investigation report.

Comprehensive "Victim's Bill of Rights" laws in some states may also ensure the victim's right to continued employment, provide medical or social support services, and appoint an "ombudsman" to protect the victim's rights during the trial.

THE ROLE OF THE POLICE

The first and all-important contact between the police and a victim is made during the preliminary investigation. It is critical that police officers be realistic with victims. If a police agency has an "early case closure system," victims should be told that nothing further can be done unless additional information comes to light. Victims should be given the case number and a phone number to call if they should obtain more information about the crime.

Victims should be told of any assistance that might be available to them and, if applicable, they should be reminded to call their insurance companies. If victims need legal advice, police officers should advise them about the legal aid office.

If a case continues under investigation or will go to court, police officers should maintain contact with victims (and witnesses). If property is recovered it should be returned to victims as soon as possible. If a case goes to court, victims should be briefed as to their roles and should be kept updated.

The President's Task Force on Victims of Crime, *Final Report* (1982) stresses:

> The police are often the first on the scene; it is to them, the first source of protection, that the victim first turns. They should be mindful that, in fulfilling their obligation to solve the crime and apprehend the criminal, they must also treat victims with the attention due them. The manner in which police officers treat a victim affects not only his immediate and long-term ability to deal with the event but also his willingness to assist in a prosecution. The foundation of all interactions between police and victims should be the knowledge that it is these citizens whom the officer has sworn to serve.

As noted by Waller (1990, p. 146): "Police officers may have difficulty in being sensitive to emotional reaction. In the course of their duties, they deal routinely with crime and severe accidents in which victims have been physically injured and must handle such situations with a professional detachment."

Skogan et al. (1990, p. 16) note: "Police are in a strategic position to assist victims in a number of ways. They can offer practical assistance to victims, including helping them deal with insurance forms and smashed-in doors, advising them on how to prevent future victimization, and protecting them from reprisal if they cooperate with the prosecutor. It is crucial that police remain in continued contact with victims, keep them informed about their case, and help them get into contact with service agencies and compensation programs."

Waller (1990, p. 151), likewise, suggests:

> The police are well situated to initiate crisis support to victims. Because they are often the first officials to talk to the crime victim, they are able to reassure and refer the victim to appropriate services in the community....

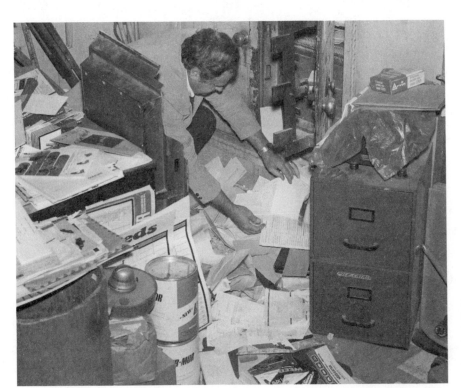

Although a thorough preliminary investigation is an important responsibility, the officers conducting the investigation must also be sensitive to the feelings and needs of victims of the crime.

The police could improve their support for crime victims by requiring the responding officer to provide the victim with a card that identifies the key telephone numbers of such services as the local distress center, locksmiths, criminal injuries compensation, the crime prevention unit, and a service that could help or refer the victim to other community services.

POLICE OFFICERS AS VICTIMS

Police officers are not immune from being victimized. Officers have been assaulted, robbed, burglarized, and victimized in all the ways civilians are, including being killed. As noted by Major (1992, p. 103): "Many officers paid the ultimate price in the performance of their duties." Table 17–13 summarizes the number of officers killed and facts related to these officers.

Police officers assaulted by gun-bearing offenders sustained the lower percentage of injuries (see Table 17–14). This is not to imply that a gun-wielding offender is not a threat to citizens and law enforcement officers. Of the sixty-six law enforcement officers killed in the line of duty in 1986, three-quarters (fifty-one officers) were killed by handguns, eight by rifles and three by shotguns. Fifteen were shot with their own service weapons. Four were intentionally run down by automobiles.

As noted by Conroy and Hess (1992, pp. 39–40):

The most obvious way officers become *primary victims* is through the physical dangers associated with the job. You may be assaulted, shot at, stabbed, or even killed in the line of duty. A much more subtle, more insidious way you become a primary victim, however, is through the psychological effects of your work. This type of victimization is far less obvious, frequently contrary to established self-image, and until recently, denied to even exist by both officers and management.

Table 17-13   Law Enforcement Officers Killed 1980-1989

- 801 were feloniously killed in the line of duty
- 104, the highest annual total, were killed in 1980
- 66, the lowest annual total, were killed in both 1986 and 1989
- 783 were male
- 18 were female
- 515 were aged 25 to 40
- 327 were attempting an arrest when killed
- 735 officers were killed by firearms
- 120 were killed with their own weapons
- 157 of those killed by firearms were wearing protective armor
- 7 out of every 10 were in uniform when killed
- 2 out of every 3 were patrol officers

Source: V. L. Major. "Law Enforcement Officers Killed 1980–1989." *FBI Law Enforcement Bulletin* (May 1991): 3. Reprinted in *Criminal Justice 92/93* (1992) by the Dushkin Publishing Group: Guilford, Conn.

Table 17-14   Use of Weapons in Assaults on Law Enforcement Officers

MEANS OF ASSAULT	PERCENT OF ALL ASSAULTS	PERCENT RESULTING IN PERSONAL INJURY
Firearm	5	21
Knife	3	27
Other weapon	9	41
Hands, fists, feet, etc.	84	34
Total	100%	100%

Note: Totals add to more than 100% because of use of multiple weapons.

Source: FBI *Law Enforcement Officers Killed and Assaulted,* 1985.

In reality, a police officer who risks his/her own life to pull a child out of a burning car, only to have that child die moments later ... is more than a secondary concerned party. They become involved victims as their initial hope is dramatically shattered within moments, replaced with feelings of deep frustration and failure.

The most common way police officers become victims, however, is as secondary victims. According to Conroy and Hess (p. 40): "You deal constantly with other people's victimization while the pain and blood are fresh and real." Over time, this can have a devastating effect on police officers.

SUMMARY

When people are victimized, they often do not report it to police. In fact, one-half to two-thirds of all crimes are not reported to police. Individuals having the highest victimization risk are young, black, unemployed males living in the city; those having the lowest victimization risk are elderly white females living in rural areas.

Households at greatest risk are those rented by African Americans in central cities, headed by younger people, and having more than six people living in the same household.

Most violent crimes except murder and rape are committed by strangers. Victims of violent crime have protected themselves by returning physical force, by verbal response, by attracting attention, by nonviolent evasion, or by brandishing a weapon.

Violent crime can affect its victim physically, economically, and emotionally. Family members and friends may become indirect or secondary victims, feeling the pain and suffering along with the primary victim.

Victims may become involved in the criminal justice system during plea bargaining, during the trial, and during sentencing. If a person is seriously injured, a victim compensation program may be available. Forty-four states, the District of Columbia, and the Virgin Islands have such programs. Most provide for recovery of medical expenses and some for lost earnings.

DISCUSSION QUESTIONS

1. Does your state have victim compensation laws? If so, how do they compare to those provided in other states?

2. Have you ever been victimized? Has a member of your family? A friend or neighbor? What were the effects?

3. Why is it so difficult for a victim of a crime to accept its consequences?

4. What one common concern do victim compensation programs all share?

5. How can prosecutors assist victims in their experiences with the criminal justice system?

6. Should victims be allowed to approve or disapprove any sentence the court places on those by whom they have been victimized?

7. When a suspect vandalizes while committing a burglary, what does that indicate to you?

8. Might a form of gun registration be beneficial in curbing crimes committed with the use of a gun?

9. Do you feel that in most cases the police in your area are sensitive to the needs of victims of crimes?

10. What type of crime victim is most likely to try to use force against a perpetrator?

TERMS

allocution, deadly force, household risk factors, indirect victim, primary victim, secondary victim, victim impact statement, victim statement of opinion.

REFERENCES

Carrington, F. and Nicholson, G. "Victims' Rights: An Idea Whose Time Has Come—Five Years Later: The Maturing of an Idea," pp. 338–343 in *Taking Sides, Clashing View on Controversial Issues in Crime and Criminology*, 2d ed., edited by R. C. Monk. Guilford, Conn.: The Dushkin Publishing Group, 1991.

Conroy, D. L. and Hess, K. M. *Officers at Risk: How to Identify and Cope with Stress.* Placerville, Calif.: Custom Publishing Company, 1992.

Davis, R. C. and Henley, M. "Victim Service Programs," pp. 157–171 in *Victims of Crime: Problems, Policies, and Programs,* edited by J. Lurigio, W. G. Skogan, and R. C. Davis. Newbury Park, Calif.: Sage Publications, 1990.

Elias, R. "Which Victim Movement? The Politics of Victim Policy," pp. 226–250 in *Victims of Crime: Problems, Policies, and Programs,* edited by A. J. Lurigio, W. G. Skogan, and R. C. Davis, Newbury Park, Calif.: Sage Publications, 1990.

Elias, R. "The Politics of Victimization," pp. 344–350 in *Taking Sides, Clashing View on Controversial Issues in Crime and Criminology,* 2d ed., edited by R. C. Monk. Guilford, Conn.: The Dushkin Publishing Group, 1991.

Finn, P. "Victims," pp. 39–42 in *American Justice: Research of the National Institute of Justice,* edited by J. Siegel. St. Paul, Minn.: West Publishing Company, 1990.

Hillenbrand, S. *"Restitution and Victim Rights in the 1980s,"* pp. 188–204 in *Victims of Crime: Problems, Policies, and Programs,* edited by A. J. Lurigio, W. G. Skogan, and R. C. Davis. Newbury Park, Calif.: Sage Publications, 1990.

International Association of Chiefs of Police. *Crime Victims Bill of Rights.* Board of Officers. Arlington, Va.: Policy Center, 1983.

Karmen, A. "The Implementation of Victim's Rights: A Challenge for Criminal Justice Professionals," pp. 46–57 in *Criminal Justice 92/93.* Guilford, Conn.: The Dushkin Publishing Group, 1992. (Reprinted from *Issues in Justice,* 46–57, R. Muraskin (Ed.) Bristol, Ind.: Wyndham Hall Press.)

Kelly, D. "Victim Participation in the Criminal Justice System," pp. 172–187 in *Victims of Crime: Problems, Policies, and Programs,* edited by A. J. Lurigio, W. G. Skogan, and R. C. Davis. Newbury Park, Calif.: Sage Publications, 1990.

Maguire, M. "Needs and Rights of Victims," pp. 363–443 in *Crime and Justice: A Review of Research.* Vol. 14 edited by Michael Tonry. Chicago: University of Chicago Press, 1991.

Major, V. L. "Law Enforcement Officers Killed 1980–1989," pp. 101–103 in *Criminal Justice 92/93.* Guilford, Conn.: The Dushkin Publishing Group, 1992. (Reprinted from *FBI Law Enforcement Bulletin,* U.S. Department of Justice, Federal Bureau of Investigation, May 1991: 2–5.)

McClenahan, C. A. "Victim Services—A Positive Police-Community Effort." *The Police Chief* (October 1990): 104.

"Mother of Slain Girl Writes Letter to Judge," *Star Tribune,* May 23, 1992, p. 12A.

Muraskin, R. "The Growth Industry of Victim Services." *Law Enforcement News,* March 15, 1992, 13.

Newton, E. "Criminals Have All the Rights," pp. 57–61 in *Criminal Justice: Annual Editions, 87/88.* Guilford, Conn.: The Dushkin Publishing Group, 1988.

President's Task Force on Victims of Crime. *Final Report.* Washington, D.C.: U.S. Government Printing Office, 1982.

Riggs, D. S. and Kilpatrick, D. G. "Families and Friends: Indirect Victimization by Crime," pp. 120–138 in *Victims of Crime: Problems, Policies, and Programs,* edited by A. J. Lurigio, W. G. Skogan, and R. C. Davis. Newbury Park, Calif.: Sage Publications, 1990.

Roberts, A. R. *Helping Crime Victims: Research, Policy, and Practice.* Newbury Park, Calif.: Sage Publications, 1990.

Siegal, M. "Crime and Violence in America: The Victims." *American Psychologist* 38 (1983): 1267–1273.

Skogan, W. G.; Lurigio, A. J.; and Davis, R. C. "Criminal Victimization," pp. 7–22 in *Victims of Crime: Problems, Policies, and Programs,* edited by A. J. Lurigio, W. G. Skogan, and R. C. Davis. Newbury Park, Calif.: Sage Publications, 1990.

Star Tribune, May 23, 1992, 12A. "Mother of Slain Girl Writes Letter to Judge."

Sullivan, J. J. and Victor, J. L. (Eds.) "Victims of Crime," p. 57 in *Criminal Justice, Annual Editions, 90/91.* Guilford, Conn.: The Dushkin Publishing Group, 1990.

U.S. Department of Justice. Bureau of Justice Statistics. *Report to the Nation on Crime and Justice.* 2d ed. Washington, D.C.: U.S. Government Printing Office, 1988.

Waller, I. "The Police: First in Aid?" pp. 139–156 in *Victims of Crime: Problems, Policies, and Programs,* edited by A. J. Lurigio, W. G. Skogan, and R. C. Davis. Newbury Park, Calif.: Sage Publications, 1990.

Wells, R. C. "Victim Impact: How Much Consideration Is It Really Given?" *The Police Chief* (February 1991): 44–47.

In Search of Justice: Our Criminal Justice System in Action

Our system of criminal justice has three interrelated components staffed by more than 1 million people: *the law enforcement community,* the *judicial community,* and the *corrections community.* Each component and its respective personnel in turn contribute to the criminal justice *process,* which is a well-defined legal continuum through which every offender may pass from detection and investigation of the criminal act; to arrest and accusation; to trial, conviction, sentencing, and possible incarceration; to eventual release.

This section looks first at our courts, (Chapter 18), our corrections system (Chapter 19) and our juvenile justice system (Chapter 20), which has some important differences from the adult system. It concludes with a discussion of critical issues facing the criminal justice system in the 1990s (Chapter 21).

Our Courts: Seeking the Truth—Innocent Until Proven Guilty

Justice is truth in action.

—Disraeli

Do You Know

How the police aid the criminal justice process?

What the typical hierarchy is within the state court system? The federal court system?

What the adversary system requires?

What abuses are most common in the prosecutor's office?

What the critical criminal justice stages are?

What purpose a preliminary hearing serves?

What the discovery process is?

What some alternatives to trial are?

What plea bargaining is?

How the defense attorney may attempt to discredit the testimony of a police officer?

What common sentencing schemes are?

How the *rule of law* and the *rule of man* differ?

INTRODUCTION

Police officers are an integral part of the criminal justice process. The criminal codes that guide police officers in enforcing laws are not a set of specific instructions, but rather they are rough maps of the territory in which police officers work and assist the criminal justice process. The officers' roles in the criminal justice process include making legal arrests; legally obtaining accurate, relevant information and evidence; writing complete and accurate reports; identifying suspects and witnesses; and providing effective, truthful testimony in court. Regardless of how sketchy or complete the officers' education or experience, in reality they are interpreters of the law and may function as judge and jury at the start of every case. If the case reaches court, the court must subsequently approve or disapprove the police officers' actions by finding the person guilty or not guilty.

For example, police officers who stop a person for speeding make a judicial decision when they give out a ticket. They might simply warn the next offender. By shooting and killing a fleeing felon who is likely to kill someone while attempting to escape, the police officer delivers a capital penalty for a crime that may otherwise have netted probation or a prison term.

Police officers aid the criminal justice process by (1) making arrests, (2) obtaining information and evidence, (3) writing reports, (4) identifying suspects and witnesses, and (5) providing testimony in court.

Errors in any of these roles may seriously damage a case or even prevent a **conviction.** In today's society it is imperative that police officers become familiar with our courts as well as each step of the criminal justice process so they can intelligently bring about desired results.

THE COURT SYSTEM

The courts in the United States operate within a highly structured framework that may vary greatly from state to state. Numerous dualities exist within this framework, the most obvious of which is the dual system of state and federal courts. These two systems will be discussed momentarily, but first some other dualities should be understood. Among the most important are those having to do with a court's jurisdiction—its authority to try a case or to hear an appeal. Technically it does not refer to a geographic area.

As noted by Waldron (1984, p. 283): "**Jurisdiction** should not be mistaken for the concept of **venue,** the requirement that the trial for an offense be held in the same area in which the offense occurred. The point to remember is that jurisdiction refers to a court's authority to take notice of and decide a case."

There are basically three levels of jurisdiction:

- Courts of limited and special jurisdiction.
- Courts of general jurisdiction.
- Appellate courts.

Another duality within the organizational structure of the courts and their jurisdiction is that of *original* versus *appellate* jurisdiction. A court with **original jurisdiction** has the authority to try cases, whereas a court with **appellate jurisdiction** has the authority to hear an **appeal** to set aside a conviction. In some cases a court has both types of jurisdiction, for example, the United States Supreme Court.

A court with the authority to try a case is often called a *trial* court, and since such courts are frequently the first to record the proceedings, they are also referred to as a *court of record*. A court that uses the record from a previous trial in considering an appeal, without calling a new trial, automatically identifies the court below as a court of record.

A **court of last resort** refers to the highest court to which a case may be appealed.

Another duality already introduced is that of civil and criminal law. Holten and Lamar (1991, p. 59) describe the fundamental division of jurisdictions between criminal and civil cases.

> Criminal cases are filed and pursued by the state rather than a private party. The process is known as prosecution. Its purpose is to deal with the question of the guilt or innocence of the persons accused and to seek the appropriate disposition of the persons found guilty. Civil cases, on the other hand, are filed by private parties—whether groups or individuals—as well as by state agents. The purpose of civil actions is to satisfy or "make whole," the alleged victims or plaintiffs by such means as awarding them damages; granting them a divorce or custody of children or of property; or enjoining the offending party from performing such harmful act.

The State Court System

Each state's constitution and statutory law establish the structure of its courts. Consequently, great variety exists in the types of courts established, the names by which they are known, and the number of levels in the hierarchy. For example, until recently, Pennsylvania had eleven different types of courts, each having jurisdiction over a specific kind of case.

The hierarchy at the state level often goes from courts of special or limited jurisdiction called justice of the peace (J. P.) courts, to trial courts or original and general jurisdiction courts, to intermediate appellate courts, to the state supreme court.

A typical state judicial system is illustrated in Figure 18–1.

The Federal Court System

Within the federal court system a further duality exists: constitutional courts and legislative courts. The constitutional courts include the United States Supreme Court as well as "such inferior Courts as the Congress may from time to time ordain and establish" (Article III, Section 1). These inferior courts include the courts of appeals, the district courts, and numerous specialized courts. Legislative courts are lower in the hierarchy and include trial courts in the United States territories, specialized courts, and the Military Court of Appeals.

The federal court system is three tiered: district courts, appellate courts, and the United States Supreme Court.

The three-tiered federal court system is illustrated in Figure 18–2.

The Supreme Court

The United States **Supreme Court** is presided over by nine justices appointed by the president of the United States, subject to Senate confirmation. The

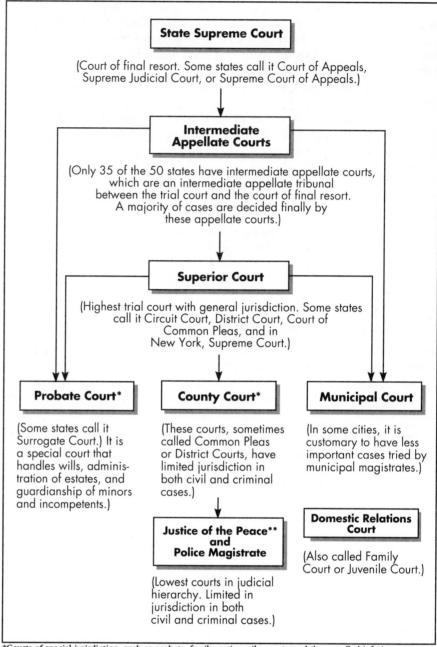

State Supreme Court

(Court of final resort. Some states call it Court of Appeals,
Supreme Judicial Court, or Supreme Court of Appeals.)

**Intermediate
Appellate Courts**

(Only 35 of the 50 states have intermediate appellate courts,
which are an intermediate appellate tribunal
between the trial court and the court of final resort.
A majority of cases are decided finally by
these appellate courts.)

Superior Court

(Highest trial court with general jurisdiction. Some states
call it Circuit Court, District Court, Court of
Common Pleas, and in
New York, Supreme Court.)

Probate Court*

(Some states call it
Surrogate Court.) It is
a special court that
handles wills, adminis-
tration of estates, and
guardianship of minors
and incompetents.)

County Court*

(These courts, sometimes
called Common Pleas
or District Courts, have
limited jurisdiction in
both civil and criminal
cases.)

Municipal Court

(In some cities, it is
customary to have less
important cases tried by
municipal magistrates.)

Justice of the Peace**
and
Police Magistrate**

(Lowest courts in judicial
hierarchy. Limited in
jurisdiction in both
civil and criminal cases.)

**Domestic Relations
Court**

(Also called Family
Court or Juvenile Court.)

*Courts of special jurisdiction, such as probate, family, or juvenile courts, and the so-called inferior courts,
such as common pleas or municipal courts, may be separate courts or part of the trial court of general
jurisdiction.

**Justices of the peace do not exist in all states. Where they do exist, their jurisdictions vary greatly from
state to state.

Figure 18–1   State Judicial System

Source: American Bar Association, *Law and the Courts* (Chicago: American Bar Association, 1974): 20. Updated information provided by West Publishing Company.

Source: J. J. Senna and L. J. Siegel. *Introduction to Criminal Justice.* 5th ed. p. 328. © 1990, West Publishing
Company: St. Paul, Minn. Reprinted by permission.

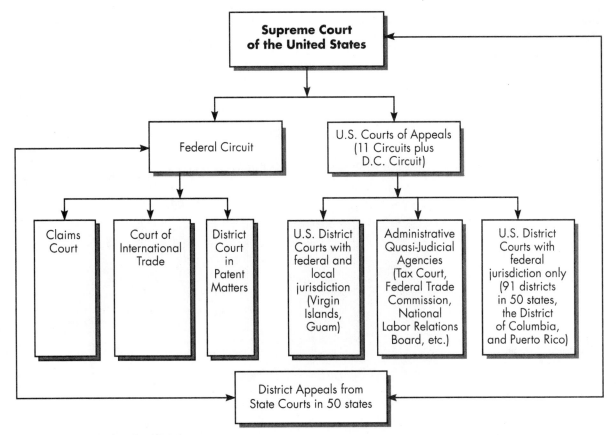

Figure 18–2   Federal Judicial System

Source: American Bar Association, *Law and the Courts* (Chicago: American Bar Association, 1974): 21. Updated information provided by the Federal Courts Improvement Act of 1982 and West Publishing Company.

Source: J. J. Senna and L. J. Siegel. *Introduction to Criminal Justice.* 5th ed. p. 331. © 1990, West Publishing Company, St. Paul, Minn.

president also appoints a chief justice, who assigns the cases to the other justices. Most have been lawyers and are from the upper class, white, male, protestant, and graduates of prestigious universities. Over half were judges prior to their appointments as United States Supreme Court Justices. As noted by Glick (1983, p. 105):

> Becoming a federal judge requires political visibility, involvement in political activity, party loyalty, and, depending on the court, sharing the political values or ideology of the administration making the appointments.... The occasional appointment of Jewish, Catholic, or black justices is a recent and rare event. President Reagan's appointment of Sandra D. O'Connor is the most recent change to occur in recruitment to the Supreme Court.

The Constitution established tenure for "life on good behavior"; therefore the only way to remove a justice is through impeachment unless voluntary retirement can be obtained.

When the Supreme Court decides to hear a case, it grants a **writ of certiorari,** which is a request for a transcript of the proceedings of the case for review. According to Senna and Siegel (1990, p. 333):

> When the Supreme Court rules on a case, usually by majority decision (at least five votes), its holding becomes a precedent that must be honored by all lower courts. For example, if the Court grants a particular litigant the right to counsel

The United States Supreme
Court is the highest constitutional court in the nation.

at a police lineup, then all similarly situated clients must be given the same right. Such a ruling is known as a **landmark decision.** The use of precedent in the legal system gives the Supreme Court power to influence and mold the everyday operating procedures of the police, trial courts, and corrections. In the past, this influence was not nearly as pronounced as it became during the tenure of the two previous chief justices, Earl Warren and Warren Burger, who greatly amplified and extended the power of the Court to influence criminal justice policies. Under Chief Justice William Rehnquist, the Court has continued to influence criminal justice matters, ranging from the investigation of crimes to the execution of criminals. There is little question that the personal legal philosophy of the justices and their orientation toward the civil and personal rights of victims and criminals have a significant impact on the daily operations of the justice system.

Figure 18–3 traces the course of a case to the U.S. Supreme Court.

Having looked at the organizational structure of our court system at both state and federal levels, next turn your attention to a concept on which our entire criminal justice system rests: the adversary system.

THE ADVERSARY SYSTEM

Our criminal justice system is based on an **adversary system**—the accuser versus the accused. The accuser must prove that the one accused is guilty. A critic of the adversary system, Maechling (1992, p. 133) asserts:

> Only the Anglo-Saxon countries cling to a judicial parody of the medieval tournament—lawyers for the state and for the defense fight for the body of the accused before a judge as umpire and a jury carefully selected for its ignorance of the personalities and issues before it.

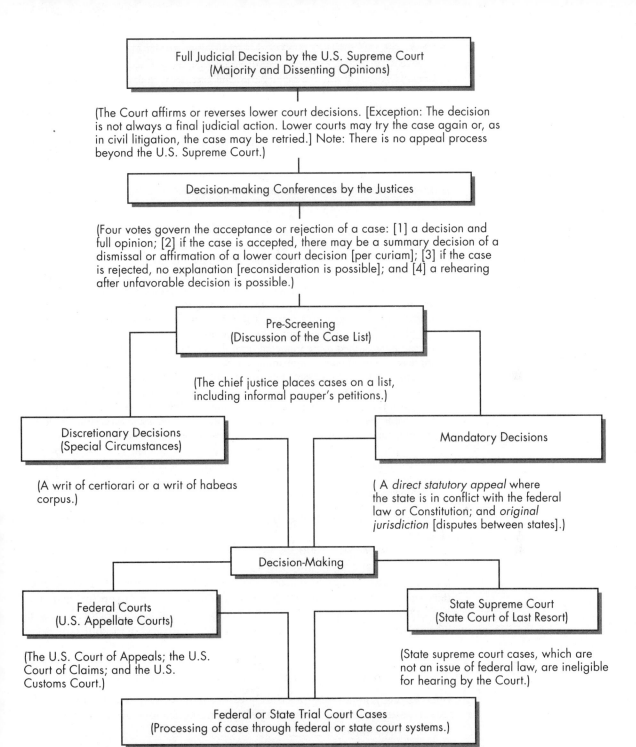

Figure 18–3   Tracing the Course of a Case to the U.S. Supreme Court

Source: J. J. Senna and L. J. Siegel. *Introduction to Criminal Justice.* 5th ed. p. 334. © 1990, West Publishing Company: St. Paul, Minn. Reprinted by permission.

In the Anglo-American system, the narrow focus on the accused, coupled with the disproportionate power and authority of the state, necessitates a bristling array of constitutional safeguards and procedural rules to level the jousting field and protect the defendant's rights. The tournament, or trial, is the supreme event.

The adversary criminal justice system requires that the accuser prove beyond a reasonable doubt to a judge or jury that the accused is guilty of a specified crime.

The assumption is that the accused is innocent until proof to the contrary is clearly established. Included on the side of the accuser is the citizen (or victim), the prosecutor, and the police officer. On the side of the accused is the defendant and the defense attorney. An impartial judge or jury hears both sides of the controversy and then reaches a decision as to whether the accuser has proven the accused guilty beyond a **reasonable doubt.** As noted by Inbau, Thompson, and Fagel (1974, p. 229):

> It [reasonable doubt] is a term often used, probably pretty well understood, but not easily defined. It is not mere possible doubt because everything relating to human affairs and depending on moral evidence is open to some possible or imaginary doubt. It is that state of the case which, after the entire comparisons and consideration of all evidence, leaves the minds of the jurors in that condition and they cannot say they feel an abiding conviction, to a moral certainty, of the truth of the charge. The burden of proof is upon the prosecutor. All the presumptions of law independent of evidence are in favor of innocence; and every person is presumed to be innocent until he is proved guilty. If upon such proof there is reasonable doubt remaining, the accused is entitled to the benefit of it by an acquittal. For it is not sufficient to establish a probability, though a strong one arising from the doctrine of chances, that the fact charged is more likely to be true than the contrary; but the evidence must establish the truth of the fact to a reasonable and moral certainty; a certainty that convinces and directs the understanding, and satisfies the reason and judgment of those who are bound to act conscientiously upon it. This we take to be proof beyond reasonable doubt; because if the law, which mostly depends upon considerations of a moral nature, should go further than this and require absolute certainty, it would exclude circumstantial evidence altogether.

Reasonable doubt means the juror is not morally certain of the truth of the charges.

Senna and Siegel (1990, p. 441) note that: "Proof beyond a *reasonable doubt* is the standard required to convict a defendant charged with a crime at the adjudicatory stage of the criminal trial." This is a more stringent evidentiary standard than is required in a civil trial where a mere **preponderance of the evidence** is standard. Table 18–1 illustrates the various evidentiary standards of proof or degrees of certainty required in varying circumstances.

The Suspect or Defendant

Until formally accused of a crime and brought to trial, a person accused is called a **suspect.** After formal accusation and court appearance, the person is called a **defendant.**

Everyone, including a person suspected of committing a crime, has certain rights that must be protected at all stages of the criminal justice process. Suspects have all the rights set forth in the Bill of Rights. They may waive these rights, but if they do, the waiver should be in writing because proof of the waiver is up to the police officer or the prosecution. The police officer must be able to show that all rights have been respected and that all required procedures have been complied with.

The Fourth Amendment forbids unreasonable search and seizure and requires probable cause. The Fifth Amendment guarantees due process; notice of

Table 18–1   **Evidentiary Standards of Proof—Degrees of Certainty**

STANDARD	DEFINITION	WHERE USED
Absolute certainty	No possibility of error; one hundred percent certainty.	Not used in civil or criminal law.
Beyond reasonable doubt; moral certainty	Conclusive and complete proof, while leaving any reasonable doubt as to the innocence or guilt of the defendant; allowing the defendant the benefit of any possibility of innocence.	Criminal trial.
Clear and convincing evidence	Prevailing and persuasive to the trier of fact.	Civil commitments, insanity defense.
Preponderance of evidence	Greater weight of evidence in terms of credibility; more convincing than an opposite point of view.	Civil trial.
Probable cause	U.S. constitutional standard for arrest and search warrants, requiring existence of facts sufficient to warrant that a crime has been committed.	Arrest, preliminary hearing, motions.
Sufficient evidence	Adequate evidence to reverse a trial court.	Appellate review.
Reasonable suspicion	Rational, reasonable belief that facts warrant investigation of a crime on less than probable cause.	Police investigations.
Less than probable cause	Mere suspicion. Less than reasonable to conclude criminal activity exists.	Prudent police investigation where safety of an officer or others is endangered.

Source: J. J. Senna and L. J. Siegel. *Introduction to Criminal Justice.* 5th ed. p. 442. Copyright © 1990, West Publishing Company: St. Paul, Minn. Reprinted by permission.

a hearing, full information regarding the charges made, the opportunity to present evidence before an impartial judge or jury, and the right to refrain from self-incrimination. The Sixth Amendment establishes the requirements for criminal trials including the right to speedy public trial by an impartial jury and the right to have a lawyer. The Eighth Amendment forbids excessive bail and implies the right to such bail in most instances.

Since our system uses an adversary process to seek out basic truths, the right to counsel is fundamental. In *Faretta v. California* (1975), however, the United States Supreme Court held that the Sixth Amendment guarantees self-representation in a criminal case, but before the court can allow such self-representation, defendants must intelligently and knowingly waive their rights to the assistance of counsel when they formulate and conduct their own defenses. A record is usually made stating that counsel is available to the defendant to prevent subsequent claims of improper waiver of counsel or lack of counsel. It has often been said, however, that "one who defends himself has a fool for a client."

The purpose of the right to counsel is to protect the accused from a conviction that may result from ignorance of legal and constitutional rights. Although defendants in all criminal cases have basic constitutional rights, often they do not know how to protect them. The right to counsel is indispensable to their understanding of their other rights under the Constitution.

Although the criminal justice system is sometimes criticized when a defendant is found not guilty because of a technicality, such criticism is unfounded. Even though a person confesses to a hideous crime, if he or she was not first told of his or her rights and allowed to have a lawyer present during questioning, the confession should not be considered legal. As noted by the United States Supreme Court in *Escobedo v. Illinois* (1964):

> No system of criminal justice can or should survive if it comes to depend for its continued effectiveness on the citizens' abdication through unawareness of their constitutional rights. No system worth preserving should have a fear that if an accused is permitted to consult with a lawyer, he will become aware of and exercise these rights. If the exercise of constitutional rights will thwart the effectiveness of a system of law enforcement, then there is something very wrong with that system.

During the past several decades many landmark decisions of the Supreme Court have extended the rights of individuals accused of a crime to have counsel at government expense if they cannot afford to hire their own lawyers.

In *Powell v. Alabama* (1932) the Supreme Court ruled that in a capital case, where the defendants are indigent and are incapable of presenting their own defenses, the court must assign them counsel as part of the due process of the law.

Between 1932 and 1963 the United States Supreme Court heard a variety of "right to counsel" cases. The Supreme Court ruled in *Johnson v. Zerbst* (1938) that an indigent defendant charged with a federal crime had the right to be furnished with counsel; however, this case said nothing about indigents who appeared in state courts.

In *Betts v. Brady* (1942) the Supreme Court ruled that an indigent charged in a state court had *no* right to appointed counsel unless charged with a capital crime. Nineteen years later Clarence Gideon, a habitual criminal, was arrested in Florida for breaking and entering a poolroom. Gideon claimed to be an indigent and asked for appointed counsel. The court refused on the grounds that Florida statutes provide for appointment of counsel only in capital cases. Gideon made his request based on the *Betts* case, but he was turned down and subsequently sentenced to the state prison.

Gideon, in a handwritten petition, took his case to the Supreme Court. In the famous *Gideon v. Wainwright* case (1963) the United States Supreme Court overruled *Betts v. Brady* and unanimously held that state courts must appoint counsel for indigent defendants in noncapital as well as capital cases.

Expanding on the "fairness" doctrine in 1972 in the *Argersinger v. Hamlin* case (1972), the United States Supreme Court ruled that all defendants in court who face the possibility of a jail sentence are entitled to legal counsel, and that if the accused cannot afford counsel, the state must provide one.

The Prosecutor

Prosecutors are officials elected to exercise leadership in the criminal justice system. They may be city attorneys, county attorneys, state attorneys, commonwealth attorneys, district attorneys, or solicitors.

Prosecutors are usually elected to a two- or four-year term at the state level. At the federal level they are appointed by the president.

Prosecutors are the legal representatives of the people and the police officers. They are responsible to the people who elected them, not to any other state or local official. They determine law enforcement priorities and are the key in determining how much, how little, and what types of crimes the public will tolerate. They serve the public interest and consider the public's need to feel secure, its sense of how justice should be carried out, and the community's attitude toward certain crimes. Sometimes a case becomes so well publicized that the prosecutor is forced to "do something about it" or face defeat in the next election.

Prosecutors are also the legal advisors for police officers; they are elected to decide what cases should be prosecuted and how. They rely heavily on the police officers' input in determining if a case should be brought to court or rejected. Often, however, misunderstanding and even ill will may result when a prosecutor refuses a police officer's request for a complaint because of insufficient evidence or some violation of a criminal procedure such as an illegal arrest. Plea bargaining may also cause ill will between a prosecutor and a police officer.

Since both police officers and prosecutors are striving for the same end—justice—they should be familiar with each other's problems. Police officers, for example, should understand what the prosecutor can and cannot do, which types of cases are worth prosecuting, and the need for and advantages of plea bargaining in certain situations. Prosecutors, on the other hand, should be sensitive to the police officers' objections to numerous legal technicalities and excessive paperwork and should include police officers in plea bargaining when possible, or, at the least, inform them when such bargaining has occurred.

Gershman (1992, p. 117) contends that: "The prosecutor is the most dominant figure in the American criminal justice system. . . . [The prosecutor has] the power to employ the full machinery of the State in scrutinizing any given individual. . . . The prosecutor's charging power includes the virtually unfettered discretion to invoke or deny punishment, and therefore the power to control and destroy people's lives." He suggests that in states with capital punishment the prosecutor has literally the power of life and death.

Senna and Siegel (1990, p. 358) suggest the following as common reasons for rejecting or dismissing a criminal case:

Insufficient evidence that results from a failure to find sufficient physical evidence that links the defendant to the offense.

Witness problems that arise, for example, when a witness fails to appear, gives unclear or inconsistent statements, is reluctant to testify, is unsure of the identity of the offender or where a prior relationship may exist between the victim/witness and offender.

The interests of justice, wherein the prosecutor decides not to prosecute certain types of offenses, particularly those that violate the letter but not the spirit of the law (for example, offenses involving insignificant amounts of property damage).

Due process problems that involve violations of the constitutional requirements for seizing evidence and for questioning the accused.

A plea on another case, for example, when the accused is charged in several cases and the prosecutor agrees to drop one or more of the cases in exchange for a plea of guilty on another case.

Pretrial diversion that occurs when the prosecutor and the court agree to drop charges when the accused successfully meets the conditions for diversion, such as completion of a treatment program.

Referral for other prosecution, such as when there are other offenses, perhaps of a more serious nature, in a different jurisdiction, or deferral to federal prosecution.

Although most prosecutors are ethical, the potential for abuses is ever present.

Abuses in the prosecutor's office most frequently occur in bringing charges, in controlling information used to convict those on trial, and in influencing juries.

Gershman (1992, p. 121) notes: "In one leading case of outrageous conduct, a prosecutor concealed from the jury in a murder case the fact that a pair of undershorts with red stains on it, a crucial piece of evidence, was stained not by blood but by paint."

Prosecutors perform one other critical function in the criminal justice process; they are responsible for protecting the rights of all involved, including the suspect. In essence they have a dual responsibility: on the one hand they are the leaders in the law enforcement community, the elected representatives of the public, and the legal advisors to the police officer; on the other hand, they are expected to protect the rights of persons accused of crimes. In *Berger v. United States* (1935) Justice Sutherland defined the prosecutor's responsibility as being "the representative not of an ordinary party to a controversy, but of a sovereignty whose obligation to govern impartially is as compelling as its obligation to govern at all; and whose interest, therefore, in a criminal prosecution is not that it shall win a case, but that justice shall be done."

Gershman (1992, p. 120) notes:

> The duties of the prosecuting attorney during a trial were well stated in a classical opinion fifty years ago. The interest of the prosecutor, the court wrote, "is not that it shall win a case, but that justice shall be done. As such, he is in a peculiar and very definitive sense the servant of the law, the twofold aim of which is that guilt shall not escape or innocence suffer. He may prosecute with earnestness and vigor—indeed, he should do so. But, while he may strike hard blows, he is not at liberty to strike a foul one."

The Defense Attorney

According to Serpe (1992, p. 111): "A public defender is an attorney appointed to aid indigent persons, usually in cases involving possible imprisonment." She notes that: "Lawyers join the public defender's office to gain trial experience and to make a positive contribution to society through public service." Many lawyers donate time to represent the indigent, called **pro bono work.** Many others, however, are reluctant to do so. Economics is not always the reason. As noted by Serpe (p. 114): "Most of the accused are not articulate and tend to be less intelligent and more sociopathic than the general population."

Lawyers who undertake to represent an accused have the same duties and obligations whether they are privately retained, serving as a legal aid in the system, or appointed by the court. They interview clients about their offenses, whether they are aware of any witnesses who might assist them, and whether they have given a confession. Lawyers investigate the circumstances of the cases and explore facts relevant to the guilt or innocence of their clients. They try to uncover evidence for their clients' defenses and organize the cases to present in court. The **defense attorney** represents the accused in court.

Although the role of the defense attorney has been glamorized by television series, in actuality over 99 percent of all criminal cases involve different kinds of lawyers and defense styles. Criminal law is not emphasized in law school, which instead concentrates on business, property, and tax law. Part of the reason for this is that clients are usually poor. In addition, the public generally has little sympathy for criminals and even less for a lawyer who "gets the criminal off."

The majority of criminal cases are assigned to public defenders or to a few private lawyers who handle such cases. Public defenders are full- and part-time lawyers hired by the state or county government to represent people who cannot afford to hire a lawyer. Like prosecutors, most public defenders see the position as a stepping-stone to private practice.

Not all cities have public defenders. In smaller cities, courts may appoint lawyers to represent poor people charged with crimes. In other cities the duty may be rotated among all lawyers practicing in the area as part of their professional obligation to society.

Most cities also have a small group of criminal lawyers who represent people who do not qualify financially for public defense. Known as "regulars," these lawyers do not intend to take these cases to court since few of the clients have much money. Instead they assist in plea bargaining with the prosecutors.

Judges

Although most people think of trial judges when they hear the word *judge,* many different kinds of judges exist. In fact, if a person comes to trial he or she will already have encountered certain levels of the court system and judges acting within that system. Glick (1983, p. 163) suggests that judges have many important functions throughout the entire judicial process:

> One of their most important jobs is to decide in preliminary hearings whether a prosecutor has sufficient evidence to justify prosecution. . . . Another important early decision for judges is whether to grant bail, if money bail is required and how much, or if the defendant can remain free without money bail before trial. Judges also make decisions to grant delays to give one side or the other additional time to prepare their case, to attend to other legal business, or to give a defense lawyer time to persuade a client to plead guilty or even to pay part of the lawyer's fee.

In many instances the judge has the key role in imposing the sentence to be served if a defendant is found guilty. And, as noted by Glick (1983, p. 177): "Judges have special status and receive great respect from everyone in court . . . their lofty position gives them an opportunity to lead others. If judges choose to exert themselves, they have practically unchallenged opportunities to influence the outcome of cases." The various types of judges and the functions they serve depend on the court to which they are appointed.

Having looked at the nature of the adversary system and the key "contestants," now consider the critical steps normally involved in the criminal justice process.

CRITICAL STAGES IN THE CRIMINAL JUSTICE SYSTEM

The criminal justice system consists of several critical stages: the complaint or charge, the warrant, arrest, booking, preliminary hearing, grand jury hearing, the arraignment, the trial, and sentencing.

The Complaint or Charge

Usually the criminal justice process begins when a police officer or a citizen approaches the prosecutor to obtain a complaint. A **complaint** is a legal document drawn up by a prosecutor that specifies the alleged crime and the supporting facts providing probable cause.

The formal complaint, also called the **charge,** contains all necessary evidence and facts to enable a magistrate to independently determine that probable cause exists for believing the offense has been committed by the accused.

The Warrant

The police officer or citizen then presents the complaint to a magistrate and, in the magistrate's presence, swears to the accuracy of the content of the complaint and signs a statement to that effect. If the magistrate, after reading the complaint drawn up by the prosecuting attorney, concurs with the charge, he or she orders an arrest **warrant** (based on the probable cause established in the complaint) containing the substance of the complaint to be issued. If the magistrate does not concur, he or she dismisses the complaint.

An arrest warrant directs an officer to bring the suspect before the magistrate. The warrant is usually directed to the sheriff or constables of a county or to all police officers of the municipality within the court's jurisdiction. The officer specified then locates and arrests the suspect if not already in custody. The officer may execute the warrant in any part of the county where it is issued or in any part of the state.

The Arrest

Requirements for a legal arrest have been discussed. When making the arrest, officers must inform the suspect that they are acting on the authority of the warrant. The suspect is entitled to see it. If the officers do not have the warrant in their possession, they must show it to the suspect as soon as possible.

The arrest may occur at other points within the criminal justice process. In a misdemeanor case, it may have occurred without a complaint or warrant, provided the crime was committed in the presence of the arresting officer. Or, as will be discussed later, the prosecutor may choose to present the case to a grand jury for indictment prior to arresting a suspect. Figure 18–4 illustrates the complexity of the criminal justice system.

The Booking

After a suspect is taken into custody, he or she is **booked** at the police station. The suspect is formally put into the police records system by the booking officer, who records on the booking sheet the suspect's name, date, time of arrest, charge, physical description, and physical characteristics. The suspect is photographed and fingerprinted. The prints are placed on file with the FBI in Washington, D.C., and the suspect has what is known as a Police Arrest Record.

Bail and Writ of Habeas Corpus

The Eighth Amendment forbids excessive bail and implies the right to bail in most instances.

One of the accused's rights is usually the right to be released from custody. Not only is this essential to the accused's immediate freedom, but it is in keeping with the premise that a person is innocent until proven guilty. After the formal booking process is completed, the suspect is usually entitled to be released on bail or on his or her own personal recognizance (**R.P.R.d**) if the

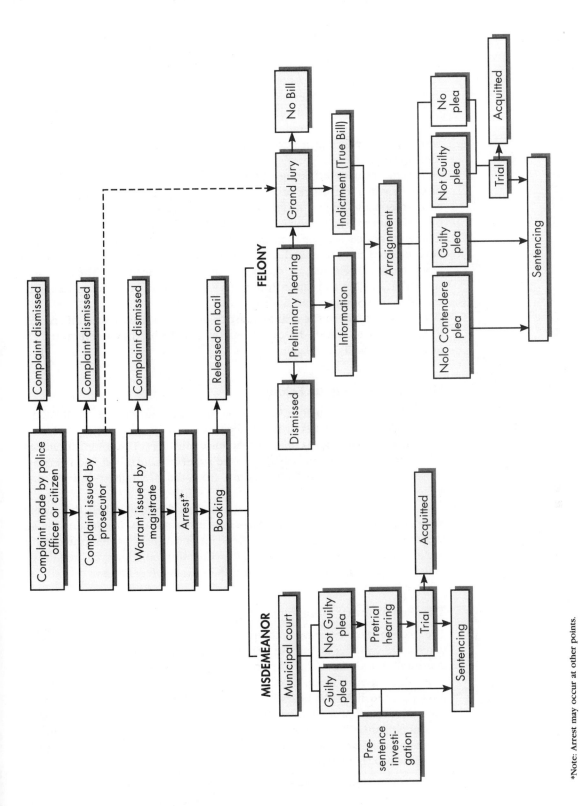

*Note: Arrest may occur at other points.

Figure 18–4 The Criminal Justice System from Complaint to Disposition

crime is a misdemeanor or released on a writ of habeas corpus or bond if the crime is a felony.

The judges decide how much **bail** (money) is reasonable as a deposit to bring the defendant into court if released. Some statutes, however, allow a judge to set a schedule for the amount of bail required for specific offenses such as violating municipal ordinances on shoplifting, driving under the influence of alcohol, and other violations.

Periodically a person in jail may be released on a **writ of habeas corpus** — a legal court order literally meaning "bring forth the body you have" — which commands that a person being held as a prisoner be brought forth immediately.

This means of determining whether the jailing of the suspect is legal is used primarily when the justice process moves slowly and a prisoner is detained for an unreasonable length of time before the court appearance. Habeas corpus often occurs when a person is arrested without a formal arrest warrant and the follow-up police investigation takes an unreasonably long time. Most states have adopted rules or guidelines as to how long a person may be jailed before being charged, released, or making an appearance in court. These rules are somewhat flexible and range from thirty-six to seventy-two hours, taking into consideration Sundays and holidays.

Up to this point in the criminal justice process, it makes little difference as to what type of crime — misdemeanor or felony — has been committed. The process is basically the same.

Misdemeanor versus Felony

Misdemeanors are usually disposed of by ticket, tab charge, or R.P.R.d, in which case the suspect is ordered to court.

Felony cases are more complex than misdemeanors. The complaint must be filed with the clerk of the district or the superior court. In a felony case the prosecutor may seek an "information" from the preliminary hearing or an indictment from a grand jury.

A formal written accusation, what has thus far been called the criminal complaint or charge, is also known as an **information.** It contains the substance of the charge against the defendant and usually is associated with a preliminary hearing. The United States Constitution, however, requires an indictment by a grand jury for most crimes against federal law.

The Preliminary Hearing

The **preliminary hearing** is the probable cause hearing. The magistrate first determines whether an offense has been committed and if sufficient evidence is presented to believe that the accused committed it.

If the accused is being held, it is important to both the defendant and the prosecutor to hold the hearing within a reasonable time. Most statutes and rules of criminal procedure require a preliminary hearing to be held within a "reasonable time." Some jurisdictions require a preliminary hearing to be held immediately after arrest, some within forty-eight to seventy-two hours, others within ten to thirty days.

The preliminary hearing seeks to establish probable cause to prevent persons from being indiscriminately brought to trial.

The magistrate in a preliminary hearing is not bound by the rules of evidence that ordinarily control a trial. A far broader range of evidence is usually admissible. The evidence need only show probable cause and reasonably and fairly tend to show the crime is as charged and that the accused committed it. The prosecutor only has to present the evidence; he or she need not prove the crime was committed beyond a reasonable doubt as long as probable cause is shown.

In reality the preliminary hearing is often a minitrial where the defense obtains as much information as possible to strengthen its case should it be bound over to a higher court. Both prosecution and defense often use this stage of the criminal justice process for tactical purposes. In some instances overwhelming evidence may lead to a guilty plea or to a request for plea bargaining.

The preliminary hearing is often a discovery tool for defendants as they hear the evidence presented. If the case went to the grand jury, the defendants would not be aware of this evidence. Some states have eliminated this element of surprise by including the discovery process in their rules of criminal procedure.

The **discovery process** requires that all pertinent facts on both sides be made available prior to the time of the trial.

Used properly, the discovery process reduces questions of probable cause and other questions normally brought out in a preliminary hearing and encourages more final dispositions before trial, thereby saving court time. Available to both the prosecution and defense attorneys, it eliminates surprise as a legitimate trial tactic.

The preliminary hearing does not determine guilt or innocence. It merely determines whether further action should be taken. At this point the magistrate usually does not rule on complicated issues of evidence.

The main intent of the preliminary hearing is to add to the checks and balances of the criminal justice system by preventing the prosecutor from indiscriminately bringing someone to trial. The preliminary hearing, one of the critical stages of due process, is a very formal proceeding insuring that all accused persons are adequately informed and that all their constitutional rights are protected.

The outcome of a preliminary hearing may be to (1) dismiss the charges, (2) present an information and bind the defendant over to a higher court, or (3) send the case to a grand jury.

The Grand Jury

The United States Constitution requires an indictment by a federal grand jury before trial for most crimes against federal law. Grand juries frequently hear cases involving misconduct of public officials, violations of election laws, bankruptcy fraud, criminal conduct, and the like.

The consideration of a felony charge by a grand jury is in no sense of the word a trial. Only the prosecution's evidence is usually presented and considered. Contrary to the popular portrayal of grand juries on television and in movies, suspected offenders are usually not heard nor are their lawyers present to offer evidence in their behalf.

A **grand jury** is usually composed of twenty-three voting citizens of the county, selected by either the district or superior judges, jury commissioners, court officials, or some designated county supervisor. These juries may be called to duty any time the court is in session. Sixteen jurors constitute a quorum, and the votes of twelve members are usually necessary to return an indictment.

Grand juries meet in secret sessions and hear from witnesses and victims of crime. Because it meets in secret session, it is an accusatory body and determines only whether enough evidence exists to accuse a person or persons of a crime.

The prosecutor usually has considerable foundation for believing an offense has been committed before taking a case to the grand jury. The prosecutor is authorized to subpoena witnesses before the jury. Usually only one witness appears at a time before the jury and is questioned under oath by the prosecutor.

In some states, by statute, a grand jury can hear evidence from suspects. In order to testify, however, the persons being considered for indictment must sign a waiver of immunity and agree to answer all questions posed in the grand jury session even though their testimony might be incriminating and lead to an indictment. Their testimony also may be used against them in a criminal trial. Their lawyers are not allowed to be present in the grand jury room if they are testifying.

After the grand jury receives all testimony and evidence, it begins its deliberations. No one else is allowed in the room during these deliberations. Before an indictment can be reached, the jurors must agree that all the evidence presented leads them to believe probable cause exists that the person is guilty of a crime. If the majority of the grand jurors (or a specified number) agree, they instruct the prosecutor to prepare an **indictment** which specifies all the facts of the case and the names of those who appeared before the jury.

The indictment is signed by the grand jury foreman and presented to the district or superior court judge, who then orders the issuance of a bench warrant for the arrest of the defendant if not already in custody. If the defendant is indicted, until arrested or brought before the court, the fact that an indictment has been found must be kept secret; it is not public information. Procedures are then implemented for the defendant's appearance in court, where a trial jury may be convened to hear the case.

Grand juries may also issue what is called a **no bill.** If, after hearing all the evidence presented and the witnesses, the jurors believe there is no criminal violation, the grand jury issues a no bill, which means they find no basis for an indictment and will no longer consider the matter unless further evidence is presented that may warrant an indictment.

Grand juries can also take action and conduct investigations on their own initiative. This is known as a **presentment** and in some jurisdictions is sufficient to support a prosecution. Some states, however, regard a presentment as mere instructions to the prosecutor to draw up a bill of indictment. If, when the grand jury reviews the bill of indictment, they agree it is a true bill, it becomes the basis for prosecution.

Table 18–2 describes which states require grand jury indictments and in what circumstances.

Critics of the grand jury process contend that it denies due process to defendants and that its main function is to serve the prosecutor.

The Arraignment

When defendants are charged with a felony, they must personally appear at an **arraignment.** As in the preliminary hearing, the defendants are entitled to counsel. The procedures of the arraignment vary in some states, but generally defendants appear before the court, are read the complaint, information, or

Table 18–2   When a Grand Jury Is Required

GRAND JURY INDICTMENT REQUIRED	GRAND JURY INDICTMENT OPTIONAL
All crimes	Arizona
New Jersey	Arkansas
South Carolina	California
Tennessee	Colorado
Virginia	Idaho
All felonies	Illinois
Alabama	Indiana
Alaska	Iowa
Delaware	Kansas
District of Columbia	Maryland
Georgia	Michigan
Hawaii	Missouri
Kentucky	Montana
Maine	Nebraska
Mississippi	Nevada
New Hampshire	New Mexico
New York	North Dakota
North Carolina	Oklahoma
Ohio	Oregon
Texas	South Dakota
West Virginia	Utah
Capital crimes only	Vermont
Connecticut	Washington
Florida	Wisconsin
Louisiana	Wyoming
Massachusetts	**Grand jury lacks authority to indict**
Minnesota	Pennsylvania
Rhode Island	

Note: With the exception of capital cases a defendant can always waive the right to an indictment. Thus, the requirement for an indictment to initiate prosecution exists only in the absence of a waiver.

Source: D. Day Emerson. *Grand jury reform: A review of key issues,* National Institute of Justice, U.S. Department of Justice, January 1983.

Source: Bureau of Justice Statistics. U.S. Department of Justice. *Report to the Nation on Crime and Justice,* March 1988.

indictment, and, if they have not received a copy, they are given one. They then enter a **plea.**

Defendants have several alternatives when they appear for the formal arraignment. **Standing mute,** that is refusing to answer, is entered by the judge as a not guilty plea.

Nolo contendere means "no contest." By entering a plea of nolo contendere, defendants, in effect, throw themselves on the mercy of the court. This plea is often used when individuals know of some forthcoming civil actions against them and do not want their pleas to jeopardize their defenses in civil trials. (A guilty plea to any criminal offense could become a part of the civil trial.)

Guilty means the accused admits the actual charge or a lesser charge agreed to in a plea bargaining session. A guilty plea has many consequences: possible imprisonment, being labeled a criminal, and a waiver of constitutional rights of all defenses. Still, 90 percent of all criminal defendants plead guilty in the United States, but most plead guilty to offenses reduced from the original charges.

Not guilty means the accused denies the charge. He or she may have a valid defense for the charge such as intoxication, insanity, self-defense, or mistaken identity. Some states require defendants to automatically plead not guilty to capital crimes such as first-degree murder.

If defendants plead guilty or nolo contendere, a sentencing time is set. Usually a presentence investigation is ordered to determine if probation is warranted. If defendants make no plea or plead not guilty, they have the choice of a trial by a judge or by a jury, who weighs the facts of the case and makes the decision of guilt or innocence. If defendants wish a jury trial, the case will be assigned to the court docket and a date set.

Before looking at the trial itself, consider some alternatives to a trial.

ALTERNATIVES TO A TRIAL

Critics of our criminal justice system note that it is overburdened and that alternatives to a trial should be available. They suggest that in many instances such alternatives would also be more equitable. As noted by Pace (1991, p. 153): "Cases filed in our courts since 1977 have increased from 6 percent to 132 percent. This increase in volume has given the term 'assembly line justice' some real validity." He further suggests (p. 155) that the number one complaint about the court system is the failure to process cases "without unnecessary delay."

Maechling (1992, p. 133) asserts:

> The American criminal justice system is breaking down. Court calendars and prisons are clogged. It can take years to execute a child murderer or put a rapist behind bars, while an otherwise harmless teenager can get a mandatory 20-year sentence for mere possession of cocaine. One Southern state recently sentenced an ignorant black youth to five years at hard labor for shoplifting a $6 item.

Alternatives to a trial include diversion and plea bargaining.

Diversion

Before clients and their attorneys go to court, defense attorneys may explore the possibility of diverting the case from the criminal justice system by using a community agency if the circumstances warrant it; for example, in cases of mental incompetence an attorney may seek to divert the case to a mental institution. **Diversion** gives defendants an alternative to a trial, for example, to obtain help from a community agency or to make restitution to the victim of the crime.

Diversion is a discretionary decision that can occur at many points as the case progresses through the criminal justice system. For example, a police officer who assumes custody of an intoxicated person and releases that person to the custody of family or a detoxification center diverts. Likewise, a prosecutor who delays prosecution while a defendant participates in psychiatric treatment diverts. In both instances, a discretionary decision is made that there is a more appropriate way to deal with the defendant than to prosecute.

As might be expected, diversion has its opponents. Some individuals feel this is "letting criminals off easy." However, major benefits can result. According to the National Advisory Commission (1973, p. 27):

Many individuals come within the language of existing criminal statutes, but their conviction and punishment would not be consistent with the intent of the legislature.... By taking the offender out of the criminal justice process before conviction, diversion imposes no stigma of conviction, and unlike screening, prevents the offender from committing future harmful acts or requires him to make restitution. Only diversion provides a means of accommodating this compromise solution. If diversion programs were made available as sentencing alternatives, the objective of avoiding the stigma of a criminal conviction would be nullified.

Colson (1992, p. 138), special counsel to President Nixon who was sentenced to prison for his role in Watergate, believes: "Diverting the nondangerous offenders from prison to work in community service would ease overcrowding in our institutions, freeing up space for the truly dangerous.... In my view, those convicted of nondangerous offenses should be working to pay back society, rather than sitting idle in expensive cells." According to Colson (1992, p. 139): "It costs an average of $15,900 to keep a person in prison for one year.... When I was incarcerated, my job was to run the washing machine. Next to me, the former chairman of the board of the American Medical Association ran the dryer. This skilled doctor could have been sentenced to provide free medical help to the poor, thus contributing to the community, rather than costing taxpayers about $16,000 a year in prison."

Another obvious benefit of diversion is economy, eliminating the necessity for what could be a costly court trial.

Plea Bargaining

The client and defense lawyer may also attempt to plea bargain their case. **Plea bargaining** is legal negotiation between the prosecutor and the defense lawyer or the client to reach an agreement that avoids a court trial. The prosecutor is seeking a conviction without going through the formality of a court trial. The defense is looking for some concessions by the prosecutor to reduce the punishment for the defendant.

Plea bargaining is a compromise between defense and prosecution that prearranges the plea and the sentence, conserving time and expense.

Basically, plea bargaining involves promises and compromises. From the prosecutor it may mean that if a series of charges are filed, the defendant would be charged with only one; the other charges would be dismissed. Or it might mean that the prosecutor would reduce a charge if only one charge is filed; for example, a charge of burglary might be reduced to breaking and entering which carries a lesser penalty.

According to Kelly (1990, p. 176): "Plea bargains and dismissals are the most common ways to dispose of cases. National estimates indicate that between 83 and 90% of all cases that remain in the system are plea bargained."

Monk (1991, p. 182) suggests that: " 'Copping a plea,' 'striking a deal,' has been a part of the American court process for at least a century." Concurring with Kelly, he notes: "Currently, approximately 90 percent of all local and state felony cases and 85 percent of federal charges are plea bargained (with sharp variations between jurisdictions)."

Walker (1991, p. 188) feels plea bargaining has some merits and argues that: "Much can and should be done about plea bargaining short of abolishing it. The most reasonable proposals call for regulation. Bargaining should be brought out of the closet, so to speak, through the requirement of a written record. Formal policy guidelines could also establish criteria for reduction and charges and sentence recommendations."

Fine (1991, p. 189), however, disagrees, asserting that: "we should not bargain with criminals . . . criminals learn they can get away with crime." He notes that: "Prosecutors like plea bargaining because trials are time-consuming, and they usually have heavy caseloads." It is also an easier way to make a living. Fine quotes a defense lawyer as saying: "A guilty plea is a quick buck." Notes Fine: "A thousand dollars is a handsome fee for two hours spent making a deal with the prosecutor."

Maechling (1992, p. 135) also criticizes plea bargaining, noting:

> Plea bargains are increasingly made with the defendant in the best position to implicate others—not with a minor accomplice to nail the ringleader. In the John Walker espionage case, for example, the mastermind of the ring was allowed to plea-bargain his way to a light sentence, while his hapless brother-in-law, pressed into service virtually against his will, received a sadistic 25-year sentence without parole for turning over one low-grade security item.

A hazard of the plea bargaining system is that it may cause police officers to feel isolated. Throughout the criminal procedures system police officers are valued; the prosecutor, the complainants, the witnesses, and society depend upon them. But when it comes to plea bargaining sessions, they are left out. Often officers will inquire about the disposition of a case of vital interest to them only to find that it has been disposed of in plea bargaining. If officers are to be part of the total system, they should have some input into the disposition of the cases or, at the least, be informed of the disposition. As criminals are placed back into society, the police officers' problems in dealing with crime grow. If police officers are to deal with these problems, they should be consulted.

The Coroner's Jury

Coroners investigate violent deaths where suspicion of foul play exists. By law, coroners may conduct autopsies as to the cause of death, and they may conduct inquests. The **coroner's jury** usually consists of six members. In some states the coroner's jury system has been abandoned and its functions performed by a professional medical examiner, usually a pathologist or a forensic expert.

THE TRIAL

The trial is the climax in the criminal justice procedure. All previously made decisions now merge in one finality. The test of how well the police officers have investigated the case, compiled evidence and reported it, and dealt with the victim and witnesses are weighed in the courtroom.

The key figures in the trial are the judge, members of the jury, the defendant and defense attorney(s), the prosecuting attorney(s), police officer(s), and witnesses.

The judge has charge of the trial and decides all matters with respect to the law. He or she also assures that all the rules of trial procedure are followed. The **jury** decides all matters of fact. The advocates are the prosecuting attorney(s) and the defense attorney(s). The trial begins with the jury selection.

Figure 18−5 illustrates another view of the progression of a typical criminal felony litigation. This progression can be repeated from a lower court to a higher court, one or more times. Notice especially the steps involved in the trial itself.

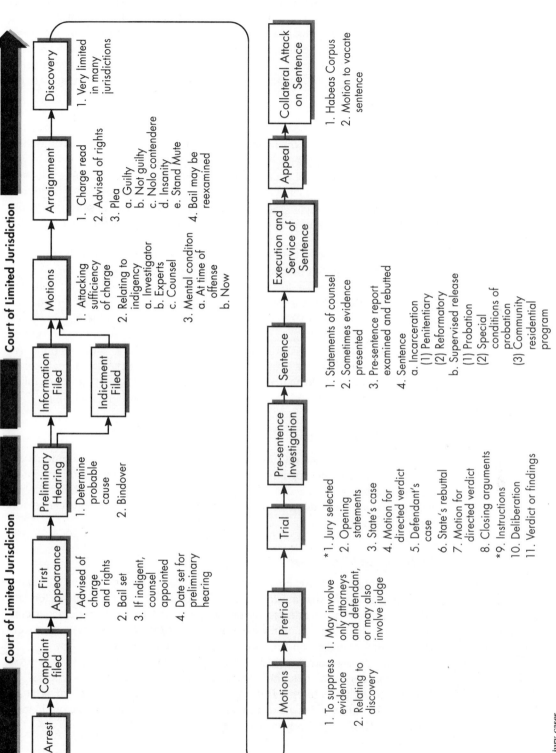

*In jury cases.

Figure 18–5   Typical Progression of Criminal Felony Litigation

Source: H. T. Rubin. *The Courts: Fulcrum of the Justice System.* 2d ed. Copyright © 1976, 1984 by Newburg Award Records, Inc., a subsidiary of Random House. Reprinted by permission of the publisher.

Jury Selection

Safeguards built into the jury selection process not only protect the rights of the defendant but also assure the public that justice is done. Trial jurors are selected at random by district or superior court judges or the commissioners of the county board. The judges or the commissioners randomly select a large group of prospective jurors and, when the trial is about to begin, call these people to the court and inform them of their duties in the particular case for which they may serve.

It is then up to the attorneys trying the case to decide which six or twelve of these individuals will be the jurors in the case. The clerk of courts draws the names of six or twelve jurors from the jury list, and these individuals take their seats in the regular jury box in the order in which their names were drawn. The defense attorney and then the prosecuting attorney question each individual as to his or her qualifications to be a juror in this case. The judge may also question the prospective jurors. The random selection of potential jurors and the careful questioning of each helps insure selection of six or twelve fair and impartial jurors.

The National Advisory Commission on Criminal Justice Standards and Goals (1975, p. 101) suggests that the twelve-person jury requirement for criminal trials that exists in most jurisdictions is an "accident of history," and that "juries of less than 12 can provide a reliable and competent fact-finding body." In *Williams v. Florida* (1970) the Court stated that the touchstone should be whether the group is "large enough to promote group deliberation, to be free from outside attempts at intimidation, and to provide a fair possibility for obtaining a representative cross-section of the community." In this same case the Supreme Court held that Florida's use of a six-person jury did not violate the defendant's Eighth and Fourteenth Amendment rights to trial by jury.

Opening Statements

After the jury is selected and instructed by the judge, opening statements are presented. The prosecutor informs the jury of the state's case and how he or she intends to prove the charges against the defendant. The defense lawyer makes an opening statement in support of the accused or may waive this opening statement.

Evidence and Testimony

The prosecutor then presents evidence and the testimony of the witnesses, attempting to prove that a crime had been committed and that the defendant did it. The prosecutor does so by using direct and indirect evidence, a confession, the testimony of witnesses, or the testimony of the police officers whose initial investigation brought the case to trial.

Through **cross-examination,** the defense attorney tries to discredit prosecution witnesses, the evidence, and the testimony of the police officers.

As noted by Maechling (1992, p. 134): "The adversarial system is at its worst in the ritual of cross-examination." He notes that cross-examination most often confuses witnesses and muddies the record.

The Police Officer in Court

Almost all officers have a day in court. Because of overloaded court dockets, cases usually come up well after the officers' investigation; therefore, officers must refer to their reports and their original notes to refresh their memories.

The notes may remind them that it was a cloudy day, a light rain had fallen and the streets were still wet, that it was midafternoon, and that clearly visible bloodstains trailed out the back door.

A court appearance is an important part of any police officer's duty. All elements of the investigation are brought together at this point: the report, the statements of the witnesses, the evidence collected, and possibly even a confession from the defendant.

The prosecution needs to establish the corpus delicti of the crime, which means it has to establish the elements of the crime by testimony of witnesses, physical evidence, documents, recordings, or other admissible evidence. This information usually comes from police officers, their recollections, their notes, and their reports. The prosecutor works with police officers in presenting the arguments for the prosecution. On the opposing side is the defense attorney.

Defense attorneys use several different techniques for which police officers should be prepared.

The defense attorney may try to confuse or discredit a police officer by (1) rapid-fire questioning, (2) establishing that the officer wants to see the defendant found guilty, (3) accusing the officer of making assumptions, or (4) implying that the officer does not want anyone else to know what is in his or her notes.

One frequently used technique is *rapid-fire questioning* with the intent of confusing the officer to obtain inconsistent answers. To counter this tactic, officers should be deliberate and take their time in answering questions. They may ask the defense attorney to repeat the question to slow him or her down and thus thwart this effort at rapid-fire questioning.

The trial of a criminal case is a very serious contest. Someone wins and someone loses. The prosecution wins if it establishes the guilt of the defendant. It must prove the defendant is guilty beyond a reasonable doubt. The defendant wins if the prosecution fails in its obligation of proof.

Proof consists of two basic elements: the evidence itself and, equally important, presentation of this evidence. No matter how much evidence exists, if improperly presented, the prosecution will fail. Presenting evidence involves credibility and believability.

In a criminal case, the defense rarely expects to gain helpful information from police officers. The main intent is usually to discredit the officers or their testimony. One common approach is to establish a motive for officers' testimony, to show the officers have a personal interest in the case, to question their candor: Is the officer being open or holding back? Is the testimony consistent? Does it contain errors? Is the officer confident and relaxed or nervous, upset, and seemingly afraid? What is the officer's general appearance? Is it the appearance of a professional doing an important, serious job?

Defense attorneys also attack a police officer's credibility by focusing on the assumptions or inferences of the officer. Assumptions and inferences are natural. We spend our whole lives making assumptions, usually reasonable ones. The law recognizes the validity of assumptions and inferences. As a matter of fact, the court will instruct the jury to make reasonable inferences. From time to time, however, a defense attorney will try to discredit police officers' testimony by asking them if they are making assumptions. If officers have, in fact, drawn inferences or made assumptions, they should not attempt to deny it.

Another cross-examination tactic used by defense counsel from time to time is to present to the jury police officers' reluctance to relinquish their notes. The police officers' notes and their reports, as a general rule, are avail-

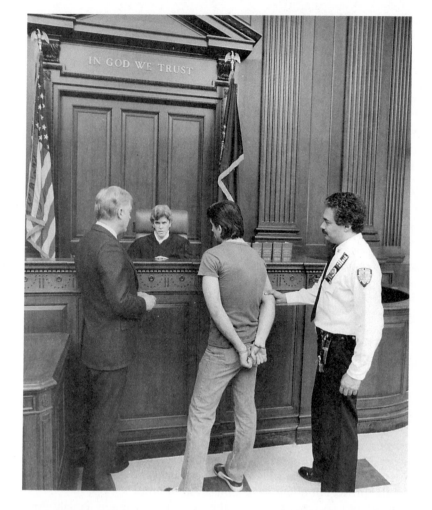

Our court system has a rich
heritage steeped in tradition. It
may be foreign and uncomfortable for defendants and for law
enforcement professionals.

able to the defense counsel in making cross-examination. When police officers
use their notes to testify, they are also available to the defense counsel.

Ten "commandments" of courtroom testimony are offered by Hope (1992,
pp. 56–60):

1. Relax and be yourself. Prepare. Be animated. Be human. Seek eye contact.
2. Answer only questions that are before you.
3. Refer to your report only when allowed.
4. Paint the scene just as it was.
5. Be ready to explain why you are remembering details in court if they are not
   in your report.
6. Avoid jargon or unduly difficult language.
7. Avoid sarcasm.
8. Maintain your detachment.
9. You don't need to explain the law.
10. Explanation of what you said is possible on rebuttal.

Closing Statements

After the advocates have concluded their presentations, the jury hears the closing statements—a contest in persuasion first by the prosecution, stating the jury
should render a guilty verdict, then by the defense attorney, concluding the
client is surely innocent or at least not proven guilty beyond a reasonable doubt.

Jury Deliberation and Decision

With the closing of the case, the judge reads the instructions to the jury. This includes an explanation of the crime, what elements constitute the crime, alternate charges, and the concepts of presumption of innocence and reasonable doubt. The jury then retires behind closed doors to deliberate their findings. They can return one of three findings: guilty, not guilty, or no verdict. No verdict simply means that no agreement can be reached; this is also sometimes referred to as a **hung jury.**

After the jury has come to a decision, the judge is notified and the jury returns to the courtroom. With everyone present, the jury foreman announces the verdict. Each juror is then polled as to how he or she voted and is asked if the verdict that the foreman has read is the verdict of the juror. If the finding is guilty, the defendant may either be sentenced immediately or may be given a sentencing date. If found not guilty, he or she is set free. If a hung jury results, the defendant may be retried at the discretion of the prosecutor.

SENTENCING

Sentences for individuals convicted of crimes vary considerably from lenient to extremely severe penalties. For one convicted of a crime this may mean the difference between probation and several years in prison.

In many jurisdictions the court has the authority to set, within limits established by state statute, both maximum and minimum sentences. Common characteristics of these schemes are summarized in Table 18–3.

Table 18–3	**Common Sentencing Schemes**
Indeterminate	Minimum and maximum terms prescribed by legislature; place and length of sentence controlled by corrections and parole; judge has little discretion over time served; goal is rehabilitation; sentence to fit offender; uncertainty and disparity in sentencing are major problems.
Indefinite	Similar to indeterminate sentence in some states; minimum and maximum terms, or only maximum terms prescribed by legislature; sentence to match offender's needs; judge has some sentencing discretion; wide disparity in sentences imposed; parole used for early release.
Definite	Fixed period prescribed by legislature and imposed by judge; goal to punish and deter offender from further crime; allows for same sentence to apply to all convicted of particular offenses; eliminates disparity; judge has no discretion over length of sentence, only over choice of sentence; offender required to serve entire sentence; no parole, inflexibility, and rigidity are major problems.
Determinate	Similar to definite sentence; has one fixed term of years set by judge; offender required to serve entire sentence where no parole exists.
Mandatory	Fixed term set by legislature for particular crimes; sentence must be imposed by judge; judge has no discretion in choice of sentence; goal is punishment and deterrence; contrary to individualized sentence; no sentencing disparity; no parole.
Presumptive	Legislatively prescribed range of sentences for given crimes; minimum and maximum terms with judge setting determinate sentence within these bounds; judge maintains some discretion; guidelines and use of mitigating and aggravating circumstances established by legislature; goal is justice, deterrence, and individualization in sentencing; "just deserts."

Source: J. J. Senna and L. J. Siegel. *Introduction to Criminal Justice.* Copyright © 1984. Reprinted by permission of West Publishing Co.: St. Paul, Minn. All rights reserved.

A presumptive sentencing scheme legislatively prescribes a range of sentences for given crimes, establishing minimum and maximum terms, with the judge using discretion within these bounds.

Common sentencing schemes include indeterminate, indefinite, definite, determinate, mandatory, and presumptive.

The alternatives available also vary and are summarized in Table 18–4. These sentences as means of "correction" are looked at in the next chapter.

Case Review and Appeal

To assure that justice is served, the court system provides for a **judicial review** of cases and for a person convicted to appeal the conviction in most instances. The National Advisory Commission on Criminal Justice Standards and Goals (1975, pp. 122–125) states: "Determining guilt and fixing punishment should not be left to a single trial court. The interests of both society and the defendant are served by providing another tribunal to review the trial court proceedings to insure that no prejudicial error was committed and that justice was done." The commission goes on to note: "Review also provides a means for the ongoing development of legal doctrine in the common law fashion, as well as a means of insuring evenhanded administration of justice throughout the jurisdiction. Functionally, review is the last stage in the judicial process of determining guilt and fixing sentence. Like the trial proceeding, it should be fair and expeditious."

What types of sentences usually are given to offenders?

Death penalty—In most states for the most serious crimes such as murder, the courts may sentence an offender to death by lethal injection, electrocution, exposure to lethal gas, hanging, or other method specified by state law.

- As of 1985, 37 states had laws providing for the death penalty.
- Virtually all death penalty sentences are for murder.
- As of year-end 1985, 50 persons had been executed since 1976, and 1,591 inmates in 32 states were under a sentence of death.

Incarceration—The confinement of a convicted criminal in a federal or state prison or a local jail to serve a court-imposed sentence. Confinement is usually in a jail, administered locally, or a prison, operated by the state or federal government. In many states offenders sentenced to 1 year or less are held in a jail; those sentenced to longer terms are committed to a state prison.

- More than 4,200 correctional facilities are maintained by federal, state, and local governments. They include 47 federal facilities, 922 state-operated adult confinement and community-based correctional facilities, and 3,300 local jails, which usually are county-operated.
- On any given day in 1985 about 503,000 persons were confined in state and federal prisons. About 254,000 were confined in local jails on June 30, 1985.

Probation—The sentencing of an offender to community supervision by a probation agency, often as a result of suspending a sentence to confinement. Such supervision normally entails specific rules of conduct while in the community. If the rules are violated a sentence to confinement may be imposed. Probation is the most widely used correctional disposition in the United States.

- State or local governments operate more than 2,000 probation agencies.
- At year-end 1985, nearly 1.9 million adults were on probation, or about 1 of every 95 adults in the nation.

Split sentences, shock probation, and intermittent confinement—A penalty that explicitly requires the convicted person to serve a brief period of confinement in a local, state, or federal facility (the "shock") followed by a period of probation. This penalty attempts to combine the use of community supervision with a short incarceration experience. Some sentences are periodic rather than continuous; for example, an offender may be required to spend a certain number of weekends in jail.

- In 1984 nearly a third of those receiving probation sentences in Idaho, New Jersey, Tennessee, Utah, and Vermont also were sentenced to brief periods of confinement.

Restitution and victim compensation—The offender is required to provide financial repayment or, in some jurisdictions, services in lieu of monetary restitution, for the losses incurred by the victim.

- Nearly all states have statutory provisions for the collection and disbursement of restitution funds. A restitution law was enacted at the federal level in 1982.

Community service—The offender is required to perform a specified amount of public service work, such as collecting trash in parks or other public facilities.

- Many states authorize community service work orders. Community service often is imposed as a specific condition of probation.

Fines—An economic penalty that requires the offender to pay a specified sum of money within limits set by law. Fines often are imposed in addition to probation or as alternatives to incarceration.

- The Victims of Crime Act of 1984 authorizes the distribution of fines and forfeited criminal profits to support state victim-assistance programs, with priority given to programs that aid victims of sexual assault, spousal abuse, and child abuse. These programs, in turn, provide assistance and compensation to crime victims.
- Many laws that govern the imposition of fines are being revised. The revisions often provide for more flexible means of ensuring equity in the imposition of fines, flexible fine schedules, "day fines" geared to the offender's daily wage, installment payment of fines, and the imposition of confinement only when there is an intentional refusal to pay.
- A 1984 study estimated that more than three-fourths of criminal courts use fines extensively and that fines levied each year exceed $1 billion.

Source: U.S. Department of Justice. Bureau of Justice Statistics. Washington, D.C., U.S. Government Printing Office, 1988.

EQUAL VERSUS INDIVIDUALIZED JUSTICE

"Equal Justice Under the Law" is emblazoned on the front of the U.S. Supreme Court building. But what "equal justice" means has been a subject of debate. Two basic approaches have been taken to interpreting this phrase, one is that of following the letter of the law, also referred to as the *rule of law,* the other that of considering individual cases, or the *rule of man.*

The rule of law goes by the book, allowing little or no discretion. The rule of man emphasizes using discretion and looking at the uniqueness of each case.

As noted by Holten and Lamar (1991, p. 21), the rule of law is rather mechanistic. It emphasizes "the values of evenhandedness, uniformity, consistency, visibility and predictability; its drawbacks include the potential for inflexibility, harshness, rigidity, complexity, formalism, and ironically inequality."

Table 18–5 **The Rule of Law and Man Compared**

IN-KIND OPPOSITES

Rule of Law (no discretion)	More law, less discretion	Roughly equal mixture of law and discretion	More discretion, less law	Rule of Man (no law or rules)

POSITIVE VALUES (ARGUMENTS FOR)

Theme: "We are a Government of laws and not of men." "No one is above the law."	*Theme:* "Discretion is the handmaiden of justice." "Discretion is the principal source of creativity in government."
1. More equal protection, evenhandedness, uniformity, consistency possible	1. More individualization and flexibility possible
2. More due process, fairness, rationality possible	2. More mercy, compassion, equity possible
3. More notice, visibility, continuity, predictability, structure, certainty possible	3. More creativity and adaptability possible
4. More centralized limits on governmental powers, generality, universality possible	4. More informality and efficiency possible

NEGATIVE VALUES (ARGUMENTS AGAINST)

Theme: "The law and justice are sometimes at odds." "Rigorous law is rigorous injury."	*Theme:* "Where the law ends, tyranny begins." "Yes, I'd give the Devil benefit of the law, for my own safety's sake."
1. More inflexibility, harshness, rigidity; mandatory legalism	1. More unequal treatment (disparity), inconsistency, nonuniformity
2. More rigidity, pigeon holing, technicality, mechanization, inequity	2. More arbitrary and capricious abuse of discretion, irrationality
3. More complexity and red tape	3. More uncertainty, invisibility, unpredictability, lack of structure and continuity
4. More blind formalism, unnecessary judicialization, and inefficiency	4. More unlimited and uncontrolled provincialism

Source: Adapted from D. Spader. "Rule of Law vs. Rule of Man." *Journal of Criminal Justice* 12, no. 4, 1984: 381, 385.

The rule of man, in contrast, emphasizes discretion. This approach, say Holten and Lamar "emphasizes the values of flexibility, mercy, compassion, informality, and efficiency. Its obvious drawbacks include the potential for unequal treatment, inconsistency, arbitrariness, capricious abuse of discretion, uncertainty, and uncontrolled provincialism." Table 18–5 summarizes the differences between the two approaches to law.

What is commonly called for is a sort of middle ground between these two extremes, referred to as **justice of dispensation.** Holten and Lamar suggest that this is "a justice ready to make exceptions when the established rules work unexpected hardship in particular cases, a justice ready to bend the letter of the law to accomplish a fair result." They also note:

> The pendulum, which had swung high in favor of individualism, has begun to swing back in favor of equalization. It accompanies the trend away from rehabilitation to a new emphasis on retribution and incapacitation and is marked particularly by attempts to restrict the discretion of judges in sentencing.

Further complicating the processes of the courts is the concept of **sociological jurisprudence.** This theory, followed by our courts, contends that the law must recognize and adapt to contemporary social conditions and that laws must adapt to a changing world.

SUMMARY

Police officers aid the criminal justice process by (1) making legal arrests, (2) legally obtaining accurate, relevant information and evidence, (3) writing complete, accurate reports, (4) identifying suspects and witnesses, and (5) providing effective, truthful testimony in court.

Our judicial system operates at both the state and federal level. The hierarchy at the state level often goes from courts of special or limited jurisdiction called justice of the peace (J. P.) courts, to trial courts or original and general jurisdiction courts, to intermediate appellate courts, to the state supreme court. The federal court system is three tiered: district courts, appellate courts, and the United States Supreme Court.

Our criminal justice system is based on the adversary system, which requires that the accuser prove beyond a reasonable doubt to a judge or jury that the accused is guilty of a specified crime.

Abuses in the prosecutor's office most frequently occur in bringing charges, in controlling information used to convict those on trial, and in influencing juries.

The adult criminal justice system has several critical stages including the complaint or charge, the warrant, arrest, booking, preliminary hearing, grand jury hearing, the arraignment, the trial, and sentencing.

The preliminary hearing is the probable cause hearing. It seeks to prevent people from being indiscriminately brought to trial. The discovery process requires that all pertinent facts on both sides be made available prior to the time of the hearing.

Not all cases go to court. Alternatives to a trial include diversion or plea bargaining. Diversion provides the defendant with an alternative to a trial, for example, to obtain help from a community organization or to make restitution to the victim. Plea bargaining is a compromise between defense and prosecution that prearranges the plea and the sentence, conserving time and expense. The case may or may not go to trial, depending on the circumstances.

Police officers' testimony at the trial is of great importance. They should be aware of tactics frequently used by defense attorneys to confuse or discredit a police officer who is testifying: (1) rapid-fire questioning, (2) establishing that the officer wants to see the defendant found guilty, (3) accusing the officer of making assumptions, or (4) implying that the officer does not want anyone else to know what is in his or her notes.

Although the police officer and the prosecutor represent the accuser, in effect, their ultimate responsibility is to see that justice is done—not to see that a conviction is obtained. If a conviction is obtained, common sentencing schemes include indeterminate, indefinite, definite, determinate, mandatory, and presumptive.

The rule of law goes by the book, allowing little or no discretion. The rule of man emphasizes using discretion and looking at the uniqueness of each case.

DISCUSSION QUESTIONS

1. Is the jury system really fair?

2. What alternatives to the jury system are there?

3. What is the best kind of notebook for police officers to use for testifying in court?

4. Can the defense attorney examine the officer's entire notebook even if it contains notes on other cases?

5. Should the victim of a crime be consulted when plea bargaining is used?

6. How can police officers be sure a person they have just arrested understands the Miranda warning?

7. Is our system truly an adversary system when the prosecutor also has to protect the accused's rights?

8. Do you believe plea bargaining is necessary? Why or why not? Do you know of cases in which it has been used?

9. Do you feel diversion is an acceptable alternative in some instances? If so, when? If not, why?

10. Which position do you tend to support, the rule of law or the rule of man? Why?

TERMS

adversary system, appeal, appellate jurisdiction, arraignment, bail, booked, charge, complaint, conviction, coroner's jury, court of last resort, cross-examination, defendant, defense attorney, discovery process, diversion, grand jury, guilty, hung jury, indictment, information, judicial review, jurisdiction, jury, justice of dispensation, landmark decision, no bill, nolo contendere, original jurisdiction, plea, plea bargaining, preliminary hearing, preponderance of the evidence, presentment, pro bono work, prosecutors, reasonable doubt, R.P.R.d, sociological jurisprudence, standing mute, Supreme Court, suspect, venue, warrant, writ of certiorari, writ of habeas corpus.

REFERENCES

Colson, C. W. "Alternative Sentencing: A New Direction for Criminal Justice," pp. 138–140 in *Criminal Justice 92/93* edited by J. J. Sullivan and J. L. Victor. Guilford, Conn.: The Dushkin Publishing Group, 1992. (Reprinted from *USA Today Magazine*, May 1991, 64–66.)

Fine, R. A. "Plea Bargaining Should be Abolished," pp. 189–192 in *Taking Sides: Clashing View on Controversial Issues in Crime and Criminology.* 2d ed., edited by R. C. Monk. Guilford, Conn.: The Dushkin Publishing Group, 1991. (Reprinted from *Escape of the Guilty: A Trial Judge Speaks Out Against Crime.* New York: Dodd, Mead, 1986.)

Gershman, B. L. "Abuse of Power in the Prosecutor's Office," pp. 117–123 in *Criminal Justice 92/93,* edited by J. J. Sullivan and J. L. Victor. Guilford, Conn.: The Dushkin Publishing Group, 1992. (Reprinted from *The World & I,* June 1991, 477–487.)

Glick, H. R. *Who Are Federal Judges.* New York: McGraw-Hill, 1983.

Holten, N. G. and Lamar, L. L. *The Criminal Courts: Structures, Personnel, and Processes.* New York: McGraw-Hill, 1991.

Hope, G. "Ten Commandments of Courtroom Testimony," *The Minnesota Police Journal* (April 1992): 55–60.

Inbau,, F. E.; Thompson, J. R.; and Fagel, J. B. *Criminal Law and Its Administration.* Mineola, N.Y.: The Foundation Press, 1974.

Kelly, D. "Victim Participation in the Criminal Justice System," pp. 172–187 in *Victims of Crime: Problems, Policies, and Programs,* edited by A. J. Lurigio, W. G. Skogan, and R. C. Davis. Newbury Park, Calif.: Sage Publications, 1990.

Maechling, C., Jr. "Improving Our Criminal Justice System: Can We Borrow from Europe's Civil Law Tradition?" pp. 133–137 in *Criminal Justice 92/93,* edited by J. J. Sullivan and J. L. Victor. Guilford, Conn.: The Dushkin Publishing Group, 1992. (Reprinted from *The Brookings Review,* Summer 1991, 22–27.)

Monk, R. C. (Ed.) *Taking Sides: Clashing View on Controversial Issues in Crime and Criminology.* 2d ed. Guilford, Conn.: The Dushkin Publishing Group, 1991.

National Advisory Commission on Criminal Justice Standards and Goals. *Corrections.* Washington, D.C.: U.S. Government Printing Office, 1973.

National Advisory Commission on Criminal Justice Standards and Goals. *The Courts.* Washington, D.C.: U.S. Government Printing Office, 1975.

Pace, D. F. *Community Relations Concepts.* Placerville, Calif.: Custom Publishing Company, 1991.

Rubin, H. T. *The Courts: Fulcrum of the Justice System.* 2d ed. New York: Random House, 1984.

Senna, J. J. and Siegel, L. J. *Introduction to Criminal Justice.* 5th ed. St. Paul, Minn.: West Publishing Company, 1990.

Senna, J. J. and Siegel, L. J. *Introduction to Criminal Justice.* 3d ed. St. Paul, Minn.: West Publishing Company, 1984.

Serpe, A. A. "Public Defenders," pp. 111–116 in *Criminal Justice 92/93,* edited by J. J. Sullivan and J. L. Victor. Guilford, Conn.: The Dushkin Publishing Group, 1992. (Reprinted from *Case & Comment* 94, no. 5, September/October, 1989.)

Waldron, R. J. *The Criminal Justice System: An Introduction,* 3d ed. Boston: Houghton Mifflin, 1984.

Walker, S. "Close the Loopholes," pp. 184–88 in *Taking Sides: Clashing View on Controversial Issues in Crime and Criminology.* 2d ed., edited by R. C. Monk. Guilford, Conn.: The Dushkin Publishing Group, 1991. (Reprinted from *Sense and Nonsense About Crime: A Policy Guide.* 2d ed. Pacific Grove, Calif.: Brooks/Cole Publishing Co., 1989.)

CHAPTER 19

Corrections: To Punish or to Rehabilitate?

At the increasing rate the U.S. is locking up offenders, over one-half of all Americans will be in prison by 2052.

—Brookings Institution Projection

Do You Know

What corrections is?

What the objectives of the correctional system are?

How jail differs from prison?

What negative characteristics are linked with jails?

What two philosophies are evident in U.S. prisons?

How the medical model differs from the justice model?

Where the United States ranks among countries of the world in number of people incarcerated?

What alternatives to jail or prison are being used?

How parole differs from probation?

What reintegration methods have been used to facilitate the transition from prison to community?

INTRODUCTION

The final stage in the administration of the criminal justice system in the United States is corrections. Corrections is the part of the criminal justice system that the public sees the least of and knows the least about. It seldom gets into the news, unless there is a prison riot, jail break, or scandal involving corruption or brutality in an institution or by an official.

Corrections is that portion of the criminal justice system that carries out the court's orders. It consists of our probation and parole systems as well as our jails, prisons, and community-based programs to rehabilitate offenders.

Compared to two hundred years ago, the methods used by the corrections component of our criminal justice system are very humane. Gardner and Anderson (1992, p. 202) show the contrast:

> The criminal punishments used two hundred years ago in England and Europe were severe. In England alone, more than two hundred offenses were punishable by death. Condemned criminals were usually hanged, although occasionally they were beheaded, quartered, or drawn (dragged along the ground at the tail of a horse). Burning continued until 1790 to be the punishment inflicted on women for treason, high or petty. In practice, women were strangled before they were burnt; this however, depended on the executioner....
>
> For lesser offenses, various forms of mutilations, such as cropping (clipping of the ears), blinding, amputation of the hand, and branding, were common. The whipping post and the pillory were often used, as were fines and imprisonment.

Eldefonso (1984, p. 5) suggests that the underlying philosophy of corrections is to serve and protect society by rehabilitating offenders: "The purpose of any correctional program is to make services available, within a client-restrictive status designed to protect society, which will enable the offender to become a useful, productive citizen." The National Advisory Commission on Criminal Justice Standards and Goals (1973, p. 222) points out, however: "Public protection is not always the sole objective of correctional programming. Some kinds of offenders, especially the most notorious, often could perfectly well be released without jeopardizing public safety. But their release will not be countenanced because public demands for retribution have not been satisfied."

The primary purpose of a correctional program is to make services available—within a restricted environment—which enable an offender to become a useful, productive citizen. Secondary purposes of a correctional program are individual deterrence, general deterrence, incapacitation, retribution, or expression of moral outrage.

The Bureau of Justice Statistics (1988) cites the following objectives of the correctional process:

- Retribution—giving offenders their "just deserts" and expressing society's disapproval of criminal behavior.
- Incapacitation—separating offenders from the community to reduce the opportunity for further crime while they are incarcerated.
- Deterrence—demonstrating the certainty and severity of punishment to discourage future crime by the offender (specific deterrence) and by others (general deterrence).

- Rehabilitation—providing psychological or educational assistance or job training to offenders to make them less likely to engage in future criminality.
- Restitution—having the offender repay the victim or the community in money or services.

The objectives of the correctional system are retribution, incapacitation, deterrence, rehabilitation, and restitution.

According to Sullivan and Victor (1992, p. 186), however: "Crowded, tense conditions make survival the principal goal. Rehabilitation is pushed into the background in the effort to manage incipient chaos."

PROBATION

A person who is found guilty of a crime may be placed on probation. Probation is the most frequent alternative to a jail or prison sentence. **Probation** is the conditional suspension of a sentence of a person convicted of a crime but not yet imprisoned for that crime. The defendant is placed under the supervision of a probation officer for a set period of time and must meet specific conditions.

Probation is most frequently used with first offenders and with crimes that are not considered heinous by society, such as many of the white-collar crimes. A first-time embezzler of high standing in the community might be given probation, avoiding the stigma of a prison record. Probation operates on a "second-chance" philosophy. Consequently, if a person is convicted a second time for a crime, that person is very unlikely to receive probation.

According to Territo et al. (1989, p. 496): "Between 60 and 80 percent of sentences meted out by the courts involve probation, and on any given day, there are about one million persons on probation in the United States." Probation is seen as a combination of punishment and treatment. It is similar to a suspended sentence, except that in a suspended sentence, there is no supervision.

CORRECTIONAL INSTITUTIONS

The first truly correctional institution in the United States opened in Philadelphia in 1790 and was called the Walnut Street Jail. This jail, unlike existing workhouses, prisons, and jails, was used exclusively for the "correction" of convicted felons.

Not until the nineteenth century was the use of correctional institutions common in the United States. The primary goal of correctional institutions is to protect society. Secondary goals may be to deter, rehabilitate, and reintegrate offenders into society.

Although corrections attempts to rehabilitate offenders, conditions cannot be such that the prison is a pleasant place to be. Inmates should dread a return. Unfortunately, however, too often our correctional institutions do not rehabilitate but actually contribute to and reward criminal behavior.

The type of correctional institution in which an offender is **incarcerated** usually depends on the type of crime committed and the offender's past record. Incarceration alternatives include local and county jails and state and federal prisons.

JAILS

The jail is an important part of the criminal justice system in the United States.

Jail differs from prison in that its inmates are there for shorter terms, usually for less serious crimes.

The court's decisions directly affect the number and type of persons sentenced to jail. The court's decisions also dictate how much involvement the jail personnel must have with rehabilitative programs. If, for example, the court specifies that an offender must participate in a work program, the jail must provide such a program.

As part of the corrections segment of the criminal justice system, the jail has an advantage over prison because it is frequently located in the community and can coordinate its services with that of the community. In addition, its offenders are usually more likely to be rehabilitated than prison inmates, many of whom are habitual offenders.

Clearly, one of the greatest problems is the variety of offenders either awaiting trial or serving sentences in our jails. Each needs different types of programs and requires different kinds of security. In most instances, the physical facility and lack of personnel make such individualization next to impossible.

Negative characteristics of jails in the United States include the following: the wide variety of backgrounds of the offenders in our jails; the problems of local control and politics; inadequate personnel; demeaning physical facilities; inept administration; failure to adopt alternative programs and dispositions.

According to Adler et al. (1991, p. 454) the United States has 3,338 jails, varying greatly in size. A jail in one state might be as large as the entire prison system of another state. They note: "Criminologists generally consider the conditions in jails to be inferior to those in prisons. Most jails are unsanitary, have few services or programs for inmates, and do not separate dangerous from nondangerous prisoners. They are often overcrowded and underfunded."

Monk (1989, p. 242) notes:

Jails are by definition holding cells, so they typically do not make any efforts to rehabilitate inmates. . . .

Because so many jail inmates are serving short periods of time for less serious offenses, jails are generally far less policed than prisons. Therefore, surprisingly to many, they are often far more dangerous than prisons. A youthful first-time offender, picked up for public drunkenness or being held for trial might be placed into a "tank" or cell with older, streetwise inmates, who feel free to have "a go" at the newcomer. Many local jails throughout the United States are currently being sued by family members of such victims. The youngsters might be badly beaten, gang-raped, or even killed.

The primary function of American jails is to enable the local police to be able to dispense instant street justice: that is, have the power to arrest folks on the street who the police feel need arresting. A jail serves as a clearinghouse for such arrests. . . .

Currently over one-half of the jailhouse population has not been convicted of any crime. These inmates are either awaiting trial, arraignment, or are standing trial.

Just as the United States has both a state and federal court system, it also has a state and federal prison system in addition to local county correctional systems.

Also, as noted by Adler et al. (1991, p. 454): "A prison normally has three distinct custody levels for inmates, based on an assessment of their perceived dangerousness":

- Maximum security prisons—designed to hold the most dangerous and aggressive inmates. Their structure is often imposing with high concrete walls or double-perimeter fences, gun towers with armed guards, and strategically placed electronic monitors.
- Medium security prisons—designed to house inmates considered less dangerous or escape-prone than those in maximum security facilities. These less imposing structures typically have no outside wall, only a series of fences.
- Minimum security prisons—designed to house inmates considered the lowest security risks. Often these institutions operate without armed guards and without perimeter walls or fences.

Controversy often arises over some of our country's minimum security prisons. Table 19–1 summarizes some of the issues in the current controversy.

***Table 19–1* Current Controversy: Should the Federal Government Run "Country Club" Prisons?**

Every time a well-known person is sentenced to a federal minimum-security prison, the issue of federal "country-club" or "Club Feds" is debated. When millionaire-stock broker Ivan Boesky was sentenced to three years at the federal prison camp at Lompoc, California,* attention was again focused on whether federal minimum-security facilities are too soft and easy. The television program "60 Minutes" did a segment asking this.

ARGUMENTS AGAINST THE PRESENT FEDERAL MINIMUM-SECURITY SYSTEM

As there are no cells for inmates nor walls around the camps, they really are not prisons or jails. One observer stated that the only restriction he could see was the "Keep Off the Grass" signs.

The system neither punishes nor rehabilitates the two most common groups sent into the federal prison system ("white-collar" criminals and persons convicted of drug-related crimes).

Persons such as Ivan Boesky can do far more damage to society by their crimes than inmates in maximum security prisons who have committed crimes of violence. (Boesky was convicted of "inside trading," which shook the financial markets and Wall Street.)

ARGUMENTS FOR THE MINIMUM-SECURITY SYSTEM

Boredom and lack of true freedom in the prison camp setting is adequate punishment even though it is not harsh.

Minimum-security camps on the average cost only half as much to operate as the more secure prisons. Population in the federal prisons is expected to nearly double to 87,000 by 1995. In the more secure federal prisons, annual costs per prisoner can amount to $30,000. The federal government now has 20 minimum-security prisons and is likely to rely more on this type of facility.

It is presumed that "white collar" prisoners do not mix well with violent prisoners. Some experts say that the camps are a necessity because sentencing a "white-collar" prisoner to a maximum security prison is (as one expert stated) "like sentencing the guy to death. He wouldn't last two days."

---

*In 1990 Lompoc federal prison camp was converted into a higher security federal prison. Lompoc was the most famous of the "country club" prisons because of the persons who served time there (Watergate's H. R. Haldeman, inside trader Ivan Boesky, and San Diego Charger star Chuck Muncie).

Source: T. J. Gardner and T. M. Anderson. *Criminal Law: Principles and Cases.* 5th ed., p. 223. Copyright © 1992, West Publishing Company: St. Paul, Minn. Reprinted by permission.

Punish versus Rehabilitate

The word *prison* usually conveys an image of rows of cagelike cells, several levels high, crowded mess halls, a "yard" where prisoners engage in physical activities, organized and not so organized, all patrolled by tightlipped, heavily armed guards.

The physical facility itself reflects the philosophy regarding the purpose of imprisonment. Two basic physical designs developed in the United States. The first design consisted of fortresslike structures containing solitary cells, each with a tiny walled-in courtyard. Prisoners were, in effect, in solitary confinement for the duration of their sentences. The second design consisted of cells built back to back and facing a corridor. Meals were eaten in large rooms, and prisoners were expected to work at hard labor. This design, often referred to as the Auburn design because it was first used in the Auburn Penitentiary constructed in 1818 in Auburn, New York, is most frequently used in the United States today.

Both of the early philosophies influencing prison design were basically punitive. Throughout the decades, however, efforts at prison reform have lead to a change in emphasis, seeking to rehabilitate prisoners rather than to punish them.

As Greenberg and Rubeck (1982, p. 214) note: "All prisons are custodial (and therefore punitive, as custody implies the loss of rights and the denial of certain comforts), but some are more oriented toward treating and rehabilitating offenders than others." They go on to cite several important differences between these two orientations. Table 19–2 summarizes the basic philosophies of punitive-oriented and treatment-oriented prisons.

Greenberg and Rubeck (1982, p. 215) conclude: "Although both punitive/custodial prisons and treatment-oriented prisons exist in the United States and although most prisons have elements of both types, most lack the physical and human resources necessary for an effective treatment orientation and, therefore, are primarily of the punitive/custodial type."

Prisons may be punitive or treatment oriented. Punitive-oriented prisons are more formal and rigid, with an emphasis on obedience. Obedience is sought through negative incentives. Treatment-oriented prisons are more informal and flexible, with positive incentives for good behavior.

Maximum security prisons confine our country's most dangerous criminals.

Table 19–2 **Philosophies of Imprisonment**

PUNITIVE ORIENTED	TREATMENT ORIENTED
Authority pattern based only on rank. For example, guards obey warden.	Authority pattern based on technical knowledge.
Very specific, measurable rules, with strict emphasis on obedience.	More general goals, more flexibility, more individualized.
Guards have limited decision-making authority, limited discretion.	Guards are encouraged to make their own decisions, use their own discretion.
Communications with inmates is very formal, usually restricted to orders.	Communications is less formal and is encouraged.
Incentives used are usually negative, for example, force and coercion, removal of privileges, solitary confinement, and the like.	Incentives used are usually positive, for example, granting of special privileges, better living quarters, furloughs, and the like.

Source: A. S. Greenberg and R. B. Rubeck. *Social Psychology of the Criminal Justice System.* Monterey, Calif.: Brooks/Cole Publishing, 1982. Reprinted by permission.

According to Schoen (1992, p. 217):

Punishing criminals is a provocative subject that arouses deep feelings of anger, compassion, frustration, and fascination. Millions of tourists have trooped through the remaining buildings of the ncw defunct Alcatraz, chilled at the thought of being caged in a claustrophobic underground dungeon, gripped by tales of escapes, and intrigued at the sight of the cells of Capone and the Birdman.

Yet as noted by Senna and Siegel (1990, p. 525):

Many examples of the treatment philosophy still flourish in prison: educational programs range up to the college level; vocational training has become more sophisticated; counseling and substance abuse programs are almost universal; every state maintains some type of early release programs and community corrections models.

A similar dichotomy in philosophy regarding the purpose of corrections can be seen in the existence of two correctional models, the medical model and the justice model.

Medical Model versus Justice Model

Pace (1991, p. 145) notes that from 1930 until 1974 our corrections system was based on a **medical model,** viewing offenders as ill and in need of help. This medical model gave way in the mid 1970s to the **justice model,** viewing offenders as responsible for their own actions and incarceration.

The medical model of corrections assumes criminals are victims of society and need to be "cured." The justice model assumes criminals are self-directed and responsible for their crimes.

Table 19–3 summarizes the basic issues involved in each model and how they differ from each other.

Trends in Corrections

Three trends can be seen in corrections in the past decades. The first, from 1960 to 1980, was the prisoner's rights movement. According to Senna and

Table 19–3 **Comparison of the Medical versus the Justice Model**

ISSUE	MEDICAL MODEL 1930–74	JUSTICE MODEL 1974–PRESENT
Cause of Crime	Disease of society or of the individual.	Form of rational adaptation to societal conditions.
Image of Offender	Sick, product of socio-economic or psychological forces beyond control.	Capable of exercising free will; of surviving without resorting to crime.
Object of Correction	To cure offender and society; to return both to health; rehabilitation.	Humanely control offender under terms of sentence; offer voluntary treatment.
Agency/Institution Responsibility	Change offender, reintegrate back into society.	Legally & humanely control offender; adequate care & custody; voluntary treatment; protect society.
Role of Treatment & Punishment	Voluntary or involuntary treatment as means to change offender; treatment is mandatory, punishment used to coerce treatment, punishment & treatment is viewed as same thing.	Voluntary treatment, only; punishment & treatment not the same thing. Punishment is for society's good, treatment is for offender's good.
Object of Legal Sanctions (Sentence)	Determine conditions which are most conducive to rehabilitation of offender.	Determine conditions which are just re: wrong done, best protect society and deter offender from future crime.
Type of Sentence	Indeterminant, flexible; adjust to offender changes.	Fixed sentence (less good time).
Who determines release time?	"Experts," (parole board for adults, institutional staff for juveniles).	Conditions of sentence as interpreted by Presumptive Release Date (PRD) formula.

Source: D. F. Pace. *Community Relations Concepts.* Copyright © 1991, p. 145. Custom Publishing Company: Placerville, Calif. Reprinted by permission.

Siegel (1990, p. 531): "Inmates won rights unheard of in nineteenth- and early twentieth-century prisons. Since 1980, however, an increasingly conservative judiciary has curtailed the growth of inmate rights."

The second trend, violence within the correctional system, has led to tightened discipline and the building of new maximum security prisons to confine the most dangerous offenders.

Third, the medical model under which corrections was to help those who suffered from some social malady gave way to the justice model with its emphasis on self-determination. As noted by Senna and Siegel: "Prisons have more frequently been viewed as places for control, incapacitation, and punishment than as sites for rehabilitation and reform."

Unit Management

Unit management is being used in many prisons throughout the country. In fact, Levinson (1991, p. 44) notes: "Along with the Federal Bureau of Prisons and the District of Columbia Department of Corrections, more than half of the state correctional systems in the United States have one or more institutions operating in accord with the unit management concept." Key components of unit management include:

- Subdividing inmate populations into homogeneous groups, that is, housing inmates with similar behavior characteristics together.
- Locating staff offices in or adjacent to inmate living quarters.
- Providing for frequent staff/inmate interaction.

Levinson suggests: "Central to the unit management concept is the notion that each unit functions as a 'mini-institution.'" He further notes: "Placing inmates who are likely to pose a threat to others in units that are physically separate from units housing their potential 'prey' reduces the incidence of violence."

Webster (1991, p. 38) notes: "Facility design directly affects the size and location of units, how office space is used, what programs are possible, whether supervision is direct or indirect, and how staff is used."

Pierson (1991, p. 30) describes the success of the unit management approach in the Missouri Department of Corrections: "Unit management has served as the organizational glue that solidified the integration of many of the department's existing programs. Its more rational, systemized approach to inmate management has proved beneficial to both staff and inmates." Among the specific benefits resulting from using unit management, Pierson lists the following:

- Closer interaction with inmates has improved security.
- The classic custody vs. treatment rivalry has been greatly toned down, if not eliminated. The experience of working in tandem—aided by the hybrid correctional classification assistant position—breaks down distrust between custody and non-security staff.
- New career ladders were created, providing promotion opportunities for both security and non-custody personnel. In addition to improving staff morale, the new system encourages staff to view corrections as a career. This decreases staff turnover, increases interest in further training and cultivates in-house expertise.
- Unit management has freed up time for top management to engage in long-range planning and other "big picture" activities such as improving the inmate transportation system and evaluating alternative medical care providers.

Women in Prison

A *Newsweek* article (1992, p. 37) notes: "Even in jail, women are breaking down the barriers to equal achievement . . . The number of women doing time has doubled to 40,000 in the last five years. The main reason is drugs." Of these women, three-quarters are mothers, many of them single parents.

Prison Gangs

Jackson and McBride (1985, p. 55) describe prison gang members as "cold, calculating and purposeful." They are also better disciplined and more sophisticated than street gangs. When a youth gang member is sent to prison, the prison gang may recruit him, as noted by Jackson and McBride (1985, pp. 55–56):

> The prison gang will wait until the youthful offender has progressed through the juvenile justice system—from probation camps, reform schools and finally to prison. At this point the recruit has become wise in the ways of penal institutions and has matured sufficiently to be recruited into the prison gang. In today's justice system only the worst of a very bad lot are sentenced to state prison, and they are the types that the prison gang is seeking. . . .

A phenomenon which both youth authorities and prison officials have noticed recently is a rift between prison gangs and the street gang members, in that the latter seem to be achieving an independence from the prison gangs....

Some prisons are reporting that a number of street gangs have so many members at a particular institution that they are a force in themselves.

The following information on prison gangs is from the executive summary of a national study of prison gangs conducted in 1983 by the Criminal Justice Institute. The study included all state prison systems and the Federal Bureau of Prisons, with 94 percent of the agencies participating.

Extent of Prison Gangs Thirty-three agencies reported the presence of prison gangs. Twenty-nine agencies identified 114 individual gangs with a total membership of 12,634. Table 19–4 summarizes the gangs in various states.

Characteristics of Gang Members The essential elements of gang member behavior are loyalty to the gang, by a code of secrecy, and an outwardly cooperative attitude to prison authority. The most frequently used tactics to maintain order, loyalty, and obedience to the gang are fear, intimidation, and

Table 19–4 **Select Prison Gangs by Jurisdiction**

JURISDICTION	GANG
Arizona	Aryan Brotherhood
	Mexican Mafia
Arkansas	Ku Klux Klan
	Aryan Brotherhood
California	CRIPs (Common Revolution in Progress)
	Black Guerilla Family
	Mexican Mafia
	Nuestra Familia
	Texas Syndicate
	Aryan Brotherhood
Federal System	Texas Syndicate
	Aryan Brotherhood
	Nuestra Familia
	Black Guerilla Family
	Mexican Mafia
Illinois	Black Disciples
	Black Gangster D's
	El Rukns
	Latin Disciples
	Latin Kings
	Mickey Cobras
	Northsiders
	Vice Lords
Indiana	Black Dragons
Iowa	Moorish Science Temple
	Bikers
	Vice Lords

threats of violence. There is a total disregard for human life. The sanctions for killing another inmate are of no consequence to the gang member who is a "true believer."

All gangs share an emphasis on power and prestige, measured in terms of ability to control other inmates and specific activities within the institution. Money, drugs, and personal property represent tangible symbols of a gang's ability to control and dominate others and of its ability to provide essential protection, goods, and services for its members.

One of the most distinguishing characteristics of the prison gang is the virtual absence of any non-criminal, non-deviant activities. Gang members engage in some institutional pastimes, weight lifting being one of the more notable, but in general their activities are criminal or deviant. The gang member is completely immersed in being a career prison gangster, leaving little time and less inclination for other than asocial behavior.

Gang relationships are on gang terms only. Members avoid contact with non-gang members except to do business with them. Doing business means taking advantage of and controlling other inmates. Because they can be controlled, they are perceived as being weak and therefore worthless. This behavior reinforces the gang member's position that he is doing nothing wrong.

Table 19–4 *(Continued)*	
JURISDICTION	GANG
Kentucky	Aryan Brotherhood
Maryland	Pagans
Minnesota	Prison Motorcycle Brotherhood
Missouri	Aryan Brotherhood
	Science Temple Moorish Faith
Nevada	Black Mafia
	Aryan Warriors
North Carolina	Black Panthers
Ohio	Aryan Brotherhood
Oklahoma	Aryan Brotherhood
	White Supremacy Family
	Black Brotherhood
Pennsylvania	Black Power Muslims
	Motorcycle Gang
	Street Gangs
	Latin American
Texas	Texas Syndicate
Utah	Five Foot Two Gang
Virginia	Pagans
Washington	Bandidos
	Gypsy Jokers
West Virginia	Avengers
Wisconsin	Prison Motorcycle Brotherhood
	Black Disciple Nation

Source: G. M. Camp and C. G. Camp. *Prison Gangs: Their Extent, Nature and Impact on Prisons.* Washington, D.C.: U.S. Government Printing Office, 1985, pp. 23–24.

Universally the prison gang tolerates the prison staff, but only barely. They avoid contact with the staff as much as possible. Assaults, some fatal, on staff have occurred with increasing frequency in the last few years. While staff appear to be a constraint that must be worked around, they, in reality, are not a serious impediment to the gang's efforts.

Prison Gang Problems   The types of problems created by gangs include the introduction and distribution of drugs; intimidation of weaker inmates; extortion that results from strong-arming; requests for protective custody status; violence associated with the gang activity; occasional conflicts between gangs (usually racial) that create disturbances; and contracted inmate murders.

Almost without exception, administrators say that the gangs are responsible for the majority of drug trafficking in their institution.

Relationship of the Gang Membership to the Outside   Twenty-six of the thirty-three correctional agencies reported that all or some of the gangs in their institutions have counterpart gangs on the streets.

Identifying Gang Members   Several agencies reported indicators that an inmate was a gang member, including the following:

- *Appearance*—tattoos, clothing, colors, acts.
- *Official reports*—case histories, other reports.
- *Self-admission.*
- *Associations*—inmates, correspondence, home address, photos, visitors.
- *Possessions*—gang material, literature and documents, hit lists.
- *Informants.*

The Burgeoning Prison Population

The United States, with more than one million citizens behind bars in 1991, ranked first in the world in the proportion and number of its population in prison (Goodman 1992, p. 437).

The United States ranks *first* in the world in numbers of people incarcerated.

A study conducted by the Sentencing Project and released in 1991 points out that from 1980 to 1990 our prison population has doubled. Among the reasons, they give the following (Gardner and Anderson 1992, p. 215):

- Drug-related crime, the biggest cause of the increase.
- Increased use by federal and state government of mandatory minimum sentences.
- More use of imprisonment and less use of alternative sentences.
- Tightened parole eligibility requirements.
- A crime rate in the United States higher than in most other countries. (The murder rate in the United States is at least seven times higher than in most European countries. There are six times as many robberies and three times as many rapes in the United States as in former West Germany.)
- An increasingly harsh public attitude in the United States toward lawbreakers.

Overcrowding may lead to riots. Goodman (1992, p. 437) notes: "One of the bloodiest prison riots in recent years took place on September 22, 1991, at Montana's overcrowded maximum-security prison, located in Deer Lodge. . . .

The small rural town of Appleton, Minnesota has built a medium-security, privately managed prison in hopes of creating jobs in the city of 1,500 and reviving its economy. The Prairie Correctional Facility could create 170 jobs in Appleton.

The facility, designed to house 750 prisoners, contained 1,078, although officials listed 'emergency' capacity at 1,135."

New York state is converting its 798-cell Southport Correctional Facility to a super-secure—"maxi-maxi" prison for inmates who committed violent crimes. Inmates at Southport are confined to their cells 23 hours a day, with one recreational hour in outdoor cages (Goodman 1992, p. 437).

According to Doyle (1992, p. 18A): "The inmate population in the United States grew by 137 percent from 1980 to 1992, faster than governments could build prisons. Currently, there are 780,000 people in state and federal facilities—118,000 more inmates than the prisons are certified to hold." Some forty states face court orders or consent decrees to ease crowded prison conditions. Some communities, like Appleton, Minnesota, hope to capitalize on this situation by building privately run medium security prisons. Since Minnesota prisons are not overcrowded, they will have to lure inmates from other states. This may be difficult, as noted by Doyle (1992, p. 18A):

> Despite swelling prison populations nationally, finding states that will rent cells isn't easy. Some states with overcrowded prisons face budget woes that make early parole or home detention cheaper than renting prison space. Others are leery of turning over a traditional state role to private operators. And as the rent-a-cell industry grew during the 1980s, competition among operators vying for prisoners became intense.

Recidivism

Approximately 60 percent of inmates released from state and federal prisons return (Sullivan and Victor 1992, p. 186). This high **recidivism** is perhaps the result of ineffective treatment and lack of training programs.

As noted by Senna and Siegel (1990, p. 523): "One of the great tragedies of our time is that correctional institutions, whatever form they may take, do not seem to correct. They are in most instances overcrowded, understaffed, outdated warehouses for the human outcasts of our society." They contend that: "It is a sad but unfortunately accurate assessment that today's correctional institution has become a revolving door," with about half of all inmates being back in prison within six years of their release. Senna and Siegel (1990, p. 531) note: "The alleged failure of correctional treatment, coupled with constantly increasing correctional costs, has prompted the development of alternatives to incarceration."

ALTERNATIVES TO TRADITIONAL PUNISHMENT

Several alternatives to confinement in a jail or prison are being used in an effort to reduce overcrowding. Table 19–5 describes some of the more common programs.

Alternatives to jail or prison include home detention and boot camp.

Take a closer look at two of these alternatives, home arrest and shock incarceration or boot camp.

Home Detention or House Arrest

As noted by Scaglione (1988, p. 26): "With a jail's daily operating costs of $35 to $125 per prisoner, home detention represents big savings for hard-pressed

Table 19–5   **Alternatives to Traditional Punishment**

With more than one million persons in jails and prisons in the United States, more than half the states (and some federal prisons) are under court orders to stop violations caused primarily by overcrowding. Recidivism rates are very high. Recidivism is often defined as rearrest and conviction within three years of a previous criminal conviction. As traditional punishments are not working well, alternatives are being used (or considered) generally in a mix with other forms of punishment.

ALTERNATIVE	DESCRIPTION OF ALTERNATIVE	PROBABLE USE
"Electronic shackles" (home arrest)	A device worn like an ankle (or wrist) bracelet that sends signals to a receiver. If the device is tampered with or if the wearer leaves home, the sheriff's office is automatically notified. Detainee is under "house arrest" or imprisoned at home.	Also used as a mixture of penalties tailored to the offender. Person must agree to "shackles" as condition of parole, probation, or work release program.
Community service sentences	Tasks such as bookkeeping, painting, carpentry, electrical work, plumbing, etc. for churches, charities, elderly persons, public places, and even the victim's property. Particularly applicable when defendant has a skill or profession.	Also used with a mixture of punishments tailored to offender. Person must agree to services as a condition of parole, probation, or work release.
Voluntary commitment to drug or alcohol treatment	Many crimes are related to serious drug or alcohol problems. Treatment programs are not effective unless participant cooperates fully.	Could be used in a mixture of punishments believed to achieve the best results. Defendants would "voluntarily" commit themselves as a condition of probation or parole.
Denver boot	The boot is a $275 device that locks on the front wheel of a vehicle and renders the car immobile until the driver pays fines owed and police remove the clamp. Generally not used until five or more parking or other tickets are unpaid. (See *Baker v. City of Iowa City,* 260 N.W.2d 427 (Iowa 1977) for case citations.)	Use of the boot frees law enforcement and court personnel for other tasks, cuts number of persons in jail, and brings in much needed funds. Use of the boot also increases the number of persons who voluntarily pay traffic and parking fines.

Table 19–5 *(Continued)*

ALTERNATIVE	DESCRIPTION OF ALTERNATIVE	PROBABLE USE
Shock Incarceration or Boot Camp	The National Institute of Justice commented as follows in their publication of June 1989: "Offenders sentenced to shock incarceration spend a relatively short period (90 to 180 days) in prison in a military style boot camp that provides a highly regimented program involving strict discipline, physical training, and hard labor resembling some aspects of military basic training. If they successfully complete the program, they are subsequently placed under community supervision. Housed separately from the regular inmates, either in an independent facility or in a separate housing unit within a larger facility, offenders spend about 6 hours a day at work and 2 to 3 hours in military drills and physical training."	Now used by half or more of the states to shock first offenders out of a life of crime and to reduce overcrowding of jails and prisons. Young persons convicted of nonviolent offenses "volunteer" for the short shock program to avoid serving a longer term of many years for offenses such as burglary.
Antabuse	A chemical that makes a person ill if he or she drinks alcohol. Used when alcohol abuse is the root of the problems and cause of criminal conduct.	Person agrees to take "voluntarily" as condition of probation or parole, usually to avoid imprisonment.
"Chemical castration"	Use of a controversial drug, Dep-Provera, which does not eliminate sex drive but does diminish it. Possible side effects include fatigue, loss of hair, itching, headaches, weight gain, and symptoms resembling female menopause.	"Voluntary" use as a condition of probation or parole after some imprisonment or to avoid any imprisonment.
"Son of Sam" Legislative bills	Some persons who commit crimes receive considerable public attention and receive money from interviews, books, films, and other money-making ventures. The name "Son of Sam" was used by a bizarre, New York serial killer who received large sums of money for stories of his killings, causing the State of New York to enact the first "Son of Sam" statute. Another example, the proceeds of the book *In the Belly of the Beast,* which tells of the brutality of prison life, is being held under the "Son of Sam" law. The author, Jack Henry Abbott, so impressed Norman Mailer that he helped in obtaining a parole for Abbott. Abbott immediately killed again and is back in prison.	Such statutes give victims and the families of victims liens against such profits and monies. Such monies would be held in escrow until claims could be filed and verified. It was reported in 1987 that 42 states had such statutes. The federal "Son of Sam" statute is found in Title 18, Chapter 232.
Drunk driving restraint	A $350 or so device with a sensor that can measure the blood-alcohol level of a person seeking to start a car (or truck). The driver breathes into the mouthpiece for four seconds for the device to test blood alcohol levels.	Could be: (1) required by state law, (2) ordered by a court, or (3) installed by spouses, parents, or relatives of problem drinkers.

Source: T. J. Gardner and T. M. Anderson. *Criminal Law: Principles and Cases.* 5th ed. Copyright © 1992, pp. 216–217. West Publishing Company: St. Paul, Minn. Reprinted by permission.

correction officials." He notes that house arrest is being used in 32 states with some 2,000 offenders involved.

Those under house arrest can be monitored by random calls and visits. Or, they may be monitored electronically. According to Senna and Siegel (1990, p. 513): "Electronically monitored offenders wear devices attached to their ankles or wrists or around their necks, which send signals back to a control office." They note that the cost of such electronic monitoring is estimated to be four times greater than traditional probation programs. In addition, they suggest:

> Electronic monitoring seems out of step with traditional American values of privacy and liberty. It smacks of the ever-vigilant "big brother" centralized state authority that we deplore in totalitarian societies. Do we really want U.S. citizens to be watched over by a computer? What are the limits of electronic monitoring? Can it be used with mental patients, HIV virus carriers, suicidal teenagers, or those considered high-risk future offenders? Our democratic principles make us recoil at the prospect of having our behavior monitored by an all-powerful central government computer.

Figure 19–1 illustrates the various points in the criminal justice process where electronic monitoring might play a role.

Boot Camps

Boot camps, patterned after the traditional military boot camps, are being used in some correctional systems. MacKenzie (1992, p. 218) states that seventeen states are using boot camps—also known as **shock incarceration.** Table 19–6 describes the existing programs.

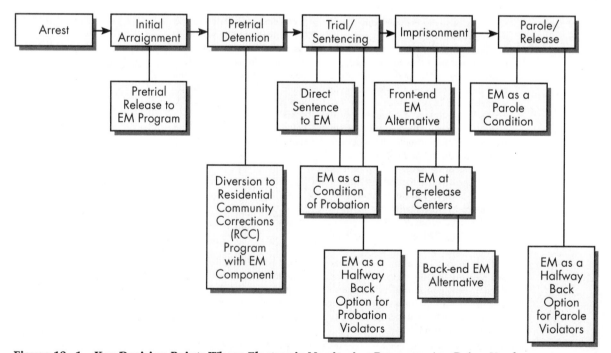

Figure 19–1   Key Decision Points Where Electronic Monitoring Programs Are Being Used

Source: J. Byrne, A. Lurigio, and C. Baird. *The Effectiveness of the New Intensive Supervision Programs.* Research in Corrections Series 2, no. 2 (preliminary unpublished draft; Washington, D.C.: National Institute of Corrections, 1989).

Table 19-6 Characteristics of Shock Incarceration Programs, May 1990

STATE	YEAR PROGRAMS BEGAN	NUMBER OF PROGRAMS	NUMBER OF PARTICIPANTS (MALE/FEMALE)	NUMBER OF DAYS SERVED	MAXIMUM AGE LIMIT	FIRST FELONY?	NON-VIOLENT ONLY?
Alabama	1988	1	127 male[a]	90	none	no	no
Arizona	1988	1	150 male[a]	120	25	yes	no
Florida	1987	1	100 male[a]	90[b]	25	yes	no
Georgia	1983	2	250 male[a]	90	25	yes	no
Idaho	1989[c]	1	154 male	120	none	no	no
Louisiana	1987	1	87 male[a] 1 female	120	39	no	yes
Michigan	1988	1	120 male	120[d]	25	no	no
Mississippi	1985	2[a]	225 male[a] 15 female	110[e]	none	yes	yes
New York	1987	5[a]	1,500 male[a] 102 female	180	30	yes	yes
North Carolina	1989[c]	1	54 male	93	24	yes	yes
Oklahoma	1984	1	150 male	90[f]	25	yes	yes
South Carolina	1987	2	98 male[a] 13 female	90	24	yes	yes
Tennessee	1989[c]	1	42 male	120	30	yes	yes
Texas	1989	1	200 male	90	25	yes	no

References
[a]Indicates increase since May 1989.
[b]May 1989: Average 101.
[c]Program new since May 1989.
[d]May 1989: Average 90.
[e]May 1989: Average 180.
[f]May 1989: Average 120.
States planning or considering programs: California, Connecticut, Indiana, Kansas, Missouri, Nevada, New Jersey, New Mexico, Pennsylvania, Wisconsin, Wyoming. States that began programs in 1990: Arkansas, Maryland, New Hampshire.
These data appear in greater detail in the September 1990 issue of *Federal Probation*.

Source: D. L. MacKenzie. " 'Boot Camp' Programs Grow in Number and Scope." *NIJ Reports,* November/December 1990.

MacKenzie (p. 219) suggests that a review of existing programs reveals a "common core based on the military atmosphere, discipline, youth of the offenders, and a common goal of providing punishment without long-term incarceration." As noted by Morash and Rucker (1991, pp. 255–256):

> The popular image of military boot camp stresses strict and even cruel discipline, hard work, and authoritarian decision making and control by a drill sergeant. It should be noted that this image does not necessarily conform to either current practices in the U.S. Military or to all adaptations of boot camp in correctional settings. However, in a survey of existing correctional boot camp programs, Parent (1988) found commonality in the use of strict discipline, physical training, drill and ceremony, military bearing and courtesy, physical labor, and summary punishment for minor misconduct.

Morash and Rucker (p. 257) are not entirely complimentary of the boot camp approach to corrections: "At least in some settings, the military model has provided a legitimization of severe punishment. It has opened the door for physiological and even physical abuse that would be rejected as cruel and unusual punishment in other correctional settings."

According to Monk (1991, p. 245): "Shock-incarceration, or military boot camp-style, prisons—in which younger inmates are housed for relatively short periods of time (frequently under six months) are somewhat novel in the United States as alternatives to traditional incarceration."

National Institute of Justice research has come to the following conclusions (MacKenzie 1991, pp. 219–220):

- Programs vary greatly, and any evaluation must begin with a description of the program and its objectives.
- There is some evidence that the boot camp experience may be more positive than incarceration in traditional prison.
- There is no evidence that those who complete boot camp programs are angrier or negatively affected by the program.
- Those who complete shock programs report having a difficult but constructive experience. Similar offenders who serve their sentences in a traditional prison do not view their experiences as constructive.
- Boot camp recidivism rates are approximately the same as those of comparison groups who serve a longer period of time in a traditional prison or who serve time on probation.
- Programs differ substantially in the amount of time offenders spend in rehabilitative activities.

Perhaps of greatest benefit is that several of those incarcerated in boot camps report getting off drugs and becoming physically fit. They change their life style by getting up early in the morning and staying physically active throughout the day.

PAROLE

Parole is the most frequent type of release from a correctional institution.

Parole differs from probation in that a person who is paroled has spent some time serving a prison sentence. It is similar to probation in that both require supervision of the offender and set up certain conditions that must be met by the offender.

According to Territo et al. (1989, p. 504): "The concept of parole has its roots in military history; the practice of releasing a captured officer on his word of honor that he will not take up arms against his captors is called *parole d'honneur*. Similarly, inmates are released to free society on their word of honor that they will not again violate the law."

Parole is a conditional release. It differs from probation in that the person on parole has served time in jail or prison. Administratively parole is part of the executive branch of government; probation is under the courts and part of the judicial branch of government.

Factors influencing whether a person serving a sentence is eligible for or, indeed, is granted a parole include the type of offense committed, the offender's prior record, and state statutes. In some jurisdictions, parole is prohibited by statute for certain crimes. In other jurisdictions, however, people sentenced to prison are immediately eligible for parole. Sullivan and Victor (1990, p. 57) note:

A spate of tough sentencing laws has extended terms for many crimes, and prison rolls have more than doubled since 1980 to 630,000. Yet penal institutions are so overcrowded that only 1 case in 6 leads to a prison term, and space limits dictate that the average time in custody remains short, as inmates are freed early to make room for newcomers. Most "life" terms end before 10 years are spent behind bars. In Los Angeles County, where the jail population of 22,000 could fill a city, inmates serve one day for every 30 days stated in the sentence.

A community's reaction to early release can be violent, as described by Sullivan and Victor (1990, p. 57):

> Much of California rose in revolt in 1987 when a convict named Larry Singleton was released on parole eight years into a 14 year sentence for raping 15-year-old Mary Bell Vincent, chopping off her arms with an axe and leaving her to die in a ditch. Singleton was forced out of six California communities by outraged citizens.

Many citizens would argue that individuals who commit such heinous murders should never get out of prison or should, in fact, be executed, to be discussed shortly.

For those offenders who are paroled it is often a condition of their parole that they participate in some program to integrate them back into society.

COMMUNITY–BASED REINTEGRATION PROGRAMS

Community-based institutional programs aimed at reintegration of the offender into society include halfway houses and restitution centers.

Halfway Houses

As the name implies, **halfway houses** are community-based institutions for individuals who are halfway into prison, that is, on probation, or halfway out of prison, that is, on or nearing parole.

Halfway houses have existed for centuries, with one of the earliest being in sixth-century France, founded by St. Leonard, who secured the release of convicts and let them live in his monastery. Williams, Formby, and Watkins (1982, p. 460) note that the first modern halfway house in the United States was founded in 1954 by the Reverend James G. Jones, Jr., chaplain of the Cook County Jail in Chicago. Since that time many halfway houses have been opened in the United States.

Halfway houses typically provide offenders with a place to live, sleep, and eat. Counselors are provided to help with reintegration into society, including help with finding a suitable job and sometimes with transportation to a job.

As noted, halfway houses may serve those who are halfway into prison, such as the misdemeanant—a person convicted of a crime requiring no more than a one-year sentence. Or they may serve persons who are halfway out of prison—those who are nearing parole or who have actually been paroled but who still need support services. Halfway houses serving those nearing parole or actually discharged from prison are sometimes called "prerelease centers."

Restitution Centers

A new variation of the halfway house is the restitution center. A **restitution center** differs from a halfway house in that in the restitution center offenders work to partially repay their victims. Like the halfway house, restitution centers offer an alternative to prison, either for those who are halfway into prison or those who are halfway out of prison.

For **restitution** to be a viable alternative, the amount of money to be repaid must be within reason and the offender must not pose an escape risk. Since persons convicted of crimes typically cannot obtain high-paying jobs, frequently some type of compromise is reached between the victim and the offender, with the agreement put into a signed contract.

Many sociologists suggest that restitution centers offer advantages to both the victim and the offender. For the victim they provide not only partial repayment, but also a sense that the criminal justice system is indeed fair and that it is as concerned with the victims of crime as it is with the perpetrators of crime. On the other hand, restitution centers may also benefit the offenders, not only as an alternative to jail or prison, but also as a means of coming to know the victim as an individual who has suffered from the crime committed. Often offenders do not think about their victims as people with the same feelings as themselves. If they can see the harm they have caused, it may assist in their reform.

Other Reintegration Methods

Several methods of reintegration into society have been used, with varying degrees of success. The most common are furloughs, work release, and study release. In all instances the possibility of escape from the directives of the criminal justice system must be considered.

Three common reintegration methods are furloughs, work release, and study release.

Furloughs Furloughs are short, temporary leaves from a prison or jail. They may be supervised or unsupervised, although generally they are the latter. Furloughs are often used as positive motivators for good behavior. They may be granted for family emergencies, for a weekend with a spouse, or for job interviewing. Many experts feel that the use of conjugal furloughs for good behavior not only is a positive motivator, but it may also reduce homosexual activity within the correctional facility.

Work and Study Release Another positive motivator for good behavior that also serves as a means to reintegrate offenders into society is release for either a job or a course of study. Often such programs are conducted through halfway houses. They may also be conducted through local jails. One problem associated with such programs is that those who are released may smuggle contraband back into the correctional facility.

The rules in work release and study release programs are usually very explicit and rigid. For example, a strict curfew may be established; going into a bar may be prohibited; and association with known criminals may be forbidden.

Individuals on work programs usually have their pay closely controlled. They may be required to pay a portion of their room and board, and, if married, to send part of their earnings to their dependents.

THE COMMUNITY

Traditionally correctional institutions were isolated from other human service agencies and were required merely to hold prisoners and to provide some form of nominal supervision for individuals on probation and parole. More recently, however, as already noted, it is expected that corrections take a more positive approach, seeking rehabilitation whenever possible. These revised expectations make it necessary to link corrections to the community in every phase of operation.

Community-based corrections require a complicated interplay among judicial and correctional personnel from related public and private agencies, citizen volunteers, and civic groups. It also requires leadership.

Community-based corrections includes any activities in the community aimed at helping offenders become law-abiding citizens. The oldest community-based correctional program is supervision under probation, a foundation on which to build a wide range of community-based services. The use of control and surveillance is basic to a sound community corrections system.

Community-based corrections includes all correctional activities that occur in the community as an alternative to confinement of an offender at any point in the correctional process. A community-based approach to corrections has three significant advantages: humanitarian, restorative, and managerial. The humanitarian aspect is obvious because no one should be subjected to custodial control unnecessarily. To help a person avoid the unfavorable consequences of prison, even though the result of the offender's own criminal actions, is humanitarian. Second, restorative measures should help an offender achieve a position in the community in which he or she does not violate the law. The accomplishment of this objective can be measured by recidivism.

Additionally, the managerial goal of cost effectiveness can often be obtained from a community-based program. Any shift from custodial control saves money; however, the primary criterion is *not* fiscal. The public must be protected. If offenders can be shifted from custodial control to community-based programs without loss of public protection, a managerial objective can be accomplished.

Further, community-based correctional programs cannot succeed without the understanding and cooperation of the police because individuals within these programs *will* come in contact with the police, and the nature of that contact will directly affect the offender's adjustment. The police can and must make affirmative contributions to community-based corrections programs. They know the resources available as well as the pitfalls to be avoided. In essence, the police are an integral part of any successful corrections program, from using good judgment in making arrests to assisting those on parole or probation to reenter the community.

Some offenders have no chance for parole, either because their sentence prohibits it or because they are sentenced to death.

THE DEATH PENALTY VERSUS LIFE WITHOUT PAROLE

As noted by Monk (1991, p. 214):

Polls in the late 1960s showed that most Americans opposed the death penalty, and virtually every other Western industrial nation had long since eliminated the death sentence or severely modified its use.

A poll in 1988 showed that close to 80 percent of all Americans supported capital punishment, and there are currently over 1,800 inmates on death row awaiting execution. . . .

The national mood is now solidly behind "getting tough" on criminals, especially drug dealers and murderers. Support and utilization of capital punishment make sense within the logic of the present cultural political situation.

Those who argue against the death penalty note that it is morally reprehensible and self-defeating. To teach that killing is wrong by killing those who do so makes no sense. Wright (1992, p. 209) suggests that "murder and capital

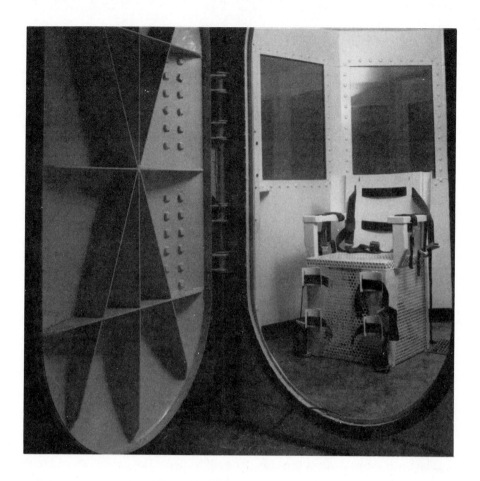

Gas chamber at San Quentin

punishment are not opposites which cancel one another." He quotes testimony of Henry Schwarzchild before Congress:

> What does the death penalty, after all, say to the American people and to our children? That killing is all right if the right people do it and think they have a good enough reason for doing it! That is the rationale of every pathological murderer walking the street: he thinks he is the right person to do it. . . . How can a thoughtful and sensible person justify killing people to teach that killing is wrong?

Greenberg (1991, p. 216), too, suggests that capital punishment as it is currently practiced should be abolished, noting: "Since at least 1967, the death penalty has been inflicted only rarely, erratically, and often upon the least odious killers, while many of the most heinous criminals have escaped execution. Moreover, it has been employed almost exclusively in a few formerly slave-holding states, and there it has been used almost exclusively against killers of whites, not blacks, and never against white killers of blacks."

Those who argue for capital punishment see it as both a deterrent and as a form of retribution. As noted by van den Haag (1991, p. 223): "We threaten punishments in order to deter crime. We impose them not only to make the threats credible but also as retribution (justice) for the crimes that were not deterred. . . . Execution of those who have committed heinous murders may deter only one murder per year. If it does, it seems quite warranted. It is also the only fitting retribution for murder I can think of."

Some criminologists argue that life without parole (LWOP) is a more fitting and punishing sentence than the death penalty. Wright (1992, p. 210) reports on a study conducted of Tennessee death row inmates and found that exactly half of the inmates surveyed consider the "penultimate penalty of LWOP a worse alternative [than execution]." Those who considered LWOP as harsher than execution asserted they would rather be put to death than "languish behind bars for thirty, forty, or fifty years."

The controversy regarding capital punishment and life without parole is likely to continue into the twenty-first century.

SUMMARY

Corrections is that portion of the criminal justice system that carries out the court's orders. It consists of our probation and parole systems as well as our jails, prisons, and community-based programs to rehabilitate offenders. The objectives of the correctional system are retribution, incapacitation, deterrence, rehabilitation, and restitution.

Many offenders, especially repeat offenders, are sentenced to correctional institutions, jails or prisons. Jail differs from prison in that its inmates are there for shorter terms, usually for less serious crimes. Negative characteristics of jails in the United States include: (1) the variety of the offenders, (2) the problems of local control and politics, (3) inadequate personnel, (4) demeaning physical facilities, (5) inept administration, and (6) failure to adopt alternative programs and dispositions.

Prisons may be punitive oriented or treatment oriented. Punitive-oriented systems have authority patterns based only on rank; rules are very specific and are emphasized; guards have limited decision making; communication with inmates is very formal and restricted to orders; and incentives are usually negative. In contrast, treatment-oriented systems stress an authority pattern based on technical knowledge; goals are more general, flexible, and individualized; guards are encouraged to make their own decisions and to communicate with the inmates; and incentives are usually positive.

The medical model of corrections assumes criminals are victims of society and need to be "cured." The justice model assumes criminals are self-directed and responsible for their crimes. The United States ranks *first* in the world in numbers of people incarcerated. Alternatives to jail or prison include home detention and boot camp.

The vast majority of people sentenced to jail or prison become eligible for parole. Parole differs from probation in that a person who is paroled has spent some time serving a prison sentence. It is similar to probation in that both require supervision of the offender and set up certain conditions that the offender must meet. Parole and probation often involve community-based institutional programs aimed at reintegrating offenders into society, including halfway houses, restitution centers, furloughs, work release, and study release programs.

DISCUSSION QUESTIONS

1. Do you feel the public accepts community-based corrections programs?

2. What are some justifications to support monetary restitution in corrections?

3. What are some obstacles in establishing prison or jail reforms?

4. Are the systems of probation and parole effective tools in dealing with law violators?

5. In our modern society, with its constant changes in corrections philosophy, do you feel that parole boards serve a useful function?

6. What are your views on home detention/house arrest?

7. Do you feel electronic monitoring presents more advantages than disadvantages?

8. Who do you feel could benefit most from a boot camp experience?

9. What are your views on capital punishment? A sentence of life without parole? Which do you feel would be the harsher sentence?

10. Why do you think the United States has the highest rate and number of people behind bars?

TERMS

boot camps, halfway houses, incarcerated, justice model, medical model, parole, probation, recidivism, restitution, restitution center, shock incarceration.

REFERENCES

Adler, F.; Mueller, G. O.W.; and Laufer, W. S. *Criminology.* New York: McGraw-Hill, 1991.

Camp, G. M. and Camp, C. G. *Prison Gangs: Their Extent, Nature and Impact on Prisons.* Washington, D.C.: U.S. Government Printing Office, 1985.

Doyle, P. "Town Hopes that Privately Run Prison Will Free It from Economic Hard Times." *Star Tribune,* May 22, 1992, 1A, 18A.

Eldefonso, E. *Issues in Corrections: A Book of Readings.* Beverly Hills, Calif.: Glencoe Press, 1984.

Gardner, T. J. and Anderson, T. M. *Criminal Law: Principles and Cases.* 5th ed. St. Paul, Minn.: West Publishing Company, 1992.

Goodman, D. "Prisons." *The Volume Library, Yearbook 1992.* Nashville, Tenn.: The Southwestern Company, 1992.

Greenberg, J. "Against the American System of Capital Punishment," pp. 216–219 in *Taking Sides: Clashing Views on Controversial Issues in Crime and Criminology.* 2d ed., edited by R. C. Monk. Guilford, Conn.: The Dushkin Publishing Group, 1991. (Reprinted from *Harvard Law Review,* 1986.)

Greenberg, M. S. and Rubeck, R. B. *Social Psychology of the Criminal Justice System.* Monterey, Calif.: Brooks/Cole Publishing, 1982.

Jackson, R. K. and McBride, W. D. *Understanding Street Gangs.* Sacramento, Calif.: Custom Publishing Company, 1985.

Levinson, R. B. "The Future of Unit Management." *Corrections Today* (April 1991): 44–48.

MacKenzie, D. L. " 'Boot Camp' Programs Grow in Number and Scope," pp. 218–220 in *Criminal Justice 92-93,* edited by J. J. Sullivan and J. L. Victor. Guilford, Conn.: The Dushkin Publishing Group, 1992. (Reprinted from *NIJ Reports,* November/December 1990: 6–8.)

Monk, R. C. (Ed.) *Taking Sides: Clashing Views on Controversial Issues in Crime and Criminology.* Guilford, Conn.: The Dushkin Publishing Group, 1989.

Monk, R. C. (Ed.) *Taking Sides: Clashing Views on Controversial Issues in Crime and Criminology.* 2d ed. Guilford, Conn.: The Dushkin Publishing Group, 1991.

Morash, M. and Rucker, L. "A Critical Look at the Idea of Boot Camp as a Correctional Reform," pp. 255–262 in *Taking Sides: Clashing Views on Controversial Issues in Crime and Criminology.* 2d ed., edited by R. C. Monk. Guilford, Conn.: The Dushkin Publishing Group, 1991. (Reprinted from *Crime and Delinquency* 36, April 1990: 204–221.)

National Advisory Commission on Criminal Justice Standards and Goals. *Corrections.* Washington, D.C.: U.S. Government Printing Office, 1973.

Pace, D. F. *Community Relations Concepts.* Placerville, Calif.: Custom Publishing Company, 1991.

Pierson, T. A. "The Missouri Experience: One State's Success with Unit Management." *Corrections Today* (April 1991): 24–30.

Scaglione, F. "You're Under Arrest—At Home." *USA Today Magazine* (November 1988): 26–28.

Schoen, K. F. "Criminal Treatment," p. 217 in *Criminal Justice 92/93,* edited by J. J. Sullivan and J. L. Victor. Guilford, Conn.: The Dushkin Publishing Group, 1992.

Senna, J. J. and Siegel, L. J. *Introduction to Criminal Justice.* 5th ed. St. Paul, Minn.: West Publishing Company, 1990.

Sullivan, J. J. and Victor, J. L. (Eds.) *Criminal Justice 92/93.* Guilford, Conn.: The Dushkin Publishing Group, 1992.

Sullivan, J. J. and Victor, J. L. (Eds.) "Victims of Crime" p. 57 in *Criminal Justice 90/91.* Guilford, Conn.: The Dushkin Publishing Group, 1990.

Territo, L.; Halsted, J.; and Bromley, M. *Crime and Justice in America.* St. Paul, Minn.: West Publishing Company, 1989.

U.S. Department of Justice. Bureau of Justice Statistics. *Report to the Nation on Crime and Justice.* Washington, D.C.: U.S. Government Printing Office, 1988.

van den Haag, E. "The Ultimate Punishment: A Defense," pp. 220–225 in *Taking Sides: Clashing Views on Controversial Issues in Crime and Criminology.* 2d ed., edited by R. C. Monk. Guilford, Conn.: The Dushkin Publishing Group, 1991. (Reprinted from *Harvard Law Review,* 1986.)

Webster, J. H. "Designing Facilities for Effective Unit Management." *Corrections Today* (April 1991): 38–42.

Williams, V. L.; Formby, W. A.; and Watkins, J. C. *Introduction to Criminal Justice.* Albany, N.Y.: Delmar Publishing, 1982.

"Women in Jail: Unequal Justice." *Newsweek,* June 4, 1992, 37–38, 51.

Wright, J. H., Jr. "Life Without Parole: The View from Death Row," pp. 204–214 in *Criminal Justice, 92/93,* edited by J. J. Sullivan and J. L. Victor. Guilford, Conn.: The Dushkin Publishing Group, 1992. (Reprinted from *Criminal Law Bulletin,* 27, no. 4, July/August 1991: 334–357.)

CHAPTER 20

The Juvenile Justice System: Caring for Our Nation's Youth

There is evidence, in fact, that there may be grounds for concern that the child receives the worst of both worlds: that he gets neither the protections accorded to adults nor the solicitous care and regenerative treatment postulated for children.
—**Supreme Court Justice Abe Fortas**

Do You Know

What four phases of development the juvenile justice system has gone through?

What is meant by the principle of *parens patriae*?

What was established by the Kent, Gault, Winship, and McKeiver decisions?

What balance the juvenile justice system seeks?

How the welfare model and the justice model differ? Which is being advocated for the 1990s?

How much discretion police have with juveniles?

What procedural safeguards should be followed if detaining or arresting a juvenile?

If youth can be fingerprinted or photographed?

What services police often provide juveniles?

How police affect the juvenile justice system?

How juvenile court differs from adult court?

What correctional facilities juvenile delinquents have?

INTRODUCTION

This chapter presents concepts related to how patrol officers or, in larger departments, officers assigned to the juvenile division deal with not only juvenile delinquents but also law-abiding juveniles. The Constitution guarantees that all citizens be presumed innocent until proven guilty. This applies to juveniles as well. The majority of the juveniles in our country are not delinquents and do not deserve to be treated as such merely because they are underage. If good relations can be established between the police and our youth, everyone will benefit.

In addition, police officers must investigate and intervene on behalf of children who are neglected and/or abused.

HISTORICAL OVERVIEW

Our juvenile justice system has had its own unique development from the time of the colonists to the 1990s. According to McCreedy (1975), our juvenile justice system has its roots as far back as the feudal period in England when the crown assumed the protection of the property of minors. When the feudal period ended, supervision of the duties previously assumed by the overlord was transferred to the king's court of chancery. This chancery court operated on a principle known as **parens patriae.** Under this doctrine, the king, through the chancellor, was responsible for the general protection of all people in the realm who could not protect their own interests. This included the children of the realm. Consequently, the king, by means of the chancery court and chancellor, assumed supreme guardianship over the persons and property of minors. McCreedy (1975, p. 1) notes: "In effect, the chancellor acted as a substitute father for those children who were abandoned, neglected, or destitute."

The doctrine of equity was used when dealing with children; that is, decisions were made based on the spirit of the law and on an attempt at fundamental fairness rather than on strict interpretation of the law. This gave much more flexibility in deciding a case.

Another principle in English common law that influenced our juvenile justice system was the belief that children younger than seven years old were considered incapable of criminal intent. Between the ages of seven and fourteen they were presumed to still be incapable of criminal intent unless it could be shown differently. After age fourteen, children, like adults, were held responsible for their acts and treated according to a strict interpretation of the law. In effect, age had a direct bearing on how someone who broke the law was treated.

The four major phases of the juvenile justice system have been (1) a Puritan emphasis, (2) an emphasis on providing a refuge for youth, (3) development of the separate juvenile court, and (4) emphasis on juvenile rights.

The Puritan Emphasis

The concept of *parens patriae* and the notion that there was an age below which there can be no criminal intent were brought by the colonists to America. From the time the colonists first arrived in the United States until the nineteenth century, however, emphasis was on Puritan values, which held that the child was basically evil. Parents were considered responsible for controlling their children who were, in effect, their property. The law dealt very severely with children who broke the law. McCreedy (1975) points out as an example that in 1828 in New Jersey, a boy of thirteen was hanged for an offense committed when he was twelve. This Puritan emphasis lasted until the 1820s.

Providing a Refuge

By the 1820s several states had passed laws to protect children from the punishments associated with criminal laws. According to McCreedy (1975, p. 2): "The first changes came in the area of institutional custody. Central to the reform effort in this area was a recognition of the brutality of confining children in the same institutions with adults convicted of crime. This awareness resulted in attempts to separate children from adult criminal offenders."

The first American institution that isolated children convicted of crimes from adult criminals was New York City's House of Refuge, established in 1825. This was, in effect, the first juvenile reformatory in the United States.

In 1869 Massachusetts became the first state to pass a law requiring an agent from the State Board of Charity to investigate all cases involving children coming to court, to attend their trials, and to make recommendations to the judge. In 1870 Massachusetts passed legislation that established separate trials for children in Suffolk County, and by 1872 this means of handling juvenile cases extended throughout the state.

Another major development in the mid-1800s was probation, instituted in 1841 by John Augustus, the first probation officer, who was authorized by judges in Boston, Massachusetts, to take into his custody adults and children convicted of crimes.

In 1884 New York passed legislation allowing a trial judge to place a child under the age of sixteen convicted of a crime under the supervision of any suitable person or institution willing to accept him or her. During this period of development of the juvenile justice system, the state took over the parents' role of responsibility for their children but not to the degree that this attitude continued into the next phase of the system's development. Table 20-1 summarizes the developments from 1825 to 1899, leading up to the development of the juvenile court.

The Juvenile Court

According to Vetter and Territo (1984, p. 497):

> The establishment (by statute) of the first juvenile court in [Chicago] Illinois in 1899 marked the beginning of an era of "social jurisprudence." Although the juvenile court was a bona fide court, its procedures were dramatically different from adult court proceedings. Prior to the establishment of juvenile court, children, like adults, were required to furnish bail or be placed in jail; they were indicted by grand juries; they were tried according to adult criminal procedure; and they were sentenced to prison or required to pay fines.

In contrast, according to Vetter and Territo (1984, p. 497):

> The court's major objective was to help the wayward child become a productive member of the community. The determination of guilt or innocence, using standard rules of evidence, was not of primary importance. Instead, ... court procedures were to be more diagnostic than legal in nature, giving major consideration to the information obtained on the youngster's environment, heredity, as well as his physical and mental condition.

Table 20–1 Antecedents of the Juvenile Court

1825	New York House of Refuge was opened, followed by houses in Boston (1826), Philadelphia (1828), and New Orleans (1845).
1831	Illinois passed a law that allowed penalties for certain offenses committed by minors to differ from the penalties imposed on adults.
1841	John Augustus inaugurated probation and became the nation's first probation officer.
1854	State industrial school for girls opened in Lancaster, Massachusetts (first cottage-type institution).
1858	State industrial school for boys in Lancaster, Ohio, adopted a cottage-type system.
1863	Children's Aid Society founded in Boston. Members of the organization attended police and superior court hearings, supervised youngsters selected for probation, and did the investigation on which probation selection was based.
1869	Law enacted in Massachusetts to direct State Board of Charities to send agents to court hearings that involved children. The agents made recommendations to the court that frequently involved probation and the placement of youngsters with suitable families.
1870	Separate hearings for juveniles were required in Suffolk County, Massachusetts. New York followed by requiring separate trials, dockets, and records for children; Rhode Island made similar provisions in 1891.
1899	In April, Illinois adopted legislation creating the first juvenile court in Cook County (Chicago). In May, Colorado established a juvenile court.

Source: L. Territo, J. B. Halsted, and M. L. Bromley. *Crime and Justice in America: A Human Perspective.* 3d ed. Copyright © 1992. Reprinted by permission of West Publishing Company: St. Paul, Minn. All rights reserved.

The Juvenile Court Act not only created the first juvenile court, it also had as a central purpose to regulate the treatment and control of *dependent, neglected, and delinquent* children. In effect, it equated poor and abused children with criminal children and provided that they be treated in essentially the same way. Most juvenile courts in the 1990s have this same multiple charge.

During this period of the development of the juvenile justice system, the philosophy of *parens patriae* was in full effect. The Chicago legislation grew out of the efforts of civic-minded citizens who saw the inhumane treatment of children who were confined in police stations and jails. The legislation, entitled "An Act to Regulate the Treatment and Control of Dependent, Neglected and Delinquent Children," included many of the characteristics of our modern-day juvenile courts, such as a separate court for juveniles, separate and confidential records, informal proceedings, and the possibility of probation.

The Chicago legislation also required that children be given the same care, custody, and discipline that parents should give them. The major goal was to save the child. This was also the first basic principle of the juvenile court—that of *parens patriae*. The state not only acts as a substitute parent to abandoned, neglected, and dependent children, but it also acts as a "superparent" for delinquent children. As noted by McCreedy (1975, p. 7): "In this role, the state can take legal control of a child away from the child's natural parents or guardians. For example, the state acts as a superparent whenever it commits a child to an industrial school or other correctional facility. The juvenile system symbolizes the state's parenthood."

The *parens patriae* doctrine made the state legally responsible for the children within that state, providing a legal foundation for state intervention in the family.

McCreedy (1975, p. 7) goes on to note:

The state, as the child's substitute parent, was not supposed to punish the child for his misconduct, but to help him. To reach this noble goal, many of the

House of Refuge collage

procedures used in adult criminal proceedings were abandoned or replaced with procedures commonly used in non-criminal (civil) court proceedings. A whole new legal vocabulary and new methods of operation were developed to reflect the new philosophy and procedures used in the juvenile justice system.

Instead of a complaint being filed against the child, a *petition* was filed. No longer was the child to be arrested in the strict sense of the term. Instead, the child was given a *summons*. A *preliminary inquiry* or *initial hearing* replaced an arraignment on the charge. The child was not required to plead either guilty or not guilty to the alleged misconduct. Instead of being found guilty of a crime, the child was found *delinquent*. Moreover, adjudication of delinquency was not to be considered a conviction. None of the liabilities attached to a criminal conviction were to apply to a child found delinquent; for example, disqualification from future civil service appointments, the inability to be licensed by the state or the right to vote.

The basic differences in the terminology used in juvenile and adult court are illustrated in Table 20–2.

The second major principle underlying the juvenile justice system, in addition to *parens patriae,* is the individualization of justice. According to Mc-Creedy (1975, p. 8): "This principle stems from the belief that children, like adults differ from one another. Each person has a different family background, mentality, physical capability, and personality. . . . As the purpose of the court is to save the child and not to punish him, it is necessary for those individuals involved in the juvenile justice system to consider the background of the child in order to treat him."

Table 20–2   **The Language of Juvenile and Adult Courts**

JUVENILE COURT TERM	ADULT COURT TERM
Adjudication: decision by the judge that a child has committed delinquent acts.	Conviction of guilt
Adjudicatory hearing: a hearing to determine whether the allegations of a petition are supported by the evidence beyond a reasonable doubt.	Trial
Adjustment: the settling of a matter so that parties agree without official intervention by the court.	Plea bargaining
Aftercare: the supervision given to a child for a limited period of time after he or she is released from training school but while he or she is still under the control of the juvenile court.	Parole
Commitment: a decision by the judge to send a child to training school.	Sentence to imprisonment
Delinquent act: an act that if committed by an adult would be called a crime. The term does not include such ambiguities and noncrimes as "being ungovernable," "truancy," "incorrigibility," and "disobedience."	Crime
Delinquent child: a child who is found to have committed an act that would be considered a crime if committed by an adult.	Criminal
Detention: temporary care of an allegedly delinquent child who requires secure custody in physically restricting facilities pending court disposition or execution of a court order.	Holding in jail
Dispositional hearing: a hearing held subsequent to the adjudicatory hearing to determine what order of disposition should be made for a child adjudicated as delinquent.	Sentencing hearing
Hearing: the presentation of evidence to the juvenile court judge, his or her consideration of it, and his or her decision on disposition of the case.	Trial
Juvenile court: the court that has jurisdiction over children who are alleged to be or found to be delinquent. Juvenile delinquency procedures should not be used for neglected children or for those who need supervision.	Court of record
Petition: an application for a court order or some other judicial action. Hence, a "delinquency petition" is an application for the court to act in a matter involving a juvenile apprehended for a delinquent act.	Accusation or indictment
Probation: the supervision of a delinquent child after the court hearing but without commitment to training school.	Probation (with the same meaning as the juvenile court term)
Residential child care facility: a dwelling (other than a detention or shelter care facility) that is licensed to provide living accommodations, care, treatment, and maintenance for children and youth. Such facilities include foster homes, group homes, and halfway houses.	Halfway house
Shelter: temporary care of a child in physically unrestricting facilities pending court disposition or execution of a court order for placement. Shelter care is used for dependent and neglected children and minors in need of supervision. Separate shelter care facilities are also used for children apprehended for delinquency who need temporary shelter but not secure detention.	Jail
Take into custody: the act of the police in securing the physical custody of a child engaged in delinquency. The term is used to avoid the stigma of the word "arrest."	Arrest

Source: L. Territo, J. B. Halsted, and M. L. Bromley. *Crime and Justice in America: A Human Perspective.* 3d ed. Copyright © 1992, p. 539. Reprinted by permission of West Publishing Company: St. Paul, Minn. All rights reserved.

Although the establishment of juvenile courts was a tremendous advancement in our juvenile justice system, it did present some major problems as well. Because children were no longer considered "criminals," they lost many of the constitutional protections of due process in criminal proceedings. In many instances, for example, delinquents were not given notice of the charge, were not provided with a lawyer, and were not given the chance to cross-examine witnesses.

Justification for the informal procedures used in the juvenile justice system prior to 1960 was set forth almost a century ago in *Commonwealth v. Fisher* (1905):

> To save a child from becoming a criminal or from continuing in a career in crimes ... the Legislature may surely provide for the salvation of such a child ... by bringing it into one of the courts of the state without any process at all, for the purpose of subjecting it to the state's guardianship and protection. The natural parent needs no process to temporarily deprive his child of its liberty by confining it in his own home, to save it from the consequences of persistence in a career of waywardness: nor is the state, when compelled as parens patriae, to take the place of the father for the same purpose, required to adopt any process as a means of placing its hands upon the child to lead it to one of its courts.

By the 1960s, however, the United States Supreme Court began to seriously question the use of *parens patriae* as the sole reason for denying the child many constitutional rights extended to adults charged with a crime, leading into the fourth phase in the development of the juvenile justice system—juvenile rights.

Juvenile Rights

In 1956 a landmark federal case was the first of a series of cases that resulted in drastic changes in the juvenile justice system. In *Shioutakon v. District of Columbia* (1956) the courts established the role of legal counsel in juvenile court. In essence, if a juvenile was to have his or her liberty taken away, that juvenile had the right to be represented by a lawyer in court. If the parents could not afford a lawyer, the court was to appoint counsel.

A second case establishing juvenile rights was *Kent v. United States* (1966). This case involved Morris Kent, a juvenile with a police record who was arrested at age sixteen in Washington and charged with housebreaking, robbery, and rape. Kent confessed to the charges and was held at a juvenile detention facility for nearly a week. The judge then decided to transfer jurisdiction of his case to an adult criminal court. Kent received no hearing of any kind; the transfer was completely at the judge's discretion and was based on several reports written by probation staff.

In reviewing the *Kent* case, the Supreme Court decreed: "As a condition to a valid waiver order, petitioner (Kent) was entitled to a hearing, including access by his counsel to the social records and probation or similar reports which are presumably considered by the court, and to a statement of the reasons for Juvenile Court's decision."

Kent v. United States established that if a juvenile court transfers a case to adult criminal court, juveniles are entitled to a hearing, their counsel must be given access to probation records used by the court in reaching its decision, and the court must state its reasons for waiving jurisdiction over the case.

According to Arnold and Brungardt (1983, p. 24): "The impact of the Kent case went far beyond the relatively narrow legal issue—conditions of waiver to criminal court—that it addressed. It served as a warning to the juvenile justice system that the juvenile court's traditional laxity toward procedural and evidentiary standards would no longer be tolerated by the highest court in the land."

An appendix to the *Kent* decision contained the following criteria established by the United States Supreme Court for states to use in deciding on transfer of juveniles to adult criminal courts for trial:

1. the seriousness of the alleged offense and whether the protection of the community requires waiver;

2. whether the alleged offense was committed in an aggressive, violent, premeditated, or willful manner;

3. whether the alleged offense was against persons or against property, greater weight being given to offenses against persons, especially if personal injury resulted;

4. the prospective merit of the complaint;

5. the desirability of trial and disposition of the offense in one court when the juvenile's associates in the alleged offense are adults who will be charged with crimes in the adult court;

6. the sophistication and maturity of the juvenile as determined by consideration of his or her home, environmental situation, emotional attitude, and pattern of living; and

7. the record and previous history of the juvenile.

The following year, another landmark Supreme Court ruling in the *Gault* case (1968) resulted in additional major changes in our juvenile justice system. Gerald Gault was fifteen years old and on probation when he was taken into custody for allegedly making obscene phone calls to a neighbor. At 10:00 A.M., when Gerald was picked up at home, his mother and father were working. No notice was left at the home that Gerald was being taken into custody nor were any steps taken to notify his parents. Mrs. Gault arrived home about 6:00 P.M. to find Gerald missing. An older brother accidentally discovered that Gerald had been taken into custody.

Mrs. Gault went to the detention home, and the probation officer told her why Gerald was there and that a hearing would be held the next day, June 9. On June 9 the officer filed a petition with the juvenile court making only general allegations of "delinquency." No particular facts of Gerald's behavior were stated.

The hearing was held in the judge's chambers. The complaining witness was not present, no one was sworn in, no attorney was present, and no transcript of the proceedings was made. At the hearing Gerald admitted to making a less obnoxious part of the phone call in question. At the conclusion of the hearing, the judge said he would take the matter under advisement.

Gerald was returned to the detention home for another two days and then released. After the release Mrs. Gault was informed by note from the probation officer that on June 15 further hearings would be held on Gerald's delinquency. The June 15 hearing was also without benefit of complaining witnesses, sworn testimony, transcript, or counsel. The probation officer made a referral report that listed the charge as lewd phone calls and filed it with the court, but it was not made available to Gerald or his parents. At the conclusion of the hearing the judge committed Gerald as a juvenile delinquent to the State Industrial School until age twenty-one. Gerald, only fifteen years old at the time, received a six-year sentence for an action for which an adult would receive a fine or a two-month imprisonment.

The United States Supreme Court overruled Gerald's conviction on the grounds that:

- Neither Gerald nor his parents had notice of the specific charges against him.
- No counsel was offered or provided to Gerald.
- No witnesses were present, thus denying Gerald the right of cross-examination and confrontation.
- No warning of Gerald's privilege against self-incrimination was given to him, thus no waiver of that right took place.

The *Gault* decision requires that the due process clause of the Fourteenth Amendment apply to proceedings in state juvenile courts, including the right of notice, the right to counsel, the right against self-incrimination, and the right to confront witnesses.

Justice Fortas delivered the opinion of the Court:

Where a person, infant or adult, can be seized by the State, charged and convicted for violating a state criminal law, and then ordered by the State to be confined for six years, I think the Constitution requires that he be tried in accordance with the guarantees of all provisions of the Bill of Rights made applicable to the States by the Fourteenth Amendment. Undoubtedly this would be true of an adult defendant, and it would be a plain denial of equal protection of the laws—an invidious discrimination—to hold that others subject to heavier punishments could, because they are children, be denied these same constitutional safeguards. I consequently agree with the Court that the Arizona law as applied here denied to the parents and their son the right of notice, right to counsel, right against self-incrimination, and right to confront the witnesses against young Gault. Appellants are entitled to these rights, not because "fairness, impartiality and orderliness—in short, the essentials of due process"—require them and not because they are "the procedural rules which have been fashioned from the generality of due process," but because they are specifically and unequivocally granted by provisions of the Fifth and Sixth Amendments which the Fourteenth Amendment makes applicable to the States.

It is clear that juveniles are to be afforded all the same rights and privileges as adults in the criminal process. The logical implications of the *Gault* decision require safeguards in the prehearing stage as well as use of the Miranda warning for juveniles, whether at the station house, in the squad car, or on a street corner.

The Supreme Court refused to rule on two questions raised on Gault's behalf: the right to an appeal and the right to a record of court proceedings.

In 1970 another Supreme Court decision expanded juvenile rights. In *In Re Winship* (1970) the United States Supreme Court examined the standard of proof in a 1967 New York case against a twelve-year-old boy who allegedly had stolen $112 from a woman's purse. The New York judge acknowledged that he had operated on the civil court principle of "preponderance of evidence," a standard of proof much weaker than the "proof beyond a reasonable doubt" required in a criminal court. In the review of the *Winship* case, the Supreme Court ruled that if adjudication might result in deprivation of liberty for the juvenile, the juvenile court must use the same standards of proof as are required in adult criminal trials.

The *Winship* decision established a juvenile defendant must be found guilty beyond a reasonable doubt.

One right of adults charged with crimes that is not afforded to juveniles charged with crimes is the right to a trial by jury.

McKeiver v. Pennsylvania established that a jury trial is not a constitutional right of juveniles.

McKeiver v. Pennsylvania (1971) involved a Pennsylvania youth charged with robbery, larceny, and receiving stolen goods. According to Arnold and Brungardt (1983, p. 24), in this case:

> The Supreme Court slowed its march toward reshaping the juvenile court to impose stronger due-process standards and formal procedures. In McKeiver, the Court, fearing that jury trials would bring delay and increased formality to the juvenile court, supported noncriminal juvenile hearings and ruled that a jury trial is not a constitutional right of juveniles.... The court felt strongly that if the formalities of the criminal adjudicative process are to be superimposed upon the juvenile court system, there is little need for its separate existence.

Arnold and Brungardt (1983, p. 24) go on to note:

> These Supreme Court decisions, taken as a whole, clearly indicate the Court's support of stronger due-process and evidentiary standards for juvenile court proceedings. However, by declining to rule on the questions of the right to a jury trial and the right to records of the proceedings in Gault, and in issuing the McKeiver decision, the Court has pointed to a fundamental dilemma it faces in its juvenile court decisions. On the one hand, the Supreme Court is alarmed by the denial of constitutional rights in juvenile courts; on the other hand, it wants to maintain something of the informality and protectiveness long characteristic of the juvenile court. It appears the movement to bring justice to the juvenile court system has been successful, although the degree to which the orientation of actual court practice has changed is highly visible.

The juvenile justice system seeks to balance the informal and protective emphasis of the *parens patriae* doctrine with the constitutional rights of juveniles charged with crimes.

In 1975, in *Breed v. Jones,* the court ruled on the issue of double jeopardy in juvenile cases. As noted by Abadinsky (1991, p. 534):

> Breed was seventeen years old when he was arrested for armed robbery, and a juvenile petition alleging armed robbery was filed. After taking testimony from two witnesses presented by the prosecutor and the respondent, the judge sustained the petition. At a subsequent disposition hearing, however, the judge ruled that the respondent was not "amenable to the care, treatment and training program available through the facilities of the juvenile court" and ordered that he be prosecuted as an adult. Breed was subsequently found guilty of armed robbery in superior court. In its decision, the Supreme Court held "that the prosecution of respondent in Superior Court, after an adjudicatory proceeding in Juvenile Court, violated the Double Jeopardy Clause of the Fifth Amendment, as applied to the States through the Fourteenth Amendment."

Table 20-3   Juvenile Justice Developments: 1646 to Present

SYSTEM (PERIOD)	MAJOR DEVELOPMENTS	INFLUENCES	CHILD-STATE RELATIONSHIP	PARENT-STATE RELATIONSHIP	PARENT-CHILD RELATIONSHIP
Puritan (1646–1824)	Massachusetts Stubborn Child Law (1646).	Christian view of child as evil; economically marginal agrarian society.	Law provides symbolic standard of maturity; support for family as economic unit.	Parents considered responsible for and capable of controlling child.	Child considered both property and spiritual responsibility of parents.
Refuge (1824–1899)	Institutionalization of deviants, New York House of Refuge established (1824) for delinquent and dependent children.	Enlightenment; immigration and industrialization.	Child seen as helpless, in need of state intervention.	Parents supplanted as state assumes responsibility for correcting deviant socialization.	Family considered to be a major cause of juvenile deviancy.
Juvenile court (1899–1960)	Establishment of separate legal system for juvenile—Illinois Juvenile Court Act (1899).	Reformism and rehabilitative ideology; increased immigration, urbanization, large-scale industrialization.	Juvenile court institutionalizes legal irresponsibility of child.	Parens patriae doctrine gives legal foundation for state intervention of family.	Further abrogation of parents' rights and responsibilities.
Juvenile rights (1960-present)	Increased "legalization" of juvenile law— *Gault* decision (1966). Juvenile Justice and Delinquency Prevention Act (1974) calls for deinstitutionalization of status offender.	Criticism of juvenile justice system on humane grounds, civil rights movements by disadvantaged groups.	Movement to define and protect rights as well as provide services to children.	Reassertion of responsibility of parents and community for welfare and behavior of children.	Attention given to children's claims against parents. Earlier emancipation of children.

Adapted from U.S. Department of Justice, Reports of the National Juvenile Assessment Centers, *A Preliminary National Assessment of the Status Offender and the Juvenile Justice System* (Washington, D.C.: U.S. Government Printing Office, 1980) p. 29, by permission of the U.S. Department of Justice.

Source: L. Territo, J. B. Halsted, and M. L. Bromley. *Criminal Justice in America: A Human Perspective,* 3d ed. Copyright © 1992. Reprinted by permission of West Publishing Company: St. Paul, Minn. All rights reserved.

The evolution of our juvenile justice system is illustrated in Table 20–3.

FURTHER EVOLUTION: A CHANGE IN MODELS?

The juvenile justice system is based on a welfare model, focusing on the best interests of youth rather than on punishment for wrongdoing. This model, however, is being called into question by some, including the Office of Juvenile Justice and Delinquency Prevention (OJJDP). As noted by Springer (1986, p. 2):

The first step in doing justice for juveniles is to revise juvenile court acts throughout the country so that when juvenile courts deal with delinquent children, they operate under a justice model rather than under the present treatment or the child welfare model. By a justice model is meant a judicial process wherein young people who come in conflict with the law are held responsible and accountable for their behavior....

Except for certain mentally disabled and incompetent individuals, young law violators should not be considered by the juvenile courts as being "sick" or as victims of their environments. Generally speaking, young criminals are more wrong than wronged, more the victimizers than the victims.

Traditionally the juvenile courts have operated under a **welfare model,** focusing on the best interests of the child. Some advocate that this model be changed to a **justice model** where youth are held responsible for their crimes and punished for them.

Springer (p. 33) suggests: "It is time that we recognize the impossible double bind our juvenile judges are placed in when they, judicial officers, are commanded to diagnose the "problem" of some young offender, when in most cases it is obvious that the criminal youth does not have a problem—he or she *is* the problem."

Regnery (1991, p. 164) is an advocate of change, noting: "Children commit nearly one-third of serious crime in America. Our system of rendering justice for their crimes, however, is antiquated and largely incapable of dealing with the offenses they commit. Disliked by the public, by those who work in it, and even by many offenders, the juvenile justice system, which is supposed to act only in the 'best interests of the child,' serves neither the child, his victim, nor society."

Regnery (p. 166) describes a University of Pennsylvania research project that found that 7 percent of the juvenile population committed over 70 percent of all serious crime and that there was an 80 percent certainty that boys arrested more than five times would continue to be arrested repeatedly well into their adult years. Because of this, he urges that the policy of sealing

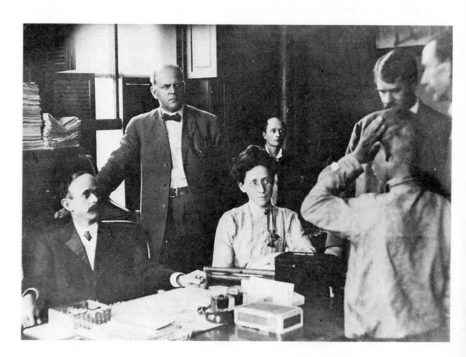

Judge Benjamin Lindsey, left, is generally recognized as the founder of the U.S. juvenile court system.

juvenile records of such repeat offenders should be changed. Regnery (p. 169) contends:

> By promising to make the record secret, or even more dramatically, by actually destroying the physical record, the juvenile justice system led the youth to believe that no matter what he did as a juvenile, or how often, it would be as if it had never happened once he reached his 18th birthday. Tight restrictions on access to the juvenile arrest and court records radically limited liability for exactly that behavior—chronic, violent delinquency—that the population at large was bemoaning.

THE JUVENILE JUSTICE SYSTEM IN THE 1990s

Just as within the adult criminal justice system, the juvenile justice system has three separate but integrally related components: the police, the court, and corrections—referred to as "Youth Authority." The normal progression of youth within the juvenile justice system is diagrammed in Figure 20–1.

THE POLICE AND THE JUVENILE JUSTICE SYSTEM

The usual flow of how police interact with youth in the juvenile justice system is illustrated in Figure 20–2.

The police usually are the youth's initial contact with the juvenile justice system. They have broad discretion and may release juveniles to their parents, refer them to other agencies, place them in detention, or refer them to a juvenile court.

The police may also temporarily detain juveniles, either for their own protection or to assure that they do appear in court. One critical aspect of the juvenile justice system is the initial contact with the law. Trojanowicz (1978, pp. 175–176) notes:

> The intake and screening process is an important aspect of the juvenile justice system. When used properly, it can effectively curtail or interrupt much delinquent behavior before it becomes serious. The intake process can also stimulate community agencies to help parents to better understand their children's behavior and the measures needed to prevent further delinquent acts.
>
> If the child is released at intake and no further processing takes place, there should still be a follow-up after any referral to a community agency by either the police or the intake unit. Follow-up facilitates not only the rendering of services to the child, but also promotes closer cooperation between the agencies involved. ... The police have a great deal of discretionary power, ranging all the way from the option of releasing the juvenile at initial contact in an unofficial manner to referring him to the juvenile court, which may result in detention.

Within this range are other options such as referring the juvenile to a community agency.

Whether a juvenile is actually arrested usually depends on a number of factors, the most important of which is the seriousness of the offense. Other factors that enter into the decision include the following (Trojanowicz 1978, p. 419):

> The appraised character of the youth, which in turn is based on such facts as his prior police record, age, associations, attitude, family situation, the conduct of his

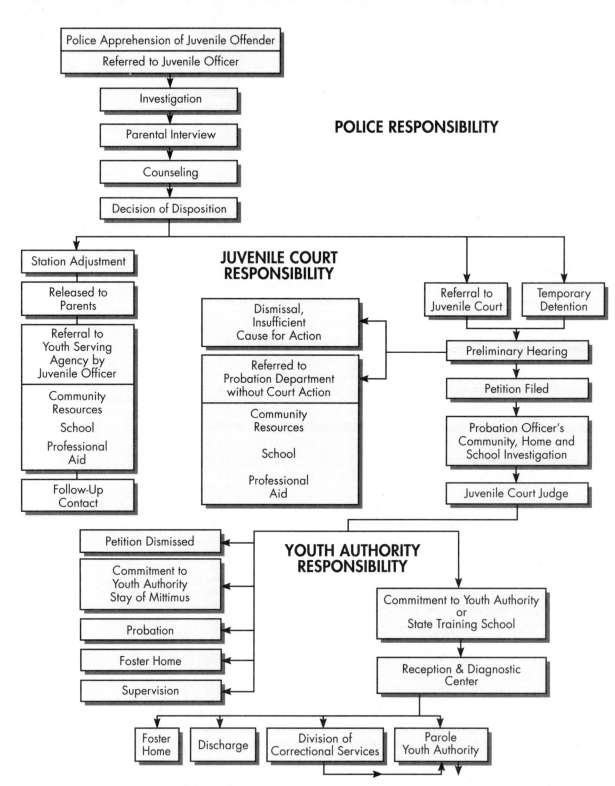

Figure 20–1 From Arrest to Disposition
Source: International Association of Chiefs of Police.

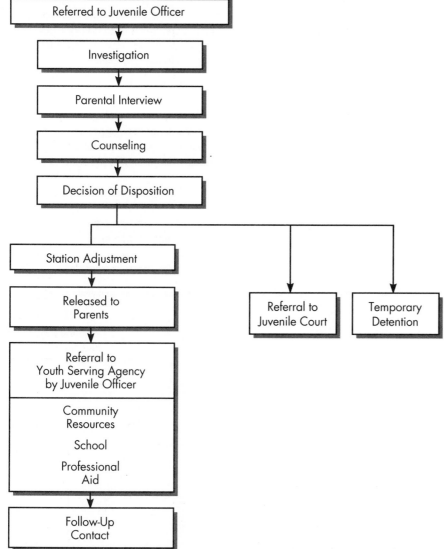

Figure 20–2   Police Responsibility

parents, and the attitude of other community institutions such as his school. The external community may exert pressure on the police department which may affect the disposition of any case. Here attitudes of the press and the public, the status of the complainant or victim, the status of the offender, and the conditions which prevail in the available referral agencies (the length of the waiting list, the willingness of the social agencies to accept police referrals) are all of consequence. Internal police department pressure such as attitudes of co-workers and supervisors and the personal experience of the officer may also play an important part in determining the outcome of any officially detected delinquent offense. These factors also indirectly determine the officially recorded police and court delinquency rates.

The amount of discretion available to police officers and the lack of criteria by which to make a decision were noted several years ago by the President's

Commission on Law Enforcement and Administration of Justice, Task Force on
Juvenile Delinquency and Youth Crime, when it stated (1967a, p. 14):

> In sum, the range of police dispositions is considerable, and the criteria for
> selection of a disposition are seldom set forth, explicitly, ordered in priority, or
> regularly reviewed for administrative purposes. Inservice training designed to
> assist police in exercising their discretionary functions is unusual.

As noted by Eldefonso (1983, p. 3): "Generally juveniles are referred to local
authorities after arrest.... In juvenile matters, probation departments provide
most of the services for the court from initial screening and filing of a petition in
behalf of the juvenile through termination of wardship (i.e., supervision and control)." Figure 20–3 illustrates the decision points in police handling of juveniles.

The probation department may or may not be part of a juvenile division.

Status Offenses

Juveniles are subjected to a conglomerate of laws and restraints that do not
apply to adults. For example, juveniles are frequently arrested for liquor law

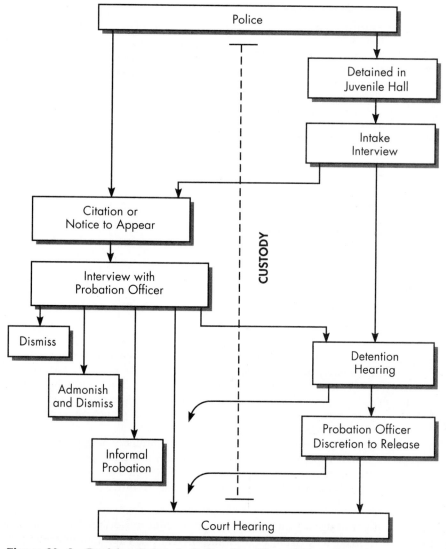

Figure 20–3   Decision Points in Police Handling of Juveniles

violations, curfew violations, absenting from home, truancy, smoking, suspicion, and incorrigibility. These are called **status offenses.**

As noted by Abadinsky (1991, p. 292): "Since, by definition, a status offender has not been accused of a crime, punitive intervention—arrest, detention, the court process, training schools—is inappropriate and the stigma is potentially harmful."

Detaining or Taking into Custody

If police officers determine that the offense is serious enough to warrant detention or that the juvenile is a threat to self or the general public, they should exercise certain safeguards.

In most jurisdictions it is mandatory that the parents of a juvenile who is detained be notified as soon as possible and that questioning of the juvenile be delayed until the parents are present. In addition to notifying the parents, police officers are also required to notify juveniles of their rights, the direct result of the *Gault* decision.

If a juvenile is detained or taken into custody the parents should be notified. In addition, as a result of the *Gault* decision, the juvenile must be told of his or her rights.

After questioning the juvenile, the police officers must determine whether the juvenile should be referred to the court or returned to his or her parents. Usually, if the offense is relatively minor, the juvenile's attitude and past record are good, and the parents are willing to provide adequate supervision and guidance, the juvenile will be returned to the parents with no further legal action taken.

If the offense is judged to be serious, if the youth has a past record of criminal activity, or if the parents appear unconcerned or nonsupportive of the police's position, the juvenile may be taken to a detention facility and may be referred to the court for a hearing. In such instances all records related to the case should be provided to the judge.

Fingerprinting and Photographing

Whether juveniles should be fingerprinted or photographed is an important issue. Some states allow one or the other but not both. Questions are often raised as to who should have access to these records and for how long. Some states have laws that require the police to purge all juvenile records when the youngster reaches age eighteen.

Some states prohibit fingerprinting or photographing of juveniles. Others permit fingerprinting and photographing, but the records are kept by the department and not released to any other agency.

POLICE SERVICES FOR JUVENILES

The police are also responsible for some specific services involving children.

Police services involving children include helping to locate missing or runaway children, conducting fingerprinting programs, and investigating reports on neglected or abused children.

Missing Children

A missing child is an extremely traumatic experience for parents. In contrast, police officers know that the vast majority of missing children show up safe and well. Frequently they have stopped at a friend's home and forgotten about the time. Despite the fact that most missing children do show up or are found, police officers must not be casual about the situation. It is a critical circumstance in the eyes of the parents.

A complete description of the child and the clothing worn should be obtained, as should a recent picture. Details regarding where the child was last seen and favorite hideaways should also be obtained. Sometimes it is necessary to call in additional help, for example, if a child wandered off into a forest. Local Boy Scout troops can sometimes be called on to assist in such situations. Dogs may also be of help. Time is an important factor because the more time that elapses, the more likely it is that the child will wander farther away or come to harm.

On October 12, 1982, President Reagan signed into law the Missing Children Act, requiring the attorney general to "acquire, collect and preserve any information which would assist in the location of any missing person (including children . . .) and provide confirmation as to any entry (into FBI records) for such a person to the parent, legal guardian or next of kin." What this means, in effect, is that parents, legal guardians, or the next of kin may have access to the information in the FBI National Crime Information Center's (NCIC) Missing Person File.

The law does not, however, require that the FBI investigate the case. It can undertake a preliminary inquiry if an indication exists that a crime has been committed and the child has been transported out of the state.

Because of this law, it is even more important that children be fingerprinted. Many schools have instituted such a program in conjunction with the local police department.

Runaway Children

The same procedures used to search for a missing child might be used to locate a runaway child. Here much depends on the child's age and reason for running away. If the child is a teenager with good reasons for running away, it may be futile to conduct a search.

Runaway children who are found should not automatically be returned to their homes. An investigation should be conducted to see if conditions there are such that they led to the youth leaving. It may be that the youth would be better off in a foster home or even staying with friends for a time.

Neglected or Abused Children

Police are sometimes called upon to investigate reports of neglected or abused children. Eldefonso (1983, p. 12) notes: "Most jurisdictions define as a crime parental abuse or neglect of children, but vary in their criteria for defining what constitutes abuse or neglect. In general, some degree of failure to feed and clothe a child is usually defined as a crime, along with some degree of failure to provide adequate shelter. Most jurisdictions establish discretionary or judgmental statutes with respect to the degree of cleanliness required in homes for children." He lists five conditions that indicate, separately or collectively, the need for action (p. 388):

- Lack of physical care and protection
- Lack of supervision, guidance, and discipline

- Exploitation
- Lack of protection from degrading conditions
- Abuse and fear of physical cruelty

Eldefonso (1983, p. 392) suggests: "The line between neglect and abuse is sometimes difficult to draw, but the two can generally be distinguished in the following way: neglectful parents usually do not consciously intend to harm their children, but through failure to meet children's health, nutritional, comfort and emotional needs, they expose their children to severe risk."

When a law enforcement agency receives a report of child neglect or abuse it may investigate on its own or with personnel from the Welfare Department. No matter what the source of the report or who does the investigating, the primary responsibility of those investigating is the welfare of the child. Any child who appears to be in danger should be removed to protective custody.

According to the Metropolitan Court Judges Committee Report (*Deprived Children* 1985–86, p. 6): "It is estimated that as many as four or five million children are neglected or physically or sexually abused each year, with an additional two million vulnerable as runaways or missing."

THE COURTS AND THE JUVENILE JUSTICE SYSTEM

The usual sequence of events within the court portion of the criminal justice system are illustrated in Figure 20–4.

Laws relating to juvenile courts attempt to secure care and guidance for each minor under the jurisdiction of the court, preferably in the minor's own home. The laws seek to protect the spiritual, emotional, mental, and physical welfare of the minor as well as the best interests of the state. Laws related to juveniles attempt to preserve and strengthen family ties whenever possible, removing minors from parental custody only when the minor's welfare or safety or protection of the public cannot be adequately safeguarded without such removal. When minors are removed from their own families, the courts seek to provide them with custody, care, and discipline as nearly equivalent as possible to that usually given by competent parents.

Juvenile court also has jurisdiction over neglected and dependent children who may suffer from abuse, malnutrition, or unsanitary conditions in the home or who may have been abandoned by their parents. The court also has jurisdiction over those persons who encourage, cause, or contribute to a child's delinquency. Because of the court's scope and clientele, laws relating to juveniles are frequently liberally construed.

Juvenile courts are more concerned with rehabilitation of the juvenile than with punishment. These courts are informal, private, and often do not follow formal judiciary procedures. Although adult courts are based on the adversary system, juvenile courts, in contrast, are nonadversary systems, even though they do have the authority of confinement.

Juvenile courts are informal, private, nonadversary systems that stress rehabilitation rather than punishment of youth.

The court may counsel children, their parents, or guardians or place them in their own homes under the supervision of a probation officer or other suitable person under conditions prescribed by the court. These conditions

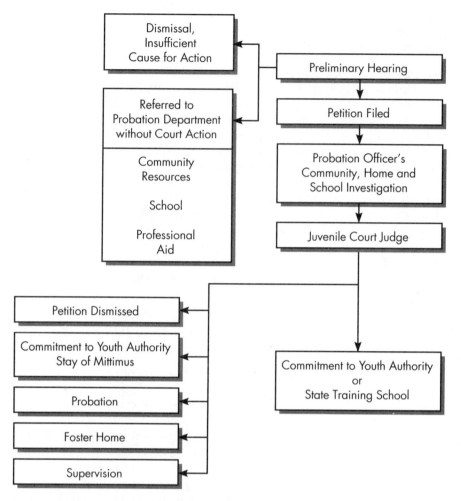

Figure 20–4 Juvenile Court Responsibility

might include rules for their conduct or that of their parents or guardian designed for the physical, mental, and moral well-being of the children.

When it is in the child's best interests, the court can transfer legal custody of the child. It may order the child placed in a foster home or a child-placing agency, committed to a youth conservation commission, transferred to a county welfare agency, or placed in a special facility if the child requires special treatment and care for physical or mental health.

Juvenile courts vary from state to state, but most begin with some sort of intake, which usually begins as a petition against the child. Frequently the petition originates with a law enforcement agency, but it can come from another source such as a school, which can refer truancy or vandalism cases, or parents who may feel they cannot control their children. The intake or initial screening is usually controlled and supervised by the juvenile court. As noted by the President's Commission on Law Enforcement (1967a, p. 14):

> Intake is essentially a screening process to determine whether the court should take action and, if so, what action or whether the matter should be referred elsewhere. Intake is set apart from the screening process used in adult criminal courts by the pervasive attempt to individualize each case and the nature of the personnel administering the discretionary process. In adult proceedings at the post-arrest stage, decisions to screen out are entrusted to the grand jury, the

Although juvenile courts are informal, private, and nonadversarial, they may still be intimidating to youth who appear there.

judge, or usually to the prosecutor. The objective is screening as an end in itself: attempts to deliver service to those screened out are rare. ... At intake in the juvenile courts, screening is an important objective, but referral is an additional goal. Thus, the expressed function of intake is likely to be more ambitious than that of its criminal law counterpart and the function is performed chiefly by persons who are neither legally trained or significantly restricted in the exercise requirements comparable to those of the criminal law.

Most referrals to juvenile court are for property crimes, but 17 percent are for status offenses.

In addition, the National Advisory Commission on Criminal Justice Standards and Goals (1973, p. 296) recommends that intake units should do the following:

1. Make the initial decision whether to place a juvenile referred to the court in detention or shelter care.
2. Make the decision whether to offer a juvenile referred to the court the opportunity to participate in diversion programs.
3. Make, in consultation with the prosecutor, the decision whether to make a formal petition in the court alleging that the juvenile is delinquent and ask that the family court assume jurisdiction over him.

At the adjudication hearing, considered to be part of the preliminary hearing, the youth is questioned about the alleged offense. The National Advisory Commission on Criminal Justice Standards and Goals (1973, pp. 302, 474) recommends the following procedures for adjudicatory hearings:

At the adjudicatory hearing, the juvenile alleged to be delinquent should be afforded all of the rights given a defendant in adult criminal prosecution, except that trial by jury should not be available in delinquency cases.

In all delinquency cases a legal officer representing the state should be present in court to present evidence supporting the allegation of delinquency.

The defense counsel should use all methods permissible in a criminal prosecution to prevent determination that the juvenile is delinquent. He should function as the advocate for the juvenile, and his performance should be unaffected by any belief he might have that a finding of delinquency might be in the best interests of the juvenile. As advocate for the juvenile alleged to be delinquent, counsel's actions should not be affected by the wishes of the juvenile's parents or guardian if those differ from the wishes of the juvenile.

At the adjudication hearing, the petition may be dismissed, or, if there is enough evidence that the child is delinquent, a court date is set for the *disposition hearing.*

Ideally, enough time should be allowed between the adjudication and disposition hearings for the probation officer to make a thorough investigation of the case, including an evaluation of the child's home and school environment, the child's attitude and behavior at home and in the neighborhood, school, and community, and the amount of supervision provided at home. Often, however, the disposition hearing is the second half of the adjudication hearing.

At the disposition hearing the judge has several alternatives. Based on the findings of the investigation, the judge may put the youth on probation, place the youth in a foster home, release the child to the parents, commit the child to an institution, or make the child a ward of the court so as to receive the required supervision. The National Advisory Commission on Criminal Justice Standards and Goals recommends that the procedures followed at the disposition hearing be identical to those followed in sentencing adult offenders.

More serious juvenile offenders have been committed to mental institutions, reformatories, prisons, and county and state schools for delinquents. Some cities, such as New York and Chicago, have set up youth courts that are adult courts using the philosophy of juvenile courts. These youth courts usually confine their hearings to misdemeanors.

Abadinsky (1991, p. 292) suggests: "Judges are often faced with few options at dispositional hearings, something that accounts for the frequent use of probation even when this is not in the best interests of the child and the community."

Adabinsky (1991, p. 292) also notes that juvenile judges need special training in dealing with youth and that "many, if not most, judges have little or no experience with children of lower-class groups, those youngsters most likely to be found in juvenile court." In addition, the juvenile court is a "bench with relatively low prestige." Because of this judges often seek transfer, having a "destabilizing influence" on the juvenile court.

Further, the role of the defense attorney is "fraught with ambivalence" according to Abadinsky because juvenile court is not based on the adversary system. The role of the defense attorney is not clearly delineated.

Waiver to Adult Court

When a juvenile has committed a series of serious crimes, juvenile courts have the legal power to adjudicate anyone under their jurisdiction as an adult. The juvenile is then charged and required to appear in an adult court.

According to the Bureau of Justice Statistics (1984, p. 61): "All states allow juveniles to be tried as adults in criminal courts." This may occur in one of three ways:

> *Judicial waiver*—the juvenile court waives its jurisdiction and transfers the case to criminal court (the procedure is also known as "binding over," "transferring," or "certifying" juvenile cases to criminal courts).

Concurrent jurisdiction—the prosecutor has the discretion of filing charges for certain offenses in either juvenile or criminal courts.

Excluded offenses—the legislature excludes from juvenile court jurisdiction certain offenses, usually either very minor, such as traffic or fishing violations, or very serious, such as murder or rape.

Abadinsky (1991, p. 291) expands on three circumstances in which juveniles can be tried in adult criminal court:

- *Judicial waiver.* All states except Arkansas, Nebraska, and New York allow juvenile court judges to transfer their jurisdiction to adult court. This discretion is limited by statutory criteria usually related to age, type of offense, prior record, amenability to treatment and dangerousness.
- *Prosecutorial discretion.* Eight states empower prosecutors to charge juveniles in either juvenile or adult courts. Again, the discretionary power is limited by statutory criteria regarding age and type of offense.
- *Legislative exclusion.* Fourteen states have statutes excluding certain crimes from juvenile court jurisdiction. For example, in Illinois, juveniles fifteen years of age or older charged with murder, aggravated criminal sexual assault, or armed robbery with a firearm are automatically tried in adult court.

CORRECTIONS AND THE JUVENILE JUSTICE SYSTEM

The usual flow in the corrections portion of the juvenile justice system is illustrated in Figure 20–5.

The philosophy of juvenile court is that ideally children should be kept in their homes pending a hearing. If detention is required for their own welfare or the public safety, it must not be in jails or police stations but in temporary quarters such as boarding homes, protective agency homes, or specially con-

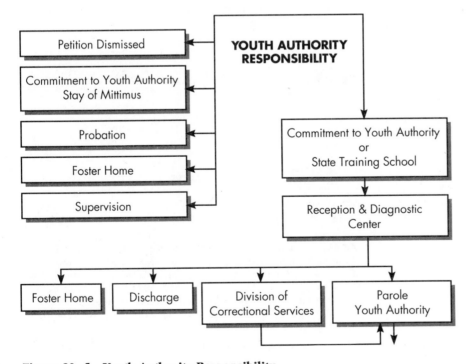

Figure 20–5 Youth Authority Responsibility

structed detention homes. The realization of these ideals of the juvenile court system, even in some of the largest United States cities, is far from complete. In many small towns and rural districts no such facilities exist. Although juvenile court acts as the protector of the child, children are still subjected to adverse publicity, criminal procedure, jail detention, and ineffective treatment because of the lack of proper facilities.

According to Pursley (1980, p. 417): "A number of federal courts are now ruling that the confinement of a juvenile in a county jail for adults is in violation of the provision against 'cruel and unusual punishment' of the Eighth Amendment."

The age at which criminal courts gain jurisdiction of youth is summarized in Table 20–4.

The disposition of juveniles and the problem of the juvenile can be partially gauged by the number of facilities existing in the United States to care for wayward youth.

Facilities other than punitive correctional institutions for juveniles include reception and diagnostic centers; detention centers; training schools; shelters; ranches, forestry camps, and farms; group homes; and halfway houses.

Reception and diagnostic centers screen juvenile court commitments and assign them to appropriate treatment facilities.

Detention centers provide temporary care in a physically restrictive environment for juveniles in custody pending court disposition and often for juveniles who have been adjudicated delinquent or are awaiting return to another jurisdiction.

Training schools provide strict confinement and instruction in vocational skills. They serve delinquent juveniles committed to them by juvenile courts or placed in them by an agency with such authority.

Shelters provide temporary care similar to that of detention centers but in a physically unrestrictive environment.

Table 20–4 **Age at Which Criminal Courts Gain Jurisdiction of Youth**	
AGE OF OFFENDER WHEN UNDER CRIMINAL COURT JURISDICTION	STATES
16 years	Connecticut, New York, North Carolina
17	Georgia, Illinois, Louisiana, Massachusetts, Michigan, Missouri, South Carolina, Texas
18	Alabama, Alaska, Arizona, Arkansas, California, Colorado, Delaware, District of Columbia, Florida, Hawaii, Idaho, Indiana, Iowa, Kansas, Kentucky, Maine, Maryland, Minnesota, Mississippi, Montana, Nebraska, Nevada, New Hampshire, New Jersey, New Mexico, North Dakota, Ohio, Oklahoma, Oregon, Pennsylvania, Rhode Island, South Dakota, Tennessee, Utah, Vermont, Virginia, Washington, West Virginia, Wisconsin, Federal districts
19	Wyoming

Source: L. A. Szymanski. "Upper Age of Juvenile Court Jurisdiction Statutes Analysis." National Center for Juvenile Justice, March 1987.

Ranches, forestry camps, and farms are residential treatment facilities for juveniles who do not require strict confinement such as in training schools. These ranches, camps, and farms allow juveniles greater contact with members of the community.

Group homes are residences that allow juveniles extensive contact with the community through jobs and schools. Seldom are juveniles placed in group homes on probation or parole.

Halfway houses provide nonrestrictive residential group living where 50 percent or more of the juveniles are on probation or parole. The juveniles are allowed extensive community contact through jobs and schools.

Treatment facilities, especially residential type facilities, for juveniles can be very expensive. Abadinsky (1991, p. 292) notes that costs for residential facilities can easily run to over $35,000 per youngster per year.

In addition to providing facilities for juveniles who have already become delinquent, many communities are attempting to meet the problem of juvenile delinquency by programs that stress prevention rather than rehabilitation, for example, police-school liaison programs as discussed in Chapter 9.

Reforming Corrections

Schwartz (1992, p. 178) notes: "Fighting juvenile crime is a multibillion-dollar business in the United States. State and local politicians and juvenile justice officials will spend approximately $1.5 billion in 1990 just to incarcerate young offenders in detention centers, youth training schools, and juvenile prisons. In spite of these expenditures, studies show recidivism rates as high as 75 percent or more.

Schwartz describes the steps taken by Massachusetts' Department of Youth Services (DYS) (p. 179) fifteen years ago:

> They closed down all of their large juvenile training schools. In their place, they developed a network of small (fifteen- to twenty-bed units) high-security treat-

Sumter County Correctional Institution "Boot Camp" in Bushnell, Florida. Here juvenile offenders experience militaristic training and discipline.

Officers can play an important
role in educating youth about
crime and its hazards. This
S.W.A.T. officer from the K-9
unit has the complete attention
of these high-school students.

ment centers for violent and chronic juvenile offenders. Today, there are only
184 secure treatment beds in the state.... For all other juvenile offenders committed to the state's Department of Youth Services (DYS), the state youth correction authority, Massachusetts developed a diverse network of community-
based programs that provide intensive surveillance and supervision, and enriched
educational employment, counseling, and other appropriate services. These programs are largely delivered by private providers under contract with the state.

Schwartz notes that the Massachusetts youth correction system was evaluated
by the National Council on Crime and Delinquency who found (p. 179):

> Juveniles placed in the custody of DYS committed "far fewer offenses after en-
> tering DYS," and for those who did commit new offenses "there was a tendency
> to commit less serious crimes." In particular, "violent and serious property of-
> fenders committed to DYS reduced the frequency and severity of their criminal
> activities."
>
> The overall rates of recidivism for DYS were as low or lower than any other
> state that the researchers compared Massachusetts with.

Utah also instituted a similar approach in 1980. It, too, was evaluated by the
National Council on Crime and Delinquency and it found (Schwartz 1992,
p. 179): "Utah's shift in policies to limit incarceration to those youth who were
violent and chronic repeaters and to manage the others in highly structured
and individualized community-based programs was cost-effective and did not
compromise public safety."

REDUCING JUVENILE DELINQUENCY

Traditionally the police officer's role was clearly defined: arrest lawbreakers and
preserve the peace. Although historically the police have been viewed as punitive and authoritarian, this view is changing. Rather than simply apprehending

and punishing offenders, police officers now also seek to educate and to promote prevention of crime. Modern approaches to juvenile delinquency take several forms, but all have in common a goal of preventing juvenile delinquency.

Knowledge of Indicators of Potential for Delinquent Behavior by Juveniles

Certain factors may indicate that a youngster has the potential for or actually is involved in delinquent behavior. Police should learn to recognize these factors and take appropriate actions, considering community resources and school and police department policies.

Police officers are in a unique position to help juveniles because they are usually the first persons of authority to confront the juvenile offender during or following a delinquent act. Additionally, police officers are often familiar with the youngsters in their patrol area whose behavior marks them as potential delinquents, and they have the authority to reprimand, release, or refer youngsters to court.

Environmental factors potentially contributing to delinquency include broken homes, criminal parents, incompetent parents, erratic discipline, economic insecurity, impoverished neighborhoods, transient populations, and racial and other tensions.

Personal factors or behavior indicating potential delinquency include unsociability, cheating, lying, fighting, temper tantrums, anxiety, guilt feelings, hostility and aggression, laziness, truancy, running away from home, and a rebellious attitude.

The environmental and personal factors may be complicated by misuses of alcohol, narcotics, and drugs, by economic factors, by physical disabilities, by sexual problems, or by numerous other factors. The result is frequently youths who show overwhelming symptoms of weakness and inadequacy. They cannot accept life as it is, cannot conform, cannot get along, cannot compete, or cannot exercise self-control.

The sooner a police officer recognizes such youngsters and attempts to work with them, the greater the chance that the juveniles will not become delinquents.

Recognizing factors that contribute to juvenile delinquency is important for all involved in the criminal justice system.

SUMMARY

The juvenile justice system has developed through four phases in the United States: (1) a Puritan emphasis with severe penalties for juvenile crime (1776–1824), (2) an emphasis on providing a refuge for youth (1824–1899), (3) development of a separate juvenile court (1899–1960), and (4) emphasis on juvenile rights (1960 to present). Important in the evolution of the juvenile justice system has been the *parens patriae* doctrine, which makes the state legally responsible for the children within that state, providing a legal foundation for state intervention in family control.

The most recent phase, that emphasizing juvenile rights, has included several landmark Supreme Court decisions. *Kent v. United States* established that as a valid waiver order to adult criminal court, juveniles are entitled to a hearing, their counsel must be given access to probation records used by the court in reaching its decision, and the court must state its reasons for waiving jurisdiction over the case.

The *Gault* decision required that the due process clause of the Fourteenth Amendment be applied to proceedings in state juvenile courts, including the right of notice, the right to counsel, the right against self-incrimination, and the right to confront witnesses.

The *Winship* decision established that a juvenile defendant must be found guilty beyond a reasonable doubt. And *McKeiver v. Pennsylvania* established that a jury trial is not a constitutional right of juveniles.

In the 1990s the juvenile system is continually seeking to balance the informality and protective emphasis of the *parens patriae* doctrine with the constitutional rights of juveniles charged with crimes.

Traditionally the juvenile courts have operated under a welfare model, focusing on the best interests of the child. Some advocate that this model be changed to a justice model where youth are held responsible for their crimes and punished for them.

The police usually are the youth's initial contact with the juvenile justice system. They have broad discretion and may release juveniles to their parents, refer them to other agencies, place them in detention, or refer them to juvenile court. If a juvenile is detained or taken into custody the parents should be notified. In addition, as a result of the *Gault* decision, the juvenile must be told of his or her rights. An additional precaution is that in some states, fingerprinting or photographing juveniles is prohibited.

In addition, police are often responsible for providing other services involving children, including helping to locate missing or runaway children, conducting fingerprinting programs, and investigating reports of neglected or abused children.

Juvenile courts are informal, private, nonadversary systems that stress rehabilitation rather than punishment of youth. Facilities other than punitive correctional institutions for juveniles include reception and diagnostic centers; detention centers; training schools; shelters; ranches, forestry camps, and farms; group homes; and halfway houses. In addition to providing facilities for juveniles who have already become delinquent, many communities are attempting to meet the problem of juvenile delinquency by programs that stress prevention, for example, police-school liaison programs.

DISCUSSION QUESTIONS

1. Do juvenile courts too often stress rehabilitation and keeping youngsters in the home?

2. Are parents required to testify against their children in court?

3. What correctional facilities are available for juvenile delinquents in your area? Your state?

4. Do you feel the process of justice should be the same for juveniles as it is for adults?

5. Do you feel juveniles should have the right to a jury trial?

6. In what noncriminal matters does the juvenile court become involved?

7. Should police officers have as much discretionary power as they have with juveniles? Why or why not?

8. Does your community have a police-school liaison program? If so, how effective does it seem to be? How popular does it seem to be?

9. What other community relations programs for juveniles are offered by your police department?

10. Does your police department have a separate juvenile division, or do police officers have the responsibility for dealing with juveniles?

TERMS

justice model, *parens patriae,* status offenses, welfare model.

REFERENCES

Abadinsky, H. *Law and Justice: An Introduction to the American Legal System.* 2d ed. Chicago: Nelson-Hall Publishers, 1991.

Arnold, W. R. and Brungardt, T. *Juvenile Misconduct and Delinquency.* Boston: Houghton Mifflin, 1983.

Bureau of Justice Statistics. *Report to the Nation on Crime and Justice.* Washington, D.C.: U.S. Government Printing Office, 1984.

Deprived Children: A Judicial Response. Metropolitan Court Judges Committee Report, National Council of Juvenile or Family Court Judges, 1985–86.

Eldefonso, E. *Law Enforcement and the Youthful Offender.* 4th ed. New York: John Wiley and Sons, 1983.

McCreedy, K. R. *Juvenile Justice—System and Procedures.* Albany, N.Y.: Delmar Publishers, 1975.

National Advisory Commission on Criminal Justice Standards and Goals. *Corrections.* Washington, D.C.: U.S. Government Printing Office, 1973.

President's Commission on Law Enforcement and Administration of Justice. *Task Force Report: Juvenile Delinquency and Youth Crime.* Washington, D.C.: U.S. Government Printing Office, 1967a.

Pursley, R. D. *Introduction to Criminal Justice.* 3d ed. New York: Macmillan, 1980.

Regnery, A. S. "Getting Away with Murder," pp. 164–170 in *Taking Sides: Clashing Views on Controversial Issues in Crime and Criminology.* 2d ed., edited by R. C. Monk. Guilford, Conn.: The Dushkin Publishing Group, 1991. (Reprinted from *Policy Review,* the quarterly publication of the Heritage Foundation, 1985.)

Schwartz, I. M. "Correcting Juvenile Corrections." pp. 178–180 in *Criminal Justice 92/93,* edited by J. J. Sullivan and J. L. Victor. Guilford, Conn.: The Dushkin Publishing Group, 1992. (Reprinted from *The World & I,* April 1990, pp. 505–507.)

Springer, C. E. *Justice for Juveniles.* Washington, D.C.: U.S. Department of Justice, Office of Juvenile Justice and Delinquency Prevention, 1986.

Szymanski, L. A. "Upper Age of Juvenile Court Jurisdiction Statutes Analysis." National Center for Juvenile Justice, March 1987.

Trojanowicz, R. C. *Juvenile Delinquency, Concepts and Control.* 2d ed. Englewood Cliffs, N.J.: Prentice-Hall, 1978.

Territo, L.; Halsted, J. B.; and Bromley, M. L. *Crime and Justice in America: A Human Perspective.* St. Paul, Minn.: West Publishing Company, 1992.

Critical Issues in Criminal Justice: Challenges of the 1990s

He who will not reason, is a bigot; he who cannot is a fool; and he who dares not is a slave.

—William Drummond

Do You Think

Some provisions of the Bill of Rights are controversial?

Some crimes might be decriminalized?

Plea bargaining is in the best interests of society?

Police are responsible for the mentally ill, the publicly inebriated, and the homeless?

Prison inmates with AIDS or who test HIV-positive should be segregated? Inmates should be provided with condoms? Tested for AIDS?

Women are being better accepted in policing?

Police have an image problem?

Police officers need a college education?

Privatization of certain responsibilities usually assumed by the criminal justice system is positive or negative?

Public and private law enforcement differ?

Civilian review boards are positive or negative?

Police departments should be unionized?

Police departments should be accredited?

Law enforcement is a profession?

INTRODUCTION

The criminal justice system has several vital issues facing it in the last decade of the twentieth century. The issues encompass law enforcement, the courts, and corrections. Several issues affect all three.

Notice that this chapter begins with "Do You Think?" questions rather than "Do You Know?" because the topics discussed have no correct answers. They are controversial issues, most of which will remain challenges for the criminal justice profession into the twenty-first century. Those who are a part of this profession should consider each issue carefully and thoughtfully.

Notice also, that some of the subjects have been introduced earlier in the text. This chapter serves as a reminder of the many issues pervading the entire criminal justice field.

INTERPRETING THE BILL OF RIGHTS

The law is a living reality that encourages the opening of new avenues of human conduct. As Oliver Wendell Holmes put it: "The life of the law has not been logic; it has been experience." People who view the Bill of Rights as an outdated document fail to see that it is the best structure so far in history for a growing society with changing institutions.

Controversial issues related to the Bill of Rights include:
Gun control—The Second Amendment.
The Exclusionary Rule and the *Miranda* decision—The Fourth and Fifth Amendments.
Capital punishment—The Eighth Amendment.

The Second Amendment is a continuing source of controversy. Those who oppose gun control state that outlawing handguns would arm criminals and

Guns are a recognized part of policing, but controversy exists over who else should be allowed to own guns, and what kind of guns.

disarm law-abiding citizens. They say the criminals will get guns anyway. The question revolves around whether the government should regulate handguns—the number-one weapon of killers. Some eighteen thousand murders occur every year in the United States, often committed by "law-abiding" people shooting other "law-abiding" people. In addition, an average of more than ninety police officers are slain by handguns every year.

Some polls consistently show that the majority of United States citizens support sensible handgun legislation. When Massachusetts held a referendum proposing to ban handguns, however, it was defeated by a 70 percent majority. Possibly they realized what New York's tough gun law has shown: if only one state outlaws guns, a person can easily get one in another state.

According to Farah (1992, p. 15A): "The L.A. riots prove that we need more guns for our protection." He notes:

> During the heat of the Los Angeles riots, some normally politically correct residents of the Hollywood Hills barricaded major entrances to their neighborhoods with automobiles, patrolled the streets with AR-15s and handed out firearms to any law-abiding homeowner who would take one. . . .
>
> Throughout Los Angeles and the nation, people cheered the defiant and courageous Koreatown shopkeepers who stood watch over their property with weapons.
>
> Suddenly, restrictive gun-control laws, 15-day waiting periods and even bans on those nasty "assault rifles" didn't seem like such a great idea any more. Could it be that the Founding Fathers knew what they were doing, after all, when they drafted the Second Amendment? . . .
>
> Would the kind of widespread looting and violence Los Angeles witnessed in the aftermath of the verdict have been likely, or even possible, if more law-abiding citizens were armed?

Controversy also exists over the Exclusionary Rule and the *Miranda* decision. Recall that the Exclusionary Rule disallows the introduction of illegally seized evidence in a trial, and the *Miranda* decision forbids confessions as evidence if the suspects have not been informed of their constitutional rights. The Exclusionary Rule has been regularly challenged in our courts. Opponents of the rule say that it penalizes society and rewards the defendant for any mistakes made by the police. When the *Miranda* decision was handed down in 1966, many people felt the criminals were decidedly given the upper hand; consequently the Supreme Court came under blistering attack from some police, prosecutors, and citizens. Since 1966 twenty-two states have sought to overturn the *Miranda* decision through the Supreme Court, but to no avail. Today's police officers are functioning and performing their jobs better than before *Miranda*; they are not hindered by it. Police officers, above all others, ought to obey the laws. Further, withdrawal of the rights provided by the Fourth and Fifth Amendments could lead to a police state.

Another controversial amendment is the Eighth Amendment, which forbids "cruel and unusual punishment." The question of capital punishment has been in the courts for the past quarter-century. In 1976 the Supreme Court ruled that states that used certain guidelines could pass laws allowing them to execute convicted murderers, but the Court reserved any decision on whether the death penalty is constitutional for any other crime. Still unresolved are such questions as how far prosecutors can go in making emotional charges in their closing arguments to a jury in a capital punishment case and whether rape can be punished by death.

DECRIMINALIZATION

The basic issues involved in decriminalization are: If a crime is victimless, is there really a crime? Can you legislate morality?

According to Williams, Formby, and Watkins (1982, p. 336): "The overreach of modern American criminal law is notorious. We have for years operated under a 'pass a law' syndrome regarding the criminalization of behavior deemed distasteful or dangerous by the lawmaking branch of government. Such a state of affairs has placed an enormous strain on all segments of the criminal justice establishment."

Obviously, the criminal justice system has limited resources. Should it not concentrate those resources on the Part I offenses such as murder, robbery, and rape?

Unfortunately, the crime-related portion of most police officers' responsibilities is devoted to lesser offenses such as prostitution or gambling. Decriminalization of certain offenses would allow concentration of resources on serious crime and might also legalize certain actions, such as gambling and prostitution, that are major revenue sources for organized crime. The acts now considered criminal might be engaged in more frequently by law-abiding citizens if they were decriminalized, however, thus lowering our country's moral standards.

Williams, Formby, and Watkins (1982, p. 337) say if "the offense so repealed is one that has heretofore created and sustained a major underground or blackmarket operation, a repeal may mean that such endeavors will ultimately cease operation because of the now legal nature of the enterprise." Legalization of drugs such as cocaine, heroin, and crack falls within this area.

Trebach (1991, p. 304), an advocate of legalizing drugs, says:

> There's no way you can have a war on a chemical. What you really have is a war on a significant segment of the American people. Roughly one in four Americans used an illegal drug within the past 12 months, so what you're saying is that we're going to go to war against 25 percent of the American people. That's a civil war.

Opponents, on the other hand, note that drugs aren't bad because they are illegal. They are illegal because they are bad. Legalizing them would make the problem worse.

Law-Abiding Citizens Select the Laws They Obey

Many good citizens disobey the law every day and justify it as "not hurting anyone else." For example, countless citizens break speed laws, drive after drinking, and pilfer from their employers.

Decriminalization would likely focus on those crimes that are now selectively enforced and would return emphasis to the more serious crimes. Offenses that would be candidates for decriminalization include prostitution, sexual activities between consenting adults, gambling, public drunkenness, certain types of juvenile delinquency (status offenses), narcotics and drug offenses, vagrancy, and disorderly conduct. This would conserve resources that have come to be overextended in many communities.

Nearly two decades ago, the National Advisory Commission on Criminal Justice Standards and Goals (1973a) recommended that the states "reevaluate laws on gambling, marijuana use and possession for use, pornography, prostitution, and sexual acts between consenting adults in private. Such reevaluation should determine if current laws best serve the purpose of the state and the needs of the public."

This recommendation is reiterated by Williams, Formby, and Watkins (1982, p. 339): "Criminal justice policymakers in the 1980s and beyond must come to grips with the criminal laws' overreach. Until such is done, we will continue to have a system of criminal law enforcement in the United States that is administratively cumbersome, selectively unjust, and economically wasteful."

Offenses that would be candidates for decriminalization include prostitution, sexual activities between consenting adults, gambling, public drunkenness, certain types of juvenile delinquency (status offenses), narcotics and drug offenses, vagrancy, and disorderly conduct.

The following extracts from the National Advisory Committee on Criminal Justice Standards and Goals (1976, pp. 230–232) summarize the arguments for and against reform or decriminalization.

General Arguments for Reform

It is not the proper function of government or the criminal justice system to regulate private morality or behavior through criminal laws; that is the role of nonlegal institutions.

The laws are ineffective. They do not deter involvement in the proscribed activities, either by organized crime or the public. Neither fines or jail rehabilitate or alter the behavior of offenders.

The laws are unenforceable. The volume of activity is too great, public support is lacking and criminal justice systems resources are inadequate.

There is no evidence that legalization/decriminalization will lead to a harmful increase in immoral behavior. The activities are already easily accessible to anyone who wants them.

The rights of individuals to live as they want, so long as they do not harm others, is a fundamental principle on which this nation was founded.

There is no proof that the moral standards of the country are declining, or that the nation as a whole is being negatively affected by victimless crimes.

The burden of proof that harm results from these crimes should rest with those wishing to impose sanctions, not with participants in the activities.

Society cannot morally declare persons to be victims when they do not see themselves as such.

Even if the law's function is to provide symbolic guidance for a correct standard of behavior, it is questionable that the laws against victimless crimes guide people in the right direction. Instead, they may engender cynicism and disrespect for the criminal justice and legal systems and for government in general.

The laws are hypocritical. They allow some activities while proscribing others that are comparable; they penalize some people involved in an activity, but not others.

More realistic and well-founded policies must be developed. Current policies are based on emotion, outdated moral norms and values, and inaccurate information. Using up-to-date information on the effects of an activity, and bearing in mind the many priorities to be met, policymakers must weigh the costs of an activity against the costs of ineffective laws. Goals and effective approaches must then be developed.

The laws have many hidden costs: creation of a class of criminals who would not otherwise be considered criminals; discriminatory, arbitrary, and selective application of the laws; unsavory and often degrading tactics employed by the police to obtain evidence or make arrests; increase in crime associated with victimless crimes; creation of subcultures of criminals who reinforce one another's behavior; overburdening the criminal justice system; creation of antagonism among minority youth toward police as a result of enforcement that hits the inner city hardest; and failure to afford constitutional rights to the accused because of efforts to process cases quickly.

There is a lack of public support for the laws.

Overemphasis on the law blunts efforts to find other solutions to abuses of the proscribed activities.

The basis on which the laws were originally promulgated no longer apply; social mores and values have changed, and new information on the effects of the activities contradicts previously held theories and assumptions.

General Arguments against Reform

The activities known as victimless crimes are antithetical to Christian beliefs and the principles on which the nation was founded.

Modification of the sanctions against these activities will result in a disastrous increase in their occurrence. This in turn will lead to a moral decline of society. The nation will become a second class power. Both the Greek and Roman civilizations were destroyed by the decadence of their citizenry.

Because morality affects the viability of a nation, it is a proper function of government to regulate morality by the use of criminal laws.

Laws are a reflection of social values and should be used, even symbolically, as a guide to proper behavior.

There has never been a serious, sustained effort to enforce the laws, so it is inaccurate to say the statutes are ineffective. A reform government backed by the public can wipe out organized crime, vice, and corruption.

Better law enforcement in terms of other crimes will not necessarily result from freeing resources by modifying the victimless crime laws, for "There is no empirical evidence that the police do a better job of protecting persons and property." (Goldberg, p. 56, 1972) Perhaps there is a limit to the amount of resources a police department can effectively spend.

There are better ways to combat corruption than eliminating the victimless crime laws. Legalization will not eliminate the temptation to corrupt, because it will involve new regulations.

It is traditional in this country for government to protect individuals from themselves. For example, the state requires motorcycle drivers and riders to wear helmets.

The fact that a law seems unenforceable is no reason to abolish it. For example, murder and theft laws are not 100 percent enforceable but are nevertheless needed. A preferable alternative to abolishing the victimless crime laws is providing more resources to implement them.

The laws do not serve as deterrents because they are not strictly enforced and the sanctions are not strong enough.

If the criminal justice system is overburdened, the answer is not to eliminate certain laws. It is to increase the resources available to it.

If the laws result in more related crime, enforcement efforts should be stepped up.

There are not enough hard facts on the impact of victimless crimes to justify modifying the laws.

THE PLEA BARGAINING
CONTROVERSY

599
CHAPTER TWENTY-ONE
Critical Issues in Criminal Justice:
Challenges of the 1990s

As previously discussed in Chapter 18, plea bargaining is a system whereby a defendant pleads guilty to a crime in exchange for a reduced punishment. According to Levine, Husheno, and Palumbo (1980, p. 214): "In many courts, more than 90 percent of criminal convictions are not obtained by the verdict of a jury or the decision of a judge. Rather, they are based upon the defendant's own plea of guilty. . . . But, many people oppose plea bargaining and argue that it provides few benefits for courts, criminal defendants, or the public. Since nearly all cases are settled short of a trial, plea bargaining is a central feature of the judicial process and we need to evaluate carefully its place in American justice."

Glick (1983, pp. 164–165) also notes:

Once a prosecutor decides to pursue a case and a judge refuses to grant motions to dismiss, *the chances of conviction are overwhelming.* Usually the crimes involved are serious or the evidence against defendants is so clear that the chances of being acquitted of a crime are extremely remote. Some readily plead guilty because they recognize the odds are against them and want to put an end to the stress and disruption. They simply want to get out of the system. Others plead guilty because they expect leniency or have negotiated specific bargains with prosecutors and judges.

The mechanics and details of bargained guilty pleas vary considerably. Arrangements may involve reducing criminal charges to less serious crimes, dropping certain charges altogether, promising light sentences for guilty pleas to original charges, and possible combinations. Whatever the arrangements, the key element to any bargain is that in return for pleading guilty and avoiding a trial, cooperative defendants expect to receive lighter sentences. Through plea bargaining, almost all cases end with convictions, but not with trials.

Plea bargaining not only involves avoiding a trial, but also the defendant surrendering such constitutional rights as the right to take the witness stand, the right to confront witnesses against him or her, the right to trial by jury, and the right to be assumed innocent until proven guilty by proof beyond a reasonable doubt. Levine, Husheno, and Palumbo (1980, p. 42) warn: "A system that encourages the waiver of such fundamental rights is defensible only if it deals justly with the person waiving those rights. On the other hand, plea bargaining also affects the police, who have accumulated evidence of guilt; the victim, who has suffered at the hands of the offender; and the public at large, who demand protection against future offenses. These interests also must be dealt with justly in the plea negotiation process, or the process is as indefensible as if it violated the rights of the offender."

A high percentage of cases are settled through plea bargaining. While plea bargaining is acknowledged to be a central part of the judicial process, some critics warn that it might not be in the best interests of society at large.

The case *Bordenkircher v. Hayes* (1978) expanded the power of plea bargaining from the prosecution's side, upholding the prosecutor's right to threaten criminal defendants with more serious charges if they refuse to plead guilty to the charges offered. In this case Hayes was indicted by a grand jury for forging an $88.30 check. In pretrial meetings the prosecutor told Hayes and his lawyer that if Hayes pleaded guilty, making a trial unnecessary, the prose-

Table 21-1   **Arguments for and against Plea Bargaining**

Pro: Allows courts to move cases quickly and efficiently.

Lightens the burden on judges, prosecutors, lawyers, and other court employees. Spares victims the stress and possible humiliation of public trial. Cooperative defendants are screened from the system and receive reduced penalties for not requiring everyone to prepare for a trial. Allows the punishment to fit the crime and the individual criminal. Few professional, hardened criminals are allowed to go free.

Con: Cheapens the image of justice by using hurried, secret negotiations to obtain convictions. The prosecutor comes out ahead by the guilty plea and the defendant gets the best deal he or she can on the sentence.Places pressure on defendants to plead guilty.Forces defendants to give up constitutional protections and safeguards.Legal errors made by police, prosecutors, or trial judges can rarely be reviewed by an appellate court.Amounts to a coerced confession, which violates the Fifth Amendment.Produces sentences that are too lenient.

cution would recommend a five-year sentence. (The sentence under Kentucky law, where the case was being tried, would have carried a sentence of two to ten years.) The prosecutor also said that since Hayes had two previous felony convictions, if he refused to plead guilty, prosecution would seek a new indictment—a habitual offender charge, which would bring a life sentence. Hayes refused to plea bargain, was convicted, and was sentenced to life. His appeal to the United States Circuit Court of Appeals was that the prosecutor's "reverse plea-bargaining" violated Hayes's due process rights. This appeal was granted, but then overturned by the United States Supreme Court, which said prosecutors must have broad discretionary powers in plea bargaining.

Glick (1983, pp. 165–167) sets forth numerous arguments for and against plea bargaining, as summarized in Table 21–1.

RESPONDING TO CALLS REGARDING "SPECIAL POPULATIONS"

Finn and Sullivan (1988, p. 205) contend: "Handling the mentally ill is perhaps the single most difficult type of call for law enforcement officers. Today, these encounters are becoming more frequent." In many instances, the police are the only ones available to deal with incidents involving the mentally ill. Most police officers have limited training in how to do so.

Likewise, the police are often called to deal with individuals who are inebriated in public. Frequently store owners or business people will call the police to remove such individuals from outside their establishments, complaining that they are panhandling or otherwise disturbing customers or clients. As noted by Finn and Sullivan (1988, p. 205):

> A recent National Institute of Justice study found that limited bed space and selective admission practices at detoxification and other alcoholism facilities have curtailed the ability of the police to transport public inebriates to health care facilities. Jail crowding and the perception that the station house lockup is an inappropriate place to take the public drunk increasingly limit other police alternatives.

Another "special population" police officers are receiving numerous calls to "handle" are homeless individuals. Finn and Sullivan note: "The homeless have a dampening effect on business, and they invite crime by creating an appearance of community neglect." The police, however, have few options available to them.

Increasingly police officers are being called to deal with mentally ill, publicly inebriated, and homeless individuals. Their options for handling such calls are limited.

Other social service agencies should provide assistance in this area. Law enforcement agencies should establish a network of support services to which they can refer individuals in need of help.

PRISON INMATES WITH AIDS

"Inside the walls of American prisons, convicts call it 'the package,' " according to Sullivan and Victor (1991, p. 205). They note: "AIDS, an agonizing, protracted form of execution, has created a new death row, more dreaded than the old."

A study by the Justice Department found only 3,136 confirmed cases of AIDS behind bars, less than 4 percent of the national total (Sullivan and Victor). This relatively low incidence may be in part due to precautions taken by the inmates, reducing such high risk behavior as unsafe sex, sharing smuggled drugs and needles, and being tattooed.

Issues related to inmates and AIDS:

■ Should inmates with AIDS or who test HIV-positive be segregated?

■ Should inmates be routinely tested?

■ Should those with AIDS be given "compassionate release" parole?

■ Should they be allowed access to condoms?

One big question for prison administrators is what to do with inmates who have AIDS or who test positive for HIV. Some administrators are using segregation, but not always without violent reactions. In an AIDS unit in the California Institution for Men in Chino, for example, fifteen HIV-positive inmates broke 220 windows to protest being segregated.

Another issue is whether inmates should be routinely tested. As noted by Sullivan and Victor, many inmates have died prematurely because prison doctors misdiagnosed their symptoms. A study conducted in New York found that the mean survival of AIDS inmates was 128 days, almost eight months less than for individuals "on the outside."

Also at issue is whether inmates with AIDS should be given "compassionate release" parole and allowed to go home to die. California and New York use such parole for their inmates with AIDS in select cases.

Allowing inmates access to condoms for "safe sex" is another very controversial issue. According to Sullivan and Victor:

> Prisons in Vermont and Mississippi, as well as New York City jails, make prophylactics available. But in Bible-belt Mississippi, where sodomy laws are still on the books, church groups protested loudly. Nationwide, prison officials are largely opposed on the ground that free condoms might encourage sexual activity, even rape, as well as create other problems. "Our security people are concerned about this," says Texas administrator Riely. "These things can be turned into slingshots. They can be filled up with a variety of items, and turned into bombs."

GENDER CONFLICTS AND SEXUAL HARASSMENT

Although women have made good headway in obtaining jobs in law enforcement, they still are not accepted in many departments. According to Senna and Siegel (1990, p. 164): "Women who prove themselves tough enough to gain respect as police officers are then labeled 'lesbians' or 'bitches' in order to neutralize their threat to male dominance, a process referred to as **defemi- nization.**" Senna and Siegel cite the observations of sociologist Susan Martin regarding policewomen. She sees most women in policing as being on a con- tinuum between *police*woman and police*woman.*

> The *police*woman gains her peers' acceptance by trying to adhere closely to the norms of behavior governing police in general and exhibits a strong law enforce- ment orientation. She tries to be more loyal, professional, hardworking, and tough than women are generally expected to be. *Police*women are not afraid to engage in physical action or take punishment.
>
> On the other end of the spectrum are police*women* who behave in a "tradi- tionally feminine manner." They make few arrests, rarely attempt to engage in hazardous physical activity, and put emphasis on "being a lady." Police*women* feel comfortable in a role of secondary importance in a police agency.

Sexual Harassment   **Sexual harassment** has become a topic of great con- cern because of the rising number of women in law enforcement and the resistance to change by many of the officers from the "old school" in a pro- fession which has traditionally been a male-dominated enclave. In addition, the number of sexual harassment cases have been increasing, and the monetary awards have been sometimes distorted, if not shocking. For example, as noted by Kopetman (1991) two ex-Long Beach policewomen were awarded $3.1 million in damages for sexual harassment.

Sexual harassment has two conditions. First, it must occur in the workplace or an extension of the workplace (department sanctioned). Second, it must be a sexual nature which does not include romance or that is mutually friendly. The harassment must be unwelcomed, unsolicited, and deliberate. According to Schrader (1992, p. 6):

> Until 1986 there were few newspaper headlines that brought the subject of sexual harassment to the public's attention. The publicity that discrimination and sexual harassment have received over the past couple years, however, speaks to a changed landscape. And, since the Clarence Thomas confirmation hearings last October, there have been numerous articles and stories written about the subject of sexual harassment. . . .
>
> One of the major problems with the issue of sexual harassment is that the courts cannot even agree on what is acceptable or unacceptable.

Senna and Siegel (1990, p. 265) suggest: "As more women enter the occu- pation, move slowly into positions of authority, and serve as role models and sponsors for other women, there is reason for guarded optimism about the future of women in law enforcement, as well as a large number of questions waiting to be addressed."

THE POLICE IMAGE

Popular and scientific literature related to the police image often identifies several personality traits of the "typical" police officer.

Police officers are frequently described as being suspicious, cynical, bigoted, indifferent, authoritarian, and brutal.

Suspicious   Police work requires a police officer to be wary of situations that are out of the ordinary, for example, a person with an umbrella on a sunny day or a person wearing sunglasses at midnight. Not only is keen observation critical to effective investigation and crime prevention, it is critical to self-defense. Danger is always possible in any situation. Police officers develop a perceptual shorthand to identify certain kinds of people as potential assailants, that is, as persons who use gesture, language, and attire that police officers have come to recognize as a prelude to violence.

Cynical   Because police officers deal with criminals, they are constantly on guard against human faults. Police officers see people at their worst. They know that people lie, cheat, steal, torture, and kill. They deal with people who do not like police, who even hate them, and they feel the hatred. Additionally, they may see persons they firmly believe to be guilty of a heinous crime freed by a legal technicality. This cynicism may also lead to paranoia.

Bigoted   Police are frequently victims of problems they have nothing to do with and over which they have no control. They are not to blame for the injustices suffered by members of minority groups: housing, educational, and employment discrimination. Yet often members of minority groups perceive the police officers as a symbol of the society that has denied them its privileges and benefits. Tension between minority group members and any representatives of "authority" has become almost a way of life in many parts of large cities. The minority group members vent their anger and frustration on the police, and some police, understandably, come to feel anger and dislike for them.

Frequently the police image is associated with violence. They are expected to protect as well as to serve. In actuality, the service function occupies a much greater portion of their time.

Indifferent   When police officers are called to the scene of a homicide, they are expected to conduct a thorough, impartial investigation. Their objectivity may be perceived by grieving relatives of the victim as indifference or coldness. Police officers must remain detached, however; one of the grieving relatives might well be the murderer. Further, a certain amount of distancing is required to work with difficult situations. Ellison and Genz (1978, p. 4) state that officers who must deal with assignments involving mutilation and death develop coping mechanisms: "These defenses, which permit one to do an important job well, often prevent him from doing the work which involves interacting with others."

Authoritarian   Effective law enforcement requires authority; authoritarianism comes with the job. Without authority and respect, the police officer could not effectively compel citizens of the community to obey the law. As noted by the French philosopher Pascal: "Justice without force is powerless; force without justice is tyrannical." The physical appearance of the police officer adds to this authoritarian image. The uniform, gun, club, and handcuffs project an image to which most people respond with uneasiness or even fear. Yet this image projects the right of the police to exercise the lawful force of the state in serving and protecting as well as in enforcing laws. The difficulty arises when the power that comes with the position is transferred to "personal power."

Brutal   Sometimes force is required to subdue suspects. Unfortunately, the crime-related aspects of a police officer's job are what frequently draw public attention. When police officers have to physically subdue a suspect, people notice. When they help individuals get into their locked cars, few notice. Sometimes, however, more force is used than is required. This, too, is easier to understand if one thinks of the other personality traits that often become part of the police "personality," particularly cynicism and authoritarianism. Police officers may use excessive force with a rapist if they believe that the probability is great that the rapist will never be brought to trial because of the prosecutor's policies on rape cases. They may also erroneously believe that violence is necessary to obtain respect from individuals who seem to respect nothing but force and power.

The eyes of the beholder determine how a police officer's actions will be interpreted or described. A person who dislikes police officers will probably perceive a specific behavior negatively, while the same behavior might be perceived positively by an individual who has a high regard for police officers. Consider, for example, the actions listed in Table 21–2 and the way each is described by an individual who feels negatively about the police and one who feels positively about the police.

Table 21–2   **Police Actions Seen Negatively and Positively**

ACTION BY OFFICER	NEGATIVE PERSON	POSITIVE PERSON
Steps in to stop a fight in a bar.	Interference.	Preserving the peace.
Questions a rape victim.	Indifferent, cold.	Objective.
Uses a baton to break up a violent mob.	Brutal.	Commanding respect.
Steadily watches three youths on a corner.	Suspicious.	Observant.

POLICE EDUCATION

The subject of police education was discussed in Chapter 3. The basic question is, does more "formal" education make for better police officers? Senna and Siegel (1990, p. 256) report on a study conducted for the Police Executive Research Forum by David Carter and Allen Sapp of state and local police agencies serving populations of more than 50,000. Six hundred ninety-nine agencies responded. Among their key findings were the following:

- 62% had at least one formal policy supporting officers pursuing higher education.
- 58% required that coursework be job related.
- 49% expressed a preference for criminal justice majors.
- 82% recognized that college education is an important element in promotion decisions.
- Only 14% had a formal college requirement for employment.
- 75% had no policy or practice requiring college education for promotion.
- 75% that supported in-service higher education did not require that the coursework be part of a degree program.

Many police agencies are now requiring some college education for employment and/or promotion. Whether such education helps the officers perform better has not been documented.

The issue of what kind of college education is most appropriate was addressed by a report of the National Advisory Commission Higher Education for Police Officers, commonly referred to as *The Sherman Report*. This report examined the findings of a national study of existing college curriculum and educational delivery systems for police education and recommended that "prospective police officers should receive a liberal education and that criminal justice courses and course materials should emphasize ethical considerations and moral values in law enforcement, not the nuts and bolts of police procedures" (Senna and Siegel 1990, p. 256).

PRIVATIZATION OF CRIMINAL JUSTICE

"Hey, guys, cops are no longer the primary protective resource in this nation!" exclaims Cameron (1991, p. 1). He offers the following facts:

> According to a new study by the National Institute of Justice, private security already outspends public law enforcement by 73%—and employs two and a half times the workforce, and is expected to increase even more over the next decade. The facts are: spending for private security is $52 billion vs. our $30 billion. And private security agencies employ 1.5 million people vs. our estimated 600,000. The average annual rate of growth in private security is predicted to be 8%, double that of public law enforcement.

Private security forces include guards, patrols, investigators, armed couriers, central alarm respondents, and consultants. These private security officers perform many of the same functions as public law officers: controlling entrances and exits to facilities; preventing or reporting fires; promoting safety; safeguarding equipment, valuables, and confidential material; and patrolling restricted areas. Businesses and educational, industrial, and commercial organizations frequently hire private security guards to protect their premises and investments.

There are, however, important differences between private and public security forces. Public police officers are salaried with public funds. They are responsible to a chief of police and ultimately to the citizens of the community. Technically they are on duty twenty-four hours a day and have full authority to uphold the law, including the authority to make arrests and to carry a concealed weapon.

Still, the public police officer cannot be everywhere. Therefore, many businesses and organizations have elected to hire special protection. Basically, two different types of private security may be hired: private patrols and private guards.

As the name implies, private patrols operate both on and off the premises of their employers and may have several customers to check periodically during a specified time period. Private guards, however, stay on the property to safeguard the premises at all times.

A further distinction exists between a security officer employed by a large industrial concern and a night guard employed by a small firm. The former are usually carefully screened, well paid, and trained to perform specific duties. In contrast, the night guard is frequently retired from a regular job (sometimes as a public police officer), needs only temporary work, or is simply supplementing a regular income by taking on a second job.

Private security forces differ from public security forces in several ways. They are salaried with private funds. They are responsible to an employer. They have limited authority and then only on the premises that they were hired to guard. They have no authority to make arrests except as a citizen's arrest, unless deputized. They have no authority to carry a concealed weapon. Their uniform and badge must not closely resemble that of a regular police officer.

The upsurge in private policing affects all facets of the criminal justice system. As noted by Trojanowicz and Bucqueroux (1990, p. 131): "In addition to for-profit prisons that house adults, we are also seeing a tremendous surge in the number of private initiatives that handle juvenile offenders. . . . Litigants in civil suits can now choose to hire a private rent-a-judge-and-jury to settle claims, virtually bypassing the public court." They also note (p. 134): "Many believe that the private sector is more efficient, more effective and less costly. Will we soon see communities subcontracting for all or part of their police service from private sources?"

This is a sobering question. According to Mangan and Shanahan (1990, p. 18): "Private security has emerged as a major player in the safeguarding of Americans and their property." Private policing or **privatization** might be attractive from another perspective—they are not bound by many of the constraints that public police officers are, such as having to give the Miranda warning to suspects. Shearing and Stenning (1987, p. 15) note:

> With contemporary corporations as the modern-day equivalents of feudal lords, reigning supreme over huge feudal estates, the search for a historical parallel leads us back beyond frankpledge to more ancient concepts of private peaces and conflicting private authorities. Indeed, the very distinction between private and public takes on a new significance that blurs, and contradicts, its liberal meanings. This is true not only because private "individuals" are engaged in the maintenance of public order but also because more and more public life is nowadays conducted on privately owned and controlled property.

The relationship between public and private police has not always been cordial. According to Mangan and Shanahan (1990, p. 19): "Police have traditionally viewed private security employees as inadequately trained and ill-paid individuals who could not find other work but were nevertheless allowed to carry a gun."

Mangan and Shanahan (p. 22) stress: "It is mutually incumbent upon both public law enforcement and private security to continue to establish and improve mechanisms at every level which will not only allow but encourage dialogue on common law enforcement concerns and challenges?"

An innovative program in Philadelphia, called Security Watch, uses over 3,000 security officers within the jurisdiction of the Central Police Division as the eyes and ears of the police department. As noted by Zappile (1991, p. 23): "With the cooperation and support of all those in the private security industry in central Philadelphia, tangible gains have been made in reducing violent crime, decreasing calls for service involving order-maintenance problems, and identifying and eliminating repeat unfounded alarms. The private security sector and the Philadelphia Police Department have formed a true partnership to establish and maintain order in the Center City area."

Bocklet (1990, p. 54) also describes the importance of police-private security cooperation:

> While many police departments must now focus their efforts on serious crimes, corporate and property crimes are being addressed more and more effectively by private security forces. Complementing law enforcement efforts, they dispose of countless incidents meeting the statutory definition of crime that would otherwise inundate the police and criminal justice system resources. Some areas of cooperation are burglar alarm response, investigation of internal theft and economic crimes, protecting VIPs and executives, terrorism countermeasures, moving hazardous materials, and crowd and traffic control for public events.

Private sector development of police stations, sheriff's stations, and jails is being advocated as a "cost-effective option for replacing outdated facilities or building new ones" according to Smith (1991, p. 28). He notes: "With private sector development, the municipality or county receives the benefits of a build-to-suit facility and pays for its use out of current revenues rather than making a major capital expenditure." Smith (p. 33) concludes:

> Private sector development is a delivery process whose time has come for a variety of economic and practical reasons. With mutual respect for each other's needs and skills, and adequate precautions taken against potential problems, private sector development can be a mutually advantageous strategy for developers and government entities, resulting in functional and secure yet cost-effective new facilities to serve the needs of our justice system.

Police Officers Moonlighting in Private Security

Closely related to the issue of the relationship between the public and the private police is the question as to whether police officers should be able to have part-time jobs as security officers. Burden (1989, p. 92) says:

> The rent-a-cop business has grown steadily over the past 30 years as the fear of crime and the demand for police service have risen. Today, in some city precincts, there are more moonlighters than on-duty officers on the street. A handful of officers earn more from their off-duty jobs than their regular salaries. The total

number of sworn police officers who hire out to private employers is unknown, but it could be as much as half the force nationwide. Probably four out of five police departments now permit off-duty employment in jobs related to law enforcement and security.

CIVILIAN REVIEW BOARDS

Civilian review, according to Walker (1992, p. 8), "is a process by which citizens' complaints about police behavior are reviewed by persons who are not sworn police officers." An article in *Law Enforcement News* (1991, p. 7) states: "Civilian review boards, intended to boost public confidence in the process of investigating complaints made by citizens against police, are an increasingly visible feature on the American law enforcement landscape, according to a recent study which found that 30 of the nation's 50 largest cities have established some type of review board."

An opposite view is taken by Sharp (1990, p. 97) who says: "Civilian Review Boards (CRBs) may soon fade into history, at least in small towns. That is good news for a lot of police administrators." He notes that 76 percent of the respondents to a poll regarding CRBs, most of them chiefs of departments in towns with populations of 25,000 or less, said they do not think CRBs are worthwhile in small communities. In addition, a "resounding" 87.5 percent of those respondents who had experience with civilian review boards reported negative results. Sharp (p. 100) concludes: "As most police administrators would agree, their jobs are tough enough without having the additional burdens of civilian review boards looking constantly over their shoulders."

Civilian review boards consist of citizens who meet to review complaints filed against the police department or against individual officers.

The *Law Enforcement News* article cites the belief of Samuel Walker, criminal justice professor at the University of Nebraska in Omaha, who predicts increased attention on police brutality and misconduct because of the videotaped beating of motorist Rodney King by Los Angeles police. As noted by Walker (1992, p. 8): "The Christopher Commission appointed by Mayor Tom Bradley to investigate the Los Angeles Police Department found that many officers who were chronic wrongdoers were never disciplined by the department." Walker (p. 10) recommends that every city create some form of civilian review, preferably a Class I system where the initial fact-finding is done by full-time, trained investigators who are not sworn officers.

Brown (1991, p. 6) looks at both sides of the argument regarding civilian review boards:

> Proponents of civilian review argue that it creates a more effective relationship with the public while providing a "safety valve" when investigating the facts of a case. Another argument is that civilians may have complaints for which there is no recourse in the courts. Supporters believe that if an officer is exonerated by the board, the decision is less likely to be second-guessed.
>
> Critics argue that civilian review not only contributes to the impairment of professional law enforcement through the harassment, weakening and usurpation of legal law enforcement procedures, but materially endangers efficient and effective police performance.

The call for civilian review boards may increase as a result of the Rodney King beating. Such boards may focus on the use of force such as that shown here in Atlanta following the King verdict.

UNIONISM

According to Cole (1983, p. 214): "For much of this century, police employee organizations were mainly fraternal associations that existed to provide opportunities for fellowship, to serve the welfare needs (death benefits, insurance) of police families, and to promote charitable activities." He notes that the 1950s saw a dramatic rise in membership in police unions, partly due to job dissatisfaction, particularly regarding pay and working conditions; the perception that other public employees were improving their positions through collective bargaining; the feeling that the public was hostile to police needs; and an influx of younger officers with less traditional views on police-employee relations. In addition, during this time organized labor was making strong recruitment efforts.

Most police officers are members of local employee organizations. Cole (1983, p. 216) feels the police unions are locally based because the key decisions related to law enforcement are made at this level. And, although most police officers have joined local organizations rather than become affiliates of the AFL-CIO or other national unions, the strength of police unions has increased in many cities.

Most police officers are currently members of local employee organizations and are not directly enrolled in a national labor union.

One common objection to unionism is the tactics commonly employed, including slowdowns, "sickouts," and strikes. Although it is usually illegal for most public employees to strike, strikes by law enforcement officers have occurred in San Francisco, California; Tucson, Arizona; Oklahoma City, Oklahoma; Las Cruces, New Mexico; and Youngstown, Ohio (Gentel and Handman 1980, p. 5). Some of the strikes lasted only a few days, but others lasted weeks. In some instances strikers lost their jobs, but in other instances they obtained raises.

Other objections raised against unionism include the fear of law enforcement administrators and public officials that unionized police employees could abuse their collective bargaining power, and that specific aspects of administration such as transfers and promotions could become bound up in arbitration and grievance procedures. Cole (1983, p. 214) states: "Many administrators view the union as interfering with their law enforcement leadership and with the officers in the ranks." In addition, police unions have resisted changes in law enforcement organizations and techniques that affect their membership. According to Juris and Feuille (1974, p. 206), the unions opposed attempts to shift from two-person to one-person patrol cars in at least two of the twenty-two cities studied. Unions have also objected to efforts to hire civilians in clerical positions, and they have resisted affirmative action efforts, seeking to maintain the status quo rather than to increase recruitment of women and minorities into law enforcement.

In discussing the future of police unions, Cole (1983, p. 217) suggests:

Clearly, collective bargaining is a concept whose time has come, and police officials are going to have to recognize this new influence on law enforcement administration. At the same time, note that in a public sector of diminished resources, state and local governments may not have the funds to increase salaries to meet inflation. Already New York City and Boston have reduced the size of their police force as one way of reducing budget deficits. But in other cities, particularly those in expanding regions of the country and in the more affluent suburbs, police unions are making greater headway and can be expected to retain their influence. There are still, however, crucial questions about the role that unions should play in determining police department policies and the methods that they can use to influence bargaining agreements.

LAW ENFORCEMENT ACCREDITATION

The Commission on Accreditation for Law Enforcement Agencies was formed in 1979 to develop a set of law enforcement standards and to establish and administer an **accreditation** process to which law enforcement agencies could voluntarily apply to demonstrate that they met professional criteria.

The commission is the combined effort of the International Association of Chiefs of Police (IACP), the National Organization of Black Law Enforcement Executives (NOBLE), the National Sheriffs' Association (NSA), and the Police Executive Research Forum (PERF). Members of these four organizations direct approximately 80 percent of the law enforcement community in the United States.

The standards address six major areas:

- The law enforcement role and responsibilities, and relationships with other agencies
- Organization, management, and administration
- Personnel administration
- Law enforcement operations, operational support, and traffic law enforcement
- Prisoner and court-related services
- Auxiliary and technical services

The standards were developed to help law enforcement agencies (1) increase agency capabilities to prevent and control crime, (2) enhance agency effectiveness and efficiency in the delivery of law enforcement services, (3) improve cooperation and coordination with other law enforcement agencies and with other components of the criminal justice system, and (4) increase citizen and employee confidence in the goals, objectives, policies, and practices of the agency.

The Commission on Accreditation for Law Enforcement Agencies was formed to develop a set of professional standards and to establish and administer a voluntary accreditation process.

Any "legally constituted governmental entities having mandated responsibilities to enforce laws and having personnel with general or special law enforcement powers" are eligible to apply. If accepted, the accreditation fee is contingent upon the size of the agency, based on the number of full-time employees. In 1989 the rates ranged from $5,500 for an agency with fewer than ten full-time employees to $20,900 for agencies with more than three thousand full-time employees. This accreditation lasts five years. Whether this cost is justifiable is strongly debated in many departments.

Supporters of national accreditation suggest that it is one way to raise law enforcement into a professional status and to assure that certain standards are met. An overview of the accreditation program (Commission Update, 1984) lists the following benefits

- Nationwide recognition of professional excellence.
- Continued growth and improvement.
- Community understanding and support.
- Employee confidence; esprit.
- State and local government officials' confidence.
- State-of-the-art, impartial guidelines for evaluation, and change, when necessary.
- Proactive management systems; policies and procedures documented.
- Liability insurance costs contained or decreased.
- Liability litigation deterred.
- Coordination with neighboring agencies and other parts of the criminal justice system.
- Access to the latest law enforcement practices.

Fulton (1991, p. 37) cites the following benefits of accreditation:

- A deterrent to lawsuits and a reduction in litigation costs and insurance coverage.
- Assurance that all departmental policies and procedures are consistent with modern, professional standards.
- Since most policies and procedures are in writing, both line and supervisory personnel know what is expected.
- Because the standards are up-to-date and professional, there is justification for required resources to be placed in the department's budget.
- More resources are available for emergencies through the required co-operation agreements with other government agencies and other police departments.
- Closer management/union relations through standardized grievance and personnel procedures.
- Better morale, and an enhanced reputation for the department and the chief.
- A better managed department.

Despite these numerous potential benefits, accreditation does have critics. Among their concerns are the following (Fulton, pp. 37, 75):

- Accreditation is voluntary, therefore the agencies that could benefit the most will be least likely to apply.
- There are regional differences in policing around the country. One set of standards discounts these differences and takes away local options.
- State accreditation programs can't work because there will be a tendency to overlook an agency's problems because that same agency will be looking at you later on.
- The standards deal primarily with the administration of a police agency, and therefore have little value in the battle to fight crime and criminals.
- It's a Paper Tiger! An agency can have great policies on paper, but be out of control on the street.
- Some administrators say they can set professional standards themselves, without having a "big brother," or another bureaucracy, watching over them.
- Accreditation will lead to the elimination or consolidation of small departments who don't have the money or resources to keep up with accreditation's mandates.

According to Gavzer (1984, pp. 3–4):

New York and Los Angeles are in states whose police chiefs' associations have reservations about the accreditation commission. "We object to a national commission as an intrusion on local government," says Joe Dominelli, executive director of the New York police chief's outfit. "We go along with standards and accreditation but want it done on a statewide basis." The California chiefs' group says standards of the Peace Officers Standards and Training Commission (POST) are good enough. It expresses a fear that the accreditation commission could lead to having to deal with a Big Brother out of Washington.

POLICE PROFESSIONALISM

Throughout this text the field of law enforcement has been referred to as a profession; however, whether law enforcement technically qualifies as a profession is extremely controversial.

Part of the problem is that definitions of professionalism vary. To some, professional means simply an important job. Sociologists, however, have identified certain elements that qualify an occupation as a profession.

The three key elements of professionalism are (1) specialized knowledge, (2) autonomy, and (3) a service ideal.

Specialized Knowledge   The time when someone could walk into a police department, fill out an application, and be hired is gone in most parts of the country. Many departments now require a two-year college degree, and some require a four-year degree. In addition to a college degree, many departments require that applicants complete some kind of "skills" training. And, as noted, most larger departments also have their own "rookie schools" where new police officers learn what is expected in a particular agency.

As technology advances and as criminals become more sophisticated, more knowledge and training can be expected to be required.

Autonomy   Professional autonomy refers to the ability to control entrance into the profession, to define the content of the knowledge to be obtained, and to be responsible for self-monitoring and disciplining.

In addition, the autonomy of a profession is usually authorized by the power of the state; for example, physicians, dentists, lawyers, and teachers are licensed by the state. These professions are, in effect, legalized monopolies.

Law enforcement does fit the criterion of professional autonomy in that requirements to be a police officer are usually set by the legislature. The growth of Peace Officers Standards and Training (POST) boards throughout the country to oversee the profession attests to this fact.

A Service Ideal   The third element of a profession, the service ideal, requires that members of the profession follow a formal code of ethics and be committed to serving the community. In this area, police officers qualify as professionals provided the department stresses the public servant aspects of police work.

SUMMARY

Numerous issues are important in law enforcement in the 1990s. Some issues in law enforcement involve interpretation of the Bill of Rights, including the Second Amendment and gun control controversies; the Fifth and Sixth Amendments and the associated Exclusionary Rule and *Miranda* decision; and the Eighth Amendment and the use of capital punishment as cruel and unusual.

Controversy also exists as to whether certain offenses should be decriminalized. Such decriminalization would allow concentration of resources on serious crime and might also legalize certain actions such as gambling and prostitution, which are major revenue sources for organized crime. On the other hand, acts now considered criminal might be engaged in more frequently by law-abiding citizens if they were decriminalized, thus lowering our country's moral standards. Offenses that would be candidates for decriminalization include prostitution, sexual activities between consenting adults, gambling, public drunkenness, certain types of juvenile delinquency, narcotics and drug offenses, vagrancy, and disorderly conduct.

Heated controversy surrounds the practice of plea bargaining. In many courts more than 90 percent of criminal convictions are not obtained by the verdict of a jury or the decision of a judge. Rather, they are based upon the defendant's own plea of guilty. Convincing arguments exist both for and against plea bargaining; however, there is general agreement that it is practiced extensively.

Also controversial is how responsible police officers are for "special populations" such as the mentally ill, the publicly inebriated, and the homeless. Correctional administrators have several decisions to make related to the threat of AIDS—what is reasonable and in the best interest of the inmates?

The questions of the acceptance of women in law enforcement and avoidance of sexual harassment are of concern in many departments as is the image of the police. How much education police officers need is another issue to be addressed as is the rapid growth of private policing and the effect this might have on the entire criminal justice field.

Finally, issues related to unions, accreditation, and professionalism must also be considered.

DISCUSSION QUESTIONS

1. Will police departments be totally professionalized?

2. Unions have played a vital role in the economic development of this country. Do they have a place in police work?

3. How much education do police officers need?

4. What role should police officers play in the plea bargaining process, if any?

5. How do police officers deal with their own lives when they spend so much time with what they may feel are the worst of people?

6. Does private policing represent a threat to public policing?

7. Do you favor or oppose civilian review boards? State your reasons.

8. Is sexual harassment a serious problem for police departments?

9. Do you support or oppose accreditation of police departments? Why?

10. Do you consider law enforcement a profession? What about the entire criminal justice field?

TERMS

accreditation, civilian review, civilian review board, defeminization, privatization, sexual harassment.

REFERENCES

"Accreditation Program Overview." Fairfax, Vir.: Commission on Accreditation for Law Enforcement Agencies, 1984.

Bocklet, R. "Police-Private Security Cooperation." *Law and Order* (December 1990): 54–59.

Brown, L. P. "The Civilian Review Board: Setting a Goal for Future Obsolescence." *The Police Chief* (July 1991): 6.

Burden, O. P. "Rent-A-Cop Business is Booming." *Law and Order* (August 1989): 92–94.

Cameron, B. W. "Goodbye Cops—Hello Security Officers?" *Law and Order* (December 1991): 1.

Cole, G. F. *The American System of Criminal Justice,* 3d ed. Monterey, Calif.: Brooks/Cole Publishing, 1983.

Daley, R. *Prince of the City: The True Story of a Cop Who Knew Too Much.* Boston: Houghton Mifflin, 1978.

Ellison, W. K. and Genz, J. L. "The Police Officer as Burned-Out Samaritan." *FBI Law Enforcement Bulletin* (March 1978): 2–7.

Farah, J. "L.A. Riots Prove that We Need More Guns for Our Protection." *Star Tribune,* May 13, 1992, 15A.

Finn, P. E. and Sullivan, M. *Police Response to Special Populations: Research in Action.* Washington, D.C.: U.S. Department of Justice, National Institute of Justice.

Fulton, R. V. "Accreditation: An Issue for the 90s." *Law Enforcement Technology* (October 1991): 34–37, 75.

Gavzer, B. "Can Your Department Pass Muster?" *Parade,* December 30, 1984.

Gentel, W. D. and Handman, M. L. *Police Strikes: Causes and Prevention.* U.S. Department of Justice. Washington, D.C.: U.S. Government Printing Office, 1980.

Glick, H. R. *Courts, Politics, and Justice.* New York: McGraw-Hill, 1983.

Goldberg, W. I. "Victimless Crimes: Should Police Preserve Community Morals." *Tennessee Law Enforcement Journal,* p. 56, reprinted from *Police Law Quarterly,* April 1, 1972.

Juris, H. A. and Feuille, P. "Employee Organizations." In *Police Personnel Administration,* edited by O. G. Stahl and R. A. Staufenberger. Monterey, Calif.: Duxbury Press, 1974.

Kopetman, R. "Long Beach Policewomen Call Sexual Harassment Endemic." *Los Angeles Times,* September, 1991.

Levine, J. P.; Husheno, M. C.; and Palumbo, D. J. *Criminal Justice, a Public Policy Approach.* New York: Harcourt Brace Jovanovich, 1980.

Mangan, T. J. and Shanahan, M. G. "Public Law Enforcement/Private Security: A New Partnership?" *FBI Law Enforcement Bulletin* (January 1990): 18–22.

National Advisory Committee on Criminal Justice Standards and Goals. *Organized Crime: Report of the Task Force on Organized Crime.* Washington, D.C.: U.S. Government Printing Office, 1976.

"Police Increasingly Face Public Scrutiny through Civilian Review Boards." *Law Enforcement News,* April 15, 1991, 7, 11.

Pursley, R. D. *Introduction to Criminal Justice,* 3d ed. New York: Macmillan, 1984.

Schrader, G. E. "Moving Away from On-the-Job Harassment." *Law Enforcement News* March 31, 1992, 6, 10.

Senna, J. J. and Siegel, L. J. *Introduction to Criminal Justice,* 5th ed. St. Paul, Minn.: West Publishing Company, 1990.

Sharp, A. G. "Civilian Review Boards May Be a Thing of the Past." *Law and Order* (September 1990): 97–199.

Shearing, C. D. and Stenning, P. C. "Reframing Policing," pp. 9–18 in *Private Policing,* edited by C. D. Shearing and P. C. Stenning. Newbury Park, Calif.: Sage Publications, 1987.

Smith, W. J. "Private Sector Development: A Winning Strategy for New Police Stations, Sheriff's Stations and Jails." *The Police Chief* (August 1991): 28–33.

Sullivan, J. J. and Victor, J. L. eds. *Criminal Justice 91/92.* Guilford, Conn.: The Dushkin Publishing Group, 1991.

Trebach, A. S. "Losing the War on Drugs," pp. 304–310 in *Taking Sides: Clashing Views on Controversial Issues in Crime and Criminology,* 2nd ed., edited by C. Monk. Guilford, Conn.: The Dushkin Publishing Group, 1991: 304–310. Reprinted from *Law Enforcement News,* April 30, 1988.

Trojanowicz, R. and Bucqueroux, B. "The Privatization of Public Justice: What Will it Mean to Police?" *The Police Chief* (October 1990): 131–135.

Walker, S. "Answers to 10 Key Questions About Civilian Review." *Law Enforcement News,* April 31, 1992, 8, 10.

Walker, S. *The Police in America: An Introduction.* New York: McGraw-Hill, 1983.

Walker, S. *Popular Justice.* New York: Oxford University Press, 1980.

Waldron, R. J. *The Criminal Justice System,* 3d ed. Boston: Houghton Mifflin, 1984.

Williams, V. L.; Formby, W. A.; and Watkins, J. C. *Introduction to Criminal Justice.* Albany, N.Y.: Delmar Publishers, 1982.

Zappile, R. "Philadelphia Implements Security Watch." *The Police Chief* (August 1991): 22–23.

Glossary

accreditation being approved by an official review board as meeting specific standards. (21)

actus reus a guilty, measurable act, including planning and conspiring. (5)

administrative services those services such as recruitment, training, planning and research, records and communications, and crime laboratories and facilities including the police headquarters and jail. (7)

administrative warrant official permission to investigate the cause of a fire after the fire has been extinguished. (12)

adversary system a system which puts the accuser versus the accused. The accuser must prove that the one accused is guilty. The criminal justice system used in the United States. (18)

affidavit a statement reduced to writing, sworn to before an officer or notary having authority to administer an oath. (12)

affirmation positive declaration, assertion; usually related to an oath. (12)

aggravated assault an unlawful attack upon a person for the purpose of inflicting severe bodily injury or death. (5)

aggravated rape having sexual intercourse through use of force, threats or immediate use of force, or taking advantage of an unconscious or helpless person or a person incapable of consent because of mental illness or a defect reasonably known to the attacker. (5)

aggressive patrol designed to handle problems and situations requiring coordinated efforts. Also called *specialized patrol* or *directed patrol.* (8)

AIDS Acquired Immune Deficiency Syndrome, a disease caused by HIV viruses that has claimed the lives of more than 126,000 Americans. A spectrum of reactions to the Human Immunodeficiency virus (HIV) which infects and destroys specific white blood cells, undermining the body's ability to fight infection. (13)

allocution a victim speaking in front of the court, explaining the personal impact of a crime. (17)

American creed the belief in individual freedom. (4)

American Dream belief that anyone who works hard and is willing to sacrifice for a while can be successful. (13)

amphetamines stimulants taken orally as tablets or capsules or intravenously to reduce appetite and/or to relieve mental depression. (15)

appeal to ask a higher court to review the actions of a lower court to correct mistakes or injustice. (18)

appellate jurisdiction a higher court with the power to hear and decide an appeal to the decision of an original court without holding a trial. (18)

arraignment a court procedure whereby the accused is read the charges against him or her and is then asked how he or she pleads. (18)

arrest to deprive a person of liberty by legal authority. Usually applied to the seizure of a person to answer before a judge for a suspected or alleged crime. (12)

arson intentionally damaging or destroying, or attempting to damage or destroy, by means of fire or explosion the property of another without the consent of the owner or one's own property, with or without the intent to defraud. (5)

assault an unlawful attack by one person upon another for the purpose of inflicting bodily harm. (5)

authority the right to direct and command. (4)

bail payment by an accused of an amount of money, specified by the court based on the nature of the offense, to insure the presence of the accused at trial. (4, 18)

ballistics a science dealing with the motion and impact of projectiles such as bullets and bombs. (10)

barbiturates depressants usually taken orally as small tablets or capsules to induce sleep and/or to relieve tension. (15)

bias crime unlawful actions designed to frighten or harm an individual because of his or her race, religion, ethnicity, or sexual orientation. (6)

Bill of Rights the first ten amendments to the Constitution. (4)

biogenic an explanation of crime that focuses on biological functions and processes and relates human behavior, specifically criminal behavior, to such biological variables as brain tumors and other disorders of the limbic system, endocrine abnormalities, neurological dysfunction produced by prenatal and postnatal experience of infants, and chromosomal abnormalities (the XYY chromosomal pattern). (14)

biometrics measuring physical characteristics such as fingerprints or voice by computer. Often used as a means of access control. (10)

Bloods well-known African American gang. Rivals of the Crips. (16)

bona fide occupational qualification (BFOQ) skill or knowledge that is reasonably necessary to perform a job and, consequently, may be a requirement for employment. (3)

booked formally entered into the criminal justice system. Includes the facts about a person's arrest and charges: identification and background information. (18)

boosters professional shoplifters. (5)

boot camp patterned after the traditional military boot camps for new recruits; a system of incarceration for youth that stresses strict and even cruel discipline, hard work, and authoritarian decision-making and control by a drill sergeant. Also called *shock incarceration.* (19)

Bow Street Runners the first detective unit; established in London by Henry Fielding in 1750. (1)

burglary an unlawful entry into a building to commit a theft or felony. (5)

burn out a psychological state that occurs when someone is consumed, rendered unserviceable or ineffectual by maximum use; exhausted or made listless through overwork, stress, or intemperance. (3)

career criminal an offender arrested five or more times as a juvenile. Also called a *chronic criminal.* (14)

case law a collection of summaries of how statutes have been applied by judges in various situations; the precedents that have been established by the courts. (4)

chain of evidence documenting who has had possession of evidence from the time it was discovered and taken into custody until the present time. (10)

charge the formal complaint against a suspect. Formal accusation of a crime. (18)

chronic criminal an offender arrested five or more times as a juvenile. Also called a *career criminal.* (14)

circumstantial probable cause incidents which taken together suggest that a crime has been or is about to be committed. (12)

civil law all restrictions placed upon individuals that are noncriminal in nature; seeks restitution rather than punishment. (5)

civil liberties an individual's immunity from governmental oppression. (4)

civil rights claims that the citizen has to the affirmative assistance of government. (4)

civilian review a process by which citizens' complaints about police behavior are reviewed by individuals who are not sworn police officers. (21)

civilian review boards consist of citizens who meet to review complaints filed against the police department or against individual officers. (21)

classical theory sees people as free agents with free will, saying that people commit crimes because they want to. Theory developed by eighteenth-century Italian criminologist Cesare Beccaria. (14)

cocaine a central nervous system stimulant narcotic derived from the Erythroxylon coca bush of South America. (15)

code of silence a pact among officers that they will not make known any misconduct of fellow officers. (5)

cognitive interview a technique to help victims or witnesses remember a specific incident. It guides people back to their original memories using an established formula. (11)

cold crime a crime discovered after the perpetrator has left the scene. (8)

common law in England, the customary law set by the judges as disputes arose; the law in force before and independent of legislation. (4)

community era (1980-present) the third era of policing. Characterized by authority coming from community support, law, and professionalism; broad provision of services, including crime control; decentralized organization with more authority given to patrol officers; an intimate relationship with the community; and use of foot patrol and a problem-solving approach. (2)

community-oriented policing a philosophy that emphasizes a problem-solving partnership between the police and the citizens in working toward a healthy, crime-free environment. Also called *community policing, neighborhood policing,* and *community wellness.* (8)

community policing see *community-oriented policing.* (8)

community relations the sum total of activities by which the criminal justice system can become a part of the community rather than being solely a punitive regulatory agency imposed upon the public it has been sworn to serve. Seeks to provide two-way communication between police and citizens to work toward achieving law and order in the community. (9)

community wellness a philosophy that emphasizes a problem-solving partnership between the police and the citizens in working toward a healthy, crime-free environment. Also called *community policing, community-oriented policing,* and *neighborhood policing.* (8, 9)

community wellness model a prototype for community-oriented policing, modeled after medicine and its preventive approach to health. (9)

complainant a person who makes a charge against another person. (11)

complaint a legal document drawn up by a prosecutor that specifies the alleged crime and the supporting facts providing probable cause. (18)

concentric fracture break forming a circular pattern around the point of force and between the radial lines. Starts on the same side as the original force. (10)

concordance a state of agreement. (14)

consent to agree; to give permission; voluntary oral or written permission to search a person's premises or property. (12)

constable an elected official of a hundred responsible to lead the citizens in pursuit of any lawbreakers. The first English police officer and, as such, in charge of the weapons and horses of the entire community. (1)

Constitution the basic instrument of government and the supreme law of the United States; the written instrument defining the power, limitations, and functions of the United States government and that of each state. (4)

constitutional law statutes based on the federal or state constitutions. (4)

contamination prints prints resulting when a shoe or tire has a substance on it, such as dirt or blood, that leaves a print on a hard surface. (10)

contraband any article forbidden by law to be imported or exported; any article of which possession is prohibited by law and constitutes a crime. (12)

conviction finding a person guilty of a criminal charge. (18)

coroner's jury an inquest, usually before a jury of six members, to establish cause of death occurring under unusual circumstances. (18)

corporate gangs gangs that have strong leaders and focus on illegal money-making ventures, often drug trafficking. (16)

corpus delicti the body of the crime, the elements making up a specific crime. (5)

corroborative supportive, tending to confirm. (10)

corruption the misuse of authority by an officer for personal gain. Includes accepting gratuities and bribes as well as committing theft or burglary. (7)

court of last resort the highest court to which a case may be appealed. (18)

CPTED acronym for Crime Prevention Through Environmental Design. Focuses on "defensible space," using access control, lighting, and surveillance as key strategies in preventing crime. (9)

crack a relatively new form of cocaine available at greatly reduced cost. (15)

crime an action that is harmful to another person and/or to society and that is made punishable by law. (5)

criminal intent a resolve, design, or mutual determination to commit a crime, with full knowledge of the consequences and exercise of free will. (5)

criminal law the body of law that defines crimes and fixes punishments for them. (5)

criminalistics the scientific study of evidence in a criminal case and of individuals involved in such cases. (10)

Crips gang with the reputation of being the toughest African American gang in Los Angeles. Rivals of the Bloods. (16)

cross-examination questioning of an opposing witness in a trial or hearing. (18)

cultural gangs neighborhood-centered gangs that exist independently of criminal activity. (16)

curtilage that portion of property associated with the common use of land, for example, buildings, sheds, fenced-in areas, etc. (12)

custodial interrogation questioning a person who is not free to leave. (4, 11)

custody state of being kept or guarded, or being detained. (11)

dangerous drugs addicting, mind-altering drugs such as depressants, stimulants, and hallucinogens. (15)

dark figure of criminality the actual, unknown number of crimes being committed. (5)

Data Privacy Act the regulation of confidential and private information gathered by governmental agencies on individuals in the records, files, and processes of a state and its political subdivisions.

de facto segregation actual separation, often geographically into ghettos. (13)

deadly force any force intended to cause death or serious physical injury.

defeminization women proving themselves tough enough to gain respect as police officers and then being labeled "lesbians" or "bitches" to neutralize their threat to male dominance. (21)

defendant the person accused in a criminal proceeding. (18)

defense attorney the representative of the accused in court. (18)

deinstitutionalization releasing into society those who have been under the care of the state. Frequently refers to the massive release of mentally ill individuals into society in the 1960s and 1970s, many of whom became homeless. (13)

delinquency actions or conduct by a juvenile in violation of criminal law or constituting a status offense. An error or failure by a child or adolescent to conform to society's expectations of social order, either where the child resides or visits. (14)

delinquent a child adjudicated to violate a federal, state, or local law; a minor who has done an illegal act or who has been proven in court to misbehave seriously. A child may be found delinquent for a variety of behaviors not criminal for adults (status offenses). (14)

deliriants volatile chemicals that can be sniffed or inhaled to produce a "high" similar to that produced by alcohol. (15)

demographers individuals who study the characteristics of human populations. (13)

deposition a written statement made by a witness under oath to be used in court.

differential response strategies suiting the response to the call. (8)

directed patrol uses crime statistics to plan shift and beat staffing, providing more coverage during times of peak criminal activity and in high-crime areas. Designed to handle problems and situations requiring coordinated efforts. Also called *specialized patrol* or *aggressive patrol.* (8)

discovery crime an illegal act that is brought to the attention of the victim and law enforcement after the act has been committed; a burglary, for example. (10)

discovery process a system that requires all pertinent facts be available to the prosecutor and the defense attorney prior to the time of trial. (18)

discretion the freedom of an agency or individual officer to make choices as to whether to act; freedom to act or judge on one's own. (7)

diversion bypassing the criminal justice system by assigning an individual to a social agency or other institution rather than bringing to trial. (18)

DNA profiling uses the material from which chromosomes are made to positively identify individuals. No two individuals except identical twins have the same DNA structure. (10)

double jeopardy being tried for the same crime more than once. (4)

due process of law not explicitly defined, but embodies the fundamental ideas of American justice expressed in the Fifth and Fourteenth Amendments. (4)

ecclesiastical law law of the church. (4)

elements of the crime the distinctive acts making up a specific crime. The elements make up the *corpus delicti* of the crime. (5)

embezzle to steal or use for yourself money or property entrusted to you. (6)

emergency situations circumstances where a police officer must act without a magistrate's approval (without a warrant). (12)

empathy understanding. Being able to see things as someone else sees them. Not to be confused with sympathy. (11)

Enforcement Index a formula calculated by dividing the number of convictions with penalty for hazardous moving traffic violations during a given period by the number of fatal and personal injury accidents occurring during the same period. An index of twenty to twenty-five is suggested. (8)

equal protection requires that a state cannot make unreasonable, arbitrary distinctions between different persons as to their rights and privileges. (4)

equity a concept that requires that the "spirit of the law" take precedence over the "letter of the law." (4)

ethics involves moral behavior, doing what is considered right and just. The rules or standards governing the conduct of a profession. (7)

evidence all the means by which any alleged matter or act is either established or disproved. (10)

Exclusionary Rule a United States Supreme Court ruling that any evidence seized in violation of the Fourth Amendment will not be admissible in a federal or state trial. (4, 12)

executive the administrative branch of government that carries out the laws.

exigent circumstances the same as *emergency circumstances.* (12)

expertise specialized knowledge and/or experience. (12)

extenuating circumstances requiring immediate action; an emergency situation. (12)

eye witnesses individuals who have observed a crime, who expect no favors from the police, and who do not exchange information for protection or act out of motives for revenge. (12)

federalism a principle reserving for the states the powers not granted to the federal government or withheld from the states. (4)

felony a major crime, for example, murder, rape, arson; the penalty is usually death or imprisonment for more than one year in a state prison or penitentiary. (5)

fence a professional receiver and seller of stolen property. (6)

field detention holding suspects with less than probable cause. (12)

field identification at-the-scene identification, made within a reasonable time after a crime has been committed. (11)

field inquiry briefly detaining or stopping a person to determine who they are and/or what they are up to. (12)

field services the operations or line divisions of a law enforcement agency such as patrol, traffic control, investigation, and community services. (7)

fighting words utterances likely to cause violence. (4)

first-degree murder willful, deliberate, and premeditated (planned) taking of another person's life. (5)

flake a more refined form of cocaine than rock, extracted from cocaine paste. It comes in flat crystals and is approximately 95 percent pure. (15)

follow-up investigation investigation after the preliminary investigation. (10)

forced entry an announced or unannounced entry into a dwelling or a building by force for the purpose of executing a search or arrest warrant to avoid the needless destruction of property, to prevent violent and deadly force against the officer, and to prevent the escape of a suspect. (12)

Frankpledge system Norman modification of the tithing system requiring loyalty to the king's law and mutual local responsibility in maintaining the peace. (1)

frisk a patting down or minimal search of a person to determine the presence of a dangerous weapon. (12)

gang a group of people that forms an allegiance for a common purpose and engages in unlawful or criminal activity. (16)

genotype an individual's genetic constitution. (14)

ghetto syndrome a vicious cycle of poverty and welfare dependency leading to inability to go to college or prepare for a well-paying job, leading to lack of motivation, leading to unemployment, poverty, welfare dependency . . . (13)

ghettos areas of a city inhabited by people of an ethnic or racial group who live in poverty and apparent social disorganization often resulting from involuntary segregation. (13)

Good Samaritan laws laws protecting those who come to the assistance of injured persons, removing them from threat of civil lawsuits. (5)

graffiti writing or drawing on buildings and walls. A common form of communication used by gang members. Marks their territories. Sometimes called the *newspaper of the streets.* (16)

grand jury a group of citizens, usually twenty-three, convened to hear testimony in secret and to issue formal criminal accusations (indictments) based upon probable cause if justified. (4, 18)

grand larceny theft of property valued above a certain amount, in contrast to *petty larceny,* a less serious offense. (5)

guilty the accused admits the actual charge or a lesser charge agreed to in a plea bargaining session. (18)

habeas corpus a judicial order to bring a person being held in custody to court. (1)

halfway houses community-based institutions for individuals who are halfway into prison, that is, on probation, or halfway out of prison, that is, on or nearing parole. (19)

hallucinogens drugs whose physical characteristics allow them to be disguised as tablets, capsules, liquids, or powders; hallucinogens produce distortion, intensify sensory perception, and lessen the ability to discriminate between fact and fantasy. (15)

hate crime unlawful actions designed to frighten or harm an individual because of his or her race, religion, ethnicity, or sexual orientation. (6)

Hawthorne effect positive effects achieved by a new program occurring because anything new initially tends to be greeted enthusiastically, but soon the novelty wears off. (8)

hearsay evidence secondhand evidence. Facts not in the personal knowledge of a witness, but a repetition of what others said. (4)

Henry system classification system for fingerprints used in most countries. Developed in 1900 by Sir Edward R. Henry. (10)

heroin a commonly abused narcotic synthesized from morphine. Physically addictive and expensive. (15)

HIV Human Immunodeficiency virus. Infects and destroys specific white blood cells, undermining the body's ability to fight infection. Often results in AIDS. (13)

homicide the willful killing of a human being by another human being; also *murder.* (5)

household risk factors the degree of danger associated with factors related to how and where people live. (18)

Hue and Cry a shout by a citizen who witnessed a crime, enlisting the aid of others in the area to chase and catch the offender. May be the origin of the general alarm and the citizen's arrest. (1)

hundreds groups of ten tithings. (1)

hung jury a jury which cannot reach a decision. The result is a "no verdict" decision which can result in a retrial. (18)

hypertension elevated blood pressure. (15)

image how one is viewed; the concept of someone or something that is held by the public. Results from the media portrayal and from everyday contacts between individual police officers and citizens. (7)

immediate control within a person's reach; also called *wingspan.* (12)

implied consent laws stating that any person driving a motor vehicle is deemed to have consented to a chemical test of the alcohol content of his or her blood if arrested while intoxicated. Refusal to take such a test can be introduced in court as evidence. (8)

impressions imprints left on a soft surface such as sand or mud. (10)

in custody not free to leave. (11)

incarcerated confined in jail or prison. (19)

incarceration being confined in jail or prison. (19)

incident-driven policing where calls for service drive the department. A reactive approach with emphasis on rapidity of response. (8)

Index Crime categories of crime used in the Uniform Crime Report; Part I or Part II depending on the seriousness of the crime. (5)

indicted accused based on probable cause, by a grand jury charging an individual with a specific crime. (4, 18)

indigent destitute, poverty-stricken, with no visible means of support. (4)

indirect victim family members and friends of victims who also feel pain and suffering along with the victim. Also called a *secondary victim*. (17)

inevitable discovery doctrine holds that illegally obtained evidence may be admitted at trial if the prosecution can prove that the evidence would have been discovered sooner or later (inevitability). (12)

infamous crime a heinous felony. (4)

informants persons who furnish information concerning accusations against another person or persons. (11, 12)

information a formal written accusation of a crime resulting from a preliminary hearing; a charging document. (18)

informational probable cause statements made to officers that can be relied upon and are generally sufficient in themselves to justify an arrest. (12)

innovator effect anything new initially tends to be greeted enthusiastically, but soon the novelty wears off. In experimental psychology this is called the *Hawthorne effect*. (8)

instrumental gangs gangs formed for the express purpose of criminal activity. They pose a greater threat than cultural gangs because they provide for a higher degree of organization. (16)

instruments of a crime the means by which a crime is committed or the suspects and/or victims transported; for example: gun, knife, burglary tools, car, truck. (12)

intent see *criminal intent*. (5)

interrogation the questioning of a suspect. (11)

interview the questioning of a witness or person with information relating to an incident. (11)

involvement crime an illegal act discovered while it is being committed. (10)

judicial review a court's power to declare a statute unconstitutional, to interpret state laws, and to review cases that are appealed. (18)

jurisdiction the geographic area within which a court (or public official) has the right and power to operate. Also refers to individuals and subjects over which a court has the right and power to make binding decisions. (18)

jury a group of persons selected by law and sworn in to look at certain facts and determine the truth. (18)

justice model in corrections, assumes criminals are self-directed and responsible for their crimes. (19) In the juvenile system, a model where youth are responsible for their crimes and punished for them. In contrast to the welfare model. (20)

justice of dispensation a middle ground between the rule of law and the rule of man, that is, making exceptions when established rules work unexpected hardships in particular cases. The ability to bend the letter of the law to accomplish a fair result. (18)

justification a sufficiently lawful reason why a person did or did not do the thing charged.

juvenile delinquency behavior by a person not of legal age (usually under age eighteen, but in a few states under age twenty-one) that violates a law or an ordinance. (14)

landmark decision a ruling of the Supreme Court which becomes a precedent that must be honored by all lower courts. (18)

Language Line a service of AT&T which offers subscribers translation for over 140 languages. Officers who encounter language problems can call a toll-free number from almost any type of telephone and request the language translation needed. (13)

larceny/theft the unlawful taking and removing of the property of another with the intent of permanently depriving the legal holder of the property. (5)

latent fingerprints prints made by sweat or grease that oozes out of the pores from little wells situated under the ridges at the ends of the fingers. (10)

law a body of rules for human conduct that are enforced by imposing penalties for their violation. (1)

lawful arrest lawfully taking a person into custody (with or without a warrant) for the purpose of holding that person to answer for a public offense; all legal standards must be satisfied, particularly probable cause. (12)

legal authorized by law.

Leges Henrici a document that made law enforcement a public matter and separated offenses into felonies and misdemeanors. (1)

liability   a broad word for legal obligation, responsibility, or debt.

limitation   a legal restriction of time or authority relating to an offense.

litigaphobia   fear of a lawsuit. (5)

loansharking   lending money at higher than legally prescribed rates. (6)

Mafia   an Italian word referring to the lawless, violent bands of criminals who engaged in kidnapping and extortion in Sicily in the nineteenth and twentieth century; used today to refer to organized crime. (6)

magistrate   a judge. (12)

Magna Carta   a decisive document in the development of constitutional government in England that checked royal power and placed the king under the law (1215). (1)

malice   hatred or ill will, disregard for the lives of others. (5)

manslaughter   accidentally causing the death of another person. No malice or intent is involved. (5)

marijuana   the most socially acceptable of the illegal drugs, derived from the cannabis plant, a hardy weed adaptable to most climates. Variously classified as a narcotic, a depressant, and a hallucinogen. Usually smoked. (15)

medical model   in corrections, assumes criminals are victims of society and need to be "cured." (19)

mens rea   guilty intent, literally, a guilty mind. (5)

mere handcuff rule   common police department policy stating that all suspects who are to be transported in police vehicles must be handcuffed. (12)

misdemeanor   a minor offense, for example, breaking a municipal ordinance, speeding; the penalty is usually a fine or a short imprisonment, usually less than one year, in a local jail or workhouse. (5)

mobility   movable; not firm, stationary, or fixed; for example, an automobile that is capable of being moved quickly with relative ease. (12)

moonlighting   working at a second, part-time job while fulfilling the obligations of a full-time position. (3)

moral law   laws made by society and enforced solely by social pressure. (4)

motive   reason for doing something. (5)

motor vehicle theft   the unlawful taking or stealing of a motor vehicle without the authority or permission of the owner. Includes automobiles, trucks, buses, motorcycles, motorized boats, and aircraft. (5)

mules   individuals who smuggle cocaine for professional drug dealers. Often tourists or students. (15)

murder   see *homicide*. (5)

narcotics   drugs that produce sleep and lethargy or relieve pain; usually opiates. (15)

NCIC (National Crime Information Center)   the computerized files of the Federal Bureau of Investigation containing records of stolen property and wanted persons. (2)

negligence   failure to exercise a reasonable amount of care in a situation that causes harm to someone or something. (5)

negligent homicide   an accidental death that results from the reckless operation of a motor vehicle, boat, plane, or firearm.

neighborhood policing   a philosophy that emphasizes a problem-solving partnership between the police and the citizens in working toward a healthy, crime-free environment. Also called *community policing, community-oriented policing,* and *community wellness.* (8)

networks   relationships, links between people as well as between people and their beliefs. (11)

nightcap   slang for a nighttime search or arrest warrant. (12)

nighttime search warrant   a search or arrest warrant issued by a magistrate that authorizes a police officer to execute the warrant during the night. (12)

no bill   issued by a grand jury if they believe that no crime has been committed. (18)

no-knock search warrant   authorization by a magistrate upon the issuance of a search warrant to enter a premise by force without notification to avoid the chance that evidence may be destroyed if the officer's presence was announced. (12)

no-knock statute   authorizes entry without first announcing the presence of the authorities. (4)

nolo contendere   "I will not contest it." A defendant's plea of "no contest" in a criminal case. It means he or she does not directly admit guilt, but submits to sentencing or other punishment. (18)

nystagmus   an uncontrolled bouncing or jerking of the eyeball when an intoxicated person looks to the extreme right or left, and up or down. (15)

oath   a legal attestation or promise to perform an act or make a statement in good faith and under a responsibility to God. (12)

observational probable cause   what an officer sees, hears, or smells; that is, evidence presented directly to the officer's senses. (12)

offense   an act prohibited by law, either by commission or omission.

offense report   a preliminary report filled out by the responding officer for all crimes, attempts, investigations, and incidents to be made a matter of record.

open fields doctrine holds that land beyond what is normally associated with use of that land, that is undeveloped land, can be searched without a warrant. (12)

ordinance a local law or regulation. (4)

ordinary care such degree of care, skills, and diligence as a person of ordinary prudence would employ under similar circumstances. (12)

ordinary law statutes passed at the federal or state level which are not based on the Constitution. (4)

organized crime conspiratorial crime involving a hierarchy of persons who coordinate, plan, and execute illegal acts using enforcement and corruptive tactics. (6)

original jurisdiction a court's power to take a case, try it, and decide it. In contrast to an appellate court which hears appeals to the decisions of the original court. (18)

parens patriae the right of the government to take care of minors and others who cannot legally take care of themselves. (20)

parish the area in which people lived who worshipped in a particular parish church. (1)

parish constable system an early system of law enforcement used primarily in rural areas of the United States. (1)

parole a release from prison before a sentence is finished. Continued release depends on good behavior and reporting to a parole officer. The most frequent type of release from a correctional institution. (19)

pat down an exploratory search of an individual's clothing. The "search" phase of a stop and frisk. (12)

PCP phencyclidine, also known as Angle Dust, a hallucinogen. (15)

perception how something is seen or viewed. (11)

petition a written request for some action. (4)

petty larceny theft of property valued below a certain amount, in contrast to *grand larceny,* the more serious offense. (5)

phenomenological point of view emphasizes the fact that reality is very much the way a given person perceives it. (11)

phenotype an individual's physical makeup. (14)

pilfer to steal or use for oneself money or property entrusted to the person. (6)

plain feel/touch doctrine related to the plain view doctrine. An officer who feels/touches something suspicious during the course of lawful activity can investigate further. (12)

plain view evidence that is not concealed and that is inadvertently seen by an officer engaged in a lawful activity; what is observed in plain view is not construed within the meaning of the Fourth Amendment as a search. (12)

plea the accused's answer to formal charges in court. (18)

plea bargaining a compromise between the defense and prosecuting attorneys that prearranges the plea and the sentence, conserving time, effort, and court expense. (14, 18)

police authority the right to direct and command. (7)

police des mouers a special police force to regulate prostitution. (1)

police power the power of the federal, state, or municipal governments to pass laws regulating private interests, to protect the health and safety of the people, to prevent fraud and oppression, and to promote public convenience, prosperity, and welfare. (4)

political era (1840–1930) the first era of policing. Characterized by authority coming from politicians and the law, a broad social service function, decentralized organization, an intimate relationship to the community, and extensive use of foot patrol. (2)

positivist theory sees criminals as "victims of society" and of their own biological, sociological, cultural, and physical environments. Theory developed at the turn of the century by Italian criminologist Cesare Lombroso. (14)

post-traumatic stress disorder (PSTD) a psychological illness which happens after a highly stressful event or series of events, commonly associated with shooting incidents. (3)

power the force by means of which others can be made to obey. (4)

precedent what has come before. (4)

preliminary hearing a court process to establish probable cause to continue the prosecution of the defendant. (18)

preliminary investigation actions performed immediately upon receiving a call to respond to the scene of a crime. Usually conducted by patrol officers. (10)

premeditated planned ahead of time, as in premeditated murder. (5)

preponderance of the evidence the greater weight of the evidence. One side is more credible than the other. Used in civil trials. (18)

presentment action taken by a grand jury which involves conducting an investigation of a case on their own. (18)

primary victim the individual directly affected by an incident, such as the person who is robbed, burglarized, or raped. (17)

privatization civilians performing duties normally performed by sworn personnel who may be volunteers, paid civilians, or private security personnel. (21)

pro bono work work done for free. Lawyers volunteer their time to be public defenders. (18)

proactive seeking to find the causes of crime and to rectify those problems, thereby deterring or even preventing crime. Acting before the fact rather than reacting to something which has already occurred. (2, 8)

probable cause reasonable grounds for presuming guilt; facts that lead a person of ordinary care and prudence to believe and conscientiously entertain an honest and strong suspicion that a person is guilty of a crime. (4, 12)

probation the conditional suspension of a sentence of a person convicted of a crime but not yet imprisoned for that crime. The defendant is placed under the supervision of a probation officer for a set period of time and must meet specific conditions. (19)

procedural criminal law laws specifying how law enforcement officers are to carry out their responsibilities. (5)

procedural due process deals with notices, hearings, and gathering evidence in criminal matters. (4)

professional model the style of policing used during the reform era, based on the thinking of August Vollmer and O.W. Wilson. (2)

prosecutors elected or appointed officials who serve as the public's lawyers. (18)

psychogenic an explanation of crime that focuses on psychological factors and understands crime to be the result of an individual's propensity and inducement toward crime. (14)

public offense any crime. Includes felonies and misdemeanors.

public relations seeks to enhance the image of police officers by helping citizens gain an understanding and acceptance of the role of the police in the community. (9)

public safety exception allows police officers to question suspects without first giving the Miranda warning if the information sought sufficiently affects the officer's or the public's safety. (11)

pure speech words without any accompanying action. (4)

radial fracture a break spreading out from the center. Starts on the opposite side of the force causing the break. (10)

random having no set pattern; by chance; haphazard. (8)

rape carnal knowledge of a woman or man through the use of force or the threat of force. (5)

rattle watch a group of night patrolling citizens armed with rattles to call for help used in New Amsterdam in the 1650s. (2)

reactive responding to crime after it has been committed. (2, 8)

reasonable sensible; just; well-balanced; good, sound judgment; that which would be attributed to a prudent person. (12)

reasonable doubt that state of a case which, after the comparison and consideration of all evidence, the jurors cannot say they feel an abiding conviction of the truth of the charge. Moral uncertainty of the truth of the charges. (18)

reasonable force force not greater than that needed to achieve the desired end. (12)

reasonable search a search conducted in a manner consistent with the Fourth Amendment. (12)

reasonable seizure the seizure of evidence or persons according to constitutional standards set forth in the Fourth Amendment.

recidivism repeating or habitual offenses. (19)

red light district area to which prostitutes were restricted within a city. (1)

reeve the top official of a hundred. (1)

reform era (1930–1980) the second era of policing. Characterized by authority coming from the law and professionalism; crime control as the primary function of law enforcement; a centralized, efficient organization; professionally remote from the community; and an emphasis on preventive motorized patrol and rapid response to crime. (2)

regulator a respectable settler of average or affluent means who joined others as vigilantes to attack and break up outlaw gangs and restore order in the 1760s. (2)

relevant having a direct relationship to the issue in question.

restitution having the offender repay the victim or the community in money or services. (19)

restitution center a new variation of the halfway house where offenders work to partially repay their victims. (19)

restraint to restrain; to prohibit; to bar further movement; to limit freedom.

reverse discrimination giving preferential treatment in hiring and promoting to women and minorities to the detriment of white males. (3)

riflings spiral grooves cut into a gun barrel in its manufacture. (10)

riot act an order permitting the magistrate to call the military to quell a riot. (1)

ritual a system of rites; a ceremonial act. (6)

ritualistic crime an unlawful act committed during a ceremony related to a belief system. It is the crime, not the belief system, that must be investigated. (6)

robbery the stealing of anything of value from the care, custody, or control of a person in his or her presence, by force or by the threat of force. (5)

rock cocaine extracted from cocaine paste. The extracted cocaine looks somewhat like rock sugar candy. Its purity varies from 70 to 80 percent. (15)

roll call the briefing of officers prior to their tour of duty to update them on criminal activity and calls for service. (7)

rookeries criminal areas of London. (1)

R.P.R.d released on own recognizance. (18)

Scandinavian-type law prohibits driving with blood-alcohol concentrations exceeding specific levels and establishes severe penalties for disobedience. (8)

scavenger gangs gangs that have few goals and primarily provide an outlet for impulsive behavior and meet the need to belong. (16)

scienter a degree of knowledge that makes an individual legally responsible for the consequences of his or her acts. (5)

search examination of a person or property for the purpose of discovering evidence to prove guilt in relation to a crime. (12)

search warrant a judicial order directing a peace officer to search for specific property, seize it, and return it to the court; it may be a written order or an order given over the telephone. (12)

secondary victim family members and friends of victims who also feel pain and suffering along with the victim. Also called an *indirect victim.* (17)

second-degree murder the unpremeditated but intentional killing of another person. (5)

seizure a forcible detention or taking of a person or property in an arrest. (12)

selective enforcement targets specific accidents and/or high-accident areas. (8)

self-incrimination being required to provide answers to questions that might convict an individual of a crime. (4)

sensorium the part of the human brain which translates what the eye takes in, into what is actually seen. (11)

sentence the punishment, such as time in jail, given to a person convicted of a criminal offense.

sexual harassment has two conditions: (1) it must occur in the workplace or an extension of the workplace (department sanctioned) and (2) it must be of a sexual nature which does not include romance or that is of a mutually friendly nature. The harassment must be unwelcome, unsolicited, and deliberate. (21)

shadow children children whose mothers were addicted to crack while pregnant. Also called *crack babies.* (15)

sheriff the principal law enforcement officer of a county. (2)

shire-reeve the top official of a shire (county)—the forerunner of our county sheriff. (1)

shires counties in England. (1)

shock incarceration patterned after the traditional military boot camps for new recruits, a system of incarceration for youth that stresses strict and even cruel discipline, hard work, and authoritarian decision-making and control by a drill sergeant. Also called *boot camp.* (19)

simple assault an unlawful attack by one person upon another, but without the intention of causing serious, permanent injury. (5)

simple rape misleading a victim into having sexual intercourse. (5)

sinsemilla marijuana grown indoors in the United States. (15)

situational testing job-related simulation exercises to assess a candidate's qualifications for a law enforcement position. (3)

social law law made by society and enforced solely by social pressure. (4)

sociogenic an explanation of crime that focuses on the environment's effect on the individual and places responsibility for crime on society. (14)

sociological jurisprudence a theory that contends that the law must recognize and adapt to contemporary social conditions and that laws must adapt to a changing world. (18)

speech plus words accompanied by some sort of action, such as burning a flag. (4)

spoils system a political system whereby "friends" of politicians were rewarded with key positions in the police department. (2)

standing mute refusing to answer as to guilt or innocence at an arraignment. Is entered as a "not guilty" plea. (18)

status offenses crimes restricted to persons under the legal age; for example, smoking, drinking, breaking curfew, absenting from home, truancy, incorrigibility. (14, 20)

statutory law law passed by a legislature. (4)

statutory rape rape without force, but still against the law, as in having intercourse with an underage female. (5)

stereotype oversimplified conception, opinion, or belief, often associated with specific racial or ethnic groups; seeing all members of a group as the same with no individuality. (13)

stop briefly detaining someone who is acting suspiciously. A stop is *not* an arrest. (12)

stop and frisk a protective search for weapons that could be used to assault police officers and others; for example, knives, guns, and clubs. (12)

strict liability intent is not required; the defendant is liable regardless of his or her state of mind when the act was committed. (5)

submission placing of one's person or property under the control of another; yielding to authority.

subpoena a written legal document ordering the person named in the document to appear in court to give testimony. (4)

substantive criminal law statutes specifying crimes and their punishments. (5)

substantive due process protects individuals against unreasonable, arbitrary, or capricious laws and limits arbitrary government actions. (4)

suppressible crime crimes that commonly occur in locations and under circumstances that provide police officers a reasonable opportunity to deter or apprehend offenders. Included in the category are robbery, burglary, car theft, assault, and sex crimes. (8)

Supreme Court the highest court in the United States and the only court established by the Constitution. (18)

suspect an individual accused of a crime before a trial begins. After the trial begins, the individual is referred to as a *defendant*. (18)

symbolic speech tangible forms of expressions such as wearing buttons or clothing with political slogans or displaying a sign or flag. Protected by the First Amendment. (4)

target hardening making it more difficult for crime to occur. For example, using access control, lighting, and surveillance. (9)

territorial gangs gangs that establish their turf and defend it. (16)

theft stealing of any kind. (5)

threshold inquiry same as a *stop,* that is, briefly detaining an individual who is acting suspiciously. (12)

tithing in Anglo-Saxon England, a unit of civil administration consisting of ten families; established the principle of collective responsibility for maintaining law and order. (1)

tithing system established the principle of collective responsibility for maintaining local law and order by organizing families into groups of ten families known as a *tithing.* (1)

tort a civil wrong for which the court seeks a remedy in the form of damages to be paid. (5)

totality of circumstances taking into account all factors involved in a given situation. (11)

traditional gangs gangs that can trace their heritage back several generations and have a strong system of tradition. (16)

turf the geographic territory claimed by a gang. (16)

typologies systematic classifications, as in styles of policing. (7)

United States attorney general the head of the Department of Justice and the chief law officer of the federal government.

venue the local area where a case may be tried. It is usually required that the trial for an offense be held in the same area in which the offense occurred. (18)

victim impact statement a written or spoken statement detailing the medical, financial, and emotional injuries resulting from a crime. The information is usually provided to a probation officer who writes a summary to be included in the defendant's presenting packet. (17)

victim statement of opinion a spoken or written statement to the judge in which victims tell the court their opinion on what sentence the defendant should receive. More subjective than the victim impact statement. (17)

vigilante a person who takes the law into his or her own hands, usually in the absence of effective policing. (2)

waiver the intentional giving up of a right. (11)

warrant a written order issued by an officer of the court, usually a judge, directing a person in authority to arrest the person named, charged with the named offense, and to bring that person before the issuing person or court of jurisdiction. (4, 18)

Watch and Ward a system of law enforcement that was used to protect citizens twenty-four hours a day; the day shift was called the "ward" and the night shift the "watch." (1)

welfare model in the juvenile system, a model focusing on the best interests of the child. In contrast to the justice model. (20)

white-collar crime occupational or business-related crime. (6)

wingspan the area with a person's reach; also known as *immediate control.* (12)

witness a complainant, an accuser, a victim, an observer of an incident.

writ of certiorari a request for a transcript of the proceedings of a case for review. Made when the Supreme Court decides to hear a case. (18)

writ of habeas corpus see *habeas corpus*. (18)

zones of privacy areas safe from governmental intrusion. (4)

Author Index

A

Aaron, T. 402
Abadinsky, H. 133, 572, 579, 584, 585, 587
Adams, T.F. 38, 40
Adler, F. 540, 541
Allard, R., Jr. 383
Alpert, G.P. 16, 25, 270
Anderson, T.M. 95, 96, 97, 98, 100, 101, 140, 145, 147, 149, 153, 403, 404, 538, 541, 548, 551
Arnold, W.R. 203, 569, 572
Austin, D. 290

B

Bailey, W.G. 23, 25
Barbour, G.R. 323
Batson, L. 466
Bayley, D.H. 296
Bennett, G. 163
Bennett, W.W. 74, 82, 84, 165, 311, 312, 322, 369, 436
Benson, C.C. 251
Bishop, D.R. 282
Bittle, L.R. 72
Black, J.K. 163, 167
Blanchard, K. 226, 229
Blumberg, M. 405
Bocklet, R. 607
Bodinger-deUriarte, C. 179, 180, 183
Boydstun, E. 247
Braaten, J. 290
Brand, L. 246
Brantingham, P. 12, 133
Braunstein, S. 227
Brewer, N. 270
Briggs, K.C. 67
Brodsky, S.L. 151
Bromley, M. 539, 554, 573
Brown, D.K. 307
Brown, L.P. 199, 227, 240, 257, 289, 296, 297, 381, 608
Brown, R. 26, 27
Bruce, T.A. 369, 377
Brungardt, T.M. 203, 569, 572
Buckley, J.P. 332
Bucqueroux, B. 606
Burden, O.P. 450, 607

C

Cameron, B.W. 605
Camp, C.G. 547
Camp, G.M. 547
Campbell, A. 462
Campbell, D.P. 67
Caplan, G.M. 334
Carrington, F. 488
Carter, D.L. 394, 395, 396, 398
Chaiken, M.R. 445
Chamelin, N.C. 131
Chapman, S.G. 17, 247
Church, G.J. 449
Clark, J.R. 398, 399
Clede, B. 382
Cole, G.F. 218, 609
Colson, C.W. 523
Connor, G. 382, 384, 385, 386
Conroy, D.L. 82, 245, 497, 498
Cope, L. 82
Couper, D.C. 278, 297, 298
Creamer, J.S. 110, 355, 363, 375, 379, 380, 381
Cressey, D.R. 130, 131, 150, 168, 175
Critchley, T.A. 16
Curry, G.D. 468, 469
Cushing, M.A. 83, 84, 254
Cusik, J. 253

D

Dash, J. 81
Davis, J.R. 457, 459, 460, 462, 463, 464
Davis, R.C. 474, 476, 492, 496
DeAngelis, F.J. 310, 311, 318, 319
del Carmen, R.V. 152, 153, 332, 376, 382
Delattre, E.J. 225
Dershowitz 426
Dickey, S. 163, 165, 166
Dodenhoff, P. 320, 321
Donaldson, J. 250
Doyle, P. 549
Drowns, R. 415, 424
Dunham, R.G. 16, 25, 270

E

Eck, J.E. 299
Eldefonso, E. 538, 578, 580, 581

Elias, R. 488, 489, 492
Ellison, W.K. 84, 604
Epps, C.A. 403
Evans, D.D. 330, 340
Evans, K.R. 131

F

Faber, S.J. 437
Fagel, J.B. 510
Fair, F.K. 227
Farah, J. 595
Farmer, M.T. 240, 241
Farmer, R.E. 82
Farrell, J.S. 423
Feuille, P. 609
Fine, R.A. 524
Finn, P.E. 399, 400, 401, 474, 483, 486, 487, 488, 600
Fiscus, C.A. 84, 85
Folley, V.L. 34, 35, 39
Formby, W.A. 254, 255, 555, 596, 597
Fralicx, R. 71
Frawley, E. 251
Fulton, R.V. 611

G

Gallagher, G.P. 151
Gardner, T.J. 11, 22, 95, 96, 97, 98, 100, 101, 131, 132, 140, 145, 147, 149, 153, 403, 404, 538, 541, 548, 551
Garmire, B.L. 422
Gavzer, B. 611
Geberth, V.J. 320, 321
Geller, W.A. 236, 238, 239, 241, 242, 257, 260, 267, 269
Gentel, W.D. 609
Genz, J.L. 84, 604
Gershman, B.L. 513, 514
Glick, H.R. 507, 515, 599, 600
Goldberg, W.I. 598
Goldstein, H. 222, 239, 240, 299
Goodman, D. 548, 549
Gordon, M. 162
Gough, H.G. 67
Graham, M.G. 442
Graves, F.R. 384, 385, 386
Greenberg, J. 558
Greenberg, M.S. 542, 543

Subject Index

633

PHOTO CREDITS

1 James L. Shaffer; 2 The Granger Collection; 7 Historical Pictures/Stock Montage; 15 The Granger Collection; 20 James L. Shaffer; 23 Brown Brothers; 24 J.D. Stinchcomb; 30 ©Norman R. Rowan, Stock Boston; 33 Owen Franken, Sygma; 39 Scott Harr; 56 AP/Wide World Photos; 58 ©Rhoda Sidney, PhotoEdit; 78 James L. Shaffer; 79 AP/Wide World Photos; 88 The Granger Collection; 94 The Bettmann Archive; 99 The Granger Collection; 102 ©Peter Vandermark, Stock Boston; 116 Library of Congress; 119 ©Hazel Hankin, Impact Visuals; 122 AP/Wide World Photos; 126 ©P.F. Gero, Sygma; 138 ©Arnold J. Saxe; 144 ©Michael Weisbrodt, Stock Boston; 158 ©Bettye Lane, Photo Researchers; 164 ©John Neubauer, PhotoEdit; 172 West Publishing Company; 174 ©Bill Powers, Frost Publishing Group; 176 UPI/Bettmann Newsphotos; 177 James L. Shaffer; 180 AP/Wide World Photos; 184 James Shaffer, PhotoEdit; 191 James L. Shaffer; 192 PhotoEdit; 213 ©Star Tribune/Minneapolis-St. Paul; 214, 234 ©Tony O'Brien, Frost Publishing Group; 245 ©Spencer Grant, Stock Boston; 246 Scott Harr; 248 ©Laimute E. Druskis, Photo Researchers; 249 James L. Shaffer; 258 Frost Publishing Group; 266 ©Star Tribune/Minneapolis-St. Paul; 268 James L. Shaffer; 276 ©Rhoda Sidney, Stock Boston; 280 ©Andrew Lichtenstein, Impact Visuals; 282 Bill Nation, Sygma; 284 Scott Harr; 286 ©Star Tribune/Minneapolis-St. Paul; 293 Scott Harr; 294 ©Michael Weisbrot, Stock Boston; 304 ©Renee Lynn, Photo Researchers; 308 ©Star Tribune/Minneapolis-St. Paul; 316, 317 West Publishing Company; 320 ©David Woo, Stock Boston; 328 James L. Shaffer; 336 AP/Wide World Photos; 343 Elena Olivo, Brooklyn Image Group; 352 ©Paul Conklin, PhotoEdit; 361 ©James Shaffer, PhotoEdit; 372 James Shaffer; 386 AP/Wide World Photos; 391 ©Felicia Martinez, PhotoEdit; 392 ©Mark Richards, PhotoEdit; 400, 401 ©Star Tribune/Minneapolis-St. Paul; 404 ©Richard Cash, PhotoEdit; 408 ©John Neubauer, PhotoEdit; 418 ©Frank Siteman, Stock Boston; 422, 430 AP/Wide World Photos; 434 ©Arthur Tress, Photo Researchers; 442 James L. Shaffer; 444 UPI/Bettmann Newsphotos; 450 ©Mark Reinstein, Photoreporters; 454 ©Esias Baitel, Photo Researchers; 456 ©Star Tribune/Minneapolis-St. Paul; 461 ©Michael Newman, PhotoEdit; 469 ©Star Tribune/Minneapolis-St. Paul; 472 ©H.L. Delgado, Impact Visuals; 476 James L. Shaffer; 490 ©Star Tribune/Minneapolis-St. Paul; 497 James L. Shaffer; 501 Library of Congress; 502 ©Spencer Grant, Stock Boston; 508 Library of Congress; 528 Russ Kinne; 530 Susan Van Etten, The Picture Cube; 536 Harry Gustafson; 542 UPI/Bettmann Newsphotos; 549 ©Star Tribune/Minneapolis-St. Paul; 558 UPI/Bettmann Newsphotos; 562 Harry Gustafson; 567 Historical Pictures; 574 Library of Congress; 583 James Shaffer, PhotoEdit; 587 UPI/Bettmann Newsphotos; 588 Jim Shaffer; 589 Bernard Pierre Wolff, Photo Researchers; 592 AP/Wide World Photos; 594 ©George W. Gardner, Stock Boston; 603 James Colburn, Photo Reporters; 609 Gamma Liaison.

Color Photos

1 ©Richard Hutchings, PhotoEdit; 2, 3 ©Michael Newman, PhotoEdit; 4 ©Stephen McBrady, PhotoEdit; 5 ©Mary Kate Denny, PhotoEdit; 6 ©Star Tribune/Minneapolis-St. Paul; 7 ©Mark Reinstein, Photo Reporters; 8 ©Stephen Wursta, Sygma; 9 ©Terry E. Eiler, Stock Boston; 10 ©Donna Binder, Impact Visuals; 11 ©F. Paolini, Sygma; 12 ©Hal Stucker, Brooklyn Image Group; 13 ©Star Tribune/Minneapolis-St. Paul; 14 ©P.F. Gero—Sygma; 15 ©Bob Daemmrich, Stock Boston; 16 ©D. Hudson, Sygma; 17 ©Mark Richards, PhotoEdit; 18 ©Rhoda Sidney, PhotoEdit; 19 ©James Colburn, Photo Reporters; 20 ©John W. Emmons, Photo Reporters; 21 ©Mark Richards, PhotoEdit; 22 ©Sygma; 23 ©William Campbell, Sygma; 24 ©Curtis Willocks, Brooklyn Image Group.